A Social
Geography
of the City

HARPER & ROW SERIES IN GEOGRAPHY

D. W. Meinig, Advisor

A Social Geography of the City

David Ley

UNIVERSITY OF BRITISH COLUMBIA

1817

HARPER & ROW, PUBLISHERS, New York

Cambridge, Philadelphia, San Francisco,
London, Mexico City, São Paulo, Sydney

Sponsoring Editor: Kathy Robinson
Project Editor: B. Pelner
Designer: Robert Sugar
Production Manager: Willie Lane
Compositor: Waldman Graphics, Inc.
Printer and Binder: R. R. Donnelly & Sons
Art Studio: Vantage Art, Inc.
Cover: *Sandlot Games,* 1967, Ralph Fasanella.
    Courtesy of the artist. Cover design by R. Bull.

Photos by the author, with the exception of Figure
    5.4 from the Vancouver City Archives.

The Dylan Thomas selection on p. 138 is from
Quite Early One Morning, London: J. M. Dent,
1954. Reprinted by permission.

A Social Geography of the City

Copyright © 1983 by Harper & Row, Publishers

Library of Congress Cataloging in Publication Data
Ley, David.
    A social geography of the city.
    (Harper & Row series in geography)
    Bibliography: p.
    Includes index.
    1. Cities and towns. 2. Social structure. 3. Geog-
raphy, Political. 4. Human ecology. I. Title. II. Series.
HT119.L49 1983   307.7′64   82-11986
ISBN 0-06-384875-9

To my mother and father,
teachers of three geographers

Contents

PART 4
THE CITY AND SOCIAL STRUCTURE

PART 5
THE CITY AS THE HOME OF MAN

Preface

Like many books, this text is a product of teaching an undergraduate course for which no satisfactory text existed that did justice to the range and diversity of an increasingly significant and popular subject matter, in this instance, that of urban social geography. Urban geography has been strongly influenced by economic theory, which, though appropriate for particular material, may be incomplete and even defective for understanding the social, cultural, and political aspects of urbanization. As a result, urban social geography has often assumed a derivative position in urban studies, representing on the one hand a development of human ecology with its asocial roots in economics, and on the other a tendency to use census data that may be far removed from the realms of human experience of the city. So, too, the urban geographer's conventional concern with spatial pattern and urban form has held back inquiry, both from a full examination of the social processes behind the map distributions and from the broader historical contexts within which form and pattern are themselves defined.

The limitations of conventional urban geography became clear during the 1970s as various new traditions in human geography, including behavioral, humanistic, and radical perspectives, directed attention to the experience, the social processes, and the broader contexts enveloping urbanization. This book attempts an integration of these perspectives with the earlier emphasis on spatial form into a distinctive social geography of the city. As such, the book contains a number of current and novel emphases. These include a treatment of the geography of everyday life in the city and the role of culture and values, not only in defining our experience of the urban environment but also in molding the pattern of urban land use. Social groups in the city, both informal groups and urban institutions, are examined systematically, and their interaction through urban politics and the urban land market are assessed. The quality of life experienced by urban residents is given special emphasis, and various explanations for its geographic variation are considered. Finally, the book begins and ends with an analysis of the broader historical contexts that surround the development of urban land use patterns and the quality of urban life. In Chapter 2, the distinctive contexts of the emergence of the industrial city, the prototype for so much urban analysis, are considered; in Chapter 11, the contemporary contexts of urbanism are laid out, and the prospects for attaining a truly livable city are assessed.

This manuscript has benefited greatly from classroom experimentation and interaction with pupils and colleagues over the past five years. It assumes that students have completed an introductory course in human geography and preferably, though not necessarily, a course in spatial analysis or economic geography. It has been deliberately written to cover a broad range of material and has taken shape as an unavoidably interdisciplinary venture, so that it would be appropriate for students in urban studies, urban planning and design, and urban sociology, as well as for geography majors. Its focus is the city in the advanced industrial nations, and concepts are applied internationally to case studies in Western Europe and Australasia, as well as in the United States and Canada.

Though the perspectives and content of the book are ultimately my responsibility, it would not have taken its present shape without the assistance of many people. My colleagues at the University of British Columbia, particularly John Mercer (now at Syracuse University), Jim Duncan, and Marwyn Samuels, have provided a sympathetic intellectual environment. Roman Cybriwsky and David Hodge offered encouragement at critical points in the development of the project. Kevin Cox, Michael Dear, Ross MacKinnon, Don Meinig, and Roger Miller all provided constructive and helpful criticisms of an earlier draft. A number of themes were clarified in discussion with my graduate students, especially David Evans, John Lowman, and Gretchen Zdorkowski. Finally, through a combination of verbal and nonverbal communications, several generations of Geography 457 students have given the assessment and response necessary to any instructor.

On the technical side, a team of typists have provided excellent support. Irene Hull, Lee McSkimming, Maureen Stone, and Helsa Wong have shown a level of patience, endurance, and skill that made the author's task much easier. At Harper & Row I am grateful for the professional, editorial, and production work of four editors and the technical staff.

To Sandy is due special thanks for her companionship and sacrifice during the years that this manuscript has been in progress; to Katy are due apologies for those absent evenings at the office. I am happy to dedicate this volume to my parents who have consistently shown me over the years how the quality of family relations helps to sustain the quality of urban life.

D.L.

A Social
Geography
of the City

Chapter 1

Introduction: Urban Society and Urban Theory

Urban geography must be a geography of human experience

(Gibson, 1970)

By the end of the 1960s urban policy in the United States was in disarray, and by any measure the American central city was in severe distress. In part, the city exemplified the failure of technical and bureaucratic management based upon abstract models and disregard for social evaluation and public consultation (Gans, 1972). Each new technical solution, it seemed, spawned a new set of problems. The freeways advocated by transportation engineers, designed to relieve acute traffic congestion, themselves became congested in a matter of years. As ever more freeways were built, the local side effects of ravaged neighborhoods and a reduced tax base were joined by the metropolitan effects of increased pollution, rapid decentralization, and accelerated neighborhood change—all with their heavy fiscal and human costs. As jobs were lost by the central city, unemployment levels in the most deprived areas exceeded 20 or even 30 percent. Meanwhile, public redevelopment, with its objectives of relieving slum housing conditions, either resulted in a shortfall of low-cost housing or else condemned the poor to ghettoized living in high-density projects. This was not only an American problem. In Glasgow, Scotland, where over 60 percent of the population lives in public housing, over 300 high-rise blocks were built by the local authority after 1945. The anonymity and sterility of the high-rise environment has helped to make them design catastrophes and breeding areas for crime and delinquency among multiply deprived households. In the United States the social pathologies of the central city reached crisis proportions with the serious urban riots of the late 1960s, which provided an indicator of the full extent of the urban malaise. In short, it was a period for intensive reevaluation of urban theory and urban policy in the face of a threatened imminent breakdown of urban society.

One cannot identify a simple relationship between urban crisis, new policy initiatives, and developments in urban theory since the late 1960s. But the connections are

1

certainly there. A major theme of urban specialists such as Jane Jacobs and Herbert Gans has been the joining of social planning to physical planning, so that to the physical urban system have been added criteria of social assessment and evaluation, invariably accompanied by degrees of neighborhood consultation in the decision-making process. There has been much greater concern with how physical development affects people. Certain forms of development have been curtailed or altogether abandoned, such as the urban freeway program and high-rise public housing. In the words of Brock Adams, the U.S. Transportation Secretary, in 1978, "We must shift from an urban highway philosophy to an urban transit policy . . . we have to face up to the fact that the automobile is no longer a good means of urban transportation." To this end there has been an investment shift from urban freeways to rapid transit and innovative bus services. In Denver, for example, ridership increased by 50 percent as a result of an experiment in offering free public transportation during nonpeak hours. The program was also good ecology, for the reduced use of private cars removed 30 tons of pollutants a day from the air.

In terms of housing and neighborhood development there has also occurred a fundamental policy change. High-rise public housing programs have been totally abandoned in many cities, to be replaced by smaller low-rise projects, self-help cooperative housing associations, and an ever greater emphasis on public and private rehabilitation and preservation. For example, in the East End of Glasgow, a multiply deprived inner city area, the 5-year housing plan from 1977–1982 calls for 2500 new housing units, but also 7300 rehabilitated units, with over 20 percent of these renovations to be carried out by neighborhood housing associations. Housing is one element of a multifaceted area-based program of preservation and revitalization for inner city neighborhoods. In Glasgow's East End, local and senior governments have allocated over $300 million to be spent over 5 years in a comprehensive program of community development incorporating components in employment, housing, health, education, shopping, transportation, recreation, voluntary associations, and restoration of the physical environment. Similar broad-scale community development for target areas was initiated in the Model Cities program in the United States and somewhat more narrowly in the more closely administered Community Development program. In Canada, also, the Neighbourhood Improvement Programme was designed to enhance the quality and preserve the stability of inner city areas, with expenditure priorities determined in liaison with community residents; in addition improvement grants and loans were available for residential rehabilitation. In 1970, 100 percent of federal loans and grants in Canada for urban renewal, home renovation, and neighborhood improvement were committed to renewal, the bulldozing of acres of property followed by massive redevelopment. By 1977, when the budget was eight times larger, 96 percent of expenditure was for improvement and renovation and only 4 percent for renewal. Conservation and preservation replaced demolition and rebuilding in part to maintain viable communities and heritage architecture. A broader sense of urban welfare now informs public policy.

In urban policy, then, greater emphasis on social evaluation and an expanded understanding of the dimensions of urban welfare have been a feature of the past 15 years. This has been a more general characteristic of national policy, as is implied by the U.S. government's landmark publication of 1969, *Toward a Social Report,* which proposed a regular national accounting of social indicators which would parallel the established inventory of economic indicators to give a more integral view of the nation's well-being.

These developments are surely consistent with a theoretical reappraisal urged upon urban geographers by authors such as Edward Gibson in 1970, namely, that urban geography should become more fully *the geography of human concerns in the city*. Gibson's short paper, presented to a small regional meeting of the Association of American Geographers, was not the only instigator of change, for its arguments were typical of sentiments shared by many human geographers that were beginning to be voiced. The paper was an expression of a broad current of opinion that was calling for a new emphasis in the geographer's investigation of the city, an emphasis well summarized by the title of Torsten Hägerstrand's address at the same time to a surprised body of regional scientists whose urban research, like Hägerstrand's own, had been imbued with abstract theory and analytic method. To this group Hägerstrand asked, "What about people in regional science?" (Hägerstrand, 1970).

The intellectual historian of the future will no doubt point to the social context of these pronouncements, for, as always, theory and society were closely intertwined. As an eminent Swedish social scientist, Hägerstrand, with other Swedish geographers and planners, had been closely involved with the state's planning policies. In Sweden, an advanced social democracy where urban and regional planning by the state is widely developed, the weakness of apparently rational planning by a bureaucracy detached from the experience of its clients was first recorded. In Olsson's words, too often the methodology and the objectives were in conflict, leading to unexpected and unwanted side effects to government policy (Olsson, 1974a). In California, where Gibson's paper was presented, there were added factors to heighten a critique of the existing nature of both theory and society. Vietnam, the environment, civil rights, unrest and police action at the Chicago Democratic Convention, the Kent State killings—the 1960s showed with remarkable clarity the dehumanizing potential of a technical-bureaucratic value-free ethos not only in the obvious ranks of the military-industrial complex but also in civil authority and government and, as it became clear, in the technically correct but morally noncommittal corridors of the university. The model of science taught in university classrooms was one that emphasized an objective, value-free stance, and yet the model of man featured in the same courses presented man in a simplified manner that downplayed his cultural and moral nature. As Herbert Marcuse demonstrated with, it seemed, rare conviction to California students, the plight of such a one-dimensional man was therefore a problem of theory as well as practice, one where "technological rationality has become political rationality" (Marcuse, 1964:xvi). It was not enough to criticize the actions of a technological society without attacking also its theory, its world view built around the glorification of technique.

Around such a critique developed a vigorous if diverse humanist manifesto. When James Parsons, the Berkeley geographer, declared in 1969 that "the humanist approach to learning may prove more congenial to the coming generation than any other viewpoint," he was simply repeating the lesson he was learning in his classroom, for at Berkeley, in particular, new social movements were sweeping the campus. New perspectives, if not yet new theory, were emerging from the critique of a society constructed on a world view whose destructive potential was starkly exposed. The message of reconstruction for both theory and society included a deeper respect for the integrity of the nature of man and his environment, a renewed emphasis on the quality of human experience, and a keener sensitivity to questions of values, in particular, the plural values and minority rights of modern urban society.

At one level, the 1980s would seem to be bringing a new period of reassessment to urban policy, as the free enterprise governments in the United States and Britain appear to be deflecting the trends of the past decade. We will examine these issues in more detail in the final chapter in surveying the contexts of urbanization in the 1980s. But for now we might note that it is unclear for how long and for how far policies of state withdrawal from the cities can be pressed. In early 1982 President Reagan is facing fierce political opposition to his current budget, while in Britain Prime Minister Thatcher has announced huge grants to hard-hit unemployment areas, primarily in the cities, following urban rioting. Indeed in Britain, the Conservative policy of deregulation and state cutbacks has not led to a decrease in government involvement in the economic and social life of the nation. By 1980–1981 government expenditures in Britain accounted for nearly 45 percent of the gross domestic product, a figure which has continued to grow steadily during Mrs. Thatcher's Conservative administration.

The pace of change in the cities has been explored in ever-diverging research by geographers since 1970, a period of lively debate and creativity in urban studies with the opening up of new perspectives, theoretical positions, and innovative empirical research which have brought the discipline into contact with much broader intellectual currents than in the past. This volume is intended as a review and partial synthesis of that work. Of course the book is written from a chosen perspective which may add originality to sections of the argument, though no doubt at the cost of a certain bias. Moreover, any integration of different viewpoints cannot be other than tentative in a field which is growing vigorously and where such a synthesis has not been made. Parts of the research I will seek to bring together have separate traditions both in subject matter and methodology, so that the integration will not always be easy. Nevertheless, however preliminary its synthesis, this book will attempt to provide the substance of a geographical understanding of the Western city as the home of man.

The Heritage of Urban Geography

But, first, where does this program fit into the conventions and traditions of urban geography? To a considerable extent a treatment of urban geography as "a geography of human experience" does not square easily with orthodox views of the discipline. Urban geography is one of the most firmly established of geography's disciplinary branches—in the United Kingdom alone the roll call of the urban-study group of the Institute of British Geographers numbered over 500 in the late 1970s, whereas in the United States it is the most popular specialty among members of the Association of American Geographers, with nearly 1200, or 20 percent, of the membership claiming an affiliation. This established status has given the field some well-developed precedents for the conduct of urban enquiry.

Most reviews of urban geography would recognize two distinct phases in the field's development up to 1970 (Berry and Horton, 1970; Carter, 1972; Herbert and Johnston, 1978). The earlier phase, identified first as settlement geography and then as urban geography, emerged slowly from the nineteenth- and early-twentieth-century notion of geography as the relationship between man and his physical environment. This viewpoint brought certain empirical questions to the fore but disregarded others. A naturalist and almost Darwinian viewpoint traced the evolution of cities as adaptations to environmental circumstances. Griffith Taylor, one of the most influential scholars of his day, was "chiefly interested in the town as an evolving organism" (Taylor, 1949:85).

This emphasis readily gave rise to a genetic or historical approach that emphasized particularly urban origins and the physical conditions around which an urban nucleus would have been founded. The city's historic location would then be "explained" in terms of some man-land relationship, such as a defensive hill site, a river bridging point, or a convergence of natural valley routeways. On another scale the details of the city's architecture and form could be related, as they were so fully in Jean Brunhes' influential *Human Geography,* to the circumstances of the local physical milieu, particularly the components of climate, topography, geology and biogeography. The orientation of build-ings, the street pattern, roof types, and construction materials could then all be tied to immediate environmental components. A particular attraction of historic explanation was that it allowed these environmental contexts to be highlighted. But there is an important consequence, for as urban evolution has approached modern times, so local physical constraints have become less binding on urban development, and the stress on the physical environment appears increasingly incomplete. As a result, this first phase of urban ge-ography is not well suited to an understanding of the contemporary city, where the factors influencing urban development are broader in scope. Although explanations favoring the physical environment might have been appropriate for urban development in the past, the environment of present urban society is more complex, including social, political, and economic dimensions as well. To some extent the modern city has been freed from the constraints of its local physical environment but faces a new vulnerability to wider economic, political, and social factors.

A second characteristic of the early phase of urban geography was its concern with morphology, the material or built form of the city. Townscape studies, with their mapping of urban form, were directed in part toward the identification of functional areas, dis-tinctive land use zones. The preparation of a land use inventory would permit a classi-fication of functional areas. This urban application of region building, traditional geography's stock in trade, was exemplified by the careful studies delimiting the extent of the central business district (Murphy, 1974). But, as subsequent critics have noted, this approach often led to a theoretical dead end. Once the inventory of urban form was assembled and the regional classification completed, inquiry was finished. As in all forms of regional delimitation, the act of region building itself does not readily address questions of theory or process. It is as if historians painstakingly established precise time intervals around a particular era and then, with the temporal boundaries firmly defined, concluded their work.

The nontheoretical nature of conventional urban geography was challenged by the development in the late 1950s of spatial analysis, a school in human geography which claimed scientific status in its pursuit of formal hypothesis testing, statistical explanation, and theory construction. This school identified itself with the methodology and philosophy of natural science, particularly the philosophical system called logical positivism (Harvey, 1969b; Guelke, 1978). Redefining geography as the science of spatial relationships (Bunge, 1966), it sought through analytic method and mathematical language to establish statistical and lawlike relationships between spatial phenomena. During the 1960s spatial analysis had supreme influence on urban geography and transformed the style of research, which aspired to a more rigorous and theoretical status. But it has become clear that this second major phase of urban geography often secured its rigor at considerable cost. The abstraction of the spatial analytic school has taken much of its work far from real problems in the contemporary city, to a fascination with technique and relationships in a logical theoretical system. But the gulf between a logical system and the empirical world has often been a broad one, and as skepticism has grown, it has been suggested that some of the relationships discovered by the spatial analyses have a reality *only* at the level of logical abstraction. Its internal logical elegance need not have any external relevance to the empirical world (Ley, 1978a).

Moreover, in some respects, the transition in urban geography from morphological townscape studies to spatial analysis shows continuity as well as departure. The preoccupation with urban form and land use patterns has not ended, though more recently in place of descriptive statements there has been an attempt to relate land use to a small set of spatial variables. The continuity is most marked in the ongoing effort to define an efficient system of urban regions; though the mathematical technique of factorial ecology (see Chapter 3) has replaced the more intuitive schemes of an earlier generation, the objective of building urban regions remains.

More fundamentally, spatial analysis retains the emphasis of morphological inquiry on the built environment. Its interest is with urban *form*—buildings, streets, land use patterns—objects which may be precisely defined and measured with cartographic or mathematical symbols. But a preoccupation with spatial form leaves unanswered the questions of underlying social *process* and *meaning* in terms of human experience. More than one originating process may result in the same form; there is not a single process, for example, that gives rise to a grid street pattern. This illustrates the more general principle that logical systems relevant for a description of form may not be appropriate for an understanding of process (Olsson, 1969). Moreover, the methodology of logical positivism recognizes no distinction between the physical and human world, the realm of objects and the realm of meanings. But this is a controversial position, for other philosophies would assert a fundamental distinction, claiming, with Olsson (1974b), that in the human world of hopes and fears, two times two does not always equal four. The world of experience, in short, does not always operate according to the same logic as the language of mathematics. Thus an urban geography attentive to human experience, to ideas, meanings, and process as well as physical form may well have to begin its investigation of the city from an alternative methodology and philosophy offering a different perspective on knowledge and understanding.

Philosophical Issues in Urban Geography

Through much of its history human geography has had relatively limited formal contact with methodology and philosophy. The commonsense, fieldwork orientation of the discipline has dismissed philosophical matters as unprofitable and unnecessary speculation. When the historical geographer Andrew Clark commented in a review of his understanding of humanism that "methodology is neither an enthusiasm nor forte of mine" (Clark, 1977), he was making a common declaration for several generations of historical, cultural, and broadly regional geographers.

Its philosophical naiveté made human geography extremely vulnerable to the enthusiastic surge toward logical positivism and its mathematical style in the 1960s. Positivism in geography established itself rapidly not so much as *a* philosophy as *the* philosophy of science, declaring all earlier work to be "prescientific" and, implicitly, unworthy of scientific status. However, if such self-confidence was initially disarming, more recently the weaknesses of the positivist program have become visible, not least to former advocates such as David Harvey, William Bunge, and Gunnar Olsson. The decade of the 1970s was a period of developing philosophical sophistication in geography which is reflected in a stream of scholarly papers and in several books critical of positivist orthodoxy and presenting alternative perspectives (Harvey, 1973; Olsson, 1975; Gregory, 1978; Ley and Samuels, 1978). A number of key philosophical questions, formerly regarded as settled or else unimportant, once again appear now as problematic. These questions, covering such matters as the nature of man, the nature of the environment, and the form geographic explanation should take, are critical to our task of constructing an urban geography that is a "geography of human experience."

The first issue to be raised queries the adequacy of inquiry that remains at the level of spatial form while largely neglecting discussion of underlying processes. The overriding commitment of spatial analysis in urban geography has been to uncover regularities in spatial relations and not to process studies. But this is to make the prior assumption that there is something in some way significant about spatial form in its own right. A recent critique by both humanistic and Marxian writers has commented that urban form in itself is not as important a category as spatial analysts have claimed, for spatial form is not an end in itself but an expression, a consequence of something else—the prevailing forces in society. Thus inquiry that remains at the level of form cannot provide an adequate treatment of urbanism, for the city does not contain its own explanation. In other words, adequate explanation should be concerned with the social processes and historical contexts that constitute and accompany urban development. Research should then shift from spatial relations to social relations, for the former is but one particular instance of the latter.

In short, an explanation of urban form requires a prior understanding of its social contexts. Similarly, the science of spatial relations says nothing about the *meaning* of urban places to their inhabitants. An inventory of land use facts or the classification of an area according to socioeconomic characteristics give little indication of the urban sense of place. To understand process and meaning, the detached stance and logical system of the spatial analyst needs to give way to an anthropocentric perspective that examines the daily activities and perceptions of the urban resident, whether he be company president or man in the street. These realizations led to a behavioral revision of spatial analysis as attention was redirected to man as a decision maker or, in Olsson's words, away from the geometric outcome of the spatial game to the decision rules employed by the actors on the gaming table (Olsson, 1969). The behavioral approach countered some of the shortcomings of spatial analysis as it grappled with issues of process and meaning. It introduced more realism, for its greater attention to empirical studies reduced the overly abstract nature of spatial theory (Cox and Golledge, 1981). But behavioralism was itself limited inasmuch as it retained the methodology of logical positivism (Olsson, 1974b; Ley, 1977b). Its approach to subjectivity and experience was overly structured, suppressing too severely the dynamism and ambiguity of everyday life. The language of numbers is rarely the language of human relationships; the imprecision and variability of perception are rarely revealed by overly formal methodologies. But behavioral geography retained many of the methods and much of the language of positivism. In its use of intrusive methodologies, laboratory settings, and student samples, it at best approximated the contexts of everyday life in which decisions were made, actions were taken, and the meaning of places was constructed. Its mathematical language created a false sense of exactness in settings more accurately characterized by their flux and indeterminacy.

As a result, geography's behavioral movement acted as a transition to the adoption of an approach that reflected more satisfactorily an anthropocentric perspective, the world of everyday life. This approach has been derived from the humanist philosophies of existentialism, phenomenology, and pragmatism. This is not the place to review these philosophies, for a number of expositions by geographers are now available (Mercer and Powell, 1972; Relph, 1970; Buttimer, 1974, 1976; Ley, 1977b; Samuels, 1978), but we might note some of their emphases. In their commitment to empirical study—to the things themselves, in the slogan of phenomenology—they are seeking the relevant social contexts that permit the understanding of an action or the interpretation of a place. Their methodologies, such as participant observation, also seek to recreate the circumstances within which decisions are made, while their language is that of nuance and subtlety rather than the unnatural precision of mathematics.

A richer model of man and of human creativity is a central theme of these more humanistic philosophies. The model of man is unlike the pallid figure of logical positivism. Man is not cast in an essentially passive role, and neither is his personality reduced to a single dimension. He is animated and treated as a culture builder; what is important is not simply his products, the buildings he constructs, but also his ideas and his experience of place. Indeed it is his world, his meanings, that we are anxious to discover and to understand. Of course the actions of urban man do not unfold in some ill-defined environment where his will is supreme. He inherits an already structured world, a biographical situation that includes an historical epoch, a location, a family, a class, an ethnicity, a culture, all of which exercise constraints upon him. These constraints are frequently social. The philosopher Merleau-Ponty has commented that history is other people, but in an urban age geography too is becoming other people. The effective environment of urban man is increasingly an interpersonal one.

An urban geography that is a geography of human concerns is likely to return to a man-environment perspective, but it will not be reductionist, with a one-dimensional model of man. Nor will it be deterministic, but will stress human creativity and the reciprocal nature of man-environment relations; nor will it be purely materialist, but will consider not only the built environment of the city but also the values, ideas, and experiences that characterize urban life; nor, finally, will it be overly abstract, but will approach its research with a fully empirical methodology, which sets urban problems within their local and historical contexts.

Urban Geography and Social Theory

Human geography has traditionally overlapped with the physical sciences, for its attention to the physical environment made knowledge of geological, hydrological, climatological, and biological conditions a necessity. But we have seen that in the contemporary city it is increasingly a social rather than a physical milieu that is uppermost. A more logical connection for our present purposes would bring human geography into contact with sociology and social theory. There is surprisingly little precedent for this liaison. Since the celebrated dispute between the followers of the geographer Vidal de la Blache and the sociologist Durkheim at the turn of the century (Berdoulay, 1978), there have been few contacts between the disciplines until very recently. The only major exception was Max Sorre's ambitious but isolated attempt to forge a synthesis, and unfortunately this peace missive has remained largely inaccessible to the English-speaking world (Sorre, 1957). Before considering what form of social theory might be relevant for the development of process studies in urban geography, we will review briefly why such integration has not occurred before.

Social geography, though popular, has always occupied a marginal *conceptual* position in the discipline. In his famous presidential address to the Association of American Geographers in 1922, Harlan Barrows correctly foresaw that economic geography would in the future provide the discipline's leading edge, from which it would follow that social geography would be peripheral and its future uncertain. As a result human geography has retained an essentially passive view of society and culture (Duncan, 1980). Earlier in the century it was the potency of the physical environment that was stressed, and so, in a 1932 overview of social geography, Stephen Visher observed confidently that "democracy is interfered with by exceptionally fertile soil" (Visher, 1932). Later, as the role of economic factors was stressed in human geography, so social geography became heavily influenced by the branch of sociology known as human ecology, even though the consistent underpinning of human ecology has been acknowledged: "To a large extent the model may be seen as one of economic determinism" (Timms, 1971).

It is significant that human ecology has been the one form of sociology to have exerted lasting influence on social geography, for it is in many ways the least *social* variant of sociology. Ecological research by urban sociologists into segregation, neighborhood succession, and the later regionalization schemes of social area analysis and factorial ecology have been replicated and, in some instances, extended by geographers (Peach, 1975; Jackson and Smith, 1981). But it is important to remember once again the underpinning of human ecology. Robert Park's alternative term for human ecology was "biological economics," a label that indicates its essentially mechanistic and nonsocial nature. A biological model is concerned with instincts not perceptions and with ethology not culture, whereas the economic model is individualistic and competitive, with its shrunken view of rational economic man. These underpinnings are inadequate for the study of social process and human experience, for they not only have an essentially limited view of social relations but also do not deal with questions of meaning and the purposefulness of action. As a perceptive human ecologist has noted, "Attitudes, sentiments, motivations and the like are omitted from consideration not because they are unimportant, but because the assumptions and point of view of human ecology are not adapted to their treatment" (Quinn, 1940).

If human ecology provides an unsatisfactory vehicle for interpreting the social milieu of the city, where then in social theory should one turn in order to understand the social processes that sustain urban form and the experience of urban life? Set against biological economics we might oppose social psychology, which treats man's purposefulness and social relations in a more fully empirical and contextual manner, especially when it is couched within such philosophies of meaning as existentialism, phenomenology, or pragmatism. In this book, especially in Part 3, we follow the theoretical guideposts of social phenomenology and, to a lesser extent, pragmatism in examining urban experience as a product of social and subcultural processes. These perspectives, with their explicitly social definition of experience, are more promising than the individualism of behavioralism and ecology for a truly *social* geography. The literature of social phenomenology and symbolic interactionism (an empirical extension of pragmatism) emphasizes the processes for the construction and maintenance of social worlds and subcultures within which attitudes and values are developed and experiences unfold.

But these processes are themselves also set within a broader social context. The old urban geography considered aspects of both site and situation in relating an urban settlement to its physical milieu. So too in our understanding of the social milieu of the city must we be aware of both immediate and more distant contexts. Besides the immediate situations of everyday life, familiar routines, people, and places, there are also less visible contexts of which urban residents may not always be aware. These include both the details of an individual's biography, which constrain his or her experience to a varying extent, and external events, including the action of other groups, which may thwart or promote his or her own purposes. We cannot consider social milieu without discussing the question of power, an individual's ability to advance his or her objectives. The conclusion, of course, is that individual opportunities are not equal; neither the biographical situation nor the power held by all individuals is identical.

In probing the social processes of the city, then, urban geographers will need to make use of social theory which both emphasizes the subcultural effects of group membership and also places social worlds within a broader societal context of access to resources. Even though a similarity of attitudes and experiences is likely to occur within social worlds, a dissimilarity of values and priorities is to be expected between groups. Inasmuch as urban resources, including such varied resources as employment, land, power, status, or public safety, are in scarce supply, intergroup relations will be inherently competitive and, to the extent that a group's fundamental aspirations are threatened, competition will contain the seeds of tension and even open conflict.

A Social Geography of the City: Outline of the Book

As should be clear from the preceding sections, this book contains some departures from the two earlier traditions in urban geography that we have discussed. The concern with perceptions and experience, as well as behavior and spatial form, draws our standpoint away from logical positivism and toward the man-centered philosophies of meaning. Theoretically, the emphasis on social context and social process challenges the economic perspective that has dominated much recent human geography and requires that connections be drawn with a broader body of social theory. At the same time the book is intended to be substantive rather than an exercise in philosophy or social theory, so that we will only touch lightly on explicit discussion of these matters. It would require a separate volume to deal fully with such topics, and this literature is increasingly becoming available.

Neither is our stance at this stage dogmatic, for much of the research effort is still in its early phases. Indeed the preliminary nature of research has been a frustration at several points in the writing of this book and has led to the use of as yet unpublished sources and also of findings that have been made in related disciplines. Nowhere is the empirical gap more evident than in our knowledge of the decision-making environment of organizations. Although social geographers have been active in their examination of informal social groups in the city, there is much less known of the formal organization and its social world. Yet urban society is increasingly a managed one, and in an era when the social environment of urban man is becoming increasingly institutional, a research agenda investigating the subculture of formal associations should have a high priority.

Our discussion opens in Part 1 with a review of some of the major themes in urban geography's study of spatial form. In Chapter 2 the more important findings of the classical land use studies are presented and are assessed in the historic context of the development of the industrial city. Some of the assumptions of this work have been challenged by recent changes in urban form which elude the rather simple-minded explanations of the industrial city that have sometimes been presented. In Chapter 3 the pervasive nature of social and land use segregation in the city is discussed together with the various attempts to classify segregated districts into coherent social areas. But it seems as if the abstract reasoning of the researcher only partially fits the experience of the urban resident. The model of social areas implied by census data is an imperfect representation of the varied meanings attached to urban space by residents.

In Part 2 we seek to correct this imbalance by moving from an overly analytical perspective to an experiential view of the geography of everyday life in the city. The view of urban space held by an analytical tradition is complemented by an anthropocentric viewpoint which examines human spatial behavior, geographical perception, and the experience of place. Chapter 4 emphasizes the partial nature of everyday life in the city. The urban resident's activity patterns and ongoing routines are restricted to a small portion of the metropolitan area. Within this small area of familiarity daily life is lived out and, as behavioral studies in geography have shown, it is this familiar district that the resident is most likely to peruse in order to satisfy such needs as shelter or employment. The selective encounter with the city inevitably places certain urban resources beyond reach and implies, too, a lag in knowledge of them. This incomplete character of the information field has generated considerable geographical research on spatial problem solving and spatial diffusion. The city is further brought to life as we consider in Chapter 5 the meanings attached to space by urban dwellers. Moreover the animation of space implies also a more faithful representation of urban man, for the personality of a place and the identity of a social group mutually reinforce each other. A set of dominant meanings attached to urban areas is outlined, and the geographical distribution of these meanings defines gradients which are increasingly of critical significance in understanding the map of land values and population movements.

Part 3 develops more fully the inherently social nature of urban life. Much of urban experience and perhaps more of urban problem solving are achieved in community. In this section there is predictably a fuller contact with sociology as we outline the processes by which a social milieu is constituted. It is likely that Chapters 6 and 7 will prove the most unfamiliar to geographical readers with limited sociological background, but they are far from a digression, for if we are serious in developing a truly *social* geography, then an understanding of the social processes implicit in the construction, maintenance, and functioning of informal groups and formal associations is a necessary step. In Chapter 6 we examine the processes involved in the formation of informal social groups, and the role of such groups in aiding personal adjustment to urban life. Chapter 7 extends the analysis to the character of formal organizations and institutions, for in an increasingly corporate society, it is important to understand the internal dynamics of organizations, whether they be multinational corporations or part of government.

In Part 4 the isolated social group is placed within its context of a hierarchy of urban communities and interest groups with differential access to the city's scarce resources. Whereas Part 3 has been concerned with the internal relations of social worlds, Part 4 is concerned with their external relations, the interactions between the city's varied communities of interest. In Chapter 8 the differential access to urban resources is discussed in terms of a household's access to the housing market and neighborhood types. Residential mobility is constrained by a family's housing class but also by its preferences, so that patterns of neighborhood change tend to be slow but also consistent and to a certain extent predictable. The orderly progression of change may be disrupted, however, by the mobility of groups who are perceived as socially distant. The dissimilarity of households may accelerate neighborhood change, but it may also retard it through community resistance to the in-migrants. Particularly in the latter circumstance exclusion is commonly accompanied by intergroup confrontation and even conflict.

Besides households there are other interest groups seeking to steer the course of urban development. The interaction of neighborhood groups with the institutional forces of government and business highlights the political basis of urban life, which is examined in Chapter 9. The city is an arena where diverse lobbyists seek to exert their will. Urban land use patterns are thereby a negotiated outcome of conflict and compromise, reflecting the changing disposition of power and alliances among private and institutional interests.

In Part 5 the discussion moves from analysis to evaluation of the city as the home of man. The quality of urban life represents the fundamental concern of a humanistic perspective, for it provides the balance sheet to a geography of human experience. Chapter 10 begins with a review of the distribution of indicators of well-being in the city; with few exceptions both objective and subjective indicators reveal the same gradients in the quality of urban life. These patterns require interpretation, and the remainder of the chapter considers explanations and policy implications offered from the ecological, subcultural, spatial, and political economic viewpoints. There are, however, still broader contexts encompassing the course of Western urbanism. In Chapter 11 we consider the city as a product of advanced industrial society, expressing societal conditions in its built form and livability, and changing in response to social change in society at large. The economic, political, and cultural dimensions of social change in the advanced industrial nations are reviewed, and their impact upon the city are assessed. Given these societal trends, the constraints and criteria for developing more truly livable cities are considered.

In this book, then, we shall see that both the spatial form and the geographical experience of the city are the product of not only choice but also constraint, the outcome of private ambitions, mutual objectives, interest-group power, and historical possibility. Spatial form and the quality of urban experience represent the meeting of human intentions and an environment with economic, political, cultural, and physical components. The task of this volume is to untangle part of this complex web of man-environment relations expressed by urbanization in advanced industrial society.

PART 1
The Spatial Form of the City

Chapter 2

Urban Form and the Urbanization Process

The conventional wisdom about the nature of urbanization processes that has been widely accepted throughout the social sciences . . . may be in need of substantial rethinking, re-evaluation and reshaping

(Berry and Kasarda, 1977:248)

In 1902, at the end of the Victorian era, which had wrought such a transformation to the geography of Britain, the novelist H. Rider Haggard undertook an assessment of the condition of rural England. Typical was his encounter with the fertile Rother Valley in the county of Sussex, where the 1851 Census had shown that 60 percent of the males were employed in agriculture and that 75 percent of these were farm laborers. Eighty years before him the essayist William Cobbett had passed through the same region on his own *Rural Rides* and had detected a sense of well-being, noting "with great delight a pig at almost every labourer's house." The agricultural society Cobbett observed had changed little in its population, settlement, and agricultural land use over the previous 1000 years. However, Cobbett's diaries recorded the final generation which would sustain this historical pattern. By 1902 rural society and rural land use had been transformed. The competition of world markets demanded extensive changes in farm practices which caused a marked reduction in the agricultural work force. But many laborers left the land voluntarily, perceiving better opportunities in the growing cities. The census takers felt a need to explain the reduction in parish populations after 1850; a characteristic footnote in the 1861 Census against one parish in the Rother Valley spelled out the process initiating the breakdown of rural stability: "The decrease in population in Rogate parish is attributed to migration to large towns in consequence of the lowness of wages, etc." Despite a subsequent doubling of the farm laborer's wage from 1871 to 1901, by the time of Rider Haggard's survey the perceived attractions of urban life had dissolved the bond to the land for agricultural laborers and had even prompted a rural labor shortage: "The labourer no longer felt tied to the soil and afraid to leave his parish . . . so great is his desire for town pleasures that he migrates at length into the town" (Rider Haggard, 1906:124, 127). One farmer in the Valley observed that "all the young men were leaving the land . . . during the previous week he had lost two unmarried carters'' (Rider Haggard, 1906:110).

These disruptive processes transformed the face of local rural society throughout Western Europe and North America and have in the twentieth century fuelled the vast global phenomenon of urbanization. For some rural migrants, the move involved a journey half way around the world and from feudalism to industrialism. In 1899 the arrival of the ''Gospel of New York'' in the farming town of Vaslui in Roumania led to the formation of a short-lived To-America-on-Foot society among the eager adolescents of the community. The excitement again dissolved the bonds of centuries: ''Suddenly America had flashed upon our consciousness and fanned our dormant souls to flames of consuming passion.'' It was not long before ''All my relatives and all our neighbors—in fact, everybody who was anybody—had either gone or was going to New York'' (Ravage, 1971:5).

Similar local incidents, multiplied millions of times, produced the massive rural depopulation which fed the unprecedented urbanization of the nineteenth century. The combination of objective circumstances and a subjective appraisal of opportunities, however irrational, created a new geography.

The Preindustrial City

The societal cataclysms of the nineteenth century transformed not only the countryside but also the city. Prior to the Industrial Revolution, towns had served as ceremonial, military, political, or mercantile centers (Weber, 1958; Vance, 1977). With few exceptions their growth had been slow and modest, and based upon regional rather than national or international functions. In Britain, London was the only city whose population exceeded 100,000 in 1800; in 1860 only 16 American cities claimed more than 50,000 residents.

In an ambitious attempt at synthesis, Sjoberg has tried to identify some common cross-cultural features of the preindustrial city (Sjoberg, 1960). Like all models claiming a wide range of application, the model of a generic preindustrial city has come under heavy criticism for its oversimplification and overextension (Wheatley, 1963; Langton, 1975). As is often the case, however, the model continues to be influential and, though not correct in many of its details, continues to serve as a standard against which individual cities are assessed. Sjoberg's model is most appropriate in circumstances where domination by a local ceremonial or traditional elite occurred. He identified three social classes: an upper class, a lower class, and a numerically dominant group treated as outcasts. Group boundaries were rigidly defined and often formally codified, and the class pyramid was translated into a distinctive spatial pattern (Figure 2.1). The elite occupied the central district around the city's ceremonial and symbolic institutions, including the religious, educational, and political structures. Interspersed within the core were the servants of the elite, but the major concentration of lower-class residences was located in a zone outside the core. The outcasts were relegated to the periphery, completing the spatial gradation of social status. Within each of the zones further differentiation occurred by occupation or ethnicity; however, there was limited segregation of distinctive land use functions.

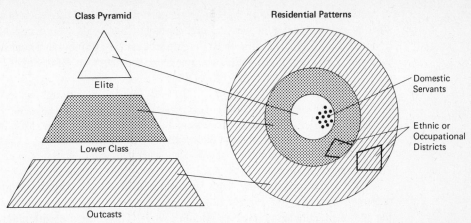

Figure 2.1   Social class and residential structure in the preindustrial city. (*Source*: J. Radford, ''Testing the Model of the Preindustrial City: The Case of Ante-Bellum Charleston, South Carolina,'' *Transactions, Institute of British Geographers* NS 4 (1979):392–410, fig. 1. Reprinted by permission of the Institute of British Geographers.)

The appropriateness of Sjoberg's model has been tested in Charleston, South Carolina, which until 1830 was the sixth largest city in the United States (Radford, 1979). The elite class could be identified with the aristocratic plantation owners, who were firmly distinguished from the white working class and slave populations. The residential patterns of Charleston in 1860 followed in general a status gradient consistent with the model. Over 50 percent of the highest-status occupations were tied to residences in the two innermost of six zones; 40–50 percent of the lowest-status occupations were clustered in the two outermost zones. These outermost zones also contained the homes of free blacks who were assigned many of the characteristics of an outcast group in antebellum society; the core, in contrast, contained the city's major ceremonial buildings. Although the trends are consistent with the model, they also indicate some deviations from it, particularly in terms of the functional specialization that already had occurred in parts of the city and a stratification by social class more complex than that allowed by Sjoberg's three-fold division. Radford concludes that Sjoberg's model, although relevant in some respects to Charleston, is ''much more partial'' than its general designation, the preindustrial city, would suggest—a conclusion that we shall repeat later in discussing a similarly overdrawn descriptive model of the industrial city.

It should be noted, however, that the model of the preindustrial city is not without support from nineteenth-century observers. In 1841, the German author Johann Kohl suggested that the typical form of the contemporary European city consisted of a series of concentric circles (Berry and Kasarda, 1977). The innermost circle was the business core containing administrative and clerical institutions, and surrounding it were four residential zones housing, in turn, the upper class, the upper middle class, the lower middle class, and the lower class. This zonal arrangement reproduces the spatial patterning of social status suggested by Sjoberg, though Kohl adds an interesting nuance. In addition to horizontal social segregation, he noted a vertical segregation in the large cities, whereby different social classes occupied separate floors of a tenement. In an era of primitive insulation, long flights of stairs, and the mediocre provision of public services such as running water, it was the higher-status households who occupied the lower or middle levels of the dwelling. In late-eighteenth-century Edinburgh a contemporary report itemized the varied households occupying one tenement on High Street (Smout, 1969, cited by Elliott and McCrone, 1980:1):

> A fishmonger's house on the ground floor, a respectable lodging house on the second floor, the rooms of the dowager Countess of Balcarres on the third floor, Mrs. Buchan of Kelly living above that, the Misses Elliots, milliners and mantuamakers above that, and the garrets occupied by a great variety of tailors and other tradesmen.

Vertical segregation by status survived in the industrial city, though perhaps in less extreme form, and was identified by Charles Booth in his massive survey of London at the end of the nineteenth century (Booth, 1967). The vertical partitioning of households by status continues as a largely unrecognized form of segregation in modern high-rise apartment buildings, though with the invention of the elevator, the piped delivery of water, heat, and power, and the contemporary premium placed on view sites, the status hierarchy has been reversed, with the most expensive units now occupying the top floors.

The Built Form of the Industrial City

The built form of the industrial city represented the onset of a substantially new constellation of social forces. The scale of demographic change was unprecedented. Whereas London was the only city in England and Wales with a population exceeding 100,000 in 1800, by 1891 this status was shared with 23 other towns. In the United States, where the era of most rapid urban growth occurred several decades later, the 16 towns with more than 50,000 residents in 1860 had expanded to 109 by 1910; in the 1880s Chicago doubled in size and Minneapolis-St. Paul tripled, while the industrial centers of Detroit, Milwaukee, Columbus (Ohio), and Cleveland all grew by 60–80 percent. Fourteen of the 19 cities with more than 250,000 inhabitants in 1910 were located in the American manufacturing belt, which extended east-west from Boston to Chicago and south to include St. Louis, Cincinnati, and Baltimore.

Urbanization was closely tied to industrialization as cities developed adjacent to sources of cheap energy, based first on water power and then on coal, and at sites where rivers, lakes, or canals permitted the assembly and dispersal of bulky raw materials and finished products, a transportation pattern later reinforced by the railroads (Borchert, 1967; Ward, 1971). So close was the relationship between industrial production and urbanization that in a review of the nineteenth-century American city, Goheen noted how "industrialization is almost synonymous with the growth of the modern city" (Goheen, 1974). This assessment was shared by nineteenth-century commentators such as Frederick Engels: "Industry and commerce attain their highest stage of development in the big towns, so that it is here that the effects of industrialisation on the wage earners can be most clearly seen" (Engels, 1958:29).

The nineteenth-century industrial city suggested an entirely new order, what one English writer in 1840 described as "a system of life constructed on a wholly new principle'' (Briggs, 1965:12). In Britain and the United States, two industrial cities in particular—Manchester in the 1840s and Chicago in the 1890s—became the epitome of the new age; both of them were also the inspiration for important schools of social theory which attempted to understand the phenomenon of the industrial city in its societal context.

Manchester and Chicago: Views of the New Industrial City

Manchester was the shock city of England in the 1840s, a city that was utterly incomprehensible by earlier standards of urban life; it presented an intellectual challenge to the observer. In *Coningsby* (1844), a novel by Benjamin Disraeli (later to be British Prime Minister), the hero is sent to ponder several days on ''the comprehension of Manchester,'' a task which takes him to ''a new world, pregnant with new ideas and suggestive of new trains of thought and feeling . . . concerning this unprecedented partnership between capital and science'' (Marcus, 1974:43). Other travellers, such as de Tocqueville, saw Manchester as a moral challenge, the coupling of the highest levels of human achievement with the lowest levels of barbarism: ''From this filthy sewer pure gold flows. Here humanity attains its most complete development and its most brutish; here civilization works its miracles, and civilized man is turned back almost into a savage'' (Marcus, 1974:66). For Engels, who wrote perhaps the most celebrated analysis of Manchester in the 1840s, the city provided both an intellectual and a moral challenge. For Engels analysis had also to imply change. The exploitation of the wage laborer was so intolerable that it contained the seeds of its own transcendence, for the more miserable the lot of the worker, the more certain was the working-class insurrection, and so ''the revolution *must* come,'' perhaps with the anticipated trade crisis of 1848, certainly not later than the next predicted economic downturn in 1852 or 1853 (Engels, 1958:335). ''The imminence of this collapse may be foretold with the certainty of the laws of mathematics or mechanics'' (Engels, 1958:26).

Manchester could scarcely have provided a more complete laboratory for the interpretation of industrial capitalism. Its growth was wholly a product of the industrial era. The cotton industry took root in the 1770s, and by the late 1780s the town had a population of 40,000. Just over 50 years later Engels claimed 400,000 inhabitants in the continuous built-up area, two-thirds of them manual workers. A dispassionate and purely calculating view on public life reached its perfection with the Manchester merchants; they appeared as the personification of economic man, as ''a walking political economy'' (Marcus, 1974:234). Moreover, within the city an archaic form of administration offered negligible constraints to the excesses of free-market processes. The first borough council did not meet until 1838, and it was some years before significant planning and regulation of development occurred and health and sanitation bylaws were enforced.

How typical was Manchester of the industrial city? Asa Briggs, a historian of the Victorian city, is skeptical: ''Manchester was the shock city of the industrial revolution, but it was not typical. Its real interest lies in its individuality'' (Briggs, 1965:113). Nor were the separate effects of the market and industrial technology in the new urban society adequately distinguished in the historical record. Was the plight of the industrial worker and the form of the industrial city only a product of market competition between merchants, or was it also a byproduct of new forms of technology requiring large sources of labor and economies of scale? Engels commonly, and surprisingly, seems to imply the latter, as for example in his introduction to the Manchester region where "can be seen most clearly the degradation into which the worker sinks owing to the introduction of steam power, machinery and the division of labor" (Engels, 1958:50). Upon this point there seems to have been a matter of permanent disagreement between Engels and Marx, as Engels continued to argue in other writings that a strict division of labor and thereby a major source of worker alienation was a necessary product of modern technology, independent of the market system (Giddens, 1973:90).

Whatever the resolution of these controversies concerning the work experience, there can be little doubt that Manchester in the 1840s represented a striking approximation to an industrial landscape constructed by rational economic men each favoring his own best interest. Fifty years later, on the other side of the Atlantic, similar perceptions were expressed of Chicago—a young, brash, industrial city—which received international attention as a result of its successful World Exhibition in 1893. The assessments of Chicago were remarkably similar to those of Manchester: a sense of awe at the spectacular scale of growth, perceptions of a precedent-making city representing an entirely new set of circumstances—judgments alternately impressed by technical progress and critical of the attendant social costs. Julian Ralph, an American writer, commented that "those who go clear-minded, expecting to see a great city, will find one different from that which any precedent has led them to look for" (Briggs, 1965:51). Rudyard Kipling was characteristically terse, observing that having once seen Chicago he "urgently desired never to see it again" (Ibid).

A few months before the opening of the World Exhibition, the University of Chicago was founded. One of many innovations befitting an institution whose declared goal was to challenge the supremacy of the Yankee intellectual establishment in New England was the formation of the first sociology department in the United States (Faris, 1970). In 1916 Robert Park and Ernest Burgess joined the department, and for the next 20 years at least the University of Chicago dominated North American sociology. From its inception in 1905 until 1936, the *American Journal of Sociology*, the premier journal in the discipline, was edited by a member of the Chicago department; from 1923 to 1934 all but four of the annual presidents of the American Sociological Society were current faculty or former students. The dominance of the Chicago department was important for two reasons. First, its best-known and most prolific studies were in the area of urban sociology; second, for these studies Chicago was invariably the field laboratory. As a result, Chicago, a young, rapidly growing, industrial city, assumed a theoretical primacy in North American urban research. It came to represent the norm in North American urbanization. Urban theory, such as it was, was heavily influenced by the city's urban form; for example, as we shall see, all three classical models of urban land use were developed on the basis of field research in Chicago.

Industrial Chicago was scarcely less governed by market principles than had been Manchester in the 1840s. The caricature of Manchester's business elite as "a walking political economy" reappeared in the Chicago school's identification of the "pecuniary nexus," monetary relations, as the characteristic social relationship of the industrial city

(Wirth, 1964). Like Engels, Park saw economic competition as a dominant factor in urban life, though his concern was not with competition between industrialists but with competitive bidding for the use of urban land; in this respect the Chicago sociologists applied the findings of early neoclassical land economists like Hurd and Haig who wrote on urban land use at the beginning of the twentieth century. Like the radical writers, Park regarded this competition as potentially if not inherently dehumanizing, and sharing with them an admiration of Charles Darwin's evolutionary principles, he labelled the competitive relations as ecological, referring to a biotic level of society where primitive forces led to conflict, both economic and on occasions physical, and so to a hierarchy of dominants and subordinates among social groups in the city (Park, 1936).

Urban Land Use: The Surviving Heritage of Manchester and Chicago

Modern conceptualizations of the city continue to be heavily influenced by the traditions represented by Engels and Park. David Harvey, for example, considers them to be authoritative figures representing two divergent views of the city that remain relevant today, adding (from his own radical perspective) that "it seems a pity that contemporary geographers have looked to Burgess and Park rather than to Engels for their inspiration" (Harvey, 1973:133). Indeed there are important lines of continuity between these early authors and contemporary formulations of the city. In the radical tradition, the texts of Marx and Engels are still treated as authoritative, while the human ecological tradition initiated by Park and Burgess continues to be a source of inspiration for urban geographers (Entrikin, 1980; Jackson and Smith, 1981).

So, too, recent land use theories by land economists have grown out of the early formulations of Haig and Hurd. For example William Alonso's theory of land value, which we shall examine shortly, showed marked continuity and conformity with much earlier writers on the industrial city (Alcaly, 1976; Goldberg, 1970). In 1903, from observations of the industrial city of his day, the land economist Hurd generalized the role of physical accessibility in generating a land value surface, summarized in his remark that "value depends on nearness." Twenty years later it was industrial Chicago that provided the laboratory for the Burgess concentric model of urban land use. In many respects Alonso drew together Hurd's notions on the costs of distance to consumers with the Burgess model of concentric land use. Inasmuch as these authors were writing 40–60 years earlier, Alonso was providing in the 1960s a retrospective explanatory model of the industrial city. In a review of the new urban economics of the 1970s, Richardson concludes that these studies have not fundamentally challenged many of the basic assumptions of older approaches following Haig, Hurd, and Von Thünen, and indeed show a continuity that "betrays their neoclassical origins" (Richardson, 1976; for a radical critique, see Roweis and Scott, 1976).

To what extent are the precedents of nineteenth-century Manchester or early-twentieth-century Chicago, youthful and rapidly growing centers of industrial production, adequate prototypes for understanding the late twentieth-century city in North America or Western Europe? Let us recall some of the features of the early industrial city. It was a city dominated by its downtown core and, in an era before the widespread ownership of motor cars, the question of accessibility was critical and the friction of distance was severe. Second, industry was frequently the dominant land use; in Victorian Toronto, ''industry was able to demand almost any land in the city. Such was its bidding power, and such was the utility which manufacturing gave to the land'' (Goheen, 1970:11). Manufacturing and goods handling were concentrated around the central business district in an industrial zone, which included port facilities and railyards, leading to high levels of air and noise pollution and heavy traffic in the inner city districts. As both Engels and Burgess noted, more affluent households took advantage of such transportation as existed to live a mile or two beyond the manufacturing zone, particularly after the development of the electric streetcar in 1888.

On a political level the early industrial city practiced either a laissez faire administration, which acknowledged the undisputed authority of business interests, or else merged imperceptibly with those interests. In the Chicago of the 1920s, the realm of ''social politics,'' the development of the welfare state at the municipal scale, was just beginning (Zorbaugh, 1929), while such policies of government intervention as active planning, including a city or regional plan, were spoken of but rarely secured. In short, the state and the political process scarcely warranted separate attention in models of urban land use, and political considerations were conspicuously absent from their formulation. So, too, there was little indication of plural values in land use decision making, for the popular mood promoted growth as an expression of progress, because growth meant full production and full employment and the appreciation of existing land values. A set of sociocultural values tied around work, growth, and progress was largely compatible with the notion of rational, economic man, which is such a feature of models of urban land use.

These then were the historical contexts of attempts to understand the built environment of the industrial city. In the following sections we shall look more carefully at the content of these models which have provided the orthodox framework around which to organize an understanding of the land use patterns of the late-twentieth-century city.

Urban Land Use Analysis

Some Basic Assumptions

Land use analysis has continuously emphasized the importance of distance and space relationships in arranging the distribution of land use types in the city. This theme has been asserted consecutively by the human ecology of the interwar years (Park, 1936), the urban geography of the 1960s (Berry and Horton, 1970), and the new urban economics of the 1970s (Anas and Dendrinos, 1976). This research has drawn much of its theoretical inspiration from two early statements of spatial structure at the regional scale, Von Thünen's nineteenth-century theory of the location of agricultural land use zones (Hall, 1966) and Christaller's central-place theory developed in the early 1930s (Christaller, 1966).

Both of these theories envisaged a dramatically simplified stage and actors. Both conceived of the environment as a flat, unbounded plain of unvarying fertility, with transportation unimpeded in all directions—the so-called isotropic plain. The actors were men and women of uniform taste and rationality, eager to minimize distance in their transactions, for distance was equated with cost. These rational men were arranged at a uniform density across the isotropic plain in Christaller's original conceptualization. In the introduction to his influential monograph *Location and Land Use,* William Alonso does not conceal the simplification of man and environment required in such theorizing:

> From this wealth of subject matter only a pallid skeleton will emerge. Both the Puerto Rican and Madison Avenue advertising man will be reduced to that uninteresting individual, economic man . . . we shall assume that the city sits on a featureless plain . . . what it does not have are such features as hills, low land, beautiful views, social cachet, or pleasant breezes. These are undoubtedly important, but no way has been found to incorporate them into the type of theory that will be presented (Alonso, 1965:1, 17).

These are controversial simplifications subject to empirical questioning, but their spirit has been the common starting point in independent discussions of the distribution of land use types within the city.

The initial assumptions concerning urban man and the urban environment are accompanied by a series of other simplifying assumptions, summarized by Richardson (1976). These include a monocentric city, marked land use segregation with downtown employment and concentric residential rings, uniform transportation access throughout the metropolis, uninterrupted land value and population density gradients falling off from a peak in the central business district (CBD), minimal planning intrusion, and a dependence on basic market processes of supply and demand to generate the land use patterns with all the built-in assumptions these concepts imply, including perfect information and consumer sovereignty in the marketplace. From our earlier discussion, at least some of these assumptions seem to be reasonable approximations of actual conditions in the industrial city. However, to what extent do they remain appropriate today?

Accessibility and Land Values

The roles of relative and absolute location have long been regarded as key factors in molding a local geography, as illustrated in such traditional geographic concepts as site and situation or access and accessibility. In central place theory Christaller deduced a stable form for a settlement pattern based in part on the differential access demanded by consumers to various urban goods and services. Similarly, within the city land value gradients have been identified as providing an equilibrium solution to the competition of varied users for a central location and optimal access to citywide consumers.

Competitive bidding for land by entrepreneurs is in part a bidding for proximity to consumers. It is argued that those enterprises that require a metropolitan market to support a specialized or high-order good will prefer a location at the point of minimum aggregate travel for their citywide consumers. These enterprises should bid for a downtown location that, with spatially centralized transportation services, represents such a point of maximum convenience. Christaller's assumption of consumer distance minimization was anticipated in Hurd's famous summary statement of urban land economics: ''Since value depends on economic rent, and rent on location, and location on convenience, and convenience on nearness, we may eliminate the intermediate steps and say that value depends on nearness'' (Hurd, 1903:13). The friction of distance and competitive bidding together "shake down" a distinctive land value gradient and associated set of land uses. As Carter (1972) has noted, this argument has become so much the orthodoxy in urban land economics that it has been raised to an economic dogma expressed in the maxim of the highest and best use for a parcel of land: "In summary one might say that the structure of the city is determined through the dollar evaluation of the importance of convenience" (Ratcliff, 1949:375).

The point of maximum convenience is the point of maximum access, and as long as transportation networks continue to be centralized, this point should continue to coincide with the central business district. Early studies showed an invariable increase in land values as downtown was approached, corresponding to the increasing accessibility of a central location. In Cleveland a transect along Euclid Avenue in 1927 showed peak land values of $15,000 per foot of frontage in the heart of downtown which declined to $5,000 per foot a mile away, while in New York the land value gradient was even more precipitous, decreasing from $22,000 per foot on Broadway at the peak-value point to less than $3,000 only half a mile distant (Mackenzie, 1933).

More recent examination of land value surfaces in Topeka (Knos, 1962) and Seattle (Seyfried, 1963) suggests that for moderate-sized cities in the United States, the central business district continued to be a major influence on the metropolitan land value surface at least into the 1950s. An isochrone map of Seattle for 1957 indicated the centrality of the CBD within the city, with no district more distant than a 30-minute drive during the rush hour even in this period prior to the construction of major urban freeways, which tended to reinforce the accessibility of the downtown core. This accessibility surface favoring the CBD was transferable to Seattle's land value surface. Using land value data for 1958, transects were taken in the four compass directions fixed on an origin of the peak-value site in downtown Seattle (Seyfried, 1963). Land values dropped off very rapidly at first with distance from the peak-value point and then more gradually. The relationship was well described by a logarithmic function, with a high correlation between land value and distance from the peak-value site, which varied between 0.80 and 0.93 along each of the four transects.

Accessibility is, however, a more complex variable than is often acknowledged. Although optimal access to a metropolitan consumer market might well be critical for retail outlets, this argument is much less convincing for office and certain manufacturing uses, where the general consumer is a much weaker locating force. For these uses it seems as if *general* accessibility to the metropolitan market is less significant than *special* accessibility to particular complementary activities (Richardson, 1971). In other words, offices and some manufacturers are drawn to downtown locations because of intense linkages with other firms who share a central location (Goddard, 1973, 1975). In light of the increasing congestion that is a characteristic of downtown travel and the emergence of suburban shopping centers, it is likely that special accessibility has been a more important factor in the recent development of the central business district than general accessibility. In downtown Detroit, for example, the opening of the prestigious new Renaissance Center in 1977 with its extensive offices and convention space coincided with the closure of Sears Roebuck's last central-city department store. There are obviously different sets of factors favoring the survival of downtown office and hotel space and the demise of retail outlets that cannot be explained by a simple accessibility argument.

Land Value and Land Use

In the city, competition for space theoretically works itself out in the marketplace, with each parcel of land passing to the highest bidder. This sequence of competition and dominance was compared by the human ecologists to the biotic processes of plant ecology: "In a plant community this dominance is ordinarily the result of a struggle among the different species for light . . . the principle of dominance operates in the human as well as in the plant and animal communities . . . the area of dominance in any (urban) community is usually the area of highest land values" (Park, 1936). In this naturalistic and rather mechanistic conception of the development of patterns of urban land use Park saw an application of what he termed "biological economics."

The sensitivity of various land users to access should lead to a distinctively concentric pattern of land use as long as the *ceteris paribus* character of the isotropic plain and other necessary assumptions are upheld. The most central user, the land use dominant in Park's terms, should have the greatest need for proximity to the point of maximum accessibility. But this same desire for proximity to the core will give it a low tolerance for sites that are removed from the core. Consequently, in addition to bidding the highest rent for a central site, its willingness to pay rent will also show a very sharp drop-off with distance from the peak of the land value surface. In a fairly coarse classification of land users, Berry (1959) identified retailing as having the greatest demand for accessibility, followed by industry and commerce, multiple-family housing, single-family housing, and agriculture. At this general scale, we can superimpose the rent-bid curves of the different uses on a graph, where the steepness of each curve shows the necessity to each user of a central location (Figure 2.2). Obviously at each site in the city the user making the highest bid will capture the location, so that assuming well-defined gradations between users in the necessity of a central location, there will emerge a characteristically concentric pattern of land uses around the peak-value point (Figure 2.2).

This extremely simple model describes reasonably well the *general* patterns in actual cities. In Chicago, for example, it provides a plausible description of the land use sequence (Browning, 1964; Berry and Horton, 1970). Streets are ubiquitous in the city, accounting for 25–35 percent of land in all zones, but other uses show more zonal variation. Commercial uses cover more than 25 percent of the downtown area, but this figure decreases to less than 5 percent in the suburbs. Transportation shows a similar gradient with over 20 percent of downtown space but only about 10 percent in the rest of the metropolis. Manufacturing reaches a peak of 10 percent in the inner city and inner suburbs. The major land user, residential, is scarcely present in the central business district, but rapidly expands to 40 percent and more in the suburbs. Both the relative proportions and the locations of the major land uses are similar in other large North American cities; private residences cover 35–40 percent of developed land, commercial

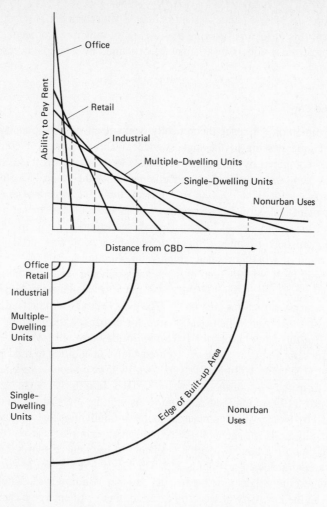

Figure 2.2   Land use and distance from the CBD.

use 3–5 percent, industrial use 4–8 percent, transportation 5–10 percent, public use 15–25 percent, and streets 20–30 percent (Bartholomew, 1955; Niedercorn and Hearle, 1964; Manvel, 1968).

In detail there are of course numerous departures from this simple typology. Through time the land value gradient responds to changing patterns of metropolitan accessibility. With increasing city size the central business district suffers from increasing remoteness and traffic congestion, and even heavy transportation expenditures may mitigate these problems only temporarily; in Los Angeles, for example, new urban expressways rapidly reach saturation level, and peak-hour travel time has doubled or tripled over a 10-year period despite new highway construction (Nelson and Clark, 1976). Outlying business centers and a whole range of topographic, historical, and planning controls guarantee that there will be no smooth gradient to the land value surface.

Perceptual factors also cause departures from the theoretical pattern. High-order specialty stores, for example, which should locate in the central business district, are often found in eccentric sites because their owners feel they are able to draw clientele over longer distances and will therefore make do with satisfactory rather than optimal locations (Leigh, 1966). In this sector of the retail trade at least it is difficult to justify the assumptions of rational behavior by either consumers or entrepreneurs. Consumers do not necessarily patronize the nearest store, and entrepreneurs are commonly guided by neighborhood image rather than by accessibility in selecting a store site. The result is eccentric store location and overlapping store market areas as consumers bypass nearby outlets for preferred but more distant competitors, behavior which clearly falls outside the predictions of Christaller- and Von Thünen-type models.

Population Density Gradients

The land value surface has implications for the density of land use as well as its type. High-cost locations in the downtown core prompt multiple-story development of stores, offices, housing, and even industry; in contrast, cheaper land on the metropolitan edge encourages much more extravagant horizontal development. Turning more specifically to the metropolitan housing market, we pass through a sequence of housing types with distance from downtown, reflecting land value and the wisdom of city planners as reflected in the urban zoning map. A city such as Edmonton, Alberta, which is dominated by a single business core, shows the sequence well (Figure 2.3). High-rise apartments cling primarily to the central area, to be followed by low-rise apartments, houses converted into multiple units, houses with single conversions, and finally single-family dwellings. The site of Edmonton, with its limited relief, simulates quite well the isotropic plain, and there is a fair symmetry of housing densities on each side of the central business district. The major exception is on the south bank of the North Saskatchewan River, where lower densities edge closer to the CBD in response to the area's lower accessibility via bridges to the central area.

Housing densities are of course mirrored by population densities. A distinctive population gradient with a downtown peak and rapid decline with distance outward has been described mathematically by a negative exponential function, which relates population density at any point, P_d, to the density at the core, P_0, the radial distance separating the two points, d, and b, the slope of the density gradient for that city (Clark, 1951):

$$P_d = P_0 e^{-bd}$$

In this relationship, P_d and d are variables; P_0 and b are fixed parameters for each city; and e is a constant, the base of the Napierian logarithms with a value of 2.718. As with the land value gradient, this modelling of population densities is only descriptive at a general level. It assumes, for example, concentric development with symmetrical densities in each radial sector from the CBD, which is unrealistic; in Chicago, for example, there is a continuous increase in sectoral densities as one passes from the north side

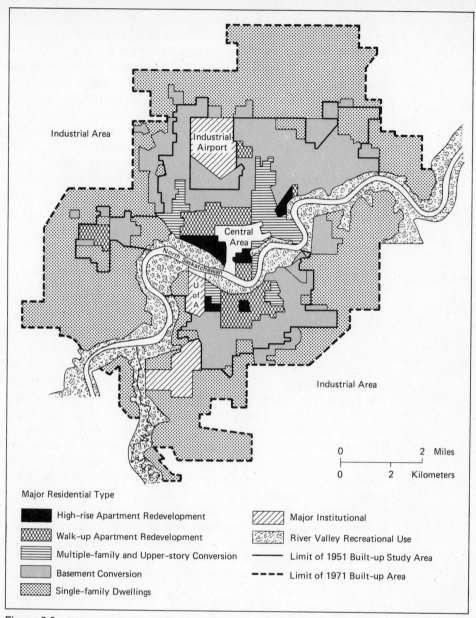

Figure 2.3   Edmonton's housing landscape. (*Source*: L. D. McCann, *Neighbourhoods in Transition*. University of Alberta, Dept. of Geography, Occasional Papers No. 2, 1975, fig. 2.1. Reprinted by permission.)

through the west side to the south side. In addition, the negative exponential rule projects a density peak at the heart of the CBD. In large cities this is never the case, for nonresidential uses preempt space in the downtown core and the resident population is very small. A more complicated mathematical function has been devised by Newling (1969) to describe more faithfully the population density trough at the center.

The central population density trough has become increasingly prevalent in succeeding decades this century, leading to the suggestion that the peak of residential densities is being consecutively displaced outward. Montreal provides a good example of this process, with a continuous decline of central densities through the 1941–1971 censuses (Figure 2.4). By 1971 the peak density had been displaced outward to a zone 3–4 miles from the core. This instability suggests a marked degree of social and land use transition near the core, and as we shall see later this instability has led to a concentration of land use conflict in and around the central business district.

The density gradient for Montreal shows a second important feature through time. Matching the decline of population at the center has been an increase in density elsewhere in the metropolis; beyond $3\frac{1}{2}$ miles from the core, densities have increased since 1961 (Figure 2.4). Clearly this involves not simply new construction on the periphery but also redevelopment or conversion of the existing housing stock. In Edmonton, for example, there has been a marked outward expansion of housing conversions between 1951 and 1971 (Figure 2.5). The location of areas with more than 20 percent converted dwellings has grown outward substantially from several nodes on the edge of the CBD in 1951. Thus in addition to the initial surge of the metropolis into agricultural land, there are secondary waves that add to existing densities through redevelopment, conversion, and the absorption of open spaces such as parks and golf courses within the built-up area.

The result of this process is a tendency toward the growing equalization of population densities throughout the metropolitan area. This is borne out by the continuous flattening of the density exponent, b; in Chicago, b has decreased from -0.917 in 1860

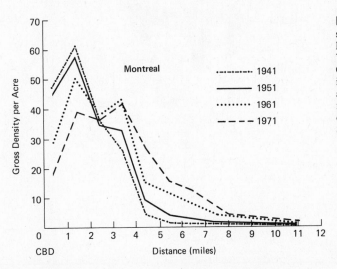

Figure 2.4 Population density and distance from the CBD, Montreal 1941–1971. (*Source:* M. Yeates, *Main Street*. Toronto and Ottawa: Macmillan and the Ministry of State for Urban Affairs and Information Canada, 1975, fig. 3.2. Reprinted by permission of the Minister of Supply and Services Canada.)

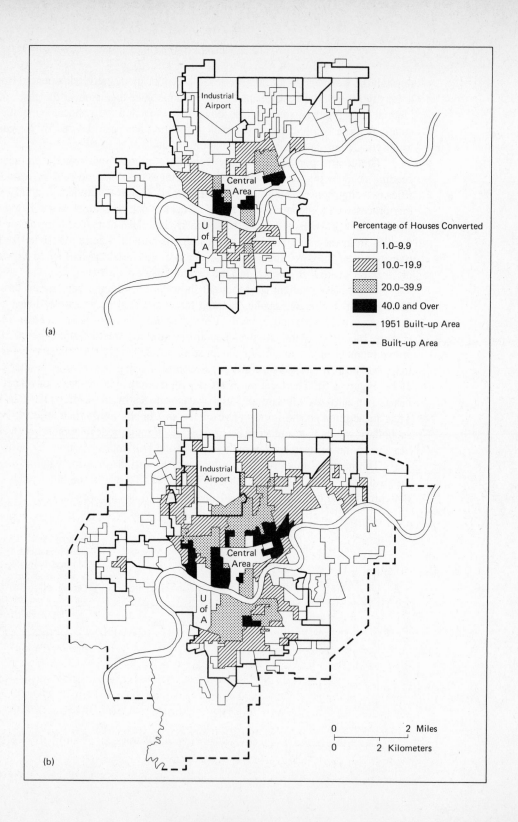

Percentage of Houses Converted

- ☐ 1.0–9.9
- ▨ 10.0–19.9
- ▦ 20.0–39.9
- ■ 40.0 and Over
- —— 1951 Built-up Area
- - - - Built-up Area

(a)

(b)

0   2 Miles
0   2 Kilometers

Figure 2.5   Housing conversions in Edmonton: (a) 1951; (b) 1971. (*Source*: L. D. McCann, *Neighbourhoods in Transition*. University of Alberta, Department of Geography, Occasional Papers No. 2, figs. 3.3 and 3.4. Reprinted by permission.)

to -0.415 in 1900 and to -0.182 in 1950 (Newling, 1966). Newer metropolitan areas with a higher proportion of twentieth-century housing stock, such as Los Angeles, typically have gentler gradients than older, East Coast and European cities with their heavy investment of older housing constructed when the friction of distance was more severe. The automobile has drastically reduced the friction of distance of the compact nineteenth-century city and has permitted more expansive development; in Lewis Mumford's terms, the urban "implosion" of the nineteenth century has been replaced by an urban "explosion" in the twentieth (Mumford, 1961).

There is a further question raised by population density which carries the argument beyond the detection of statistical regularities to the meaning of density for urban dwellers. Although there has been much speculative generalization on the detrimental effects of crowding, the situation is complex, and empirical evidence ambiguous (Wohlwill and Carson, 1972; Gad, 1973). An oft-mentioned factor is differential cross-cultural perception of crowding. In Hong Kong and Japan density rates many times higher than those in the United States are accompanied by substantially lower indices of pathologies and disorders (Lai, 1974). This question will be taken up again in Chapter 10; for now it is sufficient to note that the balance of evidence is far from the point where simple statements may be made about optimal and critical population densities and their relation to social pathologies.

Land Value Theory

An attempt to draw together population density and land values is implicit in Alonso's theory of land rent (Alonso, 1960, 1964). His general model follows Von Thünen, Haig, and Hurd in seeking to relate the intensity of land use to transportation costs, though Alonso is concerned to extend Von Thünen's model of agricultural land use to the spatial structure of the city (Alcaly, 1976). In the urban case he develops an abstract model applicable to both firms and individual households as consumers of space. Land value theory offers an answer to the apparent paradox of lower-income residents occupying expensive inner city land adjacent to the peak values of the central business district while higher-income residents occupy cheaper land near the periphery. His argument is essentially theoretical rather than empirical and shares Christaller's assumptions of an isotropic plain and rational consumers with consistent tastes and preferences.

Alonso argues that in selecting a residential unit, a household is purchasing both a site and a situation. The site can offer either positive or negative utility according to such variables as its size and condition, and the situation is similarly appraised according to its proximity to desired facilities, and particularly proximity to the place of work. Although all consumers would prefer more rather than less space, their discretionary income is limited, so that space must be traded off against other expenses. In the trade-off decision, Alonso focuses attention on the competing claims of space and accessibility to the place of work. Accessibility is held to be more critical to lower-income employees, because with their lower fixed budget the cost of commuting is relatively more burdensome. Consequently, referring back to Figure 2.2, the poor are consumers who will place a high priority on a central location near the downtown work place, and this utility will be translated into a steep rent-bid curve. But this does not of course alter the fact that a single poor household could not outbid a single rich household for the same plot of land. Though the *slope* of their rent-bid curve would be steeper, the *height* of the curve might still fall below that of a more resourceful competitor. The answer is for the poorer household to trade off space for access and to join with other poorer families so that together they can outbid their wealthier rival. By giving up space and accepting high-density living, they are therefore able collectively to outbid the rich for more expensive land near the downtown employment source.

In its style of reasoning, Alonso's land value theory has much in common with the theoretical structures of Christaller and Von Thünen. It requires a landscape devoid of gradients other than the friction of distance and consumers whose utilities rest on very few dimensions (Harris, 1968). Again it seems relevant to the residential patterns of the early industrial city with its extreme friction of distance and is consistent with the observations of Engels in Manchester and Burgess in Chicago. But have more recent trends challenged the theory's validity?

A specific shortcoming is the overdependence on transportation costs and the distance variable, which some would see as a more general fault of geographic research during the 1960s. There is little empirical evidence that the cost of commuting is as central a constraint as the model requires within broad (and it seems still broadening) limits. An examination of the housing market in Bristol, England, an older core-dominated city, queried the role of accessibility as a major trade-off variable in house selection (Ball and Kirwan, 1977). Research with the more specifically behavioral thrust of interviewing decision makers has given substance to this query. From a sample of 380 homebuyers in Toronto who were asked to account for their recent move, 32 percent placed the desire to own a house as their prime motive, 30 percent stated that their previous accommodation was too small, and 11 percent expressed dissatisfaction with their previous neighborhood. Only $2\frac{1}{2}$ percent felt that they had been prompted to move because of their distance from work (Barrett, 1973). Even amongst a poorer population, which according to the theory would be expected to be more sensitive to commuting costs, the critical importance of this variable has not been demonstrated. A citywide study of household moves in Seattle could find no evidence that access to work place was an important intraurban locating factor even in lower-income areas (Boyce, 1969). The conclusion of a Vancouver study was that the preexisting spatial structure of the city was as important as access to work in determining the choice of a residence (Wolforth, 1965). These and other behavioral studies of residential selection raise serious doubts as to the appropriateness of continuing to give too much prominence to the separation of home and work place as the key locating factor. Transportation improvements have greatly extended the geographic range of potential residence, so that factors other than the journey to work increasingly influence home selection.

Changing Land Values: Chicago and Los Angeles

We have noted certain weaknesses in models of urban land use that isolate the role of accessibility for both entrepreneur (to a market) and consumer (to a work place) in forming a spatial equilibrium of concentric land values, land uses, and densities around a downtown core. Congestion has threatened the accessibility advantages of the central business district; increasing downtown office employment seems more bound to the special accessibility of linkages to other compatible firms; the density gradient in the city is flattening out; and the role of the journey-to-work seems a less than complete explanation for the location of different social groups.

To what extent do these inconsistencies reflect small departures from the urbanism of the past, and to what extent do they transcend earlier conceptions of the city? The theoretical basis of the classical models is derived from an industrial metropolis whose retail, employment, and land use distributions were dominated by a strong central business district supported by a highly centralized transportation system. This assumption underlies the reasoning of Hurd, Burgess, Clark, and Alonso; their conceptualization was of the ''imploded'' industrial city of the nineteenth and early twentieth century. To what extent are these conditions general and to what extent are they historically determined, representing one phase alone of urban evolution?

Some clues to the changing face of North American urbanism are offered in an interesting study of the shifting land value surface in Chicago from 1910 to 1960 which reveals a steady erosion of the central business district as anchor for the distribution of metropolitan land values (Yeates, 1965). A multiple regression model incorporating six independent variables was tested against a sample of nearly 500 sites whose land values were known at 10-year intervals from 1910 to 1960. The independent variables measured population density, percentage nonwhite, and four variables incorporating distance from each site to: (1) the central business district, (2) the nearest regional shopping center, (3) the nearest rapid transit line, and (4) the Lake Michigan shore front. Two notable trends appeared in the analysis through time (Table 2.1).

TABLE 2.1 RANKING OF INDEPENDENT VARIABLES OF CHICAGO LAND VALUES, 1910–1960

	1910	1920	1930	1940	1950	1960
Distance from CBD	1	1	3	2	3	3
Distance from regional center	6	4	5	5	6	5
Distance from rapid transit	3	3	2	4	1	6
Distance from Lake Michigan	2	2	1	1	2	2
Population density	4	6	6	6	5	4
Percent nonwhite	5	5	4	3	4	1
R^2 (Explanation level)	77%	65%	37%	34%	24%	18%

Source: Adapted from M. Yeates, ''Some Factors Affecting the Spatial Distribution of Chicago Land Values, 1910–60,'' *Economic Geography* 41 (1965), 55–70, table 4, p. 65. Reprinted by permission.

First, a rearrangement occurred in the ranking of independent variables in terms of their association with the land value surface, and second, there was a continuous and marked reduction in the ability of the model to account for the variation in the map of land values; the multiple coefficient of determination (R^2) dwindled from 0.77 in 1910 to 0.18 in 1960.

This study raises a number of significant challenges to orthodox reasoning about land value and land use patterns. Population density is only significantly related to land value at three of the six time periods, and its generally low association with land value is contrary to the close relationship predicted by Alonso. Access to the rapid transit line converging on center city is predictably important up to 1950, but during the 1950s it fades markedly to last rank in 1960, by which time it is no longer a statistically significant factor. Proximity to the central business district is the leading predictor of land values early in the century, but in more recent decades it has declined to a more moderate role. Thus the two variables describing central city accessibility show only a moderate performance in accounting for current land value gradients. However, explanatory power is not absorbed by decentralized commercial areas, the regional shopping centers, which play an indifferent role as an independent variable throughout the entire time period. Perhaps of most interest to the themes emerging in this book are the changing fortunes of the two variables with direct social implications in Yeates' model. Access to the amenity frontage of Lake Michigan is the most consistent of all six variables in predicting Chicago's land values over the 50-year period. But for the 1960 surface it is eclipsed by the proportion of nonwhite population, which dramatically increased to first rank during the 1950s. That these social variables occupied first and second place in accounting for Chicago land values in 1960 encourages the hypothesis that over the past 20 years gradients of social distance have been preempting physical or cost distance in molding the form of the city. But at the same time the marked decrease of the model's ability to simulate the land value pattern, from 77 percent in 1910 to 18 percent in 1960, indicates the complexity of the contemporary distribution and checks too firm a conclusion.

Yeates' fruitful study presents one further challenge to orthodox Von Thünen-type theory when applied to the city. Orthodox theory presupposes a concentric gradation of land values around the downtown core, and in his initial model Yeates followed this convention by making no sectoral differentiation of his observations. However, in a refinement of his first model, he added a dummy variable to specify the location of his observations in one of five radial sectors converging on the Loop, Chicago's central business district. This modification caused a dramatic improvement in the predictive power of the model, with the multiple coefficient of determination (R^2) increasing from 0.18 to 0.51 for the 1960 land-value surface. It is apparent that a concentric zonal model is an inappropriate assumption for modelling land values that are more effectively described as following a sectoral pattern. The revised model also underscored the demise of the Loop in anchoring the city's land value gradient. By 1960 it was only a dominant force within a radius of 1.5 miles; indeed, in three of the five radial sectors there was a *significant increase* in land values with distance from the Loop.

It is clear that the distribution of metropolitan land values has become far more complex since the 1920s and the beginning of the automobile era. In a series of cross sections of Chicago land values, Hoyt (1933) showed that by the late 1920s the regular decline of land value with distance from the CBD was interrupted by a trough of low values in the inner city and a secondary peak in the inner suburbs (Figure 2.6). As a result, according to his data, distance from the CBD accounted for 85 percent of the variation of land values in 1857 (the best prediction) and 46 percent in the last time period of 1928, the poorest prediction (Mills, 1969)—results fully compatible with Yeates' more detailed analysis. By the mid 1960s distance from the CBD had become an insignificant determinant of residential values in Chicago, though business and commercial uses still showed a significant if decreasing negative relationship with distance (Mills, 1969). More recent data suggest that even for commercial land values "the effect of distance to the CBD is żero" (McDonald, 1981). Indeed, by 1970 retail land values, like residential values, *increased* with distance from the Loop.

In the past 20 years, the residential land value surface has undergone further evolution. A Boston study of residential values showed the inner city trough well established by 1925. By 1940 central values had fallen relative to suburban values, and by 1970 residential values actually had increased with distance from the CBD, an *inversion* of the nineteenth-century gradient (Edel and Sclar, 1975). This trend is confirmed by the average sale price of single-family houses in the city of Los Angeles in 1975 (Figure 2.7). With house prices standardized per square foot, the lowest prices occurred in the innermost single-family dwelling districts south of the downtown area. Prices then rose steadily with distance from the CBD with the principal exception of the northernmost reaches of the San Fernando Valley. Residential prices followed a well-defined sectoral pattern with the most valuable sites following the foothills of the Santa Monica Mountains north and west of Beverly Hills 6–18 miles from the downtown core, where the combination of prestige neighborhoods, view homes, a lower incidence of air pollution, and, in the west, proximity to the ocean create a high level of residential amenity. In contrast

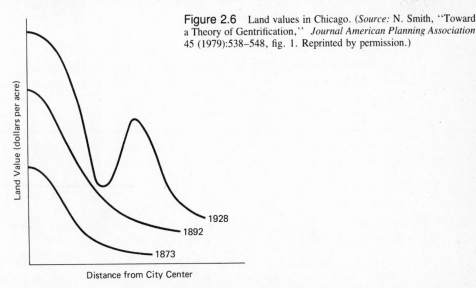

Figure 2.6 Land values in Chicago. (*Source:* N. Smith, "Toward a Theory of Gentrification," *Journal American Planning Association* 45 (1979):538–548, fig. 1. Reprinted by permission.)

Land Value (dollars per acre)

1928

1892

1873

Distance from City Center

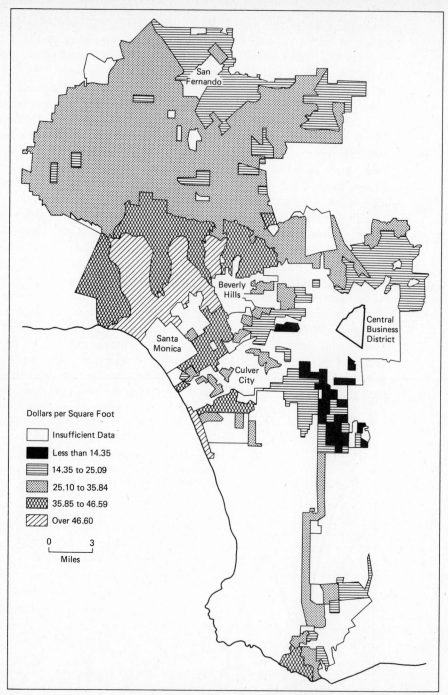

Figure 2.7   Sales prices per square foot for single-family dwellings in Los Angeles, 1975. (*Source*: City of Los Angeles, Community Analysis Bureau. *Housing Price Trends in the City of Los Angeles 1965–1975*, opposite p. 2. Reprinted by permission.)

the lowest prices coincided with the highly segregated minority areas extending 5–9 miles south of the CBD. In Los Angeles, a dispersed automobile-oriented metropolis, the downtown area provides an anchor for residential land values to an even lesser degree than in Chicago and the direction of the relationship between residential values and distance from the CBD is opposite to that predicted. Moreover, the role of amenity and social-distance gradients in influencing recent land values that was noted in Chicago is supported far more decisively by the residential data for Los Angeles. The reduction of the friction of distance is allowing factors of neighborhood amenity and disamenity to play a much larger part in organizing the land value map of the contemporary city.

Contemporary Urbanization Processes

Urbanization of the postindustrial city is characterized by explosion outward—expansive low-density use based on access to the automobile—in contrast to the urban implosion of the compact, high-density industrial city of the nineteenth century with its high friction of distance. Continuous suburbanization has prompted the fear of the coalescence of metropolitan areas and extensive megalopolitan development by the year 2000 and has aroused in response the nongrowth popular movement of the 1970s (Molotch, 1976; Hart, 1976). The coalescence of large cities that had already occurred in Britain by the 1920s is now anticipated on a massive scale in such futuristic scenarios as foresee the emergence of the triple megalopolitan structure of Boswash (Boston-Washington), Chipitts (Chicago-Pittsburgh), and Sansan (San Francisco-San Diego) in the United States, with a projected total population exceeding 150 million by 2000. Boswash, Gottmann's (1961) original megalopolis, already contained over 37 million people in 1970 within a corridor running 600 miles north-south and 50–150 miles east-west. In Canada the population of the Windsor-Quebec City axis is expected to reach between 19 and 27 million by 2001; with the latter, liberal estimate, "A sinuous strip of urban development through south-western Ontario, along the Lake Ontario shore and the St. Lawrence River, is almost complete by the year 2001 to Quebec City" (Yeates, 1975:312).

Rapid suburbanization has led to a marked redistribution of population within the metropolitan region. In England, where decentralization was vigorously promoted by government until the late 1970s, the regional population of South-East England has continued to rise while the population of the London metropolitan area has declined by a million between the 1951 and 1971 census (Hall et al., 1973; Bourne, 1975). In the United States the relative growth of suburban municipalities has been as persistent and, in some instances, almost as dramatic, even in the absence of direct political encouragement (Muller, 1981). In metropolitan areas in all regions of the United States, the suburbs commonly accounted for half the regional population and often for two-thirds by 1970 (Table 2.2). Though decentralization appears to have advanced most rapidly in the older industrial cities of the northeastern manufacturing belt, this is in part a fabrication of more compact political units, and certainly the trend is proceeding apace in every region of the country. During the 1960s the suburban population increased by 140 percent in Atlanta and 130 percent in Seattle; between 1950 and 1970 suburban Detroit grew by nearly 1.3 million while the central city suffered a net loss of one-third of a million.

TABLE 2.2 SUBURBAN POPULATION AS A PERCENTAGE OF METROPOLITAN POPULATION IN SELECTED CITIES, 1950–1970

	1950	1960	1970
Boston	64	71	76
Cleveland	39	51	62
Detroit	39	53	62
St. Louis	49	55	67
Kansas City	35	48	54
New Orleans	13	26	38
Atlanta	35	37	58
Seattle	25	35	57

Source: Adapted from N. Glenn, "Suburbanization in the United States since World War II," pp. 51–78 in L. Masotti and J. Hadden (eds.), *The Urbanization of the Suburbs.* Beverly Hills: Sage, © 1973, p. 58, by permission of the publisher.

The Decentralization of Core Activities

As population has suburbanized so it has been followed by a progression of activities formerly centralized in the downtown core (Figure 2.8). The graph shows the slope of the density gradient for different land uses for a sample of American cities since 1910. The higher the value of the gradient, the more centralized are land uses around the central business district. As the graph indicates, all activities have undergone continuous and apparently accelerating decentralization, although the onset of this process has varied through time for each activity; marked suburbanization of manufacturing and retailing occurred during the 1950s.

The movement of activities seems to have followed, not preceded, the movement of population. In *retailing,* the suburbs initially supplied only low-order goods such as foodstuffs, but since the 1930s and the opening of the early suburban shopping centers, higher-order outlets and notably department stores have decentralized. Such outlets were

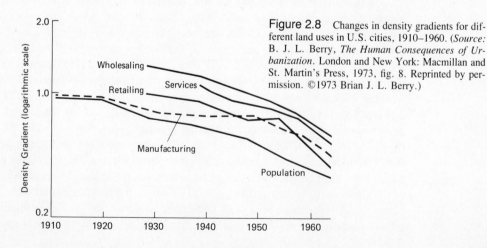

Figure 2.8 Changes in density gradients for different land uses in U.S. cities, 1910–1960. (*Source:* B. J. L. Berry, *The Human Consequences of Urbanization.* London and New York: Macmillan and St. Martin's Press, 1973, fig. 8. Reprinted by permission. ©1973 Brian J. L. Berry.)

typically location leaders in the 5000 new shopping centers opened in the United States between 1963 and 1969 (Dawson, 1974). This development has transformed the market share of center city and suburban retailing (Table 2.3). The central business district lost between 25 and 40 percent of its establishments in cities of over 250,000 from the mid 1950s to late 1960s, while the suburbs gained 30–50 percent. In terms of total sales the CBD of the largest cities has done somewhat better, though its performance still lags far behind that of the suburbs. The result was that by 1972 in a number of the metropolitan areas of the Midwest and Northeast the suburbs had captured 75 percent of regional retail sales: 77 percent in Pittsburgh and St. Louis, 76 percent in Boston and Washington (Muller, 1976a). In Canada and Australia the emergence of large suburban shopping centers did not occur until the 1960s, and in Britain and other European nations this trend was still in the initial stages in the early 1970s (Dawson, 1974).

The causes of the decentralization of *manufacturing* firms are more varied than those of the flight of retailing after its market. The most commonly stated factor is the shortage of appropriate space in the central city for expansion and new construction; other suburban advantages have included improved access on regional and ring freeway systems, tax incentives, and the provision of fully serviced industrial parks in the suburbs (Steed, 1973). The redistribution of manufacturing employment toward the suburbs is evident for all regions in the United States (Table 2.4). Relocation of central-city firms in the suburbs has been tallied for several individual cities: in 1970 there was a migration of 43 St. Louis firms to the suburbs; 68 Chicago firms moved out in 1969–1970, and also over a 2-year period Boston lost 75 companies (Berry and Cohen, 1973). Note, too, the relationship between suburban population growth (Table 2.2) and manufacturing decentralization (Table 2.4): in Atlanta and Seattle rapid suburban growth was accompanied by a marked increase in manufacturing employment, whereas in Boston slow growth was accompanied by a more modest gain in suburban manufacturing. This relationship was explored in an Australian study that showed a short lag effect between suburban growth and an ensuing expansion of manufacturing employment in the Sydney metropolitan area (Logan, 1964).

TABLE 2.3   RETAIL CHANGE IN U.S. CITIES BY CITY SIZE, 1954–1967

	Population of Metropolitan Area (in thousands)			
	250–500	500–1000	1000–3000	3000 +
	Percentage Change in Sales: Current Dollars			
CBD	−6.7	−3.7	8.3	12.1
Central city	61.4	58.4	26.8	34.3
Suburbs	193.1	209.0	175.0	132.2
	Percentage Change in Number of Establishments			
CBD	−37.6	−38.2	−26.9	−26.0
Central city	−8.4	−8.4	−23.7	−26.3
Suburbs	48.0	51.3	30.3	29.9

Source: B. J. L. Berry and Y. Cohen, ''Decentralization of Commerce and Industry: The Restructuring of Metropolitan America,'' pp. 431–455 in L. Masotti and J. Hadden (eds.), *The Urbanization of the Suburbs.* Beverly Hills: Sage, © 1973, p. 443. Reprinted by permission of the publisher.

TABLE 2.4 PERCENTAGE CHANGE OF
MANUFACTURING EMPLOYMENT FOR SELECTED
CITIES, 1958–1967

	Central City	Suburbs
Boston	−11.8	17.0
Cleveland	− 5.3	42.6
Detroit	− 1.8	47.6
St. Louis	−14.9	41.4
Kansas City	0	68.3
New Orleans	12.3	29.2
Atlanta	8.9	86.0
Seattle	−25.7	244.7

Source: B. J. L. Berry and Y. Cohen, "Decentralization of Commerce and Industry: The Restructuring of Metropolitan America," pp. 431–455 in L. Masotti and J. Hadden (eds.), *The Urbanization of the Suburbs.* Beverly Hills: Sage, © 1973, p. 440. Reprinted by permission of the publisher.

Overall the suburbs are now the major location for industrial jobs in the North American city; by 1972 the suburbs contained 53 percent of manufacturing employment in New York, 64 percent in Los Angeles, and 57 percent in Chicago, while in as stereotypically an industrial city as Pittsburgh, 76 percent of industrial jobs were outside the city limits (Muller, 1976a). Outside the clearly defined North American pattern there is some question as to how much of suburban manufacturing is a product of decentralization and how much is the result of new, in situ investment and development. In England, for example, Wood claims that the role of decentralization has been much exaggerated as a source of suburban manufacturing and that the area is in fact also a significant incubator of new firms (Wood, 1974).

Despite the suburban capture of more than half of the manufacturing jobs in the metropolis, much more parity with the central city remains in terms of overall employment patterns. Thus in 1970 the city of New York still contained 64 percent of all metropolitan jobs, and the city of Los Angeles, 46 percent. However, the employment status of many central cities deteriorated markedly during the 1970s, particularly the older cities of the American manufacturing belt. New York City lost no less than 542,000 jobs between 1969 and 1976 (Tabb, 1978). Worse than this, the decline has accelerated: in 1975 the rate of job loss was twice the average for the preceding 7 years, and over this short period almost one-third of the city's manufacturing employment had disappeared.

The central cities have been more successful in retaining and even adding to their *white-collar employment*, prospering from a remarkable boom in downtown office construction since 1965. Often this redevelopment has emerged from the initiative of individual industrial and business leaders with commercial but also symbolic stakes in the downtown core. In Detroit, for example, New Detroit Incorporated was formed after the 1967 riot to restore credibility to the central city; 3 years later under Henry Ford's sponsorship a group of businesspeople and civic leaders created Detroit Renaissance Incorporated with the same objectives (Redstone, 1976). The downtown Renaissance

Center is the first fruit of their enterprise, a 70-story hotel, surrounded by four 39-story office buildings. Similar major developments are underway in all metropolitan cores, including Philadelphia (Market Street East and Franklintown, a huge redevelopment that will cover 22 downtown blocks) and Chicago, where 8.2 million square feet of office space were added to the Loop between 1967 and 1972.

There is some evidence that the hectic rebuilding of the American metropolitan core may be short-lived and its recovery illusory, the last gasp of the expiring CBD (Muller, 1976a). In an industrial city like Detroit, where the economic base of automobiles is in severe recession, even the Renaissance Center has foundered, with reported losses of $100 million in its first four years of operation. In New York's CBD the 12 percent office vacancy rate in 1975 and the continuing erosion of Wall Street, its financial heart, are less than encouraging (Schwartz, 1979). But the post mortem is probably premature in cities with a substantial white collar service sector. Even in New York the vacancy rate in 1975 must be put in the context of an increase of 104 million square feet of office space between 1960 and 1975 in the Manhattan CBD, an *increase* substantially greater than the total office space standing in the entire Chicago metropolitan area (the second-ranking city) in 1975. Outside the United States the CBD shows much greater vitality; for example, in Vancouver, a moderate-sized Canadian metropolis with a 1973 population of 1.1 million, over 7 million square feet of office space were constructed in the central business district between 1969 and 1976; in response to this development city employment in service and public administration categories increased from 24 percent of the labor force in 1951 to 37.5 percent in 1971. The construction boom has been so vigorous that guidelines varying from advice to disincentives to outright prohibition have been introduced in certain cities in Canada, France, and Britain, respectively, to encourage a redirection of new office construction away from the central business district. But despite these directives the trend has been for decentralization to be short-range only; despite government pressures 60 percent of offices leaving central London moved less than 20 miles to inner suburban sites like Croydon, a South London suburb which is expected to contain eventually over 30,000 office employees (Daniels, 1974). A study of the location of Pennsylvania corporate headquarters indicated the same site inertia with 75 percent maintaining the same address between 1950 and 1970; in the Philadelphia metropolitan area, half of all corporate moves had both origins and destinations within the central city (Abler, 1974). Data from Toronto indicate that from 1960–1977, only 12 percent of firms moving into suburban office space originated in the downtown (Code, Morris and Wilder, 1981).

Though office decentralization has undoubtedly occurred, the downtown core is still resilient for a number of reasons, including specific access to banking and other financial services and the desire of city administrations to promote white-collar employment. It is clear that there can be a useful partnership between the civic pride and boosterism of the city fathers and the prestige and symbolic attachment to a downtown skyline for office occupants. The publicity that follows the successful quest for corporate ascendancy or distinctiveness on the downtown skyline provides some tangible return to the heavy investment of construction, and yet clearly the value of a central location is weighed by corporations along dimensions that are not simply economic. The prestige value of conspicuous centrality is illustrated in corporate competition for the skyline (Figure 2.9). Where redevelopment has occurred there is relatively little difficulty in holding office employment downtown. In Philadelphia's CBD the redeveloped Penn Square area has provided a strong magnet for corporate headquarters location, whereas there has been some attrition and suburban movement of headquarters formerly located in peripheral and deteriorating sections of the CBD (Abler, 1974).

The role of boosterism and noneconomic factors is even more apparent in recent public and private investment in civic, cultural, convention, and sporting complexes in and near the CBD and continued public support for central-city universities and hospitals. Pittsburgh, Seattle, New Orleans, and Montreal have all made large capital expenditures for in-town sports stadia since 1970. Rarely is there economic justification for such arenas, but they have nevertheless been promoted with vigor by city administrations as an important symbol of metropolitan ''big-league'' status. Similarly, the redevelopment of the forgotten CBD of metropolitan Los Angeles has been given momentum by an extensive cultural center complex built under the directive of city hall. The suburbanization of such large civic complexes has been limited; new construction such as the Nassau County Coliseum on Long Island is invariably an example of development in situ in response to the growth of a large local market. The abandonment of an in-town sports stadium is perhaps one of the ultimate stages in the potential sequence of demise of the North American central city.

Figure 2.9   Skyline competition between the Canadian chartered banks in central Toronto. From the left are the Bank of Montreal, Toronto Dominion Bank, Imperial Bank of Commerce, and the cleft gold-windowed tower of the Royal Bank.

We can see, then, that the relative status of downtown and suburb is no longer as conceptualized by the classical land use theorists. The American CBD is no longer necessarily the metropolitan anchor of the land value surface; its accessibility is weakened and the central city has lost extensive population, retailing, and manufacturing to the suburbs. At the same time downtown has become more of a symbolic focus in the metropolis, with heavy public interventions in the marketplace in image-setting civic and cultural development and with private investment in hotels and office towers. A result is that in a number of cities the downtown core is evolving away from an image of industrial workhouse and striving toward an image of postindustrial radical chic.

Inner City Revitalization

A smaller and more recent development than suburbanization has been residential changes occurring adjacent to the central business district. By the mid twentieth century a large stock of obsolete structures had accumulated in the inner city, and land began to be recycled in urban renewal and, later, in rehabilitation programs incorporating both public and private housing and redevelopment of the central business district.

The first phase of replacement involved extensive urban renewal and the construction of monolithic blocks of high-rise public housing on the downtown margins of the inner city. From the start this program had mixed effects at best on existing low-income inner city residents. Most were displaced outward through relocation, and in addition to sociopsychological costs, which were recorded in some instances, there tended to be a marked increase in housing costs. One renewal project in Detroit left 57 percent of relocatees with an increase in their monthly outlay for housing, with 37 percent experiencing an increase of over 20 percent; this situation was also common to Chicago and other major cities (Mercer, 1972).

A second phase, which began to be noticed in the late 1960s, has been more unexpected, the so-called return of the middle class to the central city. This process led to the transformation of inner city neighborhoods first in major cities like New York (Greenwich Village), Philadelphia (Society Hill), and Washington (Georgetown) but has more recently spread to smaller urban centers like Seattle (Queen Anne) and St. Paul (Crocus Hill). It has been eagerly publicized by central-city administrations. According to the mayor of St. Paul in early 1977, "Something is happening in our inner cities . . . as a result of the fuel crunch, as a result of a new life style, as a result of housing quality or residential qualities that frankly cannot be matched by new construction . . . there is a very discernible return to the cities." The same month in Baltimore, Mayor Schaefer observed that "people are starting to come back and live here . . . they're beginning to find out there is something alive here. They're coming back for . . . life, pride and activity" (Nichols, 1977). The return to center city has been encouraged by the downtown office boom and in-town institutional expansion, and has drawn a population of mainly childless households of young executives, clerical workers, professionals, and students. But it has also been expedited by new societal definitions of family life. More women are remaining unmarried; the rate of first marriages of single women between the ages of 14 and 44 has dropped 30 percent between 1960 and 1975 in the

United States. More women are entering the labor force; this figure has increased from just over 30 percent to more than 50 percent over the same time period. Reinforcing these trends has been both the increasing instability of marriage, with a tripling of divorce from 1960 to 1975, and a decrease of almost one-half in the birth rate.

The net result has been a new demand for attractive but smaller central-city accommodation. This has been supplied by the construction of luxury high-rise apartments, condominiums, and town houses downtown. Around Philadelphia's renewal area of Franklintown, for example, only 20 percent of 4000 housing units are planned for a lower- or moderate-income market (Redstone, 1976). But particularly with the incentive of government improvement grants, there has also been a movement to the rehabilitation of existing older housing stock and an encroachment into former blue-collar neighborhoods (Hamnett, 1973; Cybriwsky, 1978). Accompanying the residential transition has been a commercial transformation as blighted storefronts have rapidly passed through a retail cycle from junk to art to vogue; the nuance is captured by the status passage of furniture stores from second hand to antique.

In Toronto a transformation of the center-city demographic structure has occurred since 1961 with a large influx of young adults to new apartment districts and an exodus of families to the suburbs (Figure 2.10). Beyond the apartment zone, inner city row housing has been purchased and rehabilitated by a cohort of young professionals and executives (Lorimer and Phillips, 1971; Holdsworth, 1981). The renovation of center city housing is occurring simultaneously in North America, Western Europe, Australia, and South Africa under varied local names, including brownstowning (New York City), whitepainting (Toronto), gentrification (London), and chelseafication (Cape Town). We will consider this development in more detail in Chapters 5 and 8.

The Metropolitan Field and Rural Resurgence

In 1902 the geographer Mackinder already recognized the true breadth of twentieth-century urbanization as he commented that within South-East England ''the Metropolis in its largest meaning includes all the counties for whose inhabitants London is 'Town' '' (Mackinder, 1902:258). The metropolitan field so defined extends beyond the contiguous built-up suburbs to include outlying areas drawn within the employment and cultural orbits of a metropolitan central place. As such the metropolitan field includes rural zones of long-range commuting, part-time farming, recreational use, and summer cottages (Clout, 1974). Evidence from Australia and the northeastern United States indicated that by 1970 the recreational hinterland around major cities extended a modal range of 100–150 miles (Mercer, 1970; Ragatz, 1970). In England, London is now enveloped by a broad zone of rural farming and amenity land where new development is strictly controlled. Its picturesque settlements are more properly ''metropolitan villages'' (Connell, 1974), for they are commonly occupied by London executives; small villages south of London with populations of less than 500 might well contain a badminton club and a Conservative political association (Figure 2.11). The metropolitan orientation of such areas is indicated in their zoning bylaws which are designed to maintain amenity and to check incursion of even light industry, despite the overdependence of local employment on low-paying agricultural work.

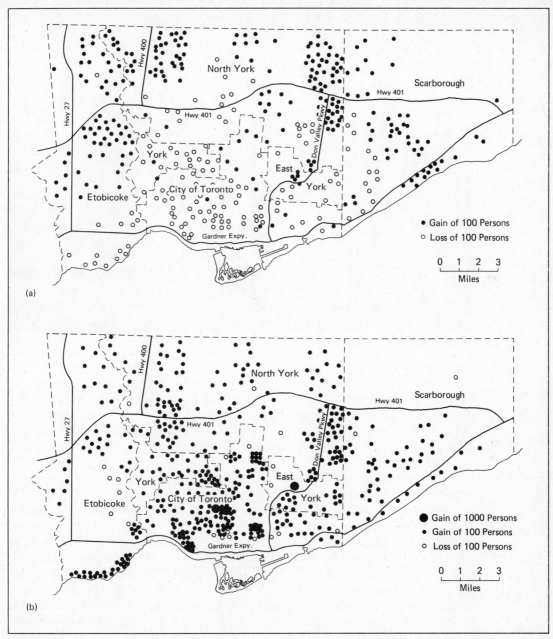

Figure 2.10   Net migration patterns in Toronto, 1961–1966: (a) ages 0–4; (b) ages 15–19. (*Source*: J. W. Simmons, "Net Migration Patterns." Pp. 138–148 in L. S. Bourne et al. (eds.), *The Form of Cities in Central Canada*. Toronto: University of Toronto Press, 1973, figs. 9.1 and 9.2. Reprinted by permission of the Department of Geography, University of Toronto.)

Figure 2.11   Rural gentrification south of London.

Such an inclusive metropolitan region has been termed a *daily urban system,* defined as the daily commuting field around a central city (Berry, 1970). In the United States in 1960 daily urban systems already covered a vast area of the nation and were home to 95 percent of the population. In densely populated regions they were already interlocking and in the sparsely settled southwestern states extended far into the semiarid hinterland.

A continuing increase in vehicle ownership and the vigorous highway programs of the 1960s have permitted further dispersion of metropolitan regions. Indeed, analysis of the 1970 census shows that for the first time this century population decline in a number of rural counties has been arrested and even reversed. In Pennsylvania the zone of net migration gain has broadened from a radius of 5 miles around a major metropolis in 1950 to a zone with a radius of 25 miles by 1970. This trend has continued since 1970 and has been joined by a second, a net migration gain in certain rural counties *beyond* the sphere of daily commuting. Although the first trend is ascribable to expanding waves of metropolitan commuting, the second is not and represents a completely new force in North American population patterns (Zelinsky, 1975; Morrill, 1980). These demographic shifts have been even more dramatic in the Pacific Northwest, for since 1970 there has been a reversal of migration flows that have been operative for at least two generations (Figure 2.12). Migration flows during the 1960s showed net circulation away from the mountains and rural areas and toward the cities and the coast, but this pattern has been substantially modified in the period 1970–1976. In this more recent period, census-

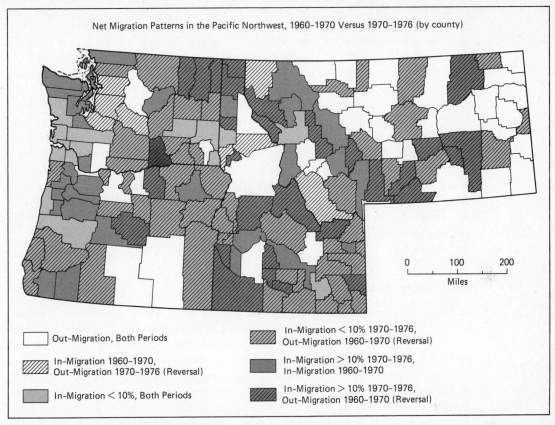

Net Migration Patterns in the Pacific Northwest, 1960–1970 Versus 1970–1976 (by county)

Out-Migration, Both Periods

In-Migration 1960–1970,
Out-Migration 1970–1976 (Reversal)

In-Migration < 10%, Both Periods

In-Migration < 10% 1970–1976,
Out-Migration 1960–1970 (Reversal)

In-Migration > 10% 1970–1976,
In-Migration 1960–1970

In-Migration > 10% 1970–1976,
Out-Migration 1960–1970 (Reversal)

Figure 2.12   Changes in net migration patterns in the Pacific Northwest, 1960–1976. (*Source*: R. Morrill, "What's Behind the Rural Recovery? Population Trends in the Pacific Northwest." Unpublished paper, Department of Geography, University of Washington, 1977. Reprinted by permission.)

defined metropolitan areas have grown by only 4.4 percent and nonmetropolitan areas by 10.9 percent; net migration increases total 1 percent and 7 percent, respectively (Morrill, 1977). In a preliminary analysis of these data Morrill identifies metropolitan spread effects as only a third-order explanatory variable; of more importance in the rural resurgence are the development of nonmetropolitan manufacturing employment and the role of amenity in the form of recreation and retirement centers. The recent growth of nonmetropolitan manufacturing is such that between 1962 and 1978 its share of U.S. manufacturing employment grew from 23.5 percent to 29 percent (Lonsdale and Seyler, 1979). In different nonmetropolitan regions the particular stimulants of growth may vary, and even in one region several diverse reasons commonly underlie in-migration; in a region outside Hartford, Connecticut, growth was associated with metropolitan spread, a high amenity setting, and rural and small town institutional employment (Meyer, 1981).

An examination of a sample of 192 nonmetropolitan counties suggests a modification of Morrill's finding for the United States as a whole (Lamb, 1975, 1977). The general rural pattern is one of heavy net out-migration during the 1950s, smaller loss during the 1960s, and significant net in-migration during the 1970s (Table 2.5, row 1). Partitioning this sample indicates the relative weight of metropolitan spread (row 2), amenity (row 3), and the size of the proximate urban center (row 4) in influencing these changing patterns. During the 1950s the size of the adjacent urban center was most clearly associated with the demographic behavior of counties. However, during the 1960s and 1970s this variable was replaced by the role of amenity and metropolitan spread effects, though by the latter period the friction of distance from a metropolitan area seemed less significant. In terms of the rate of change of net migration, counties adjacent to the smallest towns have been gaining more rapidly. Similarly, since 1970 migration to amenity-rich counties no longer seems to be as constrained by traditional distance effects. Over the country as a whole amenity seems to be in the process of becoming a dominant factor in redirecting net flows of migrants (Roseman and Williams, 1980). If this is indeed the case (and it is also Zelinsky's tentative conclusion), then it is no overstatement that such trends "reflect some deep structural changes in American society" (Zelinsky, 1975).

The Context of National Political Culture

If one set of criticisms of the traditional analysis of urban spatial structure has identified the changing nature of urbanization processes and urban form, then a second weakness would be the neglect of political forces both within states and between states. Although few urbanists have extended orthodox analysis in toto to Third World urbanization, yet even within market economies of the Western hemisphere there are significant national variations of urban spatial structure derived from differences in national policy and the distribution of power within the state.

These variations occur both in the constitutional distribution of power between the several levels of government and also in the relative roles of the public and private sectors

TABLE 2.5 MEAN ANNUAL NET MIGRATION IN 192 NONMETROPOLITAN COUNTIES

	1950–1960	1960–1970	1970–1975
1. Total sample ($n = 192$)	−1.25%	−0.35%	+1.09%
2. Location relative to metropolitan commuting fields			
Inside ($n = 96$)	−0.99	−0.01	+1.45
Outside ($n = 96$)	−1.51	−0.69	+0.74
3. Natural amenity endowment			
Amenity rich ($n = 54$)	−0.61	+0.31	+2.23
Amenity poor ($n = 138$)	−1.50	−0.61	+0.64
4. Population size of nearest nonmetropolitan urban center			
>10,000 ($n = 64$)	−0.50	−0.20	+0.97
2,500 − 9,999 ($n = 64$)	−1.35	−0.64	+0.73
<2,500 ($n = 64$)	−1.90	−0.21	+1.57

Source: R. Lamb, "Intra-Regional Growth in Nonmetropolitan America: Change in the Pattern of Change," paper presented to the Association of American Geographers' meeting in Salt Lake City, 1977, p. 10. Reprinted by permission.

within each state (Bourne, 1975). Canada and Australia, for example, have a political culture that grants considerable discretion to regional levels of government, the provinces, or states, whereas the federal government has more limited jurisdiction. In contrast, in the United States this middle level of jurisdiction has traditionally been subordinate to a strong sense of local municipal autonomy coupled with strong federal influence. In Britain centralized national government has been uppermost, whereas local jurisdiction has trailed behind. The second dimension in the distribution of power, the public–private relationship, ranges from the mixed economies of Britain and Sweden to that of the United States with its greater commitment to free enterprise and a market economy with more limited regulations. These variations in political culture make their own contribution in introducing national modifications to any general model of urban structure.

Canadian-U.S. Urban Differences

It has become common to speak of the North American city continentally as if there were no variations north and south of the forty-ninth parallel. Yet there are differences of urban form even between nations as similar as the United States and Canada (Mercer, 1979). A convenient comparison is provided by the cities of Seattle (1970, 1.4 million) and Vancouver (1973, 1.1 million), particularly as their downtown cores are less than 150 miles apart; a more controversial comparison of Toronto and Detroit is provided by Bunge and Bordessa (1975). Both Seattle and Vancouver owe their emergence in the late nineteenth century to the lumber industry and to their selection as terminal ports of transcontinental railways. Seattle is the terminus of three transcontinental rail lines and Vancouver of two (Andrus et al., 1976; Hardwick, 1974).

But despite common origins there are important differences. Seattle is more a product of the American ideology of privatism, providing a laissez faire umbrella to dispersed individual enterprise. Vancouver, in contrast, has known more centralized corporate action since its inception in 1886 when a huge land grant of over 5000 acres of prime real estate to the Canadian Pacific Railway brought a major corporate presence to the city. Today privatism is reflected in the 46 separate municipalities of the Seattle region, where overall planning direction has never been strong. Greater Vancouver consists of only 14 municipalities and has an influential regional planning body. Its history of urban planning extends back to the laying out of New Westminster by British military engineers and later to Bartholomew's comprehensive plan of 1929; the present morphology of the city in large measure represents the sequential infilling of Bartholomew's blueprint. This tradition of centralized planning has continued in the shape of closely enforced zoning bylaws and an edict by the provincial government in 1973 controlling the conversion of agricultural land to urban uses in the suburbs.

Seattle, in contrast, with less regulated private enterprise has created a more dispersed urban landscape. A freeway system was built that hastened decentralization and encouraged urban sprawl, whereas in the city of Vancouver freeways were rejected, the city in effect choosing high density over sprawl. The resultant downtown landscapes of the two cities show considerable differences. Vancouver's central business district has remained vigorous in both the retail and office sectors. Two new department stores and several underground shopping malls have been opened since 1970, whereas in Seattle apart from some government construction, downtown investment has been more sluggish. A second major difference is provided by the inner city ring. In Vancouver expanding white-collar employment downtown has led to the development of several fashionable inner city neighborhoods with highly inflated housing markets. The extensive private redevelopment of in-town high-rise and walk-up rental apartments, and luxury condominiums and townhouses contrasts with the more limited private investment in inner city Seattle, which still contains an extensive zone of deterioration, and where inner city revitalization began after it was already well established in Vancouver. Indeed, Canadian developers were among the first to venture reinvestment capital to Seattle's inner neighborhoods.

The ethnic, and particularly racial, component of the American city has up to the present distinguished it markedly from other less ethnically diverse Western nations, though it is possible this distinction may lessen in the future. Associated with the racial variable is the location of public housing (Table 2.6). In Canada, and to an even greater extent in Britain where local autonomy is weaker, suburban resistance to public housing is more easily overcome. But in the United States stronger local jurisdictions have often vetoed low-income housing so that it is more commonly concentrated in existing minority-group areas in the inner city ring; in Canada dispersion of publicly assisted units has been possible throughout the metropolis, including the cheaper land of the suburbs.

The level of commitment to government-assisted housing offers another point of international variation. In North America this type accounts for between 4 and 8 percent of the stock, but in Britain the level of local authority housing had reached 30 percent by 1972 and as much as 53 percent in Scotland (Robson, 1975). Because the prototype out-county estates clustered around London were built after 1945, the siting of these large developments has been typically, though not exclusively, on available land on the edge of the city. The suburban local-authority estate is a prominent feature of the British city, and housing tenure is one of its major differentiating variables (Herbert, 1970).

The American ideology of individualism lends itself to the nation's longstanding commitment to the single-family dwelling on its own lot (Duncan, 1981). This commitment takes fiscal expression in low-interest loans for homebuying (though these have

TABLE 2.6 CENTRAL-CITY AND SUBURBAN
PROPORTIONS OF GOVERNMENT-ASSISTED
HOUSING

	Central City	Suburbs
Toronto	29	71
Vancouver	52	48
Seattle	58	42
Atlanta	75	25
Chicago	80	20

Source: J. Mercer, ''National Policy and the Geography of Housing: Canada and the United States,'' unpublished paper, Department of Geography, University of British Columbia, 1976. Reprinted by permission.

been removed by the recessions of the late 1970s) and tax write-offs on mortgage pay-ments, which have in the past aided families in entering the private housing market. In conjunction with a vigorous highway program this has translated into metropolitan de-centralization, a landscape of low-density subdivisions with high levels of homeowner-ship. In contrast, such incentives are more limited in Canada and Britain, and with less enthusiasm for urban freeways, greater promotion of public transport, and tighter controls on urban sprawl, the pressures encourage higher urban densities and weaker pushes toward decentralization.

The net effect of these national variations is that in the United States privilege has largely decentralized, leaving a central city shorn of its traditional metropolitan preem-inence. In other Western nations this process has been retarded. The central city remains sought after commercially and residentially while government-assisted housing beyond the inner city serves to mitigate too extreme a social polarization between central city and suburb.

Conclusion

Metropolitan development since the 1920s and especially since the 1950s has wrought great changes in the involuted, high-density city of the prefreeway era with its single central business district, the anchor of land values. Extensive decentralization and the more recent return to central city fall outside the postulates of traditional land-use model-ling which must undergo considerable revision to encounter the new conditions of the postindustrial city. Indeed, some critics have argued that such modelling is obsolete and cannot make this accommodation, that the new form requires a new theory.

What would be some of the ingredients of such a new theory? Older formulations more appropriate for the industrial city emphasized rational economic man, an isotropic land surface, and the conjunction of distance, accessibility, and economic mechanisms in arranging the spatial structure. This bundle is not obsolete, particularly as the continued survival of older sections of the city is indicative of locational forces operating 30, 50, or 70 years ago. But in terms of new development and contemporary trends, the orthodox model is heavily flawed, as has been frequently illustrated in this chapter. Repeatedly we have seen that the traditional concept of the friction of distance is being eroded as a leading causal variable. Proximity of residence to workplace has not been shown to be the empirical necessity that Alonso postulated; the present growth sectors in the CBD are not necessarily located for reasons of general accessibility as Hurd suggested; it is becoming increasingly difficult to relate land values in the large American city to the distance measures Mackenzie found so useful; and beyond the built-up area, rural re-surgence is no longer as closely associated with an adjacent metropolis as the growth-pole theorists would have anticipated.

Instead, the emerging causal forces appear to be departing from this economic orthodoxy. At one level there is the new tier of values represented by the intervention of government in the marketplace with its social-welfare criteria, and with energy and strategies with national variations. But this is not all. In Chicago in 1960 the two best predictors of urban land values could be described in terms of *social*-distance gradients.

The massive exodus of white families to the suburbs in the 1960s had a similar major component of social distance, just as the more recent return to city center by young adults represents a lifestyle change and a transformed *perception* of in-town living. This is not only true for residents. In England the *Strategic Plan for the South East* could not identify significant locational advantages for manufacturers between center city and suburb, while in the United States Berry and Cohen concluded that "the massive decentralization of industry . . . was dictated more in its locational choices by social factors and prestige locations than by traditional dollars and cents" (Berry and Cohen, 1973:451). The same factors seem to hold in metropolitan office location, where Muller observes that "management perception becomes the key location variable" (Muller, 1976a). With rent and local taxes running to only 10 percent of office expenditures (Manners, 1974), and with labor costs by far the largest item, corporations are more likely to attend to employee and particularly executive well-being in their locational decision making. A study cited by Abler (1974) showed the strong role of quality of life issues in determining a suburban office relocation; indeed the advantage mentioned most frequently was proximity to quality housing for top management!

Thus there is strong and consistent evidence that the forces of social distance and quality of life factors are assuming a new significance in the postindustrial metropolis which is modifying substantially traditional interpretations of urban form. Hurd wrote that value depends on nearness. But current trends are raising new questions. What are the salient values? And along what dimensions is nearness itself now to be measured? We shall return to these questions in later chapters.

Chapter 3

Residential Differentiation in the City

The most pervasive feature of urbanization today, and the principal source of internal dynamics of the nation's daily urban systems, is segregation—of land uses and activity systems, of income groups, family types, and ethnic and racial minorities

(Berry, 1973)

Whereas Chapter 2 examined the macrospatial structure of the city, the patterning of its land uses, and trends in urbanization processes, this chapter will narrow the focus to residential differentiation in the city. We will examine the nineteenth-century origins of residential segregation, its contemporary persistence, and attempts to develop classifications of urban social areas. The emphasis will be on spatial patterns; underlying processes will be examined in later chapters. Much of the inquiry has been conducted by geographers and sociologists working in the subfield of human ecology and making use of objective census data. However, residential areas have a subjective as well as an objective identity, and people's actions and sense of well-being are dependent at least as much on their perceptions of neighborhood as on its objective status (Timms, 1976). Consequently the chapter will conclude with a short discussion of neighborhood as defined by the perceptions of residents. This section will then serve as a transition between our concern with urban spatial structure in Part 1 and our examination of the more subjective or inside view of the city in Part 2.

Identifying Residential Segregation

As we saw in Chapter 2, the preindustrial city was marked by varied degrees of social segregation. In the antebellum cities of Charleston (Radford, 1979) and New Orleans (Lewis, 1976) residential areas were defined by social class, which consisted of an overlapping set of income, status, and racial characteristics. In European and Middle Eastern cities the most pronounced feature of segregation was commonly the Jewish ghetto, but other foreign traders also formed their own urban enclaves, while cultural segregation followed linguistic and religious divisions, most notably in the four religious quarters of Jerusalem, where the adherents of the major religions clustered around their holy sites and ceremonial buildings (Ben-Arieh, 1975).

The Industrial Revolution generated a new set of principles governing the distribution of residential areas. The development of industrial sites at high-access points in and around the central business district and the primitive forms of transportation up to the middle of the nineteenth century encouraged the construction of high-density working-class accommodation near the factories and warehouses, and the slow erosion of higher-status central-city neighborhoods. The steady expansion of the commercial and industrial activities of the urban core—the central place for a rapidly growing urban population—caused pressures for higher-density use of elite areas, either for multiple-family accommodation or else for commercial and industrial sites. The declining amenity of the industrializing and working-class central neighborhoods also encouraged outward movement by wealthier families, a movement which accelerated later in the century with the introduction of the electric streetcar and the development of streetcar suburbs.

Around Boston the suburbs south of the city housed a population of 60,000 in 1870, when travel into the city was by horsecar. The installation of the streetcar allowed an outward movement of middle-class residents of a variety of occupations to occur into a landscape of detached and semidetached family homes, so that by 1900 the population of these streetcar suburbs had risen to 227,000 (Warner, 1962). Beyond the streetcar lines a zone of wealthier commuters took advantage of the commuter rail service; in Philadelphia elite neighborhoods developed in clusters along the ''main line'' railroad stations serving the northwestern suburbs. A similar, if less pronounced, pattern of social redistribution was noted around British industrial cities with the appearance of a streetcar network. Ward (1964) cites the observations of two nineteenth-century commentators in Leeds, made 15 years apart, to emphasize the release of population density made possible by the municipal streetcar service. In 1884 ''there was no tendency, active or passive, for sections of the population to move from the centre to the outskirts. There was no difficulty in obtaining good houses at a short distance from the city centre.'' However, this pattern had been transformed by 1899, when ''there were wide excellent roads and along them for about three and a half miles from the centre of the city, tramways with horse, steam and electric traction offered ready and cheap locomotion; giving to many householders the opportunity of residing away from their shops, offices and factories.''

The changing contexts of urbanization were contributing to a residential resorting of the population; the spatial patterning of social classes that had existed in the preindustrial city was in the process of being inverted, with lower-status households now occupying the inner city and more prosperous households moving toward the periphery.

Class Segregation in Industrial England

One of the first descriptions of residential segregation by social class is usually ascribed to Frederick Engels in his review of housing patterns in Manchester in the 1840s. But Engels was restating a view which had been current for some time, and which was later to be captured by Disraeli's designation of the two nations, the rich and the poor, who occupied the industrial cities of England. In Manchester the two nations were being spoken of as early as the 1780s, and by 1819 a city newspaper reported that "here there seems no sympathy between the upper and lower classes of society" (Briggs, 1965:86). Moreover such designations were rife throughout the nineteenth century. In inner London, William Booth, founder of the Salvation Army, asked, "As there is a darkest Africa is there not also a darkest England?" (Booth, 1890:11).

Engels projected this dichotomous class model onto the residential map of Manchester (Engels, 1958). He carried out an exercise in landscape interpretation, deciphering the town's urban form in order to clarify the social realities lying behind it. He identified four major landscape units: the commercial district at the core, the major radial thoroughfares lined with shops which brought middle-class commuters to work, an inner zone about $1\frac{1}{2}$ miles wide of working-class housing, and an outer zone of middle-class residences. Each inner city district was then itemized in turn, and in each one of them a picture of squalid and oppressive living conditions was portrayed. Although Engels' description of class segregation is not inconsistent with that of other contemporary observers, it is not clear how accurate it may have been or, indeed, how general these conditions were in other cities. Ward (1975) has suggested that the extent of segregation in early Victorian cities remains an open question, though the present balance of evidence suggests more residential mixing than Victorian stereotypes would imply. A detailed analysis of Leeds in the middle decades of the nineteenth century has revealed surprisingly low levels of segregation, with only the poorest and most wealthy households showing evidence of marked concentration at the neighborhood scale (Ward, 1980). Some segregation by place of employment rather than by social class alone seems to have been common, as employees grouped around the place of work, leading to some occupational mixing. Baltimore's industrial areas were located in six districts in 1860, and each cell included a distinctive mix of employees who provided the work force for the local factories (Muller and Groves, 1979). So, too, in Boston at mid century "streets of the well-to-do lay hard by workers' barracks and tenements of the poor; many artisans kept shop and home in the same building or street; and factories, wharves, and offices were but a few blocks from middle-class homes" (Warner, 1962:19). By the end of the century, London exhibited a series of residential zones, and yet heterogeneity remained from house to house in some areas, while vertical mixing where "poverty seems to go by floors" remained common (Booth, 1967:141).

Although there were certainly concentrations of the elite and the destitute in the Victorian city, "far larger areas housed a mixture of lesser professionals, petty proprietors, master craftsmen, journeymen, laborers, and domestic outworkers" (Ward, 1976). In terms of both social areas and the social structure this large and growing segment of the population confused a simple dichotomous model of social class. As Marx himself acknowledged, even in nineteenth-century England, "the stratification of classes does not appear in its pure form. Middle and intermediate strata even here obliterate lines of demarcation everywhere (although incomparably less in rural districts than in the cities)" (Marx, 1967, vol. 3:885). The imprecise categories of the social structure were repeated in a blurring of any simple pattern in the residential structure.

Ethnic Segregation in Industrial North America

The United States, unlike Britain, was a nation of immigrants, so that the residential areas of North American cities were stratified by ethnicity as well as by social class. Between 1820 and 1920, 32 million immigrants entered the United States, a quarter of them in the decade after 1900. Even in 1920 nearly 60 percent of the population of the largest cities were foreign-born or the children of foreign-born. The result was an extraordinary concentration of immigrants in the industrial towns of the American manufacturing belt. In 1890 no less than 127 of the 205 sanitary districts in New York City and Brooklyn had more than 70 percent of their inhabitants of foreign parentage (Ward, 1969).

In Boston, immigrant concentrations developed in the tenements of the North End and West End. In 1905 half the population of the West End was of Russian parentage, and 60 percent of North Enders were of Italian parentage (Figure 3.1); a generation earlier both districts had been dominated by Irish immigrants (Ward, 1968). There was considerable diversity in the semicircle of inner city neighborhoods edging the downtown core. The ethnic districts to the north were essentially stable; to the south the South Cove district was an unstable and more problem-ridden transitional area in the advancing line of warehouses and transportation terminals. Westward the South End was a district of fewer immigrants and single white-collar workers adjacent to the retail section. The ring was completed by the high-status neighborhoods of Beacon Hill and Back Bay, which had resisted business and immigrant encroachment. Each residential area had its own set of employment ties with the functional districts of the business core and existed as semiautonomous cells. The ethnic districts of the North End and West End were both substantial enough and were spared invasion from the expanding CBD, so that they were able to develop the institutional supports of cohesive community life. There was great variety within the inner city ethnic districts, including both poverty and disorganization, but community solidarity and self-help could be located also. As social scientists were to rediscover in the early 1960s, neighborhoods such as the North End and West End could at the same time contain high densities in older structures and yet also offer a positive quality of life to residents through the familiarity and security of tightly woven social networks and community institutions (Jacobs, 1961; Gans, 1962a).

As soon as their numbers passed a certain threshold, each minority settled in variably segregated quarters, in cheap rental districts close to the employment opportunities of the CBD. Segregation in part was voluntary, as immigrants clustered around kin and friendship bonds. The ethnic neighborhood acted as a port of entry, a halfway house between the new land and the old country, permitting a gradual adjustment for immigrants through the maintenance of religious and dietary customs and by shielding them from more extreme forms of culture shock and the handicap of a foreign mother tongue. Upon his arrival in New York City, Marcus Ravage entered the constricted world of the Lower East Side Rumanian community:

> The East Side Ghetto *was* my America, a theater within a theater, as it were. No, it was
> even more circumscribed than that . . . The leap in civilization from Ridge Street to Madison

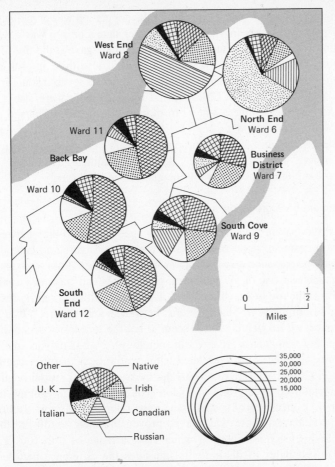

Figure 3.1   Parentage of the population of central Boston, 1905. (*Source*: D. Ward, ''The Emergence of Central Immigrant Ghettoes in American Cities: 1840–1920,'' *Annals, Association of American Geographers* 58 (1968):343–359, fig. 5. Reprinted by permission.)

Street is a much wider one than that between Philadelphia and Seattle . . . As I had come from Vaslui, it was my lot to settle in that odd bit of world which I have referred to as Little Rumania . . . of the broader life and the cleaner air of that vast theater within which this miniature stage was set I was hardly aware (Ravage, 1971:87–89).

The ethnic community had other functions. Besides being a stepping stone to acculturation, it was also a preserve for old-country loyalties and a defense against hostility or discrimination (Boal, 1976).

Large-scale immigration occurred in a series of waves beginning with northwestern Europeans in the 1840s and with a second major wave of southern and eastern Europeans starting in the 1890s. Cressey's (1938) classic study of ethnic succession in Chicago was conducted in a city in which only 21 percent of the population was of native white parents in 1900 and only 28 percent in 1930. By the latter date Chicago was already a city of some 3 million people, and its huge ethnic communities gave it the third largest Polish and Irish urban populations in the world and made it also third in rank among urban concentrations of Swedes, Bohemians, and Jews. In total, seven distinct minorities had more than 100,000 members in Chicago, and by 1930 there were also a quarter of a million blacks from the southern states. In more recent decades Chicago and other industrial cities have continued to bear the strong imprint of ethnic diversity in their residential districts (Figure 3.2). In the past 20 years new waves of Spanish-speaking immigrants, native Indians, and various Asian nationalities have added a new set of ingredients to the pluralism of inner city neighborhoods.

The Measurement of Segregation

The human ecologists in Chicago assessed the spatial relationships between the city's ethnic groups in terms of the ecological processes of concentration, centralization, segregation, invasion, and succession (Park, 1936; Mackenzie, 1968).

Segregation was one of the ecological processes which was most easily measured. Indeed, for Park, the use of statistics in sociology was justified primarily because of their usefulness in describing segregation patterns between social groups: "It is . . . because physical distances so frequently are, or seem to be, the indexes of social distances, that statistics have any significance whatever in sociology . . . it is only as social and psychical facts can be reduced to, or correlated with, spatial facts that they can be measured at all" (Park, 1926:18). During the 1950s the measurement of spatial relations between groups was systemized by a group of sociologists in the human ecology tradition who devised a series of measures of spatial association (Duncan, Cuzzort, Duncan, 1961).

Of these statistics, those which have proven the most useful are the indices of dissimilarity and segregation, both of which have a range of 0 to 100 (Timms, 1965; Peach, 1975). The index of dissimilarity measures the difference between the spatial distribution of diverse groups: for example, the dissimilarity in the residential patterning of lawyers and laborers in a city; the higher the index, the greater the dissimilarity between the two groups in question. The index of segregation assesses the dissimilarity between one group, say the lawyers, and all other occupational groups combined minus the lawyers. It measures the residential separateness of a specified group from the population at large. Unfortunately these indices are not stable with variations in the size of the spatial units for which data are collected; the smaller the spatial units, the easier it is to arrive at a high segregation index. Thus significant segregation may be demonstrated on one scale but not on another. In Belfast the Protestant-Catholic dissimilarity index rose from 50 when the base was the city's 15 wards to 71 with a microscale analysis at the level of more than 3000 street frontages (Poole and Boal, 1973).

Other useful descriptive statistics, such as the mean center and mean distance deviation, measure the spatial focus and the extent of geographical dispersion of social distributions on the map. These and other spatial statistics are discussed more fully in standard texts (King, 1969; Hammond and McCullagh, 1974; Timms, 1965).

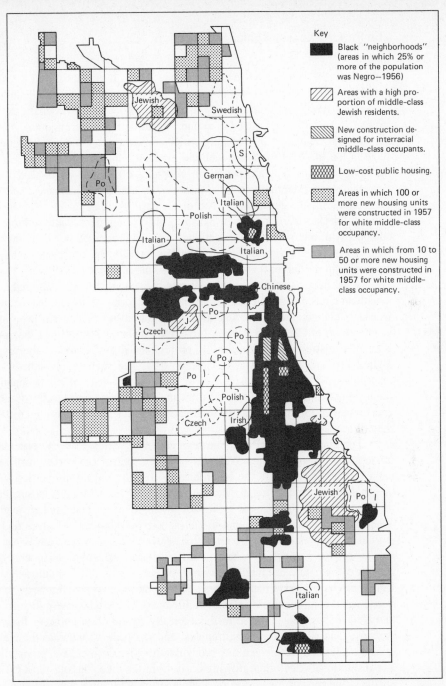

Figure 3.2 Ethnic concentrations in Chicago, 1957. (*Source*: St. Clair Drake and H. Cayton, *Black Metropolis*. New York: Harper & Row, 1962, fig. 21e. Reprinted by permission of Harper & Row. ©1962 by St. Clair Drake and Horace R. Cayton.)

The Persistence of Social Segregation

Indices and spatial statistics have permitted comparable studies to be made of segregation patterns at different periods and in different cities. It is clear that the residential segregation identified in the nineteenth-century industrial city has persisted and may well have intensified, though its form is sometimes subtle. Whereas the occupational basis of social structure is usually emphasized as a source of residential differentiation, it is also apparent that societal cleavages are far more varied, following demographic boundaries, such as stage in the life cycle and sociocultural gradients, including ethnicity and lifestyle. All the divisions that separate people in everyday life might be expected to have some expression in residential patterns. Moreover, as urban size increases, so the threshold is transcended for the separate survival of increasingly idiosyncratic social groups. Urban mass and density permit a new tribalism. This development is attested to by the growing complexity of metropolitan segregation, from a pattern based primarily on socioeconomic status to the added variations derived from stage in the life cycle, ethnicity, and, increasingly in the larger metropolitan centers, the nuances of lifestyle.

A number of studies have measured the extent of *socioeconomic segregation* in American cities using the eight occupational categories of the Bureau of the Census. The Duncans' classic study of occupational segregation in Chicago has been upheld by later examinations of Cleveland (Uyeki, 1964) and Pittsburgh (Wheeler, 1968). All have found a bimodal distribution, with class 1, professionals, and class 8, laborers, showing the highest levels of segregation; in Chicago these had segregation indices of 30 and 35, respectively, and the highest index of dissimilarity (54) of all occupational pairings (Duncan and Duncan, 1955). In contrast the middle-range categories of clerical workers and craftsmen/foremen had low segregation indices and no dissimilarity index higher than 38.

The degree of socioeconomic segregation increases with city size. In a sample of urban areas in England and Wales, over 60 percent of the variation of segregation by class was associated with the logarithm of city size and the proportion of professional and managerial employment (Morgan, 1975). This led Morgan to suggest that an increasing level of high-status white-collar employment precipitates heightened group awareness of social distance and that these sociopsychological factors find their expression in greater residential differentiation. Nevertheless, segregation is also a feature of smaller towns, particularly when the differentiating effects of socioeconomic status are reinforced by ethnic or racial pluralism (Porteous, 1974). The small towns of the American South have always had their well-defined racial quarters. Similarly, in the Canadian north, small communities like Yellowknife or even Hay River have distinctive Old Town and New Town areas. The former is typically the lakeside home of Indian people and perhaps some white old-timers, trappers, and prospectors, whereas the New Town contains the fabric of southern culture brought north—government and private housing, retail and institutional uses often growing away from the lake, the old resource and transport channel, and toward the airport or landing strip, the lifeline with the world upon which contemporary settlement depends (Ostergaard, 1975).

A second broad factor influencing the residential mosaic is *age and family status*. The urban density gradients considered in the previous chapter imply small living units near the downtown core and more expansive houses in the suburbs. The innermost residential zones are not regarded as favorable for bringing up children (Michelson, 1970). Apart from the problems of high-density living, they are high-risk environments both from heavy traffic flows and from an above-average incidence of street crime. In addition, family accommodation is in short supply near the downtown core, and redeveloped apartment complexes often advertise themselves as adult-oriented units, restricting access to families with young children. Consequently families who are able to, leave the central city; a Chicago study showed that familism was a locational factor for 83 percent of suburban migrants (Bell, 1958). There remains an undue representation of poor immigrant and disadvantaged children near the urban core; day-care facilities and elementary schools in this area commonly have a third or more of their children from single-parent households.

The potential extent of life-cycle segregation is illustrated by the age-sex pyramids for four Kansas City census tracts based on the 1960 Census (Figure 3.3). Tract 002 covers the downtown core, tract 009 an inner city neighborhood, tract 020 an inner suburb, and tract 439 a new suburb. The center-city profile shows the marked skew toward elderly males typical of skid-row districts. The inner city tract also has a high proportion of the elderly, but its pyramid is far more balanced, with an additional 15 percent of children less than 10 years old. In the inner suburb the base of the pyramid continues to broaden and its apex to narrow, whereas the new suburb is dominated by young families, with 15 percent of the population less than 5 years old and a high proportion of adults in the 25–39 age range. There is a corresponding lack of young adults aged 15–24 years. This pattern is replicated in miniature within segregated minority communities, though the pattern tends to be somewhat distorted by the fixed location of public housing projects. In the black districts of south Los Angeles, for example, there is a clear concentration of young families in a zone that is peripheral to the original core of ethnic settlement, with a gradient toward smaller households with proximity to the core (Roseman, Christian, Bullamore, 1972).

Data at the census tract level do not always capture more fine-grained segregation patterns. Golant's study of the elderly in Toronto showed ten census tracts with more than 20 percent of residents over 65 years of age (Golant, 1972). But as Golant pointed out, microscale examination would show additional institutional segregation concealed by tract data and those elderly who are in such an institutional setting lead an almost totally age-segregated existence.

Despite the emphasis on an occupational basis for segregation, the 1950 census showed that the more pronounced factor in social differentiation in Chicago was *ethnicity* and not occupation, even when the effects of race were discounted (Duncan and Lieberson, 1959). Despite the myth of the melting pot, there is evidence that Americans are more divided by ethnicity than by class. The most marked of these gradients are racial. The full extent of racial segregation was revealed by Taeuber's remarkable statistics derived from the 1960 census (Taeuber, 1965). In an analysis of 207 American cities—all those with a minimal black population for which city block statistics were available—the median segregation index was 87.8 in 1960. The index ranged from 60.4 in San Jose to an amazing 98.1 in Fort Lauderdale. The mean index had shifted only two percentage

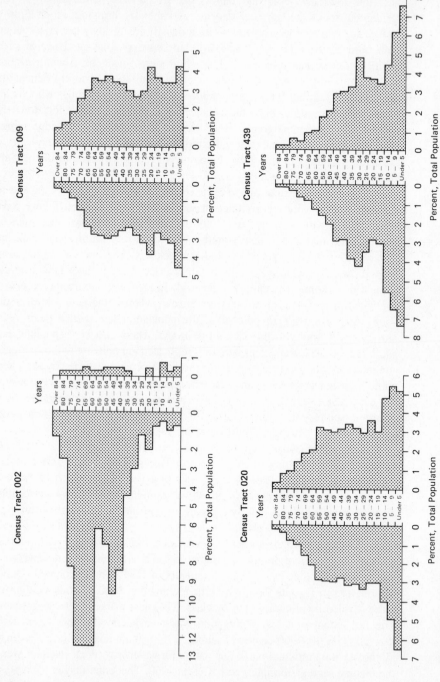

Figure 3.3 Population age structures in Kansas City. (*Source:* M. Coulson, "The Distribution of Population Age Structures in Kansas City," *Annals, Association of American Geographers* 58 (1968):155–176, figs. 3 and 4. Reprinted by permission.)

points over a 20-year period. More recent data for public school enrollment lends no support to the notion that segregation has been decreasing since 1960; in 1971, for example, it was announced that Philadelphia's school system was more segregated than that of the traditionally polarized state of Mississippi. Similarly, the racial map of elementary-school enrollment in Chicago points to an overwhelming level of racial polarity (Figure 3.4). Indeed, it is likely that racial segregation increased in the city during the 1960s (de Vise, 1972). During that decade 17 suburbs registered a decrease in their black population; whereas in 1960 the proportion of blacks living in districts more than 90 percent nonwhite was 66 percent, by 1970 this figure had risen to 78 percent.

While racial polarization in the United States provides an extreme example of sustained minority segregation, it is not unique. Other cultural variables such as language in Montreal or religious status in Belfast have served to maintain high dissimilarity indices between racially homogeneous groups. Ethnic segregation may also be more subtle and its extent revealed only by microscale analysis. Within the apparently homogeneous West Indian community in Britain, segregation is seen to exist by the Caribbean island of origin even at the coarse scale of the ward. It seems as if the smallest differentiation of ethnic status can become translated into a spatial pattern.

Superimposed onto the basic societal cleavages of socioeconomic status, family status, and ethnic status is a further array of attitudinal and behavioral characteristics that may be described as *lifestyle variation*. Each metropolitan area has its neighborhoods of dated respectability and those with an avant garde image, its slums and its ethnic villages. From the census these nuances are not apparent, but they are of marked importance in the daily experience of the urban dweller.

Several categories of lifestyle neighborhood may be identified. There are some which are associated with distinctive leisure activities, such as proximity to a boating marina or arts and cultural centers. Lifestyle differentiation is a particular feature of inner city neighborhoods undergoing middle-class resettlement in the larger metropolitan areas (Winters, 1979). A second category includes districts dominated by a major institution. The so-called youth ghettoes, such as University Hill (Boulder) or Isla Vista (Santa Barbara), which began to receive comment following the campus riots of the late 1960s, are commonly associated with a major state university (Mason, 1972). In smaller campus towns, like Ann Arbor (University of Michigan) or State College (Pennsylvania State University), students may account for one-third of the population, and the university lifestyle makes a firm impress on land use and community ambience. Medical institutions may similarly come to dominate nearby residential districts. A special case of this has occurred as a result of a policy shift that transferred mental health patients from institutional to community care. The closure and cutback of hospital facilities in the United States have led to a flooding of selected neighborhoods with released patients; in San Jose, one downtown district contained as many as 2000 such patients (Wolpert and Wolpert, 1974), while over 1200 discharged psychiatric patients live in Toronto's South Parkdale neighborhood in the vicinity of a large mental health center (Siggins, 1982). Moreover, on account of their age and housing stock the same neighborhoods are similarly suited to supply halfway houses to serve other populations, including the elderly

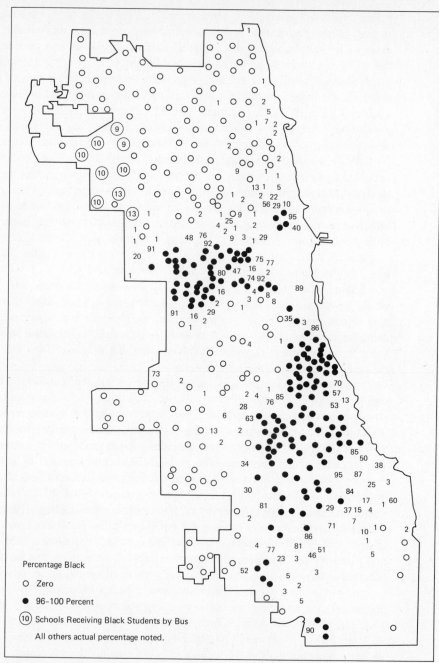

Figure 3.4   Black percentage of public elementary school enrollment in Chicago, 1968. (*Source*: B. J. L. Berry, ''Monitoring Trends, Forecasting Change and Evaluating Goal Achievements: The Ghetto v. Desegregation Issue in Chicago as a Case Study.'' Pp. 196–221 in C. Peach (ed.), *Urban Social Segregation*. London: Longman, 1975, fig. 13.6. Reprinted by permission of Colston Research Society.)

and rehabilitated criminals or drug users. The result is a district with a high proportion of transients and the handicapped; scarcely the milieu for a therapeutic community!

One factor in the present high level of social segregation is the role of government itself. Planning initiatives have commonly been reduced to the zoning map, and the goal of zoning has invariably been to enforce land use and social homogeneity. Its rationale has been the preservation of investment and the maintenance of the quality of life by blocking the encroachment of incompatible and noxious land uses. To the extent that incompatibility threatens investment, land use homogeneity has also been encouraged by financial and other institutions. Only sporadically, and invariably in opposition to market pressures, has government vigorously pursued a housing policy incorporating social mixing. Such policies, such as the American scattered-site public housing program of the late 1960s, have met with marked community resistance (Forman, 1971). In the British new towns, social mixing was co-opted more quietly, with a subsequent relocation by middle-class families to private estates and peripheral villages beyond the original publicly developed housing districts (Heraud, 1968).

The Classification of Social Areas

Classification is often advanced as the first step of the scientific method, and regionalization is but one form of classification, where the classes are spatial units identified by single or multiple criteria (Grigg, 1967). Because regions represent the continuous spatial extent of variables or clusters of variables, they imply the presence of spatial homogeneity or segregation. Thus it is of no surprise that the identification by the human ecologists of urban segregation was accompanied by the more ambitious attempt to generalize segregation patterns into citywide descriptive spatial models.

There are, however, two separate tasks involved in urban regionalization schemes. The first is the development of social areas through the selection of appropriate key variables and a decision concerning the definition of boundary limits for each variable. The second phase asks questions concerning the relative location of social areas in the city as a whole. Much of the controversy that has surrounded the classificatory models of Burgess and Hoyt has been a result of too hasty a progression to the second phase without a full exposition and justification of the diagnostic variables used. In the following section we shall look first at attempts to identify social areas and then at the classical models which aim to describe the metropolitan distribution of these social areas. Finally, more recent multivariate studies will be discussed that not only permit region building, but also provide a sounder base for developing citywide descriptive models.

Morphological Analysis

Geographers have had an abiding interest in analyzing the visible form or morphology of a city in order to arrive at a typology of distinctive urban regions. This emphasis was prominent in texts in urban geography written in the 1940s and 1950s by Griffith Taylor and R. E. Dickinson and seems to be undergoing a contemporary revival (Vance, 1977). Typically, a classification of townscapes begins with the examination of such variables as the age and function of buildings and leads to the identification of such residential categories as Victorian terraces or twentieth-century public housing. But what is frequently missing is the purpose of such a classification—the questions which it raises beyond its own construction.

Following an important methodological statement on the art of morphological analysis by Smailes (1955), work became more rigorous, based less on armchair mapping than on field research, and shifted its former "antiquarian squint" away from obscure urban origins to emphasize more contemporary phases of urban growth. This mapping was particularly popular in Britain, where there were more fastidious attempts at morphological analysis, including a study of a small English town that used 134 different townscape elements (Conzen, 1960), and even more minute classifications based on detailed elements of house style, where types were aggregated using multivariate mathematical techniques (Carter, 1972:251–257).

Morphological analysis seeks to identify distinctive regions in the city according to the functions of tangible land use types. Its method thereby isolates physical areas that may be visibly striking to the outside observer, though the classification may be much less informative in revealing salient social areas, for physical units may well straddle significant social boundaries. The method is essentially a descriptive device applied to particular cases, though like other classificatory schemes, it could be a first step to asking more taxing questions. However, because it emphasizes the architectural rather than the social fabric of the city, its usefulness as a resource for raising interesting questions for the social geographer has so far been limited—though Vance's recent volume teases much more information from the approach than has been derived before.

The Natural Area

An alternative perspective on urban regions emerged from the work of the Chicago School and the students of Robert Park. It is interesting to note that both the style and the spirit of their regional monographs had many affinities with the earlier French School of regional geography under Vidal de la Blache, and indeed the relationship might be pressed further, for the work of Vidal, Brunhes, and other geographers was known and quoted by the Chicago sociologists (Entrikin, 1980). Park's group developed the concept of the natural area, "a geographical area characterized both by a physical individuality and by the cultural characteristics of the people who live in it" (Zorbaugh, 1961).

The natural area was a higher order-concept than the morphological area, for its defining criteria included both physical and cultural features. Physically a natural area was characterized by homogeneous rather than heterogeneous land use types and was usually delimited by prominent barriers such as an industrial zone, park, or transportation arterial. Land use homogeneity was often assessed from the distribution of land use and land rents, and cultural integration was assessed according to class, ethnic, or lifestyle qualities. In this manner the city became a mosaic of well-defined natural areas, and an impressive series of regional monographs described these "atoms of city growth" (Zorbaugh), including Wirth's *The Ghetto* (1928), a study of Chicago's Jewish area, and, in New York, Carolyn Ware's *Greenwich Village* (1935). These studies, many of them conducted under Park's supervision, were regarded as a means of understanding the city objectively, while at the same time not jeopardizing its experienced reality for the sake of an arbitrary conceptual formula. Park's confidence in natural area studies was unbounded: "It is the detailed and local studies of man in his habitat and under the conditions in which he actually lives, that have contributed most to give the social sciences that realistic and objective character which they have assumed in recent years" (Park, 1929).

The strongest validation for the natural area studies was precisely this rich and detailed examination of the texture of urban life. Their empirical depth has rarely been equalled. It took Frederic Thrasher seven years to accumulate his copious case reports, interviews, and statistical records of the 1313 delinquent gangs he identified in Chicago, and Thomas and Znaniecki's exhaustive examination of the immigrant experience in *The Polish Peasant* remains a definitive statement on the social and personality effects following immigration. A classic regional study was Harvey Zorbaugh's *The Gold Coast and the Slum,* which studied two juxtaposed but widely contrasting districts in Chicago's Near North Side. Running parallel with Lake Michigan was the corridor of the Gold Coast, a narrow upper-income enclave containing in the 1920s one-third of the households in the city's *Social Register* "of good family and not employed." Behind it was a world of rooming houses and dilapidated structures "of constant comings and goings, of dull routine and little romance, a world of unsatisfied longings" (Zorbaugh, 1929:8–9). Here, indeed, in Zorbaugh's writings is the personality of place, the urban equivalent of Vidal de la Blache's twin concepts of milieu (setting) and genre de vie (lifestyle). This deftly woven contrast between highlight and shadow was sharpened by agency statistics (Figure 3.5). One square mile on the Gold Coast contained 90 contributors to the city's United Charities in 1920–1921, whereas an adjacent area of the same size to the west contained 460 poverty cases. The transition between these subareas was marked by the arterial of State Street, while the Near North Side itself was clearly defined on three sides by the lake shore and massive nonresidential land uses.

Nevertheless there were also shortcomings in the treatment of natural areas. They were heavily biassed toward the central sections of the city where unambiguous lifestyle and ethnic territories were contained within large areas of industrial and transportation land uses. The monographs were not directed to less locality-based groups or to suburban districts, where a less precise spatial articulation checked the easy demarcation of natural areas. An early criticism (Hatt, 1946) suggested that marked heterogeneity might occur within a natural area, challenging its status as a distinct sociospatial unit and Zorbaugh's claim that "the natural areas of the city are real units." This claim has also been contested by more recent critics, for reexamination of Burgess' map of the 75 community areas in Chicago indicates a certain artificiality in his attempt to keep units of approximately the same area and population, and an arbitrary hand in drawing some boundaries.

A more serious difficulty is determining the importance of the natural area in the experience of neighborhood residents, which tended to be assumed rather than demonstrated. It is likely that most residents have a far more localized view of neighborhood than the natural area, so that for them it may not be a meaningful perceptual unit. Indeed, at least one aspiring community group in Chicago had to rediscover its neighborhood name from an academic atlas! In addition a natural area may not arouse the emotional

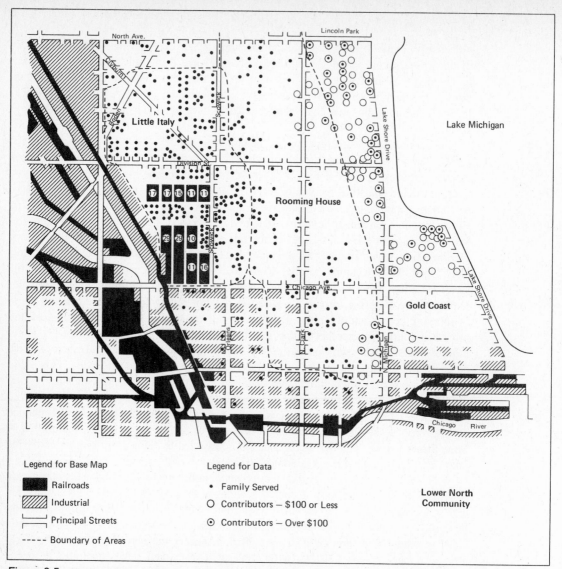

Figure 3.5 The Gold Coast and the Slum, Chicago 1929. The dots and block totals indicate the number of families receiving welfare; open circles show contributors to United Charities. (*Source*: H. Zorbaugh, *The Gold Coast and the Slum*. Chicago: University of Chicago Press, 1929, p. 175. Reprinted by permission. ©1929 by University of Chicago.)

commitment that was often implied in the local monographs, which in their emphasis on internal processes tended to work in closed-system terms and to disregard external forces and contacts. This was an oversimplification, for most neighborhoods assume an identity not only from internal transactions but also from their "foreign relations" with other parts of the city. Local ties are rarely completely binding, and a more realistic portrayal would see community as usually a "limited liability" in the lives of its residents (Suttles, 1972).

The experiential realism of the natural area studies of Zorbaugh, Wirth, and others has been extended in more recent Chicago research with a more social anthropological content (Suttles, 1968; Kornblum, 1974). But the Chicago School also moved in a different theoretical direction. As geographers had earlier built up classificatory schemes of natural regions on the basis of one or a few key indicators, such as climate or landform, so too ecologists have reduced the natural area to one or several diagnostic or key variables. The cost of this transfer was the loss of the distinctively human character of place and the tendency to generate typologies which, though suited to a specific academic purpose, created regions that were often less recognizable as lived places.

The Ecological Area: Simple Approaches

Despite its weaknesses, the natural area did attempt to identify spatial units that were expressions both of physical land use and of social occupancy. Its demarcation was usually in part intuitive and its boundaries often ill-defined. As attempts were made to introduce more rigorous standards for delimiting and classifying social areas, regionalizing procedures became more formal, using diagnostic variables derived from the census or from some other official source describing such characteristics as land value or ethnic status. Interest passed from the personality of places to the classification exercise itself and to the spatial relations of social areas so defined. It is important to note that this implied a remove from the field situation, for in using secondary sources the researcher has distanced himself from the insider's view of place. Although Zorbaugh could claim that natural areas were ''real,'' such an assertion would need to be accompanied by careful caveats in the case of ecological areas. It is something of a controversial point to argue that the ecological area offers more than a working guide for a particular problem; the skeptic might well respond that its reality is not necessarily any firmer than any other construction of the armchair researcher. One of the early uses of an ecological variable to establish social areas, Hatt's (1946) mapping of rental values in a part of central Seattle, did indeed conclude with the comment that such units were no more than an analytical convenience. Later researchers have sometimes been more ambitious in claiming a reality status for their ecological districts.

The single-variable classification has its uses as a preliminary form of regionalization. Key diagnostic variables include measures of economic status, such as land value and occupational type, or social status, such as age or ethnic composition. But these indicators do not necessarily coincide, and a more satisfactory schema would incorporate several variables. An example of such a type was a classification of social areas in Belfast using socioeconomic status and population density (Figure 3.6). Each variable was subdivided at its median, allowing a four-category classification. Such simple approaches to defining ecological areas are satisfactory for specific purposes, but it is unwise to claim a generality for them beyond the purpose for which they were established. For other purposes alternative diagnostic variables will prove more relevant, and as with all classifications no single set of criteria will fit all circumstances. In addition the regionalizing method represents an ad hoc solution to classification and does not have a firm theoretical base. We will see later that social area analysis and factorial ecology set out to meet both these criticisms.

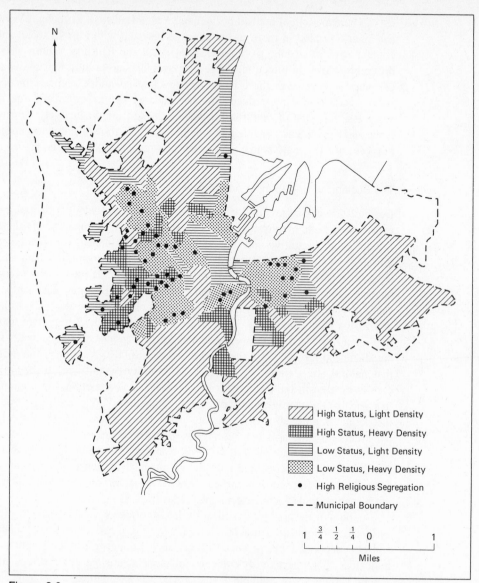

Figure 3.6 Ecological areas of Belfast. (*Source*: E. Jones, *The Social Geography of Belfast*. London: Oxford University Press, 1960, p. 205. Reprinted by permission.)

The Classical Land Use Models

The recognition of segregated social areas and distinct land use zones led to attempts to develop general descriptive models of the city's spatial structure. The two classical interwar models were those of Burgess, who stressed concentric or zonal gradients away from the business core, and Hoyt, who identified radial or sectoral gradients. The later multiple-nuclei model of Harris and Ullman recognized the dispersion of the city into specialized districts and the beginnings of decentralization of the core activities, which challenged irrevocably any simple scheme.

It has been explicit in the orthodox model of urban structure that the ideal city is dominated by a single business and employment center around which range concentric land use zones disrupted only by radial transportation lines which produce an outward bulge in the land use sequence. This pattern was formalized in the famous concentric zone model of urban structure discussed by Ernest Burgess at Chicago in the 1920s. (For extended commentary see Johnston, 1971, or Carter, 1972.) As a result of mapping demographic and behavioral data for a variety of variables in Chicago and other cities— "The students made maps of any data we could find in the city that could be plotted" (Burgess and Bogue, 1967:6)—Burgess arrived inductively at a land use model consisting of five concentric zones around the central business district (Figure 3.7a). Although concentric gradients predominated, there were also sectoral elements, such as the line of residential hotels following the amenity of the lakeshore and the elongated Black Belt, which extended through three zones. However, it was subsequently shown that the concentric arrangement was repeated within the black areas themselves. In New York City, black Harlem showed strong tendencies toward a concentric sequence of social characteristics even in the 1930s when it was still a small district (Table 3.1). The first black settlement around Seventh Avenue and 135th Street had become the business and cultural center of the community by 1930, and there was a clear gradient of demographic and social variables through five zones over a 30-block radius centered on this intersection.

By dint of the sheer number of factors that could be described by a concentric pattern on the map, the Burgess model gained immediate acceptance. But in emphasizing zonal gradients Burgess neglected radial trends along transport arteries, and an early

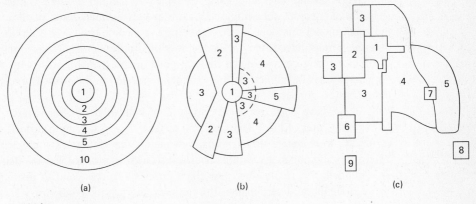

(a)   (b)   (c)

District

1	Central Business District	6	Heavy Manufacturing
2	Wholesale Light Manufacturing	7	Outlying Business District
3	Low-class Residential	8	Residential Suburb
4	Medium-class Residential	9	Industrial Suburb
5	High-class Residential	10	Commuters' Zone

Figure 3.7 Models of urban land use: (a) Burgess' concentric zone model; (b) Hoyt's sectoral model; (c) Harris and Ullman's multiple nuclei model. (*Source*: C. D. Harris and E. Ullman, "The Nature of Cities," *Annals, American Academy of Political and Social Science* 242 (1945):7–17, fig. 5. Reprinted by permission. ©1945 American Academy of Political and Social Science.)

TABLE 3.1   SOME ZONAL CHARACTERISTICS OF BLACK HARLEM, 1930–1934

Zone	Percent under 20 Years	Percent Males over 15 Years, Married	Families on Home Relief, per 1000
1	18	50	709
2	22	56	585
3	25	60	395
4	30	62	311
5	37	64	284

Source: Adapted from E. F. Frazier, "Negro Harlem: An Ecological Study," *American Journal of Sociology* 43 (1937), 72–89, pp. 80, 81, 86. Reprinted by permission of the University of Chicago Press.

criticism of his schema pointed to the juxtapositions of low-income housing strung out beside railroad lines and commercial frontage extended along business thoroughfares. A reorientation toward radial trends emerged in the sectoral land use model (Figure 3.7b), which is usually regarded as competitive with the Burgess scheme, though Hoyt himself seemed to regard them as complementary to each other (Hoyt, 1939). The sectoral model was also developed inductively, as a result of examining rental gradients in a large number of American cities. Hoyt was interested in the location of high-rent neighborhoods and their subsequent movement. Like Burgess he stressed outward expansion of land use types, arguing that high-rent areas are initially tied to the downtown office and retail district but that as the downtown expands in response to overall metropolitan growth, so the elite areas are displaced outward along radial transportation routes taking advantage of high ground and other amenities. The typical residential structure is then one of wedge-shaped class sectors superimposed onto a loosely defined zonal pattern. In contrast to the zonal model this does not leave the higher-income groups in sole occupancy of the outermost ring; indeed, Hoyt's data showed that in few cities did as much as 25 percent of the outer ring consist of the highest-rental areas. British cities, with their extensive peripheral areas of public housing, commonly refute the form that Burgess predicted for the outermost zone.

There have been extensive criticisms of both models. (For reviews see Johnston, 1971, and Carter, 1972.) They are said to lack universality both historically and cross-culturally, to overstate firm land use boundaries that do not exist empirically, to insist upon a false homogeneity within zones and sectors, to produce schema that are altogether too simplistic, to imply overly mechanistic causal forces, and to disregard significant social and cultural determinants. But the very fact that the controversy continues and the debate remains current underlines the immense value of both the zonal and concentric models in an initial examination of urban social areas.

Numerous revisions to the models have been made, the most significant by Harris and Ullman (1945), who suggested a range of factors that would modify both zonal and radial patterns. Their most important argument related to the development of special-purpose districts such as waterfront areas, airports, or medical districts resulting from particular locational needs or external economies. These achieved satellite status and their own localized land use gradients, thus challenging the dominance of the central business district as the city's only focus (Figure 3.7c). So, too, with the continued expansion of the urban area, the absorption of formerly independent settlements or the creation of new foci around regional shopping centers would contribute to a metropolis with multiple nuclei. Amongst other modifications that have added to the realism of the two major models has been the suggestion to incorporate the effects of building cycles and changing transportation technologies (Adams, 1970). As a result of fieldwork in Minneapolis, Adams argued that the size of a zone or sector is dependent on historical booms and depressions in the building industry; the density of settlement, in turn, is related to available modes of transport at the time of construction.

There is no reason to regard the concentric, sectoral, and multiple-nuclei models as incompatible, particularly as all three found in Chicago evidence to support their claims! Recent classificatory approaches to residential land use have permitted some reconciliation of the Burgess-Hoyt controversy. Each schema was developed from different criteria, Burgess using social and demographic variables and Hoyt mapping rent surfaces. The development of multivariate classifications of social areas has permitted the implications of these different criteria to be assessed more fully.

Social Area Analysis

Two of the shortcomings of early ecological classifications of social areas were their dependence on a few key variables and their lack of a theoretical base to justify use of these variables. Shevky and Bell sought to meet both these shortcomings with an elaborate multivariate classification procedure emerging from a theory of social areas which they claimed was developed prior to the method itself. Their concept of the social area implied some points of departure from as well as similarity with the natural area: ''We view a social area as containing persons with similar social positions in the larger society. The social area, however, is not bounded by the geographical frame of reference as is the natural area, nor by implications concerning the degree of interaction between persons in the local community as is the subculture'' (Shevky and Bell, 1955:20). In short, references to place and interaction were jettisoned in their concept of the social area in favor of a typology of characteristics as revealed by the census. The distancing of the researchers from the study area is thereby maintained, though the gain is the claim of rigor and generality: ''This method might be used to compare the social differentiation of one country with another, one region with another, or one city with another'' (Ibid). Social area analysis permits comparative examination of social trends in space between cities and through time.

The method is of interest because its rationale is not simply pragmatic but is alleged to be supported by a theory concerning the relationship between societal processes and urban form. The city is a product of society, and therefore ''the social forms of urban life are to be understood within the context of the changing character of the larger containing society'' (Shevky and Bell, 1955:3). Three underlying themes are identified as characterizing modern society: (1) changes in occupational structure, including increasing specialization and a reduction in the relative proportion of manual employment, (2) family lifestyles and role relationships alternative to the traditional nuclear family, and (3) the growing isolation of ethnic and other lifestyle groups, in part as a result of increasing city size which provides a critical mass for distinctive subcultural groups to form. These themes are operationalized into quantifiable indices for census tracts or smaller enumeration areas and permit a multivariate classification of urban areas to be constructed.

The procedure progresses in three stages. First, the three themes are identified by the constructs of social rank (or economic status), urbanization (or family status), and segregation (or ethnic status). Second, key diagnostic variables are selected from the census to represent each construct. Occupation and education commonly represent economic status, and the level of female fertility, women in the labor force, and the incidence of single-family dwellings represent family status. Ethnic status is assessed from measures of non-Caucasian racial status and ethnic origins outside the traditional white Anglo-Saxon Protestant core areas. Each diagnostic variable is transformed into a numerical index for each census tract. Finally, the indices are aggregated into their distinctive constructs and transferred to the map as a multivariate classification of the spatial units. The detailed procedure for transforming census tract data into a social area typology is involved, though each step is computationally simple; the interested reader is referred to the detailed exposition by Shevky and Bell.

An example of a social-area analysis is shown in Figure 3.8, which is taken from the original San Francisco study using tract data from the 1950 census. Areas are classified according to their position on a 16-category scale incorporating economic status (social rank) and family status (urbanization); in addition each category may be further designated according to its composite segregation level above or below the mean for the whole city for selected minority groups. In this manner a typology of 32 potential social areas is developed. Though the detailed distribution of social areas in the Bay Area is not simple, in general high-economic-status tracts form continuous districts in hill and view locations away from industrial and port facilities; areas of nuclear-family status are displaced away from the urban cores of San Francisco and Oakland; and areas of ethnic status have formed adjacent to the business cores and near industrial waterfront districts.

Social area analysis is a versatile form of urban regionalization, and an inventory by Timms showed its use in over 40 studies of American cities up to 1967, both as a tool for constructing a typology and as a first step in an ecological analysis of such traits as voting behavior or delinquency. The method's wide currency has invited a range of basic criticism. (For a detailed discussion see Timms, 1971.) These cover each stage of the method, including its theoretical underpinning, the extension of the theory to urban form, the adequacy of the diagnostic variables to represent the theoretical themes, and what is seen as an arbitrary computational procedure. Certainly the theoretical structure is flawed. It is, for example, overly dependent on the particular urban perspective of human ecology, and the relationship between the three theoretical themes and the accompanying three constructs is not entirely self-evident. But the niceties of the methodological debate are to some extent superfluous for geographers who are well aware of the inherent problems and limitations of any regionalizing scheme. Even if the constructs and related diagnostic variables are arbitrary, they represent a useful set in describing the North American city. As long as it is remembered that social area units are operational rather than real, there is no reason to reject the conclusion that the method as a classificatory technique "appears to fit the structure of the modern city well" (Timms, 1971:209).

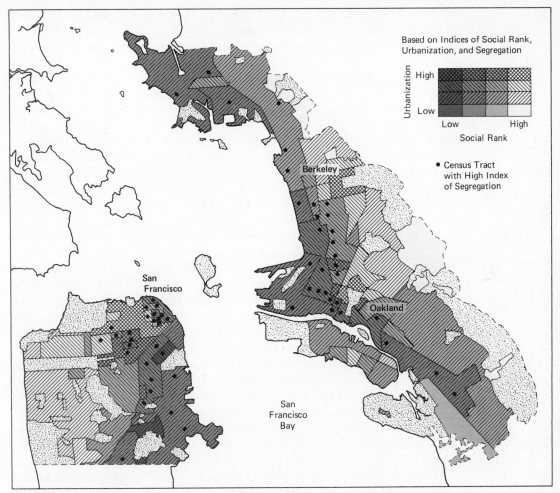

Figure 3.8   Social areas of the San Francisco Bay region, 1950. (*Source*: E. Shevky and W. Bell, *Social Area Analysis*. Stanford: Stanford University Press, 1955, fig. v-14. Reprinted by permission. ©1955 by the Board of Trustees of the Leland Stanford Junior University.)

Factorial Ecology

This conclusion is supported by the evidence of factorial ecology, the aggressive offspring of social area analysis. Since the mid 1960s there has been a profusion of studies by urban geographers and sociologists applying the family of factor analysis techniques, a multivariate statistical method, to the classification of urban census tracts (Rees, 1971; Johnston, 1976a).

Factorial ecology provides a mathematically rigorous method for constructing urban social areas. It constructs a number of more general factors or components that provide an efficient description of a far longer list of diagnostic variables drawn from the census. Each factor can be thought of as a "super variable" representing a highly intercorrelated cluster of diagnostic variables. The result of a factorial ecology is that census tracts can be scored on the higher-order factors, which presents a more general classification than would the use of a few variables. More technically, the family of factor analysis techniques collapses a large data matrix of n observations (census tracts) $\times$ m attributes (census variables) into a simpler matrix of n observations $\times$ f factors. Where before each tract was scored on a variety of individual variables, after factor analysis they are scored on a small number of factors. (For an extended discussion see Murdie, 1969, or Berry and Horton, 1970.) This exercise has some parallels with the collapsing of several diagnostic variables into a single index for each of the three constructs in social area analysis, but there are also two important differences. First, the diagnostic variables need not be limited in number as they are in the Shevky-Bell method; variable selection is still normally confined to the census, but it commonly incorporates over 30 different urban traits. Second, the somewhat arbitrary computational procedure of social area analysis is replaced by complex and formal mathematical operations performed by the computer. In this manner two of the major operational objections to social area analysis would seem to be met.

The factors or components that emerge from a factorial ecology provide a summary of the original data matrix. It is possible to uncover how much of the variance of the data matrix has been absorbed by each of the emergent factors in percentage terms. The meaning of the factors is interpreted on the basis of the diagnostic variables that they have absorbed. A factor incorporating high loadings on such variables as education, income, and occupational type could justifiably be interpreted as a general factor describing social class or socioeconomic status. Of considerable interest in light of Shevky and Bell's theory of social areas is the nature of the three general factors that most commonly emerge in factorial ecology studies of American cities. In order of absorbed variance these are socioeconomic status, family status, and ethnic status. Thus the deductive Shevky-Bell formulation, which identified the same three characteristics as basic to American urbanism, is substantiated on the basis of census data by the inductive method of factorial ecology.

Outside the United States, studies of cities in Canada, Western Europe, Australia, and New Zealand show some variation around the three basic dimensions, reinforcing the argument of Chapter 2 for distinctive national differences in urban structure among Western industrial nations. This is usefully shown in a factorial ecology of metropolitan Vancouver, a study which will also serve to illustrate the method in more detail (Patterson, 1974). Particular attention was paid to methodological questions in this study. From computer tapes of the 1961 Canadian Census, information was derived for 192 variables that were arranged against 1237 enumeration areas, permitting a finer-grained analysis than would have been possible using the 122 census tracts in the metropolitan area. This data matrix of 1237 observations $\times$ 192 variables allowed comprehensive coverage of a metropolis of less than 1 million people in 1961. The variables were transformed to a normal distribution, and factor analysis was carried out. The factor structure that emerged revealed four major independent dimensions which were interpreted according to their loadings on the original variables (Table 3.2). Together these four factors accounted for 40 percent of the variance in the original data matrix. In other words, two-fifths of the

TABLE 3.2 FACTOR LOADINGS FOR SELECTED VARIABLES ON FIRST FOUR FACTORS, VANCOUVER

Variable	Factor 1	Factor 2	Factor 3	Factor 4
7. % 5–9 years	0.86			
20. % 70–74 years	−0.88			
28. % Widowed	−0.88			
36. % Originating UK & Ireland		0.68		−0.51
40. % Originating Italy				0.48
46. % Originating Scandinavia				0.50
48. % Originating C. Europe				0.48
54. % Originating China				0.70
62. % Protestant		0.54		−0.55
63. % Catholic		−0.57		
66. % Language non-English, non-Fr.				0.53
72. % Male completing university		0.88		
89. No. persons per family	0.88			
90. % Population in families	0.81			
93. Average family earnings		0.80		
112. % Families with all children < 15	0.82			
121. % Owned single-family dwellings			0.83	
125. % Dwellings rented			−0.85	
141. Average rooms per dwelling			0.58	
144. % Owned, s-f, worth < $12,000		−0.73		
160. % Population tenants			−0.82	
186. % In managerial occupations		0.79		
	Family Status	Socioec. Status	Housing Status	Ethnic Status
% Explained variance	17.3	12.3	6.3	4.1
% Cumulative	17.3	29.6	35.9	40.0

Source: Adapted from M. Patterson, *The Factorial Urban Ecology of Greater Vancouver.* Unpublished M.A. thesis, Department of Geography, University of British Columbia, 1974, Appendix E. Reprinted by permission.

variance of the initial 192 variables has been condensed into the four most general factors. Though the three Shevky-Bell dimensions appear among these four, the relative positions of socioeconomic status and family status are reversed, and the sequence is interrupted by factor 3, housing status, which in American cities like Chicago is contained within the family-status factor (Rees, 1970). In factorial ecologies of British urban structure, housing tenure is also a major dimension, reflecting in part the distinctive role of local-authority housing (Herbert, 1968).

Scores generated for each enumeration area allow the metropolitan region to be classified according to the principal factors. The pattern for factor 1 (family status) shows a concentric distribution of factor scores with the lowest values in downtown and inner city Vancouver, the satellite town of New Westminster, and the retirement community of White Rock (Figure 3.9a). The socioeconomic factor shows a markedly different distribution, more closely described by a sectoral pattern, with a sharp north-south boundary separating the high- and low-status sectors in Vancouver (Figure 3.9b). The high-status suburbs north of the Burrard Inlet contrast with the medium-status suburbs east

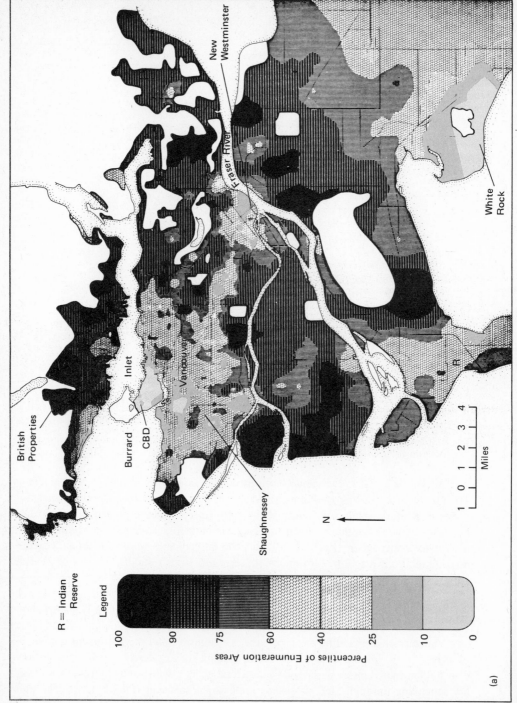

Figure 3.9 Factorial ecology of Greater Vancouver, 1961. (*Source*: J. M. Patterson, *The Factorial Urban Ecology of Greater Vancouver*. Unpublished thesis, Dept. of Geography, University of British Columbia, 1974, pp. 121, 123, 126. Reprinted by permission.)

80

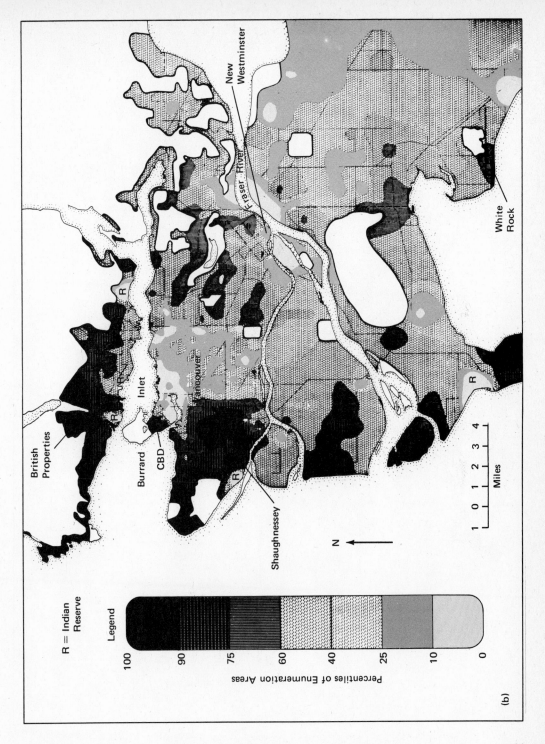

Legend

R = Indian Reserve

Percentiles of Enumeration Areas

	100
	90
	75
	60
	40
	25
	10
	0

British Properties

Burrard Inlet

CBD

Vancouver

Shaughnessey

Fraser River

New Westminster

White Rock

N

Miles
1 0 1 2 3 4

(b)

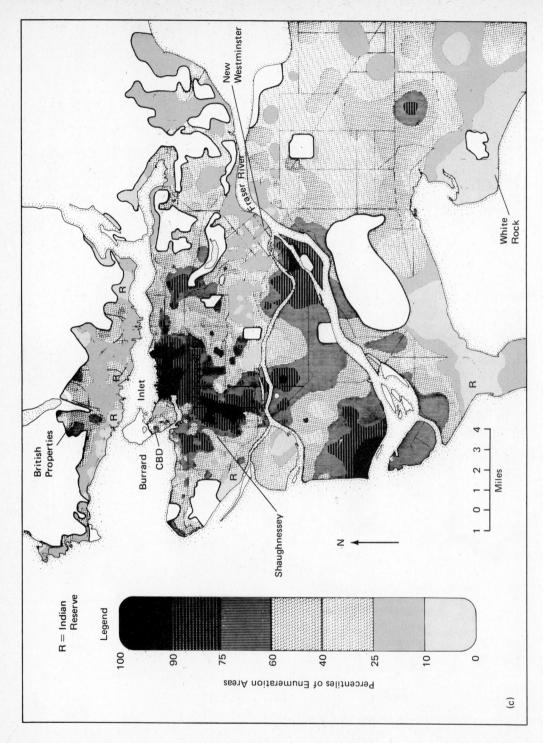

Legend

R = Indian
Reserve

Percentiles of Enumeration Areas

100
90
75
60
40
25
10
0

(c)

British
Properties

Burrard
Inlet

CBD

Shaughnessey

New
Westminster

Fraser River

White
Rock

N

Miles
1 0 1 2 3 4

R = Indian Reserve

and south of the central city. The lowest-status areas are industrial neighborhoods adjacent to downtown Vancouver and along the Fraser River and also several Indian reserves. Finally, the map of ethnic status (Figure 3.9c) reveals the presence of several minority clusters through the metropolitan areas. The two largest concentrations are the Asian and Italian clusters east of the central core, and the mixed Central European and Asian districts that form a belt southward. Smaller outlying areas consist of fishing and industrial communities along both arms of the Fraser River.

It is apparent from this description that a more comprehensive classification procedure might well permit a reconciliation of the Burgess and Hoyt models of social areas and land use. Although socioeconomic status conforms to Hoyt's sectoral model, family status is better described by the Burgess concentric model. The map of ethnic status is more ambiguous and is not simply described by concentric, sectoral, or multiple-nuclei models. A statistical analysis of these relationships has been performed in other cities applying analysis of variance to multivariate classifications of social areas. In Winnipeg, the social-area scores for economic status and family status were sampled in four zones and four sectors centered on the main downtown intersection (Table 3.3). A general similarity of economic status occurs along each sector and of family status through each zone; analysis of variance showed these trends to be statistically significant. Similar general results from factorial ecology or social area analysis have been confirmed for Chicago (Rees, 1970), Toronto (Murdie, 1969), Brisbane (Timms, 1971), and several medium-sized U.S. cities (Anderson and Egeland, 1961).

As with social area analysis, the final stage of a factorial ecology often consists of the integration of the separate factors into a higher-order classification. Census tracts or enumeration areas are consecutively grouped with neighbors with which they share similar profiles on all factors. In this manner, progressively larger urban regions are formed through the grouping of similar and juxtaposed tracts. As the regions become larger they display a decreasing level of internal uniformity. The optimal classification attempts to balance the competing claims of generality (the number of regions) and homogeneity (the similarity of tracts within each region). In the Vancouver study the 1237 enumeration districts were progressively aggregated to 122 urban regions, the same as the number of census tracts in 1961. This level was chosen to compare the efficiency of the census to factorial ecology in delimiting social areas that would maximize the homogeneity within

TABLE 3.3 SOCIAL AREA SCORES FOR SECTORS AND ZONES IN WINNIPEG

	Zones							
	1		2		3		4	
Sector	Econ. Stat.	Fam. Stat.	Econ. Stat.	Fam. Stat.	Econ. Stat.	Fam. Stat.	Econ. Stat.	Fam. Stat.
A	22	54	39	29	46	32	38	18
B	56	58	59	50	62	35	60	26
C	69	87	89	50	91	26	96	25
D	23	54	22	40	30	38	49	30

Source: D. Herbert, *Urban Geography: A Social Perspective.* Newton Abbott, U.K.: David and Charles, 1972, p. 149. Reprinted by permission.

each area. There was a statistically significant difference between methods in the degree of homogeneity within social areas, with factorial ecology proving the more efficient regionalizing scheme.

This conclusion illustrates the versatility of factorial ecology, which has led to its increasing popularity as a method of urban regionalization. But enthusiasm for the technique has recently become more muted in light of a growing number of cautions and criticisms (Hunter, 1972; Johnston, 1976a). Many of these have been technical, concerned with such matters as the interpretation of factors (Palm and Caruso, 1972) and the variations among the family of factor analysis techniques (Griggs and Mather, 1975; Davies, 1978). But a more serious question concerns the nature of the social areas themselves. They are, of course, simply an artifact of the input data, which is one reason for national differences in factor structure because national censuses are not always directly comparable in the information they collect. How real are these social areas identified by analysis following conventional mathematical assumptions of data that were collected at a particular spatial scale at a given point in time for the purposes of distant policymakers? And how valid are the variables themselves as differentiators of urban places and their users?

From Social Areas to Neighborhoods

The Cultural Critique of Ecological Areas

Inherent in ecological models is a somewhat mechanical and deterministic view of the development and evolution of social areas according to market processes that neglects, among other things, the cultural and volitional aspects of urban life. This objection was first raised in the late 1940s in a spirited debate concerning the role of noneconomic values in molding social area patterns. As a result of detailed research in central Boston, Walter Firey argued persuasively for the importance of sociocultural factors in interpreting the form of the city (Firey, 1945). He claimed that it was impossible to explain the continued existence of areas of open space and the maintenance of certain residential areas without seeing them as symbolic articulations of deeply felt social and cultural values. The Boston Common and other large open spaces like New York's Central Park and London's Hyde Park are valuable real estate and incongruous survivors in cities bent only on the maximizing of economic returns on land investment. Clearly the maxim of the highest and best use does not have a total hold on urban form.

Similarly, in-town heritage and status areas are anomalies to notions of the down-filtering of inner residential areas explicit in the Burgess and Hoyt land use models. Boston's Beacon Hill, an area of "age-old quaintness and charm" had an anomalous low-rise skyline despite its immediate proximity to the central business district. The neighborhood's extensive literary and historical associations had created an image that was vigorously defended by its community association and city bylaws. By the late 1970s Firey might have added other examples from inner city Boston, for the Back Bay and even parts of the South End, which were formerly deteriorated neighborhoods, have joined Beacon Hill in becoming fashionable for low-rise intown living. Boston's core areas have been so rejuvenated that except for some public housing in the South End "the really poor no longer live in the immediate vicinity of the Central Business District" (Winters, 1977).

Firey sought to extend his argument to certain low-income areas of Boston. He observed how the Italian neighborhoods of the West End and North End represented a distinctively European way of life. To choose to leave or to stay in these districts was as much a statement of cultural affinity as it was of economic status. This interpretation was reinforced by William Whyte's detailed participant observation research in the Italian community of Boston which showed the varied effects of "local" and "American" lifestyles in promoting local institutions and culture (Whyte, 1955). Firey's argument was also supported by a study of the changing areas of Norwegian settlement in New York City over a 100-year period that emphasized the creative role of household decision making in shaping social areas. Residential decisions "must be referred to factors that are volitional, purposeful, and personal and. . . . these factors may not be considered as mere accidental and incidental features of biotic processes and impersonal competition" (Jonassen, 1949). In his conclusion Jonassen firmly resisted mechanistic ecological arguments for the formation of social areas: "Men tend to distribute themselves within an area so as to achieve the greatest efficiency in realizing the values they hold most dear." It is implicit that values are plural not one-dimensional, that utility tradeoffs are not reducible only to economic criteria.

The creative force of social values in molding a landscape is most easily demonstrated in the history of elite social areas, the group for whom economic constraints are presumably the least limiting. Commenting on the distribution of social groups in Belfast, Emrys Jones observed that "individuals do not conform to such a pattern—they contribute to it" (Jones, 1960:267). The elite sector in southwest Belfast has grown toward preexisting high-status districts owned by the rural gentry, because the high-prestige connotation of the country estates has acted to entice patterns of residential selection by the urban elite. An apparent North American parallel has been the tendency for new upper-class subdivisions to be built adjacent to already existing exclusive golf and country clubs. In suburban Detroit over 80 percent of new elite subdivisions built between 1913 and 1967 were sited within 2 miles of an existing high-status country club (Backler, 1974). Outside the United States, gracious in-town living has survived more easily in the major cities of Canada (Seeley, Sim, Loosley, 1956; Forward, 1973), Britain (Eyles, 1968), Australia (Johnston, 1966), and New Zealand (Johnston, 1969), where the preeminent meaning of an elite address has permitted considerable neighborhood longevity.

If ecological regionalization schemes disregard the creative force of social and cultural variables, it is a moot point to ask just how meaningful they are in understanding social patterns in the city. Preliminary testing of factorial ecology classifications in the Minneapolis metropolitan area has raised some doubts as to their effectiveness in predicting social and attitudinal characteristics. Examination of the flows of telephone messages between exchange districts in Minneapolis showed no apparent relationship between the pattern of calls and the region's social areas as defined by factorial ecology (Palm, 1973a). In other words, census tracts with similar ecological profiles do not necessarily show a high level of telephone interaction; the spatial regions do not seem to be equivalent to functional regions. A second study, which probed attitudinal characteristics of ecologically defined areas, reached the same conclusion (Palm, 1973b). A random sample of households from five areas classified as ecologically different were interviewed concerning their readership preferences for magazines and newspapers. Subsequent analysis showed that there was no significant difference in reading habits between social areas that exceeded the variations within each of them. There was no attitudinal gradient, at least as measured by readership, which coincided with the ecological gradient.

Even though the Minneapolis studies were exploratory rather than definitive, they do raise questions concerning the significance and meaning of urban social areas constructed from census variables. Even with aggregate data the utility of factor scores in predicting behavioral traits is limited. In one study, factor scores from a factorial ecology of several hundred American suburban municipalities were correlated against voting patterns for the same municipalities in six federal elections (Walter and Wirt, 1972). Only one factor, socioeconomic status, showed a consistent correlation with voting patterns, and the power of the explanation was modest—an average level of 32 percent of the electoral variance was accounted for—so that there are obviously factors with a substantial effect on the behavioral traits of social areas that are omitted from the social area classification. And again, since there is no theoretical basis (apart from pragmatism) for the inclusion of variables in a factorial ecology, there is nothing in the method that allows unambiguous causal inferences to be made from those variables that are included and applied to some other phenomenon under study (Alford, 1972). It is not apparent what the precise relationship is between the spaces identified by ecological classification and the places that are real in the experience of urban dwellers (Caruso and Palm, 1973).

This query becomes even more telling when the data base is disaggregated and individual comparisons are made. In metropolitan Vancouver, Shaughnessy and the British Properties are two elite neighborhoods of single-family dwellings falling within the top 10 percent of census tracts in terms of their factor scores for socioeconomic status (Figure 3.9b). However, the similarity in income, education, and occupational standing masks subtle lifestyle variations between the two districts which give them a totally dissimilar image. Visually the differences are apparent. Though both are prestigious residential areas, Shaughnessy is older, more heavily landscaped, and characterized by dignified Tudor mansions, whereas the British Properties presents a more open landscape, with low ranch-type houses its most popular style. Interviews completed with 30 households in each neighborhood at a comparable income level and stage in the life cycle exposed the social gulf that separates these two high-status areas (Cooper, 1971). An indication of social differentiation is evident from the sample of responses reproduced in Table 3.4. The profiles that emerge contrast the establishment qualities of Shaughnessy with the less rooted character of the British Properties, with its sense of rapid mobility and weak affiliation with the bastions of Vancouver society. These marked differences are not trivial in the experience of their members but circumscribe the boundaries of two social worlds. A final question showed there to be limited interaction and almost no common friendships between residents of the two neighborhoods. Thus a common ecological structure has disguised lifestyle differences which have powerful distancing effects in the social worlds of residents.

TABLE 3.4 SELECTED SOCIAL CHARACTERISTICS IN SHAUGHNESSY AND THE BRITISH PROPERTIES, VANCOUVER

Characteristic	Shaughnessy	British Properties
1. Residential mobility		
In present house 0–5 years (%)	13	53
In present house > 20 years (%)	53	0
2. Social mobility		
In present job 0–5 years (%)	7	50
In present job > 20 years (%)	43	23
Higher-status occupation than father (%)	7	43
3. Family ties		
Relatives living in same neighborhood (%)	93	7
4. Social affiliations		
Anglican or United Church (%)	67	16
Frequent attendance of the arts (%)	67	0
Children at private school (%)	87	13
Membership at the Vancouver Club (%)	67	3
Met friends at school (%)	90	3
Met friends at parties (%)	0	57

Source: Adapted from M. Cooper, *Residential Segregation of Elite Groups in Vancouver, B.C.*, unpublished M.A. thesis, Department of Geography, University of British Columbia, 1971, Chapter 4.

The Perception of Neighborhood

Partly in response to criticisms directed against ecological areas, recent attempts have been made to demarcate social areas not only through their formal census attributes but also on the basis of their residents' activities and perceptions, revealed through survey questionnaires. An early study in Cambridge, England, showed that 75 percent of a sample of housewives were able to demarcate an area with a mean size of 75 acres, or 600 yards, radius about their home, which they identified as their neighborhood (Lee, 1968). Neighborhood delimitation was closely associated with the local activities of the women, their degree of neighboring, membership in local organizations, and shopping patterns. Interestingly, Lee did not observe any variation in neighborhood size associated with the socioeconomic status of residents or with the population density of the neighborhood. Later studies in Chicago, Philadelphia, and Paris have supported most of these findings; 70–80 percent of residents are usually able to identify neighborhood boundaries that commonly follow one or several main thoroughfares acting as a barrier to activities. The ability to make this demarcation is positively related to family size, socioeconomic status, the proportion of contacts that are local, and the length of residence (Hunter, 1974; Ley, 1974a; Melton, 1969).

However, there are a number of local variations that confuse any general rule of thumb concerning the spatial extent of neighborhood, as Herbert and Raine (1975) demonstrated in a study in the Welsh city of Cardiff. Residents were questioned on three streets in different parts of the city to assess their experience of neighborhood, revealed both by their activity patterns and by their perceptions. The locations of local friends and the intensity of visiting provided one measure of social interaction; another was the use of neighborhood services, including shops and voluntary associations. There was considerable diversity in the three areas in the degree of overlap between these two indicators of neighborhood. In district A the spatial extent of the two interaction measures was virtually identical, but in district C there was almost no coincidence at all (Figure 3.10a). A composite neighborhood ellipse was derived and plotted from the two measures of social interaction. Residents were then asked to identify their home areas on a map. This perceptual definition was itself inconsistently related to the indicators of social interaction (Figure 3.10b). In district A the fit between perceptual and interaction measures of neighborhood was close; however, in district C the overlap was minimal. In district A, where the various indicators delimit almost identical areas, we might expect that the composite ellipse offers a good approximation of the spatial extent of neighborhood. However, in district C, with virtually no overlap between the indicators, the composite ellipse is merely a statistical average with very little relation to any one measure of neighborhood. Indeed, so geographically diffuse are the various indicators that we might well doubt whether neighborhood is a salient concept in the experience of these residents.

The Defense of Neighborhood

Perhaps the best evidence of the reality of neighborhood sentiment has been the development over the past 20 years of a neighborhood political movement, lobbying city hall for community preservation against the incursions of redevelopment or demolition for freeways or other public works and also urging more effective local public services and even some control or at least consultation over their delivery. A most important inspiration of the neighborhood movement was Jane Jacobs' influential book, *The Death and Life of Great American Cities,* which was virtually a celebration of urban neighborhood. Jacobs developed her "attack on current city planning and rebuilding," arguing that it was destructive of local community (Jacobs, 1961:16). In its place she presented a set of alternative principles for the preservation and enhancement of the local neighborhood which was, she argued, an important ingredient for the quality of urban living. The rich resource offered by a viable local neighborhood has been amply documented in a number of contexts as a source of vitality and diversity (Morley and Burton, 1979), security (Jacobs, 1961), and not least, as Wolpert (1976) has noted, as a setting for volunteerism and effective support networks. The construction of community has now become a formal planning goal; in Lemon's words, "planning of the physical environment means planning communities; and this must be explicit rather than implicit" (Lemon, 1978).

The ethnic and working-class reaction in the 1960s against schemes for urban renewal that would destroy their neighborhoods, plus their lobbying for greater control over public services, was met to some extent in the United States by government grants to support community action agencies, community development corporations, and the Model Cities program with its budget of almost $1 billion (Kasperson and Breitbart, 1974). In the early 1970s this momentum for activism passed to middle-class neighborhoods (Goering, 1979; Bell and Newby, 1976). In some cities the middle-class neighborhood movement led to some changes in municipal political leadership, favoring candidates supporting neighborhood preservation (Ley, 1980; Lemon, 1974). However, potentially more important because of being more significant as a source of public funds, was a shift in the policy of central government. In Canada the Neighbourhood Improvement Programme and Residential Rehabilitation Assistance Programme provided funds to stabilize and preserve inner city neighborhoods. In Britain a wide variety of programs, including improvement grants to general improvement areas and to housing action areas, was also targeted toward stabilizing the inner city (Thrift, 1979; Eyles, 1979). The promotion of the role of local community councils and the funding of community housing associations were acknowledgments of the significance of neighborhood preservation and neighborhood interests. The neighborhood movement has, however, progressed furthest in the United States (Goering, 1979). A presidential report in 1976 recommended as a national priority ''restoration of the vitality of urban neighborhoods.'' As part of the quickening pace of federal activity at the neighborhood level in the late 1970s, a high-ranking Office of Neighborhoods and Voluntary Associations was formed in the Department of Housing and Urban Development, while neighborhood-scale legislation was built into the $4-billion Community Block Grant program.

We will see in Chapters 8 and 9 that the issue of neighborhood integrity is neither simple nor one-sided, for undesirable tendencies to beggar one's neighbor may result from successful neighborhood activism. So, too, an emphasis on neighborhood-scale problems may obscure issues that are best analyzed and responded to within broader contexts. Again, the degree of success of private and public initiatives to preserve neighborhood is a question that will require further study. However, for now we will simply note the subjective reality of neighborhood for a number of urban dwellers. Neighborhood is more than an ecological abstraction; for many people it is an integral element in the experience of urban living. The current tendencies are to rediscover the individuality of the natural area—''man in his habitat and under the conditions in which he actually lives'' (Park, 1929)—and urban policy is being redirected toward sustaining, where possible and where desirable, the urban neighborhood.

Conclusion

Following the discussion of metropolitan land use in Chapter 2, we have looked more selectively in this chapter at the residential districts of the city. Pervasive patterns of segregation occur at this scale for a wide range of social and economic variables, creating a mosaic of social areas in the city. Ecologists in geography and sociology have expended considerable effort in developing efficient classifications of urban regions resulting from this segregation and also in testing descriptive general models of the distribution of land use types and social areas within the typical city. These classical land use models still have pedagogic value, particularly when there is a clear specification of the range of criteria for which they are appropriate.

Classification is an early phase in the scientific endeavor, but nevertheless some uneasiness has arisen concerning the development of ecological regions. Ecological classification represents a distancing by the researcher from the field situation, but one suspects that the adopted view from the census volumes is based as much on pragmatism

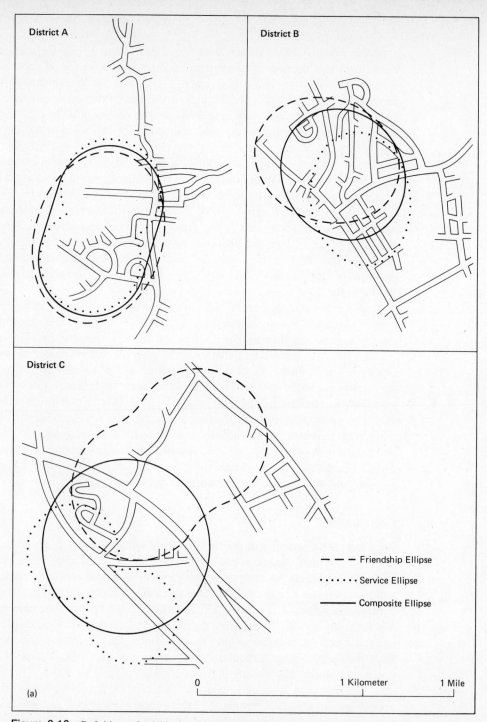

Figure 3.10 Definitions of neighborhood in Cardiff, Wales: (a) by activity patterns; (b) by perceptions. (*Source*: D. T. Herbert and J. Raine, ''Defining Communities within Urban Areas,'' *Town Planning Review* 47 (1976):325–338, figs. 2 and 4. Reprinted by permission.)

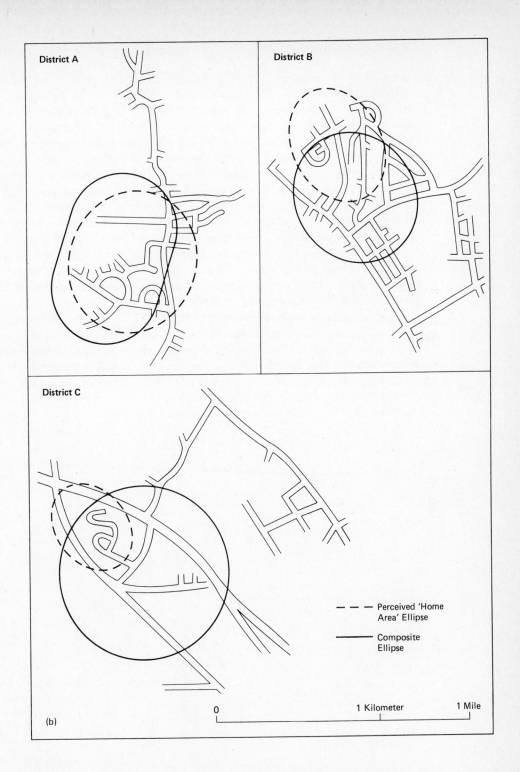

District A

District B

District C

- - - Perceived 'Home Area' Ellipse

——— Composite Ellipse

0   1 Kilometer   1 Mile

(b)

as on theory. In what sense, then, are ecological regions "real"? For one thing, it is uncertain to what extent they coincide with regions based on interaction patterns or attitudes. For another, there is the background specter of the ecological processes themselves, with their heavy debt to the irrevocable forces of social darwinism and their passive view of man. For, as Timms admits, the theory underlying social area analysis, and by extension factorial ecology, is consistent with earlier ecological thought: "To a large extent the model may be seen as one of economic determinism" (Timms, 1971).

In both the use of ecological variables and the implication of ecological processes one senses that something important has been omitted. Firey claimed that what was missing was the incorporation of social values and human initiative which may divert and block the inevitability of ecological process. We have seen that even for questions of spatial form asked by ecologists one cannot remain true to the facts and disregard the pluralism of motives and values. If we accept that there is a world of urban experience much of which eludes ecological forms of thinking, then a new posture is required of the researcher. No longer can he or she be satisfied with aggregate models alone; his or her view of the city needs animation. The status of detached observer thumbing through the census volumes is certainly useful, but it is incomplete; one must also return to the field situation itself. Although neither ecological variables nor ecological processes can ever be ignored, they provide only a partial view of the city as experienced. The resiliency and immanence of everyday life gives rise to other real worlds; within the structures of spatial form the citizen is preoccupied with constructing his or her own reality, his or her own city. It is to these matters that we shall now turn.

PART 2
The Geography of Everyday Life

Chapter 4

The City of Mind and Action

We are all artists and landscape architects, creating order and organising space, time, and causality in accordance with our apperceptions and predilections

(Lowenthal, 1961)

The static modelling of urban land use, fixed in time and space, needs to be complemented by a dynamic approach concerned with movement through space and change through time. This argument was presented as early as 1938, when Crowe challenged the morphological preoccupation in urban geography by asking if geography were concerned only with *homo dormiens*. "Town geography is already a popular branch of the science. It is a study that cries aloud for dynamic treatment" (Crowe, 1938). He advocated a theme of regional organization where the city would be conceived not only in simple land use categories but also as a functional unit with circulating movement between its parts: "A dynamic view implies that stress is to be laid not upon terminal facilities, nor on the pattern of the system, but upon men and things moving."

The transition that is called for is one that exchanges the perspective of the map for that of the airline pilot, so that to the pattern of urban morphology is added the movement of people and goods along the city's transportation corridors, which is such a clear feature when the city is viewed from the air. But the airline pilot's view has its own bias, for the view from the air is an aggregate and comprehensive one concealing the purposefulness of each individual trip. The view is different at ground level, where the urban resident lives and moves and has his being. For him the city is less comprehensive, a more partial phenomenon corresponding to his own specialized interests, experience, and socioeconomic status. Those sections to which his specialties draw him are finely differentiated, but beyond there is a merging of space to unknown districts which are rarely encountered and scarcely recognized.

There is a reciprocal relationship between spatial behavior and our mental image of the city. Although the image is constructed as a result of interaction with the environment, yet as we shall see, subsequent movement also tends to be constrained within

TABLE 4.1   USE OF DISCRETIONARY TIME IN WASHINGTON, D.C. (*n* = 1667)

	Passive Activity		Social Interaction		Other Diversions and Recreation	
	Mean Hrs.	% Discr.	Mean Hrs.	% Discr.	Mean Hrs.	% Discr.
Weekdays	2.59	44	1.40	24	1.87	32
Saturday	2.74	36	2.33	30	2.60	34
Sunday	3.57	40	2.92	23	2.41	27

Source: F. S. Chapin, *Human Activity Patterns in the City*. New York: Wiley, 1974, p. 119. Reprinted by permission.

already known areas. For both activities and imagery our experience of the city is as partial, and even parochial, as are our concerns and responsibilities. In Berger and Luckmann's words, "The reality of everyday life is organised around the 'here' of my body and the 'now' of my present" (Berger and Luckmann, 1966:22).

Urban Activity Patterns

A number of scholars have related the success of the city to its ability to generate activities. The city, writes Richard Meier, finds its rationale as a transaction-maximizing system (Meier, 1968), while Karl Deutsch equates human freedom with the availability of a broad range of transactions, concluding grandly that "if freedom is the ability to choose, then the metropolis, in so far as it is an engine for facilitating choice, is also one of liberation" (Deutsch, 1961).

However, it seems as if many urban residents tend to exercise this offer of freedom in a rather passive manner. In the city of Washington the chief claim on discretionary time is made by passive activities, primarily watching television, resting, and relaxing (Table 4.1); a national survey in 1969 showed that the average American spent almost 2 hours a day watching television. Discretionary time is itself only one element of the 24-hour day, although in contemporary society it occupies increasing significance as the workday contracts and levels of affluence rise for many households. The Washington study showed that about 25 percent of weekdays and 35 percent of weekends are spent in discretionary activities (Table 4.2). This is almost identical to the amount of time spent on the job or on homemaking by household heads and considerably more time than is spent on other obligatory activities such as shopping.

TABLE 4.2   HOURS SPENT IN MAJOR ACTIVITIES IN WASHINGTON, D.C. (*n* = 1667)

	Work and Homemaking	Other Obligatory	Discretionary	Sleep
Weekdays	7.80 (32%)	2.88 (12%)	5.86 (24%)	7.46 (31%)
Saturday	4.65 (19%)	3.52 (16%)	7.67 (32%)	8.16 (34%)
Sunday	3.30 (14%)	3.71 (15%)	8.30 (37%)	8.09 (34%)

Source: F. S. Chapin, *Human Activity Patterns in the City*. New York: Wiley, 1974, p. 118. Reprinted by permission.

Time-budget studies, in which respondents are asked to keep an activity diary specifying the duration and location of activities, are permitting to emerge a fine-grained picture of the temporal and spatial use of the city (Anderson, 1971; Chapin, 1974). The major activities are phased in time and space, with trips for other activities lagged to avoid the morning and evening rush hours of the journey to work and return journey home. Studies in several metropolitan areas have suggested that the longest trip is the journey to work; in Washington it is on average almost 11 miles, compared to a mean of 6 miles for all types of shopping and only $2\frac{1}{2}$ miles for socializing and recreation. The work trip is not only longer but also more spatially focussed, emphasizing radial trips to a central city workplace. The shopping trip, in contrast, is multinodal, making use of suburban shopping centers, whereas discretionary trips are more typically short range and, at an aggregate level, appear to be scattered randomly.

Urban Routines

A time-geography approach to spatial behavior has been developed by Hägerstrand and other Swedish geographers and promises to emerge as a useful research and policy perspective (Hägerstrand, 1974; Ellegård, Hägerstrand, and Lenntorp, 1977). With its concern with scheduling problems and differential constraints on activities, it has already proven of use in Swedish planning studies (Pred, 1977a), particularly problems concerned with household access to public services, where the task has been to minimize scheduling and distance constraints in consumer utilization of services such as child care and libraries. The time geographic model of society portrays individuals and households as following a series of daily *paths* through time and across space, with their movement broken by periods spent at a sequence of *stations,* including such settings as the home, the office, school, shops, and sites of discretionary activities such as the church or community center (Pred, 1981). One objective of the time-geography approach is to provide a systematic language and methodology for describing everyday spatial behavior, which will highlight various forms of constraint upon individual activities and clarify issues for planning intervention (Thrift, 1977).

One theoretical finding of interest has come from a time-geography study of 200 students and educators in Michigan (Stephens, 1976). Part of the investigation involved a categorization of daily activities according to their repetitiveness, and this showed the heavy predominance of *routine* activities compared to periodic or unexpected events during the typical day (Figure 4.1). A comparable study in Britain also showed the high level of routinization in the daily activities of university students (Cullen and Godson, 1975). However, student activities are still more footloose than are those of other elements of the population, and a follow-up examination of daily activities among residents of a public housing estate in inner London indicated an even greater rigidity of scheduling of places and times in everyday life (Thrift, 1977).

The activities of everyday life fall into well-defined and repetitive channels and in this way solve the problem of *information overload* in the contemporary city. A number of commentators awed by the prodigious capacity for transactions in the city have inquired how urban man is able to screen out the barrage of information inputs, particularly when

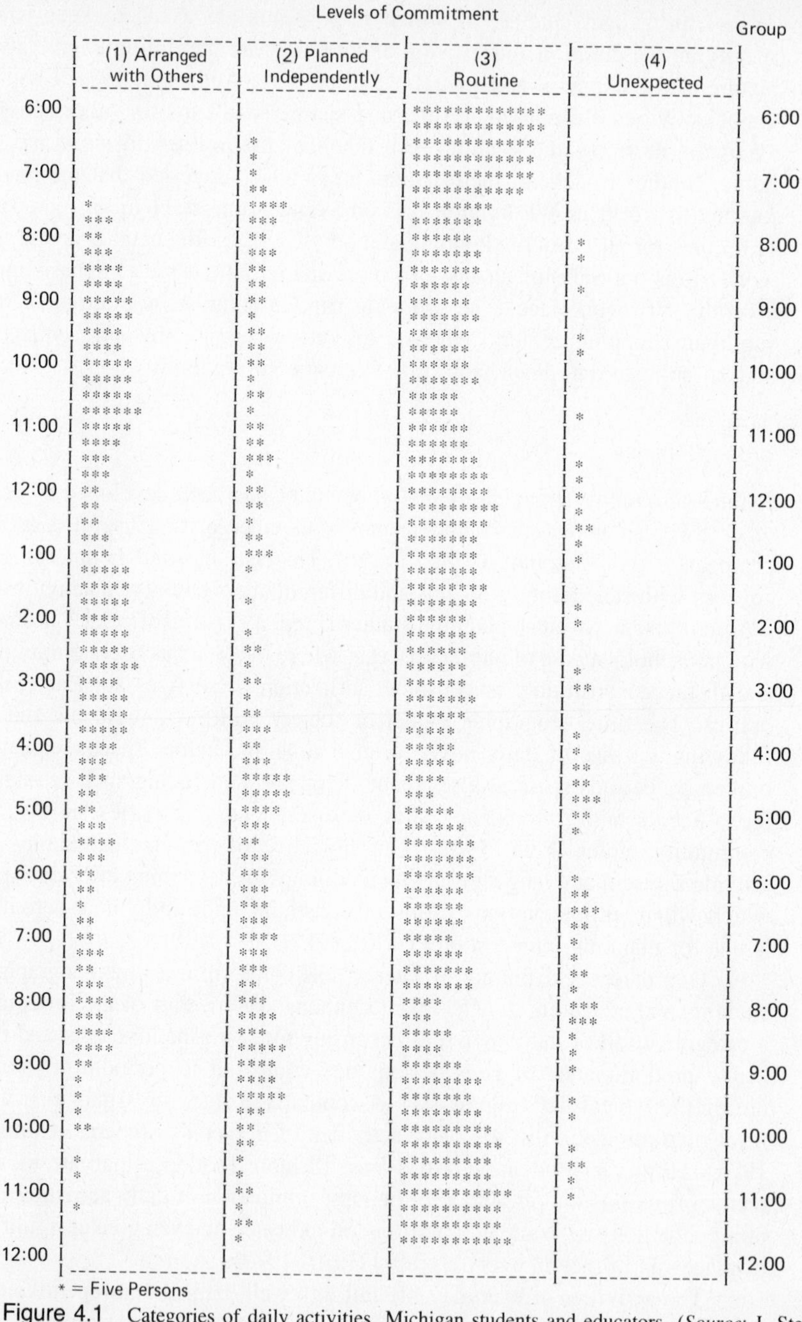

Levels of Commitment
Group
(1) Arranged with Others
(2) Planned Independently
(3) Routine
(4) Unexpected
6:00
7:00
8:00
9:00
10:00
11:00
12:00
1:00
2:00
3:00
4:00
5:00
6:00
7:00
8:00
9:00
10:00
11:00
12:00
* = Five Persons

Figure 4.1 Categories of daily activities, Michigan students and educators. (*Source*: J. Stephens, "Daily Activity Systems and Time-Space Constraints." Pp. 21–69 in B. Holly (ed.), *Time Space Budgets and Urban Research*. Dept. of Geography, Kent State University, Discussion Paper No. 1, 1976, fig. 6. Reprinted by permission.)

so many promise attractive opportunities (Meier, 1962; Lipowski, 1974). This problem tends to be theoretical rather than practical. Urban routines are strongly specialized and channelled, and divert activity from all but a few of the range of potential encounters (Lofland, 1973). In some instances nonparticipation is enforced by a failure of access, as for the suburban housewife cut off without available transportation (Palm and Pred, 1974). On other occasions opportunities are physically accessible but are disregarded because of an existing preoccupation. The repetitive, daily nature of a routine establishes a behavioral habit and an attitudinal norm from which it takes an effort to be wrenched, for urban man is a pragmatist rather than an optimizer and essentially conservative as he keeps to familiar and well-tried schedules. The routine is ongoing at the unreflected level of experience, so that a day at the beach or an evening at the club is undertaken unself-consciously, as falling naturally within the bounds of "what people like us do." Such conduct is rarely reflected on or scrutinized rationally. Indeed, such scrutiny might lead to a redefinition of the situation; a housewife might return to career employment, or a long-range commuter change jobs or residence upon conscious reflection of their existing taken-for-granted routines.

Types of Urban Routines

Urban culture, like its rural counterpart, has its rhythms, its repetitive activity patterns. Its routines are often taken for granted and apparently inconsequential, yet in cumulative form they define much of the meaning of the city to its residents and shape their own intersection with urban life (Ley, 1977b). They may seem ephemeral, and yet they account for much of the ongoing essential experience of place. For the meaning of the city to its residents is largely dependent on small, incremental, and recurrent events. In everyday life, as John Dewey observed, "Man is a creature of habit, not of reason nor yet of instinct" (Mills, 1966:453). For most of us, urban reality is an unspectacular procession of little things which together define the fuzzy outline of a friendship network, an attitudinal set, a lifestyle, a familiar place.

Social worlds and lifestyles emerge from a pattern of routines. The classical French regional geographers reported how recurrent patterns of *circulation* contributed to defining a *genre de vie,* or lifestyle, in a rural setting (Buttimer, 1971). In the Alpine valleys, for example, life was characterized by movement cycles that followed the seasons; out-migration for seasonal employment to the larger urban centers and seasonal transhumance as livestock were moved to the high summer pastures. These patterns of circulation were major components of the geography of the place and its people. In this classical tradition, circulation and genre de vie were defined in pursuit of the productive process and in relation to the rhythms of the physical environment. Today such a definition would be too narrow. In the late-twentieth-century city, man's activities are far more varied than those associated simply with the economic process, and the rhythms to which he responds are those of the human as much as the physical environment. The construction of artificial indoor environments has blurred the contrast between day and night and summer and winter. Urban rhythms in time and space are becoming far more the product of the human mind; organizing events in space and time is now more a problem of management than an accommodation to the elements of nature. In metropolitan society geography and history have been bureaucratized, reduced almost to a schedule.

Thus at one level the routines of urban life are set not by nature but by other men. Only for privileged professional groups is there freedom to define the hours of the *working day;* for most employees the shift and the time clock intimate their dependence on the schedules of management. Karl Marx was critical of this organization of time which disregarded natural rhythms, where ''men must work at night because the machines could not be allowed to sleep.'' But it is now evident that such work alienation is a product not simply of industrial capitalism but of the division of labor demanded by technology (Ellul, 1964). The shop floor specialization that so astounded visitors to a Birmingham hardware factory in the late eighteenth century has diffused equally to the high-technology industries of North America and the Soviet Union. Indeed, eastern European intellectuals recognize the continuation of work alienation springing from the demands of a technological society in the communist state. The division of labor, writes the Pole Almasi, is ''the most important social source of alienation operating under socialism as well as capitalism'' (Almasi, 1965). For some, work continues to be an absence of freedom endured, relieved only by the intense escapes of a ''Saturday night and Sunday morning'' (Frankenberg, 1966).

But such a conclusion would be incomplete for advanced Western societies. Labor legislation, unemployment insurance, the minimum wage, the increase of statutory holidays, the shortening of the working week, and above all, the power of the union movement, have transformed the culture of work. A vehicle assemblyman's wage may be comparable with that of a junior lawyer and in excess of that of a schoolteacher; indeed, it is often the white-collar non-unionized worker such as the bank clerk who is being left behind in the inflationary wage spiral. A blurring of income-based class stratification has occurred objectively and subjectively, particularly in North America where surveys show that 80–90 percent of the population now perceive themselves as middle-class. Although it would be naive to relate job satisfaction only to wages, yet a minimum conclusion would be that urban malaise could scarcely be attributed deterministically to the culture of work. This conclusion is reinforced by a series of empirical studies in Sweden, France, and the United States which have shown that urban alienation is not necessarily correlated to alienation on the job (Seeman, 1971).

Other major routines of urban life are centered around the home, the school, and discretionary activities. If the workplace has molded the identity of the male, the home has traditionally provided the routine for the woman. Though trends are changing, the *home* is the woman's world. As Loyd (1975) has indicated, Western culture has constantly identified women with the internal world of the home, whereas the male role has been fixed outside the dwelling in the competitive arena of society. This dichotomy reached its most extreme form during the Victorian and Edwardian eras with the institutionalization of elaborate protocol for polite society. Among those of ''good taste,'' the woman's social world revolved around the at-home and garden party; the man's around his business office and private club. The contemporary challenge to this role and place characterization by the women's movement is repeating in modified form the earlier argument of unionists that overidentification with one setting carries with it the seeds of alienation. The malaise of the middle-class housewife in the suburban Valium belt intimates a routine that can be as lacking in opportunities for self-expression and personal development as any factory floor (Peterson et al., 1978).

The liberal belief in the self-made man with education his avenue to social mobility has placed a premium on the *educational routine* in Western society. The critical role of education in the social structure is indicated by the manner in which structural problems are played out in the schools, and there, too, attempts are made to institutionalize solutions. In Canada the issue of national bilingualism is being fought out in part in the schools (C. Smith, 1974); in the United States school busing was a major impetus to counter national patterns of racial segregation (Lord, 1977), and in Britain the development of comprehensive schools is addressed to breaching the divisiveness of class and inequality (Herbert, 1976b). That the educational routine can play an important role in perpetuating lifestyle is indicated by the tenacity with which certain groups cling to their private education systems. Private schools reflect and accentuate the structural divisions of class, race, language, and religion (Lowry, 1973). They direct students into specific life trajectories and thereby consolidate the boundaries of social worlds; not only the British Empire but also the British class system were secured on the playing fields of Eton.

Discretionary routines comprise a fourth major routine of urban life, following the rhythm of the evening hours, weekends, statutory holidays, and annual vacations. Estimates of daily traffic flows suggest that about 15 percent of all vehicle trips are undertaken for leisure purposes; this of course excludes pedestrian and telephone contact initiated for social reasons. There is a creative regularity to the discretionary routine; in it roles and lifestyles are clarified, experience and habits reinforced, rituals and myths established. Like the other routines, the volitional has its own particular places. In industrial South Wales, if we believe Dylan Thomas, discretionary activities rotated between evening attendance at the public house, weekend attendance at chapel, and summer visits to the seashore. August Bank Holiday at the seaside was a part of the trilogy, predictable, repetitive, an integral element of industrial urban culture and transferable with local exceptions to Blackpool or Atlantic City. In the perceptive mind of the artist the essential experience of such places and times is captured. Every year, reflects Thomas:

> There was cricket on the sand, and sand in the sponge cake, sandflies in the watercress, and foolish, mulish religious donkeys on the unwilling trot. Girls undressed in slipping tents of propriety . . . Little naked navvies dug canals; children with spades and no ambition built fleeting castles; wispy young men, outside the bathing huts, whistled at substantial young women . . .Recalcitrant uncles huddled over luke ale . . . Mothers in black . . . gasped under the discarded dresses of daughters . . . And fathers, in the once-a-year sun, took fifty winks (1954:32).

Familiar people, familiar places, familiar activities, together create a subculture as roles and tastes are learned, rehearsed, and consolidated. The meanings of a subculture are often private and inaccessible to the unknowing eye of the outsider; only a native can fully savor the artist's success in recreating the essence of a place, the contours of a separate life-world, though by making the appropriate substitutions the outsider may insert his own times and places and approximate the artist's effect for himself.

Routines consolidate a lifestyle or a subculture. They involve repeated interaction with persons, places, and objects that are well-known and have a meaning to people over and above their objective features. The life-world is not an epiphenomenon, a mere detail on the urban scene. For most of us the routines of the daily round provide our effective linkage with the city, the cultural reality of urban living.

Social Space and the Daily Round

Routines have a configuration in space. The concept of social space emphasizes the group nature of the life-world and also that it has cognitive as well as behavioral dimensions. Social space is a concept that has been widely used of late in varied contexts, so much so that a precise definition is elusive. In studies of urban spatial structure the term usually refers to characteristics of land use and population as described in land use plans and the census; in factorial ecology the reference is to the distance relations between census tracts in an abstract mathematical space defined by factor scores on leading factors. More commonly, however, social space implies not structure but process and is drawn around the spatial interaction patterns of specified groups (Buttimer, 1969, 1972; Boal, 1970; Weightman, 1976). Social-space definitions commonly emphasize corporate and neighborhood-oriented activities, so that patterns involving the place of work are often, though not necessarily, omitted. Usually the social space of a group will incorporate the places identified with its recurrent routines, its daily or weekly rounds. The concept of social space is most easily illustrated for groups whose daily or weekly round is spatially constricted, including the poor (Hyland, 1970), the elderly (Rowles, 1978), and minority groups (Weightman, 1976). For example, the weekly round of a group of elderly men living in the skid-row area of San Diego was limited to a few blocks around their residential hotel (Figure 4.2). The stations on their round consisted of the restaurants, bars, and a public plaza within a two- to three-block radius, with less regular visits to the welfare department, rescue missions, and places of social activity including a library, small park, and drop-in centers. Around such stations on the weekly round, the attitudes and subcultural norms of skid-row men were constructed and reinforced (Wiseman, 1970).

However, such mapping of social space still leaves margin for ambiguity as different forms of social conduct involve different spatial orbits. In his pioneering work in Paris, Chombart de Lauwe recognized concentric tiers of social space stratified according to the activity type and its relative frequency (Buttimer, 1969). In Chapter 3, we noted that interaction patterns for different purposes in a local area do not necessarily coincide (Herbert and Raine, 1976). Similarly a study of an Appalachian community in Cincinnati showed that there was a variation in the radius of several standard ellipses drawn around the home area describing the distribution of friends, relatives, and the voluntary associations to which community members belonged (Hyland, 1970). A further distinction may be drawn between objective and subjective social space. The former is defined by the patterns of interaction on the map, whereas for subjective space the group itself is

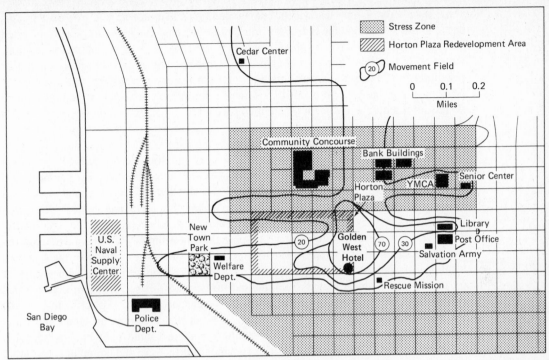

Figure 4.2 The social space of a group of elderly men in downtown San Diego. (*Source*: F. P. Stutz, "Adjustment and Mobility of Elderly Poor amid Downtown Renewal," *Geographical Review* 66 (1976):391–400, fig. 2. Reprinted by permission of the American Geographical Society.)

required to outline the perceived extent of a meaningful social area. A full discussion of social space should therefore acknowledge that it is a concept with physical, social, and psychological dimensions; to physical and social extent is added a component of meaning.

A detailed examination of the social space of American Indians in Syracuse, New York, incorporated these several dimensions, revealing how Indian urban identity was consolidated through their interaction in particular places (Flad, 1973). Using a methodology of participant observation supplemented by a limited use of questionnaires, Flad was able to demarcate the stations on the daily round for the Indian population of Syracuse. The group occupies a specialized niche within the city. Economically, there is a high occupational specialism in high steel ironworking; socially there is a high level of intragroup contact; and for recreation there is widespread enthusiasm for the native sport of lacrosse.

These specialized activities lead to a selective imprint on space. On the regional scale, Indian social space selectively highlights their concerns and status, forming around reservations and urban centers with Indian communities, particularly those large enough to support a rival lacrosse team. For a small sample of the Syracuse community over a six-month period, the two major reasons for out-of-town trips were to visit kin and to play or to watch a sports contest, invariably lacrosse. Within each city there is a parallel place specificity; as one respondent commented, whenever she arrives in a distant city, her first task is to locate the Indian tavern. Within Syracuse, Indian social space is riveted around the downtown neighborhood containing over one-third of the native population, where an Indian subculture is maintained both in a number of public settings, including restaurants and taverns, several churches, and the lacrosse arena, and in a network of private settings in neighborhood homes and on the nearby reservation. In these places shared information and common activities promote a distinctive group identity within a confined area.

A more accurate portrayal of subjective social space would regard it as a discontinuous network of significant nodes. It is scarcely appropriate to speak of an Indian neighborhood in Syracuse, for in no census tract does the group comprise more than 5 percent of the population. The spatial contiguity implied by neighborhood masks the presence of both significant and insignificant places within an identified local area. Even for working-class residents social space may not be perfectly contiguous. For the middle-class, with greater access to private transportation, noncontiguity is more probable because one's identity is shared between significant roles at home, work, and the scattered locations of friends, clubs, and other social activities. Among more affluent groups, a greater degree of one's identity may be tied to the place of work, so that occupational communities may provide important nodes of social space. A group of affluent Portland longshoremen was shown to live in dispersed residential areas free of ethnic bias, and yet they displayed a keen sense of community centered about their employment and union traditions: "The union serves as the center and focus of the community, welding the longshoremen together into a social group and furnishing them with a very real community of interest" (Pilcher, 1972). Though it may be spatially dispersed, the occupational community can develop its own distinguishable norms and subculture, its own specialized places which contribute toward the identity of its members.

Developmentally, social space is a social construction taught and learned within family and peer groups. A pilot study of 6-year-old children in Vancouver illustrates how early distinctive social-space patterns emerge. Children of different status groupings were asked to name the places that they had recently been taken by their parents. Children from wealthier families listed more public and distant settings such as the ski slope, a restaurant, or even out-of-town trips, whereas working-class children outlined a social space whose configuration was both more proximate and more private, focussed on the nearby homes of friends and relatives, neighborhood stores, and places of worship. Upper-middle-class children are being socialized into an identity that includes distance, glamour, and performance in public places, whereas working-class children, particularly those of immigrant parents, will find their identity in a more private and local world with less varied settings.

Urban Imagery

Subjective notions of social space have been explored in more detail in a series of studies in environmental perception, examining the image, mental map, or cognitive map of the city held by various groups of urban residents. Though cognitive mapping examines the perception of place in isolation, it is implied that the perceptual surface is built up through repeated encounter; in other words, the cognitive map is regarded as a surrogate measure for the spatial pattern of urban routines (Golledge and Spector, 1978).

Place Learning

The newcomer, like the child, approaches a place with some preconceptions but little structured knowledge. The tourist's cognitive map of London, for example, is typically one of isolated landmarks (Figure 4.3a). It comprises the well-known London symbols confounded only by a local effect around the tourist's place of accommodation—the university area in the case of these American high school students. With increasing time spent in the city the image begins to fill out and consolidate, attracting a growing consensus and showing also an increasing differentiation of landmarks and areas with which the tourist is most familiar (Figure 4.3b). Although the landscape edges of the Thames and Euston Road have consolidated, between them there is a growing differentiation as additional landmarks and areas are identified together with the linkages between them, particularly near the tourist's place of residence. With experience in the city *place learning* has occurred, so that to the initial isolated and stereotyped symbols of London have been added more mundane features reflecting the tourist's own activities and incipient routines.

Though the theoretical controversy over the stages and processes of spatial learning is unresolved (Hart and Moore, 1973), the developmental progression is evident. In a manner akin to the tourist's expanding image of London, Gould (1973, 1975) has shown the developmental growth of information maps of Sweden for Swedish schoolchildren. The initial discontinuous surface for young children comprising the home area and outlying highly visible points is gradually enlarged and filled out into a more continuous surface as the children grow older. The expansion of the mental map does not, however, appear to be indefinite. At least on the intraurban scale, a saturation level occurs beyond which little new spatial knowledge seems to be acquired. A Chicago study showed that after a few years residence there was no marked improvement with continued residence in an ability to name neighborhood boundaries (Hunter, 1974). Additional research in Hamilton, Ontario, indicated that there was a correlation of 0.68 between the knowledge of retail stores in the city and the length of residence (G. Smith, 1976). However, the relationship was best described by a logarithmic curve, indicating a rapid surge of initial learning which quickly tapered off after a few years residence, reaching a threshold after about 5 years in the town. There is support in these studies for the quick adoption of a set of routines in urban life that establish a pattern of habitual trips covering restricted areas in the city. There has even been a suggestion that the adoption of routines leads to a decrease in known places (Golledge and Zannaras, 1973). The initial search for facilities and routes may lead to wide-ranging trial-and-error behavior, but once routines are established, travel may cover more limited areas (Humphreys and Whitelaw, 1979).

Thus it would be misleading to suggest that in contrast to the incomplete view of

Newcomer's Image

Initially

after a few days

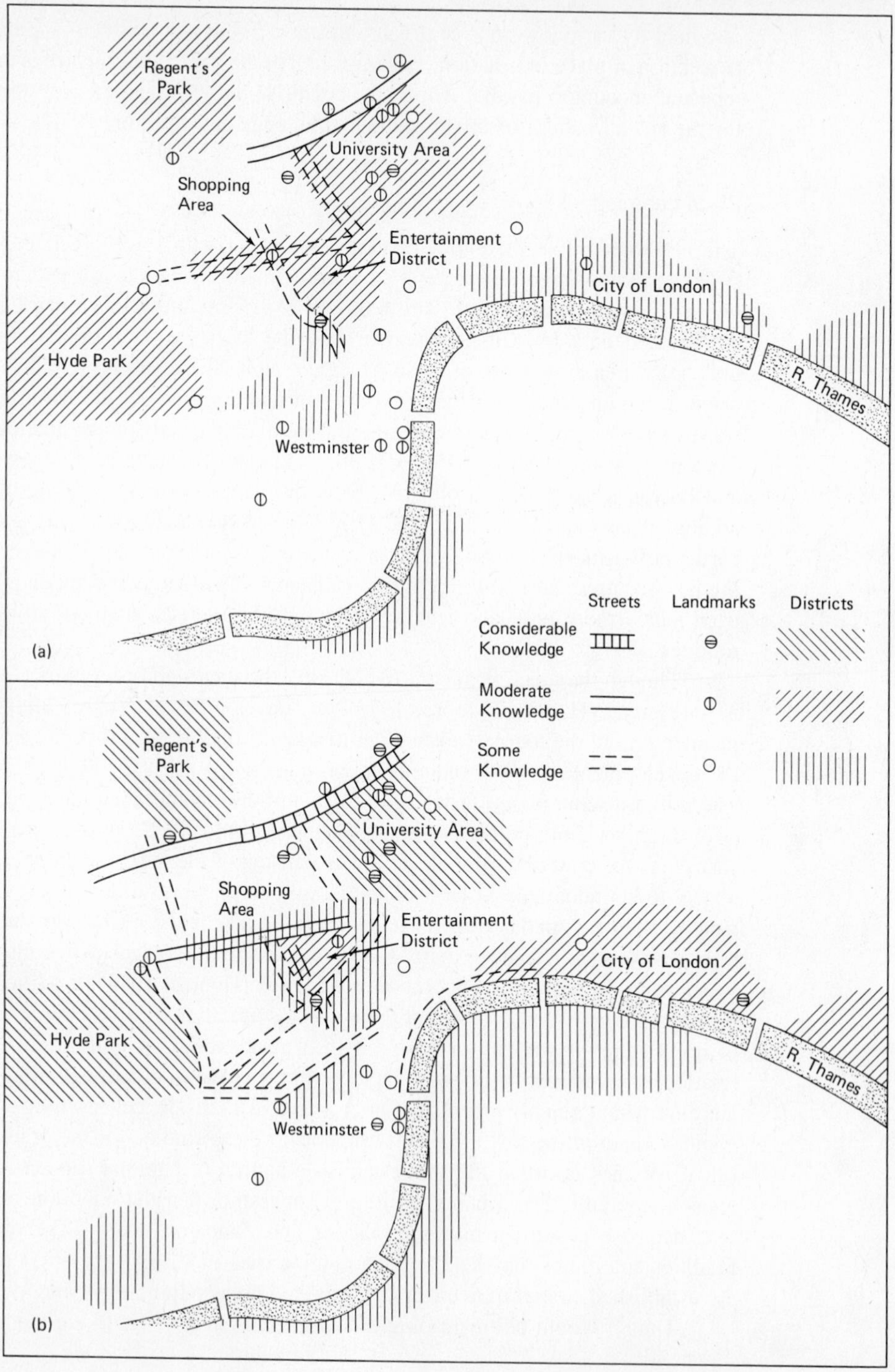

Regent's Park
University Area
Shopping Area
Entertainment District
City of London
Hyde Park
R. Thames
Westminster
(a)
Streets
Landmarks
Districts
Considerable Knowledge
Moderate Knowledge
Some Knowledge
Regent's Park
University Area
Shopping Area
Entertainment District
City of London
Hyde Park
R. Thames
Westminster
(b)

the newcomer or outsider, the insider's mental map is comprehensive and acutely differentiated. The insider's map may be equally parochial and incomplete, though within the range of his or her daily routines there is likely to be a marked knowledge of detail. The partial nature of the native's mental map was revealed by an experiment in New York in which 200 residents were asked if they could recognize slides depicting scenes in each of the five boroughs (Milgram et al., 1972). The aggregated response by this well-educated group of natives revealed that much of the city was unknown to them. Outside central Manhattan and a few familiar areas like Greenwich Village and Kennedy Airport, recognition was almost uniformly less than 10 percent. Clearly, for the native the city of the mind is also a composition of public symbols and the familiar area around the here and now of his or her everyday routines.

Urban Role and Urban Image

The earliest studies of the image of the city showed that even though certain districts were finely differentiated, others were virtually unknown. As most of the interviewees were well-educated downtown workers, downtown invariably emerged prominently in their sketch maps and verbal reports (Lynch, 1960). However, the section of the city that is known and finely differentiated depends on the perceiver's urban status and interest at hand. The psychologist Brian Little has advanced a model of man that regards urban man as a specialist, a model that highlights not only his initiative and ability but also his selectivity and limited range of competence (Little, 1972, 1976). Urban man as specialist lives predominantly in subcultural worlds of like-minded others, with specialized concerns and projects of which he has considerable knowledge and in which he invests considerable time.

His specialism is selectively channelled to certain places and certain times. The role of residential real estate agent, for example, directs activity toward the weekends and to zones of the city with high-demand levels; in contrast, the criminal role draws attention to the hours of darkness in places of familiarity and/or anticipated excitement (Carter, 1974). There are very few roles that provide knowledge of extensive areas. Real estate brokers have their familiar territories to which they selectively direct clients (Palm, 1976), and as numerous ethnographies report, inner city delinquents and petty criminals have intimate knowledge of their own neighborhoods and may easily elude police in their use of local alleys and rooftops (Brown, 1965).

All roles, however humble, lead to a focussed familiarity with a specific place. The urban tramp is a specialist in negotiating metropolitan skid rows and has developed a finely differentiated *argot* to categorize space and its resources (Duncan, 1978a). All roles imply a bias in knowledge of the city; the objective urban map is an abstraction that does not correspond with any personal or group mental map. Even roles such as police officer or taxi-cab driver, which might be expected to develop citywide familiarity,

Figure 4.3   The newcomer's image of London: (a) initial tourist impressions; (b) after a few days sightseeing. (*Source*: D. Wood, *I Don't Want To, But I Will*. Unpublished dissertation, Clark University Cartographic Laboratory, 1973, figs. 14–10 and 14–12. Reprinted by permission.)

show a much more partial urban image. Cab drivers keenly differentiate space on the basis of profitability and safety; urban boundaries are then embodied in the minds of the driver, and their perception tends to strengthen these boundaries in actuality (McDermott, 1975). In New York the licensed cab drivers typically avoid trips that terminate in high-crime inner city neighborhoods—except for Sunday morning trips to church! Their selective negotiation of neighborhoods led to the emergence of a gypsy industry serving the inner city market, but the gypsy cabs were territorially limited and had low investment levels and weak supervision, so that they offered an uneven service which often ran close to the law. In this manner the specialism and selectivity of the licensed driver's mental map was a daily reinforcement of New York's social boundaries and larger social structure. We will note in later chapters that the same processes of spatial labelling are practiced by urban institutions as well and also serve to consolidate the existing pattern of social areas in the city.

Urban Image and Social Structure

Besides the limitations of his own concerns, urban man as specialist is further constrained by the position in the social structure that he inherits. This relationship between a group's mental map and its social status was strikingly established in the well-known study of group images in Los Angeles conducted by the city's planning commission (Orleans, 1973). As small samples were taken of mental maps from a series of neighborhoods in the city, it became evident that there were consistent and systematic differences between images on the basis of social structure. For a middle-class and upper-middle-class group in Westwood, near Santa Monica and west of downtown, there emerged a composite image that showed detailed knowledge of an urban sector west and northwest of downtown (Figure 4.4a). Toward the southwest the information was more incomplete, and to the south and east the map lay almost empty. The planning commission assembled cognitive maps for several other neighborhoods, none of which equalled the spatial extent of the articulate Westwood professionals. The most remarkable contrast was with the Spanish-American neighborhood of Boyle Heights, immediately south of downtown Los Angeles (Figure 4.4b). The severely constricted maps of this Spanish-speaking population betray an extremely limited urban life-world. Their range of familiarity is confined to the immediate area and a few downtown landmarks, notably the bus depot and railway station, ports of entry for recently established immigrants. It is difficult to imagine that the groups in Westwood and Boyle Heights have drawn maps of the same city; evidently the intersection of their life-worlds is minimal.

The degree of incompleteness in the cognitive map is related directly to the relational character of the space; neighborhoods occupied by groups who are socially distant are much less likely to be known. The Westwood image is extremely incomplete not only for Boyle Heights but also for the extensive black community of south Los Angeles. This ignorance is tacitly acknowledged by city residents:

Here in Los Angeles we have a ghetto that covers more than 50 square miles, but as far as the white community was concerned, it really didn't exist. It was quite conceivable for the

white to live his entire life in Los Angeles and never interact with a Negro and certainly
not go to Watts (Fleming, 1968).

Ironically, after the 1965 Watts riot south Los Angeles emphatically *was* known, though
in the mind of the white suburbanite the entire district was typified as "Watts," the only
point where urban black experience had imposed itself on the collective consciousness
of the white world. This led to a new complaint: The press has played up Watts so as
to isolate it from the black community as a whole. But Watts is only some 30,000 of
the 250,000 black people in south Los Angeles (Jacquette, 1968). Jacquette's complaint
is informative. His protest is that south Los Angeles has been reduced to Watts and that
Watts signifies no more than a single historic event. But such, invariably, is the outsider's
view of history and geography. It is a view that scarcely respects the integrity of events
and places, insisting rather that they be rewritten to accord with the outsider's own
concerns (Ley, 1977a). In being reduced to a historical and spatial moment, "Watts"
now belongs less to its natives than it does to the white Los Angelenos who do not know
it.

Other research has replicated the Los Angeles study and has examined more specifically the relationship between social structure and the urban image. Sex does not
appear to be a major determinant of urban knowledge, though there are consistent tendencies for men to have a somewhat more expansive mental map than women, reflecting
their greater mobility (Everitt, 1976). The major differentiating factors appear to be
income and education, which may be conveniently collapsed under the rubric of socioeconomic status. A Vancouver replication compared the urban images of an affluent
westside group and a blue-collar eastside group who lived equivalent distances from the
downtown area (Figure 4.5). In less striking form the features of the Los Angeles maps
reappear. The westside group displayed the fuller mental map of the city, emphasizing
their local area and downtown streets and landmarks. Eastsiders were far more localized
in their perception and omitted the downtown entirely from their cognitive map—for
them downtown scarcely existed. As correlates of these maps, the blue-collar group had
substantially lower access to private transportation and made less use of public media as
an information source. An index of socioeconomic status was compiled from income
and education characteristics, and compared with a second index that measured knowledge of the city assessed from the correct identification of slides of city scenes and
landmarks (Figure 4.6). A very consistent linear relationship between the two indices
emerged; stratifying the sample into low, middle, and high socioeconomic status showed
corresponding mean scores on the city knowledge index of 17.2, 24.6, and 32.1, respectively.

Additional research that has confirmed this relationship between social class and
the extent of urban knowledge, even in a small country town of 10,000 people (Goodchild, 1974), could be cited. Data from Cedar Rapids, Iowa (Horton and Reynolds,
1971), Hamilton, Ontario (G. Smith, 1976), and Stockport, England (Potter, 1979)
reached the same conclusion; for a large sample in Hamilton there was a statistically
significant correlation of 0.56 between the spatial knowledge of retail stores and an index
of social class. There is abundant evidence that the spatial range of the life-world is

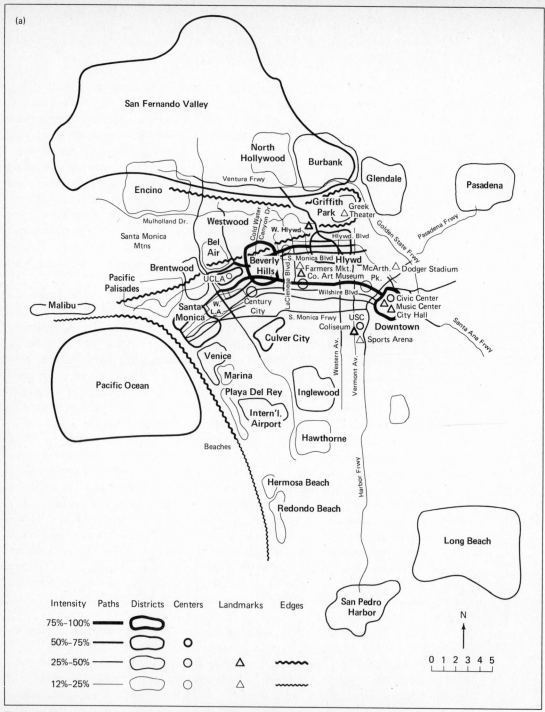

(a)

San Fernando Valley

North Hollywood

Burbank

Glendale

Pasadena

Encino

Ventura Frwy

Griffith Park

Greek Theater

Mulholland Dr.

Westwood

Cold Water Canyon Dr.

W. Hlywd

Hlywd. Blvd

Golden State Frwy

Pasadena Frwy

Santa Monica Mtns

Bel Air

Beverly Hills

S. Monica Blvd

Hlywd

McArth. Pk.

Dodger Stadium

Brentwood

LaCienega Blvd

Farmers Mkt.

Co. Art Museum

Pacific Palisades

UCLA

Wilshire Blvd

Civic Center

Music Center

City Hall

Santa Ana Frwy

Malibu

Santa Monica

W. L.A.

Century City

S. Monica Frwy

USC

Coliseum

Downtown

Culver City

Sports Arena

Venice

Western Av.

Vermont Av.

Inglewood

Marina

Playa Del Rey

Pacific Ocean

Intern'l. Airport

Hawthorne

Beaches

Harbor Frwy

Hermosa Beach

Redondo Beach

Long Beach

San Pedro Harbor

Intensity	Paths	Districts	Centers	Landmarks	Edges
75%–100%					
50%–75%			○		
25%–50%			○	△	
12%–25%			○	△	

N

0 1 2 3 4 5

Figure 4.4 Images of Los Angeles: (a) from Westwood; (b) from Boyle Heights. (*Source*: P. Orleans, "Differential Cognition of Urban Residents." Pp. 115–130 in R. Downs and D. Stea (eds.), *Image and Environment*. Chicago: Aldine, 1973, figs. 7.4 and 7.3. Reprinted by permission. Copyright 1973 by Aldine Publishing Company.)

p 110   only

(b)

City Hall   Union Station

Downtown

Brooklyn Ave.

Little Tokyo   1st St.

5th St.

Bus
Depot

Intensity	Paths	Districts	Centers	Landmarks	Edges
75%–100%					
50%–75%	▬▬▬			▲	
25%–50%	────				
12%–25%	──	⬭	○	△	

N

0 1 2 3 4 5

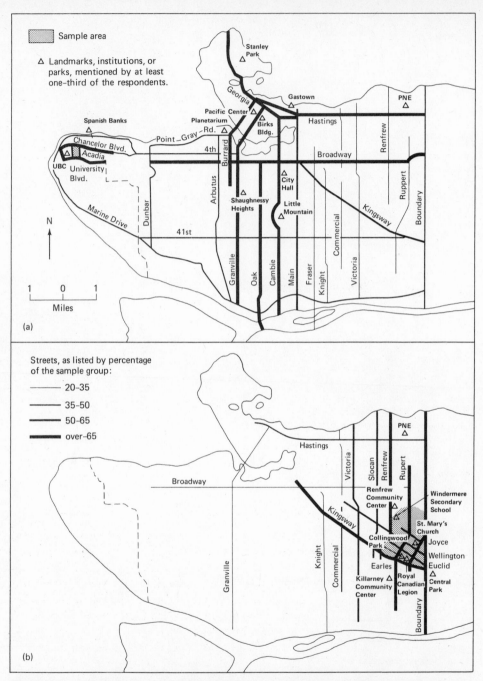

Figure 4.5 Images of Vancouver: (a) from a middle-class neighborhood; (b) from a working-class neighborhood. (*Source*: A. Hobkirk, "Eastside, Westside: Social Class Images of Vancouver." Pp. 11–24 in D. Ley (ed.), *Community Participation and the Spatial Order of the City*. Vancouver: Tantalus, B.C. Geographical Series No. 19, 1974, figs. 5 and 6. Reprinted by permission.)

112

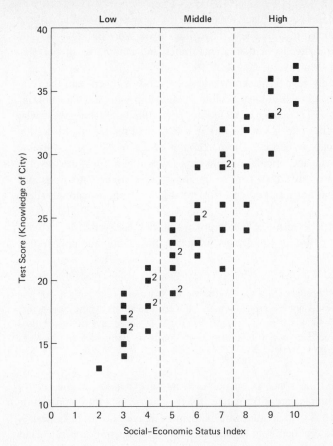

Figure 4.6   Spatial knowledge of Vancouver, by socioeconomic status. (*Source*: A. Hobkirk, "Eastside, Westside: Social Class Images of Vancouver." Pp. 11–24 in D. Ley (ed.), *Community Participation and the Spatial Order of the City.* Vancouver: Tantalus, B.C. Geographical Series No. 19, 1974, fig. 4. Reprinted by permission.)

heavily colored by the more abiding forces of social class as well as by the more temporary status of newcomer.

The Relational Nature of Urban Space

We have commented at several points on the relational nature of our experience of space. This notion of space carried unreflectively in our heads has little in common with the objective map of the city. It is nevertheless the schema that directs action in the life-world and proves itself daily to be an efficient guide to navigation and conduct.

The unreflective mental map is taken for granted and not easily analyzed. One attempt at analysis has been to devise somewhat bizarre experiments that aim to accentuate perceptual awareness by temporarily removing the use of one sense, obliging city dwellers to become much more self-conscious in their use of other senses than they would be in everyday navigation. One such experiment in Boston alternatively removed the sense of hearing and sight with earmuffs and goggles, and instructed subjects to report their perceptions through the other senses in a controlled walk in the downtown area (Southworth, 1969). Less clumsy and more common have been the use of projective techniques, notably sketch mapping and place recall tests, to uncover the contours of the city of the mind. Though such projective tests have their own shortcomings, they do seem to be efficient in eliciting recall of the salient routes and landmarks of personal geographies (Saarinen, 1973; Murray and Spencer, 1979).

Projective tests repeatedly reveal that knowledge of the city's extent and the relations between urban elements show a highly variable relationship with standard notions of space and distance (Wood, 1978). Even citywide travellers like taxi-cab drivers, who are skillful at urban navigation, conceive of the city in a relational manner that has little in common with objective map properties. The perception of distance itself is variable according to familiarity, usage, and orientation relative to downtown. Destinations that are familiar or oriented toward downtown tend to be understated in subjective distance estimates relative to those that are less known or oriented away from downtown (Lee, 1970; Briggs, 1973).

What, then, is this metric in terms of which urban space is assessed? McDermott, in his study of the space perception of cab drivers in New York, quotes the philosopher Merleau-Ponty:

> In so far as I have a body through which I act in the world, space and time are not, for me, a collection of adjacent points nor are they a limited number of relations synthesised by my consciousness, and into which it draws my body. I am not in space and time, nor do I conceive of space and time. I belong to them, my body combines with them and includes them (Merleau-Ponty, 1962).

Merleau-Ponty's argument is that space is encountered as an extension of the self or group. Here children's sketch maps are informative, for they show the child's projection into the space he or she portrays; their maps are both more naive and more honest of the natural attitude with its interpenetration of man and space, subject and object. Thus one child overestimates the width of a street separating his home from an ethnically diverse public housing project, implicating the social and spatial barrier which the street represents. His side of the street is finely differentiated, but the other side is typified as "the project" (Ladd, 1970). A second child living in a high-rise apartment draws a neighborhood map in a vertical dimension that consists of her building, its landscaping, and a vertical parking lot, revealing the more constricted world that high-rise living offers a child (Bunge and Bordessa, 1975:83). Finally, in a neighborhood sketching exercise in his school, a third child includes a hospital on his map, exaggerating its size relative to other features (Figure 4.7). There is no hospital near his neighborhood, but after recent medical treatment it remains a salient landmark of his life-world and as such is introduced "incorrectly" to the projective image of his home area. In the same exercise his friend, having recently broken a window at school and been threatened with a visit to the police, introduces on his map a police station!

These final examples are reminders that the image of the city is not fixed and that upon the relatively enduring elements representing major routines more ephemeral features are temporarily superimposed. The experience of urban form is both momentary and enduring; the existential moment captured by the cognitive map offers clues of both transitory and abiding elements of the urban life-world.

Figure 4.7   A child's image of his neighborhood.

The Mean Information Field

The image of the city revealed by various cognitive mapping techniques may also be conceptualized in a different manner which has proven extremely fruitful for the study of spatial behavior. Knowledge and information of the city have been shown to be greatest around an individual's here and now; distance in space and in time weakens information levels. Consequently, we might think of an information field anchored around an individual (or group), with increasing distance from the center leading to a decreasing probability that information from a given source will be received. There are of course many barriers to the effective transmission of information, so that it is unlikely that the probability contours of the information field will be symmetrical in all directions; within the city one major barrier to transmission may be incompatible social status. Superimposed on the simple distance decline model of the information field will be outliers of high information and inliers of low information according to the location of groups who are more or less socially compatible.

Spatial Search

The information field has proven useful as an independent variable in its own right in explaining geographic patterns of search and the spatial dimensions of problem solving in the city. It has been argued that if an individual is seeking a particular commodity, service, or relationship, then the search process will be constrained by the contours of the existing information field developed in everyday routines. The existing biasses of this field will then be reproduced in selective patterns of search and adoption (Brown and Holmes, 1971).

These principles have been applied to several empirical questions. In the case of the selection of *marriage partners*, geographers have predictably emphasized the spatial constraints of the information field, and sociologists its social constraints. Analysis of the premarriage addresses of bride and groom in Seattle and Detroit has shown the rapid and consistent decline in interaction with distance (Morrill and Pitts, 1967; Fowler and Nystuen, 1976). In Detroit two-thirds of the marriages registered in 1965 occurred between partners whose premarriage addresses were less than $2\frac{1}{2}$ miles apart; in Seattle, a newer city with lower population densities, almost one-half of the contacts were less than 3 miles. To turn these statistics to a more romantic note, the continued preeminence of the girl or boy next door seems guaranteed.

But there are of course other opportunities for contact than over the garden wall. The major divisions of social structure, including ethnicity, class, religion, and lifestyle, constrain contact probabilities and the mean information field. Gordon has reviewed a broad literature indicating the ethnic and religious constraints on marriage patterns, and argues for a pluralist model of American society (Gordon, 1964; Peach, 1980). In a mixed ethnic neighborhood of Philadelphia, data for 1968–1969 showed that 47 percent of marriages involving at least one partner from the neighborhood were ethnically endogamous; in addition, in 38 percent of the marriages both partners had neighborhood addresses (Cybriwsky, 1978). Interestingly, however, these effects were largely independent of each other, for even though 51 percent of intraneighborhood marriages were between members of the same ethnicity, there was only a small decrease, to 44 percent, in extraneighborhood pairings. The same conclusion was reached in a Norwegian study that isolated social class and distance as predictor variables of marriage linkages. Though both compatible status and proximity were strongly related to contact probability, the effects were again independent of each other (Ramsøy, 1966). Carrying this generalization further, Beshers has argued that social-distance perceptions regarding marriage may be translated into urban structure, because families select neighborhoods according to their class and religious status in order to increase the probability of "acceptable" spouses for their children (Beshers, 1962).

The bounding effect of the mean information field in problem solving has been examined more closely in the case of *intraurban migration*. Early thinking on a behavioral model of migration envisioned household moves as occurring within an area of prior knowledge (Wolpert, 1965; Brown and Moore, 1970). Once the pressures to move arose, the shape of the search process would be guided by the household's existing information field. An additional and more ambitious hypothesis was that this field had an outward directional bias, forming a sectoral wedge between downtown and the edge of the city through the searcher's existing home (Adams, 1969). This further hypothesis was based on the assumption that household movement, and thereby knowledge of the city, was concentrated along radial thoroughfares leading to downtown that would result in sectoral patterns of familiarity. Some support for this suggestion comes from image-mapping exercises, such as those reported earlier for Los Angeles and Vancouver, which for suburban locations typically show knowledge of the home area and a sectoral path converging on the central business district. There is also some evidence that the mean information field of consumers includes retail stores forming a sectoral wedge outward from the city center and through the consumer's home area (Potter, 1979).

A preliminary testing of these relationships was conducted using a small sample in Toronto (Gad, Peddie, Punter, 1973). An added interest of this study was that the information fields and search spaces for both an Italian and a Jewish group who lived in the same inner suburb were compared. Households were interviewed while in the process of searching for a new house, and despite some imperfections in the study design, some interesting if tentative conclusions emerged. The Italian information field showed a sectoral bias of familiarity inward toward downtown and outward to the new suburbs in the northwest. The space searched for a new home fell generally within this sector with some investigation due north and in the existing neighborhood (Figure 4.8a). The relationship is more clearly defined for the Jewish subgroup. Their information field followed a north-south axis in the city through their present neighborhood, and the search space revealed selective preference for the existing area and the suburbanward continuation of this sector, north and northeast (Figure 4.8b). A more thorough testing of Adams' sectoral hypothesis was carried out in Christchurch, New Zealand (Donaldson, 1973). Residents were interviewed shortly after arrival in a new home in a suburban sector of the city, and data were collected on their information fields, search space for their new unit, and the directional bias of the actual move. In each instance there was evidence of a systematic sectoral bias to both their knowledge and activity patterns.

Although directional bias constrained by the information field seems to be present in the movement of middle-class homeowners, the data for lower-income groups and tenants is much less certain. Indeed, the requirement of sectoral bias is unnecessary for the present theoretical purpose; what is more important is that search behavior be associated with information surfaces whatever directional form these should take. Here McCracken's finding is pertinent that four-fifths of dwellings inspected by movers in Edmonton fell within previously known areas and that tenants were *more* confined to familiar areas than were owners (McCracken, 1975). More impressive yet was the analysis of 380 homeowners and recent movers in Toronto of above average means (Barrett, 1973). Whereas the average distance moved was over 3 miles, the median value was less than 3, and the modal value less than half a mile. The average search profile was five to seven houses over a 2-month period in an area that was already known; another Toronto-based study indicated a median search period of 1 month (Michelson, 1977). Search behavior, in short, was far from thorough but rather "a short perusal of a familiar area" (Barrett, 1973:206). In summary there is strong evidence from research into intraurban migration for concluding that search behavior in the city is indeed constrained by the configuration of the mean information field.

Access as a Subjective Problem

Distance, although it presents some constraints to the activity patterns and information field of middle- and upper-class residents, is more binding on poorer households, which

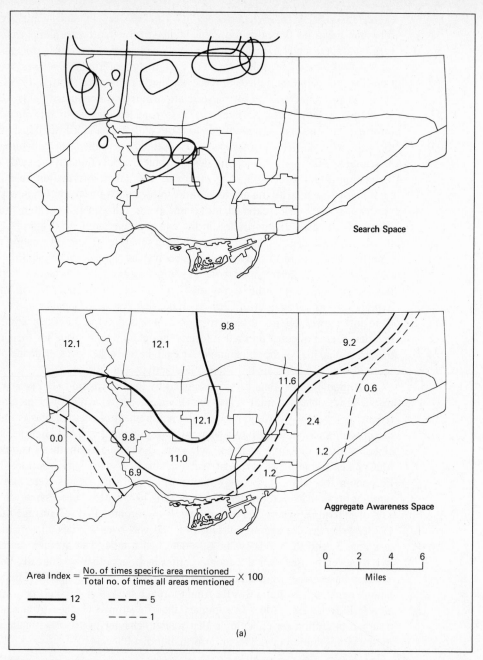

Search Space

Aggregate Awareness Space

$$\text{Area Index} = \frac{\text{No. of times specific area mentioned}}{\text{Total no. of times all areas mentioned}} \times 100$$

———— 12   — — — 5
———— 9   - - - - 1

(a)

Figure 4.8 Household information fields and search spaces in Toronto: (a) Italian sample; (b) Jewish sample. (*Source*: G. Gad, R. Peddie, and J. Punter, ''Ethnic Differences in the Residential Search Process.'' Pp. 168–180 in L. S. Bourne et al. (eds.), *The Form of Cities in Central Canada*. Toronto: University of Toronto Press, 1973, figs. 11.2, 11.4, 11.5, 11.7. Reprinted by permission.)

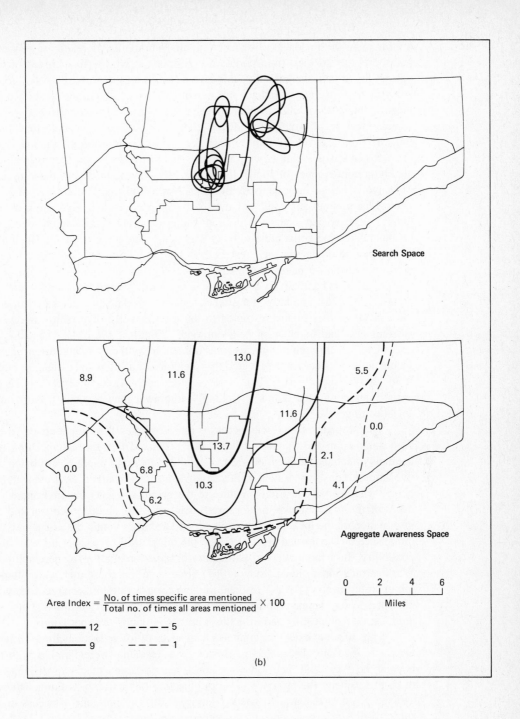

Search Space

Aggregate Awareness Space

$$\text{Area Index} = \frac{\text{No. of times specific area mentioned}}{\text{Total no. of times all areas mentioned}} \times 100$$

| ——— 12 | ----- 5 |
| ——— 9 | --- 1 |

0   2   4   6

Miles

(b)

are far more the prisoners of distance. Spatial immobility is related to economic status and the ability to make transportation expenditures, which, it is argued, discriminates against lower-paid workers. But this factor should not be pressed too far, for as Flad's study of Syracuse native Indians illustrated, lower-income groups do show a significant level of intercity mobility in their movement patterns. Short-term trips out of town are a major feature of American Indian activity patterns; to argue then that their limited intracity orbits are related only to imperfect access to transportation is too simplistic.

Space has a social as well as a physical component, and spatial immobility may also be a consequence of social disengagement. Revealing here is the comment of one of Whyte's Italian informants in Boston's North End that "fellows around here don't know what to do except within a radius of about three hundred yards" (Whyte, 1955:256). Other inner city participant observation studies have noted the same tendency for social encounters in blue-collar areas to be closely controlled and limited to a small local group of compatible others. In the West End of Boston, Gans observed that "potential peer group members are many, but their number is effectively reduced by the requirement that people must be relatively compatible in terms of background, interests, and attitudes" (Gans, 1962a:76); similarly, for street clusters in West Side Chicago, "in each group the conversation is highly restricted to the known world of persons and events in the Addams area and its adjacent neighborhoods" (Suttles, 1968:74). The school performance of Indian children in Syracuse was influenced by their parents' disengagement from school activities because they feared that prejudice or a stigmatized identity might emerge from such contact (Flad, 1973). A sense of compatibility and efficacy is necessary for social interaction, and if this is lacking, withdrawal may occur to a more comfortable social setting.

The problem of inner city access is more complex than might appear at first sight. For example, in Indianapolis it has been speculated that the juxtaposition of chronic unemployment and unfilled job vacancies in the inner city might be attributed to ineffective information flows and a limited knowledge of the urban environment among the poor: "The spatially restrictive nature of the ghetto so limits the environmental experiences of the (continuously unemployed) black that his ability to collect and assimilate information on the location of suitable job opportunities within the urban area is severely diminished" (Davies and Huff, 1972). This might well be so, but there is also another possibility. In a more detailed participant observation study of underemployed men in Washington's inner city, Liebow (1967) discovered that these men were often aware of job opportunities but did not respond to them for a variety of social reasons which from their perspective seemed rational: the jobs might be temporary or low-paying, physically arduous, or require long and difficult journeys on public transportation.

Thus to some extent the limited social space of lower-income groups might be self-imposed. As Gans discovered in Boston, few residents were familiar with the world beyond the West End, and few were concerned to extend their knowledge. This is not of course to deny the presence of more objective factors such as limited transportation and the physical distance to needed services. But the problem of access does have a subjective as well as an objective dimension.

This is well illustrated by the failure, at least initially, of some decentralized services, where storefront operation has removed the penalty of distance without, it appears, necessarily penetrating the social barriers to interaction. This was evident in a voter registration drive held in Philadelphia's inner city over several days. The project was under credible and vigorous black leadership with national and local representation; local publicity was promoted by a campaign of leaflet distribution that culminated in door-to-door canvassing and the use of a public address mobile unit. However, this widespread publicity failed to dislodge many of the thousands of unregistered voters. At the main registration office in one neighborhood, 50 percent of those who registered their names on the first day of the campaign lived one block or less from the registration point (Ley, 1974a). This pattern was unrelated to the distribution of unregistered voters; on one block face two blocks away from the registration booth, canvassers' lists showed 22 eligible registrants, but only one man added his name to the electoral list on the first day of the campaign. Though the registration booth was now a part of neighborhood space, it remained separate from the life-world of many eligible community members; in their definition of the situation, residents decided that its concerns were not theirs.

The problem of limited social participation is a handicap to inner city organization; in the words of a community member in the same neighborhood on another occasion:

> I don't know. If Bobby Seale and Huey Newton, the leaders of the Black Power organisation, came out and stood on this corner they'd get some young people and teenagers, but those people won't come out of their houses. That's how it is with the politicians. The people won't come out and vote. You know how it was when Hardy Williams (a black mayoralty candidate) and Bill Green came through here. The people stayed in their homes. I don't know if it's apathy or what. Maybe they reckon whoever's in down there won't get nothing done for the people.
>
> It's very disheartening and disappointing, but I can't say I'm exactly surprised. I don't know if it's that people are apathetic or suspicious or what exactly. But telling it more like it is, all the people seem to want is to get in some food and some drink and shut themselves in their home beside their T.V. set. . . . (Ley, 1974a:167).

More dispassionate data present the same picture. Analysis of time budgets in Washington, D.C., showed that low-income respondents spend less time away from home than do higher-income respondents and that within the home low-income and black groups spend significantly more time watching television (Chapin, 1974).

The relative immobility of inner city residents can be a penalty in their consumption of necessary services. Typically, municipal and private provision in inner city neighborhoods of such services as education, recreation, health care, and retailing are inferior to those available elsewhere in the city. The sophisticated consumer would shop comparatively for services to maximize quality and minimize cost, but this might demand considerable spatial search. As this is not always a characteristic of inner city residents, for subjective as well as objective reasons, they make do with often inferior local services. In terms of retailing, for example, prices are commonly higher and the quality lower in inner city outlets. In part these deficiencies may be compensated for by the availability of credit at local stores and the social nature of the transaction. But there are instances where these gains seem modest compared to the costs incurred.

A study among non-English-speaking immigrants on the edge of Spanish Harlem exposed a wide range of questionable retailing practices among a population whose very limited consumer knowledge compounded their handicap of limited access to a car (Caplovitz, 1963). Interviews revealed that for no commodity did purchases from discount or department stores account for as much as 25 percent of all major goods bought. The population was heavily dependent on a local network of 60 furniture and appliance stores which were aggressive in their use of door-to-door sales representatives; one small store used over 100 such representatives. The products available were invariably inferior-quality goods without price tags and with steep markups. Indeed markups were so high that name-brand products were invariably priced out of the market. Inevitably there were serious consumer problems; over half the households interviewed had consumer debts of over $100. Clearly, perfect competition was not working; the limited information field of this vulnerable immigrant group presented a near captive market to local retailers.

There is a strong implication in the literature that poor spatial access will correspond to weak political access. Those groups whose information fields are highly localized are unlikely to find their way to the appropriate council member's door in an emergency. Gans reports a forceful example from his study of the urban villagers in Boston's West End. The residents appeared to be oblivious to city hall and its plans, even though these included massive demolition and redevelopment of their neighborhood. The West Enders did not mount significant opposition to the proposals and once the work started fatalistically allowed their neighborhood to be levelled by the bulldozer. Though the forces of city hall conspired to destroy the West End, they were not regarded as immanent or salient by the West Enders until it was too late to check their impact.

The Mean Information Field and Spatial Diffusion

The concept of the mean information field was first introduced to geography in the influential research of Hägerstrand on the diffusion of innovations (Hägerstrand, 1967). To understand the spatial unfolding of the diffusion of an innovation, Hägerstrand argued that the critical process was interpersonal communication between kin or peers. Despite the extensive barrage of mass media communication, it is private information imparted by word of mouth which is more attended to, in large part because it is perceived as coming from a more trustworthy source; decisions are made in the context of a private social network whose members share common concerns. An information field is centered around this group, and because significant information is imparted in face-to-face inter-action, the field's intensity weakens markedly with distance from the group's location.

A mean information field around an area can be constructed using as surrogates a variety of interaction measures to generate a map of contact probabilities, such as friendship networks, or more easily collected approximations of interaction such as the origin and destination of household moves or the premarriage addresses of spouses. Hägerstrand assembled a mean information field about the rural Swedish settlement of Åsby using migration movements to set up contact probabilities between Åsby and adjacent areas. A matrix was constructed with each cell representing an area of 5 kilometers square about Åsby, its central cell; at a preliminary level the matrix was standardized so as to

TABLE 4.3   MEAN INFORMATION FIELD
ABOUT ÅSBY

0.0096	0.0140	0.0168	0.0140	0.0096
0.0140	0.0301	0.0547	0.0301	0.0140
0.0168	0.0547	0.4431	0.0547	0.0168
0.0140	0.0301	0.0547	0.0301	0.0140
0.0096	0.0140	0.0168	0.0140	0.0096

Source: T. Hägerstrand, *Innovation Diffusion as a Spatial Process.* Chicago: University of Chicago Press, 1967, p. 245. Copyright © 1953 Torsten Hägerstrand. Reprinted by permission of the University of Chicago Press.

be symmetrical in all directions from the center (Table 4.3). In this matrix the probabilities sum to 1.0, and values decrease with distance from the core, indicating the lower contact probability with the central cell. From this information field representing contact probabilities, Hägerstrand claimed it was possible to predict the spatial diffusion of an innovation.

Although barrier effects were considered as producing potential spatial bias during the diffusion, emphasis was on physical distance alone as a constraining variable on information and the diffusion sequence. Later research in geography included size as well as distance as a key variable; thus we can think of both *contagious diffusion,* following simple distance gradients, and *hierarchical diffusion,* where innovation adoptions pass between large centers which may be widely separated and later trickle down to lower-order settlements (Gould, 1969a; Economic Geography, 1975). For example, the diffusion of the Rotary International organization in Europe was transmitted between national capitals and other major cities and only later was adopted in contagious fashion by smaller towns around the major centers (Hägerstrand, 1965).

Many other factors besides size and distance influence the shape of the mean information field and guide the course of diffusion (Rogers and Shoemaker, 1971). Physical barriers such as mountain ranges and bodies of water are obvious examples, but at least as telling are the boundaries of the mind. Cultural barriers of race, religion, and language; social barriers of class, age, sex, and role; political barriers of nationality and ideology; and psychological barriers of attitude and personality all check the diffusion process. Indeed, barriers of language and academic temperament held back the transmission of Hägerstrand's own ideas from the English-speaking world for over a decade! All the micro- and macroforces that bring men together in groups tend also to separate those groups from each other and thereby retard the flow of information.

Intraurban Diffusion

The course of diffusion is therefore far more complicated than Hägerstrand's model under simplified conditions would allow, particularly when the scale is narrowed from the regional to the intraurban level. The probability of innovation adoption is related to a variety of factors so that within the same area there will be both early innovators and laggards, and social proximity to adopters may well be of as much significance as physical proximity. In developing a surface of adoption probabilities, social distance might well be of as much significance as physical distance. Although geographers have examined spatial effects and sociologists social effects, there has been little study of the operation of both effects jointly (Meyer, 1976).

A detailed documentation of the interpersonal as well as the spatial component of the diffusion process was attempted for a government program introduced to an inner city neighborhood in Vancouver (Phillips, 1979). The innovation was a residential rehabilitation assistance program (RRAP) for homeowners and landlords to aid home renovation sponsored by the federal government. It was made available in the neighborhood of Cedar Cottage, an area with few physical or land use barriers but with significant social barriers in the form of diverse ethnic groups speaking English, Chinese, Portuguese, Italian, German, and Punjabi as mother tongue.

A questionnaire survey of adopters and nonadopters 9 months after the beginning of the RRAP program revealed the ordered complexity of the diffusion process. Little of this order was visible on the map, however, apart from a minor concentration of early adopters around a storefront planning office promoting the program (Figure 4.9). Most of the early adopters had been involved with a citizen's committee and had received intensive exposure to RRAP. Subsequently this group acted as *opinion leaders* to their friends and neighbors as they endorsed the program and thereby provided bridges for it to enter Cedar Cottage's diverse social networks. Initial media publicity was in English and had little impact on the ethnic communities. Information was relayed to these groups later by the opinion leaders who made some house-to-house calls and contacted key ethnic institutions with which they had links of varying strength (Figure 4.10). Weak links directed the information between groups, but within groups it was transmitted through high-density networks. These networks were centered around neighborhood organizations (the community center and neighborhood house), ethnic centers (Portuguese social center, Edelweiss center), local churches (Chinese Alliance Church, Portuguese Catholic Church), and kin, friends, and to a lesser extent neighbors.

Despite the apparently unordered map of innovation adopters (Figure 4.9), the pattern of diffusion does follow an orderly, if complex, sequence. Information is received from both formal and informal channels, but far more selective attention is paid to interpersonal sources, as Hägerstrand claimed. Although awareness of an innovation may occur through the mass media, it is social reinforcement which expedites decision making in the stages from awareness to adoption. Opinion leaders act as bridges introducing the innovation, supporting the well-established hypothesis of the two-step flow of communication (Katz, 1957). Subsequently, information is disseminated through local social networks focused around neighborhood associations and kin linkages. In this process the social distance of individuals and groups from opinion leaders and early adopters influences the timing of their awareness and response to the innovation, with increasing social distance associated with a longer time lag. On the neighborhood scale the classic spatial contagious process might be only a minor factor as social dimensions of the information

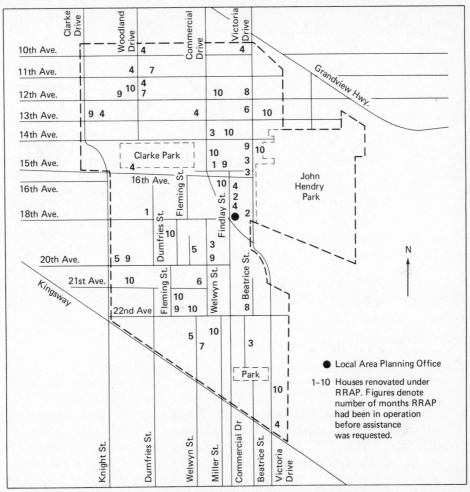

Figure 4.9 Spatial diffusion of RRAP applications, Vancouver. (*Source*: D. Phillips, "Information Diffusion within an Inner City Neighborhood," *Geografiska Annaler* 61B (1979):30–42, fig. 4. Reprinted by permission.)

field become uppermost. However, as abundant research has shown, the spatial factor assumes much greater significance on the regional scale, particularly when long-range communication is curtailed.

As an illustration of regional diffusion within the same city, we can follow the expansion of support for a new civic political party founded in Vancouver in 1968 (Figure 4.11). The party (TEAM) received most strength in the 1968 civic election in the high-status, liberal, Anglo-Canadian neighborhoods in the west and southwest of the city. In three subsequent elections TEAM support diffused east, southeast, and finally northeast as it followed the spatial gradients presented by class and ethnic distributions in Vancouver (see Figures 3.9b and 3.9c). The expanding pattern of "adopters" of TEAM

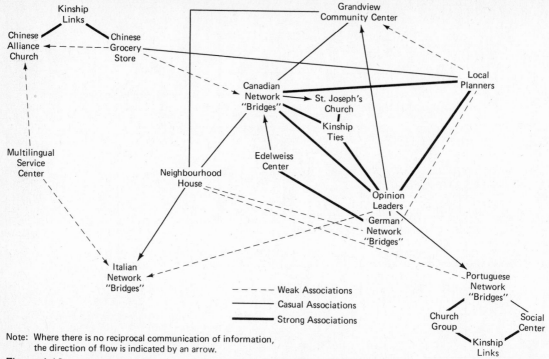

Figure 4.10   Social network diffusion of RRAP applications, Vancouver. (*Source*: D. Phillips, ''Information Diffusion within an Inner City Neighborhood,'' *Geografiska Annaler* 61B (1979):30–42, fig. 3ii. Reprinted by permission.)

policies over the map represented the diffusion of a set of political values along ethnic and class gradients through the social structure.

Connectivity of Social Groups

The degree of connectivity between diverse social groups is critical in following the course of a diffusion process. For transmission to occur, bridges must exist linking separate groups. Examination of the interconnecting paths between a family of social networks has been undertaken in several studies of the ''small world problem'' (Travers and Milgram, 1969). The experimental task is for groups of starters to convey a document interpersonally (i.e., not directly through the mails) to a specified recipient. Because none of the starters know the recipient, their strategy is to send the document to an intermediary whom they do know on a first-name basis who in turn will advance the message in a second chain to one of his or her acquaintances, so that eventually the transaction will converge on the target. One experiment set up as target a male stockholder in suburban Boston. Three groups of respondents were selected as origins, including a Boston sample, a Nebraska sample, and a stratified sample of Nebraska stockholders. Less than one-quarter of the transactions was completed with successful contact of the target.

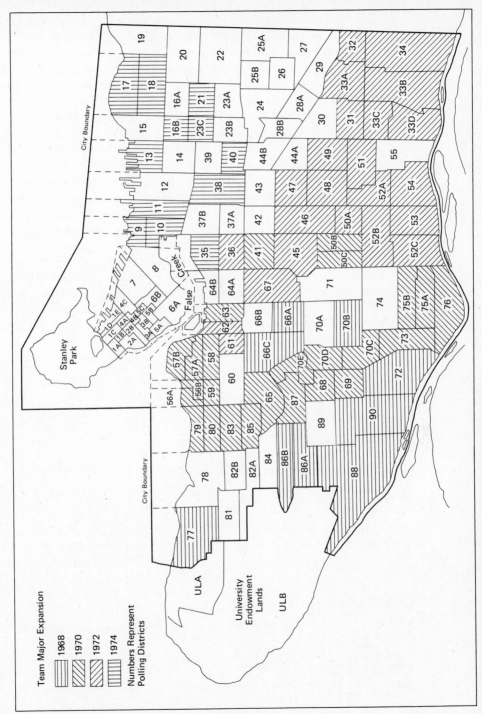

Figure 4.11 Sociospatial diffusion of a social movement, Vancouver.

127

The variables selected in this experiment permitted a comparison of spatial and social effects in transmission. The Nebraska stockholders followed occupational networks for transmission, whereas the randomly selected groups followed geographic networks. Completion rates or successful transactions varied from 24 percent (Nebraska random) to 35 percent (Boston random) of those who initiated at least the first chain; the mean number of intervening links ranged from 5.7 (Nebraska random) to 4.4 (Boston random). Spatial proximity between the target and initial senders was a greater aid to rapid completion than occupational similarity, but the completion rate was higher among those who followed occupational networks. Thus the most effective strategy was for a spatially proximate starter to search through the occupational network—additional confirmation for the pervasiveness of specialized social groups in the city. This theme also received support from the finding that there was considerable homogeneity within networks as persons tended to communicate with others similar to themselves.

The small world problem can be extended to the connectivity between groups and neighborhoods within the same metropolitan area. We might expect that the level of intergroup connectivity would reflect social-distance gradients in the city. Western's study of social groups in the small Mississippi Delta town of Houma supports this thesis (Western, 1973). For 10 social and neighborhood groups questioned in Houma, the probability of contact is clearly related to social-distance gradients (Figure 4.12a). In this fragmented community, contact between the middle-class and the socially disadvantaged blacks and Cajuns is limited to the public high schools; otherwise their networks do not interpenetrate (Figure 4.12b). In Belfast the polarized communities do not even

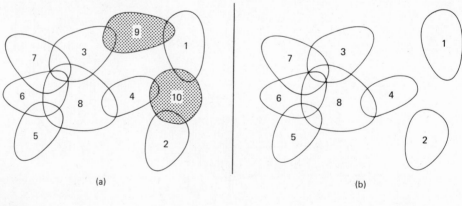

(a)   (b)

▓▓▓▓ Public High Schools

1 Blacks   6 Vandebilt Catholic H.S. Students
2 Cajuns   7 Mulberry Subdivision Residents
3 Newcomers   8 Rotarians
4 Jaycees   9 Terrebonne H.S. Students
5 Suthon Ave. Residents   10 South Terrebonne H.S. Students

Figure 4.12 Intergroup contacts, Houma, Louisiana. (*Source*: J. Western, "Social Groups and Activity Patterns in Houma, Louisiana," *Geographical Review* 63 (1973):301–321, figs. 9 and 10. Reprinted by permission of the American Geographical Society.)

share schooling. Catholic and Protestant activity patterns do not intersect; patterns of social visiting, travel, marital pairing, shopping, the use of local media, and school selection are all segregated and point to a deeply divided community (Boal, 1969).

Highly biassed transaction patterns intimate a highly fragmented metropolis. In American cities almost any measure of transactions reveals the profound racial polarization in society. In black north Philadelphia, for example, migration data showed the intense directional and distance bias of movers into one neighborhood, with 50 percent of households originating within a 45-degree sector southwest of their present neighborhood (Figure 4.13). In contrast are cities where social-network surrogates imply more direct connectivity between different neighborhoods. In Toronto, again using intraurban migration flows as a measure of neighborhood interaction, it is apparent that there is a degree of connectivity between most neighborhoods, as household moves occur far more freely across the city. Only weak regions of internalized migration flows occur within the metropolitan area, leading to the conclusion that "in the aggregate, Metro Toronto should be viewed as a single entity with considerable household movement among all locations" (Simmons and Baker, 1973). Such integrated patterns of connectivity are absent in Belfast and also in most American cities with their racially polarized interactions.

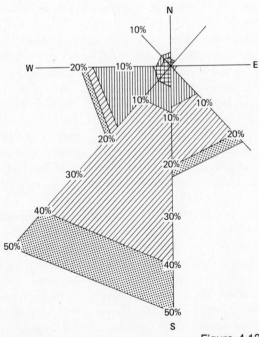

Distance from Rochester Ave. and 46th St.

⊞ 0–5 blocks   ▨ 16–30
▥ 6–15   ▦ 30+

Figure 4.13 Directional bias in intraurban migration, North Philadelphia. (*Source*: D. Ley, *The Black Inner City as Frontier Outpost*. Washington, D. C.: AAG Monograph Series No. 7, 1974, fig. 4. Reprinted by permission.)

It is tempting to relate the connectivity level between urban neighborhoods to the overall quality of urban life. Where a well-integrated pattern occurs, the theoretical requirements of Deutsch and Meier are more likely to be met for the creation of a healthy city with its wide-ranging transactions and access to opportunities. But when isolated and poorly integrated cells are common, the access of certain groups is limited; harmful stereotypes may govern intergroup relations; and there might well be tension and even fission within the city and the nation. "In America," writes Leroi Jones, "black *is* a country." However, this speculation could well be too simplistic, for there is also a contemporary movement seeking to protect rather than to dismantle the idea of neighborhood. Certainly, the experience of the ethnic neighborhood suggests that internalized transactions and local institutions can also aid immigrant adjustment to the urban way of life.

Conclusion

In this chapter we have sought to animate the static model of the city by adding to it the dynamic component of movement—the rhythms, routines, and activity patterns of everyday life. We have seen also the close interdependency between action and imagery in our encounter with the city. Though routines lead to the construction of a bounded urban image, yet subsequent activities also tend to be constrained by the existing information field.

The human map of the city that emerges bears little necessary relationship to the comprehensive accomplishments of the cartographer. The city of the mind and of action is partial and a product of the individual's role, interests at hand, and position within the urban social structure. The metropolis is always perceived from a viewpoint that influences on the one hand those neighborhoods and buildings which are known, and, on the the other, those districts where knowledge is absent or restricted to gross typifications. The mental map is relational rather than quantitative; space is assessed in terms of encounter rather than in feet and yards. The extent of the mental map is much diminished for newcomers and those of lower status who dwell in a more local life-world, but all urban dwellers have a specialized knowledge of space and are to some extent "experts" within their own domain.

The image of the city is a reflection of the activities that comprise our everyday routines. Within its bounds, social space consists of those places that the resident experiences as a group member and where interaction contributes to a sense of personal and collective identity. For low-income groups the social space may be geographically confined, though for more affluent groups, such as an occupational community, social-space nodes are often dispersed. The restricted spatial world of lower-status and immigrant groups may generate a feeling of local community but may also penalize their access to urban services and opportunities. In other forms of spatial search, such as intraurban migration, there is abundant evidence that action is constrained by the extent of the information field.

The mean information field is also a critical starting point in charting the course of diffusion in space and through the social structure. As Hägerstrand hypothesized, interpersonal communication is the most trusted information channel for adopting inno-vations, so that knowledge of the interpenetration of social networks will outline the probable path of diffusion. Transaction connectivity can also be assessed at an aggregate scale and assessment made of the level of integration between neighborhoods as a whole, as defined by household movements or other measures of interaction. According to the arguments of theorists such as Deutsch, the better integrated the metropolis and the less biassed the citywide streams of transaction, the higher will be the overall quality of urban life.

Hägerstrand's diffusion theory, with its dependence on face-to-face communication within and between social networks, draws our discussion to the pervasively social character of urban life. Chapter 6 will begin a reevaluation of urban man, as we will see that he is far from the independent, contextfree individual who has graced the pages of so much orthodox reasoning. But first we will look in more detail at the variable meaning to residents of different parts of the city, and the relationship between this sense of place and the changing map of consumer demand, population movements, and metropolitan property values.

Chapter 5

The Urban Sense of Place

A geographer is not a collector of shells which are no longer the home of a living being
(Max Sorre, 1957:199)

In Chapters 3 and 4 we noted briefly that urban neighborhoods have a subjective as well as an objective component, for besides their census characteristics they also bear a particular meaning, both for their residents and for outsiders. In this chapter we shall explore further the meaning of urban places by looking at the city and its social areas not as a distant observer viewing it from a map, an air photograph, or through the census volume but rather from the ground level, sharing as much as possible the natural attitude of everyday life in the city. The transition is one from spatial pattern to urban experience, from conceptions of space to perceptions of place.

Preoccupation with spatial patterns alone is a specialized and uncharacteristic conception of the city which is alien to the way we live our daily lives. In the words of Emrys Jones, ''Atlases of social data are rather like cases of butterflies—very pretty and telling us something, but the butterflies are dead'' (Jones, 1972). To understand the experience of city space, the physical form of the city must be animated; to the background of land use must be added the urban resident and his or her concerns. Though the point will not be labored in the text, in this chapter (as in Chapter 4) the development of such an anthropocentric perspective can usefully be achieved by such humanistic philosophies as phenomenology, existentialism, and symbolic interactionism. Unlike the physical-science orientation of human ecology, the humanistic geographer is centrally concerned with a view of phenomena as they are known in their essential meaningfulness in everyday life and with human values and creativity regarded as inseparable from the objects of the environment (Relph, 1970; Buttimer, 1976; Ley, 1977b; Ley and Samuels, 1978). As we shall see, within this analysis the relationships of man and environment are reciprocal, for whereas it is human intent and action which ascribe meaning and transform empty space to experienced place, so, too, place can act back on man and its meanings and contextual effects constrain his values and actions. We shall suggest that various parts of the city acquire specific meanings and that these meanings substantially influence population movement, patterns of demand, and land value surfaces.

Human Purpose and Urban Space

The first step in our argument is to realize that places are constructed, constructed not simply in the physical-engineering sense, but more profoundly that they are objects given meaning by a subject and that their reality is thereby socially constructed and socially contingent. It follows from this that place is an idea as well as an object and likely to have a multiple reality to groups with varied concerns.

Place as a Multiple Reality

To begin, consider the statement that Pittsburgh is a steel town. This is an objective fact of urban geography, an uncontroversial fact to which we might readily give our assent. It is a fact that has been impressed on us by high school geography classes with their black and brown arrows labelled coal and iron ore converging at the confluence of the Allegheny and Monongahela rivers. Subconsciously it has been reinforced by wide-angle photographs in back issues of *National Geographic* scanned in the doctor's waiting room or by 5-second filmclips included in dated television documentaries on air pollution. It is a fact that has been indirectly asserted in sporadic casual conversations with acquaintances who have stopped over for an hour or a day in the city. In this manner, a sediment of knowledge concerning Pittsburgh has settled in our minds; *for us* Pittsburgh has *become* a steel town.

Such sedimentation is the process whereby places beyond an individual's immediate perception become known as a stock of knowledge about them is built up (Schutz, 1970). This knowledge is unquestioned and assumed to be reliable; we rarely take account of the socialized nature of learning, including place learning, and the manner in which knowledge is the product of a particular social context. Learning always generates an incomplete stock of knowledge, derivative of a view from a particular vantage point with specified purposes and intent, so that the image of the city reflects the observer's own partialities and concerns (Ley, 1977a). In extreme form, the image is caricatured in the tourist's differentiating cliché of each city. San Francisco becomes the Golden Gate Bridge; London becomes the houses of Parliament viewed, of course, from the South Bank; Ottawa collapses to a scene on Parliament Hill (Downs and Stea, 1977; Tuan, 1974). This view is not a spontaneous one but a product of conscious promotion by travel agents and chambers of commerce, so that on the tourist's arrival he has simply to validate an image already constructed for him by others. The tourist acquiesces to a meaning of place that has been fabricated by strangers as the appropriate image for the role he has accepted. His role implies a way of looking at the world; his relationship to a place colors his perception of it.

The argument can be taken a step further, for the objective analyst also surveys the city from a particular viewpoint. For example, social scientists have long recognized what has been called the bias of exotic data. Exposure to a new subculture often leads to selective perception and a preoccupation by the researcher with the idiosyncratic and differentiating features of a place and its people. Herbert Gans detected this bias in his own perception during field research in the Italian West End of Boston. During his first visit to the neighborhood, he was impressed by the sense of difference, the unique qualities which "gave the area a foreign and exotic flavor" (Gans, 1962a:11). It was only after several weeks' residence in the West End that his perception began to shift away from features that appeared idiosyncratic to him toward more general and salient processes that aided an understanding of neighborhood life. It was only as his own position began to be redirected from that of observer and outsider to participant and insider that his initial prejudices were modified.

There are some parallels in the views of tourist and social scientist. Their point of view is essentially that of the detached outsider, separate from the daily experience of a place and dominated by their own interests at hand. They have their own set of "relevances" or concerns which sensitize them to differential and partial elements of the character of a place. These concerns are often taken-for-granted presuppositions that govern the description of a little-known place and even action toward it. Only to a nineteenth-century traveller from the forested eastern states could the grasslands of the American prairies have attracted the image of the Great American Desert (Bowden, 1976). But so, too, only for white American social scientists who have lived through the late 1960s could the black inner cities of the United States be seen as a revolutionary insurgent state in the making (Salisbury, 1971).

This argument casts our initial designation of Pittsburgh as a steel town in a new light. The description, apparently so objective, now appears questionable, for concealed within it is a point of view. It is the viewpoint of the industrial magnate, of Andrew Carnegie's ledger book, of bankers, economists, men of commerce, and also, it seems, of geographers.

But there were others for whom the steel mills had another meaning, no less partial, and no less compelling for their own behavior. For tens of thousands of eastern European Slavs at the turn of the century, Pittsburgh was a city of seductive opportunity, the immigrant's promised land. However, by 1914 this image had been tarnished, and a new perspective arose with the publication by the Russell Sage Foundation of the six-volume *Pittsburgh Survey*. This pioneering social-science inventory revealed the full meaning of Andrew Carnegie's industrial empire in the lives of working people. Its portrait of social dislocation and immigrant poverty in the industrial sectors of Pittsburgh became a symbol for a generation of social reformers, and the steel mills became the epitome less of wondrous commerce or immigrant aspiration than of the shame of the Industrial Revolution.

But times change and for other intents other buildings might now symbolize the meaning of Pittsburgh. For the historian or the defender of heritage, the city is summarized by the ruins of the Fort Pitt blockhouse, the symbol of empire named after a British prime minister and celebrating the subjugation of the wilderness and the beginnings of urban culture. For the urban planner, the city's meaning might rest with the

Golden Triangle and the remarkable success with which this land around the blockhouse was transformed into valuable downtown real estate. Other outsiders have a more humble view of the city, perhaps sharing with Paul Simon's hero in search of *America* the view of Pittsburgh through the glass doors of the Greyhound bus station; for youth culture, the city is less a destination than a place to wait for a connection elsewhere. There is one other common viewpoint of Pittsburgh for the outsider. In the spectator sport era of the last quarter of the twentieth century, Pittsburgh, with its successful football and baseball franchises, has become a major node of professional sport. For the large television sports audiences of the 1970s, the Pittsburgh image would include Franco Harris at running back and memories of Dock Ellis on the mound; a more appropriate metaphor for the city might be the aerial view of Three Rivers Stadium from the Goodyear blimp!

For each of these perspectives Pittsburgh is a city designated by a simple metaphor differentiating it from other metropolitan areas, a single structure that provides a cognitive cue, an aura around which the meaning of the metropolis is drawn. In passing from the perspective of outsiders to that of city residents, these external images with their simple typecasts are less salient. The insider's perception shows a keener differentiation, a more sensitive eye and ear to complexity and local nuances. Most important of all, for residents, Pittsburgh is home. A questionnaire directed to students living in Pittsburgh asked them to list the city's most important buildings in their experience; the most salient building by far was the structure anonymous if not invisible to the outsider, the student's own home. For the insider, the contours of localized concern are superimposed on the objective urban template.

The distinction between internal and external perceptions was demonstrated for the English industrial city of Hull (Burgess, 1974). Samples of residents and nonresidents were presented with a list of adjectives and asked to indicate which of them was descriptive of the city (Table 5.1). Perceptions fluctuated dramatically between the two groups, and statistically significant differences existed for almost half the adjectives. Although residents held a differentiated view of their city, the perception of outsiders was impoverished and unidimensional, congealing around a simple negative connotation of environmental and social deterioration.

A geographical location is not simply an unvarying object but an object for a subject, a phenomenon whose definition changes according to the perspective from which it is perceived. Place is relational to a purpose and an intent. As such, any place has a *multiple reality* for the plurality of groups that encounter it. The designation of Pittsburgh as a steel town may be factually truthful but less than fully real in experience.

The Anthropocentric Nature of Space

The social sciences have been slow to acknowledge this relational nature of space, that it is an object for a subject. Traditional urban geography did not explore far beyond the morphological form of the city, its land uses and artifacts. But behind each architectural facade, each land use zone, is the intent of an individual or group (Knox, 1982). To understand the monumentalism of Montreal's urban form, for example, it is necessary

TABLE 5.1 INTERNAL AND EXTERNAL PERCEPTIONS OF HULL
(*n* = 180 FOR EACH GROUP)

Attribute	Insiders		Outsiders	
	Number	Percentage	Number	Percentage
Good shopping center	154	85	87	48
Working-class city	152	84	154	85
Docks	147	81	162	90
Friendly	133	74	70	38
Low wages	111	61	53	29
Fishy	105	58	136	75
Redevelopment	100	55	72	40
A garden city	94	52	5	2
Isolated	90	50	24	13
Lot of potential	85	47	65	36
Historic buildings	83	46	40	22
Light industry	81	45	71	39
Unemployment	70	38	104	57
Heavy industry	53	29	121	67
Slums	46	25	115	63
Cold	46	25	102	56
Drabness	26	14	89	49
Overcrowded	24	13	80	44
Smoke	16	8	96	53
Coal mines	0	0	27	15

Source: After J. Burgess. "Stereotypes and Urban Images," *Area* 6 (1974), 167–171, Table 1, p. 169. Reprinted by permission.

to know the personal and political philosophy of Mayor Drapeau (Figure 5.1): "The ugliness of slums in which people live doesn't matter if we can make them stand wide-eyed in admiration of works of art they don't understand" (Drapeau, 1967; cited in Auf der Maur, 1976:96). It was this strategy which brought destructive freeway and subway construction to Montreal, extravagant cultural and art centers, and the excesses of Expo '67 and the 1976 Olympics, while at the same time leaving unattended the largest stock of slum housing in Canada and the continued discharge of untreated effluent into the St. Lawrence River. Similarly, Robert Forman has argued that the configuration of the black ghetto in Chicago may be traced not to anonymous ecological processes but to the conscious manipulations of the housing market by the Chicago Real Estate Board in the 1920s. In 1917 the Board established a policy stating that "it is desired in the interest of all that each block shall be filled solidly (with Negroes) and that further expansion shall be confined to contiguous blocks" (cited in Forman, 1971:60). At that time the core of what became the Black Belt in the 1920s was still close to racial parity. To guarantee black consolidation, the Board also encouraged the development of restrictive covenants ("contracts") in white areas. In a speech in 1928 a Board member described the "fine network of contracts that like a marvelous delicately woven chain of armor is being raised from the northern gates of Hyde Park . . . to all the farflung white communities of the South Side" (cited in Forman, 1971:55). In this manner, the residential

Figure 5.1   Urban monumentalism, theory and practice. (*Source*: David Wilkinson, unpublished figure. Reprinted by permission.)

distribution of the black population was constrained by the purposeful blueprint of a power elite fabricated 50 years ago.

The objective facts of the urban landscape point beyond themselves to a set of underlying values, the subjective world of an author (or authors) that give them substance. Indeed, the values are not some addendum to the spatial facts; rather, the facts are themselves the direct product of values. This is a very different conclusion to the rather sceptical dismissal of a values approach sometimes adopted by human ecologists. Whereas the physical-science orientation, which we saw to be so pervasive in the economic and ecological approaches to the city, conceives of abstract space and cannot accommodate a values approach, there are alternative philosophies for which it is basic. Phenomenological philosophers, for example, take as their starting point the world of naive experience, unreflected everyday life, what has been called the world of the natural attitude (Schutz, 1960; Gurwitsch, 1962). Within this *life-world* there is no conceptual distinction between object and subject; every object has its purpose, every place its meaning. The life-world is always anthropocentric, constructed around a group and its concerns. When portrayed in art and literature, it presents a script in which we recognize ourselves. Indeed, artists constantly animate the profile of the life-world, as in this description by

Dylan Thomas of its spatial extent for a child in South Wales during the First World War.

> This sea-town was my world; outside a strange Wales, coal-pitted, mountained, river-run, full, so far as I knew, of choirs and football teams and sheep and story-book tall hats and red flannel petticoats, moved about its business which was none of mine.
>
> Beyond that unknown Wales with its wild names like peals of bells in the darkness, and its mountain men clothed in the skins of animals perhaps and always singing, lay England which was London and the country called the Front, from which many of our neighbours never came back. It was a country to which only young men travelled (Thomas, 1954:8–9).

This is landscape viewed from the inside, anchored around the reference points of the perceiver's experience. At the heart of the life-world is a web of familiarity, predictable places and people, and some differentiation of detail—the summation of varied experiences over time. Beyond are consecutive zones where information is less complete and derived more indirectly. These are zones of decreasing differentiation subject to an increasing tendency toward *typification* as places are perceived in less richness. England is reduced to the typification of London, and the world beyond becomes no more than the Front, the only salient intersection between a child's world in South Wales and the European continent during the years of war. Though England is far more than London and Europe, far more than its typification as the Front, at that time—with his current concerns—such things were of no matter to the child.

This anthropocentric sequence of circles of familiarity and interest centered upon the group is a universal of perception in the life-world. Tuan (1974) has illustrated its character for historic peoples such as the Chinese, for whom increasing distance from the center imputed a corresponding decrease in civility and increase in barbarism. The same anthropocentrism was recorded in preindustrial Europe. Max Sorre (1957) wrote of *le patriotisme de clocher,* the manner in which the rural village or parish was the reference point of all experience for the French peasant, and in central Europe, William Thomas (1971) alluded to its Polish equivalent, the *Okolica,* "the neighborhood round about" with its spatial range "as far as a man is talked about." As a more current illustration, when a class of Harlem schoolchildren was asked to write about their city, their sense of spatial primacy was emphatic: "New York is a large modern country," wrote one child, and a second added that "the Hudson is an important ocean" (Kohl, 1968:39). And in a sense, so they are, for in the experience of these children their city is their reference book to the world.

The relationship between proximity and significance has been examined in psychophysical experiments comparing an individual's emotional involvement in an issue with the perceived distance separating him or her from the place where the issue occurred (Figure 5.2). The typical function that describes this relationship shows an exponential decrease of personal concern as the perceived distance increases. Initially there is a rapid decline in emotional involvement, but as distance increases, so the curve flattens out. The relationship shown by such experiments is of course only an average one and likely to be interrupted by a variety of social and political gradients in actual circumstances.

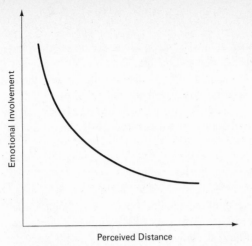

Figure 5.2   Perceived distance and emotional involvement.

Contextual Effects

The relationship between urban man and his environment is reciprocal; in Marcel's words, "a man is his place." Not only does urban man create a sense of place as we have described, but he is himself also influenced by the places he frequents and inherits. On one level the city is "a product of nature, and particularly of human nature" (Park, 1916); on another, "in making the city, man has remade himself" (Park, 1929).

The Behavior Setting

Social psychologists have formalized this relationship between microspaces and their users in their concept of the *behavior setting:* "Behavior settings and their inhabitants are mutually, causally related. Settings have plans for their inhabitants' behavior, and inputs are activated within the limits of the setting's control systems to produce the planned behavior" (Barker, 1963). Erving Goffman has discussed the characteristics of such settings minutely, examining how the physical details of the setting interact with social cues to help define a situation (Goffman, 1959). Developing a dramatic metaphor, he distinguishes between backstage, the area of preparation, and frontstage, the area of performance. Each of these elicits markedly different behaviors, as for example, the contrast between a closed meeting of a political caucus and its subsequent press conference or the transition from a salesperson's preparation for an important appointment to his or her conduct in the presence of the client.

One of the earliest studies of behavior settings was an analysis published in 1932 of the commercial dance hall in Chicago—"a distinct social world with its own way of acting, talking and thinking" (Cressey, 1971). It was a setting with elaborate conventions and interaction rules, and a specialized vocabulary, all of which provided cues for defining a situation and acting appropriately. Conformity to the code identified an insider. In the same vein Tom Wolfe has racily described some of the eccentric social worlds and behavior settings of the postindustrial city. In the affluent society, Wolfe argues, with time and money on their hands, some individuals create their own statuspheres, their own definition of reality, shared and maintained with fellow dévotés (Wolfe, 1969). The *statusphere* has its well-defined setting—the surfing beach, the discotheque, the speedway track, the ski slope—and it is here that one creates one's own world and seeks to excel in frontstage performance. Again, the cost is conformity, as vocabulary, costume, appearance, values, and action are all constrained by the norms of the setting.

Neighborhood Effects

The contextual narrowing of optional attitudes and actions has been noted for larger areal units and particularly at the level of the neighborhood. Even should initially incompatible neighbors live side by side, it is argued that with continuing interaction the weight of local opinion will cause attitudinal convergence to occur, with a much greater shift in the attitudes of the minority members. This was an early argument in favor of the social mixing of residential groups so that less-privileged groups would "upgrade" themselves through the "improving presence" of their "superiors" (Sarkissian, 1976).

Early evidence for this conversion effect was forthcoming from microstudies of residential subdivisions. Veterans' housing at the Massachusetts Institute of Technology constructed in the 1940s followed several designs, including a pattern of single-family and detached units built around a series of central courtyards (Festinger et al., 1950). An examination of friendship patterns that arose in the development showed the strong role of distance in allocating partners. The emergent cliques also tended to display a measure of attitudinal conformity with respect to local issues in each courtyard, and the closer the friendship, the more marked was the consensus. A similar finding appeared later in the suburban subdivision of Park Forest, south of Chicago (Whyte, 1957). Like the M.I.T. student housing, Park Forest was an area of high population turnover. Despite this frequent disruption of clique structures, there emerged fairly stable distance-based friendship patterns focussed around courtyards, and these were able to develop and maintain their own attitudinal nuances even though individual clique members were regularly replaced.

The role of neighborhood effects was assessed more systematically in a study of educational attitudes in Sunderland, northern England (Robson, 1969). Seven districts in the city were chosen that varied substantially in socioeconomic status. As a direct relationship between socioeconomic status and educational aspirations has been commonly asserted, it would be expected that the variation in attitudes to education would be readily traced to variations in social class. But the relationship was not this straightforward. Completed interviews with 188 parents in the seven districts showed only a moderate correlation between class and attitude to be present ($r = 0.53$). Of considerable interest was the pattern of residuals from the regression (Figure 5.3). As these were far from randomly scattered, it was clear that there were contextual forces present systematically diverting district scores away from their predicted levels. In other words, within each district a neighborhood effect was causing attitudinal similarity independent of socioeconomic status, so that families of similar class tended to hold different attitudes according to where they lived. "No matter what the area, the attitudes of individual

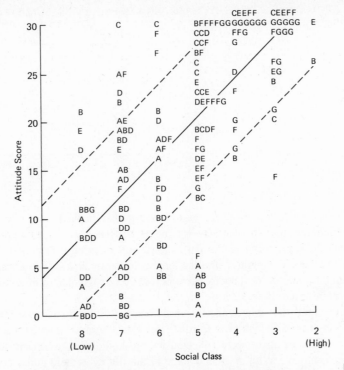

Notes: (*i*) The regression line of *y* on *x* is shown, together with lines drawn at one standard error from the regression line. (*ii*) Each entry represents one family from the following areas:

A	Deptford	E	Bishopwearmouth
B	Upper Hendon	F	Thornhill
C	Lower Hendon	G	Alexandra Road
D	Thorney Close		

Figure 5.3 Attitudes toward education by social class: the pattern of residuals. (*Source*: B. Robson, *Urban Analysis*. Cambridge: Cambridge University Press, 1969, fig. 5.1. Reprinted by permission.)

families were more similar to those prevailing around them than to those of their 'objective' social class'' (Robson, 1969:244). This conclusion is highlighted in Table 5.2, which shows the varying associations of social class and area of residence with positive attitudes toward education, which was measured on an index ranging from a minimum of 0 to a maximum of 29. In Table 5.2 there is a progressive decrease in status through classes 2 to 8; entries in the table have been filled only when derived from a minimum of five families. Despite this reduction in available data, it is evident that in both the working-class neighborhoods of Upper Hendon and Thorney Close, and the higher-status neighborhoods of Thornhill and Alexandra Road, there is a degree of homogeneity within neighborhoods across the range of local social classes.

In unravelling the neighborhood effect, Robson discovered that a key factor was the level of social interaction in each district. In the working-class neighborhoods of Sunderland, strong local integration led to attitudes reflecting class norms. Only families isolated from their neighbors had higher than expected educational aspirations. Indeed, only Lower Hendon of the four working-class areas had community attitudes that were

TABLE 5.2   ATTITUDINAL SCORES BY CLASS AND NEIGHBORHOOD, SUNDERLAND

Neighborhood	Social Class						
	2	3	4	5	6	7	8
Deptford						15.1	
Upper Hendon				12.5	10.1	11.0	10.2
Lower Hendon				23.4			
Thorney Close				17.4	14.3	10.6	15.2
Bishopwearmouth				19.0			
Thornhill		25.2	25.8	21.1	20.4		
Alexandra Road		27.4	26.6	21.8			

Source: B. Robson, *Urban Analysis*. Cambridge, England: Cambridge University Press, 1969, Table 5.10c, p. 213. Reprinted by permission.

more positive than predicted from regression, and it also displayed the weakest level of local social integration. Although small sample sizes should lead to some caution in interpretation, the clear trend of the data showed overscoring households in working-class areas to be poorly integrated into the local community and therefore immune to the attitudinal conditioning of local social networks. Only social isolation provided immunity from the neighborhood effect.

A more recent study examining the variation of attitudes by neighborhood has been carried out in a second British city, Cardiff (Herbert, 1976a). Attitudes toward juvenile delinquency and punishment were collected for areas stratified according to their level of delinquent behavior. With class and stage in the life cycle held constant, systematic attitudinal variations remained between neighborhoods in the city. Moreover, these were related to the incidence of delinquent acts. Indeed, location seemed to be the most persistent source of attitudinal variation, supporting the notion of the existence of neighborhood subcultures offering varied sanctions for delinquent behavior. Localized values and lifestyles acted independently of ecological structure to encourage distinctive behavioral patterns.

This conclusion is consistent with the basic tenet of contextual analysis, that one may describe "a member of a collectivity by using properties of the collectivity" (Scheuch, 1969:142). Contextual analysis has been taken furthest in studies of political attitudes in the city (Johnson, 1976b). Kevin Cox has examined contextual effects in studies of political-party affiliation in both England and the United States (Cox, 1969a, 1969b; Busteed, 1975). Survey results in Columbus, Ohio, suggested that neighborhood networks were more influential than regional or national sources in the choice of political-party affiliation. Voters most sensitive to these forces were newcomers and those with moderate political involvement. The partisanship of the most committed political supporters generated a self-conscious barrier to neighborhood effects, whereas those with almost no political interest were effectively shielded from contextual forces by their own lethargy.

Particularly in the literature on political contextual effects, discussion has centered on questions of causality. To what extent are the attitudes of individuals changed in situ by local effects, and to what extent is there a self-selection of households that group together precisely because of their prior attitudinal compatibility—a case of birds of a feather flocking together? The available evidence is meager but would seem to indicate the joint operation of both factors in a process of circular and cumulative causation. Although Cox has persuasively presented the argument for contextual effects, there is little doubt that most households also have a prior preference for neighbors with compatible lifestyles. The continuous opposition to proposals for social mix in housing is a cogent case in point. In suburban Levittown, Pennsylvania, it was found that as soon as cost differentials between adjacent houses exceeded 20 percent, it became extremely difficult to find a buyer for the higher-priced property (Gans, 1967).

The net result of the interaction between the desire for compatibility and neighborhood effects is the emergence in the city of distinctive communities of interest with a territorial base. Attitudes are regionalized, and there are strong tendencies for adjacent neighborhoods to share a common outlook. Illustrative data on the spatial distribution of attitudes are limited, and the most ready information comes from elections and civic referenda, which repeatedly show marked contiguity effects between adjacent electoral districts. Thus attitudes can be as regionalized and segregated as any ecological variable in the city, as communities of interest arise with a distinctive territorial expression. In the Sunderland and Cardiff studies, the relationship between local values and ecological variables was complex, and social class, for example, provided an imperfect predictor of local attitudes and their related behaviors. A neighborhood takes its character from the values and lifestyles of its residents; however, reciprocally, its personality is also a context that acts to reinforce and narrow a range of human responses.

The urban landscape itself provides cues for appropriate responses (Lewis, 1979). Ethnic neighborhoods are the most visible places expressive of group values, but for the interpretive observer all urban neighborhoods offer their own indicators: the empty storefronts of deteriorating neighborhoods, the private schools and elaborate landscaping of the rich suburbs, the sect and cult centers of the youth ghetto, the body-building gyms and billiard halls of working-class areas, the indoor plant shops and craft stores of fashionable in-town living. Such landscape features accentuate the image of a place and the identity of its residents. The personality of a place and the identity of a group mutually, cumulatively, reinforce each other.

Existential Notions of Space

Space is irrevocably humanized, both a mirror and a molder of human purposes. In Tuan's words, "Place is a center of meaning constructed by experience" (Tuan, 1975). The detached, highly abstract concept of space of the architect or regional scientist is one which has to be deliberately cultivated, for it departs from the natural attitude. Moreover, it is a posture from which even the specialist returns. The abstract space of the architect's blueprint is a universe that he holds to only during the working day, for each evening he returns to a room in a home in a neighborhood in a city in a nation, all of them spatial tiers of meaning in his life-world. His "off-duty" world is one of meaning, his encounter with space inescapably experiential (Norberg-Schulz, 1972). Inspired by the philosopher Merleau-Ponty, McDermott, a social anthropologist, argues that the city is perceived in terms of embodied neighborhoods, where boundaries are the boundaries of typical experiences. Thus the image of the city is overwhelmingly a relational one, "a spatial consequence of the kinds of relations possible with different people in different places" (McDermott, 1975:21).

Everyday life provides abundant examples of this vicarious perception of space, so that allusions to place have been found to be useful in counselling sessions as a means of discovering critical psychiatric episodes that have occurred in a patient's life. The mention of a place by a counsellor brings to the patient's mind a set of relations and experiences that took place there, which could be of significance in the patient's psychiatric history (Godkin, 1977). Places are defined in terms of typical encounters that are likely to occur there. This point is nicely made in the following dialogue from the television series *Upstairs, Downstairs,* set in an upper-middle-class London house in the early 1900s. Mr. and Mrs. Bellamy are discussing a move to a cheaper district in London in response to an economic downturn in family fortunes:

Mr. Bellamy: What about Paddington?
Mrs. Bellamy: Oh no, not north of the Park!
Mr. Bellamy: Chelsea?
Mrs. Bellamy: That's just for artists and the young.
Mr. Bellamy: Then, Kensington?
Mrs. Bellamy: Oh dear, I once had a governess who lived there.

Each district in turn takes on the character of those who live there, intimating a set of typical experiences which the household might expect to confront and which, in turn, would color its own self-image. For this status-conscious family, it is a surface of social prestige, its attendant encounters and resultant effects, which is projected onto London's residential districts.

For each social group, space is similarly embodied, characterized in terms of typical experiences. In a working-class black district of North Philadelphia, residents were asked to differentiate their neighborhood from other black areas nearby. Their responses were grouped into three major categories: evaluative, physical, and social (Table 5.3). The evaluative category contained such general comments as "It's nicer here" or "It's worse there," without explicit reference to the dimension along which comparison was being made. Though from the interview context it is likely that social factors were usually implied by such an answer, the argument is more satisfactorily maintained by the frequent explicit reference to the social environment and the manner in which neighborhood meanings were commonly defined by typical social behavior that occurred there. It is noteworthy that the incidence of teenage gang activity was the indicator most widely used in differentiating one neighborhood from another. In both the affluent world of Edwardian London and the deprived world of black Philadelphia, places were distinguished along an *existential* dimension.

A number of recent writers, working mainly in the tradition of French phenomenology and existentialism, have begun to develop existential views of space that have

TABLE 5.3   DIMENSIONS OF NEIGHBORHOOD
DIFFERENTIATION (n = 116)

Evaluative			42
Housing quality	18		
Physical condition	9	Physical environment	39
Descriptive land use	8		
Traffic density	4		
Gang activity/delinquency	21		
Quietness	16		
Violence	15	Social environment	69
Bad habits	6		
Privacy	6		
Income	5		

Source: D. Ley, *The Black Inner City as Frontier Outpost.*
Washington, D.C.: Association of American Geographers,
Monograph Series No. 7, 1974, Table 20, p. 229. Reprinted
by permission.

conceived of space in terms of the values ascribed to it and the meaning it holds for
social groups. Space is pervasively and unavoidably humanized (Matoré, 1966; Bachelard, 1969; Moles and Rohmer, 1972; Samuels, 1978). Matoré, for example, writes:
''We not only apprehend space, therefore, through our senses and especially through the
sense of sight; we live in it, we project into it our personality. Space is not only perceived,
it is experienced.'' In the same way that existential writers have confronted social realities
such as love and anxiety, so, too, an existential conception of space would look for the
relational properties of space and seek a categorization based on typical experiences. In
everyday life, the city is invariably encountered as a multidimensional topography of
meaning. What are the dimensions of this topography, and what is their distribution?
There is no real precedent for answering these questions, so that the following discussion
can only be tentative; in the absence of adequate empirical studies, some of the evidence
is necessarily fragmentary and literary. Despite this and the inductive derivation of these
dimensions, it is felt that together they provide a satisfactory animation of urban space
and highlight some of the major dimensions along which urban areas are experienced
and responded to. In Chapters 2 and 3 there were repeated suggestions that in the
contemporary city different areas were perceived in terms of a plural set of values and
that these new existential gradients were increasingly defining patterns of population
movement, market demand, and land value. We shall now attempt to identify these
existential regions of the city more systematically.

Regions of Security, Regions of Stress

The regions of security are a fundamental existential domain, and the core of secure
space is the *home* (Porteous, 1976; Rowles, 1978; Sopher, 1979). Nowhere is the di-
vergence between objective and subjective space more marked, for whereas bureaucracies
speak of houses and building starts, of geometry and dollars, home is a word of expe-

Figure 5.4   A place of their own: an early immigrant household in Vancouver. (*Source*: Vancouver City Archives. Reprinted by permission.)

rience, a word of human relationship: "A house that has been experienced is not an inert box. Inhabited space transcends geometrical space" (Bachelard, 1969:47). Home is a place of few surprises, of rooms, personalities, and routines well-known and usually well-loved. It is a private domain where one is able to be creative and to regulate his environment, particularly it seems when he is also an owner rather than a tenant. Simone Weil writes provocatively that "private property is a vital need of the soul" (Weil, 1971; cited in Hayward, 1975), and certainly in the New World, where home ownership is treated almost as a constitutional right, immigrants and newly formed households seem willing to endure heavy debts in order to have a place of their own (Figure 5.4).

Home is a multifaceted security, and its primeval meaning is that of refuge: "Life begins well, it begins enclosed, protected, all warm in the bosom of the house" (Bachelard, 1969:7). A number of writers have claimed that for the working-class for whom life may be uncertain and oppressive, the home is indeed a haven from outside exigencies (Rainwater, 1966). In a perceptive review of the meaning of home, Holdsworth (1979) quotes from a description of nineteenth-century life in the Manchester slums, where "*Home, Sweet Home,* first heard in the 1870s, had become almost a second national anthem" (Roberts, 1973:53). The home was the final bastion, the last line of defense, and thus the supreme comfort of working-class life: "Where almost everything else is ruled from outside, is chancey, and likely to knock you down when you least expect it, the home is yours and real; the warmest welcome is still 'Mek y'self at 'ome' " (Hoggart, 1958:34).

There are circumstances, however, when the intimacies of the working-class home are extended to the surrounding neighborhood. An important series of studies has highlighted the existence of cohesive working-class neighborhoods in the inner cities of large metropolitan areas. These *urban villages* have a basis in class, as in London's Bethnal Green (Young and Wilmott, 1957), in lifestyle, as in New York's Greenwich Village (Jacobs, 1961), or, most commonly in North America, in ethnicity, as in former Italian districts in inner city Boston (Whyte, 1955; Gans, 1962a; Fried and Gleicher, 1961). Reviewing these studies in the mid-1960s, Alvin Schorr concluded that for the typical urban villager the meaning of his neighborhood was "security, warmth and a sense of belonging. . . These are the things he prizes about the space around him: his possession of all of it, his being enclosed by it, its familiarity, its manageability, and its intimacy" (Schorr, c. 1964:42–43). The urban village is typically located in moderate- to high-density inner city areas and is characterized by intense local social networks, a high degree of neighboring and use of local facilities, and the presence nearby of extended family members (Jacobs, 1961). Among the dominantly Italian population of Boston's West End, 60 percent claimed all or most of their friends to be living within the neighborhood, giving it an intimacy that transcended the individual house. Indeed, the family house became simply one level of a hierarchy of secure spaces, progressing from the home to the block to the neighborhood. The strength of local support and camaraderie in such neighborhoods is evident in patriotic displays, annual festivals, and effusive block parties with each house draped in flags and bunting, such as those that welcomed home a local boy during the Vietnam War (Figure 5.5).

Figure 5.5   Mexican-American street murals, San Francisco.

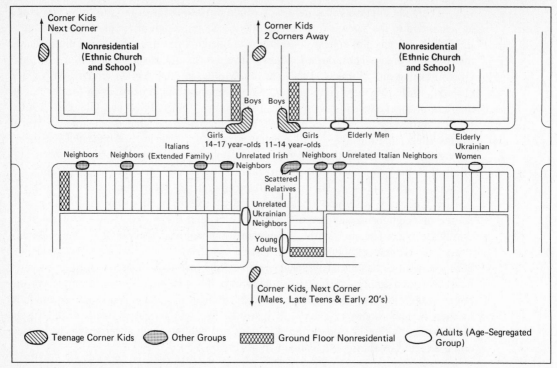

Figure 5.6   Street life in an urban village. (*Source*: R. Cybriwsky, "Social Aspects of Neighborhood Change," *Annals, Association of American Geographers* 68 (1978):17–33, fig. 4. Reprinted by permission.)

The Fairmount district of Philadelphia is a neighborhood that has exhibited many features of the typical urban village (Cybriwsky, 1978). It is a working-class district of aged row houses, with a mixed first-, second-, and third-generation ethnic stock. There is a high level of local commitment. Ninety percent of houses are owned by Fairmounters, and 75 percent are owner occupied; in addition, perhaps 40 percent of residents have relatives living elsewhere in the neighborhood. Each block face commonly contains 40 brick row houses, with corner properties having grocery or variety stores or taverns on the ground floor. As all properties commonly abut directly onto the sidewalk, a vigorous street life is common (Figure 5.6). In hot weather, peer-group, neighbor, and extended-family clusters form on the block; chairs are brought outside, food and drink consumed, and radios and on occasion even televisions are set up on the sidewalk. Intimate space extends beyond the four walls of the house, and the street becomes part of an extended concept of home.

Beyond the borders of their urban village, residents have limited knowledge of other neighborhoods and little desire to know them better. In Boston's West End, Gans found that "people were genuinely frightened at the thought of going into other neighborhoods" (Gans, 1962a:100). Stress may be engendered by intrusion into places that are at too great an existential distance from the routines of everyday life. In his examination of activity patterns in Paris, Chombart de Lauwe claimed that there were critical distance thresholds beyond which certain groups could not travel without enduring forms of discomfort and tension (Buttimer, 1969). Long-range migration may have the same stressful effects, especially when the move implies a marked culture shift. Consider the personal symbolism in the following poem written by a young West Indian immigrant shortly after his arrival in Florida (Fiddler, n.d.):

> When we had slept, we parted that morn into the wilderness—my master departing into the west and I departed into the north. Then suddenly, behold I came unto large areas of marshes stretching into oblivion, beyond nowhere the horizon expanding. There I saw horrible snakes crawling upon whatever leaves existed, and into those swamps, I also saw beasts beyond the horrible imaginations that men may think. Within that swampland, I came upon a solid piece of land which these horrible monsters inhabited. Only protected by the strong will of passion was I able to defend myself for twenty days and nights. . . .

The Kafkaesque style of the poem reenacts the immigrant's existential struggle for hard ground in an uncertain setting removed from his bases of security. After departing from a familiar relationship, the hero journeys far "into the wilderness," an unrelieved expanse of uncertainty and menace ("beasts beyond the horrible imaginations"), of indeterminable extent ("stretching into oblivion"). Finally the hero "arrives," but his refuge is itself a place of continuous struggle. More orthodox social science sources would suggest that such an existential surface is often encountered by long-range migrants who traverse cultures as well as distance (Brody, 1970).

But stress can also occur closer to home. Rediscovery of the urban village may have led to an overromanticizing of inner city life, for in most of the metropolis loyalties are more contingent and neighborhoods more nearly communities of limited liability (Suttles, 1972). In England the working-class urban village of London's Bethnal Green might be matched by a working-class wilderness such as the former slum of St. Ann's in Nottingham (Coates and Silburn, 1970). In a Chicago survey, 50 percent of residents felt little or no attachment to their local area regardless of socioeconomic status (Hunter, 1974). As might have been predicted from the urban-village thesis, the degree of local interaction was most often associated with local attachment, both in Chicago and in a nationwide study in England (Kasarda and Janowitz, 1974). Other factors adding to neighborhood sentiment are length of residence and stage in the life cycle, with child rearing and retirement the periods most conducive to local commitments such as the church, PTA, or informal contacts. The neighborhood is thus a variable component of intimate space; to many urban dwellers its claim is partial and more often potential than real.

The Chicago data revealed that black households showed less positive sentiment toward their neighborhoods than did whites. This general response can be investigated in more detail in the district of "Monroe" in the black section of North Philadelphia (Ley, 1974a). Monroe is a neighborhood that scarcely engenders feelings of warmth and solidarity. As one resident observed: "The community? Huh, what is the community? There ain't no community. People are just watching out for themselves . . . who cares about the community? Give people a meal and a can of beer and they're satisfied. They

TABLE 5.4 STRESS SCORES IN A NORTH PHILADELPHIA NEIGHBORHOOD
(*n* = 116)

Event	Stress Score (0–15)
1. A neighbor is evicted by his landlord.	9.4
2. A black police chief is appointed in Philadelphia.	8.6
3. Someone you know is left by her husband.	11.3
4. A friend's child gets hooked on drugs.	11.5
5. The local gang problem is solved.	9.8
6. Someone on the block is mugged.	11.3
7. Monroe High becomes one of the city's good schools.	8.5
8. A factory with new jobs is built in this community.	10.2
9. A house on the block is burned down.	9.9
10. A neighbor goes on welfare.	11.0
11. Neighborhood people come together to work for the future.	7.9
12. A shooting occurs on the block.	9.7
13. The police harass young people around here.	9.6
14. A neighbor's child drops out of high school.	11.2

Source: D. Ley, *The Black Inner City as Frontier Outpost*. Washington, D.C.: Association of American Geographers, Monograph Series No. 7, 1974, Table 6, p. 139. Reprinted by permission.

don't need no community'' (pp. 170–171). A survey in Monroe showed that only 37 percent of residents would offer much resistance to an urban renewal notice that would raze their block and that only 34 percent would turn down a chance to leave Philadelphia. ''I've had enough of this city—too much violence'' was a common theme in their responses. The failure of the urban village model in this ethnically homogeneous district can be attributed in large measure to the diversity and intensity of neighborhood stress. An attempt was made to assess the degree of local stress with a multivariate index incorporating such dimensions as crime, family breakdown, and unemployment (Table 5.4). On a scale ranging from a low point of 0 (no stress) to a high point of 15, residents assessed mean probability scores on 14 items. Scores toward the upper end of the scale indicated a stressful outcome, either a strong likelihood that a negative event would occur or an accompanying weak prospect that positive trends would be initiated. Close examination of the table shows the pessimistic perception of neighborhood in this area and the inappropriateness of overromanticizing inner city life. Residents are under no illusions as to the quality of the local environment, and many of them openly refer to it in the language of the urban jungle.

If secure places are those that we are drawn to, stressful places are those that are avoided. New Yorkers were offended by the French newspaper that published a map of New York classifying dangerous districts that should be avoided, but we all carry such mental maps that categorize places and influence behavior. In Monroe it was possible to map the perceived stress surface from crime by asking residents to name any blocks or intersections that they regarded as dangerous (Figure 5.7a). The contours of the stress surface played an important role in directing pedestrian movement, with residents being prepared to increase the length of their journey by as much as one-half to avoid dangerous corners (Figure 5.7b).

TABLE 5.5 SECURITY TECHNIQUES OF
HOUSEHOLDS IN RAVENNA, SEATTLE (*n* = 60)

	Yes	No
1. Always lock house even when home	60%	40%
2. Have added extra outside lighting	35	65
3. Have added extra locks, bolts, bars	57	43
4. Have an automatic lighting system	23	77
5. Belong to neighborhood block watch	37	63
6. Own a firearm specifically for home defense	12	88
7. Have installed burglar alarm	7	93
8. Have a dog primarily as watchdog	22	78

Source: Developed from data in L. Springer, *Crime Perception
and Response Behavior*. Unpublished dissertation, Department
of Geography, Pennsylvania State University, 1974, chapter 7.
Reprinted by permission.

A marked concern with invisible contours of stress, related largely to the perceived incidence of crime, is not limited to the inner city, as has been documented from an inner suburb of Seattle, chosen to be "typical of (white) urban residential communities within the inner suburban ring" (Springer, 1974; also Appleyard, 1981). The Ravenna neighborhood was safe and did not have a crime problem according to objective police statistics and subjective police perceptions. Yet Ravenna had three neighborhood-inspired anticrime programs; 60 percent of a sample of residents took some security precautions while out walking, and 20 percent carried some form of defensive device. As in Monroe, the neighborhood was finely differentiated according to its crime potential, and certain areas were avoided, particularly at dusk and after dark. Perhaps most interesting of all was the diversity of security techniques adopted by homeowners in this safe area (Table 5.5). In total, over 30 percent of households in this objectively low crime neighborhood had adopted four of the eight security techniques. Yet these precautions were consistent with both their perception and experience, for 50 of these households had been subject to 20 cases of residential burglary or theft, 22 crimes against the person, and 44 automobile-related crimes; only 60 percent of these offenses were reported to the police.

In objectively more crime-prone environments, security precautions are more elaborate. In the central city, fear of crime is much intensified; in Philadelphia, response to a poll conducted by a daily newspaper in 1972 showed that 84 percent of those polled felt crime was the city's biggest problem. Examination of a brownstone apartment building in an affluent section of Manhattan found that 17 of the 24 apartments had been burglarized at least once and that the building had become a fortress; one unit was defended by five locks, two peepholes, alarms, chains, bars, bolts, and booby traps (Thorsen, 1971)!

Geographic variability in the perceived crime surface has become a critical existential dimension of American and some British cities (Cohen, 1973). A study in Missouri is typical in revealing the perceptual differentiation between central-city, suburban, and rural areas (Table 5.6). Twenty-five percent of central-city residents regarded their neigh-

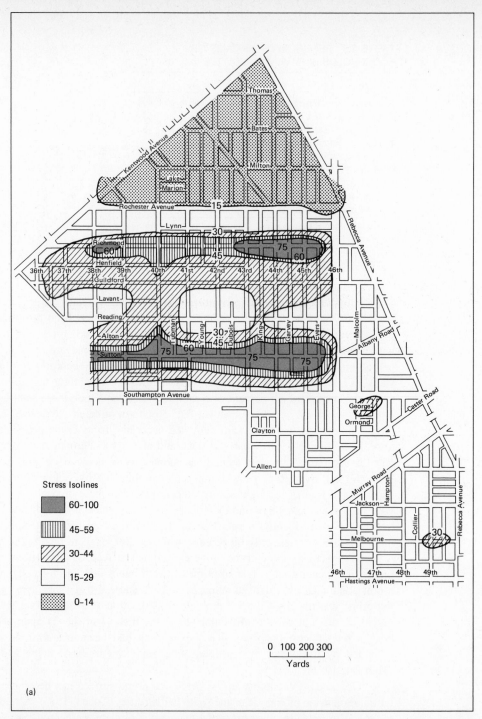

Figure 5.7 Monroe stress surface and spatial behavior: (a) spatial pattern of stress; (b) pedestrian routes between two points. (*Source*: D. Ley. *The Black Inner City as Frontier Outpost*. Washington, D.C.: AAG Monograph Series No. 7, 1974, figs. 36 and 38. Reprinted by permission.)

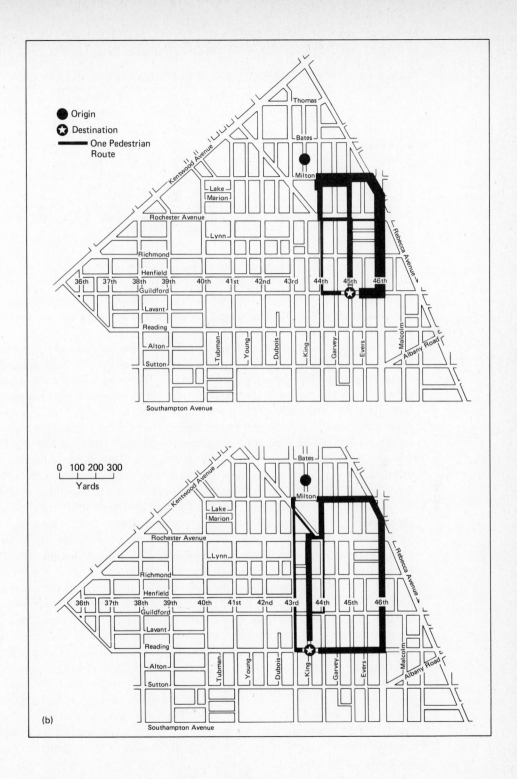

TABLE 5.6   PERCEIVED SAFETY FROM NEIGHBORHOOD CRIME IN MISSOURI

	Rural/ Small Town	Suburbs	Central City/White	Central City/Black
Neighborhood is . . .	(n = 360)	(n = 212)	(n = 200)	(n = 70)
Very safe	33.3%	34.0%	23.5%	1.4%
Safe	62.5	61.3	60.5	48.6
Unsafe	1.1	2.8	9.5	25.7
Very unsafe	2.0	1.4	6.0	22.9
Other	1.1	0.5	0.5	1.4

Source: Adapted from S. Boggs, ''Formal and Informal Crime Control,'' *Sociological Quarterly* 12 (1971), 319–327, Tables 3–4, pp. 324–325. Reprinted by permission.

borhood as unsafe or very unsafe, compared to 3 or 4 percent in the suburbs and beyond. Within the city there is further marked differentiation between white and black neighborhoods in crime perception and fear of local victimization. In objective police records and ecological analysis this relationship collapses to an association of the black population with high crime rates (Harris, 1974, 1976).

This association has become powerful in the public psyche and is one of the factors that has promoted the exodus of middle-class families from the city since the 1950s. Juxtaposition with an expanding black community has been an important trigger to white out-migration. In the South Bronx rapid and contagious out-migration occurred in a formerly stable white ethnic community in response to an advancing tide of perceived deterioration and crime (Greenberg and Boswell, 1972). Significantly there was a large movement into Co-op City, a new, isolated, and highly protected housing cooperative that would eventually house over 15,000 households. This ethnic population, unwilling or financially unable to secure safety through a move to the distant suburbs, opted instead for a nearby garrison. The relationship between black encroachment and white out-migration has been recorded in detail in Chicago (Forman, 1971; Berry et al., 1976). From a study of six varying Chicago neighborhoods, Berry and his associates conclude, ''Across the range of white responses . . . is the general conclusion that at each income level and regardless of socio-economic characteristics, a concentration of black families is perceived negatively by whites'' (Berry et al., 1976:222).

It is notable that racial transition and conflict in neighborhood schools has been identified as a critical factor in triggering the out-migration of white families to the suburbs. In one neighborhood school examined by Berry, there was a racial turnover from 25 percent to 90 percent black enrollment from the end of one school year to the beginning of the next. The suburbs, in contrast, are perceived as secure areas where child rearing and family activities can proceed peacefully, and it is they and not the city that are now the homes of white family life. An early suggestion of Wendell Bell was that it was primarily a lifestyle of familism that drew households to the suburbs (Bell, 1958). In suburban Chicago, 83 percent of householders mentioned some element of family life as prompting their move, and 73 percent added a quest for community. In contrast, themes of upward social mobility or the desire for consumerism proved relatively inconsequential.

Thus in many respects the suburbs are becoming the new urban villages, though a village based no longer on ethnicity but rather on American middle-class culture. The suburban characteristics of family life and community orientation are giving them an image as a refuge for secure living, slower paced, more certain, and more conforming than the pressures and vagaries of the central city. The suburb as refuge may be traced back to a nineteenth-century image carefully explored by Dyos in his discussion of the development of the suburbs of Victorian London: "Here was his own way out of the urban mess, a protection for his family, a refreshment for his senses, a balmy oasis in which to build his castle on the ground" (Dyos and Reeder, 1973:370; Dyos, 1961). The gregariousness of the suburbs continues to reveal itself in the range of family-oriented social organizations, such as the church or school-related associations, which are supported. Localism, another feature of the urban village, is revealed by surveys showing significantly greater local orientation in the suburbs than in the central city (Fischer and Jackson, 1976). Reisman has commented that the work of suburbia is the celebration of peace and domesticity (Schwartz, 1976). The suburban municipality has become a greater family home; the suburbs collectively are the secure regions of the metropolis. An existential surface constructed from a dimension with polar extremes of security and stress provides powerful insights into the social geography of the contemporary American city.

Regions of Stimulus, Regions of Ennui

A separate dimension, though not independent from the security-stress continuum, would distinguish regions of stimulation from regions of ennui or understimulation. The regions of security are essentially modest and private places with well-known routines and personalities. But security is not enough, particularly outside the years of child bearing. A number of social scientists would concur with the astronaut Frank Borman that "exploration is really the essence of the human spirit."

Stimulus as well as security needs to be an integral part of the urban scene. Urban designers have urged "on the one hand for sufficient order in the environment to facilitate comprehension and on the other for sufficient complexity and change to stimulate curiosity and exploration" (Carr, 1967:205). Robert Park used the analogy of the moth drawn toward a lamp to illustrate the magnetic drawing power of the city; in rather more casual language, "a metropolis is where the real action is" (Meier, 1968). Despite the well-orchestrated models that see economic opportunity as the prime enticer of rural and small-town dwellers to the city, it is possible that a primary existential surface to which young migrants are responding is one of stimulus, nurtured by a hometown social environment in which migration "is the thing that people like me do." According to one immigrant autobiography, for Roumanians at the turn of the century, "America had become, as it were, the fashionable place to go" (Ravage 1971:5). For the stimulus seeker, distance offers its own reward. Consider these statements from a group of Pennsylvania students, rationalizing their own changing place preferences and anticipated movement patterns:

> At sixteen, increased mobility now made me view Galeton as a limited, unchallenging atmosphere, instead of as the secure home territory it had been at age twelve.

I realised a world of different people and places existed beyond my tiny and now inadequate local area and city of Pittsburgh, which encouraged me to want to see more of what I hear about.

Until I am thirty I will probably hold many jobs in different cities because I will be searching for experience.

Everyone knows that California's the place to go, it's where everything's happening.

The leisure resorts of the Western world have been developed specifically for stimulus-seeking outsiders. These places are *other-directed*, having obligingly internalized the expectations of outsiders (Jackson, 1956–1957). Because the visitor is not privy to local details, there is no room for modesty in other-directed architecture. They are high-information locales, clamoring for attention and promising fantasy and new experience; the Las Vegas landscape has been characterized as the architecture of persuasion (Venturi, Brown, and Izenour, 1973). The experience industry reaches its perfection in the vacation fantasylands of Florida, Nevada, and southern California, the ultimate bonanza for experience-seeking, leisure-laden, mobility-charged consumers (Banham, 1971).

Places of stimulus are usually at a distance, spatially and sometimes socially, from the mundane everyday world. In Europe and North America, towns and even regions of vacation land are removed from the main centers of population but are yet within reach. As modes of transportation have changed, so intervening distances from population centers to resorts have increased. Thus any one resort has found favor from a sequence of social cohorts through time according to their differential access to contemporary forms of transportation. In this manner the resort towns around New York or London have experienced changes in the social composition of their visitors and therefore of their own image. The image of Atlantic City, New Jersey, has filtered down from that of a fashionable elite resort to that of a *passé* popular seaside town and, most recently, to one of the commercial entertainment of a Nevada gambling town. The action has passed further afield. A similar sequence has occurred around London, where transportation improvements have also brought phases of first seasonal visitors, then weekly guests, and finally day-trippers to resorts such as Southend, as their locations have consecutively shifted to the life-world margins of first the elite, then the middle-class, and finally the working class (Hugill, 1975). The bounds of stimulating space are expanding continuously outward; the consumer's tendency seems to be toward distance-maximization!

But within the metropolis stimulating space is also extending inward. Beyond the ennui of the suburbs and the stress of the inner city lies a new frontier to be colonized— even homesteaded—by a new generation of pioneers. The downtown neighborhoods have always offered diversion and stimulation from their intense activity, their diversity, their art and cultural centers, and their places of commercialized entertainment. Within the metropolis, downtown is where the action is. Tom Wolfe has perceptively captured the stimulus-responsive world of the young adults who frequent center city in a series of vignettes. In one essay he updates Cressey's study of the commercial downtown dance hall of the 1920s with a profile of the contemporary central-city discotheque, the setting of young office employees for whom even a lunch break is time enough to get back into sensory encounter with giddy sound, thrill seeking, *The Life* . . ..

underground at noon
    a vast black room heaving with music and human bodies. Up at one end is a small lighted bandstand. There is somebody up there at a big record turntable and rock music fills up the room like heavy water . . .
    down in the cellar at noon. Two hundred and fifty office boys, office girls, department store clerks, messengers, members of London's vast child work-force of teenagers who leave school at 15, pour down into this cellar. *Tiles* in the middle of the day for a break . . . back into *The Life* (Wolfe, 1969:78–79).

The excitement and diversity of central city has brought a more lasting encounter for communities of young adults. In the 1930s Carolyn Ware documented the transition of Greenwich Village from a cohesive ethnic community to a transient neighborhood of intellectuals, artists, and bohemians (Ware, 1935). As early as 1915, contractors were renovating old buildings, craft stores were opened, and artists and intellectuals were flooding into the district as it became the "cradle of modern American culture." By the 1920s it adopted the image of America's bohemia, then the image of a gay district, and finally attracted a distinctive criminal element supplying the excesses of liberated youth. Greenwich Village became a neighborhood of experimentation and rebellion, a bastion from which to assault the ennui of the safe suburbs and small towns from which its residents had come. At the same time in Chicago, Harvey Zorbaugh was describing inner city Towertown with its "bizarre and eccentric divergencies of behavior which are the color of bohemia" (Zorbaugh, 1929:87). Towertown had undergone a similar transition from artistic and intellectual colony to an undisciplined and indulgent bohemia of young adults seeking "escape from the conventions and repressions of the small town or the outlying and more stable communities of the city . . . (with) a genuine hunger for new experience, a desire to experiment with life" (Zorbaugh, 1929:91).

Zorbaugh's description of Towertown ends with the neighborhood's anticipated demise before the expansion of Chicago's business and apartment district. He did not anticipate its reappearance elsewhere, for he felt that metropolitan society was itself converging toward the bohemian lifestyle. But in the 1960s there was a resurgence of bohemias in the major cities of North America. Bob Dylan, as a spokesman for his generation, reinstituted the pilgrimage to Greenwich Village; in Chicago, Towertown reappeared on the North Side in Old Town; in Toronto, Yorkville became a center of youth culture; and in San Francisco the Haight-Ashbury neighborhood became synonymous with new forms of social and cultural experimentation. These hippy neighborhoods, or youth ghettoes as they have been called, restored the eccentricity of the 1920s bohemias, even if their philosophical leitmotif was now oriental transcendentalism rather than the 1920s passion for Freudian psychoanalysis.

The youth ghettoes have in turn initiated a new interest in central-city living for an entourage of lifestyles, a grouping similar to that identified by Carolyn Ware in Greenwich Village in the 1920s. The choice of central city has been associated with new office construction downtown, careerism rather than familism within the household, the initially low cost of "pioneer" housing in low-income central neighborhoods, and the newly emergent radical-chic imagery of downtowns in the major cities. Security is certainly not one of the realities of central-city living, however, particularly as rejuvenated neighborhoods are typically juxtaposed with high-crime areas. The return to center city has been in part a lifestyle move associated with an invisible surface of stimulus-seeking. In contrast to the homogeneity of the suburbs, social and physical diversity is an important objective of middle-class households settling in center city (Weiler, 1978).

The antithesis of the resurgent neighborhood is the suburb and small town, as is implied by the comments of the Pennsylvania students cited earlier. In the suburbs one buys security at the potential cost of ennui: "One renounces, in favor of a more tranquil repose, the variety and contrasts which have made the city the locus of the most colossal enterprise and ironic reconciliations" (Schwartz, 1976:335). It is the suburban condominium that has to offer its activity-starved residents a swimming pool, country club, and tennis courts; for center-city living, the address itself is enough to promise activity and diversion. The ennui of the underserviced suburb with its look-alike subdivisions has frequently been alluded to in the migration of young adults to the center city. A second survey of Levittown, 10 years after Gans' (1967) examination of the suburb built to house the American dream, showed a desire amongst youth to leave the area, with 50 percent citing frequent boredom as a significant problem (Popenoe, 1977). More recently the women's movement has pointed to another and more menacing facet of the malaise. Behind the suburban repose is the suburban Valium belt and the social costs engendered by isolation in a restrictive and understimulating setting. In ways less conspicuous than in the high-stress areas of the central city, the suburbs are the home of modern man for whom appearances may conceal realities, for whom the familiar may often turn sour, and for whom, in Harold Pinter's words, there may be "a weasel under the wine cabinet."

Regions of Status, Regions of Stigma

Cross-cutting the existential dimension, which ranges from stimulus to ennui, is a third dimension, which differentiates regions of status from regions of stigma. Just as every upper-class Victorian household had its places above stairs and below stairs, the social worlds of the drawing room and of the scullery, so the contemporary city has its prestigious Nob Hill and its more lowly East End.

Where one is from is a label in social life which may be used to define who one is and even who one is allowed to become. In class-stratified societies such as Britain, identity and place of origin are often closely interrelated via dialect and a set of social nuances that distinguish those with "class" from those who fall outside this socially defined reality. Peter Gould has brought to light Parkinson's social map of England, which is a stunning précis of the relationship between place and status, with its gradient from social desperation in the North of England to social privilege in the South (Gould and White, 1974). John Braine has explored the quiet discrimination based on class in *Room At The Top*, where upward mobility in northern England is challenged by the barrier of privilege and status. These social distinctions seem to be reproduced in residential patterns in British towns even when the data are aggregated at a coarse level.

With the labor force separated into only four occupational categories, the consistent relationship between social distance and spatial segregation remains strong in a varied sample of medium-sized towns (Morgan, 1974). In his analysis Morgan comments on the asymmetric nature of residential segregation in Britain, with higher-status households (categories 1 and 2) more segregated than lower-status households, a trend which he claims is not typical of the North American city, where dissimilarity is determined by ethnicity as well as by class. This finding is of course consistent with John Braine's appraisal of the more limited access in England to "room at the top."

In the United States, Brian Berry and his associates have argued for the importance of status differentials as a cause of white removal from expanding black residential areas (Berry et al., 1976). Although status differentials are undoubtedly a major factor in residential sorting in the United States, in the polar case of black-white differentiation a more likely existential surface is, as we have suggested, white fears of stress rather than of status deprivation. But, at a less specific level, Berry's suggestion revives an earlier theoretical attempt to link social process and spatial form in the development of urban structure (Beshers, 1962). Beshers' objective was to bring together ecological macroscale concepts of urban structure with microscale social and psychological processes in a common synthesis. In this reconciliation, social distance is a central concept, with the emergence of segregated social areas regarded as the result of initial social distancing between groups. Space then consolidates the social structure by limiting intergroup contact; friendship and marriage partners are regulated by the friction of distance, guaranteeing the separate existence of social worlds with distinctive value orientations. Space is thereby used to guarantee association with compatible others; upper-middle-class children will be more likely to meet (and marry) peers of the same social status. The reciprocal biases of space and social structure serve to separate and stabilize the position of neighborhoods along the status-stigma continuum. The egalitarian aspects of this thesis are disturbing, implying the maintenance of areas of privilege in the city that practice exclusion against "undesirables"; these intergroup relations will be examined in Part 4.

Beshers' argument clearly applies most forcibly to prestige neighborhoods of upper-middle-class and upper-class status, and his interpretation might provide one context for the considerable longevity of these areas, particularly outside the United States (Johnston, 1966; Forward, 1973). In Melbourne the persistence for over 50 years of an in-town high-status district has been related to the same forces of sentiment and symbolism that have preserved Boston's Beacon Hill. Analyzing Melbourne's social register for each decade between 1913 and 1962, it was possible to chart the residential preferences of the elite through time (Figure 5.8). The mean center of the southern elite sector following the coastline has been displaced a distance of 5 miles southward over the period, whereas the eastern sector has been more stable. The latter district, centered about the former village of Toorak, has been the more significant, accounting continuously for about 75 percent of Melbourne's high-status residents. Toorak was chosen by the State Governor for his residence in the 1850s, and other mansions and estates were added nearby. Through time these estates have been subdivided, but intensification of land use has not brought any erosion to the district's prestige. Indeed, continuing in the tradition of the

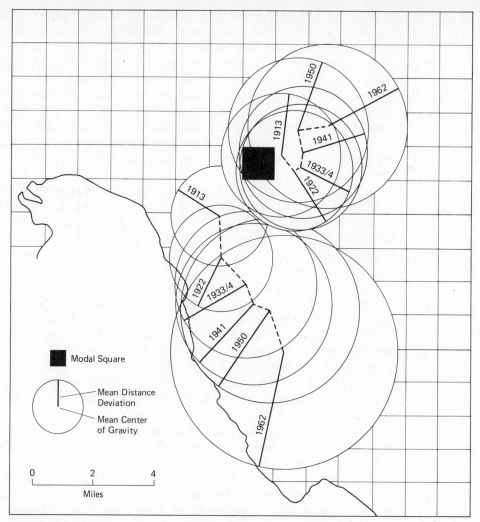

Figure 5.8 Persistence and change in the location of elites in Melbourne. (*Source*: R. Johnston, "The Location of High Status Residential Areas," *Geografiska Annaler* 48B (1966):23–35, fig. 5. Reprinted by permission.)

State Governor 100 years earlier, Australia's retiring Prime Minister purchased a house in 1965 in the final estate in Toorak to be subdivided, thereby perpetuating its continued reputation as an elite area.

Within the central city the revived status of heritage buildings means that age is becoming its own justification, as old buildings and whole blocks are benefitting from the new adage that old is beautiful (Lowenthal, 1979; Ford, 1979). The appetite to preserve the past has seen the expansion of protected heritage buildings from isolated museum sites, such as Philadelphia's Independence Square, to more mundane structures with recycled uses. The past has become marketable as entrepreneurs have invested heavily in the rehabilitation of Victorian commercial districts such as underground Atlanta, Seattle's Pioneer Square, and San Francisco's Union Street and wharf front. Stronger measures have been enacted to protect historic sites from destruction; in 1977 the city of Columbus, Ohio, was refused a federal grant of $6 million for allowing the demolition of the downtown Union Station Arcade, which had been registered as a historic site. The new-found popular concern for preservation has brought a new gentility and status to in-town living which extends beyond genuinely old structures. An in-town location is enough to justify use of an aristocratic (frequently Georgian) motif, even for new luxury high-rise condominiums.

The symbolic meaning of places can act as a form of *nonverbal communication,* conveying information about the identity of their users. Indeed, spatial form may be deliberately manipulated in order to reinforce the reality of a social hierarchy. This is a not unusual interpretation of the morphology of company towns, where systematic patterns of segregation reinforce the company's social hierarchy, with executives receiving the largest and most favored sites (Porteous, 1974). In hilly terrains there may be a morphological restatement of status in the company, with top management occupying view sites and the lowest-paid workers located in downslope hollows. This status game is replayed in downtown office towers, where position in the firm is measured by a series of spatial markers and promotion implies invariably a move upstairs, a larger office with more elaborate furnishings, or at least a desk further from the elevator shaft and nearer the window (Figure 5.9).

Status indicators in the landscape may be subtle but nonetheless binding. Groups may be categorized according to the nonverbal message given by their neighborhood or home, and social relations will be related closely to this categorization, however subtle. An illustration is provided by the distinction between elites reflecting "old money" and associated traditional cultured lifestyle tastes, and elites consisting of the nouveaux riches, whose tastes might appear more exaggerated and contemporary. In Bedford Village, a small upper-class commuter settlement in Westchester County 30 miles from New York City, the close relationship between landscape taste and social status has been reported for two such elite groups (Duncan, 1973). The traditional or "alpha" group occupies a muted rustic landscape of winding lanes, dry stone walls, and heavy landscaping, concealing houses that are set back far from the road. In contrast, the "beta" or nouveau riche landscape is more explicit, an open public setting of paved roads and highly visible and expressive colonial-style houses with accentuated artifact decorations such as colonial-style lamp posts and expensive ornamental mailboxes. Most interesting of all is the symmetry existing between landscape tastes and status claims which is revealed by membership in local social organizations. The separation in landscape taste is matched by separation in social affiliation, as the similar economic status of the two elites is overruled by social differentials that cause marked segregation in activities as well as in place of residence (Table 5.7). Social status incorporates a comprehensive mix of lifestyle variables including social affiliation, landscape taste, and preference for details of external home decoration. Within Bedford Village, alpha residents refer to the "Holy Trinity"

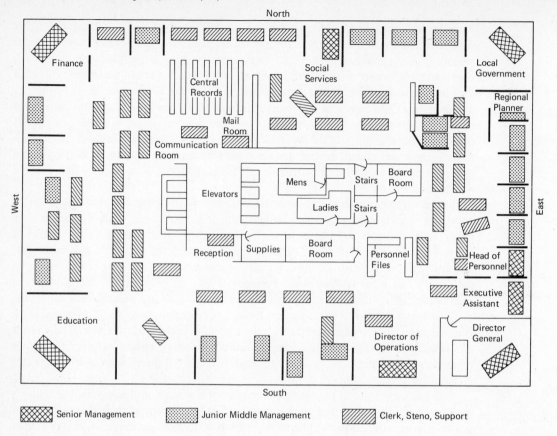

Figure 5.9 The status game in the room plan of a government highrise office building. (*Source*: P. Kariya, "Keepers and Kept: The Lifeworld Relations of British Columbia Indians and the Department of Indian Affairs." Unpublished paper, Dept. of Geography, University of British Columbia, 1978. Reprinted by permission.)

of social life—the Episcopal church, golf club, and private school—because almost 20 percent of alpha families hold membership in all three organizations.

Such status differentials reappear in many apparently homogeneous societies. Once again we see the interweaving of identity and landscape, confirming that to some degree a man is indeed his place. The routines of daily life intimate the playing out of central concerns for their actors, but once initiated they in turn consolidate the broad configuration of a lifestyle already engaged. Place is not an insignificant contributor to this culture-building process. Places both label their occupants and are in turn manipulated by them as a nonverbal expression of who they are and who they aspire to become.

Statements of identity are most clearly made in our intimate spaces. In an examination of styles of interior home decoration among an upper-class sample of households in Detroit, distinctive traditional and modern motifs were apparent (Laumann and House, 1970). Traditional themes including such items as still-life prints, artificial or cut flowers, a piano, and French Colonial furniture correlated with established, white, Anglo-Saxon

TABLE 5.7 LANDSCAPE TASTE AND STATUS INDICATORS
IN BEDFORD VILLAGE

Status Indicator	Total	Percent in Alpha Landscape	Percent in Beta Landscape
Episcopalian	254	84	16
Catholic	164	17	83
Italian	90	18	82
Garden club	76	96	4
Newcomers club	116	4	96
Golf club	213	91	9
Private elementary school	103	96	4
Social register	120	94	6
Colonial lamp post	185	25	75
Ornamental mailbox	59	14	86

Source: Adapted from J. Duncan, ''Landscape Taste as a Symbol of Group Identity,''
Geographical Review 63 (1973), 334–355, Table II, p. 346. Reprinted by permission of the
American Geographical Society.

Protestant status. In contrast, modern themes contained such contemporary late 1960s
elements as geometric drape designs, a solid carpet color, and abstract wall paintings;
this style correlated with households of recent upward social mobility, Catholic affiliation,
and southern or eastern European ethnic status. From observation of home interior decoration in metropolitan Detroit, the same social alignments as those revealed by using
exterior landscaping and voluntary association membership in the outer suburbs of Bedford Village reappeared.

Our secure spaces are the places of mastery and display, fiefdoms of personal
expressiveness. The strident dayglo posters of the adolescent hangout and the studied
permanence of grandmother's front parlor of memorabilia both supply instructive peepholes into a social personality and a way of life. The human management of place is
both contrived and unconscious, a deliberate attempt to communicate both to others and
to ourselves, and also a less conscious projection of personality into a material symbol.
In the San Francisco Bay area it was noted how extroverted, upwardly mobile business
households had a preference for ostentatious, mock colonial homes with bold expressive
design, whereas home buyers in the helping professions tended to be drawn to more
subdued, introspective styles. In this manner, the home clarifies an identity of the self
(Cooper, 1974).

But there is another side to the supportive symbols of self offered by homes situated
in rejuvenating inner city neighborhoods or prestigious suburban subdivisions, for places
can consolidate identities of stigma as well as of status. It is instructive to note, for
example, that inner city gentrification has been drawn selectively to some neighborhoods
but not to others. Landscape symbols of historical association, architectural heritage, or
environmental amenity have encouraged gentrification, but other symbols have exercised
a negative effect. A survey of 57 gentrifying neighborhoods in American cities revealed
that nearly 90 percent of them included some distinctive heritage association or environmental amenity, but none of them was near a sizable public housing project (Clay, 1979).

The label of ghetto has also become an unwelcome term of opprobrium for many inner city residents, connoting images that scarcely arouse feelings of pride or self-worth. Surveys suggest that white housing demand drops by 50 percent once an area is 20 percent black; however, perhaps more surprising is the pattern of black demand, which seems to favor an integrated and even a predominantly white neighborhood. Indeed only 17 percent of black respondents in Detroit placed an all-black neighborhood as a first or second choice for residence (Farley et al., 1978). These demand structures contribute to a more depressed land market in ghetto neighborhoods and a slower rate of new construction. In San Diego, for example, Ford and Griffin (1979) recorded a rate of infill in the suburban section of the black residential sector slower than that occurring in comparable white districts. As a result of the depressed demand levels, new middle-class homes were on average 25 percent cheaper in the black suburbs than in other parts of the city. In Hunter's study of community sentiment in Chicago, black residents gave markedly less favorable assessments of their local areas than did white residents of comparable socioeconomic status (Hunter, 1974). The most dissatisfied of all were black residents of large public housing projects.

In Britain it has also been noted how certain areas of public housing become sources of stigma rather than affection to residents, particularly when they are negatively labelled by municipal housing departments which assign them far more than their fair share of problem families (Coates and Silburn, 1970). For Wine Alley, a public housing estate in Glasgow, Damer (1974) has chronicled the development of a stigmatized identity adopted by local housing managers, by the public at large, and eventually by Wine Alley residents themselves. The typical high-density public housing project does nothing to enhance a positive self-image, and consumer surveys have repeatedly shown it to be the least preferred housing type (Cooper, 1975). Quite apart from the undesirable social and physical impact of the environment, the traditional large public housing project can be psychologically aggressive. Its austere, mass-produced, low-quality construction provides residents an unambiguous message of their status in the eyes of mainstream society. The message is reinforced by the low-cost, stigmatized locations frequently selected as public housing sites—beside the docks, industrial areas, or urban freeways (Figure 5.10). In Liverpool one area of high-rise public housing became known locally as "The Piggeries"; it was vandalized and largely abandoned before being closed down by the municipality (Economist, 1978). It is little wonder that these projects often fail so magnificently, like the much publicized Pruitt-Igoe housing complex in St. Louis, where abandonment, vandalism, and crime reached such an advanced stage that the complex was eventually evacuated and blown up by the city—a precedent since repeated in several British metropolitan areas. The identity conferred by such structures is scarcely one that residents are grateful to claim.

Conclusion: Existential Regions and Urban Property Values

In this chapter we have attempted to view the city from a new perspective, no longer that of the detached observer but rather a viewpoint that tries to recreate the resident's own definition of the situation. This anthropocentric position brings some immediate

Figure 5.10   A landscape of stigma: freeway, port facilities, and public housing in Cleveland.

changes. We see that a place is not only a phenomenon but also an idea, an object always invested with meaning. Meaning is not simply another variable tacked onto our definition of place; instead, it defines what a place is and what it can become. In this way we see that a place's meaning is socially contingent, for meanings are more mutable than objects. Not only may the status of a place change, but also at any one time it may provide a multiple reality to a plurality of social groups with different purposes.

But this is only one side of the relationship, for places can also act as independent variables, constraining the attitudes and actions of their occupants. The settings frequented by social groups begin to take on the group's own character, so that place is a reinforcing prop in developing distinctive identities. The places we frequent provide a summary of the people we see ourselves to be, for they prescribe the ongoing transactions that characterize a lifestyle. Such settings also provide a message to outsiders, for space is invariably perceived relationally, in terms of those who occupy it. Outsiders who are exposed continuously to a setting encounter social pressures to conform to its subcultural norms. These neighborhood effects have been observed in various empirical areas, including voting behavior, and encourage both attitudinal convergence and the creation of attitudinal regions in the city.

The relational perception of space implies an anthropocentrism where places are always viewed from the fixed reference point of a person's here and now. Our concern for places is highly biassed and invariably greatest for events closest to home, whereas distant places are often viewed one-dimensionally, in terms of a single concern. A closer

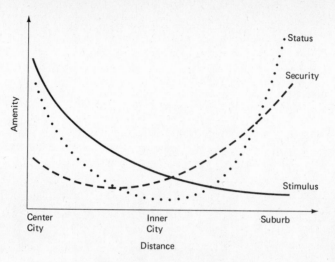

Figure 5.11 A schematic model of some components of an amenity surface in the American city.

look at the regions of meaning within the urban life-world revealed a set of existential domains. Most central are the places of security, anchored around the home, to which we constantly return, and variously located are regions of stress, regions of stimulus and ennui, and regions of status and stigma. We maintained that these existential qualities of space increasingly define the gradients and the boundaries that are important in urban life.

In an extremely tentative way, the general distribution of these surfaces is suggested for the contemporary city, particularly the metropolis in the United States (Figure 5.11). Security increases with distance from the central city, and stress decreases coincidentally. In contrast, stimulus reaches its high point in the central city and declines toward the ennui of the suburbs. Status follows a U-shaped curve, with its low point in stigmatized inner city locations. Though there will be much local departure, including sectoral variation, within these general trends, yet overall they are consistent with the preceding discussions. Furthermore, we could conceive of some combination of these surfaces as creating a new higher-order *amenity surface* in the metropolis. The weighting of the lower-order surfaces would vary for different social cohorts and in different cities. Families, for example, might be more sensitive to the regions of security, young singles to the regions of stimulus; in heavy industrial cities such as Cleveland or Detroit, the status of downtown compared to that of the suburbs would be less than in white-collar cities such as San Francisco or New York. But these local variations aside, a generalized amenity surface would, on the basis of Figure 5.11, show high to intermediate scores for the suburbs, intermediate to high scores for center city, and low scores for the inner city.

If land value curves were to follow this amenity surface, then we would expect not a continuous decrease in values with distance from downtown, as the orthodox economic accessibility model predicts, but rather a U-shaped curve with a low point in the inner city and high points near the high-amenity regions of the central city and the suburbs, the exact relationship of the latter two dependent on local conditions. Examination of the housing value surfaces for a sample of America's 20 largest cities shows exactly this U-shaped distribution (Abler and Adams, 1976). The precise relationship between suburb and central city depends on their relative amenity values. In the industrial city of Cleveland, for example, suburban housing values are on average over 50 percent higher than in the city, whereas in the high-amenity city of San Francisco, central city values are actually higher than those in the suburbs. But the more general regularity is consistent with a U-shaped amenity surface over the city. Indeed, in Chicago, where Yeates (1965) showed the steady erosion of economic accessibility as an explanation of the land value curve, the curve of housing value in 1970 is well described by an amenity gradient that has its high points along the lakeshore north and south of the central business district and in the suburbs and dips to a trough in the West Side and South Side inner city districts. Hoyt (1933) noticed the appearance of this trough in the 1920s, disrupting the smooth decline of the land value gradient with distance from the downtown core. In the past half-century the trough has steadily broadened and by the late 1960s may have approached 6 miles in width through Chicago's inner city (McDonald and Bowman, 1979).

Berry has drawn the theoretical implication from this changing pattern of metro-politan property values: "As one proceeds into the central city there is a progressive increase in neighborhood and environmental disamenities whose toll on property values is far greater than the positive contribution to value of inner city location" (Berry, 1979:444). This trend is strikingly apparent in data that trace the annual increase in sales price for single-family dwellings in Los Angeles during the inflationary period from 1965 to 1975 (City of Los Angeles, 1976). In census tracts in high-amenity areas in the suburbs and inner suburbs with view lots and high social status, home sales prices increased by more than $2 per square foot for each year of the period. Meanwhile, home values in some census tracts in the inner city actually *declined* over the decade. Although Los Angeles may not be a typical American city, it fully substantiates Berry's claim con-cerning the relative ranking of amenity and accessibility in influencing contemporary trends in property values.

In this chapter, then, we have attempted to explain substantial shifts in the meaning of place that distinguish the contemporary city from the industrial city of the nineteenth century. These distinctions were introduced in Chapter 2 but have been interpreted more fully here. The nineteenth-century industrial city was a prisoner of distance; accessibility to a central core organized its demand surfaces and spatial form. But in the contemporary American city, accessibility in this sense is challenged by patterns of amenity. We have suggested that the amenity gradient may itself be collapsed into a set of existential surfaces which bring distinctive meanings to different regions in the city. We might then suggest a more central role for a values approach to urban land use patterns than has normally been conceded in urban geography (Timms, 1971), for the property value map is a socially constructed reality, the outcome of competing and changing definitions of the meaning of urban space.

But this is not the end of the story, for the processes and contexts of this map require further investigation. How are the meanings of place constructed? What is their connection with social change and broader relations in society? However, first we must have some understanding of social relations themselves in the city. The economic analysis of urban land use which has underpinned much urban geography, human ecology, and urban economics has conceived of individual actors largely devoid of social context. So, too, has the behavioral approach to urban geography which informed sections of Chapter 4. In contrast, in Part 3 we will examine the inherently social nature of urban life, the development of formal and informal social groups, and something of the character of urban institutions. Armed with this knowledge we will then be able, in Part 4, to consider the interrelationship of these social actors and see the urban landscape and its meanings as the negotiated outcome of their interactions.

PART 3
The Social Basis of Urban Life

Chapter 6

The Geography of Informal Social Groups

Man lives a group life—even in the city

(Whyte, 1943)

Metropolitan vitality springs in part from the city's celebrated variety. The city is the exaggerator, the domain of the eccentric and the esoteric, tolerant it seems of endless innovation. The North American metropolis, with its immigrant heritage, harbors the traditions of diverse nationalities as well as the bizarre traits of the most contemporary lifestyles interlocked with the more mundane elements of New World culture. The complex but ordered intricacy of New York's social worlds impressed observers over a hundred years ago:

> No society in the world has more divisions and subdivisions than ours—more ramifications and inter-ramifications—more circles within circles—more segments and parts of segments. They begin in assumption and end in absurdity. They are as fanciful as mathematical lines; and yet so strong that they can hardly be broken, and can rarely be crossed (Junius Browne, 1869; quoted in Strauss, 1968:300).

A visitor almost a century later saw New York with the same eyes. "Each avenue," wrote Jean-Paul Sartre, "wraps around its neighboring streets its own atmosphere, but one street down, you're suddenly plunged into another world . . . All of New York is aligned this way into parallel and non-communicating concerns" (Sartre, 1955b). In Boston it was the same: "An American friend . . . pointed to the left side of a boulevard and said, 'The nice people live there.' And then, pointing to the right side, he added ironically, 'No one has ever been able to find out who lives there.' "

The city is a kaleidoscope of social worlds which, though they may scarcely intersect, each comprise for their members a large portion of the cultural reality of urban living. They form, as a result of established routines, around a set of park benches, in a tavern or social club, in a church hall, in a workplace or school room, or on a larger scale in a readily identified community. In each of these settings there is a gathering of individuals who together and often unselfconsciously define their own clique and, with ongoing communication, their own urban subculture.

In the preindustrial rural world the particular interest of the geographer was in unravelling the relations between man and his physical environment. Although the physical environment is not inconsequential in its meaning for urban man, the French geographer Max Sorre recognized that in an urbanizing age the critical forces in defining ways of life are increasingly becoming social rather than physical. The philosopher Merleau-Ponty has commented that history is other people, but we might add that in an urban age geography, too, has become other people. The salient environment for purposeful action in the city is more nearly social than physical. In this chapter we shall explore concepts some of which have not been widely used in geography. Nevertheless, these are directions implied by Sorre's observation. For the geographer to understand the city, he or she must come to terms with the social milieu of urban life in the same way that Sorre's predecessors in French geography so deftly understood the physical milieu of the rural French landscape. With this understanding the urban geographer will have a fuller appreciation of the segregated map of social areas in the city, for the formation of a social area is only a special case of the formation of a social group. How then are social groups formed? What is their implication for the behavior of urban man? And, more fundamentally, how and why does social communication itself take place?

Intersubjectivity

Intersubjectivity is a fundamental building block of social reality (Schutz, 1970). The term emphasizes the shared basis of experience within the life-world—that we can indeed have access to each other's subjectivity and meanings so that everyday life can be collective rather than solitary. Upon this concept and others may be developed a social model of man in the city.

At first sight, social communication and understanding might appear problematic, for no two people are the same. Not only do their present situations differ at least to a degree, but also their prior histories and objectives are never identical. How, then, is the gulf to be bridged for mutual understanding, rapport, to occur? Schutz explores this problem with his thesis of reciprocal perspectives. In everyday life we assume, first, that were we to change places we would perceive things similarly and, second, that the diversity of our biographies is overcome as we both adopt a common interest for the project at hand. In other words, we agree that our standpoints are interchangeable as we come to share a common concern, and this agreement may be extended to others besides ourselves whose concerns are in conformity with our own. In this manner we take it for granted that social understanding is possible.

This conception of the possible "we-ness" of interaction is foundational to mutual communication. Accepting it, we are able to share mutually another's stream of consciousness and subjective meanings; in Schutz' quaint terms, we are able to share a vivid presence and grow old together. Reciprocal identification and understanding occur most usually and easily in the immediacy of a face-to-face interaction, where time and space are shared. The mutuality of the we-relationship is the basis for a social encounter each partner might describe as "meaningful." This concept does, of course, admit of variation from its pure form. Indeed, even some cases of indirect communication can imply degrees of intersubjectivity, as for example the informed appreciation of a historical building or a piece of eighteenth-century music, which may involve the sharing of a stream of consciousness with the architect or composer, his or her subjective experience through the creative process (Schutz, 1951). However, although such a bond could be thought of as a communicative relationship, it could scarcely lead to the formation of a social group because it is not mutual except, perhaps, with other present-day admirers of the same art form who share the same experience.

The communicative relationship with an artist provides a transition from direct to indirect encounters, from the we-relationship we share with "fellowmen" to the they-relationship we share with "contemporaries." The encounter is now more limited in its vividness and richness; it is predicated on the other's existence less as a person than as a more or less anonymous type. The contemporary's stream of consciousness is beyond my knowledge; his identity to my eyes is as "one of them," so that in they-relationships we have types for partners. The more anonymous the contemporary, the more he is reduced to a type. Clearly, therefore, with increasing anonymity it becomes more likely that he will be miscast, that my typification of him will be in error.

Our social life thereby consists of interactions with others who occupy zones of increasing anonymity from ourselves, our biographic situation, and our concerns: "I live in a world of relatives, fellow-workers and recognizable public functionaries" (Berger and Luckmann, 1966:41). In this spectrum we pass gradually from direct, face-to-face communication in we-relationships, where there is still nevertheless a sharing of the subjective meanings of the other(s), to zones of increasing anonymity and increasingly indirect they-relationships in the fleeting world of contemporaries. We do not share the stream of consciousness with contemporaries, their subjective meanings. Rather we infer how they will respond as a type on the basis of our own understanding of the behavior of other members of the same or similar types in similar situations.

Although the zones of the social world usually merge imperceptibly along a continuum, empirical studies have shown that under conditions of stress there may be a much sharper definition of others and a keener dependence on the innermost zone of we-relationships. In a multi-ethnic inner city neighborhood in Chicago, Suttles noted an "ordered segmentation" both between and within ethnic minorities. In a setting of uncertainty and distrust, residents developed heavy dependence on we-relationships with a small group of others that covered a broad range of mutual concerns and sought to minimize and carefully control their encounter with more distant contemporaries:

> The central meaning attached to their slum residence, then, is a distrust, fear, and uncertainty among people so long as they rely upon public signs to establish their expectations. The first and most obvious line of development is to search out those personal signs that indicate trustworthy associates. In most cases, this means establishing a personal relation in which there is a massive exchange of information and the creation of a private morality that binds them together. When large numbers of people are involved, however, this is not a practical solution (Suttles, 1968:170).

Such persistent interaction within small neighborhood clusters leads to the sharing of subjective meaning contexts across a broad array of experience. It then becomes likely that the milieu of the we-relationship is not only the most trustworthy and credible, but also the standard both for perception and for action. A similar sharpening of ingroup and outgroup, of we- and they-relationships, has been noted in other highly stressful urban settings in inner Philadelphia (Ley and Cybriwsky, 1974; Ley, 1975b) and inner Belfast (Boal and Livingstone, 1982). In each instance, marked conformity is a feature of ingroup values and actions.

Social Distance

Whereas our contact with contemporaries is often functional and invariably tangential to our central concerns, our contact with fellow men contributes to the building of our own identity. If they-relationships tend to be those we make use of, we-relationships tend to be those we are drawn toward. In other words, as is implicit in Suttles' discussion, there is an element of personal choice in the selection of our fellow men.

Social life can be thought of in Martin Buber's terms as a twofold process of both setting at a distance and entering into relations (Buber, 1957; Samuels, 1978). Man can set objects (including other men) as separate from himself, but this detachment is simply a preliminary to selective engagement—purposefully entering into relations. Distancing thereby asserts the possibility of we-relationships, which are then actively confirmed by entering into relations. But in this twofold process, distancing is as important a statement of identity as entering into relation; to know who we are not is an important prelude to deciding who we are.

The will to relation is resolved on the basis of the perceived social distance between oneself and another. Social distance is itself a product of a similar biographical situation, including time and space, and of the sharing of common concerns. The more similar are two biographies, the closer in time, space, mutual interests, social status, and values; the smaller the social distance; and the greater the probability of a we-relationship developing between the individuals. Social distance as a concept was developed and operationalized in a crude way to measure the effects of race and ethnicity on group composition (Park, 1924; Bogardus, 1926). Later studies extended the analysis to occupational and class distinctions and changes in social perception over time (Bogardus, 1959; Triandis and Triandis, 1960); present-day studies would require further extension to more subtle attitudinal and lifestyle variations.

Bogardus sought to operationalize social distance by a graduated scale of seven hypothetical social encounters (Bogardus, 1925). Respondents were asked at which point in the sequence of successively more intimate relationships they would bar an individual of a given background. One experiment with 450 native-born white Americans showed a sequence of distance assignments to varied ethnic groups. Members of northwest European origin would be admitted to at least the fifth rank (citizenship) by almost all native-born Americans and to the first rank (kin through marriage) by some. In contrast, few respondents would admit racial minorities higher than the fourth rank (employment), and some would choose to exclude them altogether.

TABLE 6.1 SOCIAL RANKING OF ETHNIC GROUPS
BY TWO TEXAS SAMPLES

Ethnic Groups	Mexican-American	Anglo	Rank Difference
American	4	1	+3
Armenian	21	22	−1
Blacks	13	23	−10
Canadian	8	3	+5
Chinese	25	25	
Czech	20	17	+3
Dutch	12	8	+4
English	6	2	+4
Filipino	22	23	−1
Finnish	18	12	+6
French	7	5	+2
German	13	6	+7
Greek	17	18	−1
Indian (American)	9	13	−4
Indian (India)	30	29	+1
Irish	10	10	
Italian	5	11	−6
Japanese	26	26	
Japanese-American	18	19	−1
Jewish	24	20	+4
Korean	29	30	−1
Mexican	2	20	−18
Mexican-American	1	16	−15
Norwegian	15	6	+9
Polish	22	14	+8
Russian	28	27	+1
Scottish	15	8	+7
Spanish	3	15	−12
Swedish	11	4	+7
Turkish	27	28	−1

Source: Adapted from R. Brown, "Social Distance Perception as a Function of Mexican-American and Other Ethnic Identity," *Sociology and Social Research* 57 (1973), 273–287, Table 4, p. 278. Reprinted by permission.

In this manner each individual develops a hierarchy of those he considers more and less compatible with himself, a life-world of favored fellow men and distant and typified others. The usual pattern is that social distance is diminished the more similar to self another is perceived to be, or the closer he falls to a widely held cultural norm. Of course, as the reference point changes, so too does the way other groups are perceived. An experiment comparing the perceptions of Anglos and Mexican Americans in Texas indicated the differential social-distance rankings by the two groups (Table 6.1). Although there was a correlation of 0.69 between the rankings, there was a marked variation in the relative standing of certain groups, including Latins, blacks, and American Indians, who were more highly favored by the Chicanos, and minorities from northern and western Europe, who were more favored by the Anglos. In each instance other ethnicities who were perceived as similar to self in both economic and cultural terms were given a higher ranking. Ethnicities dissimilar to both of these groupings, such as Asian minorities, tended to share a common disfavored perception.

Social distance as applied by Bogardus and others provided a fairly coarse measure of differentiation within an urban population. However, the continued importance of major factors such as ethnicity and class in residential differentiation point to the concept's continued utility, and in recent years a new appreciation of it has emerged (Banton, 1960; Berry et al., 1976). Social distance does have the considerable merit of considering intergroup relations anthropocentrically, as they are perceived by urban dwellers in everyday life. It thereby exposes the purposes and prejudices that are antecedent to the formation of social groups.

The Formation of Social Groups

On the basis of intersubjectivity, social-distance perceptions, and a compatible biographical situation, relationships are established and social groups formed. These groups vary, from those that are inherited, such as the primary group of the family and kin, to special interest groups and into the realm of increasingly anonymous and fleeting encounters. Each group consists of members drawn to each other through common concerns and/or similar biographical situation. In this manner a significant degree of intragroup homogeneity is the norm for successful group cohesion.

The Sharing of Central Concerns

The individual is usually able to gauge the appropriateness of a group for furthering his own concerns by face-to-face communication. Besides the verbal assurances he or she may receive from such an encounter, there will be an array of nonverbal components, such as gestures, expressiveness, clothing, and the overall bearing of group members, which will aid in defining the situation. Indeed, such forms of nonverbal communication are often the clearest advertisement of a group's character. Such cues of group identity range beyond clothing to include cosmetic appearance and deportment as well as more general characteristics such as age, sex, class, and ethnicity, which are usually visible by observation. Together these define an individual's *impression management* (Goffman, 1959), the identity he or she consciously and unconsciously portrays to others. Other more subtle components of identity, such as the attitudes and values of a group, are intimated by observation but can be confirmed only in face-to-face interaction. Initial group associations are heavily influenced by impression management, but whether the association later flourishes into a stable we-relationship depends on the extent to which its members share central concerns.

The beginnings of these group-building processes may be illustrated in microcosm by a detailed study of the social geography of a small downtown park on the edge of skid row (Hall, 1974). Observation of Victory Square suggested that impression management amongst park users could be defined along the four dimensions of age, clothing, cosmetic appearance, and race (Table 6.2); as most park users were males, sex was not an important discriminator. A checklist of clothing items placed individuals into one of

TABLE 6.2 LIFESTYLE INDICATORS IN VICTORY SQUARE

General Age	Clothing Style	Cosmetic Management	Race
Young adult	Traditional, well-dressed	Traditional, clean	White
Middle-aged	Casual, occupational	Modern, clean	Oriental
Elderly	Mod	Unkempt	Native
			Indian
	Modern, casual		
	Modern, well-dressed		
	Mismatched, incongruent		

Source: Adapted from W. Hall, *Spatial Behaviour in Victory Square*. Unpublished thesis, Department of Geography, University of British Columbia, 1974, pp. 25–26.

the clothing categories; for example, the "uniform" of the elderly well-dressed men would include items such as a dated suit or sports coat, a shirt with a narrow tie and clasp, oxfords, and an immaculate fedora. Over a period of observation it became clear that particular sets of lifestyle attributes were invariably linked together; these sets of combined attributes defined 13 distinctive lifestyle groups who frequented the park (Table 6.3). Of these the dominant cohorts were elderly, well-dressed men, a number of them retired farmers, and young hippies, who together accounted for over half the park users. Tramps and members of minority groups, primarily native Indians, contributed another 20 percent to park visits.

As a newcomer approached the park, he would quickly scan the available seating areas and move toward a section of benches occupied by others he perceived as com-

TABLE 6.3 PARK USE BY LIFESTYLE GROUP

	Person-Visits	Percentage	Age Group Subtotals	
			Person-Visits	Percentage
Elderly well-dressed	1983	34.2%		
Elderly casually dressed	595	10.3%		
Elderly tramps	246	4.2%		
Elderly Orientals	104	1.8%		
Elderly native Indians	27	0.5%		
			2955	51.0%
Middle-aged casually dressed	437	7.5%		
Middle-aged tramps	313	5.4%		
Middle-aged native Indian	225	3.9%		
Middle-aged Oriental	8	0.2%		
			983	17.0%
Young hippies	1156	20.0%		
Young casually dressed	451	7.8%		
Young native Indians	157	2.6%		
Young mods	24	0.4%		
			1788	30.8%
Others	67	1.2%		
Total Person-Visits	5793	100.0%		

Source: W. Hall, *Spatial Behaviour in Victory Square*. Unpublished thesis, Department of Geography, University of British Columbia, 1974, p. 66.

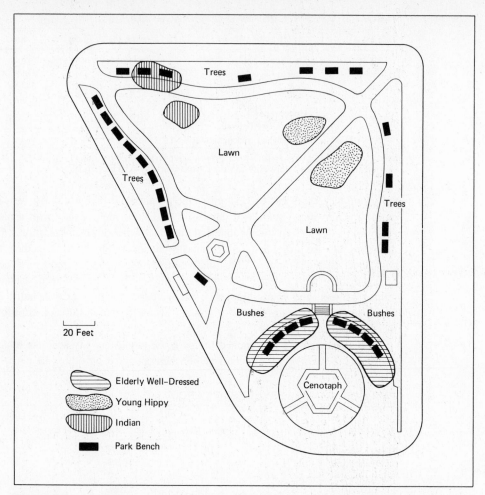

Figure 6.1 Jurisdictional areas in Victory Square, 7 A.M. to 11 A.M. (*Source*: W. Hall, *Spatial Behaviour in Victory Square*. Unpublished thesis, Dept. of Geography, University of British Columbia, 1974, fig. 4.1.)

patible with himself, who would invariably make space available for him. If an individual with an incompatible appearance approached, he would be informed by a series of body movements and microgestures that he was not welcome. Should he nevertheless select a seat, there would be a distancing effect by both parties to extend the personal space separating them. The overall effect of repeated episodes of such social distancing and entering into relation was the consolidation of jurisdictional areas in Victory Square (Figure 6.1). A well-marked spatial pattern of segregation appeared with high dissimilarity indices between groups. After more than 5000 person-visits to the park had been recorded, clearly defined segregation patterns existed between almost all groups; for example, the index of dissimilarity between young hippies and native Indians was 54.2, between elderly well-dressed men and Indians 76.5, and between the elderly well-dressed men and hippies 85.5.

The world of Victory Square could be conceived of as a social space where encounters were initiated between like-appearing individuals. A graph linking nearest neighbors on the basis of seating dissimilarity indices shows the relative proximity of the ten major user groups in this social space (Figure 6.2). With few exceptions, groups were juxtaposed with others that shared similar though not identical lifestyles. The several young adult cohorts formed one cluster, which included also the native Indians, a number of whom were of the same age. A second cluster comprised the middle-aged and elderly cohorts, incorporating the dominantly elderly Orientals. Interestingly, the link between these two generational clusters was supplied by middle-aged tramps. It suited the tramps, as a scavenger group in the park, to be dispersed rather than segregated like other park users, so that they displayed the lowest dissimilarity indices of all. The behavior of the tramps was unique in that their objectives were best met by avoidance of their own kind.

The social model of urban life explicit in this discussion is a subcultural one where like-minded individuals actively seek out associations with each other (Fischer, 1975). Those who share central concerns and a biographical situation voluntarily associate with each other; birds of a feather flock together. To what extent is Victory Square a true microcosm of group formation in the city?

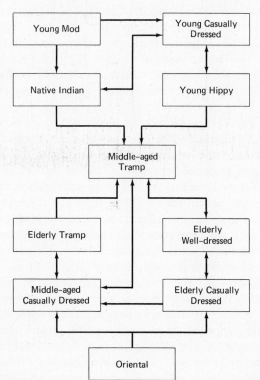

Figure 6.2   The network of nearest neighbors in Victory Square. (*Source*: W. Hall and D. Ley, "Everyday Life in Victory Square." Unpublished paper, Dept. of Geography, University of British Columbia, 1975.)

That this model is an appropriate generalization on the metropolitan scale as well as at the level of a small neighborhood park is suggested by an extensive analysis of friendship patterns in Detroit (Laumann, 1973). This study worked with a sample of 1013 native-born white males who were asked to list their three best friends. A series of supplementary questions then examined the affinities between the respondent and his named friends in terms of several attitudinal questions as well as fairly standard socio-economic variables such as religious, ethnic, and occupational status. Unfortunately these latter variables are not particularly subtle. As we saw with the plural elites of Vancouver in Chapter 3, the basis for segregation may follow lifestyle *nuances,* which are none-theless real in their distancing effects. In covering only a few major dimensions of social status, the Detroit research may have been significantly underestimating the strength of the like-minded friendships by neglecting to record the dimensions of mutual concern to the partners involved. In addition, by including only native-born white males, the study deliberately excluded the dimensions of race and recent immigration, which are known to have a strong channelling effect on the formation of social groups.

Even with these limitations, the data reveal interesting patterns. A matrix of dis-similarity indices by occupation between friends shows the extent to which individuals are constrained in their social relationships within broadly defined occupational categories (Table 6.4). The common pattern is repeated whereby the more dissimilar the occupation, the less likely is a friendship pairing; the highest dissimilarity indices in the matrix are 0.72 and 0.71, which occur between self-employed professionals (category 1) and op-eratives (category 13) and between the professionals and laborers (category 15). It is significant to note that these occupational dissimilarity indices based on *friendship* are *higher* than the 1950 Chicago indices based on *residence,* which were considered in Chapter 3. Though the data are not directly comparable, it might well be that segregation indices derived from residential structure underestimate the full extent of segregation present in urban life.

A similar pattern emerges when the data are partitioned by ethnic and religious variables. In every instance friendships established within a given ethnic or religious category easily exceed the level that would have been expected to occur by chance. Friendship networks are fairly dispersed between members of older ethnic waves from northwest Europe but are less common between this group and members of more recent immigration from southern and eastern Europe (Table 6.5). The religious data show a similar social gradient with friendships more likely between denominations with similar beliefs and most likely of all between members of the same denomination.

There are two other important findings. Using the mathematical method of smallest-space analysis, the matrix of ethnic dissimilarity indices (Table 6.5) was reduced to a two-dimensional figure (Figure 6.3). The distance between groups in this two-dimen-sional space is derived from the dissimilarity indices; groups with low dissimilarity appear close together, and groups with high indices are widely separated. From the diagram we discover, first, that the more peripheral the minority (i.e., the greater its distance from the core group of the old migration), the more probable it becomes that friendships are drawn from within the minority group itself. There is a correlation of 0.68 between the level of ethnic self-selection of friends and a minority's straight-line distance from the

TABLE 6.4 INDICES OF DISSIMILARITY OF FRIENDSHIP CHOICES FOR 16 OCCUPATIONAL GROUPS

Occupational Groups	Occupational Groups															
	1	2	3	4	5	6	7	8	9	10	11	12	13	14	15	16
1. Professional, self-employed	0.00															
2. Professional, salaried	0.47	0.00														
3. Managers and officials	0.38	0.33	0.00													
4. Sales workers, other	0.36	0.39	0.21	0.00												
5. Sales workers, self-employed	0.52	0.52	0.41	0.37	0.00											
6. Proprietors	0.41	0.39	0.25	0.27	0.28	0.00										
7. Clerical and kindred	0.50	0.34	0.27	0.33	0.46	0.30	0.00									
8. Sales workers, retail and wholesale	0.39	0.41	0.25	0.22	0.43	0.31	0.40	0.00								
9. Craftsmen, foremen, manufacturing	0.59	0.49	0.42	0.49	0.50	0.34	0.32	0.51	0.00							
10. Craftsmen, foremen, other	0.60	0.50	0.43	0.49	0.49	0.32	0.34	0.48	0.26	0.00						
11. Craftsmen, foremen, construction	0.63	0.56	0.44	0.50	0.53	0.34	0.38	0.49	0.31	0.32	0.00					
12. Operatives, manufacturing	0.69	0.57	0.49	0.56	0.58	0.42	0.38	0.58	0.23	0.30	0.37	0.00				
13. Operatives, other	0.72	0.61	0.53	0.60	0.56	0.42	0.44	0.62	0.28	0.29	0.36	0.20	0.00			
14. Service workers	0.58	0.52	0.43	0.47	0.55	0.36	0.42	0.50	0.43	0.41	0.44	0.43	0.48	0.00		
15. Laborers, manufacturing	0.71	0.60	0.58	0.62	0.67	0.56	0.37	0.63	0.42	0.47	0.50	0.33	0.44	0.62	0.00	
16. Laborers, other	0.58	0.50	0.39	0.46	0.48	0.28	0.30	0.45	0.20	0.20	0.23	0.27	0.29	0.40	0.45	0.00

Source: E. Laumann, *Bonds of Pluralism.* New York: Wiley, 1973, Table 4.3, p. 78. Reprinted by permission.

British group in Figure 6.3. However, when distance from the core group is correlated against each group's socioeconomic status, or against the percentage of foreign-born among each group's named friends, the results are negligible. Clearly, the configuration of inter-ethnic friendships is not derived from standard socioeconomic or length-of-residence variables. The clue to explaining this pattern of distancing lies in an independent national survey which examined the perceived social *status* of different American minority groups. If the ethnic rankings based on this perceived status are correlated with distance from the British group in Figure 6.3, a correlation of 0.80 results. Thus the configuration of actual friendships, though unrelated to the objective characteristics of each group, is closely associated with the perceived social status of each group and its social distance from those regarded most favorably. In short, the pattern of friendships follows a hierarchy of perceived status, with groups near the bottom of the rankings having a smaller proportion of friends drawn from outside their own number.

There are two complementary conclusions to this section of analysis. First, and supporting our earlier argument, the pattern of actual interethnic friendships is closely related to an attitudinal dimension of perceived social distance, which may be only weakly

TABLE 6.5   INDICES OF DISSIMILARITY OF FRIENDSHIP CHOICES FOR 22 ETHNIC GROUPS

Ethnic Groups	1	2	3	4	5	6	7	8	9	10	11	12	13	14	15	16	17	18	19	20	21	22
1. German	0.00																					
2. British	0.26	0.00																				
3. Polish	0.38	0.41	0.00																			
4. Do not know	0.24	0.27	0.41	0.00																		
5. Italian	0.27	0.32	0.34	0.30	0.00																	
6. Irish	0.32	0.33	0.38	0.25	0.28	0.00																
7. French	0.26	0.28	0.39	0.27	0.30	0.33	0.00															
8. Scottish	0.26	0.29	0.41	0.27	0.26	0.34	0.24	0.00														
9. Dutch	0.22	0.34	0.47	0.36	0.37	0.43	0.24	0.32	0.00													
10. Scandinavian	0.25	0.31	0.37	0.29	0.27	0.29	0.27	0.29	0.34	0.00												
11. American only	0.43	0.41	0.46	0.32	0.40	0.40	0.36	0.43	0.47	0.41	0.00											
12. Russian	0.61	0.63	0.62	0.52	0.61	0.62	0.62	0.61	0.61	0.59	0.60	0.00										
13. Slavic	0.36	0.51	0.38	0.40	0.48	0.52	0.44	0.44	0.42	0.45	0.55	0.61	0.00									
14. Hungarian	0.40	0.41	0.45	0.45	0.40	0.40	0.39	0.44	0.42	0.35	0.48	0.66	0.47	0.00								
15. Nonwhite	0.32	0.30	0.43	0.18	0.33	0.40	0.32	0.31	0.43	0.30	0.42	0.56	0.45	0.38	0.00							
16. Armenian	0.39	0.44	0.43	0.32	0.38	0.35	0.44	0.45	0.51	0.39	0.47	0.54	0.48	0.41	0.31	0.00						
17. Yugoslav	0.36	0.34	0.47	0.37	0.39	0.44	0.24	0.36	0.36	0.42	0.44	0.62	0.45	0.44	0.41	0.44	0.00					
18. Greek	0.48	0.36	0.54	0.43	0.44	0.49	0.40	0.41	0.44	0.47	0.58	0.64	0.56	0.51	0.40	0.51	0.43	0.00				
19. Jewish	0.29	0.41	0.52	0.32	0.43	0.42	0.34	0.39	0.31	0.34	0.49	0.53	0.42	0.41	0.38	0.47	0.46	0.49	0.00			
20. Arab	0.69	0.67	0.68	0.71	0.62	0.71	0.58	0.67	0.65	0.69	0.57	0.77	0.79	0.76	0.72	0.75	0.52	0.66	0.81	0.00		
21. Czech	0.43	0.56	0.65	0.52	0.55	0.58	0.51	0.41	0.40	0.49	0.58	0.72	0.50	0.44	0.62	0.56	0.55	0.62	0.46	0.85	0.00	
22. Spanish surname	0.56	0.55	0.56	0.54	0.50	0.46	0.50	0.39	0.63	0.50	0.61	0.85	0.70	0.48	0.48	0.56	0.56	0.56	0.56	0.56	0.56	0.00

Source: E. Laumann, *Bonds of Pluralism.* New York: Wiley, 1973, Table 3.3, p. 48. Reprinted by permission.

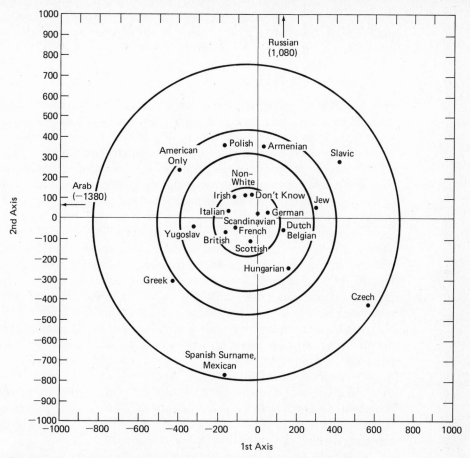

Figure 6.3 Ethnic nearest neighbors of social interaction reduced to two dimensions. (*Source*: E. Laumann, *Bonds of Pluralism*. New York: Wiley, 1973, fig. 3.1. Reprinted by permission.)

related to objective measures of socioeconomic status. Second, the greater the actual and perceived social distance between one minority and another with a perceived high status, the more likely is ethnic self-selection in terms of friendships for the lower-ranking group. The correlation between self-selection and actual social distance from the British in Figure 6.3 is 0.68, and that between self-selection and perceived social status rank on the basis of the national survey is 0.74. Socially marginal ethnic groups show a greater tendency toward selecting friends from within their own ranks.

On a more general level the Victory Square conclusions are duplicated. Although the Detroit study was unable to categorize individuals with the lifestyle nuances that were possible in the more manageable setting of a small park, nevertheless in Tables 6.4 and 6.5 the indices of dissimilarity remain high. Even within the coarse categories of occupation, ethnicity, and religion, there is marked selectivity in friendship formation as linkages are made along a social-distance continuum, with increasing similarity to the self associated with an increasing probability that contact will be made. Finally, it is likely that the level of social segregation in the city measured according to friendship patterns is a good deal higher than the more normal residential measure of segregation.

The Role of Physical Distance

The examples of group formation discussed to this point have been those where relationships have developed around the sharing of mutual concerns. However, earlier it was noted that an inherited biographical situation as well as joint concerns could stimulate group development. The area of overlap in two biographies that most consistently brings them together is the sharing of space. Of course, an overlapping spatial pattern may well be related to other biographical factors including social class and racial status. The effects of these more objective factors in forming social and spatial groupings will be examined in Part 4.

Distance has a profound influence on the formation of social relationships. Early studies of homogeneous clusters of student housing showed the effect of proximity in initiating chance encounters leading to friendships (Festinger et al., 1950; Caplow and Forman, 1950). Such findings are matched in more recent studies of friendship formation in student dormitories where statistically significant relationships are usually found between the extent of room separation and friendships that developed among students who did not know each other prior to moving in. Nuances of building design affect interaction; in dormitories and high-density housing the relative location of doors, windows, elevators, and common areas may drastically influence contact probabilities. In the public housing project of Easter Hill Village in the San Francisco Bay area, row house families living in cul-de-sacs reported visiting 40 percent more families in the project than did households in row houses lining through streets. Their visiting pattern was also more dispersed, whereas in houses parallel to streets, 40 percent of neighboring was with households within two doors on each side (Cooper, 1975).

The most divisive feature of the physical plan for social communication is the through street. In Easter Hill Village only 17 percent of all visiting was with opposite neighbors, whereas almost half was with next-door neighbors or others on the same block face. Inner city neighborhoods with their block grid present a road pattern that encourages vehicle speeding and through traffic, whereas curving and cul-de-sac road patterns, more common in the suburbs, restrict all but local traffic (Appleyard, 1981). These varied road networks have been shown to influence considerably children's socializing patterns and also the incidence of accidents involving children (Bunge and Bordessa, 1975). The elongated contact patterns of inner city children contrast with the less restrictive contacts of children in a neighborhood of curving streets with limited access to through traffic (Figure 6.4).

The extent of neighboring seems dependent once again on compatibility; the stage of the life cycle of young families seems most conducive to frequent interaction (Carey and Mapes, 1972). The restricted movement of children places a premium on local contacts and local commitment. In inner city Philadelphia, parents would not allow a child who was 6 years old or less to wander far from his house; 93 percent of children were limited to their home block, and 26 percent to within 20 yards of their own front

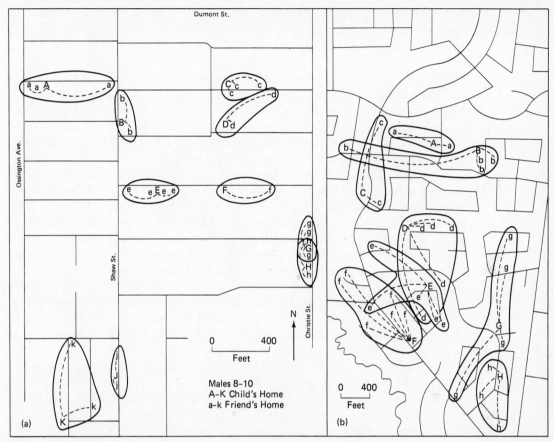

Figure 6.4   Children's play partners in: (a) an inner city neighborhood; (b) a suburban subdivision. (*Source*: W. Bunge and R. Bordessa, *The Canadian Alternative: Survival, Expeditions, and Urban Change.* York University, Dept. of Geography, Geographical Monographs No. 2, 1975, figs. 33 and 34. Reprinted by permission.)

door (Ley, 1974a). Other sources indicate that it is not until the age of 9 or 10 that a majority of parents will allow children to wander beyond sight and call (Pollowy, 1973). In these circumstances parents are particularly attentive to the local environment and local relationships. It is notable that community activism is high during the years of child rearing and that one source for the development of community organizations is the school parent-teacher association.

All of these generalizations are supported by a thorough study of social life in Park Forest, a middle-class community outside Chicago (Whyte, 1957). In Park Forest, social relationships seemed to develop unerringly from spatial proximity:

> Given a few physical clues about the area you can come close to determining what could be called its flow of "social traffic," and once you have determined this, you may come up with an unsettlingly accurate diagnosis of who is in the gang and who isn't (Whyte, 1957:366; quoted in Michelson, 1970:169).

Over a 6-month period, Whyte was able to map the addresses of residents attending a variety of social gatherings in a homogeneous, single-family home district of young families. Those activities ranged from a PTA party to a gourmet society, but in each instance the role of proximity was uppermost in drawing members; 83 guests were drawn from the same block face, 42 from the block directly across the street, and only 8 from other parts of the subdivision. Moreover, these groupings had some permanence. Although Park Forest was an area of upwardly mobile white-collar workers with a high turnover, the social groupings had some stability, for many of them were identifiable on the map in a re-survey 3 years later, although the individual families within each grouping had in a number of instances moved out and been replaced.

Such social groupings based on proximity may subsequently languish and be replaced by a less distance-biased network more closely attuned to mutual interests and compatibility. In his suburban study of Levittown, Gans (1967) observed that after 2 years of residence many relationships were developing between households that did not live on the same block. But, particularly in working-class neighborhoods, it is apparent that propinquity is a continuous molder of social groups and that the groupings may develop a semi-institutional form. For example, street-corner cliques and teenage gangs are certainly neighborhood based and may show considerable longevity. The durability of the gang structure can be strong; there are some gangs in Philadelphia which have been in existence for several decades and a few which have regrouped uptown when urban renewal has cleared their original site (Ley, 1975b). The effect of proximity on membership is evident in an example taken from a neighborhood with three active gangs in North Philadelphia; there are very few stray members living outside the group's recognized area of jurisdiction (Figure 6.5).

If the partitioning of gang space follows the familiar pattern of limiting interaction between groups, there are rare occasions when space is divided by social groups to *enhance* communication within a subculture. The early elite of Vancouver regarded themselves as a common unit, and as the city grew and their elite neighborhood of the West End expanded, they were anxious to maintain interaction in their social life. The weekly or monthly "at homes," women's tea circles in private homes, were an important feature in the continuity of the elite's social world, and with the expansion of the West End, there emerged discrete spatial groupings which held their "at homes" on different days of the week (Robertson, 1977). The "at home" landscape revealed by the 1908 *Social Register* shows the marked regionalization of at-home days which had arisen informally, with five compact spatial groupings defining the upper-class "turfs" of the city (Figure 6.6). By this management of space and time, maximum interaction between the five groupings was possible, aiding the integration of the elite world.

Group Formation: A Summary

Within the life-world, social groups are formed both by chance and by choice. They are formed by chance in the circumstances of biography beyond an individual's control, such as his or her pregiven culture, social status, ethnicity, age, and the space he or she occupies. Perhaps joint location is not truly random, for if we accept the argument that

Figure 6.5   Home addresses of street gang members, North Philadelphia. (*Source*: D. Ley, *The Black Inner City as Frontier Outpost*. Washington, D.C.: AAG Monograph Series No. 7, 1974, fig. 34. Reprinted by permission.)

there is an element of self-selection in residential location, then those who share space have already preselected themselves to some extent. Relationships consolidate around the spatial here and the temporal now; consequently, physical distance is a key variable in group formation. The argument of Melvin Webber that society has now entered a nonplace phase where community is no longer associated with propinquity is premature (Webber, 1963). Nevertheless, Webber is partly right, for relationships also form around

Figure 6.6 "At Home" territories among the elite in Edwardian Vancouver. (*Source*: A. Robertson, *The Pursuit of Power, Profit and Privacy*. Unpublished thesis, Dept. of Geography, University of British Columbia, 1977, map 7. Reprinted by permission.)

a community of interest, the sharing of central concerns, as individuals actively seek out others who are like-minded within the constraints of their biographical situation.

A number of studies of social visiting have suggested the variable effects of distance and social compatibility on interaction. In San Diego, Stutz (1973) identified three separate types of social visiting, with neighbors, friends, and relatives, each with its distinctive distance threshold (Figure 6.7). Other urban research cited by Stutz indicated that in Toronto about 40 percent of social contacts were with friends; 35 percent were with relatives; and 25 percent with neighbors. At first sight, the proportion of contacts with relatives appears remarkably high in light of traditional notions of the decline of

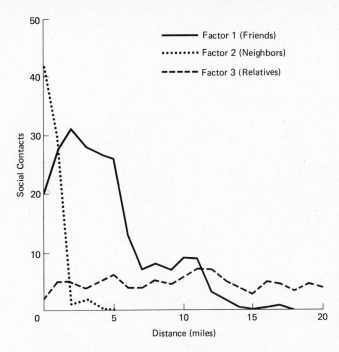

Figure 6.7 Distance separating partners by types of social interaction. (*Source*: F. Stutz, ''Distance and Network Effects on Urban Social Travel Fields,'' *Economic Geography* 49 (1973):134–144, fig. 1. Reprinted by permission.)

the role of kinship in the city. Earlier data from Lansing, Michigan, had shown that in both high- and low-income neighborhoods, 50 percent of social visits were of less than 1 mile. Beyond this range, contacts from the high-income area were selectively directed to a few other high-income sections scattered over the city (Wheeler and Stutz, 1971). This relationship is repeated in much smaller towns. In Houma, a community on the Mississippi Delta, Western (1973) discovered a distinctive spatial selectivity in visiting patterns which existed for different social groups (Figure 6.8). The Cajuns were an extremely localized group with a spatially confined life-world; in contrast, newcomers in suburban subdivisions had a more diffuse contact pattern favoring the urban periphery with its socially compatible residents.

The human condition is to form relationships, to establish groups. Group formation is a two-fold process of distancing and, later, entering into relation. We assess the social distance of others from ourselves and place them on a spectrum from direct we-relationships to indirect they-relationships according to our capacity for intersubjective relations. These perceptions are then translated into action, resulting in the formation of discrete social groups characterized by varying degrees of internal homogeneity. Social segregation is a pervasive feature of the life-world, and the map of residential segregation is simply one of its many faces.

Social Networks

Such a social model of urban life shows marked discontinuity with a number of classic analyses of urbanism. The traditional model of urban spatial structure, for example, is

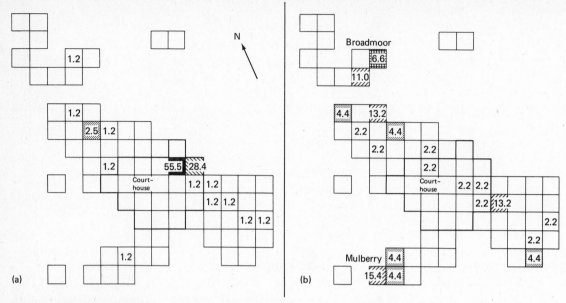

Scores = percent of total mentions (in all cells) in that particular cell.
Grid cells are 2000 feet square.

Percent of All Contacts

☐ < 2.5   ▦ 2.5-5   ▦ 5-10   ▨ 10-25   ▨ 25-50   ■ > 50

Figure 6.8   The geography of social interaction in Houma, Louisiana: (a) Cajun contacts; (b) newcomer contacts. (*Source*: J. Western, ''Social Groups and Activity Patterns in Houma, Louisiana,'' *Geographical Review* 63 (1973):301–321, figs. 5 and 6. Reprinted by permission of the American Geographical Society.)

based on competition and dominance—central notions of human ecology. In this paradigm man essentially acts singly and rationally in an economic sense. The resulting view of the city is one of disrupted social order, of disorganization and anomie. The Chicago studies of the 1920s focussing on delinquency, deviance, illness, crime, and conflict reflected an aura which was well summarized in Wirth's famous paper on ''urbanism as a way of life,'' in which he saw city life as impersonal, economically dominated, and freed of binding group relationships (Wirth, 1938).

Standing alone, Wirth's thesis is unacceptable. Several generations of participant observation studies have documented the existence of cliques and clusters, even in apparently disordered inner city areas (Whyte, 1955; Suttles, 1968). In a survey of 845 adults in Toronto's inner suburbs, 81 percent of respondents stated they had intimates whom they could turn to for emergency support, and 60 percent mentioned others who would provide everyday support (Wellman, 1976). A cross-sectional survey in Chicago of a large sample of residents who had moved to the city from outside showed that 68 percent had someone who welcomed them on arrival; 82 percent of these were relatives (Choldin, 1973). Though there are clearly urban isolates with limited support systems, the balance of evidence declares unambiguously that most people are not alone in the city but are part of a social network comprising kin, neighbors, and friends which permits orientation and adaptation to the urban setting (Smith and Smith, 1978).

The concept of the social network has been useful in exploring the social life of the city, including some spatial problems which geographers have long studied (Smith, 1980; Craven and Wellman, 1973; Connell, 1973). The concept has been popularized in social anthropology where it provided an effective approach for examining social adaptation to urbanization in the Third World. Mitchell has defined a social network as ''a specific set of linkages among a defined set of persons, with the additional property that the characteristics of these linkages as a whole may be used to interpret the social behavior of the persons involved'' (Mitchell, 1969:2). In the analysis of social networks, the emphasis is less on the individuals who act as nodes in the system than it is on the nature and implications of the linkages joining them. Techniques such as the use of directed graphs, matrices, and sociometric methods are all used to analyze communication links in a social system.

A critical component of a network is its connectivity, a property which may be illustrated either by graph or by matrix. In a graph, each node is an individual—either a person, a community, an organization, or even a city—and a link indicates a specified interaction with another node, which may or may not be symmetrical (Figure 6.9). Of interest also is the density of the network, the proportion of all possible links that are actually completed; here we may contrast the more close-knit network associated with village life and the diffuse network of the cosmopolitan life (Walker, 1977). That the former is also present in the city is revealed in Laumann's Detroit data, where he discovered that 69 percent of his male, native-born respondents belonged to high-density interlocking friendship networks and only 31 percent to low-density diffuse networks (Laumann, 1973).

A second interesting question to ask of networks is the position of individual members within them as this affects their action and status in the group. Three positions may be identified: those of conformist, bridgeman, and isolate. The conformist is the member well-included within a network, whereas the isolate is largely divorced, sharing little communication with network members. The bridgeman, although connected to the network, also has links to other networks; his position is one of intermediary between a

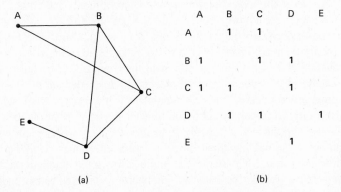

Figure 6.9   (a) Graph of social network; (b) matrix of social network.

network and the outside world, a position which may bring him some influence and authority. With these basic concepts we can now illustrate the utility of the network approach in explaining the internal social forces of a semiformal association.

Analyzing Networks: An Example

The Monroe Community Association is a community group in an inner city neighborhood in Philadelphia (Ley, 1974a). The neighborhood is predominantly black and underserviced relative to its social problems, so that there is a clear mandate for MCA both as a voluntary service agency and as an advocacy group to attract government assistance. But despite a satisfactory short-term budget and available skills, MCA is ineffective. Detailed examination of the association showed that incompatible internal cliques were one source of its failure. Participant observation isolated the critical actors at MCA, and as a result of repeated interactions over several months, it was possible to compile slowly a matrix of friendships and antagonisms between the 17 key figures. On the matrix, 1 represents a friendship, 0 an antagonism; no interaction data were recorded for some pairs (Figure 6.10a). From the connectivity matrix, a graph was formed, with each person linked to the two others with whom he or she shared the most similar pattern of friends and antagonists (Figure 6.10b). With each of the 17 actors linked to his or her two nearest neighbors, four coalitions appear within the association; a double bond indicates the symmetrical closeness of two persons. The coalition with the highest density is the Leadership Pact, a two-person clique of the association's salaried director and his assistant; it has connections with the Grassroots, another close-knit group of respected middle-aged and elderly female community workers. Both of these groups have high internal homogeneity and compatibility. A third clique was a group of Outside Professionals working on a voluntary or contract basis with MCA; as well-meaning liberals they were anxious to be responsive to the community rather than to actively initiate projects and policy. The fourth clique was the Dissidents, a loosely bonded group of isolates. They ranged from a college dropout who had turned militant Black Muslim to an upwardly mobile local entrepreneur who was also chairperson of the MCA board; all that united this diverse group was their hostility to the Leadership Pact.

There were two behavioral outcomes to this network of relationships at MCA. The Dissidents, because of the loose bonding resulting from their conflicting goals and personalities, could not present a firm front against the Leadership Pact, although objectively MCA's constitution gave several of them considerable authority. The Leadership Pact was able to resist their criticism because of its linkages with the cohesive and highly credible Grassroots and yet could not eliminate their opposition because of the constitutional entrenchment of several of the Dissidents. In this stalemate the association atrophied, and programs foundered—a state repugnant to the activist goals of the Outside Professionals. From the graph (Figure 6.10b) it is clear they were bridgemen in the MCA system of cliques, and this network position ensured that they were the only group which could coordinate the remaining three otherwise isolated cliques. Under pressure from outside funding sources an MCA steering committee was set up to direct the association's funded programs. The committee consisted solely of the Outside Professionals; ironically

From

To	CS	SS	AG	RM	LB	A	EL	DD	AL	BL	FW	DM	JP	TK	JT	CV	NV
CS		1	0	1	0	0	1	0	0	1	0	0	0	1	1		1
SS	1		1	1	0	0	1	1	1	1	0		0	1	1	1	1
AG	1	1			0		1				0		0	1	1		1
RM	1	1			0	0	1	1	1	1			0	1	1	1	1
LB	0	0	0			0	1	0	0	1	0	0			0	1	0
A	0	0		0	1		0	0			0			0			
EL	1	1	1	1	0	0		1	0	1	0	0	0	0	0	0	0
DD	0	1		1	0	0	1		0	0	0	0	0			0	0
AL	0	1		1	1		0	0		1	1				1	1	1
BL	1	1		0	1		1	0	1						1	1	1
FW	0	0		0	0	0	0	0	1			1		1		1	0
DM	0						0		0								1
JP	0	0		0			0	0									1
TK	1	1	1	1			0	0			1		0		1		1
JT	1	1	1	1	0	0	0	0	1	1			0				1
CV	1		1	1			0	0	1	1	1						
NV	1	1	1	1	0	0	0	0	1	1	0		1	1	1		

(a)

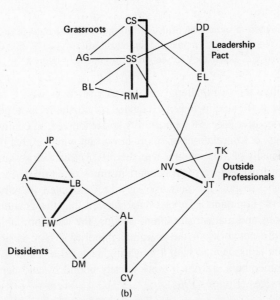

(b)

Figure 6.10 Coalitions in a voluntary association: (a) matrix of network; (b) graph of first and second nearest neighbors. (*Source*: D. Ley, *The Black Inner City as Frontier Outpost*. Washington, D.C.: AAG Monograph Series No. 7, 1974, table 16 and fig. 32. Reprinted by permission.)

the one group which had sought no more than a service role at MCA was, because of its critical bridging status, forced into the role of leadership.

The Scope of Social Networks

An important property of a social network is the extent to which an individual's life-world is contained within it. How much of his experience does it include? How much scope does it claim over him? Typically people belong to varied networks which may be only loosely connected; to switch social roles is often to switch social networks. But although plurality is perhaps the norm in urban experience, there are individuals who may be limited to a dominant role and a single network for their salient activities. For some, such containment may be enforced, the result of a marginal position in the social structure which limits access to other opportunities. Consider, for example, the self-justification of an inner city graffiti artist, notorious to the Philadelphia public for his "vandalism":

> There isn't much choice of what to do. . . . I did it because there was nothing else. I wasn't goin' to get involved with no gangs or shoot no dope, so I started writin' on buses. I just started with a magic marker and worked up (Ley and Cybriwsky, 1974).

For others, containment within one role is voluntary. In the recent words of a West Coast businessman reported in the press:

> Is there a more beautiful word in the English language than "profit"? So crisp and clean. Consider it for a moment, then repeat after me—"Profit is beautiful!". . . . sure, my wife and kids know they're second to my business interests. . . .

Typically, the occupational role gives rise to networks which are diffuse and of low density; a friendship may be equated strategically as a potential contact, so that such networks offer access to opportunity and resources. In contrast, networks based on ethnic, religious, or kin relations are more close-knit with a higher density and a higher frequency and intensity of interaction (Laumann, 1973). Such close-knit networks are more typically those of trust and personal support in times of crisis (Craven and Wellman, 1973).

The scope of a network may be associated in part with the marginality of its members. Laumann's Detroit data showed that the greater the social distance between minorities and mainstream ethnic groups, the more probable was ethnic self-selection in friendship networks in the marginal minority. There is also evidence that ethnic self-selection is associated with a much higher level of ethnic "institutional completeness," so that members are much more closely bound by and dependent on ethnic institutions and services (Breton, 1964).

Social Networks and Problem Solving

If a subcultural model of social groups is indeed appropriate for understanding aspects of urban life, and if social networks provide one appropriate framework for analysis, then it would be expected that a number of adjustment and ongoing problems in the city could be shown to be resolved as a result of interaction with fellow members of a close-knit informal network. Since the scope of social networks seems most complete for marginal members of society distant from the mainstream, researchers have often turned to minority immigrant groups to substantiate the importance of informal sources in dealing with varied urban problems.

TABLE 6.6 ETHNIC DIFFERENTIALS IN SALES PRICES OF HOUSES
1961–1972 (1967 DOLLARS)

	Intra-ethnic		Inter-ethnic	
	Avg. Price	No. Sales	Avg. Price	No. Sales
Two story	$5,769	38	$6,377	134
Three story	6,143	33	7,308	116

Source: R. Cybriwsky, "Social Aspects of Neighborhood Change," *Annals, Association of American Geographers* 68 (1978), 17–33, Table 3, p. 23. Reprinted by permission.

Nevertheless informal sources are also employed by the middle-class in problem solving. In the search for suitable *housing*, for example, personal sources are a not insignificant channel. Studies in Toronto (Barrett, 1973), Swansea, Wales (Herbert, 1973), and Philadelphia (Rossi, 1955) indicate the ranking of personal contacts and other sources in finding housing vacancies. The role of informal personal contacts increases from the middle-income buyers of Toronto and Swansea (mentioned by 25–45 percent of searchers) to the lower- and mixed-income buyers and tenants of Swansea and Philadelphia (mentioned by about 60 percent of searchers). Also computed in the Philadelphia study was an index of effectiveness which assessed the utility of each source in making the eventual selection; this index showed personal contacts to be by far the most effective.

For minority groups, not only may ethnic solidarity guide buying patterns, it also may influence asking prices. Examination of house sales in a white immigrant district in Philadelphia revealed apparent cost differentials of as much as 10–20 percent according to the ethnicity of the purchaser (Table 6.6). The existence of a housing market socially constrained by ethnic ties is even more evident for renters (Barnett et al., 1970). In the same Philadelphia neighborhood there was a pronounced pattern of intra-ethnic renting of housing; the four major immigrant minorities were all biased heavily toward landlord-tenant relationships of the same ethnicity (Table 6.7).

TABLE 6.7 ETHNIC PATTERNS IN HOUSE RENTALS

	Ethnicity of Landlords			
	Irish	Italian	Polish	Ukrainian
No. of rentals owned	47	36	23	44
No. of tenants identified by surname	30	21	19	40
Ethnicity of tenants				
Irish	20	4	3	7
Italian		10		1
Polish	1	2	13	
Ukrainian		1	1	20
Blacks				
Puerto Ricans			1	1
Others	9	4	1	11
Percent intra-ethnic renting	67	48	68	50

Source: R. Cybriwsky, "Fairmount Rules: Life in a Defended Neighborhood," unpublished paper, Department of Geography, Temple University, 1976, p. 12. Reprinted by permission.

In terms of finding *employment,* recent research is again suggesting the importance of personal connections (Sheppard and Belitsky, 1966). Studies among white-collar employees in Boston showed that word of employment vacancies was often communicated through informal channels (Granovetter, 1973). But it is for lower-status groups that the social network is preeminent on the job trail. Commonly, long-range migration has been precipitated for rural migrants by the promise of a job from a friend or relative already in the metropolis. A study of poor white in-migrants from Appalachia who had moved to Cincinnati showed that word of economic opportunity had been transmitted to them through a family network; indeed, some firms relied on such transmission in their hiring of new workers (Hyland, 1970).

For immigrants whose primary language is their mother tongue, job opportunities based on formal channels may be extremely limited, and it is the ethnic network of the extended family and ethnic institutions such as the pool hall, restaurant, and church which provide the important leads. Among a small sample of Portuguese women in Vancouver, 90 percent migrated to join existing relatives with whom they lived upon arrival in the city. They all continue to speak Portuguese at home, and their English is poor. This has constrained them both in their search for work and in the type of employment they can undertake. Ninety percent found their first job through a network of friends and relatives, but even after a number of years in the employment market, 55 percent were employed in restaurants or as janitors and cleaners, low-paying positions for which inability to speak English is not a major disadvantage.

The problem of being trapped in a low-paying and undesirable occupation has often been recognized as a particular dilemma facing the immigrant. The ordeals of the inner city sweatshop or the rural migrant labor camp seem the last to have been reached by protective legislation governing working conditions. Male immigrants have commonly moved into employment as construction laborers in firms with an ethnic employer, where the advantages of such a relationship can be mutual. The employee gains work in a setting where his language difficulties are not a shortcoming and where advice on other adjustment problems is readily available. The employer not only has met his ethnic obligations but also has gained an efficient worker, for there is a general belief that there are greater obligations on the employee in an intra-ethnic enterprise and, consequently, much weaker union influence on the construction site. Indeed, the preference of an employer for hiring employees of the same ethnicity is often the stronger, for the ethnic employees do not always regard the relationship symmetrically and prefer to escape such demanding expectations (Chimbos, 1972). Certainly the advantages of an ethnic labor force appear to give construction companies a competitive edge against their rivals (C. Smith, 1974).

There may be a danger that overdependence on the social network will jeopardize employment prospects over the long term and draw the immigrant into a "mobility trap." Among a sample of Portuguese males in Toronto, well over half were assisted in finding their first job by friends and relatives. However, for this group, at least, there was a definite (though nonsignificant) tendency for jobs secured through such sources to be lower paying than those secured through more formal sources (Table 6.8). This trend was reinforced in subsequent employment. For their present as opposed to their first job,

TABLE 6.8   CHANNEL OF ASSISTANCE AND INCOME OF FIRST JOB FOR PORTUGUESE MALES IN TORONTO

	Relatives	Friends	Relatives & Friends	Immigration Department	Union	Already Promised	Varied	Other
Sample Size	50	38	11	35	1	40	9	4
Mean Rate/Hour	$2.85	$2.52	$2.55	$2.97	$3.70	$2.88	$2.62	$2.35

Source: G. Anderson, *Networks of Contact: The Portuguese in Toronto.* Waterloo: Wilfred Laurier University Press, 1974, Table 32, p. 70. Reprinted by permission.

the males who were hired through a union or other formal sources received an hourly rate far higher (significant at 0.001) than did those who used informal sources. Nevertheless, the proportion who used informal sources actually increased after the first job (Table 6.9). For this group, access to resources through a social network does not necessarily expedite economic mobility, though it may provide compensating social benefits.

In the *migration* process itself the triggering effect of the social network cannot be overestimated, especially for long-range movement of low-income migrants (Hägerstrand, 1957). The migration from the Appalachian states to the industrial cities of the Midwest is strongly channelled and place specific: "We could almost say the streams of out-migration were running in well-worn riverbeds" (Brown et al., 1963). The cause of this place specificity is information feedback from friends and relatives, which draws increasing numbers of an extended family and friendship circle to the same center. Thousands of southern blacks were drawn north to rejoin kin and friends by letters such as the following, written in 1916, by a new migrant in East Chicago to a friend "back home" in Union Springs, Alabama:

> Let me know what is my little city doing. People are coming here every day and are find employment. Nothing here but money and it is not hard to get. Remember me to your dear family. Oh, I have children in school every day with white children (Johnson, 1930:23).

Such information, not from an avaricious employer but from a credible source, was sufficient enticement to draw migrants away from rural and small-town poverty and an oppressive social climate. The decision to migrate was contagious and diffused rapidly through social groups, as for example, the village of Vaslui in Rumania:

> In the year of my departure from Vaslui America had become, as it were, the fashionable place to go . . . All my relatives and all our neighbors—in fact everybody who was any-

TABLE 6.9   CHANNEL OF ASSISTANCE AND INCOME OF PRESENT JOB FOR PORTUGUESE IN TORONTO

	Relatives, Friends, Acquaintances	Varied	Union	Other
Sample Size	110	49	20	10
Mean Rate/Hour	$2.64	$2.71	$3.49	$3.10

Source: G. Anderson, *Networks of Contact: The Portuguese in Toronto.* Waterloo: Wilfred Laurier University Press, 1974, Table 37, p. 85. Reprinted by permission.

body—had either gone or was going to New York . . . I did not, then, as you see, come alone, to America. I came with the rest of the population of Vaslui (Ravage, 1971:5).

The process of *chain migration* often led to the re-creation of old country society in the ethnic neighborhoods of North American cities, as neighbors and extended families regrouped in discrete districts in the New World. In Detroit a large Italian community was traced back to a single migrant, joined by his family, who later drew others; in Middletown, Connecticut, an Italian neighborhood grouped around a nucleus of a sailor and a circus act (Macdonald and Macdonald, 1964)! The intricacy of chain migration is indicated by the network of several generations of emigrants who left the agricultural village of Campobasso in central Italy to join kin in North Vancouver (Figure 6.11). "Nick Fiorvento" was sponsored by a friend as a railway laborer and then a miner; after his arrival in North Vancouver, where he had heard of a municipal position from another Italian friend, he initiated a network of sponsorship which brought at least 69 relatives and friends from Campobasso to Canada (primarily to the same municipality) over a 20-year period.

Within such ethnic networks, *adjustment problems* are routinely referred to kin. It is understood, for example, that a sponsoring family will provide initial accommodation; seven separate immigrant families have been housed by a single key household in the Campobasso chain. Access to formal agencies is heavily restricted. A study of Mexican-Americans in Milwaukee indicated that it is not until the second or third generation that much use was made of social service agencies (Matthiasson, 1974). Among a largely nonimmigrant group in Toronto, only health problems drew a large proportion to professionals; for other personal, family, and employment problems, respondents confided in informal helpers or, to a lesser extent, no one at all (Tannenbaum, 1974). Widespread use of professionals and specialized agencies is restricted among the working-class and ethnic groups to social isolates who have no other support system. However, among the middle class, particularly the well-educated with "cosmopolitan" attitudes, such referral is more common (Kammeyer and Bolton, 1968).

Empirical evidence amply confirms the existence of firm links between social-network members in an urban setting. The extended family and friendship circles provide a source for problem solving for all sectors of society. Nevertheless, it appears as if the scope of social networks and dependence on informal sources may be greatest for working-class and immigrant groups, and in some circumstances, by choice, for the community elite. Middle-class society, though also dependent on informal social networks, makes a freer intersection with formal and institutional agencies in problem solving. As we turn from informal networks to more formal social groupings in the city, so the discussion passes much more to the middle-class citizenry.

Voluntary Associations

Voluntary associations occupy an intermediate social position between informal groups and urban institutions. They provide a rich fabric of secondary groupings for the urban resident; such common organizations as the PTA, Little League, Chamber of Commerce,

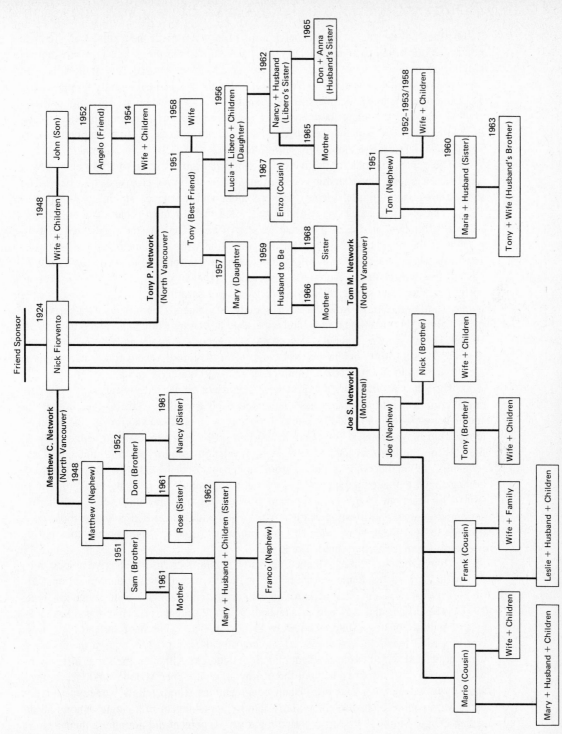

Figure 6.11 A network of chain migration from Campobasso, Italy, to Canada.

homeowners' associations, and the neighborhood church provide the texture and reference points for our urban experience. They are the bond for the individual to a broader yet still manageable community. Each of these associations is territorial, so that the voluntary organization continues to have some basis in propinquity. The community homeowners' association rarely draws members from beyond its area of jurisdiction. The neighborhood church, in contrast, contains both local and distant members who are prepared to continue their attendance to maintain cherished contacts. More esoteric lifestyle and cultural associations might draw members over long distances to seek like-minded others.

The generalizations found to exist for informal groups seem to apply also to voluntary associations. Membership is constrained along the major cleavages of urban social structure: by race, ethnicity, class, age, religion, and language (Smith and Freedman, 1972). National and local surveys have suggested that for most urban dwellers organizational affiliation reaches a moderate level. An early Detroit study indicated that 63 percent of the population had at least one affiliation with a voluntary group (Axelrod, 1956); in a later Nebraska study, the membership proportion rose to 80 percent, with 46 percent involved with three or more associations (Babchuk and Booth, 1969). Persistently, too, there is a strong relationship between organizational affiliation and socioeconomic status; if North America is a society of joiners, then this characteristic is overwhelmingly true of the middle and upper-middle classes (Smith and Freedman, 1972; Hunter, 1974). In this light it is tempting to suggest a complementarity whereby the middle class substitute such formal associations for the informal networks which we have seen described most often among immigrant and working-class groups.

Though plausible, this interpretation should not be carried too far, for it is likely that recruitment into voluntary associations is itself a result of face-to-face contact in social networks (Booth and Babchuk, 1969). In a sample drawn from a middle-class tennis club in Vancouver, for example, 90 percent of members claimed to have joined the club on the basis of face-to-face recommendation from an existing member. Consequently, as membership is drawn from preexisting social circles, it shows a certain homogeneity; tennis club members tend to be young, single professionals or semiprofessionals living in one of three rental neighborhoods within 4 miles of the club and sharing certain attitudinal and lifestyle characteristics. The club is a garden patio for those condemned to apartment living and who also prefer a "healthier" atmosphere to a bar or nightclub for meeting like-minded others.

Church membership may sometimes show similar patterns of selective association. In two juxtaposed residential subdivisions in Belfast with the same denominational affiliations, there was a marked variation in the specific churches that were attended (Boal, 1971). The differential was one of social distance. Residents of Taughmonagh, a municipal public housing estate, who were Presbyterian or Church of Ireland members, worshipped at local churches; over 70 percent of those who held a church membership were associated with the closest denominational church. Although the same institutions were also the closest for residents of the nearby affluent Upper Malone subdivision, they were bypassed in favor of more distant congregations where fellow worshippers were perceived as more compatible. Similarly, among worshippers in a single denomination in San Diego, Stutz (1976) has reported that over 40 percent did not attend their nearest denominational church.

Thus, in both formal and informal groupings there are present the dual processes of distancing in order to enter into relation. The result is a large measure of self-selection among adherents, so that individuals who come together into associations share a common biography and central concerns. As Gans observed in Levittown, "The organisations were primarily sorting groups which divided and segregated people by their interests and ultimately, of course, by socio-economic, educational, and religious differences" (Gans, 1967:61).

A Socially Defined Reality

Membership in social groups and communication through a social network imply levels of cognitive and behavioral consensus and the conscious and unconscious suppression of individualistic traits. When one of Oscar Wilde's characters declared that fashion is what one makes for oneself, the line was calculated to bring down the house before a late Victorian audience for whom conformity to social norms was a carefully practiced undertaking. Fashion—as well as comedy—presupposes intersubjectivity!

Repeated interaction with others in the routines of daily life leads invariably to a shared set of expectations; mutual communication encourages consensus and if continuous may define a distinctive subculture. Such attitudinal convergence is hastened by the selective nature of group membership. To summarize the argument presented earlier in this chapter, "Undoubtedly, the most prominent assertion in group research is that people like and interact with those who are most similar to them" (Weick, 1969:14). Initial attitudinal compatibility is accentuated by what the social psychologist Newcomb has termed a "strain toward communication equilibrium," in which interacting partners are drawn toward an increasing similarity of outlook: "Selected observations concerning symmetry as a consequence of communication are equally plentiful; there is, in fact, no social phenomenon which can be more commonly observed than the tendency for freely communicating persons to resemble one another in orientation towards objects of common concern" (Newcomb, 1966). A certain degree of conformity within a group is mandatory for its survival, for continuous disagreement will challenge the group's solidarity and is therefore countered by the expulsion of "deviant" members (Festinger, 1967). Few subcultures, whether in union halls or academic programs, reward those who rebel against an officially defined reality.

In everyday life, social order is often managed by the avoidance of potentially divisive issues. In the closely bonded social networks of Boston's West End, Gans observed that "potential peer group members are many, but their number is effectively reduced by the requirement that people must be relatively compatible in terms of background, interests, and attitudes . . . because West Enders cannot cope effectively with disagreement" (Gans, 1962a:76). Should a divisive issue be raised in the course of conversation, Gans noted how it was abruptly dropped to avert substantial disagreement. Consequently, conversational topics were limited in range both to avoid conflict and also to remain within the domain of common knowledge of the group. In this manner, social groups sustain realities which may overlap only in part.

There may emerge particular interaction styles which help to define the group. A distinctive type of joking relationship helped bound the social world of longshoremen in

Portland (Pilcher, 1972); similarly, the unique style of black street talk, or the Montreal joual dialect, contributes to the definition of the black American and French-Canadian subcultures. Such interaction styles are both inclusive and exclusionary: ''That is why black talk, especially the playful badinage of jiving, threatens the straight world'' (Abrahams, 1970:21). Each social world has its own style, its own lexicon, its own nuances, and rituals which define an in-group and an out-group. How can an American tourist understand a cricket match in London, even though baseball is second nature to him? But at least sports have formal interaction rules. Far more troubling is the status of stranger in less structured settings, for here the rules of the game are unquestioned by insiders, whereas for the stranger everything becomes problematic (Duncan, 1978b). It is only as we find ourselves in the position of stranger that we are able to ponder the social and cultural bonds of our own intimate circles, which until then have always been taken for granted. Our own social reality, our thinking as usual, is never suspended and thrown into question until it is brought to bear in a novel setting and found wanting. Then social relations become ''not a shelter but a field of adventure, not a matter of course but a questionable topic of investigation'' (Schutz, 1944).

The status of stranger can be a taxing one, well-described in the graphic concept of the marginal man (Stonequist, 1961)—the man caught between diverse cultures or social settings and for whom social relations are invariably an adventure rather than a shelter, a continuous passage between multiple realities. But learning or acculturation do occur through time, and slowly a new set of rules is learned, and a new definition of the situation, which becomes unconscious and taken for granted, is adopted.

As strangers we can suspend unwavering confidence in our own social reality to treat that which in everyday life is unquestionable and absolute as now contingent and relative. At that point we begin to see the power of our everyday social environment in molding our perceptions and routines. As G. H. Mead has observed, the self develops as a result of social interaction and ''it is impossible to conceive of a self arising outside of social experience'' (Mead, 1964:204). The emergence of the self is continuous and evolving in the light of social encounters, and to the extent that these encounters are freely chosen, so the individual charts out his or her own identity. In this manner ''our bondage to society is not so much established by conquest as by collusion'' (Berger, 1963:121).

Group membership requires cognitive and behavioral commitment, and the strength of that commitment does not seem to be weakening with rapid urbanization. The existence of large cities has permitted the emergence of plural lifestyles because, unlike rural and small-town society, population thresholds are sufficient to maintain diverse subcultures and their institutional supports. It is therefore probable that urbanization encourages divisiveness among people as each seeks the solace of his or her own cluster of like-minded peers—as Junius Browne claimed in New York over a century ago. Shortly before him, the Danish philosopher Kierkegaard had bewailed the loss of man's individuality and its replacement by the impulses of the crowd in an urbanizing, industrializing age. For Kierkegaard true man was the individual, but in the Copenhagen of his day he saw a society where men ceded their integrity by allowing other men to make their decisions for them. The same fatalistic view is taken by many contemporary intellectuals pondering the human condition in urban society. Harold Pinter, in his play *The Dwarfs,* poses the dilemma of contemporary identity: Is modern man no more authentic than the reflection of his social environment?

> The point is, who are you? Not why or how, not even what. I can see what, perhaps, clearly enough. But who are you? . . . You're the sum of so many reflections. How many reflections? Whose reflections? Is that what you consist of? (1968).

In moving from artistic insights to social science research, there is no weakening in the impression that attitudes and actions are indeed strongly influenced by immediate social pressures. Indeed, the power of in-group consensus is so great that we tend to assume it even in its absence. There is a tendency to project onto friends attitudes that are more nearly our own. In the study of male friendship networks in Detroit, it was found that whereas more objective facts such as age and occupation of friends were accurately reported, there was a tendency for the attitudinal characteristics of another to be subject to a halo effect, distorted in the direction of one's own prejudices (Laumann, 1973). The same survey reported consistent, if not overwhelming, evidence that networks consisting of more similar individuals aided in the maintenance of common group values and that this conformity was reinforced as the network's density increased, so that it became more closed than open.

Under conditions of stress and isolation there are particular pressures for the closing of ranks and the enforcement of in-group conformity (Goldstein and Rosenfeld, 1969). In these circumstances public morality may be suspended and a private morality constructed where the ends justify the means. This morality is binding on members, and in extreme situations there may be no escape from its claims. Here, most completely, a social reality is constructed, an *alternative world* enacted where attitudes and actions may develop, incomprehensible without access to the distorted logic of its members. The homicidal tendencies of juvenile street gang members cannot be interpreted without an understanding of the status rituals of adolescent subcultures in deprived inner city settings (Ley, 1975b). In North American society, such alternative worlds commonly arise among groups occupying a marginal status, and in the metropolis they are typically located amid minority ethnic and lifestyle neighborhoods in the inner city. Here aberrant cults, lifestyles, and movements find circumstances which favor their existence (Fauset, 1971), for they meet needs otherwise frustrated by the oppressive experience of marginality.

The social reality of the city is not simply given. It is also constructed and maintained intersubjectively in a semiclosed world of communication and shared symbolization. The routines of daily life create a particular view of the world and a mandate for action. It is the unself-conscious, taken-for-granted character of the life-world that makes it so binding on its members, that ensures its realities will remain secure. It is only when the "thinking as usual" of the close-knit social network is decisively challenged that there is a chance that its unself-conscious values may become problematic and questionable.

Conclusion

In this chapter we have penetrated the spatial structure of the city and examined the social worlds that lie behind it. The segregation revealed in maps of social areas is just one example of a dominant characteristic of everyday life in which groups that contain a high degree of internal homogeneity form. The segregated map of social areas matches the voluntary friendship networks in the life-world; indeed, it seems as if segregation by residence is more limited than segregation that occurs informally by choice.

With few exceptions urban man is pervasively social and not an isolate, as economic and ecological models have suggested. His relationships are not simply impersonal and contractual but also consist of rich and differentiated ties with selected others. His perception of social-distance gradients leads to both separation and association. Intersubjectivity permits we-relationships with others with whom he shares concerns and a similar biography, including a shared location. Thus, social groups form as a result of inheritance (relatives), proximity (neighbors), and a community of interest (friends). With increasing socioeconomic status, these relationships are more likely to be formalized in voluntary organizations.

Because of the social nature of urban life, it is not surprising that problems are often solved in community. Social networks are often the most important single channel for resolving typical urban problems, such as finding employment or accommodation, and the most important source of support in difficulty and crisis. Moreover, within our intimate circles both an identity and a world view are molded, incrementally and often unself-consciously. The social milieu of the city provides an environment which is a human construction but one which also acts back upon its members. In this manner the relationship between man and his environment is more fully reciprocal in the city than in the countryside, for, in Park's words, "In making the city, man has remade himself" (Park, 1929).

Chapter 7

The Life-World of Urban Institutions

The objectivity of the institutional world, however massive it may appear to the individual, is a humanly produced, constructed objectivity

(Berger and Luckmann, 1966:57)

The Industrial Revolution and nineteenth-century urbanization emerged in a context of liberal individualism. Government was limited both in the size of its bureaucracy and in its intervention in economic and social life. In 1793 the Treasury Department of the British government employed just 37 people; the industrial city of Manchester had no proper town council until 1838 (Daniels, 1975; Briggs, 1965). In the economy, the industrial scene surveyed by Engels in Manchester was one of cut-throat competition between individual mill owners and merchants. In the Western nations this era of individualism has largely passed, to be replaced by public-sector centralization and private-sector oligopoly, so that some authors are referring to the coming of corporate society, to the appearance of *corporatism* in political and economic life (Winkler, 1976, 1977; Pahl, 1979).

Certainly it is not hard to document the growth of large institutions in the private and public sectors. In Britain, 67 leading manufacturing organizations employed over 4 million people in 1972 and the five major banks over a quarter of a million more; the same year in the United States the top 1,000 industrial firms and the top 300 financial and other business organizations accounted for 22.5 million jobs (Pred, 1974). At the same time the different tiers of American government employed some 13.5 million public servants. Moreover, employment is becoming more concentrated in large organizations, one indicator of the growing scope of public and private organizations in contemporary society. The data reviewed by Pred show that jobs provided by the 500 largest American industrial firms increased by 5.5 million, or 60 percent, from 1960 to 1972, and in Britain the proportion of private-sector assets controlled by the 100 largest organizations rose by 18 percent to 62 percent in the decade ending in 1963. By 1970, in 20 of the 22 major industrial sectors in Britain, an average of only three firms controlled half or more of the market; despite the existence of over 640,000 firms, more than half the manufacturing output is the product of 100 companies (Winkler, 1977). The power and resources of the large firm are concentrated in the multinational corporation; up to 1980 the annual sales of General Motors, for example, exceeded the net national income of all but a dozen countries.

The growth of the public sector has been equally impressive, even in the United States with its free-enterprise heritage. Over the past two decades government employment in the United States has more than doubled, and the government's share of the nation's consumption of goods and services has risen from 11 percent in 1929 to over 20 percent by 1970. In the mixed economies of western Europe, governmental participation in the economy and society is even higher. In Britain the ratio of public expenditure to the gross domestic product was about 60 percent by the late 1970s (Pahl, 1979).

Any examination of the contemporary city cannot overlook the pervasive role of formal organizations, whether private or public, in the processes of urban development. There are of course some significant differences between modern organizations, both between the private and public spheres, the industrial and service sectors, and between public administration and public industrial enterprises. Nevertheless, in an increasingly interdependent society where government is an economic force as the corporation is a political force, these boundaries are rarely as firm as they have been in the past. More telling and often transcending these differences is the insidious growth of an organizational consciousness expressed in this postindustrial technocracy which has an equivalent hold on the parliamentary or party chamber and the corporate boardroom (Bell, 1976a). Consequently, in the preliminary analysis of organizational action in this chapter, few systematic distinctions will be observed between private and public institutions. This convention has been well-established by a number of important attempts to forge administrative and business studies into a broader theory of organizations (March and Simon, 1958; Silverman, 1970). The differences between the ranges of organizations will be highlighted in Chapter 9, where we will examine their interaction in the city and their impact on the patterns of urban development. However, in this chapter we will be concerned with the internal behavior and subculture of institutions in their own right.

There has been a tradition in urban studies to view urban organizations as monolithic and faceless entities standing over man, seemingly mechanistic in their response and rudderless in their actions. The urban organization has been viewed as other than a human construction. This tendency is easily understood and to a degree well-founded, for the urban resident's encounter with the institution is invariably as an outsider, perceiving and experiencing it categorically. Moreover, in the role of client, the resident is himself responded to as a type, as a category who falls within certain preestablished guidelines established by the institution. Thus resident and organization interact with each other as *contemporaries,* in the reciprocal they-relationships of strangers who meet with only their own socially constructed typifications to guide the encounter.

But in the same way that it is not enough to typecast social groups only as ecological entities without values or intentionality, so it is an incomplete analysis which sees the organization only in ecological terms, as an object devoid of internal behavioral and cultural attributes. Znaniecki commented in the 1930s that even as inert an institution as the Bank of England had its ''humanistic coefficient.'' Besides its objectivity, it had a subjectivity as a socially constructed reality; its objective status was the product of an intersubjective sanction—an interconnected series of experiences, understandings, and agreements:

> The Bank of England as an economic system exists only in so far as numbers of people in England and elsewhere perform certain economic activities and have certain experiences, owing to which ''the Bank'' has a reality and exercises an influence upon human life; the student of economics must take it as he finds it within the sphere of experience and activity of those people, with all it means to its shareholders, directors and employees, agents, correspondents, debtors and creditors (Znaniecki, 1969:138).

The proof of Znaniecki's argument rests in his example, for today fewer social scientists would identify the Bank of England as quite as impressive a case of an inert institution as it was 50 years ago. The solid rock has become shifting sand, as the intersubjective consensus which gave the Bank its reality has been steadily eroded. Its decreasing (though still substantial) influence in international money markets has resulted from the appearance of vigorous competitors and the ailing state of the British economy. As the typical experiences of the varied actors who sustained ''the Bank'' has shifted, so, too, its objective status has changed dramatically. Thus there is a reciprocal relationship surrounding institutional life. Although the organization is usually perceived as an object impacting human experience, it is itself the product of collective actions and experiences.

In Part 4 we shall consider organizations as they are usually conceived, as objects with considerable power in the urban arena. But in considering the city at ground level, we must also include the internal life-world of the organization. The goal of this chapter is to begin to lay bare the often taken-for-granted world of the urban organization which lies behind its massive facade, to consider it not simply as a given social fact, but in life-world terms to examine its actions and intentions, the manners in which its reality comes to be enacted. In this process we will see that a number of the generalizations concerning the actions of informal groups which we have already discovered in earlier chapters are even *more* appropriate in describing the actions of organizations.

Such a perspective on the organization has begun only recently in some behavioral approaches to geography (Hamilton, 1974) and has scarcely been developed in its full theory of action implications even in sociology (Silverman, 1970). Consequently there is a shortage of empirical studies in this area, and the examples in the chapter have of necessity been culled somewhat eclectically. This complaint concerning the geographic literature was also voiced by March and Simon (1958) for the organizational literature more generally, in their own pioneering attempt to develop a behavioral examination of organizations. In part, the dearth of examples reflects the difficulty of access to the internal world of urban institutions. Although institutions are well able to mount surveys and detailed studies of the urban population, they are reluctant to provide access to their own everyday activities. We are only now realizing the importance of reversing research energies and understanding the reality-building processes of the urban organization; in the words of one constantly surveyed Canadian Indian band, ''What about a survey of the Department of Indian Affairs?''

The Behavior of Urban Organizations

The Orthodox View

Traditional analysis of urban organizations has made much of the analogy of the organization as a machine or a system. In this view, which invariably coincides with the views of management, productivity is seen as central, and the organization is conceived of in terms of inputs, throughputs, and outputs. Organizational personnel are simply extensions of the productive process, passive elements who respond automatically to commands and other organizational stimuli. This approach was highlighted by Frederick Taylor's scientific management movement early in the twentieth century. Taylor's group was much concerned with questions of capacity, speed, time and motion studies, and other issues of organizational efficiency. This movement had an impact not only on the functioning of the business firm but also on reform in local government in North America. In Chicago, for example, the Chicago Bureau of Public Efficiency was established and between 1910 and 1920 published a number of reports critical of the inefficiency spawned by a multiplicity of local governments. In a 1911 report it commented cryptically on the disarray surrounding the administration of public parks in the city: "Concerning the seven smaller park districts within the City of Chicago, there is little to be said, except that their Boards are sequestered bodies of which the taxpayers know little. It was with difficulty that the Bureau was able to gather the main facts about these bodies and their business affairs" (cited in Stetzer, 1975:88).

The inauguration of scientific management was a key ingredient of the reform movement of local government carried out in the early twentieth century during the so-called Progressive era. Urban administration was redefined as an "elaboration of the processes of rationalization and systematization inherent in modern science and technology" (Hays, 1964). A centralized bureaucracy of specialists at City Hall promoted rationalism and scientific administration; economics and efficiency were the major criteria in decision making. An article in the *Canadian Engineer* for 1923, entitled "Reasons for Town Planning," emphasized the successful formula: "Good city planning is not primarily a matter of aesthetics, but of economics. Its basic principle is to increase the working efficiency of the city" (cited in van Nus, 1979).

The orthodox view of the organization has assumed that it follows a model of scientific management with well-defined and consistent objectives and an optimal capacity for gathering information and reaching decisions. As such, the orthodox perspective has more often been normative than descriptive, its analysis favoring idealized interactions between large units which examine only a few key variables (Cyert and March, 1963). The theorizing has more often been abstract than empirical, and little attention has been given to detailed examination of actual decision-making processes and actions in the organization. From Max Weber's theory of bureaucracy much attention has been given to the rationality of the organization, resulting from Weber's somewhat exaggerated belief in the superiority of bureaucracy to earlier forms of administration.

As it had in economics, the concept of rationality in geographic research has become synonymous with that of economic man. Many of the same sets of assumptions that we examined in Chapter 2 as basic to orthodox land use analysis recur in studies of economic organizations. Of these, two in particular have been implicit in economic geography: first, profit maximization by the firm and, second, access to perfect information concerning behavioral options coupled with a faultless capacity for making decisions. These frequently implicit assumptions find their explicit spatial expression in the selection of optimal locations for the organization to achieve profit maximization. For the public sector organization, rationality cannot be reduced to simple economic measures as neatly. However, if government bureaucracies are not bent on maximizing profits, or more probably minimizing costs, presumably they have some other criterion which they are seeking to optimize. Geographical research has given some attention to the question of rational locational strategies for public services and, in particular, to the problem of identifying the location which minimizes the net travel time for users (Scott, 1971; Massam, 1975, 1980). Both for economic and administrative organizations, then, rationality is translated into some optimal performance in spatial decision making.

The Question of Rationality

To what extent are the normative assumptions of orthodox theory parallel to what actually happens in the everyday life-world of organizations? A particular shortcoming of orthodox theory is its neglect of contextual realities. In the same way that Alonso's land use theory entertained only a "pallid skeleton" of man and a "featureless plain" for the environment, so organizational studies make the same abstractions from the everyday world. In Simon's words, the theoretical treatment of rationality "possesses considerable normative interest, but little discernible relation to the actual or possible behavior of flesh-and-blood human beings" (Simon, 1965:xxiii). Do the contextual realities thereby omitted simply represent small error terms, "a 'residual' domain of events which cannot be handled by the normative . . . theories" (Harvey, 1969a)? In contrast, Cyert and March (1963) argue that these "internal attributes" are not "irrelevant artifacts" but exercise a considerable degree of control over the organization's actions. Might such contextual effects, then, perhaps even overturn the predictions of abstract theory?

An instructive case study emphasizing the internal processes involved in arriving at a locational decision in the public sector has been provided by Kasperson (1971). In 1960, a decision was made in the state of Massachusetts to construct a new medical school; the location of the school was left to its dean and the Trustees of the University of Massachusetts in the hope that it could be determined rationally, outside the arena of parochial political interests, for a new medical school represented an attractive addition for any town. It would provide improved medical services and new jobs, act as an economic multiplier and yet be a clean, nonpolluting facility. From among the many claimants for the medical school the Dean examined 12 locations which he narrowed to 4 main contenders: Amherst, Boston, Springfield, and Worcester. Boston had the advantages and disadvantages of a large metropolis that was already moderately well-serviced, whereas Amherst, which was the main campus for the University of Massachusetts, had the assets and drawbacks of a semirural location in a small town. Worcester and Springfield were cities of moderate size that could demonstrate a need for improved medical services. The dean's recommendation was, as his first choice, Amherst, which he felt offered the best linkage with the University's existing facilities. An independent consultant's report endorsed this recommendation, ranking Springfield as second choice, Boston as third, and Worcester, which had offered a small site and was far from any existing campus of the University, as fourth. Amherst, then, was the "rational" locational site.

The trustees were split over this recommendation, a number of them feeling that the site should be in a larger urban area that could better utilize the school's services. Amherst was the single most favored location, but the agreed-on voting procedure delayed a final vote until only two candidates remained. In the first two rounds of voting Boston and Springfield were eliminated, but in the final round the pro-urban lobby united, and Worcester was selected over Amherst by a vote of 12 to 11. In the words of the *Boston Herald,* a first-rate medical school was awarded a fourth-rate location! Worcester was far from an optimal site, but then the determining criterion for selection proved to be not rationality but expedience. The "internal attributes" surrounding the decision-making process conspired to produce a result that few had wanted but that the majority would tolerate. Expedience and compromise overturned rational behavior; contextual realities upset a normative prescription.

It is not difficult to demonstrate the elusive nature of rationality in institutional decision making. Indeed, "the central concern of administrative theory is with the boundary between the rational and the non-rational aspects of human social behavior . . . of the behavior of human beings who satisfice because they have not the wits to maximise" (Simon, 1965:xxiv). The appropriateness of extending Simon's concept of the bounded rationality of administrative man to economic organizations also has been demonstrated in Cyert and March's (1963) empirical study of decision-making processes in several business firms. They concluded that the uncertainty of the external environment, the potential for conflicting goals in the internal environment, and the organization's own decision-making fallibility severely challenged the usefulness of normative theory. Contextual realities mean that the organization is constantly adapting to immediate, short-term pressures. The firm is adaptively rational rather than omnisciently rational, and as several geographers have suggested, this conditional rationality will have an effect on locational strategies (Pred, 1967; Webber, 1972). Rather than there existing a single best location for the firm, a more realistic concept is that of a spatial margin to profitability which recognizes that location can occur anywhere within a discretionary area whose size will vary according to the quality of available transportation and the type of business in question, among a range of other noneconomic factors (Smith, 1970; Blunden, 1972).

The Meaning of Space

In addition to its simple understanding of rational behavior, orthodox theory has also retained an idealized view of the organization's spatial context, viewing it primarily as an isotropic plain, an undifferentiated surface with equal access in all directions. For the economic organization, space is therefore regarded as a barrier to be overcome in cost- and distance-minimizing strategies; for the public administrator, space is a homogeneous surface to be partitioned efficiently so that the distance from a public facility to its users

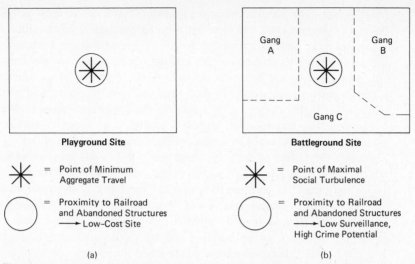

Figure 7.1   Planning a playground location: (a) the site in physical space; (b) the site in social space.

is minimized. But how "rational" is such a strategy and the view of space which underlies it?

An illustration derived from an actual planning decision will show the questionable basis of such an assumption in decision making for even a small locational problem. It was decided in the early 1960s to build a playground in a densely populated section of North Philadelphia suffering from an appalling lack of recreation facilities, with a mere 0.75 acres of recreational open space for each 10,000 residents (Ley, 1974a). The decision was made at City Hall and the first step in implementation was to find a suitable site within the neighborhood. The site decision was made according to the administrative principles of locational centrality to maximize overall access and the use of cheap available land to minimize costs. Patterns of land value and ownership were contained within the city's own assessment files; a central location was readily determined from the map. Consequently a site was selected, and the playground was built (Figure 7.1a). Note that the spatial decision was perfectly logical *on the basis of the criteria selected to determine it*. But note, too, that these criteria emerged from the abstract view of space held by a detached outsider. The locational decision could well have been made without leaving City Hall (perhaps it was!). The planners' viewpoint was one that conceived of the city as a spatial pattern whose only characteristics were cost and accessibility gradients superimposed onto an abstract space. The landscape fact, the playground, emerged as a result of a particular set of professional values.

But the neighborhood had a personality as well as a location. Closer examination would have shown the existence of three persistent teenage street gangs in the district with well-defined territories. The gangs were sporadically violent, and several incidents between rival gangs had led to serious injury and some fatalities. The site chosen by City Hall for the playground coincided with the intersection of their territories, so the playground rapidly became a battleground (Figure 7.1b). It also was along a convenient border zone at the point of minimum aggregate travel for all three gangs. The planning desire to minimize costs had identified a broadly triangular block with a railway viaduct along one edge and an abandoned apartment building along a second. Consequently, there was limited surveillance of this isolated site by community residents, which further encouraged delinquent behavior and delayed the reporting of disorders to police. Predictably, parents refused to allow their children to use the playground, which they rightly perceived as highly dangerous! Not only did the playground fail as a community facility, but by providing a convenient gang battleground, it may also have added to community problems. Disregard of the *meaning* of neighborhood space contributed to a case of bad planning. The failure of the playground was not so much an error of faulty logic as it was of basic assumptions—an inappropriate conception that space was indeed homogeneous and capable of partition following the irresistible geometry of a master blueprint.

Urban organizations have recently been able to relax decision-making rules based on simplistic views of space as a barrier. For economic organizations this is in part a result of extensive highway building and other communications changes in the 1950s and 1960s, which have substantially broadened the spatial margin of profitability. In a more mobile society, distance with its cost implications becomes much less of a constraining variable. A number of behavioral studies of industrial location decisions have noted that market access for firms, although it may differentiate site selection between cities, does not discriminate between sites within a single metropolitan area (McDermott and Taylor, 1976). For organizations, space is now assuming meanings other than that of accessibility and separation. The existential meanings of space reviewed in Chapter 5 have a bearing on organizations as well as on individuals. The gradients of stress and security, and status and stigma provide contours to which organizational decision makers are attentive; in the postindustrial state they are particularly responsive to quality of life and amenity issues (Sternlieb and Hughes, 1975). Recall some of the findings from Chapter 2 which showed that economic factors have only partly explained the decentralization of industry and services from the CBD and inner city, and need to be seen in the light of perceptions of metropolitan crime, locational prestige, and quality of life factors for key organizational decision makers.

The new regions of amenity are only slightly connected to orthodox views of space and distance minimization, though of course they remain compatible with cost constraints. Services and industries are tending to follow the amenity-directed migration of their market and labor force, and to a smaller extent they are leading that movement. In both instances footloose industries and professions are moving along amenity gradients, particularly when these coincide with more conventional locational factors and profitability constraints. This argument is not hard to sustain in the case of professional and high-technology employment. In 1979, Inmos, a computer chip firm generously financed by the British government, moved its U.S. headquarters from Dallas to Colorado Springs in a move interpreted as an attempt to match the high-amenity environment offered to highly skilled engineers by its silicon chip competitors in California (Guardian, 1979). In complete contrast is the disinvestment in industry and commerce occurring in inner city Belfast as a result of the high levels of stress in an environment of urban violence and terrorism (Murray and Boal, 1979). Two less exotic examples from Chicago will illustrate these themes further.

The medical profession provides one useful illustration, for in Chicago there has been extensive out-migration of medical services from the central city since 1950. By 1970 Chicago had only as many private physicians as in 1907, when the city was half the present size (de Vise, 1973). The number of physicians practicing in the city declined by 100 a year between 1950 and 1970—a loss of over one-third over the two decades. The loss has been associated with the declining status of the inner city and particularly, it seems, the onset of racial change. In neighborhoods of racial transition the loss has been double the city average; in the extreme cases of Woodlawn the decrease was from 125 physicians to 37, in West Garfield Park from 161 to 12, and in East Garfield Park from 65 to 2, over the period 1950–1970 (de Vise, 1971). In contrast, the Chicago suburbs gained heavily in practicing physicians, by 238 percent, during the same period. Within the suburbs there was a systematic pattern of change (Figure 7.2). Gains were strongest in the inner suburbs and particularly in the northern suburbs, the communities with high-status lakefront locations in a line north from Chicago's prestigious Gold Coast, studied by Zorbaugh in the 1920s. These districts made the greatest gain in the number of physicians, from 1.63 to 1.95 per thousand of the population, although they had already the highest proportion in 1950. Over the 20-year period the 10 most affluent communities had an increase from 1.78 to 2.10 in their physician ratio; in contrast, the 10 poorest communities had a stunning decrease in physicians from 0.99 to 0.26 per thousand of the population.

A separate study of industrial decentralization from central Chicago demonstrates that the movement of industry is following a gradient similar to that of services. Christian (1975) examined the destination of 1011 firms who relocated from the black districts of Chicago in the period 1965–1971 (Table 7.1). The sheer size of the movement is remarkable with the loss of over 1000 firms and over 50,000 employees over a brief 7-year period. It is pertinent to note that this period straddles the turbulent race relations of the late 1960s. Between 1965 and 1968 Chicago had one of the nation's worst records for racial strife with seven major riots and civil disorders during which there were over 700 injuries suffered, almost 4000 arrests, and widespread looting and arson, which caused $10 million worth of property damage at 1968 dollar rates in the riot of April 1968 alone (Committee on Government Operations, 1968). It is against this context that the instability of industrial location in the black inner city might be viewed. From Table

TABLE 7.1   INDUSTRIAL MIGRATION FROM CHICAGO'S BLACK COMMUNITY, 1965–1971

Movement Destination	Relocated Firms	Percent	Relocated Jobs	Percent
Same district	135	13.4	5,397	10.8
Other black district in city	150	14.8	4,379	8.7
Nonblack district in city	346	34.2	16,239	32.4
Suburbs	345	34.1	22,285	44.5
Outside SMSA	35	3.5	1,819	3.6
Totals	1,011	100.0	50,119	100.0

Source: Adapted from C. Christian, ''Emerging Patterns of Industrial Activity Within Large Metropolitan Areas and Their Impact on the Central City Work Force,'' pp. 213–246, in G. Gappert and H. Rose (eds.) *The Social Economy of Cities.* Beverly Hills: Sage, 1975, Table 1, p. 233. © 1975. Reprinted by permission.

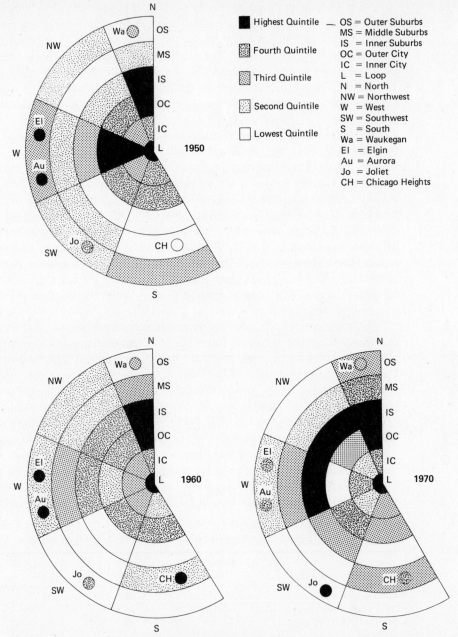

Figure 7.2 Location of physicians' offices in Chicago in 1950, 1960, and 1970 in quintiles, per 1000 population. (*Source*: P. de Vise, *Misused and Misplaced Hospitals and Doctors*. Washington, D.C.: AAG Commission on College Geography Resource Paper No. 22, 1973, fig. 7. Reprinted by permission.)

7.1 it is clear that fewer than 30 percent of firms relocated in other black areas of Chicago. As these firms provided less than 20 percent of the jobs, it is clear that they were the smaller firms which perhaps did not have the resources for longer-range movement.

In contrast, 34 percent of businesses relocated in nonblack areas of Chicago, and another 34 percent moved to the suburbs. The latter were the larger firms accounting for over 44 percent of jobs. The circumstantial evidence for suggesting that out-migration was an attempt at distancing from perceived low-amenity areas is strengthened by examining the place specificity of the destinations within the suburbs (Figure 7.3). Firms rarely moved to suburban sites adjacent to their former city location; only 16 percent of firms moved less than 6 miles to the suburbs, whereas 54 percent moved more than 10 miles. Again the smaller businesses seemed to be the least mobile, for only 6 percent of the jobs accompanied the 16 percent of firms with shifts of less than 6 miles. The directional trend of outward-moving firms has favored the northwestern suburban sector. Not only is this area of a higher socioeconomic status, but also it has almost no racial mixing; the municipalities of Des Plaines and Franklin Park, the largest recipients of new jobs, had no apparent black population at all in 1970. Berry's (1975a) maps of racial change in the Chicago SMSA during the 1960s indicate that suburban areas that were facing possible racial transition in the foreseeable future tended not to be selected as destinations by decentralizing firms.

There may well have been more conventional location factors at work, both triggering the out-migration of firms and selectively directing them toward the white suburbs in the west and northwest, but the timing of this massive out-migration during a period of racial turbulence and the racially specific choice of destination strongly suggest that the movement was not color-blind. De Vise (1976) has noted that the suburban communities of northwest Cook County were the major recipients of new employment, gaining 149,000 jobs and 223,000 new residents, during the 1960s; of the population growth, only 180 new residents were black! He further suggests that "there is strong evidence to support the contention that many households and firms locate in certain outlying suburbs to maintain a separation of 10 to 20 miles from existing black areas."

Although much of the causal argument here is inferential, the data are consistent with an interpretation that postulates the migration of organizations away from perceived low-amenity districts and toward higher-amenity districts within a permissive economic climate, where the spatial margin of profitability has broadened considerably, enabling the social evaluation of sites to become a major differentiating factor. This argument is reinforced by the institutional inertia of public organizations which, for reasons of social policy, are assuming increasing importance in low-amenity areas being abandoned by private organizations. The interface between the CBD and the inner city is increasingly becoming the preserve of public institutions like the universities and hospitals in the face of the exodus of private organizations. In Chicago, for example, much inner city health care has passed from private physicians to the expanding teaching hospitals (de Vise, 1973).

Finally, on a national scale, the differential effect of amenity may also be demonstrated. In Britain, the so-called drift to the South, in Canada, the rapid growth of Alberta and British Columbia, and in the United States, the development of the West

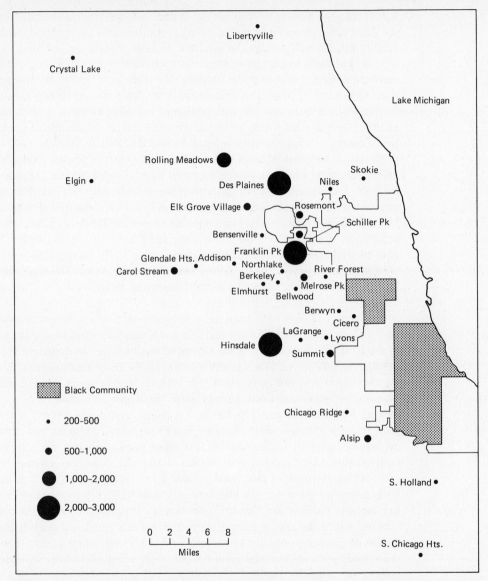

Figure 7.3   Suburban relocation of inner city jobs in Chicago, 1965–1971. (*Source*: C. Christian, "Emerging Patterns of Industrial Activity within Large Metropolitan Areas and Their Impact on the Central City Work Force." Pp. 213–246 in G. Gappert and H Rose (eds.), *The Social Economy of Cities*. Beverly Hills, Cal.: Sage, 1975, fig. 6. ©1975. Reprinted by permission.)

and resurgence of the South, all point to the migration of population and organizations alike along a gradient that is frequently defined by amenity as well as by more conventional locational factors such as labor differentials, servicing costs, and resource availability (Liu, 1975). The total net in-migration between 1970 and 1973 to American metropolitan areas with a population of between 1 and 3 million was more than accounted for by the three amenity regions of Miami-Fort Lauderdale, Tampa-St. Petersburg, and Phoenix, Arizona (Barabba, 1975). De Vise (1973) has shown that the national distribution of doctors in the United States is not related to the mean family income of metropolitan areas but rather to the presence of a prestigious medical center or a high level of amenity. The losers are the regions of ennui and stigma; the gainers the regions of stimulus and status. In medical migration, Illinois' loss is California's gain; more Chicago medical graduates move to California than remain in Illinois to practice. In Detroit, corporate recruiters have to offer executives a salary increment of 20–30 percent above the industry mean to offset the deterrent of the city's negative image, with its unattractive physical environment and grim record of 600–700 murders a year. The most recent data on the location of corporate headquarters show a similar trend, with reductions in headquarters sites in a number of the older cities of the northeastern industrial belt and a matching growth among the sun belt cities of the West and Southwest (Stephens and Holly, 1977).

For private organizations, locations are chosen in a competitive labor market not only because they are profitable but also because they are pleasing; in response, public institutions are increasingly associated with regions of privation.

Organizational Goals

In light of the qualifications that we have had to make to orthodox views of rationality and the spatial environment in organizational behavior, it might be expected that the normative perception of organizational goals might also need some amendment. The orthodox view of profit maximization has been heavily criticized for some time on a number of grounds (Cyert and March, 1963; Pred, 1967). One alternative suggestion has been that the fundamental organizational goal is that of survival, so that organizations are inherently cautious and make decisions that preserve their security. Cyert and March suggest five major objectives for the business firm that represent goals in production, inventory, sales, market share, and profit. They recognize that the attainment of these goals may well lead to internal conflict and that organizational actions will involve compromise and the establishment of satisfactory rather than optimal performance levels.

Bounded rationality does not imply action that is not purposeful but recognizes that in reality purposeful behavior has to chart a course between plural goals which are usually competing. De Vise (1973) observes that American doctors may select from four major lifestyle goals. They may desire to maximize their income, seek professional status and social prestige, establish contact within a circle of other physicians with similar specialties, or place a premium on the quality of family life. Most doctors would claim to maximize all four goals, but in practice they are often conflicting, and this is well demonstrated by the variable locations which best allow each goal to be pursued.

Moreover, goals are rarely stable over the long term, for the adaptive organization must continually attend to a changing environment. New skills need to be recruited and new strategies devised to meet new circumstances, and an organization that cannot make these adjustments faces extinction. An examination of the annual reports of a Canadian federal ministry, the Department of Indian Affairs, showed the changing priority areas of the administrators (Kariya, 1978). A space count of five different program areas in annual reports over a 10-year period revealed a marked shift in Department priorities (Figure 7.4). Some program areas, such as education, displayed year-to-year fluctuation but little overall change. In contrast, the area of native land claims made its first appearance in the 1972 report and has risen meteorically until by 1975 it received more space than any other single program area. This is a particularly striking example of organizational response to a changing environment. Increasing activism by native Indians during the early 1970s culminated in widespread demonstrations, occupation of Indian Affairs offices in 1975, and demands for the dismantling of the Department. The organization has adjusted its goals to accommodate this threat, and has sought to change its image from "administrator" to "consultant." At least superficially it has given the impression of more accountability to Indian demands. Recently, Indians have been appointed to senior positions, and the treatment of land claims has finally been admitted as a major goal.

Such a rapid change in organizational goals is inevitably accompanied by internal conflict. New skills and strategies require new appointments, the reapportioning of priorities and budgets, and changing status and authority relations between subgroups of the organization. Although a consensus concerning organizational goals usually has been assumed, a far more normal pattern within the organization is that of a differentiation of goals which can lead to potentially disruptive conflict. A good deal of organizational energy is consequently given to the anticipation and checking of conflict (March and Simon, 1958).

A common source of goal conflict is incompatibility between explicit organizational goals and the satisfaction of implicit organizational agendas. An example which has received recent attention and some notoriety has been the decentralization of mental health care in the American city into community mental health centers (Graziano, 1972; C. Smith, 1976). There is rarely a rational location for such centers, for siting is often opportunistic or a compromise between conflicting objectives, and "the shortrun resolution of these multiple objectives typically compromises the effectiveness of the facility system" (Wolpert, Dear, Crawford, 1976).

For the community mental health profession, survival was indeed a primordial goal. The development of satellite centers was an organizational decision and had to be justified and continuously rationalized in organizational terms; a need had to be demonstrated, and a strategy of meeting it devised before funding could be secured. Consequently the distribution of centers was in part a commentary on the expertise of professional promoters. But once good ideas had been rewarded, clients had to be found. The initiative was bureaucratic, so that rather than clients seeking programs, programs sought clients; in the words of one cryptic commentator, "In the mental health industry, illness is our most important product" (Graziano, 1972). Contributing to this disarray were the career aspirations of the professionals, whose advancement was tied to the success of a program they had campaigned for. The need for "results" was an internal, socially construed goal of the professionals which sometimes had only loose connections with the objective goals of treating clients. The outcome often tended toward an overdiagnosis of mental

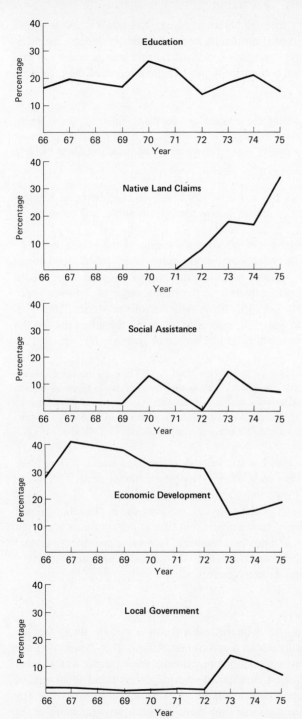

Figure 7.4 Changing goals and priorities of the Department of Indian Affairs. (*Source*: P. Kariya, ''Keepers and Kept: The Lifeworld Relations of British Columbia Indians and the Department of Indian Affairs.'' Unpublished paper, Dept. of Geography, University of British Columbia, 1978. Reprinted by permission.)

illness and insensitive care which stressed numbers rather than quality. Internal and external goals were in conflict, and program failure became common. Indeed, an organization founded as a problem solver became to its clients a problem generator; in one Philadelphia inner city neighborhood a community news bulletin recorded the local program's erratic history:

> This has been a confusing, frustrating and dramatic year for the Community Mental Health Center. It has been filled with administrative conflicts, communications problems, personnel shifts, community sit-in demonstrations, and a ransacking of the Guildford Street building (Ley, 1975a).

A preoccupation with internal goals and a relative disregard for neighborhood realities by the center aggravated the very problems it was created to solve and prompted a community revolt.

Too much attention to internal goals has commonly diluted the effectiveness of public service programs. Certain organizations become introverted and respond to an internal arena, expending energy on actions which are inappropriate for the achievement of external goals but are directed primarily toward the maintenance of the emotional, status, or career needs of members (Ley, 1974b). A reviewer of the Model Cities programs, designed to reinvigorate the American inner city following the urban riots of the late 1960s, identified internal status conflicts as one source of program failure:

> In fact, Model Cities is psychodrama on the highest level . . . (There is) the unmistakable impression that the program exists in a world dominated by only three types of human beings—loud, stout, buxom black women who are definitely in command; thin, meek, effeminate-looking white men who take orders without talking back; and stridently militant, domineering black men who flit around like street corner peacocks . . . (Mallowe, 1973).

This cast plays out its roles in a socially constructed and internalized world: ''They seem to be acting out roles and reinforcing each other's deepest emotional needs . . . There are thousands of chiefs in Model Cities and practically no Indians.''

The paucity of detailed accounts of the everyday world of the organization should limit speculation as to the generality of such a conclusion. But at the very least we might conclude that organizational goals can rarely be accepted at face value and that contextual factors in both the external and internal environment challenge and even compromise the apparent stability of formal declarations of objectives.

The Information Environment

In conferring rationality upon the organization, orthodox theory was maintaining that the firm had perfect access to information (March and Simon, 1958). This assumption has been repeatedly criticized for its patent unreality; one example among many was a recent survey of British firms which revealed considerable misinformation and ignorance of government policy and incentive programs available to industrialists in special development areas (Green, 1977). But at the same time there has been no weakening in the central role which information is seen to play in organizational behavior (Taylor, 1977; Harrison, et al., 1979). In a review of decision making in organizations, Dicken (1971) concluded, ''It is perhaps through the study of perception and information flows that progress can be made in understanding the process whereby organizations adapt to their changing environment.''

What, then, is the nature of the organization's informational repertoire? Once again there is a marked shortage of empirical studies to provide an authoritative answer, but it is clear that informational channels are biassed, centered on the organization's own location and central concerns. In this manner the organization is little different in qualitative terms from an informal social group. Its life-world is essentially anthropocentric with broad areas of ignorance enclosing a specialized information environment. In the words of the editor of the Kansas City *Star,* ''The farther away from Kansas City it is, the less it is news'' (Byerly, 1961).

Thus we can think of a mean information field centered on the organization, with decreasing knowledge coinciding with increasing distance along both social and spatial gradients. A useful indicator available for assessing organizational information fields is the map which is recovered from a content analysis of organizational records. A convenient illustration is provided by newspapers. The press, like any other adaptive organization, will retain information it regards as most useful to its own concerns; indeed, as specialized information gatherers, we might expect the press to come most closely to the ideal theoretical status of perfect access to information. In this light it is disappointing to observe the parochialism which accompanies even major newspapers. A content analysis of 13 issues of the Montreal French-language newspaper *Le Devoir* revealed a heavily biassed information field (Figure 7.5a). Over 50 percent of column inches reported news originating in the province of Quebec; only 2 percent originated in Ontario (the same level as for the whole of Central and South America); and only 1 percent for the four Canadian provinces west of Ontario. An instructive comparison with *Le Devoir* was provided by the information field of the English-language *Montreal Star* (Figure 7.5b). Like *Le Devoir,* only about 15–20 percent of the *Star*'s news had a source outside North America, but within North America there were marked variations, with the *Star* providing substantially more exposure to the rest of Canada outside Quebec and to the United States. Within the city of Montreal the same contrast was maintained, with *Le Devoir* giving more restricted and specialized coverage, emphasizing news emanating from French-speaking districts. Of course, with its French-speaking Quebec readership, *Le Devoir* is scarcely a typical North American daily. However, the circulation of Canadian news in general shows highly biassed spatial patterns reflecting local concerns, political centers, and the population size of more distant places (Kariel and Rosenvall, 1978).

The extent to which the parochial information fields of the media are generalizable to all organizations is unknown. But it is extremely probable that parallels exist, for information retrieval is costly of time and energy, and there is little incentive for organizations to collect information that is not pertinent to their central concerns. The existence of specialized information services for firms, such as the Location of Offices Bureau set up by the British government and its private-sector equivalents in North America, testifies to the unmet informational needs of the organization. Certainly when we examine

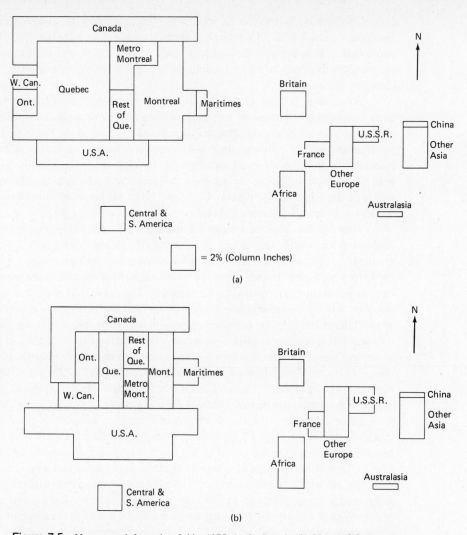

Figure 7.5 Newspaper information fields, 1975: (a) *Le Devoir*; (b) *Montreal Star*.

their patterns of contact and search, which are closely related to the configuration of existing information fields, there are no grounds for assuming organizational familiarity with more than a small area—even though this area will probably comprise a set of smaller points more scattered in space than is true for the media with their greater attentiveness to local consciousness (Pred, 1974).

Organizational Search

When confronted with a problem, the search behavior of organizations, like individuals, is concerned with a short perusal of a familiar area. Search patterns are routinized like other sectors of organizational decision making, and decision making "is concerned with the discovery and selection of satisfactory alternatives; only in exceptional cases is it concerned with the discovery and selection of optimal alternatives" (March and Simon, 1958:141).

Search and decision making are characterized by simple rules and proximate decisions. To be acceptable, solutions need be only feasible or satisfactory, rarely optimal, and information that supports an available feasible solution is likely to be perceived selectively. As Cyert and March observe, "An organizational coalition does not require either consistency or completeness in information; in fact . . . consistency or completeness would, at times, create problems in finding feasible solutions" (Cyert and March, 1963:78).

Search patterns are far from random, being directed through preexisting networks following simple rules. One of the few systematic records of organizational search is Wood's (1971) study of problem solving by municipalities in southern Ontario. At the turn of the twentieth century, the important innovation of municipally owned electric power systems was diffusing through the region, and individual municipalities were confronted with the need to make a decision on adoption. To aid their decision, towns sought information from other centers in the region either by mail or by personal visits (Figure 7.6). The spatial pattern of search showed a number of regularities. First, the largest centers, like Toronto and Hamilton, initiated the most contacts, 20 or more,

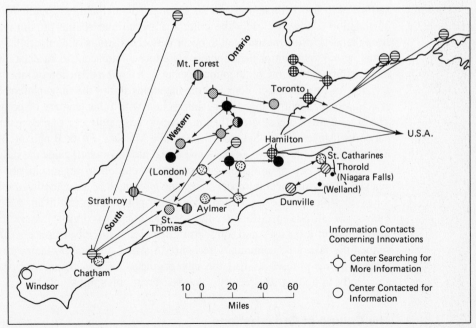

Figure 7.6 The pattern of organizational search among Ontario municipalities. (*Source*: C. Wood, "Some Characteristics of Searching by Municipal Governments," *Geografiska Annaler* 53B (1971):138–145, fig. 4. Reprinted by permission.)

whereas the smallest towns, like Thorold, sent out only 1 or 2 requests. Second, there was a marked preference for consultation with centers of a comparable size even though this might mean bypassing a closer settlement that had also adopted recently. Thus, from Figure 7.6, the small settlement of Thorold sought out the compatible community of Dunville and bypassed three larger centers that were closer and had already adopted the innovation. But at the same time the pattern in intermunicipal contact was for centers smaller than the originating settlement to be avoided, as administrators moved up the urban hierarchy to seek advice if they could not find it in a similar-sized town. The third generalization proceeds from the other two. There was a distance threshold to search that varied systematically with settlement size in a logarithmic manner, so that the largest centers initiated by far the most spatially wide-ranging contacts in their quest for information. Whereas small centers usually confined their search to a radius of 100 miles, the cities sent out requests to centers of up to 1000 miles distant.

The constraints of organizational compatibility and a distance threshold allow some predictions to be made of the diffusion of adoption decisions through a system of organizations. We would expect that an innovation would move between similar organizations, and the smaller the organization, the more contact would be constrained by physical distance. In other words, organizations will mimic the decisions of others close to them in terms of social and spatial proximity. An illustration of these processes has been the diffusion of the city manager form of government in metropolitan Montreal (Mercer, 1974). The system was introduced in the municipality of Westmount in 1913, and by 1970 had been adopted in 30 Montreal municipalities (Figure 7.7). The pattern of adoption followed closely the criteria of social and spatial proximity. There was a strong tendency for transmission to occur between districts of comparable socioeconomic status, and 60 percent of the adopters were located adjacent to an existing city manager municipality at the time of adoption. Evidence from the diffusion of innovations through a variety of formal associations and organizations shows the same pattern of local spatial effects, coupled with longer-range interaction with other centers of compatible status. The exact form of any single diffusion seems to be heavily tied to preexisting professional networks (Meyer, 1976; Spector, Brown, and Malecki, 1976; Bingham, 1977). As with informal groups, the biases of particular social networks often guide the diffusion process.

The strategy of imitation is a common solution to organizational problems. An analysis of environmental impact statements presented by city administrations to support a new highway proposal revealed widespread plagiarizing (Sullivan, Montgomery, and Farber, 1973). Seven different cities used identical wording to assess the relationship between short-term uses and long-term effects, and the city engineers of St. Louis described the favorable community response to a new highway in their city in exactly the same glowing phrases as had the city engineers of Omaha in a prior submission—apparently in finding satisfactory solutions, great cities think alike!

The Culture of Organizations

In the preceding section we have repeatedly illustrated how the everyday impact of contextual factors constantly diverts the optimizing goals suggested by the normative

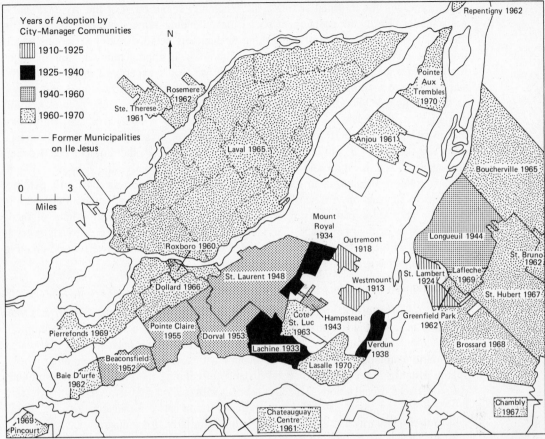

Figure 7.7   The diffusion of city manager administration in metropolitan Montreal. (*Source*: J. Mercer, "City Manager Communities in the Montreal Metropolitan Area," *Canadian Geographer* 18 (1974):352–366, fig. 5. Reprinted by permission.)

model of the organization. The normative model is a deductive abstraction which has been subject to limited empirical testing. Indeed, a repetitive complaint in the literature is the limited number of detailed examinations of the ongoing *life-world* of the organization. Such an inductive approach would give much more attention to the everyday contexts out of which organizational actions emerge, to the actual meanings of events to organizational members which lie behind their initiatives and responses (Silverman, 1970). In paying attention to the organization's own definition of situations, we would be identifying it as a social world, a potential culture builder whose boundaries are set by the limits of effective interaction among its members.

This perspective on the organization is similar to the view of informal social groups taken in Chapter 6. Indeed, in many ways, this perspective is *more* appropriate in an examination of institutional life, for within the organization codes for action are far more thoroughly systematized and enforced than they are in informal groups. Second, whereas there may continue to be debate as to whether the individual or the group is the more appropriate unit for informal settings, the inherently *social* basis of the organization is indisputable. Third, the problem of social understanding—intersubjectivity—is met by the organization's ingenuity in prescribing to members detailed role descriptions which imply not only typical actions but also typical motives. In approaching our bank manager for a loan we encounter none of the uncertainty we would experience in addressing the same request to a stranger, for we know the limited range of actions and motives available to him in his role. Fourth, the organization prescribes schedules, repetitive tasks, and activities, so that each member has a set of *routines* to which he or she continually returns. The repeated performance of a limited range of prescribed actions and interactions and the use of a common vocabulary with unchanging others quickly help define an organizational lifestyle and eventually a subculture. Finally, the *concerns* of any organization are formalized in its charter or its market behavior, so that in its external relations its transactions are heavily biassed toward other organizations with compatible interests; an institutional measure of social distance is easily defined. Many of these characteristics of the organization are taken for granted, but as we have already seen, it is precisely in the realm of taken-for-granted experience that the powerful and creative forces of a *genre de vie* are themselves constructed.

Communication

In the case of informal groups we saw that interaction was associated with common concerns and geographical proximity. Physical separation is not insignificant in prompting organizational communication, but as Wood demonstrated in his analysis of spatial search by Ontario municipalities, it must be associated with social compatibility; in other words, spatial distance is secondary to social distance in defining the probability of communication between organizations. This is consistent with several studies reviewed by Massam (1975) which suggested that interaction and cooperation between municipalities are closely tied to their similarity in socioeconomic status. Similarly, for industrial enterprises it is a commonplace of geography to discuss the specialized linkages between firms in the same industrial sector. Indeed, linkages might well determine the geographical clustering of industrial and administrative office activities; compatibility and entering into relation may have a spatial counterpart for the firm as well as for informal groups.

This relationship is illustrated in the distinction between special and general accessibility which a downtown location offers certain firms. What is significant to them is less the general market and labor accessibility provided by a central site than the specialized linkages with related downtown firms. In Swedish cities, 40–50 percent of organizational contacts are localized in the immediate area, and in Stockholm, 75 percent of contacts are absorbed within the city. For a sample of enterprises in Toronto's CBD, between 22 percent and 84 percent of all face-to-face contacts were located in the central area, with the mean value just under 50 percent (Gad, 1979). In Britain, business contacts are similarly clustered, with 70–80 percent of organizational meetings involving journeys of less than 30 minutes (Goddard, 1975). In Central London, the degree of specialization and clustering of offices is such that a third of all meetings are associated with journeys undertaken on foot.

The daily contact routines of Central London businessmen were assessed by examining three-day contact diaries kept by persons from a cross section of firms (Goddard,

1973, 1975). These businessmen kept records of their telephone and face-to-face contacts with other business sectors. Over the three-day period businessmen recorded an average of 10 contacts each, three-quarters of them by telephone. The large matrix of interactions was simplified using factor analysis, and a number of interaction clusters was identified on the basis of similar contact patterns. One group separated out by Goddard was labelled civil engineering, including such firms as consulting engineers, architects, and various construction companies, and other major groups identifiable by their contact patterns included banking and finance, and commodity trading. For six major business clusters distinguished in this way, contacts within the cluster accounted for an average of 54 percent of telephone transactions and 60 percent of business meetings. Though discrete groups may be demarcated, there is also some interaction between most sectors, so that, in detail, linkage patterns are complex (Figure 7.8). The major linkage groupings are

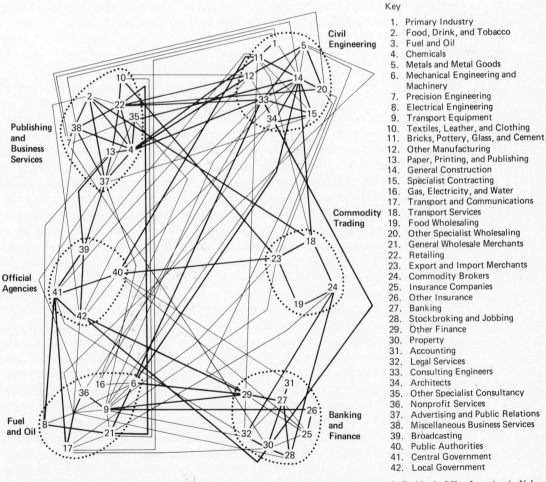

Key

1. Primary Industry
2. Food, Drink, and Tobacco
3. Fuel and Oil
4. Chemicals
5. Metals and Metal Goods
6. Mechanical Engineering and Machinery
7. Precision Engineering
8. Electrical Engineering
9. Transport Equipment
10. Textiles, Leather, and Clothing
11. Bricks, Pottery, Glass, and Cement
12. Other Manufacturing
13. Paper, Printing, and Publishing
14. General Construction
15. Specialist Contracting
16. Gas, Electricity, and Water
17. Transport and Communications
18. Transport Services
19. Food Wholesaling
20. Other Specialist Wholesaling
21. General Wholesale Merchants
22. Retailing
23. Export and Import Merchants
24. Commodity Brokers
25. Insurance Companies
26. Other Insurance
27. Banking
28. Stockbroking and Jobbing
29. Other Finance
30. Property
31. Accounting
32. Legal Services
33. Consulting Engineers
34. Architects
35. Other Specialist Consultancy
36. Nonprofit Services
37. Advertising and Public Relations
38. Miscellaneous Business Services
39. Broadcasting
40. Public Authorities
41. Central Government
42. Local Government

Figure 7.8   The pattern of telephone contacts between firms in central London. (*Source*: J. Goddard, *Office Location in Urban and Regional Development*. London: Oxford University Press, 1975, fig. 3.2. Reprinted by permission.)

also associated with spatial clustering, so that information flows are often related to geographical proximity between firms. A subsequent study in Toronto took the argument a stage further by examining the decentralization potential of firms in terms of the proportion of their business linkages that were with other offices located in the CBD (Gad, 1979). The contact data suggested that, contrary to common opinion, head offices could be decentralized with least damage to their transaction patterns. Trading functions with associated financial and legal services were most tightly linked to business contacts in the downtown area.

From his Central London data Goddard concluded that "the continuing interconnection between functional linkages, location, and movement within the city centre cannot be denied" (Goddard, 1975:34). Note the correspondence with our statement in Chapter 6 that interaction and group formation are a product of common concerns and a similar biography, particularly spatial proximity. The next question to be asked is, to what extent does this selective pattern of interaction create and sustain a shared world view within the organization as it does within informal groups?

The Organization as a Social World

In his study of office contact patterns in Central London, Goddard described over 95 percent of telephone messages as programmed, of a repetitive and routine type, and mainly between members of "a well-established contact network involving straightforward questions and answers between acquainted individuals" (Goddard, 1973:197). The selective and repetitive execution of such routines might be expected to encourage an "organizational climate," a social milieu of shared understandings, to emerge. In the same way that we saw that repeated interaction in behavior settings and in informal groups generated contextual effects and promoted the convergence of attitudes, so within organizations there might be expected to develop distinctive ambiences which would impact newcomers and encourage their socialization to organizational norms. In short, "Institutions not only select persons and eject them; institutions also form them . . . the key mechanism . . . involves the circle of significant others which the institution establishes" (Gerth and Mills, 1953:173).

This proposition is intuitively appealing, but its testing can only be piecemeal in the absence of illustrative studies in the geographic literature, although in sociology it has been explored in various organizational settings by the work of the Chicago School, including such authors as Everett Hughes and Howard Becker (Silverman, 1970). At its most extreme, this position might be represented by the model of the organization man, the individual wedded to and molded by a career role. The events of the Watergate break-in and the disclosures surrounding President Nixon's eventual resignation suggest that the ideal type of the organization man is not entirely an academic fabrication. The Nixon White House provides perhaps the most finely documented example of the processes of culture building within an institutional social world. Within the Nixon "team" a group of compatible men was brought together which continually interacted and insulated itself from outside influences. Behind the frontstage of public performance these men constructed a backstage reality, an alternative world where the ends came to justify the means, and the goal of in-group survival was mistaken for the goal of national government. Public morality was suspended for a private morality which became binding on members, so that eventually a number of governmental aides became acculturated to this socially constructed and socially sustained reality. Not uncommon are similar, if less dramatic, examples of the power of contextual effects within an organization to mold individual attitudes. Lorimer (1972) recounts the common story of the co-option of reform politicians to establishment alliances, and another common example is the changing posture of "watchdogs" set up in the public interest whose attitudes over time frequently begin to converge with those of the organization they are set up to monitor. As Peter Berger has observed, "Social affiliation or disaffiliation normally carries with it specific cognitive commitments" (Berger, 1963: 120).

These conclusions are reinforced by detailed observation of specific institutions. Closed institutions such as prisons and mental hospitals, which hold their charges over long periods, tend to impose on them an identity consistent with their status in the institution. Prisons often reinforce the status of criminal on their inmates, and asylums reinforce a self-identity of being mentally ill (Goffman, 1961). Recognition of the power of the institutional environment to mold personality has led to the recent deemphasis on institutional confinement and a policy of treatment in halfway houses where a more varied social environment might ease the transition from institutional to mainstream status.

But this implicitly deterministic influence of the organization should not be pressed too far. There is also a considerable self-selection involved in organizational membership, for, as in informal groups, there is a strong tendency for birds of a feather to flock together. Student surveys have shown a clear association between the personal and social values of students and their subsequent career aspirations: "Values exerted a powerful influence on choice of occupation . . . young people expressed occupational preferences congruent with their personal values" (Cotgrove, 1980). Certain preexisting traits selectively draw individuals to certain organizational affiliations and not to others, so that the internal homogeneity of an organization is the result not only of organizational pressures but also of selective recruitment. For example, the founding of a new civic reform party, The Electors' Action Movement (TEAM), in Vancouver in 1968, was primarily the initiative of a specific group with common concerns and a similar biography, whom we might label members of the Canadian establishment (Ley, 1980). In the 1972 city election there was a remarkably high correlation between TEAM support and establishment traits (Table 7.2). The correlations show that support for TEAM followed very closely ethnic, religious, educational, and occupational divisions of the population. The TEAM party was the articulation as a political organization of a preexisting subculture associated with a shared establishment status in Canada.

Such elite subcultures are invariably associated with organizational membership, for the elites are by definition those in control of political, economic, and cultural institutions. Vancouver's elite at the turn of the century shared comparable social and cultural status with TEAM members in the 1970s. They also controlled the city's institutional life, for the prominent businessmen who were presidents or vice-presidents of the Board of Trade were the same figures who were key members in the city's influential social clubs and who also shuffled into the arena of city politics as mayors and aldermen (Figure

TABLE 7.2 CORRELATES OF TEAM ELECTORAL
SUPPORT, VANCOUVER, 1972
($n = 68$ tracts)

Variable	Correlation*
United Kingdom ethnicity	0.78
University degree	0.75
Sales occupations	0.73
Managerial and administrative occupations	0.73
Less than grade 9 education	−0.67
United Church affiliation	0.67
Median household income over $20,000	0.65
Asian ethnicity	−0.65
Roman Catholic affiliation	−0.59
Medical and health occupations	0.58

Source: D. Ley, ''Liberal Ideology and the Postindustrial City,''
Annals, Association of American Geographers 70 (1980), 238–
258, Table 3, p. 249. Reprinted by permission.
*All correlations significant at 0.001.

7.9). At a national level the degree of interconnection between directors of different organizations suggests that it may be appropriate to conceive of a distinctive culture of power elites. Clement (1975) has shown the degree of interpenetration between major economic corporations in Canada. By examining the pattern of interlocking directorships between the largest economic organizations, one can see the extent to which Canadian economic life is controlled by a single network of elite members (Figure 7.10). These elite members are recruited selectively from upper- and middle-class backgrounds and are born primarily in central Canada of Anglo-Canadian parents and Protestant heritage; 40 percent are educated at private schools, and of those attending university, 43 percent graduate from the University of Toronto and McGill. Following graduation over half of the economic elite join one or more of six private clubs in Ontario and Quebec.

These channelled biographies are a reminder of the human construction of an organization, that it consists of decision makers who are also culture builders. The organization does not veer along in some blind and mechanistic manner but is directed purposefully within an intersubjective context. Organizational members are both self-selected and preselected by organizational recruitment. Once they enter the organization, they are introduced to a social world of ongoing routines and like-minded others. Within this context there are rewards and sanctions which both commend and disapprove the attitudes and actions of members, and have as a result a capacity to promote an organizational subculture and lifestyle—what the old French geographers might have regarded as an organizational *genre de vie*.

Organizational Perception and Labelling

In passing from institutional behavior to institutional culture we are placing more emphasis on the creative aspects of the organization, remembering that it is from a socially sustained milieu of values and typical experiences that actions emerge. The culture of organizations establishes a set of more or less fixed perceptions and ways of looking at

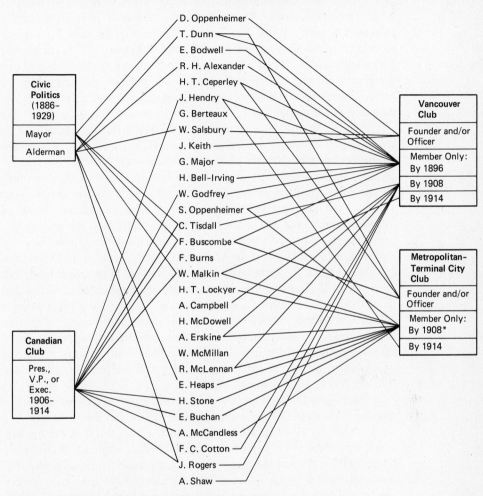

1887–1914 Board of Trade Presidents and Vice Presidents
(In Order of Service)

*Complete membership listings for an earlier period not available.

Figure 7.9 Overlapping elite networks: the Board of Trade, high-status social clubs, and civic politics, Vancouver 1887–1914. (*Source*: A. Robertson, *The Pursuit of Power, Profit and Privacy*. Unpublished thesis, Dept. of Geography, University of British Columbia, 1977, fig. 1. Reprinted by permission.)

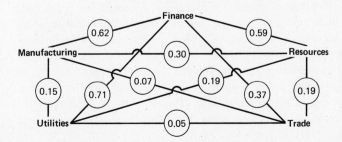

Figure 7.10 The interlocking nature of Canadian business corporations, 1972. The figures represent actual interlocking directorates as a proportion of the maximum possible. (*Source*: W. Clement, *The Canadian Corporate Elite*. Toronto: McClelland and Stewart, 1975, fig. 1. Reprinted by permission of Gage Publishing Limited.)

the environment, and these may differ even between various departments of the same organization as each develops its own social world with varying traditions and norms. In a Connecticut study, 30 criteria to be considered in transportation planning were presented to panels which included officials of both the state highway department and the state regional planning authority (Weiner and Deak, 1972). The highways personnel, with their training in cost-effectiveness and efficiency, ranked highly criteria that promoted economic development. In contrast, the planners chose as criteria more intangible factors concerned with health and safety, and sociopsychological criteria which comprised a quality of life theme.

The perceptual filters of organizations are far from incidental, for they often have the power to transform their visions into realities, including of course the realities of landscape forms in the city. Geographical landscape facts are not simply given but are created, and in a very real way facts are brought into existence by underlying values. As one philosopher has written, ''Value is not a layer atop the facts, but facts are reduced values'' (van Peursen, 1972: 38). Some of these values are recognized and lead to intended effects, but others are more hidden and rarely acknowledged. In particular, organizations share the common human problem of being unselfconscious of the side effects of their own view of the world. But in the process of their thinking-as-usual, their categories reduce the complexity of the outside world to simple labels, and their action proceeds on the basis of these taken-for-granted typifications. A consideration of unintended side effects from social planning in Sweden led Olsson to be critical of the dogmatic reasoning of policymakers, which was undermining their intended reforms. Their taken-for-granted perceptual categories and their ''thinking-as-usual'' were themselves being translated into public policy with real-world effects: ''Given this conception of reasoning, the role of any language is not to describe reality so much as to shape it'' (Olsson, 1974a; also Lowman, 1982).

Numerous studies have shown how the taken-for-granted perceptions of key bureaucrats and their interpretation of public policy can influence the social and spatial form of the city (Prottas, 1978; Knox and Cullen, 1981). In the English city of Hull, where 40 percent of the city's 100,000 households are tenants in local-authority housing, Gray (1976) examined the process by which prospective tenants were allocated to particular districts of public housing. In understanding the assignment process, it was necessary to determine the organizational definition of the situation, the everyday rules by means of which the administrators negotiated their task. The department had set up an elaborate series of in-house rules and categories for determining the eligibility of tenants, their priority on waiting lists, and their eventual allocation to a particular housing district. These intersubjective understandings within the organization governed the applicant's chances of success: ''The local authority managers are the independent variable which determines a household's access to council housing'' (Gray, 1976). Some of the descriptions of tenants made by departmental officials are revealing of bureaucratic categories; they included such phrases as ''excellent tenant, suitable for new property'' or ''poor type, will need supervision—suitable for old property.'' On the basis of such impressions, applicants were assigned to one of six administrative categories. As is implied by the descriptions, a systematic relationship existed between the labelling of applicants and

TABLE 7.3   TENANT STATUS AND HOUSING ASSIGNMENT, HULL

Housing Characteristics	Local-Authority Grading of Tenant		
	"Poor" or "Fair Only" (n = 24)	"Fairly Good" or "Good" (n = 137)	"Very Good" or "Excellent" (n = 28)
Average gross rateable value	£176.7	£201.9	£209.9
% Households occupying dwelling, by dwelling age			
1919–1944	62.5	13.9	10.7
1945–1965	29.2	38.0	28.6
post-1965	8.3	23.4	17.9
new	0.0	24.8	42.9

Source: F. Gray, "Selection and Allocation in Council Housing," *Transactions, Institute of British Geographers* 1 (1976), 34–46, Table 2, p. 42. Reprinted by permission.

their assignment to a particular housing district. From a sample of prospective tenants, Gray was able to show an overrepresentation of low-status applicants in older housing and an accompanying overrepresentation of well-regarded applicants in new housing, significant at the 0.001 level (Table 7.3). The outworking of these administrative categories has had the unintended effect of concentrating problem households in common areas, a situation which can only compound their existing difficulties. Bureaucratic perceptions of the quality of districts and the status of households, and their implicit matching of each, will do little to lessen social and spatial inequalities. Indeed, from our earlier discussion of the reinforcement of contextual effects within informal groups, it is far more likely that polarization would be increased.

It would be easy to add further examples to Gray's penetrating analysis of the creative potential of institutional subcultures and the capacity of key administrators to make over reality as a reflection of their own categories. In North America the notorious Pruitt-Igoe public housing complex in St. Louis is a famous example. When it was built, Pruitt-Igoe won architectural prizes and received the acclamation of planners. But in the daily experience of its residents, this product of tidy minds was a grotesque failure that was largely abandoned and heavily vandalized before it was eventually blown up by the city's housing authority after an unexpectedly short life. For Pruitt-Igoe was the product of a bureaucratic mind set whose categories did not exceed far enough beyond geometry and dollars, and these dominant concerns of the bureaucratic life-world were transposed too directly and inappropriately into the built environment. We shall consider further effects of labelling, such as redlining by banks and finance companies (the restriction of loans to certain districts), in Part 4, where we examine more centrally the role of urban institutions in molding the urban landscape.

The mental categories of key decision makers have effects in reality; their word can become our world. The conjunction of power and everyday bureaucratic routines can give public expression to the private life-world of the organization. The simple problem-solving conventions of the organization may not be subtle enough to accommodate the complexity and ambiguity of real-world problems, but the authority granted to the organization enables its simplified categories nevertheless to be realized in practice, whatever the side effects. The danger of this trend, as Olsson (1974a) sees it, is that "we may well be left with a society which mirrors the techniques by which we measure it and echoes the language in which we talk about it." This triumph of organizational consciousness will be no less oppressive for being entirely unintended.

Conclusion

In this chapter rather than accept the institution as a given of the urban scene, we have treated it more problematically and have examined some of the internal processes of the organizational life-world. We immediately saw that orthodox normative views of the institution and the firm are too inflexible as soon as discussion leaves an abstract plane and examines empirically the everyday actions of organizations. A behavioral position was helpful here in examining the organization as adaptively responding to constantly changing contextual effects whose origins are internal as well as external. But the behavioral perspective, useful as it is, does not do full justice to the organization's tendency to develop as a cultural entity, a social world, with its own capacity to construct realities. We have illustrated some of the unintended effects in the real world which may result from the systematic bias of values, rules, and reasoning which are a taken-for-granted part of the organizational subculture, so that the "is" of administrative language is unselfconsciously translated to the "ought" of administrative policy.

This final section reaches an extremely important transitional point in our argument. Though we have seen that there are many similarities in the internal relations of both the social group and the institution, there is also a significant differential, the reality of power. Although every social group in Chicago may have held its own private fantasies for its city, there was only one Mayor Daley who could translate his private agendas into action. The question of power carries our argument away from the internal relations of the life-world and toward external relations, the urban arena in which the different values of informal groups and organizations intersect and often conflict.

Chapter 8

The Urban Housing Market

The incentive to exclude appears to be one of the true universals, and the habit is addictive

(Wolpert, 1976)

From Life-World to Biographical Situation

In the earlier parts of the book we began by noting the more or less segregated pattern of social areas in the city, and then we sought to animate these residential patterns on the map by adopting an inside view of the geographical life-world of the urban resident. We saw the repetitive processes of reality construction that comprise the immediate geographical experience of individuals and groups: the pursuit of familiar routines, the frequenting of well-known places, patterns of repeated social interaction, membership within informal social networks, the development of social worlds, and in all of this, a conception of urban space as inherently meaningful, the meanings covering a range of dimensions, each with its own spatial distribution over the city. These regularities form the imminent, taken-for-granted realms of urban life. Together they define a set of internal relations for an individual, a group, an organization, or a community.

But besides its internal relations, a group also has a set of external or "foreign" relations. Society consists of more than intimate groups of like-minded others in informal or formal association. Although such "congregations" (J. E. Vance, 1976) form the texture of our experience of urban life, they are themselves located in a broader set of contexts. The individual- and group-centered world of everyday life rarely encourages such self-consciousness, an opportunity for a group to see clearly its own *biographical situation,* its position within a citywide or even national pattern of social stratification. As a result, urban dwellers tend to disregard as less immediate external groups and their own position in a broader social structure. But such introspection and neglect of structural relations are misleading to the researcher and may prove counterproductive to the group itself. We must now examine more problematically the biographical situation of urban residents and note the various factors of social stratification which allow them differential access to the city's neighborhoods and social areas. In a market-oriented society, unequal market power as a result of unequal incomes provides a major sorting of households. Thus there is a differential balance of choice and constraint in residential decision making. Certain social groups have numerous constraints on their freedom of choice in finding a place to live (Duncan, 1976a). Single-parent families, for example, frequently have very few housing opportunities outside government units (Lee, 1977), whereas wealthier households have a much broader range of choice. Whereas earlier behavioral studies of the housing market followed the neoclassical economists' view of consumer sovereignty and exaggerated the degree of choice, recent radical analysis tends toward the opposite error of exaggerating the constraints (Hamnett, 1977). Empirical studies have shown that even for poorer groups some trade-off choices remain (Couper and Brindley, 1975).

Moreover, a household's position in the housing market is not fixed by income factors alone. Preferences such as those concerning tenure type, family size, and the proportion of income to be spent on housing will separate households with identical incomes into different neighborhoods (Couper and Brindley, 1975). In addition, attitudinal and lifestyle factors, such as those discussed in earlier chapters, serve to sort the population. For example, Wendell Bell (1958) noted the association between the lifestyle of familism and suburban residence versus careerism with its in-town locational setting; in inner-city Boston affiliation or disaffiliation with traditional ethnic ties led to differing decisions by Italian Americans as to an appropriate neighborhood in which to live (Firey, 1945; Whyte, 1955). But the most important status (as opposed to income) differentials in the North American housing market are associated with race, for racial minorities have been, and continue to be, denied access to a neighborhood on the grounds of prejudice even though they could otherwise afford to buy a home there; so profound is this cleavage that a number of authors refer to a dual housing market based on race in the American city (Berry, 1975b, 1979).

In this chapter we shall consider the importance of social stratification in the city in terms of a household's access to the urban housing market. Three related topics will be discussed: residential mobility, neighborhood deterioration and revitalization, and the effects of and responses to a change in a community's social mix. In each of these areas we will note the variable effects of market power, broad status differentials, and also the intervention of government agencies (Bourne, 1981). In this manner we will see how the spatial structure of the city is repeatedly an expression of the social structure of the nation in which it is located.

Residential Mobility

Residential mobility is a central facet of urban social geography, for it provides a spatial expression of the link between the individual household and the social structure, between the household's life-world and its biographical situation, between internal culture-building processes and the spatial template of the city. The residential choices of individual households in aggregate define the social areas of the city. The rapid transformation of American central cities and the plight of their dwindling fiscal base was caused in part by the massive migration of middle-class families to the suburbs in the 1960s. Similarly, the anticipated revitalization of the downtown areas of some cities in the 1970s has been brought about by the reverse migration of childless professionals to "gentrified" central neighborhoods. But there is a two-way relationship between individual and aggregate levels, for at the same time the individual's pattern of choices is itself constrained by the preexisting set of spatial opportunities in the city and the household's own biography—those characteristics of income, stage in the life cycle, ethnic status, and lifestyle which will close off certain housing options to it and substantially reduce its range of choice. Consequently, over the past 10 years there has been considerable research by geographers and others to understand more fully the processes and implications of intraurban migration, a phenomenon which in its widest sense brings together urban experience and urban structure (Adams and Gilder, 1976; Quigley and Weinberg, 1977).

Residential stability has not been a norm of the North American city. Rapid growth and the arrival of repeated waves of immigrants have been major trends, and the period of massive population redistribution has not passed; between 1970 and 1975 there were 39 metropolitan areas in the United States with populations of over 200,000 that grew by more than 10 percent, and 9 of these were already million cities. In addition, there is much internal rearrangement of households within urban areas each year. About 18 percent of American families move annually, the figure varying according to a city's economic base and the type of neighborhood; inner city rooming house and apartment districts commonly show turnovers of 70 percent each year. Residential relocation rates are higher for tenants than for owners, for unattached singles than for families, and often for immigrants and minority groups than for established natives. Within Seattle's black rental market during the local economic recession at the end of the 1960s, when a number of these factors worked together to accelerate movement, there was a 50 percent annual turnover in rental units. Mobility rates are also highly variable by age and stage in the life cycle. Data from a large survey in Green Bay, Wisconsin, showed that mobility rates could be described by a u-shaped curve, peaking during the early twenties, reaching its lowest level in middle life, and reaching a secondary peak in old age (McCarthy, 1976). Nearly 70 percent of young, single-person households had moved in the previous year in the Wisconsin study, whereas this was true of fewer than 5 percent of middle-aged nuclear families. Finally, residential mobility also varies by region (Yeates and Garner, 1980). In the United States, the proportion of people who have moved in the previous 12 months may be twice as high in the rapidly growing cities of the South and West, like Houston (25.1 percent) or Los Angeles-Long Beach (22.4 percent), as in the older industrial metropoles, like Pittsburgh (11.3 percent) or Cleveland (14.3 percent).

The Decision to Move

Intraurban migration begins experientially, with a personal decision by a household to move. There are, of course, occasions when migration is forced and a family is spared this sometimes difficult process of decision making. Eviction, compulsory purchase and subsequent demolition, and unemployment or some other source of change in household income produce circumstances when migration is not voluntary. An early study of migration in Philadelphia which included a number of tenants among its sample identified 23 percent of moves as involuntary (Rossi, 1955), but more recent results have suggested that the figure is usually lower, particularly when owner-occupancy is predominant. Evidence from Toronto (Barrett, 1973) showed that 8 percent of a sample of home buyers had been involuntarily displaced from their previous residence.

Several geographers in the behavioral tradition have devised conceptual schemes which, though not fully operational, do throw light on the sequence of stages in the decision to move. Initially they envisage that stress is created for households by a change in the relations between a family's housing needs and the properties of its housing environment (Wolpert, 1965, 1966). The mismatch may be brought about by a change in the household's size or its aspirations, or, alternatively, by a deterioration in the condition of either its home or the local neighborhood. When the stress reaches a critical threshold, which will of course vary among households, some adjustment has to be made. Various strategies are now available (Brown and Moore, 1970). The family might adopt a strategy of tolerance, lowering its aspirations to accommodate the changed circumstances. Alternatively it may attempt to restore its diminished level of satisfaction by changing the housing environment, making physical additions and improvements to the home, or less likely by seeking in a cooperative effort with neighbors to divert the elements of neighborhood deterioration and attract neighborhood improvements. The final option, and perhaps the most common in North America, especially in the rental market, is a decision to move.

The precise factors that prompt a need to move in the first place are readily discernible in general, though in detail they are confused during interviews by rationalizations after the fact, memory lapses, and the inherent weaknesses of all approaches utilizing survey questionnaires. These biasses would include a desire to present socially acceptable motives to the questioner; respondents, for example, are unlikely to admit to a move on the grounds of racism, and neither would potential mortgage borrowers inform their bank manager that their interest in a new home was occasioned by eviction from the last! Perhaps the most convincing demonstration of such operational distortions concerning housing attitudes was provided by a study of preferred residential environments conducted with residents living in North Carolina (Wilson, 1962). From photographs the respondents generated a list of desired neighborhood qualities; in order of importance, the five most favored residential characteristics were spaciousness, beauty, a setting good for children, exclusiveness, and a countrylike character. A majority of respondents preferred their own neighborhood to any others shown in the photographs. The particular features of their own area that they found compelling were its friendliness, homeliness, quietness, greenery, and cleanliness. These were not the characteristics previously cited as important; indeed, they rated their own areas as less than satisfactory on four of the five qualities that they had regarded as of top priority! Such apparent attitudinal irrationality should lead to caution in interpreting questionnaire responses and may well explain in part the diversity that exists in detailed results between different studies.

With these caveats in mind, the findings of empirical studies in the United States, Canada, and Britain might be noted. Rossi found that 45 percent of moves in Philadelphia were triggered by life cycle changes in the family which made the size of the home no

TABLE 8.1 REASONS FOR MOVING FOR TORONTO HOMEOWNERS (*n* = 380)

Reason	No. of Times Mentioned	% of Respondents
Forced	16	4
Life cycle/house size	138	36
Tenure/house-style attitudes	138	36
Neighborhood attitudes	37	10
Cost	44	12
Accessibility	14	4
Other	4	1

Source: Computed from F. Barrett, *Residential Search Behaviour*. Toronto: York University, Geographical Monographs No. 1, 1973, p. 256. Reprinted by permission.

longer compatible with the needs of the household, and more generally it seems as if 50 percent of moves or more are associated with life cycle adjustments (Simmons, 1968); from his Wisconsin data McCarthy (1976) considered that 6 or 7 of the 10 moves made by a typical North American during adult life are probably associated with life-cycle needs and changes. A more detailed breakdown of home buyers in Toronto showed that besides life cycle factors, the desire for home ownership and other attitudinal preferences was an equally major contributor, with cost and neighborhood factors of somewhat lesser importance (Table 8.1). The same motives were cited by home purchasers in the smaller city of Windsor, Ontario (Dzus and Romsa, 1977), and by a sample of owners and tenants in the English city of Bristol (Short, 1978). Although the categories are not identical, there are some interesting comparisons revealed by an earlier British survey of over 3000 households. Over 1000 of these volunteered reasons for wanting to move (Table 8.2). Despite the blurring of categories, it can be seen that the major issues identified in both the British and the Toronto studies are associated with life cycle and

TABLE 8.2 REASONS FOR WANTING TO MOVE FOR BRITISH HOUSEHOLDS (*n* = 1066)

Reason	Household Tenure (Percent)*					
	Owns/is Buying *n* = 329	Rents from Council *n* = 225	Private Rental, Unfurnished *n* = 447	Private Rental, Furnished *n* = 48	Other Rental *n* = 17	All Households
Forced	2	4	16	6	6	9
House size/life cycle	33	30	28	21	30	30
Tenure attitudes	1	10	9	23	18	7
Neighborhood/house quality	47	31	50	25	12	43
Cost	3	3	3	4	1	3
Personal	18	25	13	6	12	17
Other	20	18	12	25	41	17

Source: Adapted from J. B. Cullingworth, *English Housing Trends*. London: Bell, 1965. Cited in P. Sarre, ''Intra-Urban Migration,'' pp. 65–106, in *Social Geography*. Bletchley: The Open University, 1972, Table 6, p. 83. Reprinted by permission of the Trustees, Social Administration Research Trust.
*With multiple reasons, columns do not sum to 100 percent.

space needs, and attitudes and preferences in terms of neighborhood quality, housing style, and tenure.

But, as the British results show, these priorities may not be constant across different housing tenure groups. The aspiration for home ownership might be a matter of some concern to tenants, but not of course to existing homeowners, who may be more sensitive to design and style details. Similarly, a forced move strikes tenure groups unequally, with private tenants more vulnerable to demolition orders and other forms of displacement. Over 20 percent of movers in the St. Pauls neighborhood of Bristol had been forced to move; no other single factor ranked as more important in this district of low socioeconomic status with its high proportion of tenants (Short, 1978). A more detailed inventory assembled by Bird (1976) of over 5000 answers given for moving by council (public housing) tenants in London identified the familiar linkage of housing size and life cycle changes as the leading cause (23.3 percent of the answers). This was followed by complaints directed against neighbors and the immediate neighborhood (22.9 percent), accessibility issues (20.0 percent), problems with housing design and facilities (16.8 percent), alternative tenure preferences (10.3 percent), housing quality (5.6 percent), and the cost of renting (2.1 percent). The differential weighting of a number of these factors by the public housing tenants showed that they experienced greater difficulties with neighbors and accessibility than did homeowners. These irritants were mentioned as reasons for moving over 40 percent of the time by the tenants but less than 15 percent of the time by the Toronto homeowners. While homeowners might carefully investigate the compatibility of neighbors and the desirability of proximity to regular contacts, the biographical circumstances of public housing tenants may not offer them this freedom. Indeed, inasmuch as they are allocated to units by housing managers, they may well exercise very little choice, at all, over their place of residence (Gray, 1976).

Housing Submarkets

The variable position of different families in the city's social structure and their differential access to housing has given rise to the notion of housing class (Rex, 1968) and the related concept of housing submarkets (Bourne, 1976a; Palm, 1978). The major biographical characteristics of income, life cycle stage, ethnicity, and lifestyle sort households into different housing classes which in turn imply a form of tenure, either rental (private or public) or home ownership. Family size adds locational biasses according to housing densities in different parts of the city. Thus households exhibit a bundle of attributes that assign them to a housing class and to circulation within a distinctive submarket. Implicit in this notion is a degree of closure within submarkets, so that movement between any two is limited and changes in the housing stock in one area may only imperfectly be transmitted to others. Consequently, any households seeking new accommodation are likely to limit the search to a well-defined range of options. In an examination of aggregate migration flows in Milwaukee, Clark (1976) suggested that housing options could be successfully identified by reference to income and cost variables alone. In other words, the constraint of income is the decisive determinant of access to a particular housing class. Certainly income was one major discriminator in Rex's original seven-fold classification of housing classes in Birmingham (England), which included outright owners, mortgage-paying owners, homeowners with lodgers, council tenants, council tenants in slum houses, private tenants, and, finally, lodgers. Clearly, there will be some diversity in the variables selected for a classification of submarkets in different cities, though income, stage in the life cycle, and, as we will see, minority status consistently appear to be the major criteria. These major factors are confused further by attitudinal and lifestyle preferences (Couper and Brindley, 1975).

Information on the circulation of households within and between submarkets was compiled in England for over 3000 households in 1958. Newly formed households moved primarily into a private rental market, though a surprising number (nearly 30 percent) assumed immediate owner-occupancy (Figure 8.1). The unfurnished rental market is clearly a major staging point in a family's housing career as a time to amass a down payment, for there is a large movement from this tenure type to owner-occupancy. Indeed, at the time of the survey the transition from tenancy in an unfurnished unit to ownership was the single major movement in the English housing market. A much smaller flow led from unfurnished rentals to council (public) tenancy. In contrast to the previous, temporary status of the unfurnished rental market, ownership and public tenancy represent terminal states, with a low ratio of movement out of these submarkets relative to circulation within them. Fortunately these housing types in England also showed high levels of resident satisfaction, with over 90 percent of owners and over 80 percent of public housing renters satisfied with their homes; in contrast, only 72 percent of private unfurnished rental tenants were satisfied with their accommodation, intimating their greater propensity for mobility into another housing category.

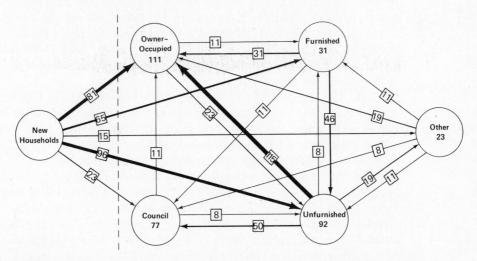

Figure 8.1   Household mobility between tenure types per 1000 population in England. (*Source*: B. Robson, *Urban Social Areas*. London: Oxford University Press, 1975, fig. 3.1. Reprinted by permission.)

The Spatial Implications of Household Mobility

The latent and actual circulation of families is projected onto a complicated preexisting spatial pattern of housing opportunities which varies according to the unique characteristics of each city. In general, however, the housing stock will include central city high-rise and low-rise apartments, inner city and inner suburban zones of duplexes and converted dwellings, and outer suburban and fringe areas of single-family units (compare Figure 2.3). Interspersed among the areas of private ownership are large blocks of public housing, scattered throughout the urban area in western Europe and Canada but more solidly limited to inner city neighborhoods in the United States. The general spatial pattern of household mobility should therefore show a predominant movement of new households into central city districts, followed by subsequent outward movement into other housing submarkets and lateral and local movement indicating circulation within the same submarket. The net pattern of outward movement is substantially the same as that conceptualized in the early formulations of Burgess and Hoyt.

Though census data are not sufficiently disaggregated to show these trends in detail, an examination of intraurban migration in London has shown the major directions of movement to be as expected. London's central boroughs have the highest level of private and public rental units and the lowest level of home ownership; these relative proportions vary in the intermediate and fringe suburbs (Johnston, 1969a). These same central boroughs are a major reception area for new households entering the system, though smaller immigrant totals also enter the intermediate and fringe zones from outside London (Table 8.3). Aside from this, however, the predominant movement is outward; despite a number of local anomalies and a frustrating amount of incomplete data, another part of the analysis suggests that outward migration exceeds inward migration by an average of 50 percent. The major trend of out-migration shows households from the central boroughs moving to outer London and households in the intermediate suburbs having some movement bias to destinations outside London, a tendency which is pronounced for households already resident in the fringe suburbs. However, though this outward tendency is uppermost, there are numerous exceptions to it, reinforcing the notion of the plural nature of housing classes and submarkets.

The outward pulse of migration is overwhelmingly sensitive to distance. Because spatial distance and social distance are so closely intertwined, incremental shifts in social status usually imply short-range movement. Although there are those rare individuals who win the national lottery, most households improve their housing status more gradually, so that without a major change in their routines, such as a new job, movements are local. As we saw in Chapter 4, existing routines and the location of familiar areas often impose a spatial inertia, adding to the constraints on migration outside a limited range. In the United States over 25 percent of moves began and ended in the same neighborhood (Butler et al., 1969); in England over one-third of moves occurred over a distance "normally covered on foot" (Sarre, 1972). A biographical situation of low income, tenant status, and membership in a minority group add to the effects of distance on the length of a move. Among a sample of black households that included both owners and tenants in North Philadelphia, marked spatial constraints were evident in answers to

TABLE 8.3   MIGRATION PATTERNS IN LONDON, 1960–1961

	Percent In-Migrants From			Percent Out-Migrants To		
	Outside London	Inner London	Outer London	Inner London	Outer London	Outside London
Central Boroughs						
Bermondsey	34	9	43	5	50	11
Hackney	32	31	16	10	43	9
Kensington	55	15	13	20	30	19
St. Marylebone	41	19	15	21	30	19
Intermediate Suburbs						
Edmonton	24	30	23	17	23	19
Feltham	31	35	5	32	10	31
Hornchurch	21	55	8	23	21	25
Malden	36	33	5	11	12	39
Wembley	25	37	17	14	19	30
Wood Green	23	42	11	16	14	26
Woolwich	25	38	12	17	26	22
Fringe Suburbs						
Banstead	32	24	0	18	0	47
Bromley	25	32	13	22	11	41
Chigwell	20	44	3	27	5	51
Rickmansworth	42	9	18	0	29	38
Woking	39	17	3	9	12	65

Source: R. J. Johnston, "Population Movements and Metropolitan Expansion," *Transactions, Institute of British Geographers* 46 (1969), 69–91, Table 6, p. 85. Reprinted by permission.

a question concerning their last address in the city (Figure 4.13). Over 80 percent of respondents had moved less than 30 blocks to their present address. In addition there was a marked directional bias to their moves, with half the households having had a previous location within a 45-degree sector oriented toward the central business district.

The corollary of short-range movement is incremental change in social status, and it is likely that about 80 percent of moves occur between census tracts of the same or similar status. For each household, only one of the eight or nine moves that might be made in a lifetime is associated with a change in socioeconomic status (Simmons, 1968). The nature of household mobility in Minneapolis between 1960 and 1961 supported this claim (Adams and Gilder, 1976). For each census tract in the city and suburbs, a position in a hypothetical "community space" was defined consisting of its socioeconomic and life cycle characteristics. The aggregate movement of population between tracts in this space was then assessed (Figure 8.2). The result was a dramatic decline in linkages between tracts as the distance between them in community space broadened. A reexamination of mobility patterns for the more recent 1970–1971 period showed substantially the same trends, as households moved between tracts of comparable status in terms of class and family size. The only exception to this generalization was the tendency overall for some limited upward social mobility and a net transference of some households into neighborhoods with higher levels of familism.

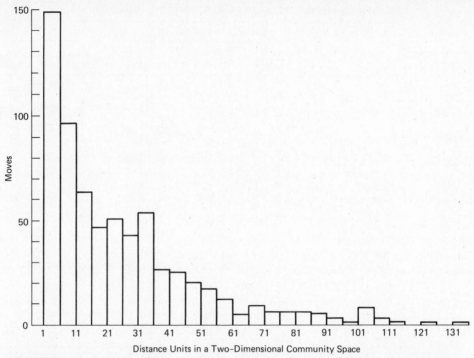

Figure 8.2   Distances of household moves in community space for Minneapolis, 1960–1961. (*Source*: J. Adams and K. Gilder, ''Household Location and Intra-Urban Migration.'' Pp. 159–192 in D. Herbert and R. Johnston (eds.), *Social Areas in Cities*. Vol 1. London: Wiley, 1976, fig. 5.3. Reprinted by permission.)

In terms of intraurban migration, therefore, once again we see that birds of a feather flock together. The same patterns of channelled interaction and spatial segregation which we earlier identified for individuals at the microscale reappear at the macroscale level of aggregate demographic movement, though in the case of housing, segregation is a product of varying levels of both choice and constraint. The effects in each instance are the heightening of within-group homogeneity and the limiting of interaction as the social distance between groups is magnified.

Vacancy Chains

Although residential mobility typically takes place over relatively short distances and is circumscribed within areas of similar social status, each move still has repercussions beyond itself. Any change in household status or the size of the housing stock will send out ripples through the housing market. Migration permits the release of one unit which will then become available for a second household, who will in turn vacate their own unit making it available for occupancy, and so on. A chain of mobility is triggered in this way by the removal of a household or by the construction of new housing, both of which will open up an additional unit of accommodation.

Each move involving two households and two addresses creates a link in a *vacancy chain,* so that the length of a chain provides some measure of the impact of a single housing vacancy. The transmission of such a vacancy chain is terminated by the demolition of existing housing units or by the establishment of a new household. The formation of a new household might have a number of causes: marriage, divorce or some other separation of an existing household, immigration, or the purchase by a family of a second home. In the 1970s, a number of major cities, despite losing population, nonetheless registered a net gain in households, the result both of the loss of families with children to the suburbs and also of the growing propensity of young adults to make—and break—new one- and two-person households. With such an increase in new-household formation, the length of a vacancy chain is likely to be shortened, for a newly formed household will occupy a vacated unit without itself giving up a vacancy. Although we have seen that most moves are local, a job transfer might involve more distant migration. The displacement of a vacancy chain beyond a regional housing market to all intents and purposes also implies the termination of its local effects.

Housing surveys in a number of Western nations suggest that the typical length of a vacancy chain varies from 1.5 to 3.5 links (Bourne, 1976a). Systematic variations exist in the length and in the termination of chains in different housing submarkets. In the Glasgow region, chains that were initiated in the private ownership market were terminated primarily by the formation of new households (45 percent), to a more limited extent by immigration (18 percent), and scarcely at all by demolition (3 percent). In contrast, demolition was by far the major factor to truncate chains initiated in the public housing submarket. The effects of these differential histories were that the average chain stimulated by new construction for home ownership consisted of 2.1 links, but that construction of public housing stimulated a smaller multiplier effect of only 1.6 links for each vacancy (Watson, 1974).

According to data from Minneapolis, a similar situation would seem to exist in North America (Adams and Gilder, 1976). The building of new public housing for the elderly stimulated vacancy chains with an average length of 1.6 links, with many of the chains localized and ending near the site of new construction. The shortness of these chains is again associated with the high probability of demolition of units vacated by the elderly poor. In contrast, varied samples of new private housing in Minneapolis generated longer chains, and these chains were more extensive for single-family dwellings than for fourplexes, and smaller yet for townhouses. An important related finding, based on a large sample of moves in the United States, was that as the cost of housing increased, either by purchase or through renting, so, too, was there a systematic extension of the length of vacancy chains (Lansing et al., 1969). Apparently, then, it would seem as if a large number of people will be able to change, and presumably improve, their housing status by the construction of more expensive single-family dwellings. Such an interpretation invoking the filtering down of high-income units to poorer households has long been influential in North American housing policy and continues to find its advocates (White, 1971).

But this interpretation begs the critical question as to whether longer chains imply the crossing of submarket boundaries or simply an extended circulation and termination of vacancies within a single or closely related housing class. If it is the latter condition which is dominant—and certainly extremely long chains would be needed in most cities for the transmission of vacancies from the affluence of Nob Hill to the poverty of the East End—then it is unlikely that vacancies generated by high-priced construction would percolate down far enough to benefit households whose housing needs are the most desperate. Evidence from Windsor, Ontario, supports this argument, for although construction of higher-priced houses stimulated longer chains than did lower-priced units, most chains were terminated by in-migration or by the formation of new households, without penetrating the poorer housing submarkets (Dzus and Romsa, 1977). Against this, policymakers and politicians are no doubt tempted to offset the limited multiplier effect of public housing against the larger number of households who will benefit from incentives to private housing construction.

Filtering

In one sense the concept of the vacancy chain is limited, in that it carries no implication for *qualitative* as opposed to *quantitative* changes in housing status, for as we have seen, an extended vacancy chain does not necessarily mean any change in residential quality for the most deprived housing classes. In contrast, *filtering* has major implications for the changing quality of both the housing stock and the residential environment of each household. As originally formulated, an inherent property of filtering is a continuous decline in the condition of the housing stock over time and a corresponding increase in the quality of accommodation occupied by individual households; as housing deteriorates, so each family can improve its lot. The process is stimulated by the construction of housing for the better off on the urban fringe. The migration of more affluent households from their existing aging properties into this new source of supply creates vacancies for less-wealthy groups, and so the process perpetuates itself, and improvement in housing status filters down to the most deprived groups. In this way, then, there is a theoretical correspondence between the aging and deterioration of the housing stock, and the continuous improvement in residential quality for all groups, including those with more limited bidding power in the marketplace. There is great intuitive and policy appeal in such a process, so that it is little wonder that housing programs have made frequent reference to filtering as a beneficial form of readjustment of the housing stock.

However, the simplicity of the process disappears on closer examination (W. Smith, 1971). Part of the difficulty is definitional. What precisely does filtering refer to? The monthly cost of accommodation? The value of the property? Or the improving welfare of households? The concept has implications at all three levels, but it is abundantly clear that there is not always a direct relation between them. For example, conversion of a property to apartments might well increase the value of property and yet at the same time admit lower-income households. Therefore the aging of a property, although it might allow entry to poorer households, will not necessarily be accompanied by a decrease in housing value.

Filtering was emphasized by Hoyt as an important temporal process in his discussion of the changing location of higher-status neighborhoods in the city (Hoyt, 1939). In a city with continuous in-migration, new subdivisions on high-amenity sites would draw elite groups away from more central locations, leaving behind their homes for conversion to lower-income groups. The factors prompting the movement of higher-status families are more problematic but are likely to be associated with both the decreasing status of the neighborhood and perceived obsolescence in the interior design or architectural style of the home relative to newer properties. Certainly this pattern is common in the central city and has been frequently noted both for older industrial cities such as Detroit (Backler, 1974) and for more recent West Coast centers like Los Angeles or Vancouver (Robertson, 1977).

The erosion of Vancouver's West End, its first elite neighborhood of single-family mansions, was rapid and was associated both with the encroachment of higher-density uses and with the construction of the nearby high-status suburb of Shaughnessy Heights, which was elegantly designed and landscaped, sited on a ridge with fine views, and protected by thorough bylaw zoning that excluded all commercial uses (Figure 8.3).

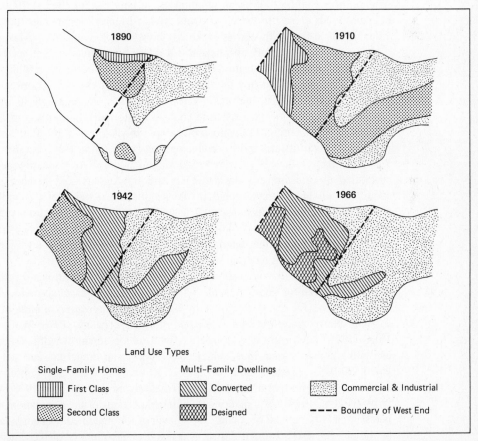

Figure 8.3   Down-filtering in Vancouver's West End, 1890–1966. (*Source*: A. McAfee, "Evolving Inner City Residential Environments: The Case of Vancouver's West End." Pp. 163–181 in J. Minghi (ed.), *Peoples of the Living Land*. Vancouver: Tantalus, B.C. Geographical Series No. 15, 1973, fig. 2. Reprinted by permission.)

Shaughnessy was aggressively marketed by the Canadian Pacific Railway, the city's major landowner, and a rapid relocation of the city's elite occurred over a period of 15 years. In 1908, the city's *Social Register* indicated that 86 percent of the elite lived in the West End. In 1912, the Shaughnessy subdivision was opened, and by 1927 only 20 percent of names in the *Social Register* had a West End address; indeed, almost one-third of the 1908 elite had moved out by 1914. Over 50 percent of those families who left the West End reestablished a home in Shaughnessy; the remainder moved to other new suburbs. The West End meanwhile underwent a period of rapid conversion and apartment redevelopment for a less-wealthy group of citizens, culminating in 1927 in a new bylaw that did not allow for single-family dwellings.

This pattern of down-filtering of elite areas has been repeated in most cities, but the process is not mechanistic, and local anomalies in both the *rate* and also the *direction* of filtering are numerous. A major revision of the filtering thesis is certainly required in light of the abundant evidence of *up-filtering* that has occurred in many central city neighborhoods since 1965 in an inflating urban land market (Berry, 1980). In Toronto, neighborhoods closest to the downtown core experienced the greatest increase in market value of single-family dwellings in the city between 1953 and 1971 (Maher, 1974). This need not necessarily imply up-filtering, for as we have already mentioned, it could have been accompanied by a transition from single to multiple occupancy, which would permit poorer households to occupy the unit. However, other evidence (Lorimer and Phillips, 1971; Holdsworth, 1981) and the increase in values in stable, single-family areas where little or no conversion has occurred indicate that, indeed, up-filtering is present. An assessment of changing occupations on sample blocks in two different Vancouver inner neighborhoods illustrates more convincingly the up-filtering that has taken place (Figure 8.4). Occupations have been scored according to an objective standard index (the Blishen scale) that allocates higher scores to an increase in job status. The increase in occupational scores for all blocks represented in the sample since the 1950s is indicative of the movement of higher-status households into these neighborhoods. As a result of the movement of higher-status households into inner city units, the Vancouver Planning Department (1979) concluded that filtering could no longer be regarded as a welfare mechanism, improving the housing quality of poorer groups.

Indeed, the exact opposite is occurring, for poorer households are being displaced by the renovation or demolition of their inner city units. *Displacement* has emerged as a major dilemma accompanying the up-filtering or revitalization of parts of the inner city in some North American and European cities (Cybriwsky, 1978; Weiler, 1978; Ley, 1981). It has been most severe in cities with major downtown office employment and escalating housing prices like London, New York, San Francisco, and Toronto. The full extent of displacement is unknown, though a survey of over 1250 households in Seattle indicated that 7 percent of all households that moved during 1977–1978 did so involuntarily (Hodge, 1979). Among certain vulnerable groups of the population, the figure was much higher; 25 percent of tenants, 27 percent of low-income households, and 34 percent of the elderly who relocated did so as a result of involuntary displacement. The simultaneous creation of higher-priced inner city housing through the replacement of lower-priced units in an inflating, high-demand, regional market (and *not* as a result of new construction on greenfield sites), has transformed filtering into a socially regressive mechanism for allocating housing to different social groups.

Another query concerns the differential rate of filtering in urban neighborhoods. Clearly there are at work factors that accelerate filtering in certain sections of the city but delay it in others. Inasmuch as age is a major independent variable in the filtering schema, one would expect older neighborhoods to be associated with diminishing status. Here, McCann's detailed analysis of the Edmonton housing market is informative (McCann, 1975; Smith and McCann, 1981). The housing histories of the 35,000 units in the built-up area in 1951 were analyzed in terms of the transition of single-family dwellings to one of several forms of conversion, and subsequent transitions were monitored between the converted units themselves, from, for example, basement conversion to multiple-family conversions. Conversion is clearly one form of filtering because it implies a household turnover with the addition of at least one household to an existing dwelling. It was precisely this mechanism which Hoyt identified as following the out-migration of wealthy households, as their units were subdivided to accommodate poorer families.

There were present some strong correlations between enumeration areas in which conversion (filtering) had occurred and other housing, socioeconomic, family, and ethnic characteristics (Table 8.4). The age of properties was strongly associated with conversion, but so were other housing variables, particularly those that were measurements of size. However, housing quality was only weakly, negatively related with areas favorable to conversion. There were some predictable links between conversion and family status variables indicative of small households, shared owner-renter occupancy, transiency, and immigrant status. Perhaps most interesting was the absence of significant correlations

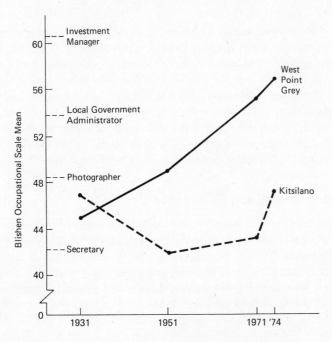

Figure 8.4 Up-filtering in two neighborhoods in inner Vancouver, 1931–1974.

TABLE 8.4 CORRELATION BETWEEN HOUSING CONVERSION AND SELECTED VARIABLES, EDMONTON, 1961

	Variable	Correlation Coefficient
Housing Characteristics	Single-family dwellings	−0.916*
	Average age	0.617*
	Average floor area	0.246*
	Average rooms	0.662*
	Bungalows	−0.169*
	Two-storey houses	0.577*
	Good construction	0.003
	Poor construction	−0.148*
	Needs minor repairs	0.227*
	Distance to CBD	−0.610*
Socioeconomic Characteristics	Median house value	0.037
	Average rent	−0.351*
	Owner-renter joint occupancy	0.795*
	Attended university	0.056
	Income over $10,000	0.023
Family Characteristics	Nonfamily households	0.721*
	Persons per family	−0.591*
	Women in labor force	0.415*
	Less than 1 year occupancy	0.457*
Ethnic Characteristics	Born outside Canada	0.503*

Source: Adapted from L. McCann, *Neighbourhoods in Transition.* Occasional Papers No. 2, Department of Geography, University of Alberta, 1975, Tables 4.1, 4.4, 4.5, 4.6. Reprinted by permission.
*Significant at 0.05 level.

against measures of social status, suggesting strongly that this form of filtering operates indiscriminately of the socioeconomic level of neighborhoods. There is some indirect support for this assertion from a longitudinal study of Cleveland and 12 other metropolitan areas in the United States which was able to detect only a minor relationship between housing age, which we know to be related to filtering, and the socioeconomic status of neighborhoods (Guest, 1974). But if filtering, which Hoyt and others regarded as synonymous with decreasing neighborhood status, is in fact only mildly associated with neighborhood status and housing quality, what then are the factors linked to the notorious decline in the status of so many inner city areas in the United States?

Neighborhood Decline and Resurgence

In Chapter 5 we suggested that neighborhood transition might be understood in terms of the typical experiences that residents and decision makers subjectively ascribe to different urban neighborhoods. Typical experiences related to such existential surfaces as those of stress, security, status, stigma, stimulus, and ennui would encourage different behavioral responses, which in turn become translated into aggregate demand surfaces, land values, and population movements within and between metropolitan areas. In this section we will reexamine these subjective interpretations in light of more objective constraints and more conventional explanations of neighborhood deterioration and resurgence. The subjective meanings ascribed to places, which we argued commonly provide the decision-making milieu concerning investment and disinvestment for residents and, to a lesser extent, for entrepreneurs, will themselves be situated in a broader context.

Decay and Abandonment

A repetitive factor in accounts of neighborhood decline is said to be the deteriorating effect of an aging housing stock (Muth, 1969). But the filtering studies we have reviewed have been unable to demonstrate a strong relationship between the aging of the housing stock and the socioeconomic status of neighborhoods. As we will see, there is good reason for suggesting that age is equally ineffective as an explanation of deterioration.

Nourse and Phares (1975) have advanced a model of neighborhood deterioration that isolates the income level of residents as the critical factor. Initially they envisage a situation of high in-migration to the central city of poor households who encounter a diminishing stock of low-income housing as a result of demolition, freeway construction, and other public works. This makes it profitable for higher-status housing stock to be subdivided and filtered to poorer households, though the proximity to better neighborhoods will maintain (and perhaps inflate) house prices. Meanwhile, aided by freeway construction and suburban development, the more affluent are able to withdraw to more distant neighborhoods; indeed, their willingness and ability to vacate will speed the transition process. In this light, it is instructive to note the common juxtaposition in cities such as Cleveland and Philadelphia of heavily Jewish areas and lines of black advance (Adams and Sanders, 1969). The rapid upward social mobility of Jewish communities permits an acceleration of the filtering process as their residents move into more distant and expensive suburban neighborhoods.

The continued advance of the boundary between the more and less affluent districts will, however, undercut the desirability of filtered blocks formerly on or near the status boundary. Those poorer families who are able to, will move again toward the higher-status areas, and so a filtering process will be initiated within the poorer housing class itself until eventually a unit is occupied by its poorest members, exerting a depressing effect on property values. Decreasing returns to the landlord will discourage upkeep and maintenance and accelerate the natural course of aging and deterioration. This transition toward the poorest households will also be associated with an increase in the demoralizing local effects of the subcultures of poverty. The end result of these combined processes will be abandonment and the emergence of the dead centers of metropolitan areas like the notorious South Bronx. With the advance of the low-income sector, this zone of blight and abandonment will pass wavelike through adjacent neighborhoods. The transition hypothesis was tested in the St. Louis metropolitan area, where the occupational and income profiles of 15 neighborhoods of varying class, racial composition, and age of construction were traced over a 45-year period. Downward shifts in house values were taken as a measure of housing deterioration and were related in turn to the age of housing, racial change, and a change in household incomes. On the basis of their analysis, Nourse and Phares claim that downward income transition rather than housing age or race is the determining factor in neighborhood deterioration. However, closer examination of their data suggests more ambiguity. Their conclusion is acceptable in terms of the age of the housing stock, for only neighborhoods more than 50 years old showed consistently lower housing values in 1970. In property built since 1920 no discernible pattern of values emerged. But the data do not permit a thorough testing of the effects of racial change, for only 6 of the 15 neighborhoods included more than 20 percent nonwhites by 1970. Moreover, in each of these 6 neighborhoods, the largest relative decrease in housing values in any decade (relative to the St. Louis metropolitan median) coincided with the advent of racial change. In most of these instances there was also a decline in the relative income level of neighborhoods within the same decade. Examining relative changes in housing values in all neighborhoods shows that a decline in income levels and racial change are equally effective in predicting a relative downturn in property values. Because the neighborhoods were in the inner city and inner suburban rings, increases in housing values at a rate faster than the metropolitan median were more limited and tended to occur in earlier decades. These earlier positive price changes were invariably accompanied by income increases; in no instance was there a nonwhite population present before or immediately after positive changes in house values.

In summary, although the St. Louis study dispelled the myth of a strong association between housing age and deterioration, it did not negate the frequently imputed factor of racial transition. It is unfortunate that a more discriminating methodology which might have isolated the independent effects of race and income was not used. In a statistical examination of Cleveland and other cities, the age of a neighborhood was also shown to bear little relationship to declining occupational status, but this was not the case when there was occupancy by nonwhite racial groups (Guest, 1974).

Evidence from North Philadelphia offers some additional insight into the Nourse and Phares model (Ley, 1974a). It is generally accepted that the first cohort of minority migrants into a neighborhood are not of a socioeconomic status lower than that of the previous residents (Bunge, 1971). This was true in the ''Monroe'' neighborhood of North Philadelphia, where the in-migrating black households in the 1950s and early 1960s had income and education levels comparable to or slightly in excess of the preexisting level among white residents. At that time Monroe was a good place to live, as one black homeowner reflected in 1970:

> When I came here eight years ago this was a good neighborhood. Move now? Well, there's really no point. I've been through all this before. In my experience you move into a neighborhood and the decay follows you. You have to make up your mind to stay and make a stand (Ley, 1974a:163).

Implicit in this resident's comment is a rapid deterioration in neighborhood status *after* black migration was already well underway, which would accord with the stage of down-filtering following initial settlement, as the boundary between higher- and lower-status areas retreated northward. His perception of deterioration was accurate, for in 1970 there were 350–450 abandoned houses in his neighborhood, or 4–5 percent of the housing stock. Clearly housing demand had slumped badly in Monroe over a 10-year period. Why?

It is clear from census data that demand levels in Monroe have declined, especially for ownership. If we accept Nourse and Phares' notion of demand being greatest during the early period of transition (though it should be class rather than racial transition according to their argument), then Monroe was passing through this period in the late 1950s and early 1960s. By 1970 the line of racial transition had passed far to the north, and with it had shifted peak demand levels. Recall (see Chapter 5) that the highest level of black residential demand is in racially integrated neighborhoods and that there is very low demand for all-black areas. At the same time there is almost no white demand for housing in black neighborhoods (Farley et al., 1978). Consequently the ranking of Monroe dropped on a status-stigma continuum as it fell progressively further from the location of integrated neighborhoods. When new properties came onto the market, there was limited ownership demand; the options for the seller were either to rent or to leave his property vacant. At the same time, the closure of shops and factories in Monroe created nonresidential vacancies and contributed to a decreasing neighborhood image. The hard-core ghetto poor, displaced by urban renewal nearer the central business district, began to occupy rental units, bringing with them welfare, crime, and drug problems and adding to unemployment and welfare rolls. Though it is obviously an oversimplification to associate deterioration solely with the in-migration of lower-class tenants, this was an association commonly made by Monroe homeowners themselves. At a neighborhood meeting attended by local homeowners to plan for the redevelopment of a derelict block, there was strong opposition to a housing mix of single-family units and three-story apartments. As one woman put it: ''We don't want apartments, period. Just up the road apartments have fallen through in three years that should have lasted a hundred.'' In neighborhood minds, the transition from ownership to tenancy was synonymous with deterioration. Thus the blighting forces in Monroe had their source in large measure outside the neighborhood, in more general patterns of metropolitan change: the northward movement of the boundary of racial transition with its high demand levels, and the displacement of disadvantaged residents by urban renewal to the south.

This analysis is consistent with a review of changes in the North Philadelphia housing market (Dear, 1976) and with a more detailed examination of house-price changes in Chicago from 1968 to 1972 (Berry, 1976b). Indeed, neighborhoods like Monroe were subject to even more-distant regional influences. Even conservative census data indicate that abandonment has been more pronounced in older industrial cities like Philadelphia in the American manufacturing belt than in newer cities in the South and West (Table 8.5). Moreover, the pace of abandonment has accelerated markedly since the conservative estimates of the census were amassed, and probably so, too, has the regional differentiation. Twelve Standard Metropolitan Statistical Areas (SMSAs) (including Philadelphia) of over 1 million lost population from 1970 to 1975, and nine of these are in the manufacturing belt. Against this sluggishness, suburban housing construction continued apace, encouraged (as we shall see in Chapter 9) by government policy, and accounted for 88 percent of all new housing in the Philadelphia SMSA in the 1960s. In the Chicago SMSA, 482,000 new housing units were built between 1960 and 1970 although only 285,000 new households were formed—an excess ratio of 1.7 of supply to demand (Berry, 1976b). The inevitable conjunction of stagnant demand and increasing supply is

TABLE 8.5 ABANDONMENT IN SELECTED CITIES ACCORDING TO THE 1970 U.S. CENSUS

Central City	No. of Units Vacant 1 Year or More	Percentage of Housing Stock Vacant > 1 Year
Northeast		
Baltimore	2636	0.86
Boston	2112	0.90
New York	9938	0.35
Washington, D.C.	1696	0.06
Midwest		
Chicago	7491	0.62
Cleveland	2394	0.90
Detroit	3778	0.71
St. Louis	2851	1.19
South		
Atlanta	499	0.05
Dallas	1870	0.58
New Orleans	1750	0.84
Miami	238	0.19
West		
Los Angeles	3101	0.27
San Francisco	981	0.31
Seattle	983	0.44

Source: M. Dear, "Abandoned Housing," pp. 59–99 in J. Adams (ed.), *Urban Policymaking and Metropolitan Dynamics*. Cambridge, Mass.: Ballinger, 1976, p. 90. Copyright 1976. Reprinted by permission.

a high vacancy level at the bottom of the housing stock. In the inner city, where the poorest housing is located, down-filtering leads finally to abandonment (Figure 8.5). One estimate, almost certainly an exaggeration, listed over 36,000 long-term vacant structures in Philadelphia in 1972. Similar inflated figures have been reported for other northern and midwestern cities since the 1970 census. One assessment placed abandonment in New York City as high as 100,000 units in 1973; yet more staggering data suggest the abandonment of 15,000 units a year in New York from 1964 to 1970, increasing to 20,000 units a year through the 1970s, for a grand total of 260,000 units from 1964 to mid 1978 (Hartshorn, 1980: p. 249). By 1978 the tax arrears on abandoned property in New York amounted to an astounding $1.5 billion, substantially worsening the city's fiscal crisis. In each city there is a clustering of abandoned structures in the inner city ring, including both dominantly white and nonwhite neighborhoods, although emphasizing districts that have undergone racial transition in the past. Much of the inner city has become a functional vacuum. Behind the physical abandonment is a psychological abandonment: "the utter loss of confidence in the recuperative power of the inner city housing market" (Dear, 1976). Substantially, this is the conclusion reached earlier in our examination of the existential regions of the city and their aggregation into an amenity or demand surface (Figure 5.11).

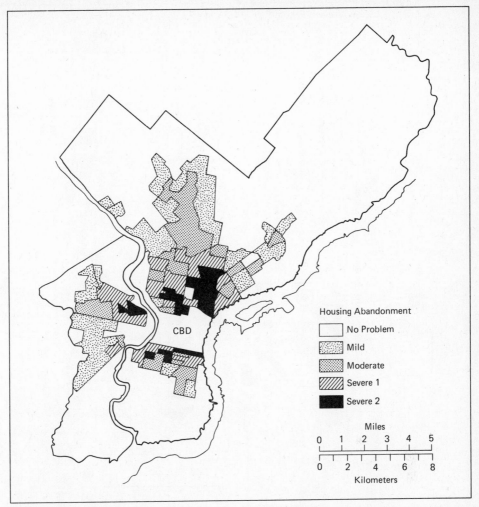

Figure 8.5 Abandoned housing in Philadelphia, 1972. (*Source*: M. Dear, ''Abandoned Housing.'' Pp. 59–99 in J. Adams (ed.), *Urban Policymaking and Metropolitan Dynamics*. Cambridge, Mass: Ballinger, 1976, fig. 3.7. Copyright 1976, Ballinger Publishing Company. Reprinted by permission.)

Neighborhood Resurgence

One of the dramatic social contrasts in the central city has been between the adjacent neighborhoods that Zorbaugh (1929) called the gold coast and the slum—the zone of high-density apartments for the wealthy, usually on a lake front or some other amenity site, which merges very rapidly with deteriorated inner city neighborhoods in less favored locations. Many of these high-status apartment districts underwent an uneasy stability until the mid 1960s, when the beginning of the downtown office boom, in conjunction

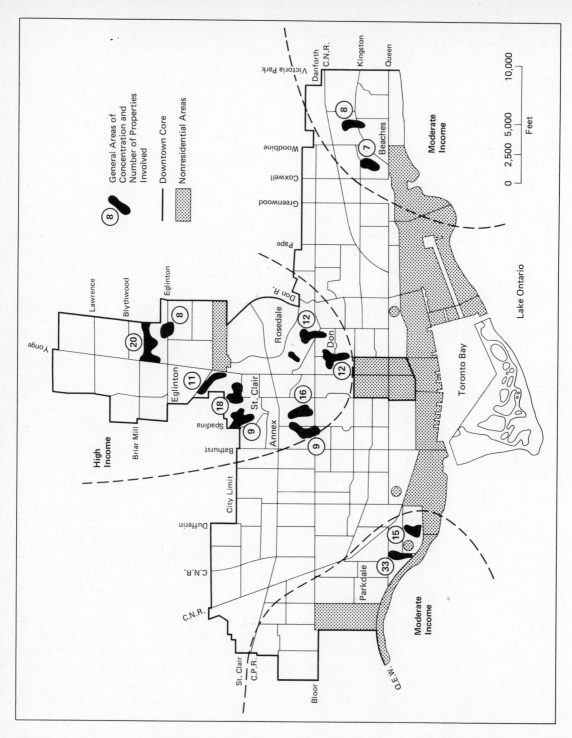

with more individualistic patterns of household formation and a taste for central city living, encouraged a new round of privately financed apartment construction which brought revitalization to some central neighborhoods. These initial units were primarily high-rise apartment blocks, in part because of land costs but also to provide views to tenants and, not least, to guarantee higher levels of personal security. More recently public taste has turned against the high rise, and their construction has been curtailed in some cities in response to citizen pressure to downzone (Lemon, 1974). As a result, a more recent landscape of the resurgent inner city neighborhood has become that of low-rise condominiums, town houses, and renovated Victorian terraces in varying stages of transition with more deteriorated uses.

A statistical analysis of the early phase of this resurgence examined the changing status of central city neighborhoods during the 1960s in America's 20 largest metropolitan areas (Lipton, 1977). By 1970, New York, San Francisco, Washington, D.C., Boston, Seattle, Minneapolis, and Houston led the field with more than one-quarter of their central city census tracts showing educational levels above the metropolitan median. According to this index of gentrification at least, these were the cities in which resurgence was most advanced by 1970. They have some important common attributes. Of these, the most significant seems to be the development of a major white-collar component to downtown employment, for a very high correlation of 0.94 was found between the presence of higher-status central neighborhoods and the amount of downtown office space. Negative correlations occurred between central resurgence and both the extent of local manufacturing and the size of the blue-collar labor force. Interestingly, race did not appear as a major factor in the correlation. The implication is clear: Resurgence accompanies the development of tertiary and quaternary white-collar employment, and such employment is selectively directed toward centers free of the stigma of heavy industry.

Several Canadian studies have examined the locations favored for privately redeveloped apartment areas. In Toronto during the 1950s and early 1960s, and prior to the major development boom on either side of 1970, 56 percent of the floor area added in redevelopment consisted of apartments and offices; during the last 5 years of this period apartments and offices accounted for 75 percent of the total (Bourne, 1967). Apartment location was strongly site specific, occurring in nodes that offered good access to the CBD and that followed in particular the high-income residential sector north from the core (Figure 8.6). Office location was more centralized but also paralleled the development of apartments through the high-status northern sector along the line of the new subway. The pattern seems to have been very similar for apartment construction in Edmonton (McCann, 1975). Parliament Hill and Oliver, the two major areas of high-rise apartment development, are adjacent to the CBD in what had formerly been the core of the city's high-rent sector; redevelopment has avoided poorer residential areas. Indeed, high-rise apartments show their strongest positive correlations with rent and income levels "confirming the earlier generalisation that these developments seek out prestige neighborhoods" (McCann, 1975:89). This finding seems to be general to Canadian cities,

Figure 8.6 Apartment concentrations in Toronto, 1952–1962. (*Source*: L. Bourne. *Private Redevelopment of the Central City*. University of Chicago, Dept. of Geography, Research Paper No. 112, 1967, fig. 28. Reprinted by permission.)

applying also to Montreal, Vancouver (McAfee, 1975; Ley, 1981), Calgary (P. Smith, 1971), and even to a smaller urban area like Victoria (B.C.), where high rises have been drawn to high-amenity waterfront sites near downtown. Though these units with high-amenity sites in Victoria have above average rents, they consistently show the lowest vacancy rates in the city (Murphy, 1973). As in Edmonton, lower-status districts zoned for apartments have been neglected by developers even though they offer equal access to the downtown core.

The second major wave of central city resurgence, which has occurred in many cities only since 1970, has been more experimental in the locations it has favored. A survey of in-migrants to Washington, D.C., in the period 1970–1974 found a number of general traits to be typical of this new wave of movers (Grier and Grier, 1977):

1. Newcomer households were predominantly small and childless; nearly half consisted of only one person, and only 20 percent included children.

2. The majority of household heads was unmarried.

3. About two-thirds of household heads were younger than 35 years of age.

4. Nearly half of household heads were employed in professional, technical, managerial, or administrative positions.

5. A majority of household heads had received four or more years of college education.

6. Despite the youthfulness of households, incomes were mainly high or moderate, and only a minority earned low incomes.

7. Nearly two-thirds of in-migrating households were white.

During the period 1970–1974 the central city of Washington was receiving about 10,000 new households annually, though with the movement of other household types to the suburbs, the city's household total remained constant. Nevertheless, this stability in overall numbers maintained a high level of demand in Washington's housing market; one indicator of this was the abnormally low level of housing abandonment in Washington relative to other cities on the eastern seaboard (Table 8.5).

The housing selected by this group of newcomers has taken two forms. High-density and, usually, high-cost accommodation in or adjacent to the core has continued to be popular, reflected in such projects as Chicago's Marina Towers and Philadelphia's Franklintown. These are high-cost rental units within walking distance of the core, consisting of high-rise and, more recently, low-rise and town house redevelopments. The second housing form has been more innovative, consisting of the renovation of existing row house structures which were often in an advanced stage of dilapidation. In addition to their central city location, renovated areas are anchored around architecturally attractive or historically significant buildings, attractive older commercial areas, counterculture enclaves or artists' colonies, and stable ethnic neighborhoods (Weiler, 1978). Indeed, each of these types may give rise to a distinctive local ambience, so that in the larger American cities nuances are emerging in the subcultures of different resurgent neighborhoods (Winters, 1978).

Revitalization through renovation has been more incremental, advancing block by

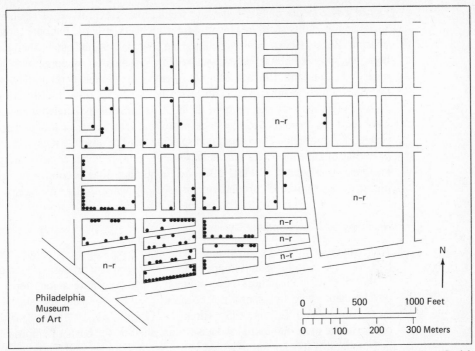

Figure 8.7 Extensively renovated row houses, Fairmount, Philadelphia. (*Source*: R. Cybriwsky, "Social Aspects of Neighborhood Change, "*Annals, Association of American Geographers* 68 (1978):17–33, fig. 5. Reprinted by permission.)

block into what were often low-income neighborhoods (Figure 8.7). Unlike the larger redeveloped projects, it has more usually been undertaken by small contractors and individual home purchasers. Although true urban pioneers seeking bargains and speculators seeking windfall profits have purchased houses a few blocks in advance of the main wave of renovation, most purchasers have bought or rented properties on the same block as other renovators. Thus at the block scale there is a marked contagion effect as renovation diffuses through a neighborhood. This diffusion often proceeds from a fixed landmark that gives the neighborhood its fashionable and stylish reputation. In the Fairmount district of Philadelphia, shown in Figure 8.7, up-filtering has progressed from a node in the southwest which includes the city's art museum and two high-priced rental towers; significantly Fairmount is becoming increasingly referred to as the Art Museum District. Similarly, revitalization, both through redevelopment and renovation, that has been underway in the Upper West Side of Manhattan since the late 1960s has diffused from well-identified nodes like the Lincoln Center for the Performing Arts and has brought a new status to formerly deteriorating districts (Winters, 1977).

In the same way that psychological abandonment by investors, homeowners, and tenants alike characterizes an advancing wave of blight moving through inner city neighborhoods, so too a compensating, if as yet weaker, wave of revitalization is progressing through districts that can make some legitimate claim to status or style. If the psychological components of blight include stigma and stress, those of revitalization include status and stimulus seeking as well as, for pioneers at least, the opportunity for cheaper housing (Berry, 1980). However, this stage soon passes, and established gentrified neighborhoods such as Philadelphia's Society Hill, Washington's Georgetown, Toronto's Cabbagetown, London's Chelsea and Kensington, and similar neighborhoods in New York and San Francisco now include some of the most expensive housing units in the city. As we saw in the previous section, the housing inflation associated with such up-filtering has been very damaging to the stock of low- and moderate-cost housing and has led to severe local problems of population displacement. The absolute incidence of deterioration or revitalization in a single city is dependent on its regional context and particularly on its association with an older, often declining industrial economy or a buoyant post-industrial economy built around amenity-seeking white-collar employees.

Neighborhood Development Cycles

The sequential waves of blight and revitalization passing from neighborhood to neighborhood represent the spatial impress of a longer temporal process of land use adjustment in the city. Several authors have attempted to reconstitute a long-term neighborhood development cycle by identifying consecutive stages of land use succession in urban areas (Hoover and Vernon, 1959; Birch, 1971; Andrews, 1971). The major implications of one of the more influential models, established on the basis of empirical investigation in New York City, are summarized in Table 8.6 (Hoover and Vernon, 1959). A neighborhood is conceived of as passing through five consecutive stages, each stage accompanied by adjustments in the type of housing, population, density, and household composition. Following the initial stages of construction and in-filling, the third stage of conversion indicates the beginnings of deterioration and the blight-abandonment syndrome that is accentuated in the fourth stage before a final phase of renewal inaugurates a new cycle, if at a higher overall density than the first. This model would appear to provide a fair intuitive description of the land use changes we have noted, especially for older American cities in the East and Midwest. Stages 3 and 4 are consistent with the deterioration-transition model of Nourse and Phares and stage 5 with the onset of public and private redevelopment.

However, the model appears to be inappropriate for the Canadian city. In Edmonton a simpler three-phase process has occurred, with distinct periods of conversion and then redevelopment being grafted onto an initial landscape of single-family houses (McCann, 1975). The blight-abandonment syndrome of stage 4 has not taken place and neither has extensive public redevelopment—unlike the experience of the American inner city, where public initiatives have become necessary as a result of the withdrawal of private investment. In Canada, neither conversion nor apartment redevelopment has been necessarily associated with the deterioration of older neighborhoods as the evolutionary cycle implies. Indeed, we noted earlier that in Edmonton and other Canadian cities, apartment redevelopment has occurred in areas whose status, whether measured in terms of income or the quality of housing stock, tends to be *above* average.

From McCann's Canadian study we can see that in broadening the contexts of

TABLE 8.6 STAGES IN A NEIGHBORHOOD DEVELOPMENT CYCLE

Stage	Physical Changes				Social Changes		Other Changes
	Dwelling Type (Predominant Additions)	Level of Construction	Population Density	Family Structure	Social Status, Income	Migration Mobility	Other Characteristics
1. Suburbanization (new growth), "homogeneity"	Single-family (low density multiple)	High	Low (but increasing)	Young families, small children, large households	High (increasing)	High net in-migration, high mobility turnover	Initial development stage; cluster development; large-scale projects, usually on virgin land
2. In-filling (on vacant land)	Multifamily	Low (decreasing)	Medium (increasing slowly or stable)	Aging families, older children, more mixing	High (stable)	Low net in-migration, low mobility turnover	First transition stage—less homogeneity in age, class, housing; first apartments; some replacements
3. Downgrading (stability and decline)	Conversion of existing dwellings to multifamily	Very low	Medium (increase slowly) population, total down	Older families, fewer children	Medium (declining)	Low net out-migration, high turnover	Long period of depreciation and stagnation; some nonresidential succession
4. Thinning out	Nonresidential construction—demolitions of existing units	Low	Declining (net densities may be increasing)	Older families, few children, nonfamily households	Declining	Higher net out-migration, high turnover	Selective nonresidential succession
5. Renewal	(a) Public housing	High	Increasing (net)	Young families, many children	Declining	High net in-migration, high turnover	The second transition stage—may take either of two forms depending on conditions
	(b) Luxury high-rise apartment; town house conversions	Medium	Increasing (net)	Mixed	Increasing	Medium	
		Low	Decreasing (net)	Few children	Increasing	Low	

Source: L. Bourne, "Housing Supply and Housing Market Behaviour in Residential Development," pp. 111–158 in D. Herbert and R. Johnston (eds.), *Social Areas in Cities.* Vol. 1, Table 4.5, p. 139. London: Wiley, 1976. Reprinted by permission.

explanation, a further spatial scale needs to be incorporated in a discussion of neighborhood land use change. In addition to the intraurban factors of neighborhood status or stigma and the regional factors of economic performance and population growth, there are clearly also national factors making their own specific contribution to the distinctive evolution of urban structure.

Social Change: Conflict and Exclusion

Invariably a change in the housing stock also implies some transition in the social composition of a neighborhood, although such transition is normally a slow process. Several factorial ecologies examining urban changes over 10-year intervals have indicated only minor adjustments in the profiles of individual census tracts (Murdie, 1969; Johnston, 1976a). Patterns of intraurban migration similarly indicate that the mover's origin and destination are generally neighborhoods with similar attributes; recall that 80 percent of moves occur between census tracts of comparable status (Figure 8.2). Moreover, research in urban history has suggested continuity in neighborhood status for much longer periods (Davis and Haller, 1973).

Where more rapid social change has occurred it has often been associated with shifts in ethnic status or, less frequently, with class transition. We have already noted several examples of more rapid neighborhood transformation involving filtering, both up and down, and minority in-migration. Commonly the succession process is orderly even when rapid, as continous housing construction and upward social mobility enable the out-migration of one social cohort to better housing, thereby creating housing vacancies for a newer cohort. However, if demand exceeds supply, the transition process may be resisted. Supply is not necessarily measurable only by the quantity of the housing stock but more importantly by its cost and quality. The semi-impermeable boundaries of housing submarkets do not guarantee that increased supply in one submarket will mitigate high demand levels in another. Moreover, a neighborhood and its housing stock may have symbolic values, perhaps, of amenity, or established community sentiment, or prestige, which cannot easily be replaced. In such circumstances transition will be resisted both overtly and covertly, and neighborhoods and municipalities will attempt to practice exclusion. Resistance to transition and the adoption of exclusionary practices have often been a source of grievance and conflict in the North American city. It has been asserted, for instance, that the urban riots and racial strife after the First World War and again in the 1960s were associated with high levels of black in-migration from the Southern states, accompanied by sluggish down-filtering and a supply in the housing stock of the cities of destination insufficient to meet these demand pressures (Forman, 1971; Adams, 1972).

Invasion-Succession

Rapid social change in urban neighborhoods has typically been associated with the arrival of new waves of immigrants, so that the North American city, with its rich immigration history over the past century, provides a perfect laboratory for examining this process. The maintenance of the first ethnic enclave depended on the continuous arrival of new immigrants and a cultural lag between these and the host society. As acculturation and upward social mobility occurred, the ethnic core would be abandoned and, either singly or in groups, minority members would seek better housing opportunities further from the CBD. Drawing from the established vocabulary of the Chicago School, Cressey (1938) labelled this the first phase of *invasion*. It was led by more successful immigrants who "desire to improve their social status by moving into an area of greater prestige." In time, these pioneers were followed by others, and ethnic transition occurred with the recession of the original residents. Cressey noted that this process might be accompanied by conflict if there were marked variations in the status of the two groups; as examples he cited penetration by blacks and Jews. Once initiated, succession would proceed more rapidly the greater the status differences between incoming and outgoing groups. Finally, community reorganization would take place with the reestablishment of daily life and its institutional supports in the new setting.

By 1930, ethnic decentralization in Chicago was most advanced for the minorities of the early immigration from northwest Europe. The median point of the German population was almost 6 miles from the Loop (the CBD) by 1930, and the Irish and Swedes had similarly moved far from their first point of entry. Minorities of the later migration, Czechs, Poles, Italians, and Jews, were still occupying inner city and inner suburban districts 3–5 miles from the CBD. Cressey noted that among more recent migrants, eastern European Jews were the group who had moved most rapidly through the urban structure. This observation has been made in many other cities. In Montreal (Figure 8.8) the Jewish community has migrated over a period of only 30 years from its port of entry in the immigrant corridor, adjacent to the city's core, into the high-status inner suburbs and, by 1971, north of Montreal Island into the new suburb of Laval. Life in the immigrant corridor is already a memory, relived primarily now in the novels of Mordecai Richler, the group's literary historian—though he has himself made the climb from St. Laurent Boulevard in the immigrant corridor to high-status Westmount.

The Jewish community has been unusual in that its decentralization has not lessened its spatial clustering. In the three census tracts of Laval occupied by Jews during the 1960s, they continued to number over 40 percent of the population in 1971. For northwestern European minorities, in contrast, movement away from the port of entry has invariably been accompanied by ethnic dispersal (Jakle and Wheeler, 1969). Spatial dispersal is an expression of a changing notion of social identity, so that acculturation to mainstream norms renders the ethnic grouping unnecessary. The Jews here provide an interesting contrast, for the community's regrouping in the suburbs represents a self-conscious attempt to maintain a distinctive cultural identity. Rosenthal (1961) has identified residence in a high-status district as an important element of the Jewish strategy to avoid assimilation. The stigma usually associated with ethnic segregation is felt to be mitigated when settlement is clustered in prestigious districts.

The close relationship between cultural identity and residential segregation may be illustrated by the changing locations of six ethnic groups in Winnipeg (Driedger and Church, 1974). A comparison of ethnic districts in 1941 and 1961 revealed the dispersal of the German and Scandinavian districts, the erosion of areas of Ukrainian and Polish settlement, but the survival of distinctive areas for the Jewish and French populations,

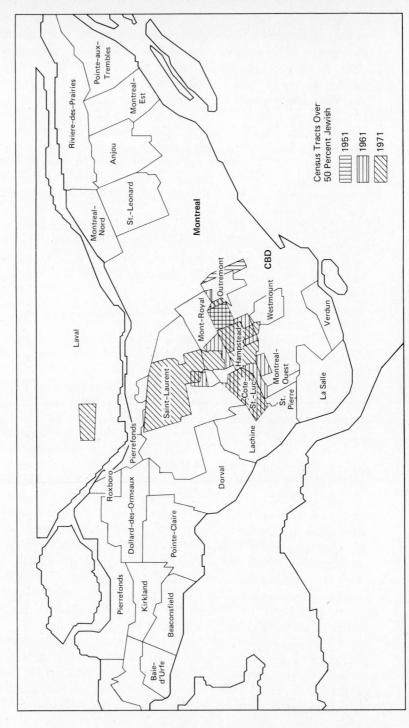

Figure 8.8 Suburbanization and persistence of the Jewish community in Montreal, 1951–1971.

including the emergence of a high-status Jewish suburb detached from the main community. These varying patterns were not related to population size, for the Ukrainian and German groups were the most numerous, and the Scandinavian and Jewish the smallest of the six minorities. But the spatial pattern was reinforced by the continuing strength of Jewish and French cultural institutions, particularly religious and educational agencies, compared to their weaker status for the remaining minorities.

Clearly, minority groups pass through variable assimilation histories. Some minorities rapidly abandon their cultural roots, and their identity merges with that of the majority group, whereas others voluntarily maintain their separateness. For a third category, for whom ethnic differences are often compounded by racial diversity, segregation is enforced not only voluntarily but also by the hostility of the host culture. Until 1950 and the beginning of the "Asian success story" (Journal of Social Issues, 1973), Oriental minorities had experienced continuous discrimination in North America. In Canada, anti-Chinese prejudice was institutionalized by the Immigration Act of 1923, and only about 50 Chinese entered Canada until the declaration of the more liberal Citizenship Act in 1947. As a result of this discrimination, clustered and inward-looking Chinese ethnic settlements developed in Canadian cities. The largest Chinese population was in Vancouver, but in 1961, after an existence of 75 years, over 50 percent of Vancouver's Chinese community still resided in Chinatown. Social ostracism helped to preserve spatial cohesion.

There has been a stable and repetitive sequence in the ease of dispersal of immigrants in North American cities. The greater a minority's social distance from the white Anglo-Saxon Protestant mainstream, the slower has been its assimilation into the majority culture (Duncan and Lieberson, 1959). Race has consistently provided the greatest distancing effect; racial minorities have suffered the most from involuntary segregation, exclusionary and discriminatory practices, and conflict accompanying expansion of their neighborhoods. We saw in Chapter 6 that increasing social distance decreases the probability of interaction between individuals and thereby retards the transmission of information. Whereas local communities may be well-known and finely differentiated, socially distant communities are more subject to distortion and may be evaluated on the basis of gross typifications. Such stereotypes or typifications also color intergroup perception, for in the absence of face-to-face interaction, mutual perceptions are derivative and represent little more than the culturally prescribed idiosyncracies of each group. As Alfred Schutz put it, in out-group interaction with socially distant others, we commonly have "types" for partners (Schutz, 1970).

Stereotypes prejudicial to minorities are often sustained by the media, for the communications industry typically upholds mainstream values and biases (Ley, 1974a). During the 1960s, when black Americans held only 100 out of 50,000 white-collar jobs in the newspaper trade, the press reflected the disinterest and typifications held by white society. In 1963, only 11 out of 20,000 display advertisements in the liberal New York Times included an unequivocal black profile, and as a Times correspondent admitted, "I agree . . . we tend to cover Harlem as a police beat" (Sitton, 1967). The same predisposition is shared by the Canadian press. The recent immigration from the Indian subcontinent has quickened media interest since 1970 in the East Indian community in

TABLE 8.7 THEMES OF CANADIAN
NEWSPAPER AND MAGAZINE STORIES ON
EAST INDIANS, 1948–1977 (*n* = 157)

	Percent
Racism-discrimination-conflict	74.5
Marriages of convenience	7.0
Immigration	4.5
Sikh culture	7.6
Other news	6.4

Source: D. Singh, ''The East Indian Community of
Vancouver.'' Unpublished paper, Department of
Geography, University of British Columbia, 1978,
p. 6.

Canada. But news stories probe a very limited range of East Indian life (Table 8.7). The
message communicated to Canadians presents East Indians in a negative and problematic
light. The image portrayed is one likely to heighten social distancing.

Racial Transition

Negative stereotypes, aggravated by the mass media, have solidified the resolve of many
white North Americans to live in racially segregated neighborhoods (Clark, 1980). Census data amply confirm the conclusion of the Kerner Commission's report on civil disorders in 1968 that there were two Americas, black and white, separate and unequal, for
examination of racial distributions in 207 American cities in 1960 revealed a remarkable
median segregation index of 87.8 for black Americans (Taeuber, 1965). This segregation
was not a result of the generally lower incomes of black families but of discrimination
in access to housing; Taeuber estimated that on the basis of income distributions the
black segregation index in Chicago should be 10, whereas in reality it was 83. This ratio
was repeated for 15 other cities that were studied. The purposeful segregation imposed
on black Americans has led a number of authors to identify a dual housing market existing
in the United States (Berry, 1975b, 1979).

　　　Until 1910 nearly all black Americans lived in the rural South, and up to 1880 the
largest urban populations were in St. Louis and New Orleans (Morrill and Donaldson,
1972). However, opportunities for employment in the industrial cities of the manufacturing belt (particularly during the First World War), together with the repressive social
milieu of the South and the perception of a more liberal atmosphere in the northern states,
triggered a huge out-migration after 1910. The black population of the Northeast and
Midwest increased in size by nearly 7 million between 1920 and 1970, and 95 percent
of the present population are urban dwellers. The result has been a steady expansion of
black residential areas through a process of invasion and succession of contiguous districts
(Figure 8.9). The regular distance-bound nature of black advance has permitted fair

Figure 8.9　Expansion of black residential areas in Chicago 1920–1960. (*Source*: B. J. L. Berry, ''Monitoring Trends, Forecasting Change and Evaluating Goal Achievements: The Ghetto v. Desegregation Issue in
Chicago as a Case Study.'' Pp. 196–221 in C. Peach (ed.), *Urban Social Segregation*. London: Longman,
1975, fig. 13.1. Reprinted by permission of Colston Research Society.)

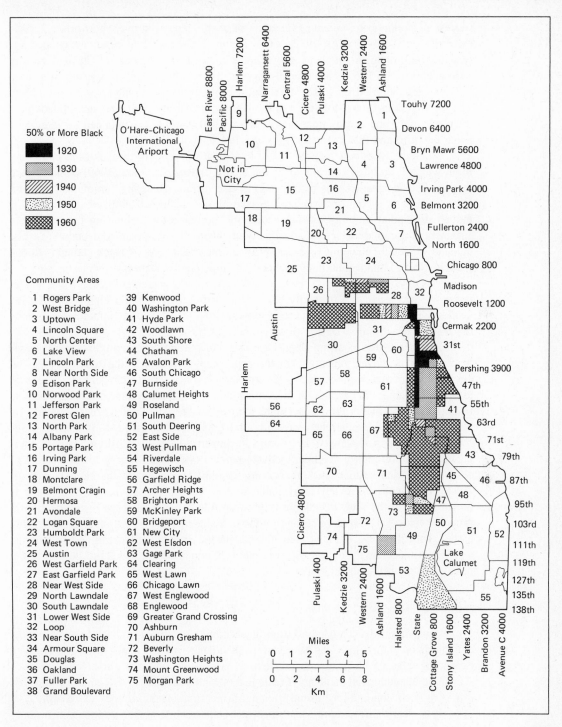

50% or More Black

- 1920
- 1930
- 1940
- 1950
- 1960

Community Areas

1 Rogers Park	39 Kenwood
2 West Bridge	40 Washington Park
3 Uptown	41 Hyde Park
4 Lincoln Square	42 Woodlawn
5 North Center	43 South Shore
6 Lake View	44 Chatham
7 Lincoln Park	45 Avalon Park
8 Near North Side	46 South Chicago
9 Edison Park	47 Burnside
10 Norwood Park	48 Calumet Heights
11 Jefferson Park	49 Roseland
12 Forest Glen	50 Pullman
13 North Park	51 South Deering
14 Albany Park	52 East Side
15 Portage Park	53 West Pullman
16 Irving Park	54 Riverdale
17 Dunning	55 Hegewisch
18 Montclare	56 Garfield Ridge
19 Belmont Cragin	57 Archer Heights
20 Hermosa	58 Brighton Park
21 Avondale	59 McKinley Park
22 Logan Square	60 Bridgeport
23 Humboldt Park	61 New City
24 West Town	62 West Elsdon
25 Austin	63 Gage Park
26 West Garfield Park	64 Clearing
27 East Garfield Park	65 West Lawn
28 Near West Side	66 Chicago Lawn
29 North Lawndale	67 West Englewood
30 South Lawndale	68 Englewood
31 Lower West Side	69 Greater Grand Crossing
32 Loop	70 Ashburn
33 Near South Side	71 Auburn Gresham
34 Armour Square	72 Beverly
35 Douglas	73 Washington Heights
36 Oakland	74 Mount Greenwood
37 Fuller Park	75 Morgan Park
38 Grand Boulevard	

success in attempts at computer simulation of ghetto expansion over short-time intervals (Morrill, 1965; Rose, 1970, 1972). Once begun, the invasion-succession sequence has typically been rapid. Eight elementary schools on the advancing edge of Chicago's South Side ghetto in the 1960s had a racial turnover of 75–100 percent in 5 years; in a more affluent neighborhood on Lake Michigan, the number of nonwhites rose from 152 in 1960 to 18,407 in 1966 (Molotch, 1969). Overall, in Detroit, Cleveland, and Philadelphia there was only one census tract that between 1940 and 1960 maintained an integrated racial balance, and that lasted for only one decade (Forman, 1971).

Although transition may be rapid, it does not necessarily provoke the panic and flight which is so often caricatured by the media. Indeed, Molotch (1969) demonstrated that the housing market was more stable in one racially changing community in south Chicago than in a comparable all-white lakeside neighborhood north of the CBD. Although residential mobility did not accelerate, normal rates of housing turnover were sufficient to accomplish racial transition. What this implies is a marked decrease in white demand in racially changing areas offset by an increased level of black demand. In one affluent North Philadelphia neighborhood, a 60 percent reduction in white housing demand was discovered when the black population reached 5 percent; the same white market resistance was found in a primarily blue-collar district in West Philadelphia (Rapkin and Grigsby, 1960). These behavioral responses are consistent with the attitudinal responses of whites interviewed in Detroit (Farley et al., 1978).

Another source of misunderstanding is associated with the vexing issue of changes in house prices during transition, for the popular myth of price reductions has received very little empirical support. In a detailed examination in West Philadelphia, it seemed as if black in-migration actually firmed up a relatively soft market; the perceived increase in neighborhood status for blacks more than offset the decreased status perceived by whites. Similarly, a comprehensive study of 10,000 housing transactions in three cities over a 12-year period showed an increase in property prices of transition areas as compared to those of control neighborhoods 44 percent of the time, parity for 41 percent of comparisons, and relative price reductions for only 15 percent of the cases (Laurenti, 1960). A government review of available studies reached the conclusion that "there is no substance to the view that minority group residency inevitably leads to a decline in property values" (U.S. Commission on Civil Rights, 1973:11). However, as we noted earlier, once the wave of racial transition has passed through an area, there may well be a subsequent decline in demand by potential black homeowners, and at this point housing prices will in all likelihood be depressed.

Racial Exclusion and Confrontation

White fears of an advancing ghetto front, undermining security and challenging perceived neighborhood status, have led to a variety of attempts to block black infiltration. The expanding edge of black residential districts is not uncommonly girded by a zone of social conflict and racial incidents (Figure 8.10). In this section we will consider informal efforts at exclusion and take up institutional forms of exclusion in the next chapter.

It is clear that there are social pressures within white neighborhoods constraining owners against selling or renting property to racial minorities. A number of homeowners

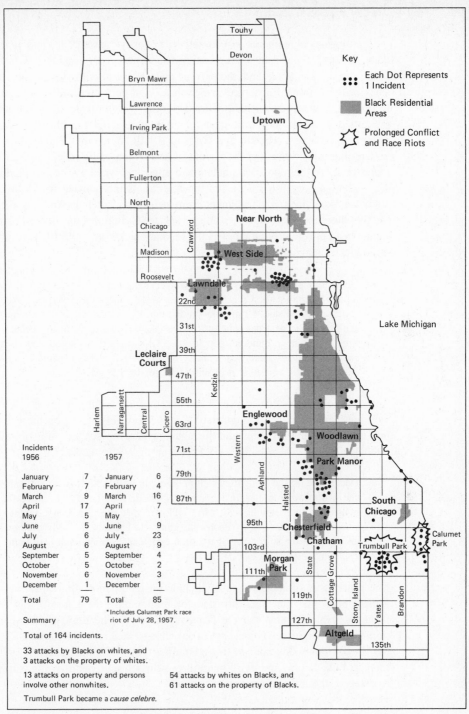

Key

··· Each Dot Represents 1 Incident

▓ Black Residential Areas

✦ Prolonged Conflict and Race Riots

Touhy

Devon

Bryn Mawr

Lawrence

Irving Park

Belmont

Fullerton

North

Chicago

Madison

Roosevelt

22nd

31st

39th

47th

55th

63rd

71st

79th

87th

95th

103rd

111th

119th

127th

135th

Uptown

Near North

West Side

Lawndale

Leclaire
Courts

Englewood

Woodlawn

Park Manor

South
Chicago

Chesterfield

Chatham

Morgan
Park

Altgeld

Lake Michigan

Trumbull Park

Calumet
Park

Crawford

Kedzie

Harlem

Narragansett

Central

Cicero

Western

Ashland

Halsted

State

Cottage Grove

Stony Island

Yates

Brandon

Incidents
1956   1957

	1956		1957
January	7	January	6
February	7	February	4
March	9	March	16
April	17	April	7
May	5	May	1
June	5	June	9
July	6	July*	23
August	6	August	9
September	5	September	4
October	5	October	2
November	6	November	3
December	1	December	1
Total	79	Total	85

*Includes Calumet Park race riot of July 28, 1957.

Summary

Total of 164 incidents.

33 attacks by Blacks on whites, and 3 attacks on the property of whites.

13 attacks on property and persons involve other nonwhites.

54 attacks by whites on Blacks, and 61 attacks on the property of Blacks.

Trumbull Park became a *cause celebre.*

Figure 8.10 Location of racial violence in Chicago, 1956–1957. (*Source*: St. Clair Drake and H. Cayton, *Black Metropolis*. New York: Harper & Row, 1962, fig. 21d. Reprinted by permission of Harper & Row. Copyright 1962 by St. Clair Drake and Horace R. Cayton.)

make informal agreements not to sell to minority households, and reneging on these commitments has alienated long-lasting friendships; on occasion sellers have asked for police protection to defend them from angered neighbors. Consequently, involuntary sales or the action of absentee owners has often permitted the first minority household to occupy a block. In an area of transition in West Philadelphia, one-third of the first entrants purchased their home from an absentee owner, more than twice the normal rate in housing transfers (Rapkin and Grigsby, 1960). In another Philadelphia neighborhood undergoing transition, over 80 percent of houses rented by blacks were held by absentee owners outside the local area, including a minority owned by the city (Cybriwsky, 1978).

Though very few of the first black entrants interviewed in Rapkin and Grigsby's study admitted to any harassment from neighbors, such hostility is common in both middle-class and working-class areas. The following account of harassment was given by the head of a family which was the second black household to move into an all-white middle-class neighborhood in Detroit:

> On the day preceding moving day, Delores and I were confronted by Mr. Lux, the attorney for the Puritan Park Civic Association, which felt I did not have a right to be in this home . . . So I said, "I am moving in here. Can I expect violence?" He said, "Yes, you can" . . . The next day when we moved in, a crowd of curiosity seekers gathered. There were at least a hundred people on the corners . . . The attacks became quite frequent . . . mostly there was breakage of windows . . . they became organised in their picketing and even worked at it in shifts (Bunge, 1971:71–72).

This provocation lasted for over 3 months, but the family held out. However, in some working-class areas harassment may take the form of attacks on the person, and fewer households are able to withstand this abuse. Black newspapers in major cities frequently publicize experiences which rarely appear in the white media:

> Declaring that she "might as well be living in Hell," Mrs. Anna Hill said Wednesday that she will move from her predominantly white neighborhood. . . . Since she moved into the house . . . four months ago, Mrs. Hill said that she has been a target for the abuse of surrounding whites. . . . "People just can't live like this. . . . My children have to run back and forth to the store. They have been threatened, stabbed and now burned. . . ." (*Philadelphia Tribune*, October 31, 1970).

The same issue of the newspaper included a report of an Italian homeowner in South Philadelphia who had been arrested for firebombing the home of his black next-door neighbor. Nine months later the *Tribune's* front page headline provided another illustration of the tension accompanying racial change in South Philadelphia: "Whites Attack Six Black Homes, Threaten to 'Burn Families Out' " (Tribune, July 6, 1971). Meanwhile in West Philadelphia, the third major area of black settlement, white gangs were seeking to preserve the racial boundary:

> Black residents of Southwest and West Philadelphia are calling for action in the wake of a six month rampage of murder and assault by white gangs in the Southwest area. Since

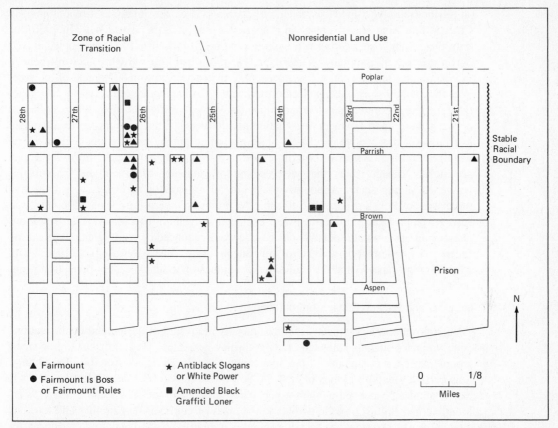

Figure 8.11   Territorial graffiti and racial transition in Fairmount, Philadelphia. (*Source*: D. Ley and R. Cybriwsky, "Urban Graffiti as Territorial Markers, "*Annals, Association of American Geographers* 64 (1974):491–505, fig. 11. Reprinted by permission.)

December, two blacks have been killed, two mutilated and one youth severely beaten during this reign of terror (*Tribune,* May 11, 1971).

Yet it has been claimed that "Philadelphia has had a particularly good reputation for its handling of residential race relations" (Forman, 1971:75).

Such volatile social relations are associated with the uncertainty of a moving racial boundary rather than with the absolute proportion of blacks on a block. In Mrs. Hill's former neighborhood in North Philadelphia, aggressive wall graffiti with such slogans as "White Power" were concentrated in one quadrant that represented the line of black advance (Figure 8.11) even though there were more abrupt—but stable—racial gradients elsewhere in the neighborhood (Ley and Cybriwsky, 1974). As Mrs. Hill discovered, the display on the walls was not idle sublimation but a real threat that promised physical consequences.

Forman (1971) has reported many other cases of violent resistance to racial transition in suburban as well as inner city settings since the infamous firebombings in Chicago following massive black in-migration during the First World War. In 1968, the only black family in Dearborn, a Detroit suburb of more than 100,000 people, moved out in the face of continuous harassment. Dearborn had a mayor who "doesn't believe in integration"; on election to his *thirteenth* term in office he won 87 percent of the vote. Wealthier suburbs organize exclusion more subtly. An elaborate point system was practiced in Grosse Pointe, one of suburban Detroit's most prestigious areas, where collusion between the property owners' association and local real estate brokers led to a detailed evaluation of prospective purchasers. Information on purchasers was amassed, and they were graded on a number of criteria related to a "typically American" lifestyle; if they accumulated enough points, they were eligible for admission. Moreover, the "pass mark" was on a sliding scale. Although a score of 50 provided a normal pass, prospective purchasers of Polish descent had to score 55 points, southern Europeans 65 points, and Jews 85 points. Racial minorities were excluded altogether. This remarkable institutionalization of an elaborate social-distance scale was denounced by civil rights investigators. Indeed, as Forman wryly adds, Grosse Pointe property owners were so preoccupied with external appearances, that they admitted a number of wealthy leaders of Detroit's underworld!

Montreal and Belfast: Ethnic Confrontation

Though prominence is typically given to racially motivated exclusion and confrontation, other variables such as language or religion may generate sufficient distancing between groups that conflict becomes a possible eventuality. In 1871, for example, the Orange riots between feuding groups of Irish in New York caused 33 deaths (Headley, 1971). Nor is ethnically induced conflict a peculiarly American trait (Glass and Obler, 1977). Montreal and Belfast provide two stark examples of ethnic incompatibility and tension, though the expression of the former conflict is primarily political and the latter primarily violent.

Montreal historically has been a linguistically segregated metropolis (Figure 8.12). French Canadians have formed a plurality in the city of Montreal and the eastern municipalities, and English Canadians have dominated the high-status suburbs on the western half of the island (Lieberson, 1965; Joy, 1976). Through time English-speakers who were not bilingual have moved steadily westward; by 1971 residents who could not speak French were in a minority even in the traditionally high-status English inner suburb of Westmount. In 1971 two-thirds of metropolitan Montreal consisted of French-speakers. The contact line between anglophones and francophones in the central section of Montreal Island has been the location of an immigrant corridor, a string of ethnic neighborhoods which have included Jews, Italians, Greeks, and Chinese. These immigrants have comprised the major group entering the province of Quebec; in 1970, 20 percent of immigrants into the province were from francophone countries, 34 percent from anglophone countries, and 46 percent from other countries. This majority group with a mother tongue that was neither French nor English was therefore critical for the future linguistic balance of Montreal, and 70 percent of them have preferred English over French as the language of instruction for their children.

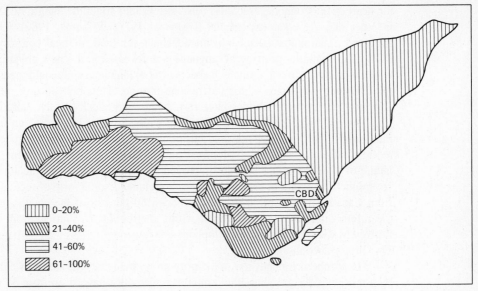

Figure 8.12   Population speaking English only, Montreal Island, 1971.

The assimilation into anglophone culture has led most ethnic minorities into a spatial trajectory westward from the immigrant corridor (Figure 8.8). However, with their greater cultural similarity, a number of Italians have moved east into francophone Montreal. This invasion process led to a violent demonstration in the eastern suburb of St. Léonard in 1969 over the language question (C. Smith, 1974). Italians began to move into St. Léonard in 1961 and by 1969 accounted for about 30 percent of the population. However, their influence exceeded their numbers, for they assumed an important commercial role and won effective control of local politics. Latent conflict became overt when Italian parents demanded that education of their children be in English and no longer bilingual—a concession wrested a few years earlier. This demand was perceived as a provocative symbolic threat to the core of francophone identity within the French heartland of Montreal Island. The earlier concession of bilingual instruction was withdrawn, and French was made the obligatory language of instruction. Such a taunt escalated ethnic tension, and in September 1969 a riot that included street fires, attacks on police, and the damaging of Italian stores broke out.

The Québecois have been placed in a double bind, for not only has French-speaking cultural, political, and economic influence been incommensurate with the size of the French-speaking population, but even French numerical superiority faced attrition in the future as immigrants chose to assimilate into anglophone culture. The second-class status of the French language, as perceived by many francophones, stood revealed in its inability to penetrate Montreal's central business district, where the language of commerce continued to be English—a source of frustration to many white-collar and professional francophones. Montreal is the major center of French culture in North America and yet its downtown core was outside the French cultural realm; symbolically this usurption of the heart of francophone ''sacred space'' throws into doubt the integrity of French culture in other than a dependency status (Laponce, 1977; Williams, 1980). This frustration triggered a nationalist social movement which assumed political control of Quebec in 1976. The symbolic primacy of language was revealed in the new government's Bill 1, which would have made French Quebec's official language and would thereby undermine the bilingual guarantees of the federal constitution. Thus both locally, in St. Léonard, and provincially francophones have responded energetically to the cultural invasion of English-speaking minorities. The province-wide response has led to an increasing out-migration of both anglophones and businesses since the nationalist crisis of 1970 and to a deteriorating climate in both Montreal and Quebec for further investment. The polarized nature of ethnic relations was not improved by the defeat of a provincial referendum for sovereignty association, seen by many as a prelude to some form of secession by Quebec from Canada, in the spring of 1980. Though 60 percent of the electorate turned down the referendum, the no vote varied within metropolitan Montreal from 96 percent in D'Arcy McGee, a West Side anglophone constituency, to less than 50 percent in several East Side francophone ridings.

In Northern Ireland, too, a majority group perceives the threat of cultural invasion by a more rapidly growing ethnic minority. Catholics have risen from 35 percent of the country's population in 1961 to 37 percent in 1971; at the present rates of change a Catholic plurality is foreseeable in less than 40 years (Compton, 1976). There are, however, two major differences in Northern Ireland's ethnic conflict. First, social distance is nominally measured by religion (in effect a label for economic, political, and historical dissimilarities), and, second, economic control is more firmly in the grasp of the majority than in Quebec.

As in St. Léonard and neighborhoods of racial transition in the United States, conflict in Northern Ireland has been concentrated at the spatial interface of ethnic residential areas (Boal and Livingstone, 1982; Murray and Boal, 1979; Mitchell, 1979). In Belfast, urban conflict has erupted on 12 separate occasions since the early nineteenth century, prior to the most recent round of ''troubles'' which began in 1969. Since 1969, segregation levels in some areas have approached 100 percent as members of both groups have withdrawn from ethnic contact zones into their own religious heartland; population movements associated with the troubles have involved between 35,000 and 60,000 Belfast residents (Boal, 1978). A territorial imperative has taken over. Territorial control is advertised on the walls by nationalist graffiti; streets near the ethnic interface have been abandoned; and exclusion has been carried to its limits by the erection of 12-foot high fences and street barricades, forming a euphemistically named ''Peace Zone'' separating the hostile factions.

Resistance to Social Mix

The industrial city saw the sharpening of the edges of class-based segregation, and in the postindustrial city to class have been added the further distancing effects of lifestyle (J. E. Vance, 1976). Despite the pervasiveness of segregation in practice, ethical and theoretical statements repeatedly have been made in praise of the integration of areas by class and lifestyle. Advocacy of social mixing has been traced back to the late nineteenth century, including such Quaker industrialists as the Cadbury family and their planned village for employees at Bourneville, near Birmingham in England. George Cadbury selected some of the early residents himself with the goal of "gathering together as mixed a community as possible applied to character and interests as well as to income and social class" (Bourneville Village Trust, 1956, quoted in Sarkissian, 1976). The idea of mixing social groups gathered momentum through the garden city movement and, later, in the development of new towns. It was vigorously promoted in Lewis Mumford's influential writing; as late as 1974 Mumford asserted that "I regard *mixture* as one of the three essential functions of the city . . ." (Sarkissian, 1976). In the past 30 years, the planning notion of the socially balanced neighborhood (Jacobs, 1961) and, in the United States, the political pressures toward racial desegregation have assured continuous if controversial prominence for the concept.

The resiliency of arguments for social mixing is more remarkable in light of the pervasive trends toward homogeneity and segregation in social areas and opposition to any proposal that would infringe this principle. Neighborhood social compatibility seems to be a general objective of individual taste. In suburban Levittown, for example, as soon as the price differential between adjacent homes exceeded 20 percent, developers found that the higher-priced unit became virtually unsaleable (Gans, 1967). In the English new town of Crawley, the government's attempt to integrate housing types and social classes was undermined by the middle class, who tended to move once new housing was available in private subdivisions and nearby villages (Heraud, 1968). Any mingling of varied housing classes leads to some social unease. When the projects are on a large scale, such as typical public housing sites, or in some other manner introduce a perceived stigma into an area, such as occurs with the introduction of community halfway houses for delinquents, the mentally ill, or addicts, opposition becomes more strident (Dear, 1977a).

Against this discouraging record, there is one contemporary countervailing force that would seem to favor the emergence of more integrated social areas. The urban philosophy of Jane Jacobs (1961) has done much to advertise the livability of central city neighborhoods and encourage the return of white-collar workers to the urban core. One of Jacobs' key ideas is the desirability and utility of neighborhood *diversity*. From their apparent preference for often dilapidated blue-collar areas for settlement, it has been inferred that diversity is indeed an objective of the returning professionals. One reviewer of neighborhood resurgence has made the claim that "diversity is probably on its way to becoming an accepted part of the middle class lifestyle and value-system, at least for urban reinvestors" (Weiler, 1978).

However, there are material consequences of central city resurgence which might challenge so optimistic a forecast and its implications for socially mixed areas. It is becoming clear that middle class reinvestment in working-class communities causes inflation in the local housing market which forces out poorer residents and dislocates the neighborhood ambience. In Philadelphia's Society Hill, house prices increased from $13,000 in 1963 to $87,000 in 1975; at the beginning of 1978, monthly rentals in high-rise apartments in the area varied from $300 for a studio to over $1,050 for a four-bedroom unit (N. Smith, 1979). The most spectacular price changes belong to the primate cities. In London, the Ivory House in St. Katherine's Dock, formerly the center of the Port of London's ivory trade and adjacent to the Tower of London, has been converted into luxury apartments, renting in 1979 for over $1,000 a *week*. In this setting, without some form of government intervention, the survival of lower-cost accommodation is a pipe dream (Hamnett, 1982a). Only on its advancing margins does Society Hill retain appreciable social diversity. Elsewhere a new homogeneity has emerged in the classical tradition of invasion and succession, and as with other forms of invasion and succession by an incompatible out-group, resistance is mounting to this middle-class takeover (Cybriwsky, 1978). Vandalism against renovated dwellings has been widely reported, and in 1977 there were the first and as yet isolated cases of firebombings in resurgent neighborhoods in San Francisco and Philadelphia. Resistance to middle-class gentrification has developed in Canadian cities, where the transition rarely has ethnic nuances (Ley, 1981). In London, a demonstration and march against tenant evictions led by the local Member of Parliament is said to have slowed the rate of renovation in the borough of Islington (Pitt, 1977). Elsewhere in London, a number of boroughs controlled by the Labour Party are resistant to office development, fearful that it will encourage a local irruption of gentrification and working-class displacement (Damesick, 1979).

Conclusion: Open and Closed Communities

The American city, commented Jean-Paul Sartre, has no more permanence than "a camp in the wilderness . . . Detroit and Minneapolis, Knoxville and Memphis were *born temporary* and have stayed that way" (Sartre, 1955a:107, 109). Rapid change in the city challenges the conservatism of ongoing routines and the closure of social worlds, and reveals the position of households and neighborhoods within the broader social structure. But the social structure is not a single, open system allowing equal and free access and circulation to all families; it is stratified by socioeconomic status, stage in the life cycle, minority status, and lifestyle. Households inherit a niche in this system, and their position, their biographical situation, is a strong influence on their choice of neighborhood; some authors would be more emphatic and state that a household's niche inevitably consigns them to a neighborhood and its attendant range of urban experiences.

The unequal distribution of opportunities presents a narrower range of neighborhood options to some households than to others; there is a differential in choice and constraint among social groups. Although all might prefer to live in the most prestigious and safest districts, not all have the same bidding power in the urban housing market. On the other hand, very few would choose to live in the most stressful and stigmatized locations. In a situation where the regional housing supply exceeds the demand, these least-favored districts will show a high number of vacancies and signs of abandonment as they are occupied by the poorest housing classes, and as deterioration is hastened by a combination of limited maintenance and a growing level of neighborhood pathologies. In contrast, in cities where there is strong regional demand, private redevelopment will seek out areas of potential status and character in the inner city which will undergo upward-filtering and revitalization. The balance of abandonment and resurgence is related to the changing proportions of different housing classes. In San Francisco, with its high proportion of downtown white-collar employment, resurgence is in the ascendancy; in blue-collar St. Louis or Cleveland, it is not. Most cities find themselves in an intermediate position; Philadelphia juxtaposes its revitalization neighborhoods like Society Hill with three traditional ghetto areas.

Residential mobility and hence neighborhood change tend to be incremental, with most moves covering a short distance into districts of comparable status. This limited mobility reflects the fixity of the preexisting spatial structure in the short term and the stability of an inherited social structure. Once again we see the powerful inertia effects on change beyond a certain range, the tendency toward closure rather than openness in housing opportunities. When rapid social change occurs in neighborhoods, it is usually a function of ethnic or racial transitions, and it is not unusual for this abrupt transgression of social distance gradients to be resisted, sometimes violently. Thus the threat of in-migration by groups perceived as socially dissimilar is met by exclusionary practices. Exclusion may be strong enough to act as a further force for division in the social structure, thereby creating an additional set of housing classes. In the United States, exclusion based on race is pervasive enough to have created a dual housing market. Similar multiple markets exist in Belfast and, to a lesser extent, in Montreal.

Together, all of these factors promote closed rather than open communities in the short run. The biographical categories of income, age, and family and ethnic status consign households to housing classes from which there is only partial short-term mobility. Neighborhood change is incremental and if it occurs too rapidly or brings together socially incompatible groups, is resisted. Though the North American city may appear impermanent to Sartre's European eye, yet land use transition and social change are typically gradual and highly ordered, reflecting the spatial management of stratified social relations.

Chapter 9

Power and Politics
in Urban Land Use

Coalitions, not communities, are the characteristic urban collectivity

(Williams, 1975)

Market power, minority status, and lifestyle preference are not the only ingredients shaping intergroup relationships and the development of residential areas and land use patterns in the city. In the advanced societies, the variable level of state regulation implies that every important locational decision may be subject to political and legal scrutiny. So, too, in an era when the allocation of many services and consumption items is administered by the state, access to key public decision makers is an important necessity in preserving and expanding one's welfare. The city consists of an arena of political coalitions including individuals, interest groups, institutions, communities, and the various agencies of government, and the changing spatial form of the city is in part the negotiated outcome of their interaction in the field of urban politics.

For many neighborhood organizations, community solidarity is often attained in large measure through a common political response to some externally induced change with positive or negative connotations as, for example, a proposal by some level of government to construct a freeway or some other undesired facility within its field of care (Suttles, 1972). Thus the neglect of its "foreign relations" with the rest of the city may well have serious consequences for a neighborhood. Gans (1962a) noted how the Italian residents of Boston's West End had strong local contacts but were isolated and disinterested in their interaction with other Boston communities and interest groups. As a result they were unprepared for a proposal initiated by the city to demolish their neighborhood as part of an urban redevelopment master plan. The failure of the West Enders to prevent the destruction of their community is an instructive example of the true importance of political relations in the city. First, though political activity may be infrequent, it may nevertheless be dramatic and promote fundamental change; second, the parochial perception of residents may be an incomplete indication of the presence of wider forces and of their own biographical situation within them. The destruction of the West End illustrates how broader political relations are often revealed in the processes of urban change.

The various political actors in the city have diverse values and criteria for action: besides economic advancement, such concerns as social welfare, ecology, aesthetics, or some other form of public interest may prompt intervention in a land use issue. In each instance dominant values create new land use facts. The city is therefore often a place of conflict, as opposing interest groups seek to impose their values on the urban landscape. The interest group with the greatest power, either market power, status authority, or political legitimacy, is able to exercise its will over competing claims. This competition does not, of course, occur in an institutional vacuum, for private and public institutions are frequently initiators of urban land use change to which residents' groups subsequently respond. Both the interest groups and the alliances established between them are shifting, as different issues threaten the objectives and values of the groups concerned. Nor is the institutional presence a monolithic one, for diverse organizations have their own agendas, which are not always in agreement.

In this chapter we shall examine the relations between urban residents and the agents of urban organizations concerned with social area and land use change. To some extent the institutional presence often reinforces other inequalities between individuals, for those with limited market power also commonly exert little political power in land use controversies. However, this situation may be reversed by the entry of more powerful allies, including government agencies with their social welfare criteria, to restore greater bargaining power to the poor than their market status would allow.

Urban Development: The Managers

Traditionally, urban geographers have taken the urban landscape as given, or at least as the outcome of anonymous forces in the marketplace, and have then gone on to describe and to establish functional relations between the given spatial structure and various ecological variables. Even behavioral approaches emphasizing consumer choice have not treated urban land uses as problematic and socially constructed. But a more complete analysis would view the urban landscape as the *negotiated outcome* of a complex series of perceptions, actions, and interactions between a variety of urban actors, including landowners, speculators, developers, financiers, planners, politicians and real estate agents, each of them operating under constantly changing degrees of freedom. Together, these development agents exercise considerable discretion over emerging patterns of land use, and their decisions, however arbitrary, provide a legacy etched in brick, asphalt, and concrete for later generations of urban dwellers.

This thesis was proposed in an innovative paper by W. H. Form (1954). In the 1940s, a vigorous debate in human ecology that contested both the ecological and economic preoccupation of urban research had arisen. Walter Firey was a central contributor to this critique, with his argument (reviewed at the end of Chapter 3) that greater attention should be paid to social and cultural values and actions in an explanation of land use patterns. Form did not dispute Firey's argument but added to it a mandate for inquiry to include also the social organization of the land market in place of deference to a set of abstract and mechanical ecological processes: "It is apparent that the economic model of classical economists from which these processes are derived must be discarded in favor of models which consider social realities" (Form, 1954). These realities consist of a set of concrete social interests that are highly organized and purposeful, and anything but anonymous and mechanistic, present in the marketplace. Four major interest groups were identified: the property industry, major business and other industries, the varied departments and levels of government, and individual land users. Each of these interest groups had different functions, economic power, internal organization, decision-making environments, and values and objectives, but whether in concert or in conflict, their actions together determined land use patterns. Land use was therefore a negotiated and socially constructed reality, neither haphazard nor inevitable in its form.

This argument has been taken up more recently in what has come to be called the managerial or gatekeeper thesis of urban development (Pahl, 1969, 1977, 1979; Williams, 1978b). This concept, like that of housing classes, has a pedigree derived from Max Weber's theories of advanced society. In Western society Weber saw a gradual extension of the power of bureaucracy as a form of mediation in the distribution of societal resources. Access to resources, whether they be shelter, health care, or education, become increasingly a product of bureaucratic rules and taken-for-granted norms, which may never become explicit but are nevertheless highly structured in their effects. Inevitably the increased intervention of the state, with its avowedly rational objectives based on scientific knowledge, increases the discretionary power of bureaucracy and institutions as mediators of urban reality. This research program draws attention to the intended and unintended effects which are a result of the culture-building processes of urban institutions. Among these varied social worlds, the "*crucial* urban types are those who control or manipulate scarce resources" (Pahl, 1969). As Gunnar Olsson has noted, these professionals, businessmen, and bureaucrats are those whose word can become our world; in the outworking of their daily routines they contribute to either the remolding or the ossification of social and spatial structures in the city.

The Land Development Industry

The land development industry consists of an assortment of builders, subcontractors, architects, marketing agents, land assemblers, and speculators, together with their legal and financial consultants. But of these the major actor is the developer himself who coordinates the other parties and is finally responsible for new construction.

The *developer* is a specialist. Some entrepreneurs emphasize a type of development, either commercial, residential, or office construction; some specialize in central city as opposed to suburban development; and all but the largest developers have highly biassed mental maps and particular areas of familiarity in the city (Bourne, 1976b). This spatial specificity is a result of past experience, proven contacts with public agencies, and perception of future opportunities. Tradition weighs heavily in the developer's perception, so that there is often a marked locational inertia in his site selection (Baerwald, 1978). Locational conservatism is in part an effort to minimize risk by adopting sites that have already been tested by previous market response, for the marketing phase of development is the most unpredictable, and developer projections are generally intuitive and unsystematic. For this reason marketing factors rather than production costs are foremost in site selection; a review of developers in North Carolina showed that the "social prestige level" of a site was "clearly the most important" locational characteristic (Kaiser and Weiss, 1970).

At periods of higher market demand or inflationary costs, developer priorities are likely to switch toward production concerns. The North Carolina data were collected in the mid 1960s, but by the mid 1970s builders around Minneapolis were showing as much concern over the cost of short-term loans in financing construction as over marketing (Baerwald, 1978). In the high-demand period of the early 1970s, the major preoccupation of Toronto developers was with land ownership and land availability; marketing issues such as neighborhood quality were then a secondary consideration (Bourne, 1976b).

The action of government and other public agencies is a major factor in the decision-making milieu of the developer. Zoning regulations and the provision of serviced land are important locational factors. Any potential bylaw instability in local jurisdictions increases uncertainty and makes investment less attractive. Municipalities with lengthy and taxing standards for evaluating construction proposals are avoided as are neighborhoods where there is community resistance and a poor climate for development. A change in government may also create uncertainty and limit investment confidence. In British Columbia, the election of a provincial government with socialist leanings in 1972 is said to have hastened a transition in construction activity away from rental units, with their relatively long-term returns and vulnerability to rent controls, and toward the fast cash returns offered by residential condominiums (Goldberg and Ulinder, 1976). Similarly, in Britain it has been claimed that government-imposed rent controls have led to the virtual disappearance of the private rental market (*The Economist,* 1980; but see Hamnett, 1982a).

The development industry has traditionally favored the entry of small builders and subcontractors as well as the persistence of larger corporations. In Victorian Edinburgh, Elliott and McCrone (1980) noted how large landowners operating in national capital markets were frequently responsible for the construction of substantial middle-class housing according to their own specifications, whereas working-class housing was more commonly the product of small builders and local financiers and was altogether a more precarious enterprise, susceptible to local economic fluctuations, particularly the availability of credit and the variations in demand. In Victorian London as well, Dyos (1978) found that the uncertainties of anticipating market demand "made every function a speculative one." Moreover, participation in the city's land market was an idea that "caught on not only among men of capital but among men of enterprise but no capital." The evidence for Victorian London assembled by Dyos suggests that although there were a few large integrated builders, the small firm with a handful of men and use of the varied services of subcontractors was the more typical arrrangement. Fewer than 10 percent of the builders enumerated in the 1851 census employed more than 50 men; in the last quarter of the century, a third of all London house builders raised only one or two houses a year. As in Edinburgh, these small jobbers were financed from a variety of local sources, including solicitors and estate executors, though in London the building societies seem also to have been important. Despite the stereotype of the speculative builder, there is remarkably little evidence of complaints against the quality of construction from the early residents of London's Victorian suburbs.

The entry of the small firm continues to be a feature of the building sector, for in the United States 65 percent of all builders produced fewer than 25 units a year during the early 1970s. However, in recent years there has also been a marked "rationalization" in the development industry with the enlarging of individual companies through takeovers and mergers. Vertical integration of companies has occurred, so that varied operations from landholding to materials supply, construction, and property management are carried out by subsidiaries of the same company. For example, Genstar, a North American subsidiary of the largest investment corporation in Belgium, has its own subsidiaries in land assembly, subdivision servicing, house construction, and a wide variety of materials products, including precast concrete, asphalt paving, a prefabrication plant, and a gypsum wallboard plant (Gutstein, 1975). Perhaps the largest Canadian developer is Cadillac-Fairview, formed by the merger of two Toronto-based companies, the Cadillac Development Corporation—an apartment developer and owner—and the Fairview Corporation—an owner and manager of suburban shopping centers. At the end of 1973 this conglomerate had assets of over $0.75 billion. In the mid 1970s, like many other large Canadian developers experiencing a softening market in Canada, Cadillac-Fairview became a multinational corporation, extending its investment and development activities into the United States (Figure 9.1). By 1978, these American investments were already accounting for up to 25 percent of the revenue of some Canadian companies, and by 1981 for as much as 75 percent. Canadian developers have become particularly active in central city redevelopment and renewal, and have shown more investment confidence in the CBD than American developers, derived no doubt from their astuteness in rebuilding the CBD in the Canadian city. This experience has given the Canadian developer a competitive edge in winning central city contracts in the United States; the most notable examples to date have been Cadillac-Fairview's successful submission in 1980 to the Los Angeles city council for a $1 billion mixed-use development in the downtown area, and Olympia and York's Battery Park City proposal, begun in 1981, for developing at the tip of Manhattan another $1 billion mixed commercial-residential project.

A number of these large development corporations made huge profits during the period of rapid inflation in the housing market in the 1970s. The total assets of Daon Development, one of Canada's largest developers, rose from $13 million in 1969 to $1.22 billion in 1979, and its earnings per common share rose sevenfold from 1975 to 1979; the 1978–1979 increment was 153 percent. The company owned or held options on more than 25,000 acres of land around metropolitan areas in Alberta, British Columbia, and several western states in the United States (Daon, 1979). It is not surprising that there have been charges and countercharges of profiteering and oligopoly practices within the housing sector (Spurr, 1976; Markusen and Scheffman, 1977). In the six townships on the developing fringes of Toronto, four principal developers held effective ownership of as much as 60 percent and no less than 40 percent of the total supply of developable land. These proportions would consistently rank as high to medium levels

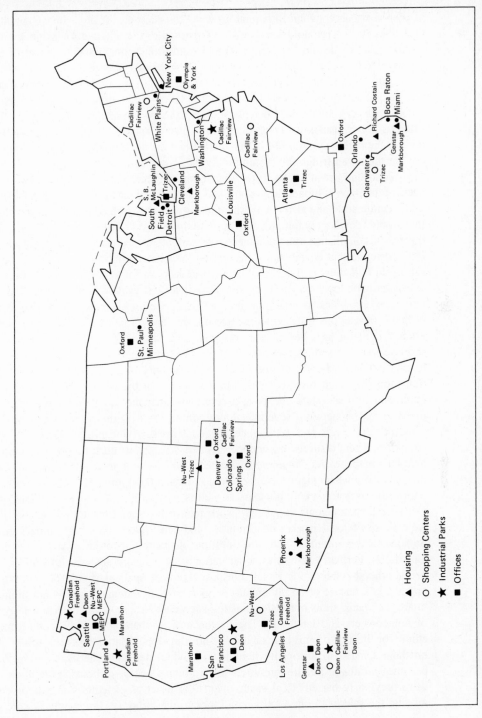

Figure 9.1 Major investment by Canadian property developers in the United States, 1977. (*Source: The Financial Post*, Oct. 15, 1977, pp. 12–13. Reprinted by permission.)

of economic concentration in several different classifications of oligopoly (Gunton, 1978). Over the whole Toronto urban fringe, as opposed to the separate township submarkets, the four leading developers have effective control of as much as 31 percent of the land acreage likely to be utilized up to 1986. The relations between such concentration in ownership and the price of new suburban houses are important but controversial ones. One economic model suggests that land speculation on the urban fringe raises per capita social costs between 3 and 7 percent for a net charge to the consumer of $50 million to $120 million a year in a city of 1 million people (Capozza, 1976). Other serious issues involve the high level of profit in this market and the destabilizing effect of land speculation on the urban fringe for farming and other land uses.

A second set of actors in the development industry are *real estate agents*. These agents often have a broader role than sales alone. They may operate as small speculators in the land market and also have a share in the assembly of land parcels for development. In Toronto, developers found it necessary to do relatively little assembly themselves, for this was accomplished by middlemen, and particularly real estate agents; indeed, Bourne (1976b) found that developers were offered far more assembled parcels than they could act on. In Philadelphia, land speculation in areas of racial transition was not infrequently associated with local real estate agents (Rapkin and Grigsby, 1960). The first black home purchaser on a block invariably paid an inflated price for his house. An undue proportion of these transactions were with absentee owners, and 75 percent of them involved a real estate speculator as seller. These entrepreneurs, who had held the property for only a short period, grossed an average of 35 percent on their resales and 50 percent on sales to the first black family on the block. Such activity is not limited to zones of racial transition. In an inflationary market in Vancouver in the early 1970s, some properties purchased by real estate agents in a resurgent inner city neighborhood were sold five times in 1 year between several holding companies with the *same* owners in order to force up rent levels and manipulate the local market (Gutstein, 1975; Ley, 1981). In similar resurgent districts in London, agents have also moved from professional to commercial enterprise. As *The Economist* noted: "Since estate agents now know much about finance, about what other people are doing and about the arithmetic of investment . . . the temptation to become entrepreneurs as well is very strong" (cited in Williams, 1976).

Real estate agents commonly work relatively limited territories, so that they are well aware of local market opportunities and sensitivities. It is unfortunate that some brokers have resorted to ethically questionable tactics in order to capitalize on local conditions. Forman (1971) has some particularly macabre accounts of *blockbusting* in neighborhoods undergoing racial transition—though again it should be noted that this practice is a feature of an inflationary market with high demand and is not limited only to areas of racial transition. Blockbusting succeeds because of the discriminatory beliefs of homeowners and landlords. Their reluctance to share space with certain minority, ethnic, or lifestyle groups limits available housing opportunities for these groups, forcing up their demand to artificially high levels. When demand reaches a certain level, it becomes profitable for the minorities to be granted access to housing from which they were previously barred. Real estate agents often act as expediters in this process, arranging the sale of the first units on a block to the minority. Frequently this initial sale is enough to generate concern among existing homeowners and to stimulate sales, while at the same time effectively reducing demand among nonminority buyers. Attitudinal data from Detroit suggest a 25 percent reduction in white demand levels with the arrival of the first black household on a residential block (Farley et al., 1978).

In a sense the blockbuster is merely providing housing to groups that are discriminated against in the open market. But his actions are commonly more pernicious—though it should be stressed that such conduct is not inevitable and that only a minority of agents are usually opportunistic in this way (Rapkin and Grigsby, 1960). The blockbuster capitalizes on the fears of residents and exploits them to his own advantage. In a situation of anxiety, homeowners may be enticed to sell their property at below-market prices to the agent who then resells it to an eager minority household at a healthy profit. A variety of tactics are employed to heighten residents' fears, including the erection of conspicuous ''For Sale'' and ''Sold'' signs. In one New Jersey community:

> The ''battle of the signs'' was in progress. Real estate agents erected FOR SALE signs in letters as high as three feet, on the front lawns of houses listed with them. After a sale, they would replace it with a gigantic SOLD, that might remain for several weeks until the new Negro took possession. It was a psychological warfare technique designed to panic whites into selling . . . One could measure the tension of a street by the number and size of its signs (Damerell, 1968:160–161).

Blockbusting is not uncommon in North American cities. It has been claimed that there were operating in Chicago during the 1950s and 1960s over 100 blockbusters who were responsible for ''busting'' two or three blocks a week. This small minority of realtors might have triggered the blockbusting of 70,000 white families over a decade (Forman, 1971). If displacement was a source of hostility, then blockbusting could generate considerable racial ill will, which would be reciprocal if in-migrating black households faced resentment and harassment.

The ambivalent professional standards of real estate brokers are illustrated by the conduct of ethical, as opposed to unethical, agents. The real estate profession has reflected the prejudices of mainstream society in its belief that racial integration is neither possible nor desirable; indeed, white and black brokers in the United States have even formed separate national associations. In their sales practices, agents have therefore selectively directed clients to socially and racially compatible neighborhoods. The Chicago Real Estate Board (Hughes, 1971) has been an explicit enforcer of segregated housing, establishing a policy in 1917, prior to the consolidation of the city's black areas, that ''it is desired in the interest of all that each block shall be filled solidly (with Negroes) and that further expansion shall be confined to contiguous blocks'' (Helper, 1969:225). In the 1920s the Real Estate Board spearheaded the development of restrictive covenants in Chicago's white neighborhoods in order to maintain the contiguous, segregated character of black residential areas (Figure 9.2). Covenants that prohibited the sale of property to certain minorities were strategically organized over no less than half the white-occupied neighborhoods and, in particular, over those adjacent to existing black districts (Brown, 1972).

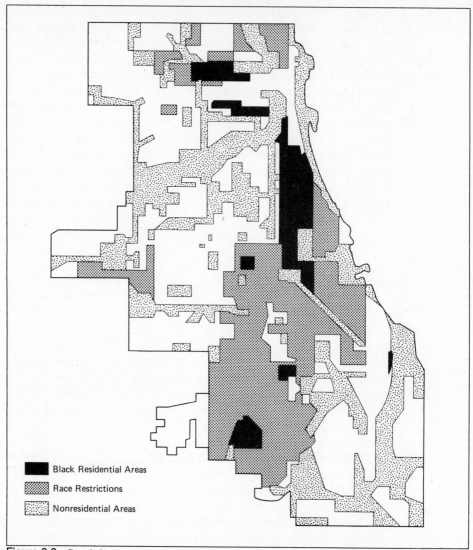

Figure 9.2   Restrictive covenants in interwar Chicago. (*Source*: W. Brown, ''Access to Housing: The Role of the Real Estate Industry,'' *Economic Geography* 48 (1972):66–78, fig. 1. Reprinted by permission.)

Helper's study of attitudes among agents in the mid 1960s showed that this ''exclusion ideology'' remained a taken-for-granted element of their day-to-day practice. A number of misrepresentations and obstacles were consistently placed in the way of prospective black purchasers to steer them away from established white areas (Forman, 1971). The mental categories of the broker were translated in practice into the firm racial divisions found in North American cities. From his research in New Jersey, Damerell concluded: ''Realtors as a group wield a social power so tremendous that it is probably second to none. They steer Protestants, Catholics, Jews, and Negroes into their respective ghettoes . . .'' (Damerell, 1968:80).

This role of the real estate agent as a gatekeeper is not restricted to minority-group segregation. Knowledge of a metropolitan market is extremely uneven between different companies, though most of them have well-specified territories where their sales are concentrated (Figure 9.3). This specialized spatial knowledge biasses the recommendations realtors give to home purchasers. A large sample of brokers in Minneapolis and San Francisco were asked to suggest suitable neighborhoods anywhere within the metropolitan area for potential clients with a range of occupations who worked in the downtown core. Consistently brokers failed to recommend neighborhoods outside their company's normal operating territory (Figure 9.3). In Minneapolis, over 75 percent of brokers showed marked partiality in recommending their own local areas to a hypothetical purchaser who was a dentist, bookkeeper, and delivery man, and over 90 percent shared this bias in expressing favoritism for local areas to an accountant. An intriguing proposition is that realtors' perceptions can become self-fulfilling; as purchasers are selectively steered toward districts on the basis of the broker's image of them, so those neighborhoods increasingly take on the form of the image. As Palm concluded: ''Those households which are dependent on realty salesmen for information on neighborhood characteristics are making use of a highly structured and spatially limited information source'' (Palm, 1976).

Financial Institutions

A second major group of managers of urban development are associated with financial institutions. These intermediaries have become increasingly important with the decline of private rental housing and the rise of home ownership. In the United States owner-occupancy has increased from 44 percent of dwelling units in 1940 to 63 percent in 1970 (Harvey, 1975), whereas in the United Kingdom levels have risen from 28 percent in 1953 to 54 percent in 1976 (Williams, 1978a). At the same time there has been a corresponding increase of institutional mortgage indebtedness; in 1900 only 50 percent of mortgages were held by institutional investors, but by 1970 this figure had risen to 90 percent. Moreover, in 1970 the residential mortgage debt in the United States was equivalent to 35 percent of the gross national product, and by the mid 1970s it had exceeded $500 billion.

Like developers, financiers are cautious and conservative in confronting risk and uncertainty. Since these business realities are differentiated over the urban area, financiers are spatially discriminatory in their lending practices. Inevitably the geographical variation in the availability of investment funds will have a significant impact on the location of both new construction and also on maintenance and improvements to existing structures.

Financiers have another important influence in their decision-making environment; they are particularly sensitive to their public image, and at least overtly are anxious to avoid practices that would be inconsistent with the desires of their clients. ''Public relations'' was a commonly used rationale to explain the reluctance of banks in the past

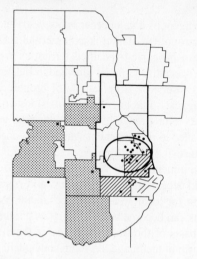

(a) **To the Dentist**

By All Agents, Taken Together

By Agents of Company 35

Standard Deviation Ellipse for Company 35

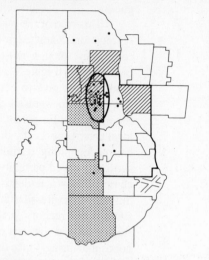

(b) **To the Accountant**

By All Agents, Taken Together

By Agents of Company 24

Standard Deviation Ellipse for Company 24

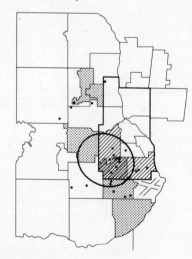

(c) **To the Bookkeeper**

By All Agents, Taken Together

By Agents of Company 29

Standard Deviation Ellipse for Company 29

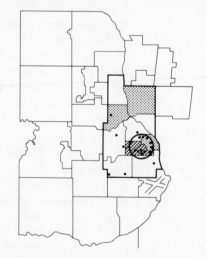

(d) **To the Deliveryman**

By All Agents, Taken Together

By Agents of Company 14

Standard Deviation Ellipse for Company 14

to lend money to black families intending to purchase housing in white neighborhoods. In San Francisco, and in the United States in general, bank lending to blacks was based on the twin criteria of residence in ''an established Negro neighborhood'' and in a ''good'' area (McEntire, 1960). The effects of such a policy have been, in the words of a 1969 federal Civil Rights Commission, that ''banks dictate where the Negroes can live'' (Forman, 1971). Thus the practices of financiers, like those of ''ethical'' real estate brokers, are a reflection of the attitudes of the society in which they are set.

There were also more direct economic reasons for discriminatory lending. Banks were anxious to protect property values in white neighborhoods where they held mortgages and other investments, and shared the common belief that racial transition is accompanied by declining values; at the very least there was uncertainty over the longer 15–25 year term over which most mortgages run. Civil rights legislation enacted since 1968 has prohibited such lending practices, though as with all civil rights laws, enforcement and the demonstration of discrimination based on race is not always easy.

The challenging of racial prejudice by the courts has not, moreover, affected other discriminatory practices. In a market society, financial institutions seek to minimize risks and maximize returns in their investment practices. When returns on investments are low and interest rates to depositors are depressed, financial agencies inevitably become unattractive to investors. There is a remarkably symmetric relationship between the size of investment funds and interest levels offered to depositors. Consequently, once again there is a susceptibility of financial agencies to broader factors in their decision environment. They respond by minimizing uncertainty, investing their funds in projects perceived as safe, and avoiding risky ventures.

This policy leads to systematic spatial biasses to their involvement in the housing market. We noted earlier how in Victorian Edinburgh national finance markets made loans for middle-class housing, whereas working-class housing depended on a variety of small, local lenders (Elliott and McCrone, 1980). So, too, in an instructive examination of the Baltimore city housing market, Harvey has shown how various financial agencies have fragmented the city into a series of submarkets by their lending preferences (Harvey and Chatterjee, 1974; Harvey, 1975). Each institution occupies a specialized niche in the housing price structure (Table 9.1). For the lowest-priced housing, either private arrangements or else state savings and loan companies were mortgage grantors in 80 percent of sales transactions. The higher perceived risks in low-income areas kept the banks and the larger savings and loan firms out of this submarket. Many of the state savings and loan companies are small and ethnically based; their role as an ethnic community service (often they are exclusionary toward other clients) means that they will accept lower profit margins than the more ''rational'' firms.

There is a geographical corollary to this systematic pattern of lending (Table 9.2). The inner city market was heavily dependent on cash transactions and money raised from private sources; typically these ranged from family lenders to usurous private investors. In the working-class ethnic districts of East and South Baltimore, the small savings and

Figure 9.3 Overrecommendations in real estate territories, Minneapolis. (*Source*: R. Palm, ''Real Estate Agents and Geographical Information,'' *Geographical Review* 66 (1976):266–280, fig. 4. Reprinted by permission of the American Geographical Society.)

TABLE 9.1 PERCENT MORTGAGE LENDING IN PRICE CATEGORIES BY FINANCIAL AGENTS, BALTIMORE, 1972

Lending Institution	Under $7,000	$7,000– $9,999	$10,000– $11,999	$12,000– $14,999	Over $15,000
Private	39	16	13	7	7
State S&Ls	42	33	21	21	20
Federal S&Ls	10	22	30	31	35
Mortgage Banks	7	24	29	23	12
Savings Banks		3	5	15	19
Commercial Banks	1	1	2	3	7
% of Sales in Category	21	19	15	20	24

Source: D. Harvey, ''The Political Economy of Urbanization in Advanced Capitalist Societies,'' pp. 119–163 in H. Rose and G. Gappert (eds.), *The Social Economy of Cities.* Beverly Hills: Sage, 1975, Table 8, p. 141. Copyright 1975. Reprinted by permission.

loan companies were extremely active, whereas in the middle-priced inner suburbs mortgage banks were the major lenders, supported by risk-free government-insured mortgages. The government FHA-insured mortgage program flourished for 4–5 years and made home ownership possible to lower-middle-class (and mainly black) families who may not previously have qualified for mortgage financing. They purchased homes particularly in areas of racial transition. (Note the high turnover levels in neighborhoods

TABLE 9.2 LENDING PATTERNS OF FINANCIAL AGENTS IN BALTIMORE NEIGHBORHOODS, 1970

	Sales per 100 Properties	% Transactions by Source of Funds								% Sales Insured		Average Sale Price ($)
		Cash	Pvt.	Fed. S&L	State S&L	Mtge. Bank	Comm. Bank	Savings Bank	Other	FHA	VA	
Inner City	1.86	65.7	15.0	3.0	12.0	2.2	0.5	0.2	1.7	2.9	1.1	3,498
1. East	2.33	64.7	15.0	2.2	14.3	2.2	0.5	0.1	1.2	3.4	1.4	3,437
2. West	1.51	67.0	15.1	4.0	9.2	2.3	0.4	0.4	2.2	2.3	0.6	3,568
Ethnic	3.34	39.9	5.5	6.1	43.2	2.0	0.8	0.9	2.2	2.6	0.7	6,372
1. E. Baltimore	3.40	39.7	4.8	5.5	43.7	2.4	1.0	1.2	2.2	3.2	0.7	6,769
2. S. Baltimore	3.20	40.3	7.7	7.7	41.4	0.6	—	—	2.2	0.6	0.6	5,102
Hampden	2.40	40.4	8.1	18.2	26.3	4.0	—	3.0		14.1	2.0	7,059
West Baltimore	2.32	30.6	12.5	12.1	11.7	22.3	1.6	3.1	6.0	25.8	4.2	8,664
South Baltimore	3.16	28.3	7.4	22.7	13.4	13.4	1.9	4.0	9.0	22.7	10.6	8,751
High Turnover	5.28	19.1	6.1	13.6	14.9	32.8	1.2	5.7	6.2	38.2	9.5	9,902
1. Northwest	5.42	20.0	7.2	9.7	13.8	40.9	1.1	2.9	4.5	46.8	7.4	9,312
2. Northeast	5.07	20.6	6.4	14.4	16.5	29.0	1.4	5.6	5.9	34.5	10.2	9,779
3. North	5.35	12.7	1.4	25.3	18.1	13.3	0.7	15.9	12.7	31.5	15.5	12,330
Middle Income	3.15	20.8	4.4	29.8	17.0	8.6	1.9	8.7	9.0	17.7	11.1	12,760
1. Southwest	3.46	17.0	6.6	29.2	8.5	15.1	1.0	10.8	11.7	30.2	17.0	12,848
2. Northeast	3.09	21.7	3.8	30.0	19.2	7.0	2.0	8.2	8.2	14.7	9.7	12,751
Upper Income	3.84	19.4	6.9	23.5	10.5	8.6	7.2	21.1	2.8	11.9	3.6	27,413

Source: D. Harvey, ''The Political Economy of Urbanization in Advanced Capitalist Societies,'' pp. 119–163 in H. Rose and G. Gappert (eds.), *The Social Economy of Cities.* Beverly Hills: Sage, 1975, Table 9, p. 142. Copyright 1975. Reprinted by permission.

receiving substantial numbers of FHA-insured mortgages.) Indeed, community opposition to racial transition and scandals associated with opportunistic real estate practices in these areas led to the program's demise by 1972–1973. Finally, the larger savings and loan companies and savings banks limited their lending policies to higher-priced houses.

There are some important implications to this geographically structured pattern of lending, especially as financial intermediaries have assumed an increasing role in the housing market. In the United States, savings and loan companies are responsible for almost half the value of residential mortgages, and in the United Kingdom building societies are in an even stronger position, granting 77 percent of the residential loan value in 1975. A most serious outgrowth of the underinvestment by these financial institutions in blighted inner city districts is a policy conventionally known as *red-lining*. We have already noted the avoidance of the inner city in Baltimore by the federal savings and loan companies; a series of detailed studies of building society practices has similarly documented red-lining in a number of British cities (Boddy, 1976; Duncan, 1976b; Williams, 1976, 1978a). In Newcastle, building society lending favored single-family and semidetached houses and discriminated against older, terraced structures. When mortgages were granted on older houses, they were for small advances and shorter terms, increasing the level of monthly repayments and therefore limiting the access of poorer households who could only afford such cheaper units. The distribution of a sample of mortgages granted between 1973 and 1975 showed a de facto red-lining policy in operation as substantial sections of the city received no or very few awards; indeed, societies explicitly mentioned some districts where they would not make loans (Figure 9.4). These were older, inner city neighborhoods in various stages of blight or where renewal or some other major land use change was possible. In contrast, new suburban subdivisions both inside and beyond the city boundary were awarded building society mortgages (an example is in the northwest corner of the map) and so, too, were more substantial privately owned homes in Newcastle. Here the nature of the neighborhood, the size and condition of the homes, and the characteristics of the borrowers all contributed to making a loan a virtually risk-free proposition. Government local-authority mortgages take up some of the slack, venturing into somewhat more uncertain transactions than the private sector, particularly into government-declared general improvement areas and some areas of local-authority housing (Figure 9.4). But there still remain substantial spaces on the map where neither institution will make loans (see also Bassett and Short, 1980). In such districts usurous and exploitative private sources are not an uncommon last resort (Duncan, 1976b).

The conservatism of building societies and their preoccupation with investment security lead them to lag behind changing market trends. In Islington, a rejuvenating borough in London, the caution of building societies has retarded their response to favorable market conditions (Williams, 1976). Similarly, in Society Hill in Philadelphia, resurgence has passed through several phases, and in each phase a separate investment source was dominant; first speculators, then state savings and loan companies, then federal savings and loan companies and banks, and most recently the large banks have played the role of key investors (N. Smith, 1979). In this manner different financial institutions have entered the investment market as their own minimum threshold of

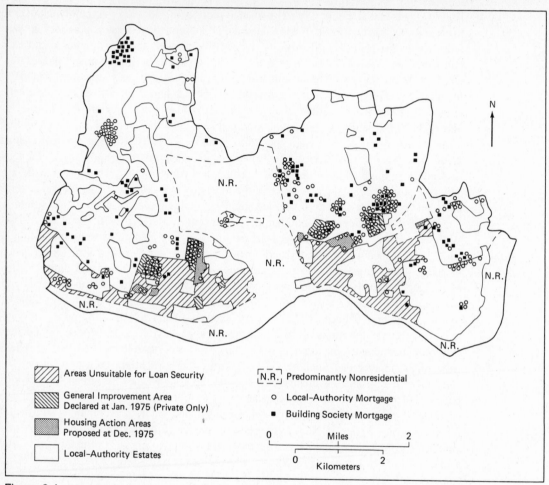

Figure 9.4 The pattern of mortgage financing in Newcastle, England. (*Source*: M. Boddy, "The Structure of Mortgage Finance," *Transactions, Institute of British Geographers* NS 1 (1976):58–71, fig. 6. Reprinted by permission.)

tolerance for uncertainty has been reached; we should note the symmetric relationships between increasing demand levels, rising property prices, and investment confidence on the part of financial intermediaries. The other face of increasing neighborhood amenity for consumers (as we discussed it in Chapter 5) is decreasing market uncertainty for institutions.

In the United States, the Home Mortgage Disclosure Act of 1975 was passed in an attempt to check red-lining by making lending agencies disclose publicly their geographic pattern of mortgage awards. However, where market conditions prevail, it is difficult to envisage how there could be other than an uneven allocation of funds reflecting differential investment insecurities and opportunities. Certainly, some preliminary indications suggest that this act has not brought about an equalization in lending practices over the city. Even in the smaller metropolitan area of Sacramento, California, some census tracts in 1976 continued to receive less than 20 percent of the loans received in other neighborhoods that were newer, of a higher status, and did not contain substantial numbers of members of minority groups (Dingemans, 1979).

Government Agencies

The role of the different levels of government and their various departments and officials in the construction of social areas has already been mentioned in passing in the preceding sections. The place of government in the housing market and in urban development more generally is so pervasive and wide-ranging that we can only illustrate its effects here. Daniel Bell has claimed that ''the power of the state . . . is the central fact about modern society'' (Bell, 1976b:228). The accuracy of this statement can perhaps be gauged by the extent of the direct involvement of the state in urban housing. In England and Wales almost 30 percent of all dwellings are owned by local authorities, and in Scotland over 50 percent; in the United States, 8.5 million housing units have resulted from federal housing programs between 1935 and 1970, with a net gain of some 7 million after demolition for renewal and public works have been accounted for. Even at the surface level of residential morphology, the Western city is a powerful testimony to the energy of state housing policy (Figure 9.5). Fiscally, state intervention is enormous. In Britain in 1978 it has been estimated that approximately $11 billion was committed to state redirection of the housing market (*The Economist,* 1980).

The managerial role of government in urban development may be separated into policies of regulation and policies of providing incentives. Regulatory functions would include code enforcement, the compilation of bylaws, and the development of a zoning map. Incentives would include the supply and maintenance of urban services (note, for example, the importance of already serviced lots in site selection for new suburban development), the provision of infrastructure such as urban transportation, the availability of grants and loans for particular programs, and the existence of various tax concessions and write-offs. Regulatory powers invariably devolve to local government except where there is a high degree of centralized planning. In contrast, powers to initiate change more often lie with senior governments, in large part because of their greater fiscal resources.

Zoning is perhaps the most familiar regulatory instrument of local government policy. Indeed, the apparatus of urban planning often reduces to the zoning bylaws, especially in the United States: ''Zoning *is* planning . . . communities do not really plan at all; they just zone'' (Linowes and Allensworth, 1973:66). Although there are some cities where zoning is virtually absent (of which Houston is the largest), a normal feature early in a city's development has been the establishment of a municipal planning bureaucracy, the preparation of a comprehensive plan, and the enactment of zoning maps and bylaws. Zoning plans are far from unique; Harland Bartholomew, the most successful commercial planner of his generation, followed a repetitive basic blueprint, and with small concessions to local conditions, this blueprint was imposed on a hundred urban centers between 1920 and 1948, primarily in the Midwest (Johnston, 1973).

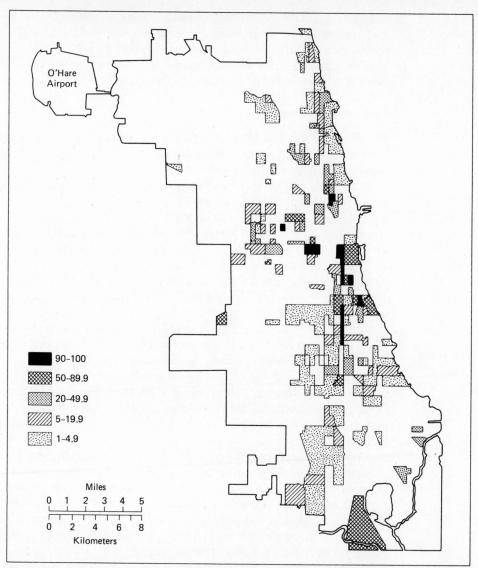

Figure 9.5   Subsidized housing as a share of all units, Chicago 1972. (*Source*: J. Mercer and J. Hultquist, "National Progress toward Housing and Urban Renewal Goals." Pp. 101–162 in J. Adams, *Urban Policy-making and Metropolitan Dynamics*. Cambridge, Mass: Ballinger, 1976, fig. 4.26. Copyright 1976, Ballinger Publishing Company. Reprinted by permission.)

The major objective of municipal zoning has been the regulation of uncontrolled market forces at the local level. The zoning map has added stability and security to landowners with the assurance that future incursions of nonconforming land uses will be checked, thereby safeguarding existing investments. The necessity of separating nonconforming uses has often provided the initiative for the establishment of zoning. In New York the momentum that eventually led to zoning controls in 1916 arose out of such a problem. Garment manufacturers chose to locate their lofts as close as possible to their customers, the retail and department stores. But this led to undesirable social mixing in the minds of the store owners, for during the lunch hour and at the end of the working day, both prime shopping periods, hundreds of low-paid garment workers thronged the streets adjacent to fashionable stores, creating a social association not conducive to prestige shopping in the minds of wealthy patrons. The merchants appealed to the Manhattan borough president for a separation of garment making from garment retailing, and the result was the eventual appointment of a zoning commission in 1913 (Makielski, 1966).

The separation of incompatible uses usually has been argued as a major advantage of zoning. A second is that land use control is exercised by the local municipality, so that owners and residents have some discretion over development that affects their interests; homeowners' associations have traditionally made heavy use of zoning ordinances to promote a desired neighborhood image. Zoning has now passed far beyond its simple origins as a control of building height to a sophisticated and flexible body of land use regulations, incorporating such policies as density controls, bonussing systems for socially beneficial designs, and trade-offs between air rights and ground development.

However, zoning can be a two-edged sword and is open to abuse and socially undesirable effects. Changes in zoning might contribute to speculative windfall profits (sometimes in conjunction with municipal corruption, or at least a conflict of interests), or alternatively, the anticipation of a future rezoning to a more lucrative use may lead to the abandonment or dereliction of existing land parcels. But perhaps the most severe weakness of zoning is its role in legitimizing exclusionary practices, its implementation to give substance to an ideology of exclusionary privatism. As we shall see, in this capacity zoning has been a major weapon of the suburbs in preserving their privileged status vis-à-vis the central city.

The effectiveness of government planning in accomplishing major redirection of urban development in Western nations has been a source of some controversy (Hall et al., 1973; Bourne, 1975). Certainly at the municipal level exemptions to existing zoning policy have been granted with some regularity in many American cities. Nevertheless, the municipal civil service has had a marked effect on the urban experience of many residents even in the United States, for the mental categories of these gatekeepers have continuously been translated into real effects in the landscape. Jane Jacobs (1961) has noted how Boston planners labelled an inner city neighborhood as a slum, justifying subsequent urban renewal simply on the basis of age and density variables recovered from the census, which gave a misleading impression of its actual quality of life. The power to designate can grant formidable powers to civic bureaucrats to construct realities (Dennis, 1978). They have been authorized, for example, to define not only "slums" but also inner city districts designated as Model Cities areas in the United States, Neighborhood Improvement Areas in Canada, and General Improvement Areas in Britain. Such a designation can bring financial windfalls to neighborhoods. In the early 1970s the Model Cities program in Philadelphia was allocated $75 million for neighborhood improvements, and in total nearly $1 billion of Model Cities money was promised to 163 urban areas.

Extensive government intervention in the housing market in North America began in the 1930s, and there is scarcely a single area of the city's social geography which has not been affected significantly by a number of direct and indirect government policies. American suburbs have benefited from government's ideological commitment to home ownership and the single-family dwelling, reflected in low mortgage interest rates, guaranteed mortgages, and tax write-offs. In 1973 tax deductions on mortgage interest and property tax payments amounted to $6 billion (Harvey, 1975). But the suburbs have mushroomed also as a result of the federal policy to promote the building industry as a stimulant for the national economy (Clawson, 1971). As Carolyn Adams has observed, "National housing policy ever since the 1930s reflects an unmistakable preference for new construction as the single most important object" (Adams, 1978). Even the 1968 Housing Act extending benefits to working-class families favored production, for 90 percent of all subsidized units between 1968 and 1972 consisted of new construction. In part as a result of federal housing programs, 1.3–1.4 new units were built for every new household that was formed between 1960 and 1975. Here, then, is a still broader context for the problem of inner city abandonment which assumed such alarming proportions during the 1970s.

In the less favored inner city areas, government policies have only recently shifted from "slum" clearance and redevelopment to rehabilitation; in Chicago only 2 percent of urban renewal expenditure up to 1974 was spent on rehabilitation. The old policy of demolition/redevelopment gave rise to the celebrated high-rise public housing projects. As a whole these projects have not been a success and rate consistently poorly on evaluations by users or potential users (Cooper, 1975). In part, this is because they have not reduced the incidence of social pathologies that it was hoped they would cure and, indeed, through high-density and anonymous, alienating design, may even have accentuated social problems. Chicago's Taylor Homes is a massive project throwing together 25,000 people, with 75 percent of the households classed as broken families (Mercer and Hultquist, 1976). In New York robbery rates in public housing projects increased from a rate of 2.6 per 1000 people for six-story buildings to a peak of 11.5 per 1000 for projects 19 stories high or more (Newman, 1972). Furthermore, government programs have not broken up existing patterns of racial segregation; it was not until 1950, for example, that FHA loans were withheld from areas where restrictive covenants were in force. The locational strategy for siting public housing has guaranteed that existing racial patterns have been perpetuated. In Chicago (Figure 9.5) in the mid 1960s, tenants in 50 of the city's 54 housing projects were 99.5 percent black, and tenants in the remaining four complexes varied from only 1 to 7 percent black. Subsequent attempts to produce a more scattered distribution, the result of federal prodding and a court order, have been strenuously resisted in white neighborhoods.

By the mid 1970s rehabilitation had become a significant aspect of inner city housing programs. In Canada the Residential Rehabilitation Assistance Program and Neighborhood Improvement Program aimed to stabilize rather than demolish inner city neighborhoods (Phillips, 1976); in the United States some monies from the Housing and

Community Development Act of 1974 have been channelled into up-filtering areas to consolidate emerging trends; and in Britain a series of Housing Acts since 1969 has established General Improvement Areas and, since the 1974 Act, Housing Action Areas in which various grants for home repairs have been made available (Thrift, 1979).

Both directly and indirectly government action has aided "gentrification" of the inner city. In New York the revitalization of the Upper West Side has diffused outward from the new Lincoln Center for the Performing Arts and the West Side Urban Renewal Area (Winters, 1977). In Philadelphia, the city's Redevelopment Authority played a major role in triggering the resurgence of Society Hill, developing a master plan, acquiring property, and investing almost $40 million in the success of the project (N. Smith, 1979). An assessment of expenditure patterns from the Community Development Act in almost 150 American cities from 1974 to 1977 showed that very little public money was being invested in low-income areas and that by the second year of operation almost 40 percent was being directed to upgrade and consolidate existing middle- and high-income neighborhoods; in contrast, only 10 percent was expended in low-income census tracts (C. Adams, 1978). A similar bias seems to have befallen improvement grants allocated in British cities. In Bristol, grants for home improvement have not been disbursed (nor applied for) in areas where housing is most deteriorated, but there has been considerable use of such monies in a few better districts for conversion of older rented units to rental and self-owned flats; by the early 1970s, 40 percent of improvement expenditure was utilized for conversions (Bassett and Hauser, 1975). A similar pattern has been identified for parts of London (Hamnett, 1973), though it now seems that demand levels for selected inner city neighborhoods are high enough to make the improvement grant simply icing on the investor's cake.

Managerial Coalitions and the "Manipulated City"

It is an abstraction to isolate the various urban managers as we have done in the preceding discussion, for in reality their strategies are closely interdependent, with each group acting as a major component of the decision environment of the others. Their interests frequently collide; sometimes they overlap. A recent trend in urban research has extended the theory of political elites to metropolitan development, arguing that urban form is the outcome of a conscious manipulation by an alliance of elite interests with social power. Simply put, "Spatial organisation is seen, therefore, to arise out of the behavior of institutions within the urban environment" (Gale and Moore, 1975:xii). Sometimes this literature can become rather shrill, and its polemical—and politically activist—reform position has diverted a number of academic commentators, particularly in Canada where it has been institutionalized in the value-explicit pages of *City Magazine*. Nevertheless this literature is more sound than some critics have allowed. It has a firm base in elite theory and a strong empirical tradition—unlike some other positions which might claim more intellectual sophistication. As we will see, the reality of elite coalitions is inescapable; what is more problematic is gauging the extent of the empirical effects of such alliances and the completeness of the theoretical argument.

At the most self-evident level, a number of biographies have shown the effects of dominant managerial personalities on the urban landscape. For over 30 years in New York City, Robert Moses was an unchallenged administrator whose policies and programs had an enormous effect on New York's landscape (Figure 9.6). Although he humbly portrayed himself as "working for the people" (Moses, 1956), his biographer more aptly saw him as a "power broker" whose whole life "has been a drama of the interplay of power and personality" (Caro, 1974:4). As Park Commissioner, Construction Coordinator, Planning Commission member, to name only his major responsibilities, Moses had supreme authority in molding the spatial form of New York. In Lewis Mumford's assessment: "In the twentieth century, the influence of Robert Moses on the cities of America was greater than that of any other person" (Caro, 1974:12). There have been a number of other celebrated personalities who have self-consciously shaped the city according to their own vision, including such "machine" mayors as Richard Daley of Chicago (Royko, 1971) and Jean Drapeau of Montreal (Auf der Maur, 1976; Aubin, 1977). Drapeau was first elected mayor of Montreal in 1954. After reelection in 1960 he committed the city to a vast program of urban monumentalism that culminated in the financial fiasco of the 1976 Olympics; the cost of the games could have provided 120,000 units of low-rent housing in the city which has the worst slums in Canada. Drapeau's authoritarian control of the Civic Party in Montreal gave him free reign to develop the city according to his own agenda, and it was not until 1974 that he encountered any opposition in city hall.

From its earliest days the North American city has often operated as a coalition of an elite of businessmen and municipal politicians. There was no need for this relationship to be covert, for it was a widely held ideology that progress and growth were synonymous, and who better to run the business of city government than businessmen themselves? The Progressive reformers at the turn of the century believed that "their concept of the city's welfare would be best achieved in the business community controlled city government" (Hays, 1964). This myth has enjoyed remarkable longevity: the mayor of Edmonton dismissed the credibility of an electoral rival in 1976 with the argument that "he has no business experience. He's been a school teacher. I've worked in business all my life, and we're running a business" (Anderson, 1979).

The evolution of a commercial-political coalition and the supremacy of the business ideology in city planning have been traced in detail in a number of metropolitan areas including Winnipeg (Artibise, 1975), Vancouver (Bottomley, 1977), and Pittsburgh (Lubove, 1969). In Pittsburgh, the reform movement burgeoned in the early twentieth century in part as a response to the Pittsburgh Survey, which laid bare the immense social costs of the city's industrial enterprise. The direction of reform was reflected in the presence of the Chamber of Commerce as one of the advocacy groups in the forefront of more efficient government. In the 1940s a succeeding business coalition was developed around the powerful Mellon family, a major corporate presence in the city, to initiate and oversee the Pittsburgh renaissance, the renewal and redevelopment of the downtown Golden Triangle. Business interests felt that such initiatives would symbolize a strong and favorable image for the city, which would in turn draw in fresh investment to reinforce the aging economic base of the steel industry. This business lobby had access to immense power and prestige with all levels of government. In enticing a major insurance company

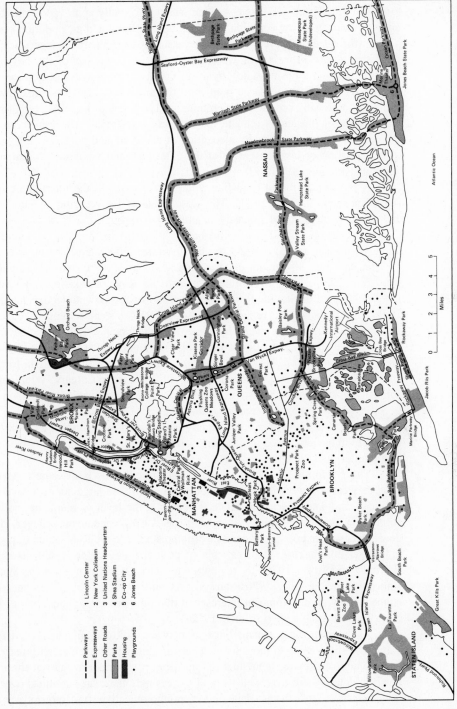

Figure 9.6 New York landscapes shaped by Robert Moses. (*Source:* R. Caro, *The Power Broker: Robert Moses and the Fall of New York.* New York: Alfred A. Knopf, 1974, inside front cover. Reprinted by permission.)

to build in the Golden Triangle—which was not formally approved by the City Council until 4 years after—the coalition promised county flood and air pollution control, which had not then been achieved, and long-term leases for 60 percent occupancy in the company's projected office tower were guaranteed by a number of the largest Pittsburgh corporations. This business hegemony in urban development was not challenged until the rise of neighborhood-based politics in the mid 1960s. Even the coalition's eventual attention to housing programs was rationalized in terms of the effects improved housing would have on the city's climate for business investment. The Pittsburgh renaissance was a stunning achievement by a coalition of corporate and political managers "in terms of mobilisation of civic resources at the elite level and wholesale environmental intervention" (Lubove, 1969:137).

A number of recent Canadian studies have exposed the interlinking coalitions of urban managers into the 1970s. The close relations between the development industry and financial institutions is easily demonstrated through the existence of interlocking directorates (Figure 9.7). Such linkages are logical in terms of the mutual business interests of each group; in 1969 the life insurance companies, the largest property financiers, had over 40 percent of their total assets in property mortgage holdings. There were four interlocking directorates between the Royal Bank—one of Canada's three largest chartered banks—and Trizec—one of the largest downtown developers (Gutstein, 1975). This association is reflected in the Royal Bank's status as a major tenant in prestige downtown office towers owned by Trizec in Vancouver, Calgary, and Montreal. There was also a key interlocking directorate with the Bank of Nova Scotia, another of Canada's major chartered banks. This liaison also has had its expression in urban form, as Trizec and the Scotia Bank are partners in major office towers in Calgary, Winnipeg, and Saint John. The bank in each instance provides construction capital and upon completion becomes a major prestige tenant (Aubin, 1977). The specialized common interests of financiers and developers are sufficient to forge such associations; as with the informal social groupings discussed in Chapter 6, so too with major corporations we see that birds of a feather flock together.

The economic and social power of such coalitions is awesome. At the national level they form powerful political lobbies and will spend large sums to have sympathetic political candidates elected to office. But it is at the level of municipal politics that the connection is most obvious. As recently as 1971, Vancouver's mayor, a real estate developer, was exposed in a conflict of interest charge while in office (Gutstein, 1975); in smaller communities the dual role of politician-developer is still taken for granted (Lorimer and Ross, 1976). A review of the city councils of Toronto, Winnipeg, and Vancouver in the early 1970s showed that about half the aldermen had occupational connections with development interests; at that time prodevelopment parties held control of city hall in each case (Lorimer, 1972).

Aside from these blatant linkages between political, financial, and development managers, there are also more indirect relationships. Inasmuch as all three groups share an ideology of growth, their interests must be intertwined, at least at the most general level; in detail, there may well be, and increasingly there are, conflicts over the distributive effects of growth, as social and economic objectives are frequently in opposition.

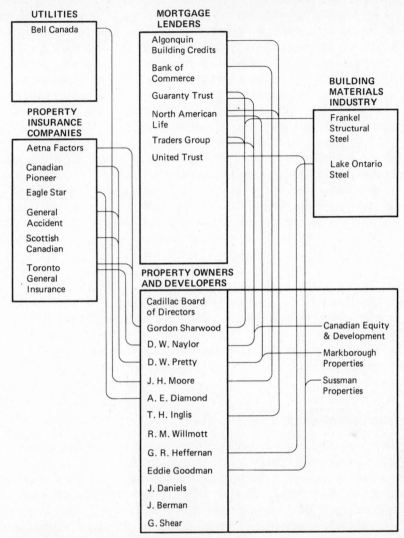

Figure 9.7   Overlapping directorates between Cadillac Development Corporation and other property interests and financial institutions. (*Source*: J. Lorimer, *A Citizen's Guide to City Politics*. Toronto: James Lewis and Samuel, 1972, p. 54. Reprinted by permission.)

For example, we have noted the manner in which the construction industry has been viewed by government as a regulator for stimulating a depressed economy. In the United States, where the value of new construction accounts for about 10 percent of the gross national product, the government's commitment to the production of new housing units has had a major effect on the pace of suburban development and the financial success of private developers.

However, although public and private interests may perhaps coincide in this facet of the suburban housing market, such convergence is by no means assured. The fiscal crisis of the central city, in contrast, may easily be cast as a conflict between the financial community and the public interest. In New York, the city overextended its borrowing in the late 1960s, in anticipation of increased tax revenues and government aid (Tabb, 1978). The severe loss of jobs and the economic downturn of the early 1970s then created a revenue gap which was met by the expensive solution of short-term borrowing in excess of constitutional limits. According to some interpretations, this gave the financial community tremendous leverage to manipulate the city's finances, and when, recognizing its fiscal overcommitment, they flooded the market with New York City bonds in 1974–1976, the city's financial credibility was destroyed. When fiscal crisis management was formed to save New York from defaulting, the financial community was firmly involved in the management process and benefited from the still higher interest on emergency loans. By 1977, 20 percent of New York's budget was committed to interest payments. In other economically impoverished central cities in the United States, the power of the business lobby may be equally awesome. In Cleveland, an oligopoly of business interests centered in the powerful Cleveland Trust Company, which has interlocking directorates with major local steel, coal, utility, and banking companies, presented an ultimatum to the city in 1978. It would organize a loan in return for certain concessions including, it is alleged, sale of the city-owned electric light utility, a competitor with a private utility enterprise with corporate linkages to the Cleveland Trust Company (Cockburn and Ridgeway, 1979). In this and in other ways, the business sector is able to use its economic power in a fiscally weak city as a political weapon to wrest further economic advantages. In an unequal contest, the financial managers are able to exercise close to monopoly power.

The Politics of Externality Control

In an important conceptual paper, Harvey has underscored how urban politics can bring about income redistribution by interpreting "much of the political activity of the city as a matter of jostling for and bargaining over the use and control of the 'hidden mechanisms' for redistribution" (Harvey, 1971). In other words, through urban politics, various interest groups lobby in order to enhance or at least protect their economic, social, and symbolic investments. These lobbyists include the institutions we have already considered as well as private citizens. Moreover, the citizens themselves are not a uniform group but have differential access to the corridors of power according to income, education, lifestyle, and ethnic characteristics.

Land use change leads to a redistribution of net costs and benefits to urban residents. For example, the construction of a new bridge over a river will improve accessibility to the whole population, may inflate local land prices, but will also create additional noise, pollution, and congestion problems for households in the bridge's immediate vicinity. Alternatively a new park paid for out of a city's general revenue will benefit particularly urban dwellers on nearby blocks. In each instance there has been an unequal distribution of costs and benefits; in the first case local households have lost excessively, and in the second they have gained excessively. Thus we can see that changes in the city's spatial form have the capacity to redistribute the real income of individuals through not only direct effects but also unpriced fringe benefits and uncompensated fringe costs. Such changes are often the outcome of political decisions by key decision makers, whether the decision be the acceptance of a rezoning application adding windfall profits to land-owners or an agreement on a freeway alignment which may devastate a neighborhood. Whatever the example, it is often *change* which exposes the bidding power of lobbyists and makes possible a redistribution of assets.

The more insidious effects are those which are indirect, a sometimes unintended spillover from a development. Such *externalities* are unpriced but may be major con-stituents of the quality of life in a neighborhood. Little is known of the spatial extent of externality fields, though they are obviously of importance in understanding the distri-bution of costs and benefits to urban dwellers. Moreover, the shape of externality fields is invariably the outcome of political decisions. In Vancouver the city has expended considerable money in developing parks and beach access. Most of this activity of late has been on the west side of town, benefiting particularly neighborhoods that already enjoy the highest status in the city. In contrast a review of native Indian reserves in the metropolitan area shows them to be juxtaposed to such uses as a sewage plant, a regional shopping center, industrial port facilities, major bridges, a gravel pit, and a mental hospital. Most of these sites were located as a result of a process of public decision making. Clearly the native Indians did not enjoy the same access to political bargaining in shaping their own externality field as that enjoyed by members of wealthier commu-nities. Inevitably property values will be influenced by adjacent uses, and as long as these are noxious, land values will be depressed, whereas the addition of amenity uses in an externality field will inflate local prices. The political status of Indians was reflected in the successful opposition by members of Vancouver's Chinese community, living in the two poorest census tracts in the city, to a proposal to construct an Indian friendship center in their neighborhood. This example also points to the reality of localism in municipal politics, the mobilization of neighborhoods to protect existing externality fields.

Localism

Change in the city is invariably propelled by forces that operate at scales beyond the neighborhood. The agents of change may represent public or private interests, but this does not necessarily affect their status in the eyes of residents as potential disruptors of community stability. Whereas the resources and investments of institutions are diffuse, residents typically have much more localized concerns for their home and neighborhood. The size of a homeowner's social, economic, and symbolic investment in his or her home makes residents alert and resistant to most forms of change. Thus localism is the homeowner's typical political response; existentially, it is a matter of defending one's own.

The salience of local concerns was recognized in the old-style ward politics. For all its patent corruption—of which Whyte (1955) offers a most colorful account con-cerning Boston machine politics in the late 1930s—there was something of a local ac-countability. The boss delivered the goods; local corruption was financed by local patronage.

Although machine politics were opportunistic and conservative inasmuch as they bred a quiescent electorate, they did provide a low level of access to political and economic mobility for immigrants (Whyte, 1955). Ward politics have been heavily criticized for their transparent complicity with business interests, and yet it is not clear that the reform politics of the Progressive era were any less favorable to a commercial and corporate elite while at the same time diluting working-class electoral power through at-large elections in which only candidates who could afford citywide campaigns were successful. The nonpartisan politics and at-large elections that characterized the reform movement of the early twentieth century served to concentrate civic power with higher-status groups and higher-status neighborhoods (Newton, 1978). In Vancouver, for example, with its at-large civic elections, 80 percent of aldermen are typically residents of the prosperous West Side (see Table 7.2).

A more recent trend has been the rediscovery of neighborhood politics, as neighborhood control is seen as a necessary antidote to reform elitism (Kotler, 1969; Mollenkopf, 1978). In San Francisco, Wirt has noted the rise of community groups since the mid 1960s:

> Associations—both temporary and permanent—named for hills and valleys, ethnic and occupational groups, age and sex distinctions, sprang up during the last decade. . . . There has appeared an almost sudden politicisation, so diverse and fragmented that observers unanimously insist that a ''new politics'' has appeared (Wirt, 1974:63).

By the mid 1970s this political fragmentation and localism were strong enough that, as a result of referendums in 1976 and 1977, San Francisco returned to a ward system, though more recently this victory has once again been reversed. Other cities also have returned to ward politics or, as in the case of Toronto, have revised their existing ward system in the wake of neighborhood demands.

In the United States localism has traditionally turned about three repetitive issues: property values, neighborhood schools, and public safety and security (Cox, 1978). To these might be added the more recent concern with maintaining an existing neighborhood ambience, with its argument for the conservation of existing landscapes and resistance to development (Lemon, 1974). This issue first appeared in elite neighborhoods with distinctive status reputations. Firey (1945) has described the activity of the Beacon Hill Association, founded in 1922 to uphold the symbolic values and historic landscape of its prestigious upper-class neighborhood, only a 5-minute walk from downtown Boston. This homeowners' association resisted the encroachment of ''more rational'' land use, such as hotels and high-rise apartments, through active revision and enforcement of local zoning and bylaws. Its success may be gauged by the net increase in upper-class households residing in Beacon Hill that occurred between the 1890s and the time of Firey's research, despite the suburbanization of elites that had occurred in the city as a whole.

The maintenance and enhancement of a neighborhood derives in part from constant vigilance to potential changes in externality fields. Wolpert and others (1972) have illustrated a household's potential response to a range of facilities that might be located in its neighborhood (Table 9.3). Facilities are responded to along what Wolpert calls a

TABLE 9.3   THE RANKING OF SELECTED FACILITIES ON A PRIDE-STIGMA CONTINUUM

	On Your Block	On a Neighboring Block	Within Rest of Neighborhood	Within Neighboring Community
Hospital	2	1	1	1
Office Building	5E	5E	4	4
Police Station	3	2	1	1
Delicatessen	2	1	1	1
Gas Station	6D	5D	3	3
Supermarket	5E	2	2	2
Day-Care Center	2	1	1	1
Public Library	1	1	1	1
Park	1	1	1	1
Theater or Movie House	6E	5E	2	2
Community Recreation Center	5E	2	1	1
Oil Refinery	7A	7A	7A	6C
Urban Expressway	7A	6C	5D	2
Sewage Treatment Plant	7A	7A	7B	5

Source: Adapted from J. Wolpert, A. Mumphrey, J. Seley, *Metropolitan Neighborhoods: Participation and Conflict Over Change.* Washington, D.C.: Association of American Geographers, Resource Paper No. 16, 1972, pp. 45–47. Reprinted by permission.

pride-stigma continuum—which we suggested in Chapter 5 to be one of the critical existential dimensions of urban space. Facilities are ranked from 1 to 7 in terms of their desirability, and for undesirable or noxious facilities interviewees could add a response category ranging from A or B, vigorous opposition, to E, no opposition. The single return in Table 9.3 shows the equivocal relation of the functional and symbolic meanings of facilities. The more stigmatized the facility, that is, the greater its negative externalities, the more vigorous the resistance and the greater the distance at which it would be tolerated. Yet at the same time many facilities may be functionally necessary, such as public housing or an urban expressway. The solution, of course, is to tolerate and, indeed, support the construction of an expressway in somebody else's neighborhood. In this manner the degree of control that a neighborhood can exert over local development will evidently influence strongly the location in the city of public and private facilities with their attendant externality fields. Neighborhood associations will use a variety of tactics to regulate change in their area of jurisdiction, including strict zoning and bylaw control and the cultivation of formal representatives and informal allies in city hall. Inevitably, politically weaker districts will fare poorly in such maneuvering.

Suburban Exclusion

In the suburbs there is a much more explicit strategy for defending one's own. Suburban localism carries with it political legitimacy; the result is that neighborhood interests assume a political form (Evans, 1980). The suburb thus has veto power over its externality field, both in terms of land use and, indirectly but no less deliberately, in regulating the entry of social groups. Political fragmentation therefore permits exclusion to be practiced by suburban municipalities. In this manner the suburbs are essentially conservative, dedicated to the status quo. The Polish inner suburb of Hamtramck, an autonomous municipality entirely surrounded by the city of Detroit, is perhaps a metaphor of the inward-looking suburban mind, organized to uphold a distinctive way of life and to keep out any groups who could not or would not subscribe to its definition of urbanity (Wood, 1955). Fragmentation and local autonomy are the essence of suburban, and perhaps of American, life. Newton (1978) has observed that the "proliferation of politically auton- omous suburbs during the first half of this century may have played as important a part in social and political life in the U.S. as the growth of the joint-stock company has played in the development of its economic life."

The extent of fragmentation is staggering. Los Angeles, far from the most balkan- ized of metropolitan areas, is not one city but more than 70, containing more than 600 separate taxing bodies, and Greater New York has its celebrated "1400 governments" (Wood, 1961). The effects of such fragmentation include the wasteful duplication of municipal services, taxation inequities, and an incapacity to deal with metropolitanwide problems. In addition there are a number of local anachronisms such as changing street names and variable local codes and bylaws.

Zoning is the great exclusionary weapon of the suburbs, the monopoly tool for sustaining the suburban ideal (Danielson, 1976). A common tactic is large-lot zoning, thereby ensuring high lot and housing prices which will squeeze lower-income groups out of the market. One study of suburban house prices around 13 metropolitan areas in the Northeast and Midwest of the United States concluded that restrictive residential zoning might lead to housing price differentials of as much as 50 percent (Hamilton, 1978). In suburban Cuyahoga County, outside Cleveland, two-thirds of available land zoned for single-family dwellings was assigned to a minimum of half-acre lots, whereas in neighboring Geauga County, 85 percent of residentially zoned land was in lots of at least an acre (Cox, 1973). Around Boston an elaborate network of restrictive zoning serves the same exclusionary purpose in the suburbs that have developed since 1950 (Figure 9.8). The widespread residential restriction on multiple-family units and duplexes (two-family units) together with minimum lot size requirements impose a near monopoly control on the character of new households who may enter the suburbs. This "country club" ideology engenders a landscape where first arrivals are heavily favored over later entries as the excess of housing demand over supply sustains an inflationary land market (Bergman, 1974). Zoning out multiple-family buildings is of course a means of barring the poor. In a celebrated case outside St. Louis, the small community of Blackjack rapidly incorporated itself as a municipality and produced a discriminatory zoning plan in order to block a proposal by the Methodist Church to construct low-density racially mixed housing in multiple units on land it already owned (Forman, 1971).

Another side of exclusionary zoning is fiscal zoning as municipalities seek to attract only high "ratables" while at the same time minimizing their overall provision of services. Large lot zoning contributes to such selective recruitment, for it admits a small, affluent population requiring limited municipal services while excluding lower-status groups with their heavier call upon public services. In this manner the suburban ideology of defending one's own easily turns into a reality of "beggar my neighbor" as more vulnerable communities find themselves burdened with an excessive share of needy residents. In-

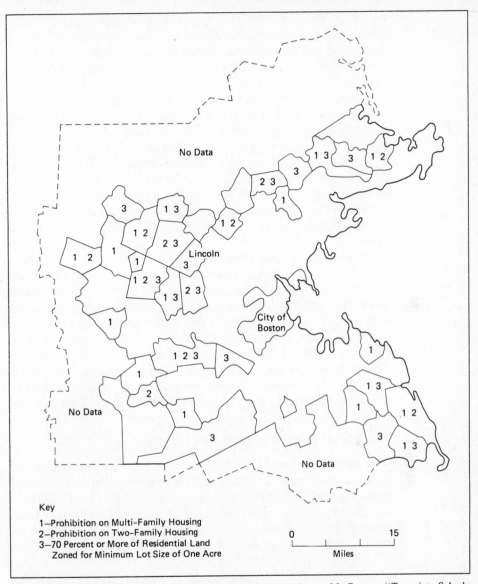

Figure 9.8   Restrictive residential zoning in suburban Boston. (*Source*: M. Conzen, "Town into Suburb: Boston's Expanding Fringe." Pp. 37–49 in C. Browning (ed.), *Population and Urbanized Area Growth in Megalopolis, 1950–1970*. University of North Carolina at Chapel Hill, Dept. of Geography, Studies in Geography No. 7, 1974, figure 1d. Reprinted by permission.)

asmuch as the inviolability of suburban space is predicated on the strength of the zoning controls, zoning frequently provides the basis of suburban politics: "Zoning holds the suburbs together, it props up social classes, it literally keeps the city out, and it excludes all of the influences of the city as well" (Linowes and Allensworth, 1973:65).

Since the mid 1970s, the misuse of legislation protecting the environment has delivered a new weapon to the arsenal of suburban exclusion. A no-growth movement has emerged in a number of wealthy suburbs and small towns such as Petaluma and Palo Alto outside San Francisco (Frieden, 1979; Evans, 1980). Although claiming the legitimacy of the protection of environmental quality, such an ideology also serves the purpose of excluding entry to new residents, not simply the poor but also new middle-class households. In suburban Boston, a number of the same wealthier suburbs that practice restrictive zoning (Figure 9.8) have been most active in acquiring land for conservation purposes, thereby securing it against future development (Conzen, 1974). The suburban community of Lincoln, one of the richer suburbs, had 70 percent of its residential land zoned for single-family residences with a minimum lot size of 1 acre; in addition the town had acquired over 1000 acres of land for conservation purposes. Not surprisingly, it had also failed to construct any low- and moderate-cost housing despite a state fair housing act that required a 10 percent target for more affordable housing in each community.

Protection of open space, heritage sites, and the green belt has also provided a rationale for exclusionary practices in British cities, particularly in the suburbs around London. The British suburbanites fear the loss of environmental amenity and increases in local taxes to support lower-income householders, but most of all they seem to fear a "status loss" from the construction of local public housing (Young and Kramer, 1978). The preservation of this status of "favoured residential areas" is the task of suburban politicians. In the United States it has also been suggested that concern over status loss by suburbanites is a major impediment to an open housing market in the suburbs (Berry et al., 1976). Once again, we see the potency of the existential surfaces reviewed in Chapter 5 in ordering the social and political geography of the city.

The Spatial Pattern of Land Use Change

With such a motley cast of coalitions as finance and property entrepreneurs, the different levels and departments of government alternately promoting economic growth and social welfare objectives, and residents' groups committed to local benefits, where does land use change occur in the city and what form does it take? In this section we shall first examine the spatial distribution of change and, second, place this pattern within the context of the city as an arena of groups with different access to influence and power.

The Geography of Urban Development

The geography of land use change has been comprehensively described for Toronto, which for present purposes we may regard as broadly representative of other metropolitan centers in North America (Bourne and Doucet, 1973). During the 1960s there were some marked changes in the land use composition of the metropolitan area, even allowing for a certain caution in interpreting the data. The proportion of undeveloped land fell by over a quarter, and there were significant increases in all land use categories except open space. Residential uses increased by over 6000 acres, and institutional and industrial uses by about 2000 acres apiece. In percentage terms, major expansion categories included universities and schools, government, and apartment and row housing. The relatively small change in office space is a function of both the use of ground level acres rather than floor space in the data and the 1968 endpoint, which predates the period of most rapid office construction. Standardizing land use change revealed those categories to have expanded more rapidly than the population itself. Educational and governmental uses and also land under high-density housing grew at a faster rate between 1963 and 1968 than did the population for the metropolitan area.

Equally informative is the geographical distribution of change during the 1960s (Figure 9.9); a subsequent extension of the analysis up to 1971 did not suggest any discordant spatial trends (Bourne, 1976b). The pattern of change was complex, but certain regularities are evident. The major area of transformation was the suburbs, where in some census tracts over 30 percent of the land changed uses, primarily from undeveloped uses to single-family dwellings and retailing and institutional facilities. Second, there was core area redevelopment: the expansion of office, commercial, and apartment space and transitional uses such as parking, with the demolition of older structures. In some tracts adjacent to the CBD, 10–30 percent of the total area changed uses in only 5 years. The remaining major change categories were not as locationally specific. They included the construction and expansion of urban infrastructure—parks, expressways, and utilities—and finally the expansion or decline of specialized nucleated land use types (Bourne and Doucet, 1973).

A major distinction can be drawn between the two major sequences of change in the metropolitan area. The first, peripheral development, involves mainly the conversion of vacant land primarily at the city's advancing edge. The second category, redevelopment, involves a recycling of existing urban uses. Within the city of Toronto, land use succession during the 1950s consisted of the conversion of vacant land on 25–50 percent of land parcels; thus succession implied a recycling of urban uses for 50–75 percent of parcels (Bourne, 1971). Obviously these proportions would shift in the case of peripheral development. Both forms of development might well achieve a redistribution of costs and benefits to urban interest groups, both directly and through the modification of externality fields.

The Political Channelling of Spatial Change

The impact of urban change since 1950 from urban renewal and freeway programs alone has been immense; during the peak years of the federal highway program in the United States, upward of 50,000 people were being displaced annually. Consistently it has been in poorer and minority inner areas where these impacts have been felt most heavily. Poorer districts have been less sophisticated politically in protecting local interests, being less likely to seek information, organize, or resist redevelopment (Cox and McCarthy, 1980). In Los Angeles, the placing of grievances before the city's highway department had a high positive correlation with income ($r = 0.88$) and a negative correlation with nonwhite status ($r = -0.73$); clearly there is not equality of access in the distribution of protest (Schneider, 1973).

Figure 9.9 Index of land use change, metropolitan Toronto, 1963–1968. (*Source:* L. Bourne and M. Doucet, "Components of Urban Land Use Change and Physical Growth." Pp. 83–103 in L. Bourne et al. (eds.), *The Form of Cities in Central Canada.* Toronto: University of Toronto Press, 1973, fig. 6.1. Reprinted by permission.)

> 30%
10–30
3–10
1–3
0–1

Miles

0   1   2   3   4   5

One result has been that poorer neighborhoods have borne an undue share of direct and externality costs of the freeway program. In Cleveland, the interstate freeway system dislocated an aging immigrant district; 60 percent of a resident sample claimed they were "very upset" at having to move, and in a re-survey several years later, 39 percent held to this response. The most penalized were the poor and the elderly, for after displacement lower-income residents found it three times more difficult to establish new friendships as did higher-income residents, and older households experienced six times more difficulty than did younger households (Colony, 1972). The social costs fall where they can least easily be borne. Nonwhite neighborhoods have suffered a disproportionate share of dislocation, with blacks accounting for almost 20 percent of dislocated people in 1970. Seley (1970) has described the notorious dismemberment of a black business district in Nashville by a kink added as an afterthought in the alignment of Interstate 40. This freeway section eliminated Jefferson Avenue, the main business thoroughfare in North Nashville, together with 650 homes and 27 apartment buildings. When the alignment was referred (too late) to the courts, the State Highway Commissioner declared he had attached total credibility to his own engineers' reports and had not carried out an economic impact analysis for North Nashville, even though I-40 had been detoured elsewhere in response to the lobbying of various commercial groups.

Indeed, it was only when more powerful communities and lobbyists resisted freeway encroachment that opposition began to be successful. The introduction of professionals—lawyers, academics, community workers, planners—into the freeway debate shifted the balance away from the major proponents, big business and big government (Pendakur, 1972). It has been claimed that the outcry against Toronto's Spadina Expressway, which successfully led to its abandonment, arose only when Spadina threatened middle-class neighborhoods. Evidently there is a hierarchy of neighborhood power in Toronto as in other cities. Bunge has suggested that a surrogate measure of local power is provided by the degree of absentee ownership and nonconforming land use (Figure 9.10). It is worth noting that the only inner city district emerging strongly on this index is Rosedale, a high-status "establishment" neighborhood, comparable to Boston's Beacon Hill, with strict zoning enforcement. Rosedale was also the only inner city district in Toronto where no appreciable land use change was registered during the 1960s (Figure 9.9).

In contrast to the Rosedales and Beacon Hills with their establishment political connections are inner city districts occupied by minorities. It is instructive, for example, to ponder the fate of North America's Chinatowns. In Montreal, the combination of federal government growth and Mayor Drapeau's civic boosterism led to the demolition of a section of Chinatown and the threatened encroachment of federal office towers (Louder, 1975). In Vancouver, Chinatown was selected for the alignment of a 120-foot-wide freeway in 1967; this proposal, which was defeated after middle-class opposition, stimulated a civic reform movement in the city. The Oriental community of Seattle was less fortunate, for its old International District is now the site of the city's domed stadium. Even the large Chinese community in San Francisco, with its significant tourist function, has not been spared the ravages of core expansion; symbolically, the Chinese cultural center is now a second-floor office in a new Holiday Inn (Figures 9.11, 9.13).

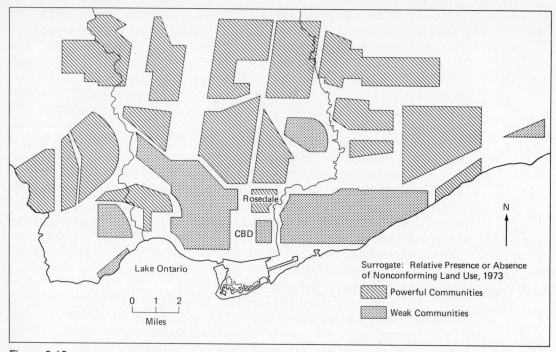

Figure 9.10 A measure of neighborhood political strength in Toronto. (*Source*: W. Bunge and R. Bordessa, *The Canadian Alternative: Survival, Expeditions, and Urban Change*. York University, Dept. of Geography, Geographical Monographs No. 2, 1975, fig. 13. Reprinted by permission.)

Inner city communities have only limited jurisdiction over their neighborhoods and little ability to check the expansion of downtown commercial uses. The downtown corporate and commercial interests often form a tightly bonded oligopoly with the expertise, resources, and informal connections that can out-maneuver a loose coalition of citizens, especially if these are from minority districts. In San Francisco, as elsewhere, these development boosters are interwoven in a formidable oligarchy of interlocking directorates and overlapping board representation (Figure 9.12). They have provided an imperious presence in civic politics and development decisions and, when their interests are at stake, have had a capacity to be invariably on the winning side in issues of public decision making (Table 9.4). Although the Municipal Conference, a coalition of property owners and downtown businessmen, was selective about the civic issues in which its members were overtly involved, their endorsements were successful over 90 percent of the time, whereas citizens and labor groups had an appreciably lower success rate of 50–60 percent.

The resolution of these variable political forces in urban land use development may be illustrated in any number of urban renewal projects. We will conclude this section by a more detailed examination of one such project which had received $46 million in federal grants (excluding indirect subsidies) by 1974—the Yerba Buena redevelopment in San Francisco (Hartman, 1974; Hartman and Kessler, 1978; Wirt, 1974). The Yerba

Figure 9.11   Commerical encroachment: the Holiday Inn, incorporating the Chinese Cultural Center, China-town, San Francisco.

Buena project represents the southward expansion of the commercial core, just as en-croachment into Chinatown represents its westward expansion (Figure 9.13). Market Street has formed a traditional boundary between social groups in the city: to the north are the retail and financial districts of the downtown core, and to the south an entourage of cheap hotels, which provide permanent accommodation to an aged male population, and a supportive network of stores and social service agencies. The Yerba Buena proposal envisaged a dramatic incursion across this boundary. It was to be one of North America's largest urban renewal developments, a half-billion-dollar project spilling over 12 city blocks and displacing 4000 residents and over 700 businesses (Hartman, 1974). In their place would be constructed a convention center, a sports center, and hotel, office, and retail facilities.

The Yerba Buena Center was a scheme of big business and big government. The proposal was conceived by corporate and financial groups associated with the Bay Area Council (Figure 9.12). In addition to the Bay Area Council, the boosters of Yerba Buena also worked through the San Francisco Planning and Urban Renewal Association (SPUR). Although SPUR was designated by the mayor as an official citizen's group, it was in fact dominated by big business interests with linkages to the major banks and utility companies (Figure 9.12). The case for Yerba Buena was taken up by the powerful San Francisco Redevelopment Agency (SFRA), which renewed the earlier vision of a down-town hotelier-developer for a major redevelopment south of Market Street. Supporters

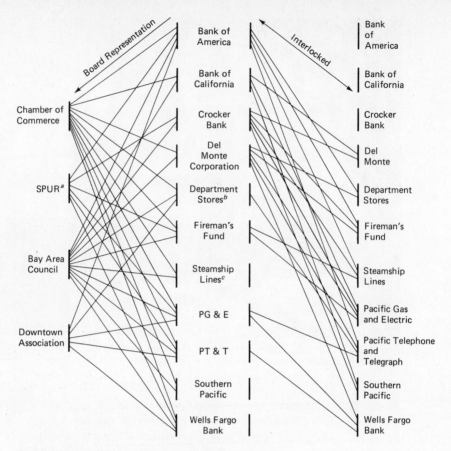

Board Representation

Interlocked

Chamber of Commerce

SPUR[a]

Bay Area Council

Downtown Association

Bank of America

Bank of California

Crocker Bank

Del Monte Corporation

Department Stores[b]

Fireman's Fund

Steamship Lines[c]

PG & E

PT & T

Southern Pacific

Wells Fargo Bank

Bank of America

Bank of California

Crocker Bank

Del Monte

Department Stores

Fireman's Fund

Steamship Lines

Pacific Gas and Electric

Pacific Telephone and Telegraph

Southern Pacific

Wells Fargo Bank

[a] SPUR—San Franciso Planning and Urban Renewal Association

[b] Emporium-Capwell complex of 28 stores

[c] Natomas, Pacific Far East, and American President Lines

Figure 9.12   Overlapping corporate linkages in San Francisco. (*Source*: F. Wirt, *Power in the City: Decision-making in San Francisco*. Berkeley, Cal.: University of California Press, 1974, fig. 8. Reprinted by permission.)

of the proposal were banking and corporate interests; hoteliers, restauranteurs, and other members of the tourist industry; construction unions; both city newspapers (which have headquarters near the site); and Mayor Alioto, the candidate of the business lobby, after his election in 1967. Funding from the federal government was authorized in 1969 after the project blocks had been designated as "blighted," less as a result of their structural condition than in order to expedite renewal and qualify for HUD support.

Critical to redevelopment was the removal of existing residents and land uses. This was rationalized by SFRA in another example of organizational labelling. Just as the area had been defined as "blighted," so its residents became "transients," "winos," and "bums." Surveys by opposition groups showed both sets of labels to be self-serving

TABLE 9.4 RATE OF SUCCESSFUL ENDORSEMENTS BY LOBBYISTS IN SAN FRANCISCO REFERENDA

Recommender	1968		1969		1970		1971		TOTAL	
	N	% Won	N	% Won	N	% Won	N	% Won	N	% Won
Municipal Conference[a]	1	100	4	100	2	100	4	75	11	91
Civil Service Ass'n.	5	80	1	0	4	75	5	80	15	73
Chamber of Commerce	9	100	4	25	7	57	4	75	24	71
Downtown Ass'n.	6	83	—	—	7	43	2	100	15	67
Labor Council	20	80	11	27	13	46	16	62	60	58
Citizen Committees[b]	5	20	4	50	7	100	7	43	23	56
Mayor Alioto	14	79	12	25	14	43	18	67	58	55
Municipal Improvement League[c]	1	100	4	25	—	—	6	67	11	55
Liberals[d]	2	100	2	0	1	100	1	0	6	50
League of Women Voters	3	67	4	25	1	0	2	0	10	30

Source: F. Wirt, *Power in the City: Decision-Making in San Francisco.* Berkeley: University of California Press, 1974, Table 8, p. 62. Reprinted by permission.
[a]Organization of apartment house and building owners and managers, retailers, realtors, and the Downtown Association.
[b]Ad hoc groups, usually not active across two elections.
[c]Organization of 18 city employee groups.
[d]Either groups like NAACP or recognized liberal names.

rather than accurate; fewer than 10 percent of hotels were substandard; alcoholism was a problem of only 15 percent of the population; and more than one-third of residents had lived in the district more than 10 years (Hartman, 1974). But according to the perception of SFRA, they had no place in the area; in the words of its director: "This land is too valuable to permit poor people to park on it." In 1969, the Tenants and Owners in Opposition to Redevelopment (TOOR) was founded in the south of Market area to contest the project, supported by liberal lawyers, academics, and community organizers. Their strategy was to carry the issue to the courts and to claim there that the rights of American citizens guaranteed by law were being infringed by the demolition, displacement, and relocation practices of SFRA.

Recourse to the courts has proven unexpectedly fruitful to the opposition groups. The project has been challenged and delayed, and significant concessions have been won by TOOR, including injunctions against SFRA displacement practices and a court charge that compensatory housing must be built, including a certain number of units in the south of Market area. The political and legal jockeying since 1970 has included the appearance of Mayor Alioto in court as a special counsel in support of SFRA's policies, condemnation by one of the city's newspapers of the judge ruling in favor of TOOR, and separate suits taken out against the project on environmental grounds. The Yerba Buena controversy has forced into the open the interlocking coalition of the city's power elite and exposed for critical discussion both its taken-for-granted assumptions concerning "the public interest" and the dubious logic on which those assumptions are based.

From a broader perspective the controversy over the Yerba Buena Center highlights the strongly political character of urban land use change, and the power of business interests and local government to act as change agents, effecting a net redistribution of direct and indirect costs and benefits to the social groups who are involved. In the case

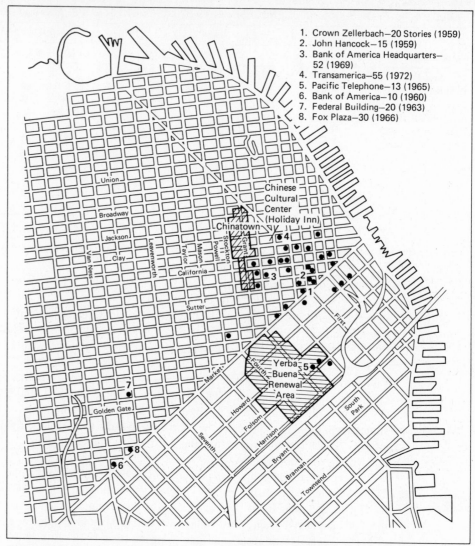

1. Crown Zellerbach—20 Stories (1959)
2. John Hancock—15 (1959)
3. Bank of America Headquarters—52 (1969)
4. Transamerica—55 (1972)
5. Pacific Telephone—13 (1965)
6. Bank of America—10 (1960)
7. Federal Building—20 (1963)
8. Fox Plaza—30 (1966)

Figure 9.13   New office construction and core encroachment in San Francisco. (*Source:* Adapted from Jean Vance, "The Cities by San Francisco Bay." In J. Adams (ed.), *Contemporary Metropolitan America,* Vol. 2. Cambridge, Mass.: Ballinger, 1976, fig. 18, p. 284. Copyright 1976 Ballinger Publishing Company. Reprinted by permission.)

of Yerba Buena, this initiative did not pass smoothly to consummation as it had so often before; most commentators are agreed that had the project been implemented 5 years earlier, opposition would not have arisen. It remains to be seen whether the Yerba Buena Center will symbolize a landmark in a trend to a more just and equitable management of urban development or simply a temporary interruption to the inequitable tradition of elite-initiated and elite-dominated land use change.

The Geography of Land Use Conflict

The Yerba Buena controversy illustrates the close relationship between land use change and land use conflict. Much of the geographic literature on locational conflict has been concerned with externality effects associated with the siting or expansion of a public facility, varying from an urban expressway to a community mental health center (Cox and Reynolds, 1974; Dear, 1977a). This literature has provided a profusion of empirical case studies which have clarified the nature of decision-making processes in the public sector and has also advanced useful policy and welfare suggestions. But at the same time it offers an incomplete dossier on urban land use conflict. The effects of private, as opposed to public, development and direct, as opposed to indirect, costs have been underemphasized. Nor has the amassing of case studies yet advanced discussion of theoretical issues; one attempt to extend Ralf Dahrendorf's conflict theory to locational conflict ended inconclusively (Seley, 1974), and a second attempt to present the issue in a Marxian framework is equally unpersuasive (Harvey, 1978). In sum, the partial nature of the locational conflict research leaves it too divorced from questions of the social distribution of power; it is this conceptual and theoretical gap which, as Evans (1976) has noted in a perceptive review, betrays the origins of much of this research in neo-classical economics.

Consequently this chapter has taken a broader perspective, assessing both privately and publicly initiated change and relating these to the differential access to power of various social groups in the city. But if this is a more complete position conceptually, it remains to generate a fuller *empirical* inventory of land use conflict. Figure 9.14 shows an attempt to compile such an inventory, describing all land use conflicts occurring in Montreal in 1975 as reported in the daily issues of the *Montreal Star*. Such a compilation of conflicts, derived from a detailed content analysis of newspapers (or from the minutes of city council meetings), does supply a fuller picture of overall patterns. However, the data are mediated by these gatekeepers and are subject to potential distortion; in the case of Montreal, for example, analysis of an English-language daily will not give a conflict pattern identical to that in a French-language newspaper. In addition, there are the normal coding difficulties which are encountered with the method of content analysis.

Nevertheless, such analysis does offer the best surrogate for the overall incidence of land use conflict. The method also allows a classification of issues by land use type and a rough ranking of the salience of issues in terms of the amount of newspaper coverage they receive. Such an examination can reveal the short-term flux in conflict issues. In 1975, disputes over the new Mirabel airport provided the major land use controversy in Montreal, to be succeeded in 1976 by the Olympic stadium; in the former year more conflicts were concerned with redevelopment than with any other category, but in 1976 preservation issues ranked first. Table 9.5 shows that conflicts were particularly associated with the conversion of land from low-density uses (single-family residential, open space) to higher-density uses (multiple-unit residential, transportation). This is consistent with the claim that freeway and high-rise development were the major irritants prompting community opposition in Toronto (Lemon, 1974). The actors involved in these conflicts show a predictable grouping (Table 9.6). The proponents of change were invariably the development industry and government; with the traditionally weak

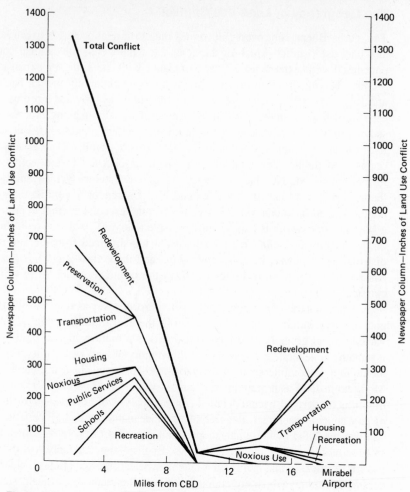

Figure 9.14   Location and type of land use conflict in Greater Montreal, 1975. (*Source*: Compiled from *Montreal Star*.)

status of elected officials other than the mayor in Montreal, Mayor Drapeau's civic bureaucracy was a more significant initiator than were the city's aldermen. In contrast, the opponents of change were typically householders, neighborhood groups, and voluntary organizations (compare Janelle, 1977; Ley and Mercer, 1980). From these groupings we might suppose that the net effect of proposed changes would have been to worsen the lot of local citizens while favoring institutional interests—which may or may not have coincided with some broader public interest. An assessment of which groups were successful in implementing their will (Max Weber's definition of power) cannot be stated simply, for the redistributive effects of change may be complex, and conflict resolution itself may take several years. A preliminary evaluation of Montreal conflicts that terminated in 1976 suggested surprisingly that city hall was most likely to secure its ob-

TABLE 9.5 LAND USE CHARACTERISTICS OF CONFLICT SITES IN
MONTREAL, 1975–1976

	Present Land Use	Proposed Land Use
Single-family dwellings, duplex	19%	4%
Multiple-dwelling units	14.5	20.5
Condominiums	5	9
Government-subsidized units	0	2
Industrial	0	0
Commercial/retail	8	13.5
Transportation	8	23
Parks and recreation	7	13.5
Public institutional	16	9
Public utilities	4	4
Agriculture	2.5	0
Open space	16	1

Source: Compiled from *Montreal Star*, 1975–1976.

jectives, followed by citizens, and finally the development lobby. If this conclusion is
correct, then it represents a considerable shift from the situation even a few years ago
(Aubin, 1977). The arrival of a modicum of participatory reform in the city may be
attributed to the emergence for the first time of an opposition reform party, which won
one-third of the seats in city hall in 1974; in addition, several citizen victories in preservation issues were attributable to the direct intervention of the provincial government
to save heritage sites.

   On the basis of a detailed analysis of land use conflict in London, Ontario (Janelle
and Millward, 1976; Janelle, 1977), a schema for the distribution of locational conflicts
has been suggested (Figure 9.15). Although this schema has a rather passive view of
power, it does integrate the forces for change with a responsive land use pattern. As in
Montreal, redevelopment and preservation issues in the downtown core attracted major
coverage; in the suburbs, key issues were the provision of public services and schools,
and the encroachment of noxious facilities. Between these high-profile regions, the inner
suburbs are more tranquil areas of limited land use conflict, in large measure because
they represent landscapes in early maturity, where little physical change is occurring. In
London it appears that city hall serves a more significant role as land use broker than in
Montreal, acting as a somewhat more frequent opponent of development proposals (Ja-

TABLE 9.6 LOBBYISTS INVOLVED IN LAND USE CONFLICTS
IN MONTREAL, 1975–1976

	Proponents	Opponents
Households	5%	23%
Neighborhood Groups	0	23
Civic Organizations	7.5	18.5
Developers/Entrepreneurs	33	12.5
Elected Officials	26	11
Administrative Officials	28	12

Source: Compiled from *Montreal Star*, 1975–1976.

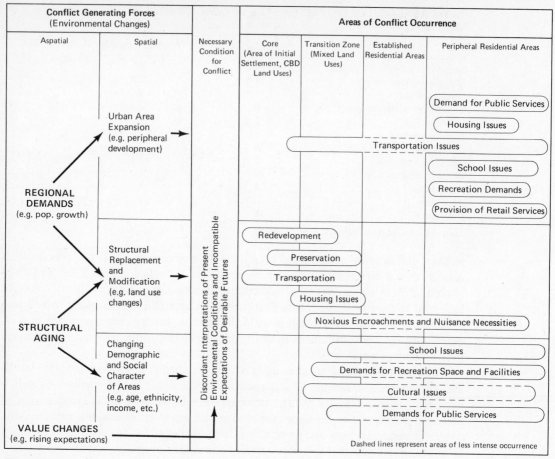

Figure 9.15   A schema for locational conflicts in the city. (*Source:* D. Janelle and H. Millward, ''Locational Conflict Patterns and Urban Ecological Structure,'' *Tijdschrift voor Economische en Sociale Geografie* 67 (1976):102–113, fig. 1. Reprinted by permission.)

nelle, 1977). A number of comparative studies are needed to extend Janelle's innovative research to larger cities, where some of these relationships may be tested more fully. In addition, it remains necessary to place the empirical record of conflict in a broader theoretical context linking it with processes of social change in society (Ley and Mercer, 1980). We shall attempt such an integration in Chapter 11.

Conclusion

In this chapter we have examined the actions and interactions of distinctive interest groups in the city and the implications for patterns of land use change. The social groups we considered in Part 3 have a configuration of external as well as internal relations, and the make-up of the former determines a system of coalitions and conflicts in the city as an arena. The three major sets of actors represent entrepreneurial, governmental, and local community interests, and much of urban politics consists of bargaining between these groups for discretion over land use stability and change. Access to power will give a victorious coalition far greater authority than its market position alone would allow.

In this arena the positions of entrepreneurial and local citizen interests are relatively consistent and predictable. More equivocal, and therefore both more decisive and more theoretically interesting, is the stand of government, itself highly differentiated into several levels, each with a myriad of departments. Traditionally, municipal government has been particularly sympathetic to business interests, as indeed has a majority of citizens, including labor unions, for whom growth means high employment and wage levels. But more recently, municipal government has been showing increasing sensitivity to community as well as to business needs, goaded by more senior governments with their longer commitment to welfare criteria and also by a more active enforcement policy in the courts. A more thorough theoretical discussion of these trends will be taken up in the final chapter. But before that, a more detailed reckoning is necessary of the consequences of social stratification, including the distribution of power and the effects of externally induced change, for the quality of life experienced by various groups of city dwellers.

PART 5

The City as the Home of Man

Chapter 10

The Quality of Urban Life

These crowded cities have done their work: they were the best that a society largely based on selfishness could construct, but they are in the nature of things entirely unadapted to a society in which the social side of our nature is demanding a larger share of recognition

(Ebenezer Howard, 1965:32)

The quality of life experienced by an urban household is a product of the opportunities available for securing those resources which its members hold most dear for their own welfare. In any society there will be constraints on the degree of access to those opportunities, constraints resulting from scarcity and constraints also resulting from the household's position in the social hierarchy. In Chapters 8 and 9 we examined three major sets of constraints that generate a hierarchy of life chances in the advanced nations: the constraint of social class and market power, the constraint of minority ethnic or lifestyle status, and the constraint of access to power. Inequality of life chances is therefore a universal in the city; there is a differential in the relative roles of choice and constraint in the decision making of various social groups.

However, a household's quality of life is not an invariable consequence of its life chances or biographical situation, for access to opportunities is mediated through the value structure of the life-world. Objective life chances take on substance in a milieu where they may be modified, diverted, or amplified by such factors as the nature of personality and attitude, the quality of social support systems, the level of individual aspirations, the extent of community sentiment, and religious or other values which provide alternative definitions of the ingredients that contribute to individual and social well-being. What, then, comprises the quality of life? Maslow (1970) has identified a needs hierarchy that progresses from such basic survival needs as food, health, and shelter to more intangible qualities like the satisfaction of mental and emotional states. These "higher needs" are no less essential for the satisfactory fulfillment of our personal and social nature. A survey in the industrial town of Dundee, Scotland, showed that family and neighborhood stability was placed second only to health in a ranking of perceived needs, and ahead of employment and housing (Knox and MacLaran, 1978). Among

American college students, for whom the basic needs are most likely secured, satisfactory interpersonal relations and spiritual needs were placed in first rank, and a variety of other personal and interpersonal needs were placed ahead of more material objectives (D. Smith, 1979). There is some variability among social groups in the perception of needs and problems; residents with higher socioeconomic status in Fresno and Denver showed greater sensitivity to environmental quality than did lower-status and minority respondents, who predictably isolated employment and public service provision as of greater concern (D. Smith, 1979; Lovrich, 1974). The Dundee study also showed that significantly different ratings were recorded between neighborhoods for the importance of 9 out of 11 indicators of well-being (Knox and MacLaran, 1978).

An assessment of the quality of life is not as straightforward as it might seem, for there are separate problems in identifying relevant indicators, in measuring them, and in utilizing them in intergroup comparisons. Data on qualitative or subjective dimensions of well-being are particularly elusive, and there is a tendency to disregard them in favor of agency statistics only because they are inaccessible, not because they are unimportant. Moreover, even with objective indicators, ''more'' may not mean ''better,'' for the meeting of needs may not lead to the satisfaction of wants (Leiss, 1976). In this context one may observe the paradox of an increase in supply of a specified good leading to a decrease in satisfaction, if aspirations have simultaneously risen.

This chapter will begin by reviewing the contributions of urban indicators to an assessment of quality of life in the city. But indicators provide only the first step, for a map of livability isolines demands explanation. Several interpretations of the unequal distribution of life chances in the city will be examined, together with policy responses which follow from each of the perspectives.

The Development of Social Accounting

Since the mid 1960s a major concern with assessing and monitoring national levels of what has variously come to be known as social well-being, livability, or the quality of life has arisen both in government and in the academic community. This movement is associated in part with a changing national perspective away from a single-minded focus on economic success to a more plural set of objectives and underlying values. In recent years, even economic growth has been challenged in some circles, and serious discussion of no-growth or steady-state economics has occurred. This trend has been fuelled by a series of historic events which have precipitated repeated crises over fundamental social values: the movement for civil rights in the United States and in the late 1970s their stark suppression in the Soviet Union and elsewhere; the question of the ethical legitimacy of the Vietnam War; the crisis of faith in national government following the Watergate scandal; the prospect of ecocatastrophe, ''the crisis of the planet,'' as a result of mindless exploitation of the environment; the moral ambivalence of the wealth of Western nations in the light of pervasive famine in the Third World; the very definition of life itself in the disputes over abortion and euthanasia; and, not least, the irony of a society whose technology could probe the secrets of outer space but whose civil order was wrought by division and violence, culminating in urban riots that in the United States led to nearly

200 deaths and almost 14,000 associated cases of arson between 1965 and 1968. While the Apollo space program carried global history into a spectacular new age, the American city was being put to the torch by its own alienated citizens: first by minorities, mainly blacks, and second by middle-class university students, the children of the technocrats.

There were other, less cataclysmic, reasons to encourage social scientists and governments to become more self-conscious social accountants. Beyond the alienation of the inner cities, the growing wealth of the suburbs suspended concern with basic needs and transferred attention to the higher levels of Maslow's need hierarchy and particularly to the pursuit of self-actualization. The convergence of increasing real wealth and more leisure time created new opportunities for consumption and constructive forms of self-fulfillment. The growing proportion of elderly and retired citizens in the population formed in part a new leisure class. For some, at least, there was a new "humanistic concern for what living was all about" (Liu, 1976:2). It is a characteristic irony of our society that this humanistic metaphysic is to be diagnosed by technological paraphernalia; the first step in understanding greater livability is that quality should be quantified!

Clearly, qualitative change has become a managerial problem. Michael Springer, one of the leaders of the social accounting movement, has written a paper with the illuminating title "Social indicators, reports and accounts: toward the management of society" (Springer, 1970). Government is taking a renewed interest in the lives of its citizens across an ever-growing range of dimensions, a trend which has received critical as well as positive commentary (Gross and Straussman, 1974). For some, the notion of "a technology of human ends" (Flax et al., 1975) might be a daunting proposition. In 1969, the U.S. government produced a seminal document, *Toward a Social Report* (U.S. Department of Health, Education, and Welfare, 1969), in which it proposed for the first time a systematic accounting of the nation's social health to complement the traditional monitoring of economic indicators. Since then similar reports have been published in other Western nations; in Britain, a collection of indicators with the title *Social Trends* began to appear in 1970. Even the Organization for Economic and Cultural Development (OECD) has broadened its single-minded economic horizons "to devote more attention to how the extra wealth which the growth process creates may be better directed to improvements of the quality of life and the meeting of social aspirations" (quoted in Coates, Johnston, and Knox, 1977:56). In this debate, geographers are playing a not insignificant role, with contributions ranging from research monographs to policy recommendations and from social criticism to technical methodology (Harvey, 1973; D. Smith, 1973, 1977; Knox, 1975; Berry et al., 1974; Berry, 1976; Coates, Johnston, and Knox, 1977).

Urban Indicators

Most attempts to develop systematic assessments of life in the city have made use of variables retrieved from government publications. Although such retrieval may be both laborious and frustrating—with forays into various public agencies which often hold noncomparable data inventories—it can provide comprehensive coverage with the possibility of interregional comparisons. But this advantage is also a major shortcoming, for the variables collected may well be fortuitous in their availability. Worse, as critics frequently charge, there is no basis for believing that such indicators necessarily act as significant factors in the experience of urban residents nor, indeed, that interpersonal comparisons of diagnostic variables may even be made. The adequacy of an efficient public transport system has a meaning for an elderly inner city resident different from that for a two-car suburban family; so, too, climatic data may have different implications for sun-seeking tourists and moisture-seeking farmers. Evidently there may be something of a theoretical gulf between objective and subjective assessments of the quality of urban life.

Objective Indicators

As we saw in Chapter 2, response to the industrial cities of Britain and North America in the nineteenth century was a curious blend of awe at the level of technical achievement and outrage at the conditions of social life. Even though inequality has always been a feature of urban life, the era of industrial capitalism in its purest form led to stark contrasts of poverty and affluence. In Manchester during the 1840s, Little Ireland was one of the most foul slum areas. The land uses adjacent to this area of perhaps 4000 residents, mostly Irish, testified to the externality field of a social group at the bottom of the pecking order in terms of social class, status, and political power (Figure 10.1). Interspersed among the rows of cottages were cotton mills, an iron foundry, a gasometer, and other industrial premises; bounding it to the north was a railway track; and on the other three sides Little Ireland was enclosed by a meander of the River Medlock, a "coal-black, stagnant, stinking river" (Engels, 1958:71). Engels took some time to describe the foul conditions in this low-lying slum:

> The cottages are very small, old and dirty, while the streets are uneven, partly unpaved, not properly drained and full of ruts. Heaps of refuse, offal and sickening filth are everywhere interspersed with pools of stagnant liquid. The atmosphere is polluted by the stench and is darkened by the thick smoke of a dozen factory chimneys. A horde of ragged women and children swarm about the streets and they are just as dirty as the pigs which wallow happily on the heaps of garbage and in the pools of filth (Ibid.).

Engels estimated an average of 20 people was living within each house, with its two rooms, attic, and wet cellar, with one privy for each six houses. Conditions that were little improved were reported in New York in 1890 (Riis, 1971), in Pittsburgh by the six-volume Pittsburgh Survey in 1914, and in other North American industrial cities. The skewed distribution of life chances in New York afflicted the young in particular, and from 1810 to 1870 the infant mortality rate virtually doubled to a rate of one death for every four births. In the first decade of the twentieth century the Pittsburgh Survey revealed a fourfold differential in mortality rates between different wards in the city (Kellogg, 1914).

The Chicago human ecologists developed further the widespread mapping of social indicators that had been introduced in the social surveys. Their research reports, covering such diverse problem areas as mental illness, crime and delinquency, poverty, vice, and

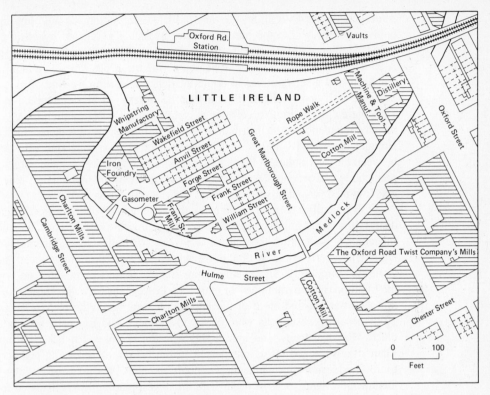

Figure 10.1   The district of Little Ireland, Manchester, 1849. (*Source*: T. W. Freeman, *Pre-Famine Ireland*. Manchester: Manchester University Press, 1957, fig. 8. Reprinted by permission.)

family breakdown, showed a repetitive spatial gradient across the city. The distribution of diagnosed schizophrenia in Chicago, for example, was closely related to the city's ecological structure (Dunham, 1937). Analysis of 7000 cases indicated that rates were 10 times as high in a rooming-house zone of unstable family relations adjacent to the Loop as they were in the suburbs. Delinquency rates followed a similar gradient (Shaw and McKay, 1972), with a regular reduction in levels with distance from the CBD, from nearly 10 percent of adolescents in a zone of up to 2 miles from the Loop to less than 2 percent in the outermost zone. It was on the basis of such consistent distribution maps that Burgess conceived his concentric ring model of urban communities.

These polarized distributions remain substantially unchanged in more recent studies of the geography of crime and health care. The medical geography of Chicago continues to display the same sharp gradients between inner city and suburb (Pyle, 1969). Intercity comparisons between Philadelphia, St. Louis, and Dallas revealed that in the newer, more sprawling Dallas SMSA, health indicators followed a more even distribution with smoother gradients than they did in the older metropolitan areas; in the latter, low-income minority neighborhoods in the inner city had a disproportionate share of deaths from a broad range of medical causes (Megee, 1976). Though the various causes of death show some geographical variation, the most afflicted zones coincide with low-income house-holds, and abrupt income transitions are invariably paralleled by an improved health status. Similar gradients describe the geography of crime (Harries, 1974; Herbert, 1982). A compilation of violent crime in Seattle during the 1960s revealed a familiar downtown emphasis and a sectoral bias in crime incidence following the line of blue-collar neigh-borhoods east and southeast (Figure 10.2). Similarly, crimes committed in Cleveland in 1971 were clustered into a corridor passing from the CBD through the city's East Side, which coincided with the distribution of poor minority groups centered upon the notorious Hough ghetto (Pyle, 1976). In Cleveland, statistical associations were found to exist between the distribution of homicides, rapes, assaults, robberies, and burglaries and some predictable socioeconomic factors describing areas of unemployment, blue-collar work-ers, low-income and poverty families, and the proportion of blacks.

This familiar correlation points to the geographical clustering of indicators of acute distress into what might be called an ecology for evil (Sanford and Comstock, 1971). A fundamental element of this cluster is poverty. In Belfast, male unemployment had the highest intercorrelations with a set of other indicators describing social malaise (Boal, Doherty, Pringle, 1978). On Manhattan island, pockets of poverty are concentrated in the traditional immigrant ports of entry, the Lower East Side and Harlem, where in 1971 up to 40 percent and more of the population were receiving welfare (Figure 10.3). In 1971 these neighborhoods were occupied by racial and linguistic minorities, primarily blacks, Puerto Ricans, and immigrants who did not have English as a mother tongue. Their disadvantaged status reappeared in the results of a reading test administered to fourth-grade pupils in elementary schools in 1969. The map of reading proficiencies identifies the same areas of need, with the lowest reading levels assessed for elementary schools in Harlem and the Lower East Side (Figure 10.4). The interlocking character of urban problems is suggested by simple correlation: moderate but significant correlations exist between reading scores and minority status (Puerto Rican -0.47, black -0.40), and the highest associations occur against poverty (median family income 0.59, percent families below poverty level -0.67), and neighborhood education levels (median school years completed 0.61, percent high school graduates 0.72). Children's reading skills are evidently associated with a broad socioeconomic context into which they are born, an inherited biographical situation which strongly influences their life chances.

Bunge has dramatically illustrated the asymmetric distribution of life chances over the city with his map of infant mortality in Detroit (Figure 10.5). There is a fourfold range in infant death rates between the central city and the suburbs. Central city rates are comparable with those of Third World nations; an American born in central Detroit has the same chances of survival as an infant born in Guyana. In contrast, a suburban child may experience a survival rate comparable to Norway's, which is 50 percent higher than the American average. This same suburban child in Detroit will breathe air that contains one-quarter the dustfall and one-quarter the sulphur dioxide of his inner city counterpart, and his neighborhood will have noise levels at least one-third lower (Jacoby, 1972). His home districts will also contain substantially more recreation space, better equipped schools and libraries, and he will run a lower risk of being struck by a car while at play. He will experience a far lower probability of being a crime victim and of

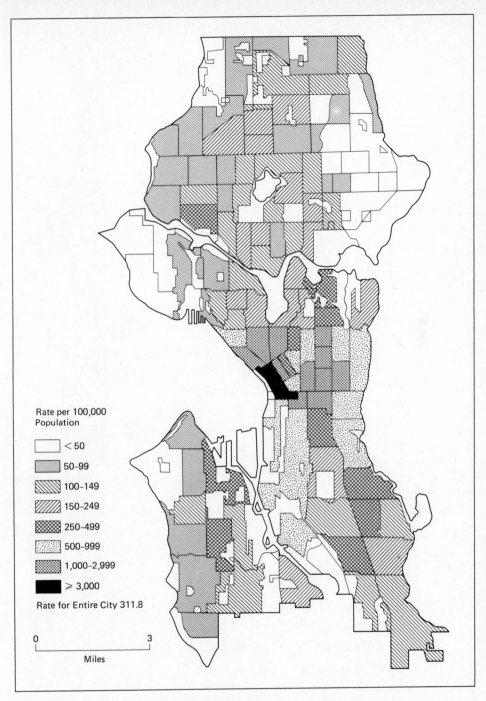

Figure 10.2 Total violent crimes reported in Seattle, 1960–1970. (*Source*: C. Schmid and S. Schmid, *Crime in the State of Washington*. Olympia, Washington: Law and Justice Planning Office, Washington State Planning and Community Affairs Agency, 1972, p. 143. Reprinted by permission.)

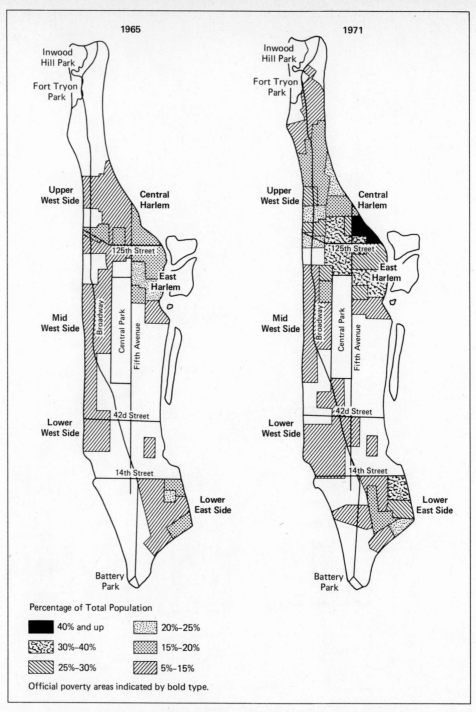

Figure 10.3 The distribution of welfare recipients in Manhattan. (*Source: The New York Times*, April 10, 1972, p. 40. Copyright 1972 by The New York Times Company. Reprinted by permission.)

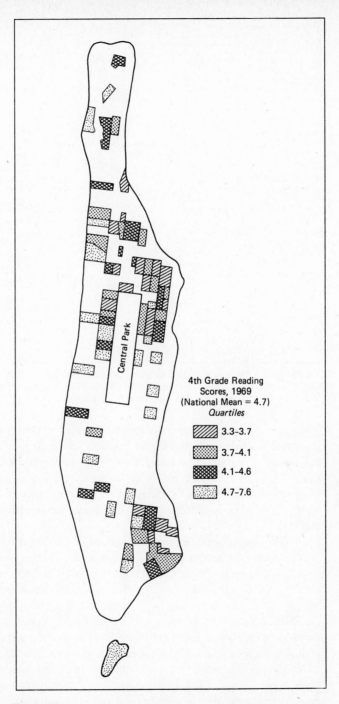

4th Grade Reading
Scores, 1969
(National Mean = 4.7)
Quartiles

▨	3.3–3.7
▨	3.7–4.1
▨	4.1–4.6
▨	4.7–7.6

Central Park

Figure 10.4 Fourth-grade reading scores in Manhattan primary schools.

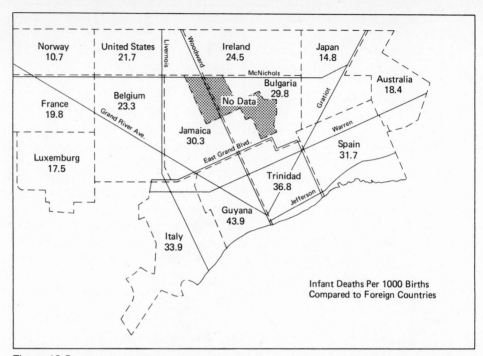

Figure 10.5   The map of infant mortality in Detroit. (*Source*: W. Bunge and R. Bordessa, *The Canadian Alternative: Survival, Expeditions, and Urban Change*. York University, Dept. of Geography, Geographical Monographs No. 2, 1975, fig. 143. Reprinted by permission.)

being introduced to a criminal subculture. Such a skewed distribution of life chances prompted the federal Kerner Commission to revive Benjamin Disraeli's imagery of the two nations, separate and unequal, to describe the worlds of the inner city and the suburb in the United States. Certainly there has been little improvement this century in the map of inequality; the fourfold differential in the geography of infant mortality in Detroit around 1970 was no different from the spatial range observed in Pittsburgh 60 years earlier.

The sharp inequalities in the quality of life within urban areas have been illustrated by a number of attempts to derive a composite livability index. Such an index would need to incorporate a broad range of a household's urban experience, and there has been considerable disagreement over which dimensions should be included in an aggregated assessment and how they should be combined. The policy emphasis on the inner city by the Department of the Environment in Britain has drawn attention to the definition of deprivation areas, and a number of methods to identify areas of need has been adopted, including forms of factor analysis using small-area data (Herbert, 1975b; Holtermann, 1975; Boal et al., 1978). But particularly at the intraurban scale, theory has commonly given way to pragmatism in both the selection of variables and their subsequent integration. At this scale, data availability is a serious constraint, and in developing their index most researchers have followed a simple procedure of adding standardized scores to arrive at a composite value. A quality of life study in Atlanta made use of 11 variables which were reduced to five factors representing the standards of health, public order, housing, socioeconomic status, and density present in each of the city's census tracts in 1970 (Bederman, 1974). These factors were combined by a simple additive procedure that ranked each tract relative to a base value for the city as a whole. A highly polarized quality-of-life surface resulted from the computation (Figure 10.6). The lowest ranking area was grouped around the CBD and in a sector extending east and west. This region of need closely outlined the distribution of the black population; chi-square analysis indicated a relationship between race and quality of life significant at the 0.001 level.

The construction of a quality-of-life index at a more macro scale increases the availability of diagnostic indicators (Smith, 1973). An early assessment of major American cities was made using 14 indicators that represented such additional dimensions as community concern, citizen participation, air pollution levels, and drug addiction—a measure of social disintegration (Flax, 1972); a larger set of 32 indicators was assembled in a comparison of Canada's 22 metropolitan areas as defined by the census (Stewart et al., 1975). Even more ambitious schedules are projected. An environmental impact assessment schedule proposed by the Battelle Institute incorporates items under the headings ecology, environmental pollution, esthetics, and human interest. Included within these latter categories are such criteria as historical significance with five items, and even "mood-atmosphere significance" with four items. The difficulty, of course, is to be able to treat such variables with any form of rigor, quite aside from the intractable problem of developing a standard criterion of values such that interpersonal (or even interregional) welfare comparisons would be possible. Thus, for example, although Liu (1976) seeks to construct a metropolitan quality-of-life scale that is a function of both objective and psychological inputs, the latter based in part on Maslow's qualitative needs hierarchy, in practice his model is largely a product of objective inputs.

Nevertheless, the Liu model does offer one of the most comprehensive comparative quality-of-life reviews of American cities. His assessment of the livability of the 243 SMSAs in the United States in 1970 is a product of over 120 separate indicators, including the major categories of economic, political, environmental, welfare (health and education), and social criteria. The distribution of the aggregate index for the largest SMSAs appears in Figure 10.7. The regional character of quality-of-life scores is evident, with the highest values recorded on the West Coast and in some of the smaller metropolitan areas of the Northeast and the Midwest. No necessary correlation occurred between each of the major factors; the economic component in particular tended to be independent of the others. The most differentiated factors are those of welfare and social life. On both dimensions southern cities perform poorly, and cities of the Northeast are close behind; in contrast, the West Coast cities have high scores, followed by the Midwest. Indeed, for every major category except the economic, a majority of West Coast cities were classed as outstanding or excellent in 1970.

Subjective Indicators

Several criticisms have repeatedly been levelled against objective indicators. At one level the accuracy of the data themselves is in question, for there are systematic biases in the

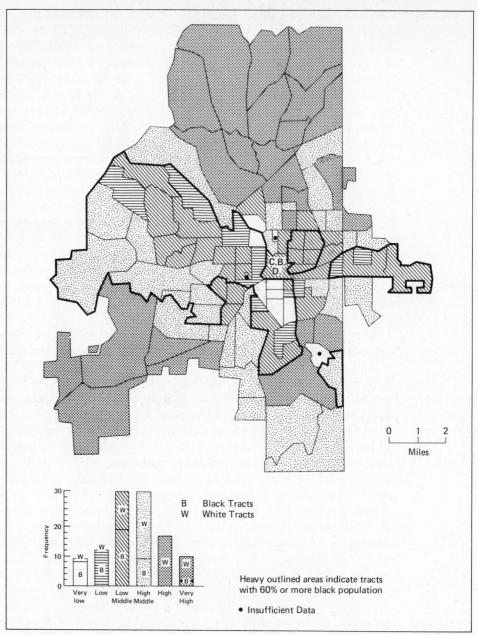

Figure 10.6 The quality of life in Atlanta. (*Source*: S. Bederman, ''The Stratification of 'Quality of Life' in the Black Community of Atlanta, Georgia,'' *Southeastern Geographer* 14 (1974):26–37, fig. 2. Reprinted by permission.)

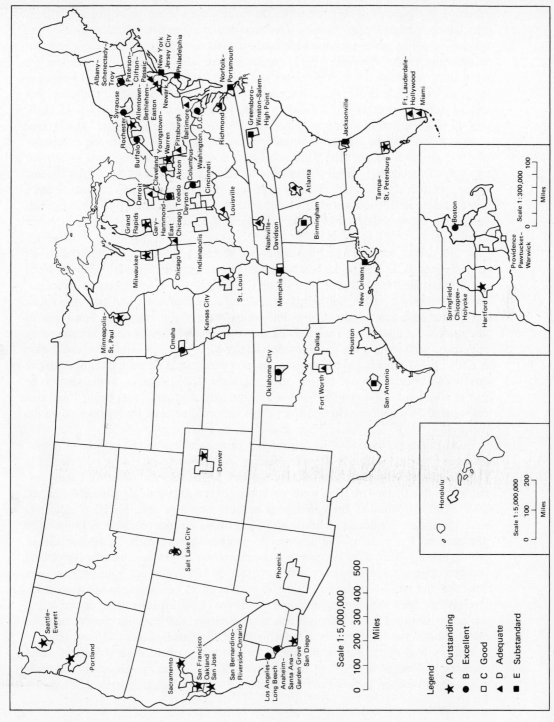

Figure 10.7 The quality of life in large American cities. (*Source:* Ben-chieh Liu, *Quality of Life Indicators in U.S. Metropolitan Areas.* New York: Praeger, 1976, p. 224. Reprinted by permission.)

reporting of a number of social statistics. In many ways a crime index, for example, is a socially constructed reality, for it is a function of such subjective influences as decisions concerning police patrol densities, enforcement levels, and the responsiveness of citizens in reporting crimes (Lowman, 1982). A second criticism concerns the procedure for combining indicators. There is no theoretical justification for either the equal weighting of variables or their linear, additive combination. Liu (1976) discovered that there was limited stability to quality-of-life rankings for American cities when he employed a factor analytic combination of indicators rather than a simple additive procedure. Third, there is no certainty that the indicators themselves have subjective validity in the experience of urban residents. Jacobs (1961) has noted how Boston planners designated some inner city neighborhoods as blighted and suitable for renewal on the grounds of their age and high population densities. But research more sensitive to the subjective nuances of place revealed these neighborhoods to be ''urban villages'' with high levels of livability. Their demolition led to considerable distress and some psychosomatic illness among former residents.

But despite these well-founded criticisms, objective and subjective assessments are certainly related, at least at the national scale. In an experimental study, Gould (1969b) has demonstrated the existence of a strong relationship ($r^2 = 0.61$) between students' mental maps, their preferential ratings for different American states, and indices of social welfare for each state representing an integration of 93 original variables. For a smaller sample of states it seems as if there are indeed consistent relationships between *subjective* preference surfaces and net migration flows (Lloyd, 1976). Supporting this conclusion is Liu's (1975) claim to have detected significant correlations between a set of *objective* quality-of-life indicators and net interstate migration. The conclusion would seem to be that at a national level objective and subjective indicators are intercorrelated and that consequently a judicious selection from either set could account for regional migration patterns.

At the intraurban scale the relationship between objective and subjective assessments of livability appears to be more complex. A detailed Scottish survey conducted in Dundee showed an overall compatibility between perceptions and objective conditions, but within this framework there were a number of contradictions (Knox and MacLaran, 1978). Only one-third of the correlations between objective and subjective indicators were statistically significant, whereas one-sixth of the correlations were negative. The disagreement was more marked in some life domains than in others. In the domains of health, housing, leisure, and access to urban amenities, there was substantial agreement between objective and subjective indicators, but there was far less symmetry between objective and perceived characteristics for employment, education, personal security, levels of affluence and consumption, and the degree of participation. Both objective and subjective measures have advantages and much discussed shortcomings conceptually and methodologically, but the general convergence of their assessments and their intuitive plausibility lead one to have some confidence that they provide a useful form of social accounting. A major shortcoming of subjective indicators is that they are costly and time-consuming to collect, for a sample size of at least several hundred is generally necessary to give satisfactory spatial coverage of a city. In addition, they are subject to the normal potential biasses of any questionnaire survey.

Nevertheless, there are some useful surveys of subjective assessments of the metropolitan quality of life which have been completed. For inner city areas the participant observation and questionnaire research conducted in Boston around 1960 was particularly significant, both theoretically and in terms of its effect on new policy initiatives (Jacobs, 1961; Fried and Gleicher, 1961; Gans, 1962a). This work challenged the professional perceptions of physical planners concerning urban renewal and gave a strong impetus to more humane social planning. In Boston's West End, physical indicators were deceptive pointers to the local quality of life, for in this cohesive ethnic community there were elaborate social support systems; 25 percent of residents had been born in the West End, and 75 percent harbored positive feelings toward the place and its people. The neighborhood's destruction by urban renewal caused a marked sense of uprootedness and disorientation for a number of residents.

These findings have been reinforced in a number of comparable urban villages. In Mowbray, a formerly racially integrated inner suburb of Cape Town, the displacement of about 200 "coloured" families as a result of Apartheid legislation led to considerable suffering (Western, 1978, 1981). Mowbray was an old, established agricultural village prior to its incorporation in Cape Town, and residents had deep roots both with the place and through extensive kin networks; most had been born in the village, and a survey of 50 percent of displaced families showed that the average length of residence for household heads had been over 30 years. But in the early 1960s, Mowbray was declared an all-white area, and colored families were removed to racial ghettos over 5 miles away. Interviews conducted more than 10 years after displacement revealed that removees continued to grieve for a lifestyle that had been shattered by legislative decree. They had been separated from kin and were more distant from their place of work, recreation, worship, shopping, and urban services. Removal brought deep regret:

> But they were hard. I remember going down to the city to plead for more time and I was praying "Please God give me some help" and you'd go in and they wouldn't even look up or say anything to you. And they came round to my house to tell us to get out and looked at it—I'd done it up nice and had a bathroom put on and things—and one said "D'you know, I wouldn't mind living in one like this." Then they said they'd got a place for me in Bonteheuwel, and now they'd got that, we'd *have* to go. But I was scared of that place, especially for my daughters who I'd brought up nice and who were then teenagers. . . . So I sat down and wrote a really sad letter, telling them everything—oh, it was a shame—and you know it must've touched one of them because they came and said I could stay for a while (Western, 1978).

Mowbray has since become a fashionable white inner city district.

But other inner city neighborhoods generate far less residential satisfaction. In an area of deteriorated housing in Glasgow, a majority of tenants preferred to leave the district altogether even if extensive home improvements were undertaken (English, 1973). In American cities the zones of greatest objective disparity are also areas of very low residential satisfaction. A survey of owners and tenants in a deteriorating black section of North Philadelphia indicated little commitment to the neighborhood and a large majority who would prefer to leave the city altogether (Ley, 1974a). Most residents expected that conditions would worsen, and consequently they said they would offer no resistance to hypothetical urban redevelopment. Demolition of their property would mean compensation from the city and a chance to move out. If confronted with a compulsory purchase order, some homeowners would be delighted: "I'd pull it down myself," volunteered one man! Their major complaints were directed at the neighborhood's social problems of delinquency and street gangs, drug addiction, crime, and drunkenness. Here, then, are the weighted experiential interpretations of objective indicators. It was the social environment rather than physical or economic dimensions that residents regarded as most aggravating and damaging to their quality of life. In the limited satisfaction they expressed lies one answer to the low demand levels for inner city housing and the rising rate of abandonment and dereliction.

The preferred places of residence for these inner city dwellers would be the suburbs or small nearby towns. The suburbs continue to provide the material substance of the American dream to most families, and surveys indicate consistently positive evaluations of suburban living. Gans' (1967) detailed assessment of the huge Levittown development of over 17,000 single-family dwellings outside Philadelphia suggested a generally satisfied citizenry. After several years residence, two-thirds of the households had no plans to move, and those that did were primarily moving to a larger house as a result of upward social mobility. Although there was some nostalgia for the Philadelphia neighborhood they had left and some of the suburbanite's typical criticism of public transportation and the rising level of local taxes, yet these shortcomings were more than offset by a high level of satisfaction with their single-family dwellings and the social environment of compatible neighbors they had joined. In summary, Gans found that "whatever its imperfections, Levittown is a good place to live" (Gans 1967:432). The only real criticism of the community came from teenagers who found it tedious and socially unstimulating. Whereas 85 percent of adults responded favorably to Levittown, this was true of less than 40 percent of adolescents. A re-survey 10 years after Gans' investigation suggested that although community satisfaction had been sustained for adults, adolescent discontent might well have intensified (Popenoe, 1977).

Levittown was an innovative effort at planned development which has come to be a popular suburban model. Legislative incentives in 1968 and 1970 quickened the adoption of this model, and government officials in the United States anticipated the construction of up to 10 "new communities" a year during the 1970s. In general these developments have been planned for socioeconomic groups higher than the predominantly lower-middle-class residents who were the first arrivals in Levittown. In 1970, over 40 percent of families living in Columbia and Reston, new towns 15 miles outside Washington, D.C., had both partners with university degrees and had median family incomes of nearly twice the national average (Zehner, 1972). The concept of a new town, its services, its accessibility, and the compatibility of neighbors were all characteristics cited as attractive by residents before they moved in. Satisfaction in these communities was very high, with over 90 percent of families making assessments of "excellent" or "good," the top two categories on a five-point scale. The quality of local services, accessibility, and the environmental quality of the community contributed to sustain this high degree of endorsement. At a more local scale, resident satisfaction in their immediate home area was correlated most strongly with the perceived friendliness and similarity of neighbors and the level of home maintenance. Here, too, satisfaction levels were clustered in the highest category.

An extension of this inquiry to a sample of over 5000 adults and almost 1000 teenagers in 13 privately developed suburban communities and 2 federally assisted communities revealed comparable results (Zehner, 1977). On the whole these suburban districts contained an upper-middle-class population who enjoyed a high level of well-being. Overall, their perceived quality of life was most highly associated with their standard of living, use of leisure time, and nature of family life. Environmental characteristics were assessed as of secondary importance. Significantly, in each of the three major life domains there was no difference in the expressed quality of life between residents of planned communities and other suburbanites in nearby subdivisions. Differences did appear in the evaluation of community and neighborhood, but these variations should not conceal the high level of livability experienced by both groups: 49 percent of planned community residents as compared to 42 percent of residents in more conventional subdivisions rated their district as "excellent." The best predictor of community satisfaction was a strong endorsement of the immediate neighborhood around the home, and the degree of home maintenance was the major factor influencing local satisfaction.

In summary, these suburban studies reinforce a number of our earlier statements. The phenomenology of the suburb reveals a localism which reduces primarily to the home and the houses that are immediately adjacent. Aspirations and energies are focused on the home as a place of child-raising and the forging of an identity of happy domesticity. Suburban families regard the dwelling unit as their major priority, followed by neighborhood characteristics, and consider location as least important; in contrast, central city families place a much higher premium on location, with the dwelling unit second, and the neighborhood last (Michelson, 1977). In the suburbs, neighbors are expected to uphold a status compatibility, and the community around to provide essential services and particularly a strong school system. In these undertakings, the suburb succeeds well for the young family. Both planned and relatively unplanned suburbs offer a high quality of life to their middle-class residents, though, as Zehner observes, the greater a household's income level, the higher, too, its community and overall life satisfaction. In the American planned community there appear to be relatively few parallels to the "New Town blues" and associated levels of mental and social maladjustment which have been reported in British new towns (Chave, 1966). The malaise of the suburban housewife does not seem to be as widespread from survey research as has sometimes been implied; in Levittown, less than a quarter of residents experienced boredom more often than "about once a month," though this was a problem for women nearly twice as much as for men (Gans, 1967). There is, however, a definite source of understimulation for a high proportion of suburban adolescents.

Thus our survey of the urban quality of life reveals a general complementarity between objective and subjective indicators. Before examining some interpretations of these gradients, we will note the results of several studies that have undertaken a livability assessment more comprehensive than the evaluation of a single neighborhood type alone. In Des Moines, Iowa, a standardized questionnaire administered to a cross section of urban residents revealed that residential satisfaction generally increased with distance from downtown (Ermuth, 1974). In Chicago, about 40 percent of respondents presented a positive evaluation of their local community and expressed some attachment to it (Hunter, 1974). A favorable evaluation of the local area was correlated with social class and white status. Residents were able to discriminate between a *positive evaluation* of their neighborhood and *personal attachment* to it. Thus although length of residence was unrelated to the identification of positive attributes, there was nonetheless a strong association between length of residence and local area attachment; specifically among the white population, although the number ascribing positive attributes to the local area hovered around 50 percent independent of length of residence, neighborhood attachment increased sequentially from 13 percent of newcomers to over 60 percent of residents with over 20 years' tenure. Here, then, is a disjuncture between objective and subjective states: given time citizens can become attached to unlovely neighborhoods as they invest more of their own identities in them. Similarly, attachment increases as a greater proportion of an individual's routines—the workplace, shopping patterns, place of worship, and formal and informal leisure activities—is spatially confined to the local area, a finding consistent with the urban village thesis (see also Rowles, 1980). However, in contrast, the lowest levels of both evaluation and attachment were expressed in low-status black districts, areas that would coincide with the slums of despair. These subtle but critical nuances distinguishing a positive evaluation from personal attachment to an area emphasize the care that is needed in generating subjective data and the vulnerability of quality-of-life surveys to an imprecise phrasing of questions.

Finally, it is important once again to recall the role of *national* variations. In the Scottish city of Dundee, the highest level of perceived well-being on 11 indicators was expressed in a mixture of inner city districts, new owner-occupied suburbs, and areas of older public housing with primarily elderly households; in contrast, the greatest dissatisfaction was voiced in privately rented inner city districts and in some of the peripheral public housing estates (Knox and MacLaran, 1978). Indeed, suburban public housing areas with large families registered the lowest overall scores of perceived well-being. Thus the relationship between location and the quality of life is dependent on other factors; a suburban location is not sufficient to offset other disadvantages, and with greater problems of accessibility to work, friends and relatives, shops, and schooling, there may even be a deterioration in the quality of life compared with higher-density central areas (Young and Willmott, 1957). Just as the British suburbs have disadvantages for public housing residents, so the Canadian central city may be highly endorsed by high-status families. In Toronto, residential satisfaction was expressed by close to 95 percent of families of above-average income whether they lived in single-family houses in suburban or central city neighborhoods (Michelson, 1977). Although families in high-rise apartments tended to be less satisfied with their homes (especially those in the suburbs), approval rates were only 10–15 percent below those of single-family dwellers. Evidently in Toronto, central neighborhoods still retain a high livability for families; indeed, Michelson concluded that families "in downtown houses give evidence of satisfaction with all the major dimensions constituting the residential context" (Michelson, 1977:279).

Bearing in mind the variable relation between intraurban location and the quality of life, in the remainder of this chapter we shall discuss different explanations which have been suggested to account for the inequitable distribution of life chances in the contemporary metropolis as described by urban indicators. We will see, too, that each perspective has enjoyed a period of popularity when it has contributed to distinctive policy formulations that have attempted to bring greater equality to urban residents. Although the relationship between an interpretation of the unequal quality of urban life and a policy prescription is not always clear-cut, nonetheless certain policy options do follow more or less logically from a particular interpretation of the nature of the problem.

An Ecological Interpretation

It was no accident that the school of urban ecology emerged in the 1920s, toward the end of the period of industrial urbanism that had transformed the geography of Europe and North America since 1800. By the early twentieth century, the human casualties of rapid urbanization had become fully apparent, and a wide-ranging chorus of condemnation had emerged from sources as disparate as Christian reformers like Jacob Riis and William Booth (founder of the Salvation Army), the philosopher-planners Ebenezer Howard and Patrick Geddes, and the socialist followers of Marx and Engels. Rapid urbanization seemed antithetical to civility. In response, liberal social movements arose to challenge the human devastation of the industrial city, including the settlement house movement and the harsh criticisms of the social reformers who ushered in the Progressive era of urban reform around 1890.

This was the intellectual context in which the Chicago school of human ecology was established. True to its pragmatist roots, the Chicago school had a strong applied focus, and its members were involved in social programs to combat the social disorganization they identified as so rampant in the immigrant industrial cities of North America. It was no wonder, then, that they held a certain skepticism and fatalism about urban life, for their dissertations and research monographs were constantly revealing its destructive effects on stable societal norms. As Burgess' concentric ring model described so well, the more heavily urbanized sections of the city were also those with the most extreme social problems. The more complete the urbanization, the more devastating, it seemed, were the pathologies. In his introduction to Frederic Thrasher's careful analysis of the adolescent gang in Chicago, Robert Park first wondered whether gangs might be regarded as "predetermined, foreordained, and 'instinctive,' and so quite independent of the environment" but then continued more forcefully:

> They spring up spontaneously, but only under favoring conditions and *in a definite milieu* . . . It is not only true that *the habitat makes gangs,* but what is of more practical importance, *it is the habitat which determines* whether or not their activities shall assume those perverse forms in which they become a menace to the community . . . The gangs here studied are not a *product* of the city merely, but they are at the same time *the product of a*

clearly defined and well-recognized area of the city, particularly of the modern American
city. It is the slum, the city wilderness, as it has been called, which provides the city gang
its natural habitat. (Thrasher, 1963:viii–ix, emphasis added)

Gangs, then, are a product of a particular setting; behavior is shaped by a distinctive
environment, "its natural habitat." The "spatial pattern" of the city has profound implications for its "moral order" (Park, 1926).

This central theoretical assertion of the human ecologists, that social disorganization is a product of city environments, was summarized in Louis Wirth's famous paper
on "urbanism as a way of life" (Wirth, 1938; Fischer, 1972). Wirth began his argument
by drawing on the psychology of Georg Simmel, one of Park's instructors in Germany,
concerning the information overload of urban living. Before an unmanageable battery of
stimuli, urban man must feign indifference to attain successful mental adjustment. Disengagement becomes a coping strategy as interpersonal bonds are loosened. At the same
time, the rule of the marketplace dictates the formation of specialized social groups and
specialized land uses. The range of social contacts promotes role-specific behaviors and
weakens the holding of a coherent value system and the formation of strong social ties.
The result is an enfeebling of social norms and the dilution of social bonds, a condition
that leads ultimately to anomie, a state of normlessness and isolation—exactly the dis-
organized moral order that had been exposed by a generation of urban research in Chicago.

City Size and the Quality of Life

If the city is essentially disorientating, then the larger the city, the greater should be the
disorientation. Ecologists have made good mileage of the controversial Midtown Manhattan study, which claimed that 80 percent of a sample of nearly 2000 residents in
central New York were beset by some form of mental illness (Langner and Michael,
1963). However, a more comparative survey of American mental health showed the
lowest rate of self-reported distress occurred in the largest cities of over 3 million, whereas
rates reached their peak in small urban areas of less than 50,000 inhabitants (Srole,
1972). Similarly inconclusive is the available evidence concerning differential rates of
alcoholism and suicide, other indicators of anomie, between rural and urban areas.

Nevertheless, there is still a fascination with exposing the peculiar maladies of the
large metropolis (Appelbaum, 1976). Australian research has tried to establish a relationship between a city's size and growth rate and the development of segregated areas
of need (Stilwell and Hardwick, 1973). But the absence of segregation of the poor in
smaller towns does not mean an absence of poverty. Among Canada's 22 census metropolitan areas, whose size ranged from 100,000 to over 2.7 million in 1971, significant
correlations between city size or growth rate and a set of 32 urban indicators occurred
for fewer than one-third of the pairings (Table 10.1). From these it is not at all evident
that the quality of life is low in the largest or fastest-growing cities. Although the major
metropolitan areas have disproportionately fewer hospital beds and more serious air
pollution, they also have higher incomes and occupational status. Similarly, a high urban
growth rate, though it is associated with lower levels of educational achievement and

TABLE 10.1   THE RELATIONSHIPS BETWEEN URBAN INDICATORS AND POPULATION SIZE AND GROWTH RATES IN CANADIAN CITIES

Indicator	City Size Correlation	Growth Rate Correlation
1. Number of Juveniles Charged	−0.14	−0.05
2. Criminal Code Offenses	0.01	0.17
3. Percent Offenses Cleared	0.03	0.28
4. Number of Missing Persons	−0.21	−0.13
5. Illegitimate Births	−0.24	−0.16
6. Educational Achievement	−0.19	−0.37*
7. Public Cultural Opportunities	0.26	0.05
8. Public Library Usage	0.18	0.17
9. Social Opportunities	0.08	−0.16
10. Percent Living in Province of Birth	−0.39*	−0.48*
11. Ethnic Prominence	−0.06	0.28
12. Number of Major Ethnic Groups	0.61*	0.35
13. Percent Canadian-Born	−0.42*	−0.35
14. Population Turnover	−0.17	0.41*
15. Number of Hospital Beds	−0.48*	−0.30
16. Voter Turnout	−0.23	−0.37*
17. Income (Nonadjusted)	0.51*	0.40*
18. Income (Adjusted for Housing)	0.49*	0.27
19. Occupational Status	0.43*	0.38*
20. Female Labor Force Participation	0.25	0.43*
21. Unemployment Rates	−0.15	−0.36
22. Annual Strike Days Lost	0.34	0.08
23. Costs, New Single Detached Dwellings	0.31	0.47*
24. Percentage Dwellings Owner-Occupied	−0.32	−0.19
25. New Housing per Added Household	−0.01	−0.46*
26. Proportion Apartment Units	0.33	−0.04
27. Apartment Vacancy Rates	0.21	−0.01
28. Children in Apartments	0.33	0.00
29. Public Transit Ridership	0.63*	0.22
30. Air Quality: Particulates	0.57*	0.24
31. Air Quality: SO_2	−0.06	−0.28
32. Hazard Index	0.18	0.27

Source: J. Stewart et al., *Urban Indicators: Quality of Life Comparisons for Canadian Cities*. Ottawa: Ministry of State for Urban Affairs, 1975, p. 84. Reprinted by permission of the Ministry of Supply and Services Canada.
*Significant at 0.05.

higher housing costs, also implies more favorable incomes and occupational status and lower unemployment, including increased female participation in the labor force. It is noteworthy that there are no significant correlations between urban size or growth rate and any of the indicators of social pathology, including crime.

In contrast, in the United States there is a persistent increase in crime rates with growth in city size. Metropolitan areas of over 250,000 experience a murder rate 3 times as great as that of rural areas (and 6 times that of small towns), 5 times the rate of property crimes, 10 times the rate of violent crimes, and nearly 50 times the rate of robbery. In addition, cities harbor less conventional attitudes and lifestyles; national surveys repeatedly display that permissive attitudes toward sex, drugs, and other liberal activities and social movements are more widely held in the largest urban areas. The question remains, however, as to whether these empirical regularities are determined by urban environments, by some other variables, or whether indeed it is selective migration of certain personality types to urban areas that accounts for the city's eccentricity.

Urban Crowding and the Quality of Life

Equally contentious is the interpretation of the correlation which the ecologists invariably discovered between urban pathologies and population density. The concentration of pathologies in the inner city neighborhoods and their limited incidence in the suburbs suggested that crowding was a leading precipitant of social disorders. After population size, Wirth suggested that high population densities were a dominant characteristic affecting the quality of urban life.

Over the past 15 years, research on the effects of urban crowding has become a major preoccupation, stimulated in part by the alarming results of ethological experiments that subjected rat populations to abnormally high densities (Calhoun, 1962). It has been tempting to extrapolate these results to urban populations, and indeed some writing that speculatively treats the city as a "behavioral sink" has appeared. The disengagement from social responsibility by urban dwellers has given rise to the peculiarly metropolitan phenomenon (or so it is implied) of bystander apathy, the failure of onlookers to become involved personally in an emergency (Milgram, 1970). Of course, the parable of the good samaritan indicates that this is not necessarily behavior of a particularly modern vintage!

Any relationship between crowding and pathologies seems to be culture specific. The high densities in Hong Kong, exceeding those of any North American city, are accompanied by far less social malaise—only 10 percent as much psychiatric hospitalization as in the U.S. and half the rate of serious crime (Lai, 1974). Nevertheless, in North America the correlation between density and pathology is unambiguous; what is controversial is its interpretation. Apart from a few carefully argued studies like Schorr's (1964) discussion of the relations between housing quality, density, and health, there is a major theoretical and causal gap between the environment (the stressor) and human stress (Gad, 1973). Indeed, the balance of current research is reaching the conclusion that once other variables such as social class, age, race, and family history have been taken into account, density alone has minimal effects: "The more recent and methodologically sound investigations of areal and in-dwelling densities reveal only negligible effects of density on morbidity, mortality, crime and emotional disturbance" (Kirmeyer, 1978). A detailed survey of objective and perceived crowding among over 800 family members in Toronto revealed that only 14 percent of the relationships that were tested were significant (Booth, 1976). There was no consistent indication that neighborhood crowding levels were harmful (there were as many positive as negative consequences that were statistically significant), and high densities within the home had only minor effects. A thorough examination of the implications of crowding for physical and mental health, family relations, community life, and political activity concluded that for the range of conditions present in Toronto, "crowded conditions seldom have any consequences, and even when they do the effects are very modest" (Booth, 1976:100).

Policy Consequences

Ecological arguments have played a significant role in the formulation of social and, especially, housing policy in the city. The persistent correlations that the human ecologists uncovered between the "spatial pattern" and the "moral order" firmly promoted a form of spatial determinism on the basis of which it was felt that if only the physical environment could be renewed, then social problems might speedily be remedied. A review of housing age and density statistics has in the past often served as a prelude to urban renewal programs involving demolition and the construction of public housing. The folly and fate of much postwar public housing in the United States and Britain have severely challenged such speculation. It has also been discredited by comparative studies of families in poor-quality and public housing. Whereas there may be some improvement in household health levels after relocation to public housing, there has been no improvement in the incidence of social pathologies (Wilner et al., 1962).

Nevertheless, there are some consistent relations between the physical environment and human behavior, and these have been examined by environmental psychologists (Proshansky et al., 1970), behavioral geographers (Porteous, 1977), architects (Canter and Lee, 1974), and some sociologists (Michelson, 1970). In extreme form this literature may suggest a type of design determinism. For example, Studer (1972) advocates a process of "behavior-contingent physical design," whose first two stages involve: "(a) delineate the system of behaviors required in a particular human organisation; (b) specify the precise characteristics of the physical system required to realise the behavior system delineated." This rather blunt form of environmental programming ends squarely in Skinnerian determinism, because it espouses positive and negative "design reinforcers" as instruments for the operant conditioning of behavior.

Scarcely less controversial have been the substantive arguments of the architect Oscar Newman, whose concept of defensible space "examines one aspect of how environment affects behavior" (Newman, 1972:xiii). Newman is nothing if not exuberant over the contributions he feels environmental design can make to solving the ills of urban man: "For urban residential settings, for low and moderate income population in particular, defensible space design may be the last stand of the urban man committed to an open society." Newman's argument is that the sheer size, density, and anonymity of American public housing projects are antithetical to residential satisfaction and promote a high level of vandalism and crime—an argument remarkably akin to the Wirthian ecological thesis. Newman, however, is not only a theoretician. Statistics from projects built according to his design proposals are strongly suggestive that pathologies may indeed be tempered by more humane design strategies that heighten resident identification with their buildings. The work of Newman and less controversial proponents of a more humanistic design such as Jane Jacobs (1961), Robert Sommer (1974), and Christopher Alexander (1975) have become important influences on social planning and urban design in the 1970s.

A Subcultural Perspective

The studies of social disorganization conducted by the Chicago school allowed two interpretations. The first, the ecological, emphasized the effects of the physical environment. But human ecology was simply one dimension of the Chicago school, albeit that portion best known to human geographers; more significant was the examination of the effects of the sociocultural milieu. The study of social worlds represents a major tradition—some would claim *the* major tradition—in North American urban sociology (Rose, 1962).

   More recently, this tradition has developed a criticism of ecological explanation that is predicated on sociocultural factors (compare Chapter 3). The critique begins with a more or less explicit refutation of Wirth's (1938) thesis: "His characterisation of the urban way of life applies only—and not too accurately—to the residents of the inner city," and even in the inner city, the "population consists mainly of relatively homogeneous groups, with social and cultural moorings that shield it fairly effectively from the suggested consequences of number, density, and heterogeneity" (Gans, 1962b). In criticizing the emphasis on social disorganization by the ecologists, Whyte (1943) used the provocative title "Social Organization and the Slum" to introduce his study of the social worlds of an Italian inner city neighborhood in Boston. With small modifications, the argument has been pressed further in a subcultural theory of urban life (Fischer, 1975) that essentially restates Robert Park's description of the city as a mosaic of social worlds (Short, 1971).

   This thesis, which we elaborated in Chapters 6–7, has found some support in human geography. J. E. Vance (1976), for example, has suggested the concept of *congregation* as a counterfoil to segregation in an examination of the city's social geography. The congregation, or social world, is a group of like-minded individuals who are drawn together by common interests and a similar biographical situation. The sociocultural world that they construct and sustain collectively meets a number of their perceived needs and shelters them from the anonymity of urban life. At the same time a set of attitudinal and behavioral norms to which group members conform is established. Each social world has "its own ways of acting, talking, and thinking. It has its own vocabulary, its own activities and interests, its own conception of what is significant in life . . ." (Cressey, 1932:31). The subcultural thesis, then, presents a more optimistic outlook on urban experience, portraying adaptation and consensus rather than anomie and conflict as characteristic social traits.

   How, then, does the essential optimism of subcultural theory come to terms with the unequal distribution of urban pathologies and life chances? On one level it argues that the city consists of a plurality of social worlds and that those with the greatest power, including market power, will have the best access to a high level of social well-being (compare Chapters 8 and 9). A second argument is that the size of the city allows the gathering of a critical mass of individuals who sustain distinctive subcultures, including those which are pathological. As Fischer has put it, "Criminals are found everywhere, but cities permit them a full-time specialisation and provide them with helpful associates. Thus, cities produce underworlds" (Fischer, 1976:199). Subcultures of crime are therefore self-sustaining and to some extent a "natural" consequence of urbanization.

The Culture-of-Poverty Debate

There is, however, a dangerous fatalism about such an extension of the subcultural thesis, which was well illustrated in the often bitter debate over the "culture of poverty." Oscar Lewis, one of the major protagonists of the culture-of-poverty argument, claimed that social problems were an outcome of a poverty cycle in which individuals were trapped. Continued adaptation over time to conditions of poverty created a milieu and a set of norms that were themselves pathological; in this way the culture of poverty became self-perpetuating (Lewis, 1968). This argument, which asserts that social problems are in large measure a *product* of the subculture in which they occur, promotes a fatalism that can paralyze intervention. If the fault of the pathologies that accompany poverty lies *wholly* with those who experience a poor quality of life, then what can be done? One logical conclusion becomes a policy of "benign neglect." As several critics have noted, such an extreme interpretation of the subcultural thesis represents a sociological determinism as uncompromising as the physical determinism of the ecologists (Wrong, 1961; Carveth, 1977).

Policy Consequences

An etiology of pathology that directs attention to the demoralizing effects of the social environment leads to a remedy that would abstract individuals from that environment. This is one keystone of the philosophy of the inner city rescue missions; the transformation of lifestyle requires a change in the social environment. At an early time, the strategy of the Salvation Army was to set up rural and overseas colonies where a Christian social environment could aid the development of new attitudes and habits (Figure 10.8). A more secular response was institutionalization of society's deviants. In the nineteenth century there was a genuine expectation that asylums and reformatories would provide a therapeutic community and not simply a punitive or caretaker facility: "Create a different kind of environment, which methodically corrected the deficiencies of the community and a cure for insanity was at hand" (Rothman, 1971:133). Today we know better; too often asylums prepare patients for a career of mental illness, and prisons provide apprenticeships for a life of crime. Ironically, the power of the social environment exceeds that of the physical environment; the removal of deviants to an isolated physical setting simply relocates their social environment without weakening it. Thus the same reasoning in the 1970s has now led to a de-emphasis of institutional confinement; the transfer of detainees from the institution to the halfway house represents an attempt to introduce them to a therapeutic environment in the community and to divert them from acculturation to the demoralizing social world of the institution (C. Smith, 1976). One problem with this strategy is that the stigmatized identity conferred by institutional confinement makes residents reluctant to accept the siting of halfway houses in their neighborhoods. Consequently group homes tend to be clustered in certain locations where community resistance is low; what is occurring, as the Wolperts have noted in San Jose, is a transition from asylum to ghetto (Wolpert and Wolpert, 1974; Dear, 1977b).

Similar difficulties have beset two other major initiatives in the United States to disperse underprivileged households into more privileged social environments: the poli-

Figure 10.8 The geographic strategy of the Salvation Army's urban mission. (*Source*: W. Booth, *In Darkest England and the Way Out*. London: The Salvation Army, 1890, frontispiece. Reprinted by permission.)

cies of school desegregation and the construction of government-assisted housing outside traditional low-income and minority areas. Underlying both of these policies is the philosophy that the exposure of underprivileged residents to more advantaged social environments will enhance their own educational and social development.

A climax of the civil rights activism of the 1960s was the battle for school desegregation and the dispersion of poorer black students from their inadequate inner city schools to a social environment of higher achievement in outlying school districts. Initial court action was directed against Southern school boards where segregation had been legislated in 17 states prior to 1954 (Lord, 1977). Some dramatic changes occurred: in Texas the percentage of blacks attending integrated schools increased from 0 in 1954 to 8 in 1964 and 45 in 1966, while in the border states between North and South even more marked shifts occurred. Indeed, by 1972 the core area of segregation had moved to the Northern states, and particularly the Northern cities; in 1971 the Philadelphia School Board was embarrassed to learn that its schools were more segregated than those in Mississippi.

The progress of school desegregation was inversely related to the size of the local nonwhite population, so that it was in the Northern cities with their massive concentrations of nonwhite students that change was slowest and most strongly resisted. In Boston a federal court ruled in 1974 that the city's schools were segregated and called for the busing of 26,000 students, almost 30 percent of the student body, within 2 years to achieve desegregation. Widespread opposition to the court's decision was expressed; in 1971 a survey that divided Boston into 10 neighborhoods found that the antibusing lobby formed the majority in each neighborhood (Massey, 1976). An index of resistance to desegregation constructed from attitudinal surveys, electoral results, and school boycotts showed the differential response throughout the city (Figure 10.9); the range of the index fluctuated on both sides of zero, the mean level for the city overall. Resistance was highest in South Boston, a cohesive neighborhood of Irish Catholic blue-collar workers. In South Boston and Charlestown opposition to two-way busing with black high schools has been persistent and violent, for in these Irish communities violation of the principle of neighborhood schooling is perceived as equivalent to violation of an inward-looking neighborhood way of life. In conjunction with strongly held racial stereotypes widespread in white ethnic areas (Binzen, 1970), the ingredients for violent opposition to busing were present.

In contrast, in middle-class white communities resistance has been more passive and has taken the form of either transferring children to private schools or else moving to a separate school district. In one Mississippi county, 24 new private schools for white students were opened between 1963 and 1970 (Lowry, 1973). The effect of desegregation on white migration is controversial (Pettigrew and Green, 1976), but in Pontiac, Michigan, where busing was fiercely resisted, the decrease in the number of white children in elementary schools tripled in the first year of the desegregated school system. In Nashville, 20,000 white students were lost to the school system the year that desegregation was implemented (Lord, 1977). The rate of white transfer seems to be strongly correlated with the proportion of nonwhite children in the school district.

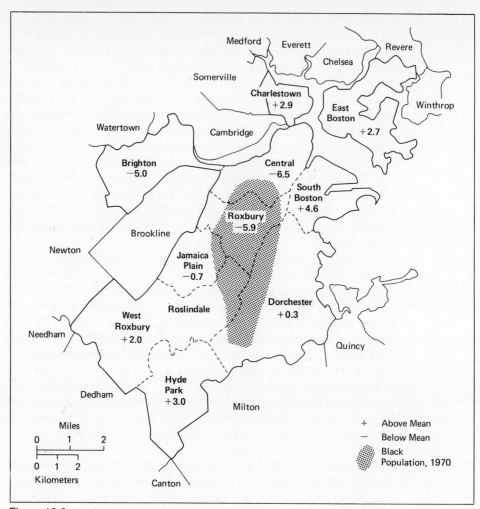

Figure 10.9   An index of resistance to school desegregation through busing in Boston. (*Source*: D. Massey, ''Class, Racism and Busing in Boston,'' *Antipode*, 8, no. 2 (1976):37–49, fig. 2. Reprinted by permission.)

Experience with the second major initiative for inner city dispersion in the United States, the scattering of government-assisted housing, has been equally daunting. Attempts by a number of housing authorities to construct scattered-site housing outside traditional poverty areas during the 1950s and 1960s ran into determined community opposition (Forman, 1971). In New York by the early 1970s, plans had been annulled for 8 out of 13 scattered-site projects; typical was the Forest Hills suburb where the residents' association demonstrated vociferously against the erection of three 24-story buildings (Cuomo, 1974). In Chicago, a court decision ordered the city to build new public housing units outside a buffer zone enclosing black residential areas that had received almost all previous construction. Public outcry, especially during a civic election campaign, caused the housing authority to be tardy in drawing up plans for dispersion and very conservative in the degree of scatter it eventually proposed (Mercer and Hultquist, 1976).

More successful in penetrating beyond traditional black residential areas have been the subsidized rental and subsidized home ownership programs included in the American Housing Acts of the 1960s. Typically these programs have provided middle-class housing and have avoided the imposition of monolithic projects in existing communities. Nevertheless, they do not seem to have brought about lasting residential integration as was intended. The neighborhoods where the housing subsidy programs are concentrated have since undergone rapid racial turnover and seem to be merely redefining the bounds of traditional racial areas without achieving integration (Leven et al., 1976). Indeed, Harvey (1975) has reported that in the Baltimore inner suburbs, programs introduced in the 1968 Housing Act were used by realtors to mount a lucrative blockbusting operation.

A Spatial Access Viewpoint

In interpreting quality-of-life gradients in the city, geographers have been particularly attentive to the spatial relations between residential groups and urban facilities and services (Cox, 1973; Harvey, 1971; Pinch, 1979). They have emphasized problems of physical *access* to urban services in the inner city, both the existing low quality of neighborhood services and also the physical distance separating often needy residents from facilities.

In education, for example, the low level of student achievement in urban schools (Figure 10.4) is associated not only with the nature of the child's social milieu but also with public service levels in his or her neighborhood (Herbert, 1976b). The ratio of pupils to teachers commonly varies from 25–30 in city schools to 18–22 in the suburbs; in Chicago, a city ratio of 28 contrasted with a ratio of 18 in Evanston, a northern suburb. Moreover, the unattractive qualities of an inner city teaching career have limited the ability of urban school boards to hire the most qualified and experienced instructors. Even within a single school board district, ghetto schools are rarely able to attract the most competent instructors; teachers in Chicago high schools that were in the most deprived districts had less than four years median teaching experience in the 1960s, whereas those in the most affluent areas were better qualified and more experienced with a median of over 12 years teaching. The schools in needy areas are also older and poorly equipped. Sexton's review of school facilities in poorer and more affluent districts revealed striking disparities (Table 10.2). Moreover, urban schools are both older and often overcrowded, so that split and even triple sessions are held. Inevitably achievement levels will be low. In a section of North Philadelphia, ghetto elementary schools fell 17–21 months below the national reading standard, and by the time of junior high school the deficit had risen to 31 months (Ley, 1974a). The local high school was on split sessions, with the morning and afternoon shifts of students together numbering 4300 in a facility built to accommodate 2400 pupils. The students supplied their own evaluation of their education; every day one in three of them was an absentee. Associated with absenteeism was a high dropout rate. Over the five school years 1966–1971, the twelfth grade class

TABLE 10.2 SCHOOLS WITH INADEQUATE FACILITIES, BY INCOME OF LOCAL AREA

Facilities	Major Income Groups				Income Halves	
	Group 1 $3,000	Group 2 $5,000	Group 3 $7,000	Group 4 $9,000	A Below $7,000	B Above $7,000
Science	50%	46%	3%	0%	47%	2%
Conservatory	67	50	6	6	54	6
Art room	11	11	4	0	11	4
Library	11	16	15	11	15	14
Instrumental Music & Speech	78	95	59	39	91	56
Speech	83	88	84	89	86	85
Store room	6	18	6	6	15	6
Men's & Women's Restrooms	61	68	40	16	66	30
Auditorium	5	16	2	6	14	3
Auditorium Activities Room (backstage)	78	95	52	39	91	50
Office	0	11	2	0	8	2
Clinic	17	21	11	11	20	11
Kitchen	44	55	31	17	53	28
Air Raid Shelter	67	61	25	6	62	21

Source: P. Sexton, *Education and Income.* New York: Viking, 1961, Table 8, p. 125. Copyright © 1961 by Patricia Cayo Sexton. Reprinted by permission of Viking Penguin Inc.

averaged little more than half the size of the tenth grade class, and in the twelfth grade, females outnumbered males by a ratio of two to one. A poll conducted at the high school showed that 80 percent of students would not want younger brothers or sisters or their own children to attend the school.

Parallel deficiencies exist for a broad range of urban services including health care and police protection and the administration of justice (Shannon and Dever, 1974; Harries, 1974). The geography of health care has received particular attention in the United States by virtue of the unequal availability of private and public treatment. The urgency for optimal *spatial* strategies in health care delivery, among other necessary reforms, is highlighted by the claim that spatial inequities in medical care in Chicago contributed to 1000 unnecessary deaths a year (de Vise, 1971; Gross, 1972). The inability of poorer patients to pay for private medical services channelled them to the relatively few public hospitals, even though these may have been inaccessible. Whereas over half of suburban Chicagoans frequented the nearest hospital for treatment, this was true of only 20 percent of those living in the central city; indeed, in 1965, 57 percent of inner city residents sought care beyond the two closest hospitals (Morrill et al., 1970). Indicative of this apartheid health system, as de Vise (1971) has labelled it, were the extended journeys of black patients who travelled twice as far for treatment as they would have if they had enjoyed equal access to all existing hospitals. Because they could not afford to pay for care, a large number of these patients travelled long distances to the Cook County Hospital, "an enormous, congested and unfriendly institution, removed from large portions of the black ghetto by a long and arduous journey" (Morrill et al., 1970). Despite its inaccessibility, the Cook County Hospital complex received nearly a third of all emergency care visits made to Chicago's 80 hospitals in 1970. Half the patients had no health insurance, and 40 percent were children or infants; the *average* waiting time was 2 hours. Yet dependence on such institutions was great, for in 1970 fully half of the central city population had no family doctor (de Vise, 1971). The existing private system of health care serves private ends which are rarely compatible with the needs of a large minority of disadvantaged citizens.

Cox (1973) has developed a multivariate index that assesses the central city-suburban disparity for a range of urban goods and services in the largest American cities during the 1960s. These assessments are in general agreement with a similar hardship index devised by Nathan and Dommel (1977) from the 1970 Census. The higher the index score, the sharper was the gradient between a needy and underserviced central city and its well-endowed suburbs; a score of 1.0 would indicate city-suburban parity (Table 10.3). As we have noted with a number of other quality-of-life indicators, there is also a marked contrast between the newer sun belt cities of the South and West and the older cities of the industrial belt in the intrametropolitan distribution of public services. Central city hardship is more concentrated in the historic manufacturing belt.

Another area which, from a welfare perspective, is generating increasing spatial injustice is the journey to work. The suburbanization of blue-collar employment opportunities in the United States has not been accompanied by a decentralization of blue-collar homes. As we have seen, suburban exclusion has barred entry to poorer workers especially when they are members of a racial minority. The result has been a growing problem of reverse commuting for central city blue-collar workers, including an extended daily

TABLE 10.3 DISPARITY INDEX BETWEEN CENTER CITY AND SUBURB FOR SELECTED U.S. CITIES

Metropolitan Area	Disparity Index
Newark	4.01
New York	3.71
St. Louis	3.35
Cleveland	3.35
Washington, D.C.	3.00
Chicago	2.80
Philadelphia	2.66
Detroit	2.47
Miami	2.46
Minneapolis	2.10
Houston	1.83
Los Angeles-Long Beach	1.56
San Francisco	1.39
Dallas	1.28
San Diego	0.96

Source: K. Cox, *Conflict, Power and Politics in the City.* New York: McGraw-Hill, 1973, Table 3.7, p. 41. Reprinted by permission.

journey to work. In Detroit, Deskins (1972) has claimed that by 1965 black workers had longer journeys to work than whites in seven out of eight occupational categories, a pattern which had only recently emerged with the suburbanization of job opportunities. In Chicago, de Vise (1976) has noted the spatial disequilibrium in the emerging pattern of employment and residence. Whereas most new jobs in the suburbs have been for blue-collar moderate-income workers, most new suburban housing is for affluent white-collar households. Whereas blacks have been essentially blocked in their access to suburban housing, central city employment is increasingly favoring skilled white-collar occupations. The net product of this spatial incompatibility is that ''the typical work trip for white suburbanites is a 20-mile ride on an air-conditioned train to do a downtown desk job paying $17,000 a year. A typical work trip for a black reverse commuter is a 30-mile ride in a car pool to an $8,000 factory job'' (de Vise, 1976).

The access problem has been blamed in part for the alarming increase in unemployment in the inner city, with its persistent linkages with the poverty and pathology syndrome. A survey of almost 5000 job applicants from poverty areas in Indianapolis showed that over 80 percent of them depended on public transportation to get to work (Davies and Albaum, 1972). But as in almost all cities, the bus system was radial, focussing on the CBD, and was not well suited for morning journeys outward to the suburbs. Slow bus speeds, a number of transfers, and poor connections combined to make a journey against the commuter flow laborious and time-consuming. In addition, the limited early and late bus service was useless for shift work. These accessibility problems worked against job retention, and the average job duration for bus riders in the Indianapolis sample was only about 3 months.

There is, however, a wide range of both objective and subjective factors affecting the rate of inner city unemployment; these have been discussed in a perceptive participant observation study of underemployed men in Washington, D.C. (Liebow, 1967). Contrary to the common wisdom, variations in central city underemployment in Atlanta were *positively* correlated with accessibility to job centers (Bederman and Adams, 1974); the nearer the jobs, the higher the underemployment. This finding led to the interpretation that job creation and retraining programs would be more effective than transportation improvements in countering poverty. However, this conclusion should be qualified because of the undue weighting given to the CBD as a job source in the Atlanta study and the relative underweighting of rapidly growing peripheral job centers from which the Atlanta poor are becoming increasingly separated.

Policy Consequences

Consistent with the spatial paradigm dominant in the 1960s and 1970s, geographers have emphasized problems of spatial disequilibrium in their interpretation of the quality of urban life (Pinch, 1979). A preoccupation with locational variables in the diagnosis has led to a locational emphasis in the remedy, with suggestions that difficulties of physical access be treated by the introduction of more wide-ranging welfare criteria in the provision of public transportation (Muller, 1976b), the location of public facilities (Morrill, 1974), and in overcoming the separation between residence and workplace (de Vise,

Figure 10.10   Black capitalism in North Philadelphia: the Progress Plaza shopping center.

1976; Berry, 1979). Although few geographers would claim a spatial determinism, that
the improvement of physical access alone would be sufficient in problem solving, yet
spatial relations are those that their training commonly draws them to. Notions of an
"optimum geography" (Alao, 1976), a locational geometry derived from welfare assumptions, would juxtapose urban services with urban needs (through decentralization
or the relocation of existing services) and eliminate socially costly accessibility problems
through improved public transportation. Implicit in such formulations is a high level of
government planning in locational decisions. However, we saw earlier (Chapter 4) that
access has both an objective and a subjective component and that geographical proximity
need not imply social participation.

A second strategy involves the *enrichment* of existing areas of need. Enrichment
in situ has been a major policy initiative since the mid 1960s, reflected in broadly based
efforts at community development including such programs as job creation and retraining,
the encouragement of local "black capitalism" (Figure 10.10), and innovative school
and preschool programs like Head Start, all culminating in the apparent largesse of the
Model Cities funds released for a wide range of community improvements following the
urban riots of the 1960s. Since the demise of the Model Cities experiment, more focus
and accountability has been added to inner city funding. However, if in a somewhat
different guise, inner city enrichment policies continue to be pursued, for example, in
the commitment to inner city housing rehabilitation by senior governments in the United
States, Canada, and Britain. The 1974 Housing and Community Development Act offered
American city administrations considerable flexibility in promoting a broad range of

community improvements, and in Britain, policy initiatives concerning the newly discovered inner city problem also intimated a new round of government measures to achieve inner city consolidation and revitalization. In Canada, Neighborhood Improvement Areas are selected inner city districts for which government grants and loans have been made available to promote community stability, with planning priorities designated by the residents themselves. Similar were the General Improvement Areas introduced in the 1969 Housing Act in Britain; more recently the 1974 Act has initiated improvement policies in small Housing Action Areas suffering from more acute deprivation.

The Perspective of Political Economy

It is noteworthy that all the government programs of grants and loans for inner city enrichment previously mentioned have come from senior governments. One of the major reasons for the low quality of urban services has been the fiscal poverty of the cities. One striking illustration of the impoverished state of city exchequers is their lowly credit rating in the major capital markets (Table 10.4). A number of the largest cities of the manufacturing belt have poor bond ratings, including New York (Caa), Buffalo (Ba), and Boston, Detroit, Philadelphia, and Newark (Baa). By 1980, over one-third of Northeastern cities had a credit rating below category A; this status was shared by 13 percent of cities in the South, 3 percent of cities in the North Central states, and only 1 percent of cities in the West (Zeigler, 1981). The rating of Northeastern cities has fallen substantially in recent years. In 1960, almost half of them enjoyed a bond rating in the two most favored categories, but by 1980, this number had dropped to 24 percent.

The fiscal crisis of the cities is multifaceted in its origins. We saw in Chapter 9 that the immediate precedent of financial crisis in New York was that the city overextended its borrowing in anticipation of increasing taxes and government aid which did not materialize as expected. A decreasing tax base was set against the context of the

TABLE 10.4 MUNICIPAL BOND RATINGS OF
AMERICAN CENTRAL CITIES, 1977

Rating	Number of Cities	Percent
Aaa	29	11.1
Aa	99	37.9
Al	65	24.9
A	45	17.2
Baal	8	3.1
Baa	13	5.0
Ba	1	0.4
B	0	—
Caa	1	0.4
Ca	0	—
C	0	—
	261	100.0

Source: John Mercer, unpublished data, compiled from *Moody's Municipal and Government Manual,* 1977.

decentralization of taxable businesses and residents to the suburbs and interregional migration to the growth states of the South and West. On another level, there is the crippling effect of a concentration of the nation's poor. New York City contained 44 percent of New York State's population in 1966 but 70 percent of its welfare recipients. The proportion of the city's population receiving some form of public assistance has increased since then; in areas of Harlem and the Lower East Side in Manhattan, where welfare levels were less than 15 or 25 percent of the population in 1965, they had exceeded 30 and even 40 percent by 1971 (Figure 10.3). In the city as a whole, 770,000 people had been *added* to the welfare rolls between 1965 and 1971; in portions of the South Bronx, where welfare loads accounted for over half the local population, there had been an increase of 900–1000 percent in recipients over the 6-year period (Burks, 1972). Overall, by 1971, New York City was dispensing $1.7 billion a year in welfare aid.

The poverty syndrome brings with it a high crime rate and a stock of aged and abandoned buildings which contribute to a high fire risk. Thus the cities have a heavy tax burden for welfare, police, and fire departments which incapacitates them for major outlays in other public services. By 1965, in the largest metropolitan areas, education expenditures for each pupil in the suburbs were already running 25–30 percent higher than those in the central city. In the 1970s, the fiscal crisis of the city deepened. In Detroit and Philadelphia, the school year threatened to end prematurely because the school board exhausted its budget before the year was completed, and in New York impending bankruptcy has been the major political issue during the decade.

In addition, the cities have a declining tax base, because the suburbanization of factories and stores is removing high taxables from the rolls. In Chicago, the tax base increased 22 percent during the period 1962–1972, but this was far behind the inflationary cost of services. Urban renewal and the highway program have also removed taxable properties and often replaced them with tax-delinquent uses such as transportation arteries or temporary vacant space; as long ago as the early 1960s, $20 million of assessed property was removed by a 3-mile stretch of freeway in Cleveland. The loss of commercial property has transferred the tax load to residents, and in a number of older American cities, tax rates might be twice as high as a proportion of per capita income as in the suburbs. A major preoccupation of big-city mayors is to find new tax sources to bolster their sagging tax base; their efforts range from former Mayor Rizzo's enactment to tax out-of-state commuters from New Jersey who worked in Philadelphia, to former Mayor Daley's challenge to civic employees in Chicago to return their residence from the suburbs to the city or else risk dismissal.

Moreover, in the growing fiscal crisis of the cities, corporate managers are able to exert considerable pressure to secure favorable tax concessions on their center city properties. At the same time as they were negotiating new high-interest loans for New York City, a number of the financial institutions were able to exact a lowering of taxes on their own downtown property (Tabb, 1978). In Cleveland, the National City Bank, an affiliate of the powerful Cleveland Trust Company, was able to exact a tax abatement for its new downtown office building that would save it $14 million in property taxes over a 20-year period (Cockburn and Ridgeway, 1979).

The City-Suburban Relationship

The failure of metropolitan government to be developed as a challenge to the existing pattern of fragmentation in the United States accentuates the fiscal crisis of the cities, as higher-income groups are able to abandon the city and retreat behind their suburban autonomy. A thesis of the suburban exploitation of the central city that is beginning to find some empirical validation has been advanced. A tentative analysis of Detroit around 1970, suggested that a suburban family of four received net benefits in services from the city that exceeded their compensatory payments by between $7 and $50 a year, depending on the extent of their use of the city's facilities (Neenan, 1973). The relatively small size of this subsidy for an individual household assumes much more significance when we recall that in 1970, 63 percent of the metropolitan population of 4.2 million lived in suburban municipalities. Extrapolating from Neenan's estimates would suggest a transfer payment of between $5 million and $35 million annually exacted from Detroit by its suburbs in the early 1970s. Assessment of interarea transfer payments is extremely complicated, so that these figures can only be speculative; nevertheless, they are illustrative of suburban exploitation of the city. Nor are poor areas in central cities exclusive welfare recipients, contrary to the general myth. In 1966, these areas received only about 20 percent of the expenditure of major welfare programs granted to the 12 largest metropolitan areas; indeed, social security unemployment payments made to the suburbs were more than four times *greater* than public assistance payments made to central city poverty areas (Pfaff, 1973).

Whereas the overall effects of net transfer payments remain in large part conjectural, there is more certainty concerning the unanticipated urban consequences of some major government programs. We noted in Chapter 9 how federal housing legislation has consistently favored new construction in the suburbs over the central cities. In 1962, various housing subsidies to the poor provided benefits valued at $820 million, whereas housing subsidies to middle-class homeowners in the form of income tax deductions amounted to no less than $2.9 billion. Even more striking are Schorr's estimates that the $820 million conceded to the poorest 20 percent of Americans was overshadowed by a figure of $1.7 billion in tax concessions granted to the wealthiest 20 percent (Schorr, 1968). Equally decisive and regressive have been the effects of the Federal Highway Act, which has provided a vast subsidy for the private automobile over public transportation. During the major period of urban highway construction, the federal government offered 90 percent funding for expressway construction. In 1969, government spending on highways amounted to over $4 billion against $150 million for transit, the transportation mode of the poor. The highway program has been socially regressive in benefitting unduly middle-class suburban dwellers and land developers at the cost of the central city whose tax base and neighborhood quality of life have been simultaneously eroded—by public programs using taxes that central city dwellers themselves have paid.

Politics Inside the Central City

Aside from city-suburban differences, there are significant political inequities within the city itself. We reviewed in Chapter 9 the unequal access of interest groups to power and the way in which elite coalitions have enjoyed excessive influence in land use decision making. In contrast, inner city neighborhoods, especially those with a minority population, have been essentially disenfranchised. Although the $75 million expended in the large Model Cities area in inner city Philadelphia is popular knowledge, it should be remembered, too, that almost $40 million of public money has been spent to develop a high level of amenity for upper-income residents in the much smaller Society Hill neighborhood. As Kasperson and Breitbart (1974) have observed, "Elite groups are, in short, successful in capturing the gatekeepers" (pp. 9–10). Moreover, large visible subsidies to poverty areas need not necessarily mean large net benefits. In a ghetto neighborhood of over 80,000 in Washington, D.C., a tentative estimate suggested that the net inflow of public services, including health, welfare, education, and police benefits, was just *exceeded* to a value of $0.8 million by the outflow of taxes and contributions (Mellor, 1973). Again, although the precise arithmetic can only be approximate, the relative size of the balance is suggestive.

In addition to the direct favoring of higher-status areas which we have already reviewed, there are at least two other political tactics that have contributed to the disenfranchisement of disadvantaged districts: gerrymandering and a process of municipal nondecision making. Gerrymandering involves the manipulation of electoral boundaries in order to assist a particular party and its associated social, economic, and ethnic interests. It is initiated by a party in power that wishes to consolidate or add to its majority at the next election by designing political units with a spatial configuration that will optimize its electoral strength.

Gerrymandering has been a relatively common tactic to undermine the democratic process to the advantage of a ruling party in American cities and elsewhere; in Northern Ireland, for example, Busteed (1975) has noted its use to limit Catholic political strength in Londonderry. A striking illustration of gerrymandering was provided in 1971 by a proposal from the majority Democrats for a reapportionment of boundaries of electoral districts for the State House of Representatives in Philadelphia (Figure 10.11). Though the Democratic legislature emphasized the equal population of each proposed district, the irregular, attenuated shape of the proposed units strongly suggests partisan politics; note districts 183 in South Philadelphia, 171 and 174 in the Northeast, and 202 and 203 in the Northwest. Most striking of all is District 196 in North Philadelphia, which snakes 4.5 miles north-south, without ever exceeding a half mile in width. Its intent is to submerge the Republican vote of the inner suburbs beneath the vote of the inner city. Such partisan forms of apportionment are not unusual. A review of selected boundaries in eight American cities showed an underrepresentation of 50 percent in areas with a black majority in the actual electoral districts when compared to a set of ideal districts derived by an objective algorithm (O'Loughlin, 1976). Such gerrymandering contributes to the underrepresentation of blacks and other minorities in elected office (Table 10.5), with an attendant neglect of their interests. Minority underrepresentation is also invariably accentuated on city councils where there is a nonpartisan, at-large political system (Sloan, 1969).

The disqualification of the legitimate interest of groups who do not enjoy a position of power may be achieved by a number of methods more subtle than gerrymandering.

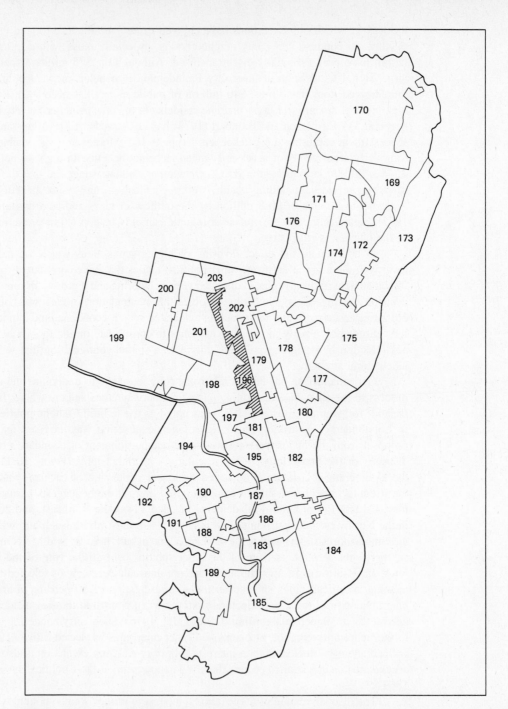

Figure 10.11   Gerrymandering in proposed reapportionment plan, Philadelphia.

TABLE 10.5 REPRESENTATION OF BLACKS IN ELECTED OFFICE, 1968

City	Type of District	# of Districts	# with Black Rep's.	% Represented by Blacks	% of City Pop. Black	Proportion of Ideal Representation by Blacks
New York	U.S. Congressional	19	2	10.5	21.2	0.50
Philadelphia	State Senate	9	2	22.0	33.6	0.65
Chicago	U.S. Congressional	9	1	11.1	32.7	0.30
Milwaukee	State Senate	7	0	00.0	14.7	0.00
Atlanta	City Council	8	1	12.5	51.3	0.24
New Orleans	City Council	5	0	00.0	45.0	0.00
Los Angeles	U.S. Congressional	14	1	7.1	17.9	0.39
Seattle	State Senate	9	0	00.0	10.0	0.00

Source: J. O'Loughlin, "Malapportionment and Gerrymandering in the Ghetto," pp. 539–565 in J. Adams (ed.), *Urban Policymaking and Metropolitan Dynamics.* Cambridge, Mass.: Ballinger, 1976, p. 563. Copyright 1976. Reprinted with permission.

A study of Baltimore politics showed that through *non*-decision making, concerns important to some groups were ignored or suppressed and failed to appear on political agendas (Bachrach and Baratz, 1970). Thus it is not simply the overt conflicts that we discussed in Chapter 9 that reveal the disposition of power but also issues for which conflict does not occur because of the maneuvering of influential lobbyists. Strategies that blunt the intervention of opposition groups and help to create a nonissue include the withholding of information or the presentation of ambiguous information concerning land use proposals (Seley and Wolpert, 1974) and also the co-optation of an opposition by the conferral of visible but inconsequential concessions (Ley, 1974b).

Policy Implications

The most obvious policy response to the imminent bankruptcy of the American central city is a form of metropolitan government that, through suburban-city transfer payments, would move toward an equalization of metropolitan indebtedness. But in the face of strong suburban resistance, there has been no progress in such a strategy of opening up the suburbs. Some commentators have claimed that although there have been no de jure changes, there has been a de facto slowing in the polarization of city and suburb (Glenn, 1973). Indeed, it has even been suggested that central city renewal plus the gradual expansion of urban problems into the suburbs will contribute toward a much closer equalization of income levels by the year 2000 (Thompson, 1973).

Meanwhile, the federal government has to some extent intervened to underwrite urban indebtedness. Between 1961 and 1975, there was almost a tenfold increase in federal aid to America's standard metropolitan statistical areas (Burkhead, 1975). In 1972, a revenue-sharing program was introduced that made block grants to cities, to be used according to the needs perceived by local administrations; this program was renewed in 1976. A number of cities have used these funds to bolster existing programs and to stabilize or even reduce taxes. By the late 1970s, the most hard pressed cities of the historic manufacturing belt were receiving additional special funds for their "urban crisis conditions'' of slow growth, aging buildings and services, and high concentrations of the poor. The emerging trends suggest that ''many cities will be receiving large shares of their operating budgets from the federal government on a more or less permanent basis'' (Brookings, 1977). But here, too, the fiscal issue is not independent of political realities: the most hard pressed cities have been losing population and, through reapportionment, their political representation in Washington, to the rapidly growing cities of the South and West. The latter regions have historically fallen victim to the dominant influence of the Northeast, and their regional loyalties might well limit their largesse in diverting special funds to their erstwhile superiors. So, too, like all welfare programs, federal aid to the cities is vulnerable during periods of national economic recession, and has been under severe scrutiny from the Reagan administration.

On the intrametropolitan level, inequality in the access to power has been challenged by a number of popular movements since 1965. By the mid-1970s, a number of cities had experienced greater community participation in the form of a decentralization of urban services and even some experiments with neighborhood control, the emergence of new urban reform parties, increased local accountability in the shape of a reinvigorated neighborhood and ward base to city politics, and a more articulate and aware citizenry (Kasperson and Breitbart, 1974; Mollenkopf, 1978). White migration to the suburbs and greater black political consciousness had allowed black mayors to be elected in Los Angeles, Detroit, Cleveland, and Atlanta, as well as in over 130 smaller centers. However, this progress was not uniform, and the momentum of citizen participation in neighborhood and city politics has certainly weakened since the early 1970s. But, as Lemon (1978) has noted in Toronto, the activism of the early 1970s has in part been institutionalized; certainly there is a much more acute perception by urban residents of ''the real world of city politics'' (Lorimer, 1970).

Conclusion

The development of social indicators has forcefully documented intuitive beliefs concerning the geography of the quality of urban life. But, as important, these indicators have on occasion revealed distributions that are counterintuitive. The discordance which was discovered between objective and subjective indicators concerning inner city urban villages prompted policy initiatives of enrichment to replace those of demolition. Again, relationships between indicators on one scale are not necessarily repeated on another; the positive correlation between environmental and economic indicators on the intrametropolitan level largely disappears on the national level. Thus, despite its measurement problems, the indicators movement is not as superficial or redundant as some critics claim. In a period of government identification with social accounting, indicators also provide a useful monitor and evaluation of government programs over a period of time.

Nevertheless, by themselves, indicators are mute. Cartographically, they present distributions which beg interpretation; socially, they portray grievances and inequities that demand action. We have noted that the several interpretations have tended to generate their own remedial policies. The ecological emphasis on the physical environment has led to design solutions; a subcultural emphasis on the invidious effects of the social environment has encouraged efforts of dispersion, to expose citizens to more wholesome social settings; the spatial emphasis on problems of access has led logically to strategies of greater locational equity and local enrichment programs; finally, the perspective of political economy, revealing urban poverty and political weakness, has demanded greater fiscal intervention in the city by the central government and the opening up of political access to disenfranchised groups, whether they be minority groups within the central city, or central city administrations in their bargaining with suburban municipalities and state legislatures.

The various policy initiatives accompanying each analytical perspective have generally been complementary rather than competitive. Nevertheless, they have not always proven consistent in their effects; for example, the initiatives toward decentralization and community control have proven contradictory to the policy of racial integration, especially in terms of neighborhood schooling. Nor have the programs been strikingly successful; some, such as the opening up of the suburbs, have been wholly ineffective. The theoretical fragmentation underlying our understanding of the city and the inconclusive results of much urban policy have stimulated attempts to develop a more synthetic theoretical formulation which sees urban life in the broader context of national (and even international) social relations and processes of economic, sociocultural, and political change. In concluding our discussion, it is to these arguments concerning the widest contexts of contemporary urbanism that we now turn.

Chapter 11

The Contexts of a Livable City

The human factor is something more than the works-of-man. It includes ideologies as well as technologies

(Watson, 1957:468)

(Jesus) came closer to the city and when he saw it he wept over it

(Luke 19:41)

The city has never been without its prophets, and rarely has it heeded them. In a provocative if somewhat melancholy thesis, Jacques Ellul (1970) claims to have traced a persistent antiurbanism through the pages of the Old and New Testaments. The first murderer, Cain, was also the first city builder, Ellul reminds us, and this grim precedent is followed through the pages of scripture until it is reversed in the final apocalyptic vision of the New Jerusalem. In this interpretation, Ellul is joining a broad tradition, for since the Enlightenment intellectual response to the city has been equivocal at best. For poets such as Blake and Cowper, the city was not only the "genial soil of cultivated life" but also:

> In cities foul example on most minds
> Begets its likeness. Rank abundance on
> Rank abundance breeds in gross and
> pampered cities sloth and lust. And
> wantoness and glutonous excess
> (Cowper, 1785).

As the nineteenth century progressed, antiurban sentiments developed into a torrent, fuelled by such literary figures as Charles Dickens and the Romantic movements in Britain and America. The mood of the men of letters was the mood also of scholars and other intellectuals (Schorske, 1963; White and White, 1962). Dickensian passion against the modern city has been upheld in the prolific and influential writings of Lewis Mumford, and in much urban sociology, especially that derived from the Chicago school of human ecology. Intellectual hostility toward the big city has extended also to the suburb, so that in his Levittown study, Gans (1967) found it necessary to challenge the generally critical suburban literature that had been written in the preceding 15 years. Overall, intellectual thought harbors a pervasive antiurbanism; indeed, its persistence has led Hadden and Barton (1973) to speak of a tenacious antiurban ideology biassing academic and professional judgment of the city.

Ellul's interpretation of the human degradation accompanying urbanization shares an important characteristic with the view of a number of urban scholars, including the human ecologists of the Chicago school. Common to each of them is a critique directed against the city as a fact in its own right, rather than against the specific attitudes and actions perpetrated within its boundaries. The city is regarded as a social *fact* largely divorced from its inhabitants, not a social *construction* sustained by particular groups and the product of a distinctive historic period. This view, shared by Ellul and the ecologists, among others, is one that offers at best a partial insight (Fischer, 1976). As we have indicated repeatedly in earlier chapters, an analytic preoccupation with urban form alone is theoretically incomplete. Urban morphology is constructed, sustained, and redirected by the ideologies and practices of social groups acting within a range of contexts, demarcated historically and geographically. Except for rare occasions, this does not imply, as we have seen, that men and women are totally at liberty in defining the city according to their own purposes. But to regard spatial form as one component of a complex interaction of meaning, activity, and constraint is not the same as viewing it as some transcendent given that impacts men, women, and children in some more or less unvarying fashion. A preoccupation with the city as a spatial object may divert analysis from the city as the home of man, that is, as a complex of interest groups, value systems, routines, and activities set in the built environment and situated within a broader range of contexts. Indeed, it could be argued that Ellul's interpretation of the city as an object over man is inconsistent with Christ's weeping over Jerusalem, not as built form but as a symbol of a covenant that had been broken, as evidenced by his denunciation of the habitual practices and attitudes of men which were current within its walls, and by his anger against the elite who sanctioned and benefited from such conduct (Luke 19:41–47).

If historical analysis of the city implies an understanding of past meanings and actions, then how much more eloquent to the interpretive geographer are contemporary urban landscapes of present values and constraints (Gibson, 1978). Speaking of the city, Henri Lefebvre (1976) has commented that ''space is political and ideological. It is a product literally filled with ideologies.'' In a striking if somewhat tongue-in-cheek illustration of the relations between townscape and ideology, Bunge has reproduced a plan for Toronto as designed by Duke Redbird, an Ojibwa Indian (Bunge and Bordessa, 1975:355). Business and industry are displaced to the urban periphery in Redbird's Toronto (there is a PBD, or peripheral business district!), and at the city core is a central *meeting* district surrounded by low-density communities of craftsmen and agriculturalists.

What Lefebvre and Bunge are both telling us is that the city does not contain its own interpretation but is a reflection of broader values and relations in society, though in urban form these relations are expressed and reinforced. Particularly in Western society, where the population is so heavily urbanized, it is too limiting to confine attention to explicitly urban categories when effective theory requires a more complete synthesis of trends in society itself. In this concluding chapter, we shall continue our interrogation of urban form (Part 1). The geography of everyday life, including the subjective meaning of place (Part 2), has already been considered against the contexts of intersubjective social worlds (Part 3) and the broader context of a system of social stratification (Part 4). In conclusion, we shall expand the contexts of urban form and urban experience still further, to assess the actual and potential livability of the city in light of the dominant economic, political, and cultural factors operating at the national level within an advanced industrial society.

From City to Society

For geographers, an appealing feature of Engels' interpretation of Manchester in the 1840s was his methodology of reading off key relations of industrial society from the land use pattern of the industrial city. The form of the city was an indicator (as well as a reinforcement) of the social order; spatial form and social relations were closely intertwined. What Engels perceived was a city and a society that were sharply polarized. From his viewpoint the nexus of society rested in the *economic* realm, in the exploitative relationship between the industrial owner and his work force, in which the owner controlled the means of existence of his work force while regarding them in a purely calculating fashion as ''hands'' in the manufacturing process. The concentration of capital in a small group of owners who were often in cutthroat competition ensured that the relationship would be a highly exploitative one. The work force was vulnerable to market trends and, in particular, trade cycles, when unemployment and destitution would accompany a downturn in production. Manchester was the embodiment of industrial capitalism, a city whose population had expanded tenfold in 50 years in response to the spectacular growth of the textile industry, with two-thirds of the work force employed as manual workers.

The era of industrial capitalism was also the era of liberal capitalism, and laissez-faire was an integral element of liberal government in the early nineteenth century. Thus Engels felt no need to treat the role of the state or of the *political* realm in any detail in his study of Manchester. From his other writings it is clear that he regarded the state as an extension of the ruling commercial class (Marx and Engels, 1970). As for the local state, municipal politics scarcely existed in Manchester in the 1840s; the city did not return a Member of Parliament until 1832, and its first council met only in 1838. On a visit to the city in 1835, de Tocqueville observed: ''At every turn human liberty shows its capricious creative force. There is no trace of the slow continuous action of government'' (Marcus, 1974:61). In the realm of *culture* and values, Engels identified a rational, calculating, and purely economic ideology as guiding the public life of the middle-class industrialist; they were a ''walking political economy'' (Marcus, 1974). The culture of the working-class is interpreted as both noble and uncivilized; in a number of places Engels, like other nineteenth-century writers, seems to subscribe to a variant of the culture of poverty thesis in describing less wholesome aspects of working-class life.

Although one could not challenge the data Engels presented, one might dispute the selectivity of the material that was both included and excluded and the interpretation made of it. But for present purposes the more important point is to note the manner in which the form and experience of the industrial city were related to the configuration of an industrial society of which the city was both a creation and a reinforcement. Connections were drawn between the land use map of the city, the individual experience of the mill laborer, and the larger picture—the sociohistorical context within which the built environment and everyday life were located.

In the remainder of this chapter we shall outline the intersection of contemporary urban trends with the economic, political, and cultural milieus comprising the larger society in the advanced industrial nations. Robert Park noted how the major city acted as a laboratory and that within it social processes were accelerated. Today, in a yet more urban society, the city is still more a concentrate of contemporary social processes. We have noted, for example, the state's use of construction and urban development as a stimulant of the national economy. But at the same time, the condition of the national economy has a reciprocal influence on the urban land market, with trends in the national economy having a cyclic effect on urban property values (Johnston, 1976c). And, as we shall see, investment in the built environment, prompted by high profit margins, is likely to divert investment from other sectors of the domestic economy, particularly manufacturing, with potentially serious consequences for the national balance of payments (*The Economist*, 1979). These interactive relations within the economic and political sectors will in turn draw further responses and initiatives from government and the public at large. Rapidly inflating housing costs and recession in manufacturing will trigger popular anxieties and resistance which in turn will feed back, through state response to opinion polls and labor militancy, into the economic sector. Thus the economic, political, and cultural components of national society, though they may be treated as distinct entities conceptually, strongly interpenetrate each other in practice. Moreover, while these macrolevel factors generate constraints and tendencies for each urban household, national trends are transmitted through a range of local circumstances which may variously accentuate or divert their local impact. In looking at the complex of relationships surrounding a household's experience of the urban environment, the researcher is well advised to seek not laws but tendencies. An understanding of the relations between the contemporary city and the society in which it is situated will usually reveal a far more complicated picture than the one Engels claimed to read off from the landscape of industrial Manchester. Just how complicated these relations can be will become clearer as we examine in turn national economic, political, and cultural milieus of the contemporary city.

The Economic Milieu

National and regional economic trends provide an environment critical to the health of cities. In this section we shall consider some of the changing traits of the economies of the advanced nations; later in the chapter the effects of these trends on urban development will be examined.

Growing Concentration

As we saw in Chapter 7, a principal ingredient of the economic milieu of the contemporary city is the growing concentration of economic activity in fewer and larger decision-making units. Recall that in Britain by 1970, in 20 of the 22 major industrial sectors an average of only three firms was controlling the market (Winkler, 1977). Even in land development, which has traditionally provided easy entry for small operators, concentration is proceeding apace; in Chapter 9, we noted that one-third of developable land around metropolitan Toronto is in the hands of just four development companies, representing a medium to high concentration ratio according to several measures of business oligopoly (Gunton, 1978).

The rise of multilocal or multinational corporations has had a range of significant effects. Fierce competition between numerous producers has been replaced in some sectors by more variable relations between a corporate oligarchy. On one level the rise of the multinationals has contributed to an awesome concentration of economic power. But it is a concentration which probably remains nonetheless more diffuse in terms of ownership than if judged by nineteenth-century standards. Marx observed that the rise of the joint stock company would make the capitalist irrelevant (Giddens, 1973), and the stock market has indeed generated some dispersion of market power to stockholders and shareholders, and the substantial replacement of owners responsible only to themselves by managers responsible to their shareholders. Moreover, through the operation of insurance and pension funds, the identity of capitalist and worker has become still more blurred. In Britain, for example, the largest investing institution is the Post Office Superannuation Fund, which invests on behalf of 40,000 contributing members and 110,000 Post Office pensioners (Ambrose and Colenutt, 1975:52). In 1974, a property investment group called the American Property Trust was coordinated by the Post Office, British Rail, British Steel, the Electricity Supply Industry, and a chartered bank to invest pension fund income in suburban office complexes and suburban shopping centers around the growing cities of the southeastern United States.

Technology and Economic Growth

At the same time the two-class polarization identified in the nineteenth century has been modified by other factors. There has occurred a steady fracturing within the working class itself, with growing numbers of skilled and semiskilled workers separating out objectively, subjectively, and often politically from the unskilled segment. Almost 50 years after his study of Manchester, Engels condemned and thereby acknowledged the innumerable gradations and subcultures within English society that precluded any unified class consciousness. Substantial real growth has occurred in the material condition of a broad segment of the population: in contrast to the hovels occupied by the Manchester textile workers and their vulnerability before avaricious landlords, over half the work force in Britain, the United States, and Canada are homeowners; in Britain, especially, the private rental sector of the housing market is much diminished. Under sustained pressure from labor unions and their allies, responsive government legislation, and sustained economic growth, a qualitative shift occurred in the material condition of the work force up to the mid 1970s. A shorter working day, extended holidays, pensions, and health and unemployment benefits have substantially modified the culture of work.

The containment of the size of the unskilled segment of the labor force has been attained in part by technological advances permitting extensive automation of tedious, routine, assembly line jobs. The introduction of mechanized robots in motor vehicle assembly represents the most recent of a long sequence of technological innovations that have removed monotonous industrial jobs—though, as we shall see, with its implications for higher unemployment, such innovation can be a double-edged sword. Nonetheless, within the economy of the Western nations a major trend over the past century has been the growing dependence of the business sector on scientific knowledge and technological innovation. Technology has become a dominant force in production; rather than the factory, Bell (1976a) suggests that the university and research establishments have become leading institutions. The major industrial states now expend 2–3 percent of their GNP on research and development. Indicative of the role of science was President Carter's statement, in presenting his 1979 budget to the U.S. Congress, that science policy be viewed in conjunction with economic policy and that research allocations be regarded not as expenditures but as long-term investments with a guaranteed high return (Kucharczyk, 1978).

The economic future of the advanced industrial state rests increasingly on high-technology enterprise. Over the past 25 years in the United States, employment in high-technology industry grew nine times faster than in low-technology industry, and productivity was twice as great. High-technology products generated a trade surplus of $25 billion, whereas since 1969 the low-technology sector has accumulated a trading deficit of $16 billion (Kucharczyk, 1978). Technology is a major producer of real wealth, a development with theoretical as well as practical consequences, for the leading role of technology and science severely challenges a labor theory of value (Habermas, 1970:104). In a highly automated industrial plant it is incongruous to ascribe the generation of surplus value to an absent body of unskilled labor. Instead, Bell places theoretical knowledge capable of solving problems and improving efficiency in a central position in contemporary Western society: "In capitalist society the axial institution has been private property and in the post-industrial society it is the centrality of theoretical knowledge" (Bell, 1976a:115).

Increasing efficiency contributed to a rapidly expanding economy at least up to the mid 1970s. From 1945 to 1973, the annual per capita production of goods and services more than doubled in real terms in the United States, while the index of output in manufacturing per man hour, set at a base of 100 in 1967, rose from 64 in 1950 to 127 in 1973. Overall productivity growth in the private sector was about 2.5 percent a year for the first half of this century, rising to about 3 percent for the following 25 years. The postwar era up to the early 1970s was a time of sustained growth in the world economy; even in Britain the period saw higher rates of growth in Gross National Product (GNP), per capita income, productivity, and exports than for any preceding 25 years in the country's history (Thrift, 1979). In continental Europe, productivity gains in manufacturing were even more marked; for Belgium, France, Germany, Italy, and the Netherlands average annual gains fluctuated from 3.5 to over 7 percent from 1955 to 1973 (Brown and Sheriff, 1979).

Occupational Shifts

The rapid ascendancy of research and development and factory automation has contributed to a transformation of the occupational categories of the advanced industrial state. Increased productivity has released increasing numbers of the work force for jobs that are not directly associated with the extraction and processing of raw materials. The growth of government has added a large professional work force to public services such as health, education, and welfare as well as a large clerical segment to all government departments. In 1900, 18 percent of Americans were employed in white-collar occupations, whereas twice as many (36 percent) were classified as blue collar; in 1950, the proportions were 37 percent and 41 percent, and by 1974, they were 49 percent and 35 percent. Including the large and diverse services component, the American white-collar sector accounted for 64 percent of the labor force in 1977 (Ginzberg, 1979). As we might expect, the job category that has shown the quickest growth has been the professional and technical class, which in the United States has surged from less than 1 million employed in 1890 to over 12 million in 1974. This category has been expanding at about twice the rate of the national labor force; the number of natural and social scientists alone virtually doubled from 1960 to 1975. In Britain, too, white-collar employment accounted for 57 percent of the work force in 1976, and the most rapid job growth had been in professional and scientific services, which had gained 1.5 million positions in the previous 15 years (Brown and Sheriff, 1979). The pattern is much the same in Canada, where white-collar employment increased by 26 percent from 1971 to 1975, when, including the services category, it included 62 percent of all jobs. A further subdivision within white-collar occupations showed much higher rates of job growth among the quaternary activities—the senior white-collar categories of professional, technical, managerial, and administrative positions—than among the tertiary sector of clerical, sales, and service jobs. Indeed, quaternary employees now account for 20–25 percent of the work force in the United States and Canada. Virtually unaccounted for in some nineteenth-century discussions of urban society, the quaternary sector represents a group in ascendancy that enjoys both market power and social influence.

The major implication of these figures for national employment is the transition from a goods-producing to a service-consuming society. By 1977, over 70 percent of the nonagricultural jobs in the United States were service-related and less than 30 percent goods-related; this represents a reversal of the proportions for 1900. Similar trends are evident in Britain, where manufacturing employment declined by over 1 million from 1965 to 1974, while almost 700,000 new jobs were added in services (Sant, 1978). In part, these figures indicate the higher levels of productivity and automation which characterize manufacturing in the postindustrial state. Industry is capital-intensive and not labor-intensive, so that major new investment may produce relatively few jobs. Indeed, even within the United Kingdom there was a 16 percent gain in manufacturing output from 1965 to 1977 (Cairncross, 1979).

Deindustrialization

But this is not the whole story. In Britain from 1960 to 1975 the contribution of manufacturing to the Gross Domestic Product (GDP) in current prices declined from 36 percent to 29 percent (Brown and Sheriff, 1979). Moreover, the British experience is shared, if to a less acute measure, by a number of industrial nations, leading economists to speak of a process of *deindustrialization* underway in Britain, the United States, and

TABLE 11.1   KNOWN JOB LOSSES FOR INDIVIDUAL BRITISH FIRMS,
JULY 22–AUGUST 23, 1980

Industry	Redundancies	Short Time
Automobiles, Trucks, Motorcycles & Components	15,485	34,790
Steel	—	19,800
Engineering	3,294	3,000
Industrial Machinery, Metal Goods	3,566	—
Paper Products, Printing	3,320	—
Textiles, Clothing, Shoes	1,741	—
Food Products, Brewing	1,370	—
Consumer Goods	1,020	1,300
Electronics	1,100	—
Construction Supplies	396	1,800
Chemicals, Plastics	256	3,000
Wood Products	280	—

Source: Assembled from data in *The Guardian*, August 28, 1980, p. 4.

a number of other advanced industrial nations (Singh, 1977; Blackaby, 1979). In the United States the contribution of manufacturing to the GDP declined (in current prices) from 28 percent to 23 percent from 1960 to 1975; in Canada the drop was also five points over the same period.

Deindustrialization is most evident in the industries that powered the industrial revolution: textiles, steel, and heavy engineering, including shipbuilding. In the European Economic Community 200,000 jobs were lost in the steel industry between 1974 and 1980, or one-quarter of the total work force. The industrial recession has been most serious in Britain; in 1975, it was regarded as unthinkable that unemployment should exceed 1 million, but in July 1980, the figure passed 2 million, and by early 1982 it touched 3 million. This represents an unemployment rate in excess of 12 percent, a figure which is also being approached in the United States and Canada; as recently as 1974 the British rate was only 2.5 percent. Jobs have been lost particularly in steel, automobile construction, engineering, and textiles, as suggested by redundancies declared by individual firms over a 1-month period in the summer of 1980 (Table 11.1). This listing is not exhaustive, but it does highlight the industrial vulnerability of a number of the Western nations, admittedly in Britain in its most acute form. Job loss has progressed beyond such typical nineteenth-century industries as steel and textiles to include automobiles and, to a lesser extent, chemicals and electrical engineering (Gillespie and Owen, 1981). However, notable is the absence of the service sector from the casualty list. The erosion of employment in manufacturing and the continued job growth in the service sector have prompted economists to speak of deindustrialization, and other social scientists to refer to the emergence of a postindustrial society in the advanced nations.

The process of deindustrialization might not matter if, first, industrial output were to be maintained by increasing productivity and, second, if the employment slack in the economy were taken up by a vigorous service sector. We have seen that in Britain, at least to 1977, not only productivity but also total output continued to rise. However, this prospect is less cheery when the share of world markets is examined, for even in sectors where output increased, its growth was at a much slower rate than that of competitors. For example, Britain's share of manufacturing trade between the advanced industrial nations declined from 25 percent in 1950 to 9 percent in 1977; the U.S. decline was from 27 percent to 16 percent, whereas impressive gains were registered by Germany and Japan (Brown and Sheriff, 1979). Equally grave has been *import penetration,* the loss of the domestic market to foreign competition; in automobiles this had become so serious by 1980 that major corporations (Chrysler and British Leyland) were surviving only through massive government financing. In Britain, a rough estimate of import penetration suggested that imported manufactured goods took about 8 percent of the domestic market in 1968 but over 20 percent by 1976. The shifting trade balance is in part the product of changing fortunes among the industrial nations themselves, favoring Germany and Japan at the expense of Britain, the United States, and Canada. But a new factor is the rise of the industrializing nations outside Western Europe and North America which, following Japan's example, are developing competitive labor-intensive industries in such areas as steel, heavy engineering, and textiles. Western Europe's share of world shipbuilding has dwindled from over 80 percent in 1950 to 37 percent in 1977, and in terms of raw steel, the combined production of the United States and Western Europe accounted for 74 percent of world supply in 1950 but only 40 percent in 1977. It is only expensive government subsidies which are maintaining ailing industries at even their present levels. The nationalized British Steel Corporation, one of the worst economic liabilities in Western Europe, lost over $4 million a day in 1977; by 1980, the economic recession caused a limit to be set to government aid and prompted a further round of job losses and short-time work (Table 11.1).

In contrast, the service sector of the economy in the advanced nations is showing more buoyancy. In Britain, gross share profits for firms in the service sector remained relatively constant between 1966 and 1976, whereas share profits in the manufacturing sector dropped substantially; according to some calculations, by 1976 the average share in the service sector was grossing a return up to eight times higher than the percentage profit on a manufacturing share (Brown and Sheriff, 1979). This relatively strong performance of the service sector has been accompanied by continuing job growth and the diversion of investment away from manufacturing, thus deepening the problems of industrial production. However, even in Britain the traditionally strong performance of invisible earnings, associated in part with the financial services offered by the City of London, does not compensate fully for the decline of manufacturing for several reasons. In terms of the export market, even in Britain the volume of overseas trade in manufacturing continues to be double the value of overseas credit from the service sector (Singh, 1977), so that the role of manufacturing in the national economy continues to be critical, and its decline could not be fully compensated for by services. Second, it is generally held that economic growth in a nation is closely related to the growth of its manufacturing sector, which therefore occupies a particularly strategic place in the economy. In part, the dynamic role of manufacturing is associated with its level of productivity and its capacity for further improvement. Despite the unsatisfactory state of British manufacturing, there was an average productivity growth of over 3 percent a year between 1960 and 1975, compared to an increment of less than 0.5 percent in the whole private and

public service sector excluding transportation and distribution (Brown and Sheriff, 1979).
Thus a simple switch of economic energy from manufacturing to services leaves unanswered significant problems induced by deindustrialization.

The local causes of manufacturing recession vary from nation to nation, but several general themes are apparent. First, there has been a geographic shift in economic advantage in the mix of factors that provide inputs to manufacturing. One input with variable costs is labor; in the textile industry, 1978 wage rates of $7–$8 an hour in Western Europe compared with less than $1 an hour in Hong Kong or South Korea. Another variable factor is energy. The American automobile industry, with the low fuel performance of its larger motor cars, has been more seriously affected by the escalating price of world oil since 1973 than have its Japanese and European competitors with their established expertise in small, energy-efficient vehicles. As a result, the deepening oil crisis has heightened the import penetration of foreign automobile manufacturers into the domestic U.S. market. Second, in the case of the United Kingdom at least, there appears to be a greater income elasticity of demand for foreign goods by the British market than there is for British goods by foreign markets. It seems as if both Britons and foreigners have a greater preference for non-British goods, leading to a broadening deficit in the national balance of payments.

Why then is there such deflated demand? There is growing support for an interpretation that emphasizes consumer resistance to low quality, poor design, and delivery delays—in other words, shortcomings that might be described as nonprice characteristics in the manufacturing process. In part, these might be linked to low levels of investment, but this is not the only set of relevant factors. Equally or more important are such inputs as the climate of worker-management relations, the role of trades unions, the quality of management, and even the lowly social status ascribed to engineering and other occupations in the manufacturing sector (Singh, 1977; Brown and Sheriff, 1979). In short, there are important influences in the cultural and political milieu of a nation which act on its economic performance (Hall, 1980). The economic milieu of cities in the advanced nations therefore cannot be understood independent of effects transmitted from their political and cultural contexts; indeed, some would speak of the necessary discovery of the "social and cultural foundations of economic success" (Hall, 1980).

We will note shortly the variable geographic impact of these national economic trends on urban development, for they are contributing to markedly unequal patterns of metropolitan growth and decline.

The Political Milieu

A second range of contexts of contemporary urbanization is associated with political relations and the policies of national, regional, and local government.

The Scope of the State

World recession and deindustrialization in many of the advanced economies have reopened the issue of scarcity and severely tempered some of the optimism of the early

1970s that the Western nations were entering an era beyond scarcity (Gershuny, 1978). Increasing unemployment, decreasing economic growth, and both the prospect and the occurrence of a decline in real income have made the distribution of national wealth a matter of some urgency, and, increasingly, questions of the disbursement of scarce resources have been referred to the state. The allocation of goods and services is now a joint responsibility of the marketplace and political decision making. Symptomatic of the complex and often confusing relations between the state and the marketplace are the varied terms used in social theory to describe the contemporary Western nation, with labels such as ''advanced capitalism'' or ''neocapitalism'' stressing continuity as well as change and phrases such as ''post industrial'' or even ''postcapitalist society'' highlighting the significant breaks that have occurred with the industrial capitalism of the nineteenth century.

Daniel Bell considers that ''the power of the state . . . is the central fact about modern society'' (Bell, 1976b:228), and the critical role of the state in contemporary life has been argued by social theorists displaying a range of political sympathies (Saunders, 1979). The scope of government may be assessed in a number of ways. In the United Kingdom, including nationalized companies, 25 percent of the labor force are government employees (Broadbent, 1977), compared to 16 percent in the United States. The fiscal role of government is even more substantial, with state purchases of goods and services amounting to around one-third of the GNP of the United Kingdom by the mid 1970s and over 20 percent of the American GNP in 1970. More impressive yet has been the rate of growth of government expenditure in the postwar era, from $45 billion in 1950 to $210 billion in 1970, when it represented $1000 a year for every American citizen. The state itself is not a monolithic entity but consists of multiple departments and agencies with their own, and sometimes conflicting, agendas and a hierarchy of levels between which there has often been bitter conflict over jurisdiction (particularly in Canada and Britain) during the past decade. In Britain, local government has an employment slightly larger than that of central government, though its expenditures are only about half as big. Nevertheless, the bounty of local levels of government remains immense; in Edinburgh, for example, the 1974–1975 council expenditure for a city of less than half a million amounted to approximately $140 million (Elliott and McCrone, 1979).

The State and Production

It is the increasing involvement of the state in economic and social life that has prompted a number of observers, as we saw in Chapter 7, to refer to the emergence of a corporate society. Corporatism is evident in the realms of production, with management of the private sector, within certain limits, via state fiscal policy and with direct state control of production in nationalized firms. Deindustrialization provides an important context for state involvement in production, for rationalization of a higher level than may be accomplished by the private sector is necessary in the face of declining margins of profit, shrinking investment coupled with the need for new technology, and growing international competition (Winkler, 1977). The state's role in production is thus multifaceted. It is committed to supporting vulnerable industries ailing under foreign competition (such as Chrysler and British Leyland) and to amalgamating small or obsolete industrial plants into a concentrated and less inefficient national industry to take advantage of economies of scale (British Steel). Indeed, the European steel industry, which has proven highly vulnerable to foreign competition, provides an instructive example of the present extent of corporatism, for regulation occurs not only from national governments but also from the European Commission in Brussels which, for example, requested a 10 percent cut in steel production in all member countries of the Common Market for the second half of 1980. The state is also involved in the promotion of strategic high-technology industry where, in sectors such as aerospace or energy, the risks and costs of research and development may be too high to be borne by private enterprise.

Winkler's thesis of corporatism suggests that state control grows without the necessity for a parallel growth of bureaucracy, for the state is able to direct the economy through quasi-governmental public bodies and through its strategic control of much of the decision-making environment of major corporations. Whatever the truth of this argument, the fact of a burgeoning state technocracy is inescapable. Inevitably the more centralized is national government, the stronger is bureaucratic control and the more certain is the making over of society into a reality that expresses the technocrat's world view. In the advanced Western nations the increasing state management of society heightens the danger that we become what we model.

The State and Consumption

At this point corporate and managerial views of the state converge, for the other side of the corporate state presence in production is its managerial presence in consumption (Saunders, 1979). We saw in Chapter 7 how the practical rules of the life-world of the urban bureaucracy impinge on the urban experience of residents in the allocation of public services such as housing. Even though the local government administrator is clearly subject to constraints imposed by central government (particularly in the size of his operating budget), nonetheless even the street-level bureaucrat has considerable discretion in, for example, allocating tenants to particular public housing projects, with all of the implications this carries for the tenant's subsequent quality of life (Prottas, 1978; Gray, 1976). The role of the state in public consumption, that is, in the allocation of social services, has passed beyond the provision of health, education, and social assistance to encompass the most varied elements of consumption; it constructs housing, monitors pollution, builds roads, saves historic sites, subsidizes ballet companies, and provides skateboard parks. In recent years such social consumption expenditures have accounted for up to one-half of public spending in Britain. Citizens readily recognize the value and desirability of enhanced public consumption and are never remiss to present politicians with a shopping list. In 1978, the Vancouver metropolitan area had a population of 1.2 million, but its modest size was exceeded by an immodest appetite for new capital developments, as a variety of transportation, recreational, commercial, and cultural projects being lobbied for in the city would have amounted to $1.5 billion in public expenditure if funded (Ley, 1982). High personal taxation is the inevitable accompaniment to the growth of public services; in Britain, for example, income tax for an average married man rose from 10 percent of his income in 1960 to 25 percent in 1975 (Broadbent, 1977).

Whereas the state's production decisions are determined in large measure by a broad national interest (the need to create/save jobs, environmental issues, a national energy policy, balance of payments concerns, etc.), its consumption decisions are more open to factional lobbying (Cawson, 1977; Saunders, 1979). It is in the resolution of consumption issues, therefore, that various interest groups may participate and seek to divert the allocation of consumption items in their favor. The political system of the advanced economies contains both a corporate sector and a pluralist sector (Cawson, 1977). What this amounts to is a variable influence of different political groups on urban policy according to the issue concerned. In an assessment of British urban policy since 1945, McKay and Cox (1979) note the shifting role of five principal political actors: the central government politicians, organized interest groups, popular protest groups, central government bureaucracies, and local (including urban) bureaucracies. In some issues, such as industrial location, elected central politicians were the key actors in initiating policy; in other areas, such as land use planning, organized interest groups had an important influence, especially early in the period, whereas in transportation, specialized interest groups, protest movements, and government bureaucracies, both local and national, have all exerted significant pressures.

The State and Political Interest Groups

The changing influence of different political groupings by issue and by time period complicates any simplistic view of the state as consistently supporting one faction over another or, more directly, as being a mouthpiece for one dominant or ruling class. The commitment of the state to economic growth need not imply a simple identification with dominant economic interests. Even in the 1840s Engels observed how in the British Parliament: ''Every parliamentary session sees the working classes gain ground, while the influence of the middle classes declines'' (Engels, 1958:25). The persistence of this incrementalism over the intervening 140 years has greatly complicated the relations between the state and the private sector. As a result there are some ironic reversals of nineteenth-century relations between government, owners and managers, and the work force. It is notable, for example, how in the late 1970s in mixed-economy nations like Canada and Britain both labor unions and management stood opposed to government regulation of wages and prices in the ''public'' interest. The urging of union leaders that market processes including collective bargaining be allowed to operate *freely* is a reminder of how far social and political relations have shifted since the rise of the industrial cities in the Victorian era. A society moving toward corporatism is not necessarily egalitarian, but at the same time benefits such as home ownership and a high level of public services are sufficiently dispersed and accessible to a large number of citizens that a majority of the population continue to be willing supporters of the status quo. Such conservatism is enhanced when government is accessible to popular pressure over consumption issues, as seems often to be the case, especially in North America, where government by opinion poll is not an entirely fanciful assessment.

Thus any ruling-class thesis of the state is an oversimplification in describing the disposition of power in contemporary Western nations. However, according to our argument, interest-group lobbying will be most active and effective for the political allocation of consumption items, and it is in this area that we might expect to find varying degrees of activity and success among different social groups in the city (Williams, 1975; Harvey, 1971). These were precisely the findings we discussed in Chapter 8 and 9, where we saw repeatedly the favored position of consumers with market power, social esteem, and political authority in manipulating externality costs and benefits to their own advantage. At the same time, in North America at least, the local state has been more diffident than national government in managing market trends, in part because of its weaker bargaining power but also because of implicit or explicit conflicts of interest between local officials and powerful economic groups. We noted in Chapter 9 the frequent intertwining of political and entrepreneurial interests in urban government during the era of ward-based machine politics and during the succeeding progressive reform era. In local administration can be found the most transparent association between an economic elite and political authority, and it is evident that this alliance has not been fully eliminated.

Nevertheless, in the 1960s opposition by civic and community groups to a one-dimensional ideology of business growth and technical efficiency at city hall became widespread, as the plural values of national lobby groups began to be expressed at the urban level, in part no doubt because it was increasingly in the cities that national issues were being worked out. Efficiency or equity? Segregation or integration? Private or public transportation? Growth or conservation? Boosterism or aesthetics? Bureaucracy or participation? The plural goals of national lobbyists now have a metropolitan presence, as has been noted in cities as diverse as San Francisco (Wirt, 1974; Mollenkopf, 1981) and Pittsburgh (Lubove, 1969). Increasingly, in urban patterns of consumption, goal achievement is an exercise in political persuasion as well as in market power: "We have become a communal society, in which many more groups now seek to establish their social rights—their claims on society—through the political order" (Bell, 1976a:364).

Vancouver offers an interesting illustration of the new politicization of urban interest groups (Ley, 1980, 1982). The city had been governed since the 1930s by a party that was a classic example of a business-dominated council evolving from nonpartisan, at-large civic elections—named appropriately, but misleadingly, the Nonpartisan Association (NPA). During the late 1960s, marked politicization over urban development occurred, and with it there emerged two new civic parties, which contested the 1968 civic election. The first of these, The Electors' Action Movement (TEAM), represented the politicization of a liberal, professional, white-collar lobby, and the second, The Committee of Progressive Electors (COPE), was a municipal socialist party. TEAM assumed control of the city council in 1972 on a reform platform of careful environmental management, the abandonment of freeway plans, and neighborhood participation to check relentless urban development—their program, in a word, would sustain "a *livable* city." For our present purposes there are two consequences of TEAM's victory we might note. First, it signalled the arrival in power of professionals and the demise of businesspersons. As recently as the 1970–1972 council, a majority of NPA aldermen were occupationally linked to the property industry (Lorimer, 1972), whereas in contrast, in five elections since 1968, 75 percent of TEAM's candidates have been professionals. Second, the new plurality of interests has led to considerable disagreement with business groups over land use development. Between 1973 and 1975 there were almost 100 conflicts in the city over a land use change, but on only 10 occasions did a council majority find itself in harmony with the business lobby (Ley and Mercer, 1980). Vancouver offers a good example of the increasingly communal nature of urban politics, as the city has become an arena for the politicized value systems of plural interest groups which often bear a blurred relationship to historic forms of social stratification. A proposal for a downtown convention center largely financed by public funds pitted developers, hotel and restaurant interests, and labor unions representing the construction industry on one side, and on the other side, members of the design profession concerned with urban planning and aesthetics and spokespersons for low-income groups who might suffer displacement—alignments essentially similar to those that faced off over the Yerba Buena project in San Francisco (Chapter 9).

The political rules of the game shifted once more in the late 1970s, when an urban electorate sensitized to rising inflation and the higher taxation needed to support the level of public services implied by TEAM policy shifted its allegiance back to the fiscal caution and market sympathies of the NPA. Increasingly, urban conflict is being focused on issues of consumption, and the important political alignments are those defined by the politics of consumption (Elliott and McCrone, 1979; Dunleavy, 1979; Ley and Mercer, 1980).

Culture and Consumption

It may not be too much of an exaggeration to state that consumption is the dominant public culture of contemporary advanced societies. The centrality of consumption issues represents both a response and a stimulus to economic and political conditions. It is a response to growing national prosperity and the rising real income enjoyed by workers in the Western nations through the twentieth century and particularly in the postwar period. It is a response also to the growing part played by the welfare state as a supplier of public consumption items and to the role of state fiscal policy in directing the consumption of private sector goods and services toward the management of the national economy.

Location and Consumer Values

At the same time, improvements in transportation have contributed to permitting a broader spatial margin of profitability for entrepreneurs and more extensive spatial options in residential choice for workers. What all this has amounted to is a broader range of consumer choice in, among other things, locational selection in the period up to the mid 1970s. (It is too early to say how irrevocably the processes of deindustrialization and world recession in the late 1970s and early 1980s have deflected this trend.) Particularly in the postwar era, these events have liberated the force of consumer demand in the housing market. But demand may no longer be reduced only to fairly simple variables, notably Alonso-type tradeoffs between distance from work and amount of living space.

In this book we have claimed a more dynamic role for human values which argues both for their plurality and also for their emergence, that is, their capacity for spontaneity and change. In Chapter 2, for example, we saw how the predictions of conventional land value theory with its simple definition of demand are challenged by, among other things, the recent preference of some professionals for small, center city housing units; prior value commitments to a lifestyle type—for example, to one of Bell's (1958) typology of careerism, consumerism, and familism—carry with them a preferred residential location. In Chapter 3, we joined Firey's criticism of a purely ecological analysis of the formation of urban social areas, suggesting a more multidimensional view of neighborhood as consisting of a range of meanings, including the symbolic as well as the economic. In Chapter 5, this argument was extended, and an urban demand surface was reconstituted in terms of three existential factors which together ascribe a meaning to urban space. In understanding contemporary population movements and land value gradients within the city, we saw that places embody meanings such as status or stigma and that such meanings are increasingly projecting a critical topography onto urban life. In short, the culture of consumption is throwing up a new mix of factors as relevant in patterns of spatial choice. Factors of locational amenity and disamenity, including such consumption items as differential social status (as in the arbitrage model of Chapter 8), are proving increasingly discriminatory in directing consumer demand.

These effects are now strong enough that they are beginning to be incorporated in formal urban modelling. For example, in the conclusion of an analysis relating migration to climate, the economist Graves (1980) notes that "existence of mountain scenery, ocean or lake recreational access and the like may indeed be important as may certain manmade, but location-fixed goods, such as symphonies, sporting events, and so on." This theme, which has been illustrated repeatedly in this book, is a familiar one to geographers, for as Ullman (1954) pointed out 30 years ago and as Gottman (1966) later reemphasized, space is a commodity, a product at the level of meaning. This view of space may be lost in conventional economics or political economy, where it is usually regarded only as an objective entry in a production or cost schedule. But space offers more than its own dimensionality: as *place* it is humanized; it becomes both objective and subjective, and thus may be regarded as pointing beyond itself to a set of meanings that may be appropriated. In the earlier chapters we have attempted to show how the typical experiences that consumers anticipate facing from place to place influence the changing geographical patterns of urban demand and thereby urban form.

Political Consequences of Consumption

As a final element in our discussion of the constitutive nature of human values, we saw in Chapters 6 and 7 the capacity of the social worlds of both informal groups and formal organizations to construct and sustain their own realities—realities which could have profound effects not only in the experience of the groups themselves but also in lifeworlds external to their own. This discussion led to an important transition in the argument, for in introducing the notion of external effects, we had also introduced the issues of competing interests, asymmetric life chances, and power relations (Chapters 8–10). Choice is never unconstrained, and in moving through the social hierarchy one is moving from households that practice substantial choice to households suffering under substantial constraint. But even for disadvantaged households constraints are rarely complete. Thus, ironically, Berry (1980) claims that inner city "abandonment may be viewed as a measure of the success we have achieved in our housing policy," for it shows that even the poorest households have exerted choice in rejecting the worst housing—though, of course, there are other dimensions to consider in an assessment of abandonment.

The societal balance of choice and constraint in consumption forms a potentially important input in the political system, and at this point the culture of consumption becomes cause rather than effect. The legitimacy of the state rests to a significant measure on the satisfaction of consumption expectations, so that a challenge to consumption standards may generate a legitimacy crisis for national and local government (Habermas, 1976). We have seen how land use conflict is repeatedly associated with consumption issues, and increasingly a mobilized consumer movement may direct its displeasure against the various tiers of government—the manager of public services. Access to enhanced levels of consumption is a primary goal of the electorate, and obstacles to its achievement may well lead to political change. The middle-class taxpayer's revolt, which began with the Proposition 13 referendum in California in 1978, has altered the allocation rules for public officials. But at the same time middle-class resistance has limited political ends, attempting a revision of taxation and allocation rules rather than more far-reaching social change. So, too, labor militancy is largely contained within a narrow set of economic objectives concerned with market power and enhanced consumption rather than with radical reform (Parkin, 1979). Indeed, the most acute social crises are associated with the failure of people to win access to the material and symbolic satisfactions of consumption. The urban riots in American cities in the 1960s have been interpreted as a result of "blocked opportunity," "the consequence of the prolonged exclusion of Negroes from American economic and social life" (Caplan and Paige, 1968). Symptomatic, according to this interpretation, was the widespread looting of consumer goods, which seemed to be a principal aim of the rioters. The significance of symbolic as well as material appropriation in consumption should not be underestimated; as we stressed earlier, the importance of commodities—and places—lies in their meanings as well as in their functions. Several reviews of working-class life have noted that it is not only the market power but also the culture and status of middle-class households that the working class aspires to (Diggins, 1977).

Consumption and the Socioeconomic Order

There are also areas where the relations of contemporary culture more squarely impact the socioeconomic order. As we saw earlier, there is a developing argument that social and cultural values provide a milieu that shapes the conditions for economic success. For example, geographically variable attitudes toward work and the relative prestige of industrial versus service occupations are two important ingredients affecting the quality of the labor force and influencing industrial productivity (Hall, 1980).

A second issue is the argument that social exploitation has been displaced away from the realm of production and into the realm of consumption (Gartner and Riessman, 1974). Extensive workplace legislation in the advanced industrial nations has mitigated the excesses of worker exploitation recorded in the nineteenth century. Of course, monotonous, assembly-line jobs with low wages remain, but, nonetheless, as a result of worker resistance and government legislation, a qualitative change has taken place in the culture of work. However, the realm of consumption is not as closely guarded, and defective products, built-in obsolescence, misleading advertising, and manipulation of supply and demand by oligarchies in the private sector are all indicative of new forms of exploitation. The activism of consumer groups since the 1960s is an indicator of both the extent of this exploitation and public laxity in providing adequate regulation. In the housing market, for example, the full force of market processes is felt with limited diversion by government regulation. The effects of distant speculators are transmitted directly into inflationary price cycles with disruptive social effects on local consumers seeking housing and with sometimes rapacious impacts on downtown and inner city neighborhoods, as viable communities have been destroyed to make way for new development (Ambrose and Colenutt, 1975; Lorimer, 1972). The displacement of lower-income households in inner city gentrification is a contemporary expression of the power of profit over need, and the domination of exchange value (''what the market will bear'') over the use value of affordable housing (Ley, 1981). It is in such realms of consumption that one sees most clearly in the mixed economies of the Western nations the closest parallels to the dispassionate dehumanizing of the work force in the Victorian factory.

And yet the equation is not this straightforward, for the social costs of redevelopment emerge from a broader system of relations in the property market which implicate a majority of the population, including the 60 percent of North Americans who are homeowners. As the National Association of Realtors in the United States noted, ''In recent years homeownership has provided the average family with an unparalleled vehicle for accumulating savings, earning a respectable return on equity and providing protection against inflation'' (National Association of Realtors, 1977). One dollar invested in 1967 would in real terms have yielded $.80 in 1977 if invested in common stock, $.93 if placed in a savings account, but $1.23 if invested in a single-family home. In the property business the majority of us are willing conspirators. But we are also victims, for the cost of this involvement is a crippling mortgage indebtedness, and here, in the infamy of the money lender, is one area to which exploitation has been displaced in postindustrial society. The prosperity of the finance and property sectors of the economy is not independent of the escalating land values that are removing the prospect of affordable housing from future generations of aspiring homeowners.

The high demand for home ownership is related to its pivotal role in everyday life, both as a secure hearth for family nurture and as an economic investment (Hamnett, 1982b). The owner-occupied single-family dwelling is a consummation of objective economic returns as well as subjective cultural goals. As such, tenure represents both an economic and a status division in society, broadening both material and symbolic boundaries between social groups (Saunders, 1978, 1979; Pratt, 1982). Housing provides a powerful example of the role of consumption issues in mobilizing interest groups into political action, for one of the key ingredients of the popular urban protest movements of the past 20 years has been the role of homeowners' associations clamoring to protect or enhance the quality of the neighborhood environment. In addition to the divisions attendant on housing tenure, systems of class stratification are also fragmented by the role of such status differentials as ethnicity and sex, which are independent of production relations in their origins but which feed powerfully into patterns of economic inequality (Berry, 1979; Wekerle et al., 1980). Social divisions emanating from the realm of culture and consumption are no less effective than those originating in economics and production in generating real effects and interest groups who may assemble political strength. Indeed, as we saw in Parts 2 and 3, at the subjective levels of everyday life, the relations, norms, and prejudices of our subcultural social worlds become paramount reality, the immanent context within which intentions are conceived and actions are born.

The Aesthetic Lifestyle

Despite the undisputed importance of material rewards, an essential ingredient of the culture of consumption is its claim to meet symbolic needs, which in the past were usually the province of tradition and religion. The "right" consumption choice is translated by advertisers into companionship, prestige, or even patriotism. In its more developed forms, consumption offers a quickening of experience, a more aesthetic lifestyle; it is the patron of the pleasure principle. The celebration of the realm of meanings and the quality of experience expressed by the 1960s counterculture has been appropriated by broader segments of society, for to a marked degree "the values of the sixties are being institutionalised in everyday life" (Gartner and Riessman, 1974:93). In a primitive form, Habermas noted in the original counterculture how "the lifestyle of protest is defined by sensuous and sensual qualities" (Habermas, 1970:33). Bell, too, observes that "the search for the modern was a search for the heightening of experience in all dimensions" (Bell, 1976b:118). But he carries the assessment still further, asserting that hedonism is a fundamental trait inherited from the counterculture: "The cultural, if not moral, justification of capitalism has become hedonism, the idea of pleasure as a way of life" (Ibid.:21). In contemporary society there is a heightened aestheticism, a greater attentiveness to all the senses. Urban pollution, for example, is an offense not only against the sense of smell but also an offense against the eye and the ear. The nonaesthetic, which in the past could at least have been admired for its efficiency, its power, or its embodiment of progress, is now scorned. The growing pursuit of sensuousness is permitted by increased leisure time and, with rising real incomes and the satisfaction of basic needs, the opportunity to pursue what Maslow (1970) called the higher need of self-actualization. Moreover, quality of life concerns are beginning to infiltrate the workplace; a Canadian employment survey conducted in 1978 found that over 30 percent of those interviewed identified self-fulfillment rather than conventional economic goals as their major occupational objective. In short, both commodities and activities are being increasingly perceived in symbolic terms and evaluated on a scale incorporating such categories as amenity, quality of life, and self-actualization.

Social Change and the Geography of Urbanization

Current trends in the economic, political, and socio-cultural milieus of the advanced industrial nations represent a departure from nineteenth-century contexts on urbanization and, as such, are molding new patterns of urban growth and livability (Bourne, 1980).

Economic Development and Urban Livability

Profound geographical adjustments at the regional and metropolitan levels are occurring in response to shifts in the economy. The regions of heavy industry that flourished during the Industrial Revolution are being stripped of their economic base and are undergoing at best slow growth and at worst rapid decline. In the United States, this has led to the new regional division of the sun belt cities of the South and West and the snow belt cities of the North and East, the latter incorporating the nation's historic industrial heartland (Figure 11.1). Between 1970 and 1975, 12 metropolitan areas of over 1 million suffered an absolute loss of population; 9 of these were east of the Mississippi, and 8 were north of the fortieth parallel. In contrast, 39 SMSA's of over 200,000 grew by at least 10 percent over the same period; of these, 23 were located west of the Mississippi, and *35* were south of the fortieth parallel. Similar, if more muted, trends have occurred in Canada, where British Columbia and Alberta have been the fastest growing provinces in the censal periods 1966–1971 and 1971–1981. In Britain, comparable shifts have been a source of public concern and the stimulus for regional policy for over a generation; aside from population loss in central London, a broadening zone around the South-East and Midlands has been the prominent growth area since the 1930s (Champion, 1976).

It is at the metropolitan level where the changing nature of the economy is most pronounced. Studies conducted by the Brookings Institute "have increasingly come to the view that the problem of these old, declining, and isolated core cities is the domestic problem of the United States" (Nathan and Dommel, 1977). These cities are the centers of a large industrial labor force and high unemployment. Urban land is severely underutilized; in the British industrial cities of Glasgow, Liverpool, and Birmingham, 12 percent, 10 percent, and 7.3 percent, respectively, of inner city land lies derelict. This is a result not only of the decentralization of plant to the suburbs but also of industrial morbidity. Factory closures are the metropolitan expression of national deindustrialization. Inner Manchester suffered a net loss of over 30,000 manual manufacturing jobs during 1966–1972; 80 percent of them were the result of firm closures (Lloyd and Mason, 1978). In South-East London, manufacturing employment declined by 25 percent in 5 years (1966–1971); of over 350 firms of all types that closed down from 1970 to 1975, three-quarters were a result not of relocation but of morbidity (Gripaios, 1977). The inner city is becoming the graveyard of manufacturing plants established during the Industrial Revolution (Thrift, 1979). The social cost of these economic changes is high, with unemployment levels of 20–40 percent now common in inner city neighborhoods of decaying industrial centers, and, as we saw in Chapter 10, urban unemployment is often the most accurate predictor of a range of social problems. Overlapping maps of social pathologies suggest that economic obsolescence brings with it multiple deprivations, with the appearance of an inner city population dependent on public assistance (Wolch, 1980).

In contrast to the slow decay of these old industrial centers is the construction activity in service-dominated cities like Dallas or San Francisco or the towns of South-East England, which have 75 percent of corporate head offices and 80 percent of research and development installations in Britain (Broadbent, 1977). Morrison (1974) has drawn the distinction sharply in his comparison of the San Jose SMSA, which tripled in numbers

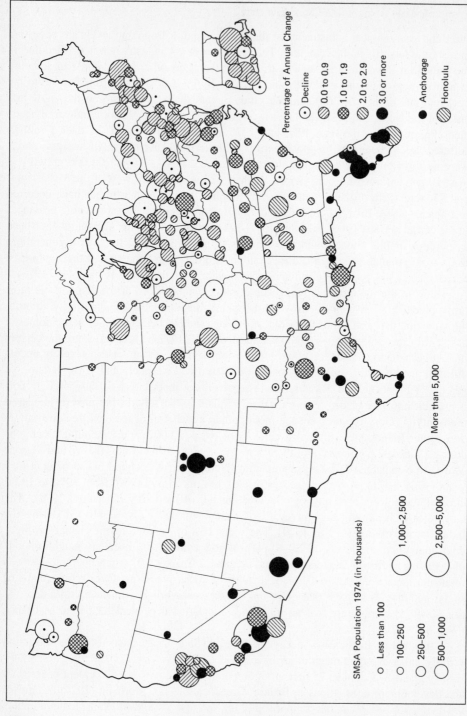

Figure 11.1 Population change in U.S. metropolitan areas, 1970–1974. (*Source:* P. Phillips and S. Brunn, "Slow Growth: A New Epoch of American Metropolitan Evolution," *Geographical Review* 68(1978):274–292, fig. 2. Reprinted by permission of the American Geographical Society.)

Percentage of Annual Change

- Decline
- 0.0 to 0.9
- 1.0 to 1.9
- 2.0 to 2.9
- 3.0 or more
- Anchorage
- Honolulu

SMSA Population 1974 (in thousands)

- Less than 100
- 100–250
- 250–500
- 500–1,000
- 1,000–2,500
- 2,500–5,000
- More than 5,000

from 1950–1970, in part through growth in its service and aerospace sectors, and the old industrial city of St. Louis, which declined in size by 27 percent over the same period. In a few of the largest cities the industrial and postindustrial economies are starkly juxtaposed; in its East End, the historic London docks are being filled in, and two-thirds of the dockers (15,000 men) have been laid off in the past 10 years, whereas a few miles to the west in the vigorous City of London not even the explosive development during the office boom of the early 1970s has challenged office rental levels, which remain the highest in the world (Damesick, 1980).

The concentration of employment growth within the service sector has created a highly biassed geographical pattern of economic development, for skilled quaternary employment in particular is segregated not only in metropolitan centers but in highly selective metropolitan centers (Pred, 1977b). Paris contains the headquarter offices of 90 percent of France's major corporations and half of its national civil service jobs; so complete is the control from Paris that branch managers in a regional center such as Nantes complain that even their ball-point pens have to be ordered through the head office in Paris (Mesnard and Vigarié, 1979). London's primacy is equally marked, for it is the location of 62 percent of Britain's top 500 industrial corporations, including 88 percent of the top 25. This bias toward the largest firms implies that with a continuing sequence of mergers and takeovers, the dominance of the primate city is likely to be accentuated. In 1971 London's quaternary employment was four times as great as the *combined* total for the remaining five British conurbations, and despite government policy, the forces for concentration do not seem to be contained. London's quaternary employment growth between 1966 and 1971 of 35,000 was 12 times greater than the total of only 3,000 for the other five conurbations combined (Daniels, 1977). The primate cities are receiving a disproportionate share of high-status job growth in senior white-collar occupations.

In federal nations, regional competition often reduces the level of concentration in a primate city. In the United States, New York included 29 percent of American industrial corporate headquarters in 1974, and the top 10 cities contained 60 percent, a figure that has been slowly declining. National concentration, though remaining substantial, clearly falls below that of non-federal nations. However, at the state or regional level, the dominance of a single metropolitan center is again apparent. In Australia, between 70 and 90 percent of the total of their state's quaternary occupations are centralized in the four state capitals of Perth, Adelaide, Melbourne, and Sydney (Alexander, 1979).

The concentration of quaternary occupations is no less marked at the intrametropolitan scale, where the preeminence of the central business district is pronounced. Even in the United States, where corporate decentralization from center city has been observed for some time, 78 percent of top industrial corporations in 1970 and 95 percent of leading financial corporations continued to have a downtown address (Burns and Pang, 1977). In Britain, 70 percent of the top 100 industrial enterprises are directed from central London, and in Melbourne and Sydney, the two largest Australian centers of quaternary employment, 80–85 percent of new office buildings, by value constructed, in recent years have been located in the central area. Especially outside the United States, where decentralization of service employment from the CBD has occurred, it has been primarily of routine and low-priority activities or of businesses serving a local suburban market. The enormous boom in downtown office construction during the 1970s (see Chapter 2) is the manifestation in urban form of the extreme spatial concentration of the quaternary sector. The combination of such spatial selectivity with, first, the high rate of new job creation and, second, the high incomes of quaternary workers contributes to an extremely biassed geographic pattern of economic opportunity, favoring some cities and penalizing others, and some neighborhoods but not others.

Government Policy and Urban Livability

It is evident that the state has not been innocent in its participation in these trends (Bennett, 1980; Johnston, 1981; Simmons, 1982). Governments have been a primary client of downtown office space. Washington, Ottawa, London, and Paris are cities sustained to varying extents by a government presence, and predictably their urban regions have experienced rapid growth. Smaller communities have also flourished under government largesse; Huntsville, Alabama, grew from a small town of 16,000 in 1950 to a metropolitan area of over 200,000 after being selected as a major development center by the National Aeronautic and Space Administration. Browning (1973) has produced an interesting review of the geographic pattern of government spending in metropolitan areas for the fiscal year 1968 (Figure 11.2). Marked regional variation in expenditures occurred, from \$662 per capita in cities in the Great Lakes region to \$1138 in metropolitan areas in the Southwest and Far West. Three years later in 1971, 18 of the 20 cities receiving the highest per capita outlay (over \$1650) were located in the sun belt states, and 13 of the 20 metropolitan areas with the lowest outlays (under \$500) were in the snow belt. Further analysis showed insignificant correlations between disbursements and urban size or income level, but significant correlations against manufacturing employment ($r = -0.36$) and service employment ($r = 0.19$). Indeed, 43 percent of manufacturing towns were in the bottom quintile of government spending. We see, then, that during the 1960s and early 1970s federal expenditure strongly encouraged, if perhaps unwittingly, the creation of a postindustrial economy by disproportionately supporting metropolitan areas that had service economies and were located in the sun belt.

By the late 1970s, this state of affairs had changed, with federal recognition of the special problems of the snow belt cities resulting in large direct grants. In 1978, the urban budget of the federal government was estimated at \$53 billion, an eightfold increase in real terms over 1967 (Goldsmith and Derian, 1979). In this manner the American government is now more squarely following the direction of British urban and regional policy since 1945 of state support for economically weak urban areas. We cannot reexamine here the details of state policy toward the cities (see Bourne, 1975; Broadbent, 1977; Eyles, 1979), though several summary comments may be made. First, the policies represent, particularly in Britain, the extension of the state's role from facilitator to manager of social and economic development. Through its support of social services, fiscal incentives to entrepreneurs, and ownership of declining manufacturing firms, the state has become a major presence particularly in the inner city. Second, state policy has favored area-based rather than household-based aid, especially in the inner city program.

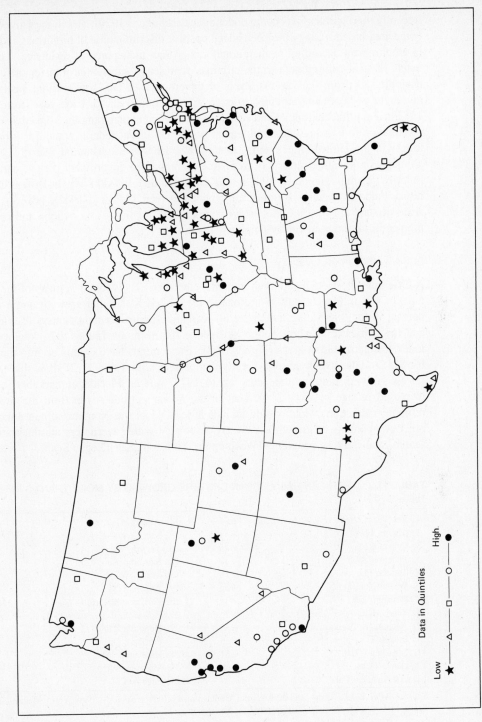

Figure 11.2 The geography of federal government per capita expenditures to U.S. metropolitan areas, 1968. (*Source:* C. Browning, *The Geography of Federal Outlays.* University of North Carolina at Chapel Hill, Dept. of Geography, Studies in Geography No. 4, 1973, fig. 3. Reprinted by permission.)

Recently this emphasis has come under attack (Hamnett, 1979), and in the United States, to the area-based strategy has been added positive discrimination of minorities and women in employment according to their status rather than their place of residence. Third, the extent of state commitment to the city may represent a substantial transfer of funds; for example, aid from the various levels of government to Glasgow's ailing eastern inner city areas in Scotland amounted to over $65 million a year for each year from 1977 to 1982 in a multifaceted social and economic development plan ranging from environmental reclamation to housing and employment policies. Current federal grants for urban rapid transit in the United States and Canada are much more substantial than this. Fourth, although significant effects may well have accompanied government policy, particularly in terms of employment (in 1968 it was estimated that 300,000 jobs in Britain had been redistributed to regions of industrial decline between 1945 and 1965), nevertheless the scale of state aid has not adequately compensated for the losses of jobs and economic momentum brought about by deindustrialization.

Amenity and Urban Livability

A different set of social and environmental characteristics is found in many of the growth cities. Of the 26 metropolitan regions in the United States that grew by more than 20 percent in the 1960s, the first 5 are all recreation and retirement centers (Table 11.2), and the entries as a whole score well above the mean on Liu's (1976) quality-of-life index for metropolitan areas (Figure 10.7). These trends have continued into the 1970s, for SMSA data (which are not directly comparable with Table 11.2) show that the three fastest growing metropolitan areas up to 1975 were in Florida; remarkably, all three increased in size by over 28 percent in the 5-year period. Aside from the recreation/retirement function, which would include at least 11 of the 26 metropolitan regions, the other components of growth are clearly associated with government administration, research, and military programs (Washington, Houston, San Diego, Seattle, Portsmouth/

TABLE 11.2   AMERICAN DAILY URBAN CENTERS GROWING BY MORE THAN 20 PERCENT, 1960–1970

1. Las Vegas, Nev.	+91%	14. Atlanta, Ga.	+28%
2. Miami, Fla.	+48	15. Sacramento, Cal.	+28
3. Orlando, Fla.	+45	16. Tucson, Ariz.	+27
4. Phoenix, Ariz.	+39	17. San Francisco, Cal.	+27
5. Tampa, Fla.	+38	18. Seattle, Wash.	+26
6. Washington, D.C.	+36	19. Austin, Tex.	+24
7. Houston, Tex.	+34	20. Portsmouth/Norfolk, Va.	+23
8. Reno, Nev.	+34	21. Pensacola, Fla.	+22
9. Anchorage, Alaska	+33	22. Honolulu, Haw.	+22
10. Dallas, Tex.	+33	23. Portland, Ore.	+21
11. San Diego, Cal.	+31	24. Huntsville, Ala.	+21
12. Denver, Col.	+30	25. Madison, Wisc.	+21
13. Los Angeles, Cal.	+29	26. Pueblo, Col.	+20

Source: After B.J.L. Berry and J. Kasarda, *Contemporary Urban Ecology.* New York: Macmillan, 1977, Table 14.1. Copyright © 1977. Reprinted by permission.

Norfolk, and Huntsville), the oil industry (Anchorage and the Texas cities), other private white-collar employment (Atlanta, San Francisco), and university centers (Austin, Madison). These metropolitan areas are primarily oriented to services and white-collar employment. *Not one* of the 26 urban regions is a part of the historic manufacturing belt. It is not simply retirement and recreation activities which are drawn to aesthetic settings but also the increasingly footloose world of white-collar employment, for as Lipton's (1977) analysis showed, there is a significant negative relationship between downtown office employment and the presence of manufacturing and a blue-collar labor force. Predictably, the major white-collar centers score well above the average on Liu's livability index.

These shifts in urbanization patterns are in part the landscape expression of the dynamic nature of consumption. The centers of growth are also in large measure centers of consumption, places that allow the appropriation of values that are regarded as self-fulfilling. People are interested in what places will do for them; it is a matter not simply of space but also of experience.

The cities that will do most in terms of aestheticism and amenity are those that are most valued, bringing about a distinction within the growth area of the sun belt itself. The cities of the South, with their petrochemical, textile, timber, and port functions, score modestly on a quality-of-life scale, with half of their major metropolitan areas falling into the bottom quintile of Liu's quality-of-life index. In contrast, two-thirds of the cities of the West occupy the top quintile (Figure 10.7). The liberation of an enhanced aestheticism in consumption has brought increasing significance to such differentials. Whereas in 1968 the average sales price of a single-family home in the South was the same as the national norm at around $22,000 and houses in the West were selling for $3,000 more, by 1978 a huge gap had appeared, with the Southern mean of $51,000 slightly below the national figure and the mean purchasing price in the West soaring to $76,000, a full 40 percent above the U.S. average. Moreover, as we have repeatedly noted, these amenity differentials are also expressed at an intraurban scale. Among a cross section of Los Angeles households, the most valued residential characteristics were shown to be air quality and personal and property safety rather than more conventional accessibility measurements (Robinson et al., 1975). In the high-status, hillside neighborhoods of Los Angeles, house prices rose by an average of over $3,000 each year from 1965 to 1975, but a few miles away in low-amenity inner city districts there was an absolute *decline* in sale prices over the decade. The *meaning* of space is setting the price gradient. The geographical differentiation of the postindustrial state and its system of cities is increasingly being defined by contours that measure the quality of consumption.

Prospects for a Livable City

Granted the character of contemporary societal trends and their consequences for urbanization, what should be the policy initiatives during the 1980s to create more livable cities? For an analysis that would end this book with a portrait of contented consumers riding their mechanical buggies on the golf courses of Palm Springs or inertly worshipping the sun on the Florida beaches would be seriously incomplete. Such a picture is not fully misleading, for the satisfaction of the consumptive appetite is one of the major legitimating forces of the advanced industrial state. But it is incomplete, for it gives a mistaken sense of consensus and equilibrium when in fact serious crisis tendencies exist at each of the economic, political, and cultural levels, tendencies which, though they have their own dynamic, are also intimately linked (Habermas, 1976).

The planning dilemma is twofold. On the one hand, there are only certain degrees of freedom available to urban planners at least in the short term, for there are many extraneous factors beyond their immediate control, including the size of their operating budget and the extent of their political power. On the other hand, there is the intractable problem of devising an optimal urban strategy across objectives that may be incompatible. For example, an assessment of Chicago's 1990 transportation plan highlighted the incompatibility of optimizing the twin objectives of more efficient movement around the city and enhanced environmental quality as long as the private automobile remained a substantial element of transportation planning. The development of new freeways to expedite movement was bound to bring deterioration to the environment (Rothman, 1973). What then are some of the economic, political, and cultural limits to the attainment of a livable city in the advanced nations in the late twentieth century?

Economic Limits

Unlike the optimistic assessments of the early 1970s, it is now clear that neither national economic growth nor the prosperity of cities can any longer be assumed. Factors external to the advanced industrial nations, including the OPEC energy cartel and industrialization in the developing Third World, have contributed to a new and alarming economic climate in many cities whose prosperity has been dependent on labor-intensive industry with relatively simple levels of technology. In these cities slow growth, no growth, and decline are already realities (Phillips and Brunn, 1978). The arguments of the early 1970s for a no-growth or steady-state economy have found less favor in the face of economic recession. In part, such arguments, especially when extended to urban development, have often provided a rationalization for the maintenance of privilege; exclusive suburbs have clamored for no growth more to preserve their own status than to be idealistic (Frieden, 1979). But it is also clear that economic growth is required both to maintain existing levels of public services and to provide the opportunity for social and economic betterment for deprived groups in the population (Gershuny, 1978). Thus the lobbyists for economic growth in urban areas are not only the local chamber of commerce but also labor unions and spokesmen for the unemployed and other deprived groups.

But those who pressure for economic growth in metropolitan areas do not provide answers for any of the disturbing effects of growth. Gains in productivity have provided a major impetus to economic growth in the advanced societies, but as we have seen, the transition to a service society seems to introduce definite limits to productivity improvements (Brown and Sheriff, 1979). In addition, if increasing manufacturing efficiency implies automation and job loss, then productivity gains are secured at a serious social cost. Aside from this are the ecological costs of growth, incorporating both rapid resource depletion and environmental damage on a grave scale (Leiss, 1976). In a number of major metropolitan centers in the United States, even water is a depleting resource, and the continued provision of fresh water over the next 20 years will involve expensive capital outlays. The incidence of air pollution, derived substantially from vehicle emissions, is already a health hazard and an important factor of neighborhood differentiation in Los Angeles and other cities (Robinson et al., 1975).

Another set of problematic relations involves the land market in cities undergoing substantial economic and population growth. The declining profitability of industrial investment has drawn capital into the money markets and into the profitable property sector. By 1978, 35 percent of all lending by financial institutions other than banks in Britain went into housing (*The Economist,* 1979). This investment in the urban land market has been fuelled by international capital seeking a secure and profitable haven, bringing, for example, Middle East investment to London and other British cities, and Asian capital to the West Coast cities of North America. In total, the effects of rapid population and economic growth plus speculative investment have stimulated inordinate levels of demand in the land market of service-oriented metropolitan areas. In Atlanta, Honolulu, Dallas, Phoenix, San Francisco, San Diego, Los Angeles, and Washington, D.C., house prices tripled in six years during the late 1970s (Stutz, 1982). The inevitable consequence of relatively unconstrained market processes in land use development has been the production of striking inequalities in access to housing between old, established residents and recent arrivals and between high-income and low-income citizens. As housing costs rise faster than family incomes, particularly in expanding service-based cities, a growing proportion of the population is disqualified from ownership of a single-family home. Between 1970 and 1976, the increase in the cost of a new house in the United States was double the gain in family incomes (Frieden, 1977). As a result, by 1976, less than one-quarter of all families could afford to purchase such a home, a substantial reduction from the level of almost one-half of families in 1970. In Canada by 1981, and at current mortgage interest rates, only 14 percent of tenants in metropolitan areas could have afforded an average-priced house (Tsang, 1981). The struggle for a home in the city is entering a new era of increasing household indebtedness, opportunism by corporate financiers and developers, conflict over neighborhood change, the disappearance of affordable housing, and perhaps the erosion of political legitimacy as consumers are denied access to what they have come to expect as a right of middle-class citizenship.

Political Limits

The housing question has always provided a mandate for state action to reduce inequalities in the city through the provision of subsidized units. In an urbanized society where people are stratified by such factors as market power and social status, inequality in life chances is endemic. But social mobility does occur, especially between generations. The Chicago sociologists showed in the industrial centers of the United States how in consecutive censuses minority groups were locating further and further from the CBD. Implicit in the spatial transfer from the inner city to the suburbs was a social transition from the rank of immigrant to the rank of middle-class American. But although individual immigrant groups moved gradually through the social hierarchy, this did not remove the fact of inequality, for the inner city slum remained the home of the newly arrived and the destitute heavily dependent on the largesse of the state—a function the slum continues to serve today (Wolch, 1980). Moreover, particularly in Europe, intergenerational social mobility was marked by greater closure; in Britain, about one-quarter of top professionals and managers had fathers in the same category (Parkin, 1979), and those who know have observed that one-sixth of the 1948 graduating class from Eton, England's premier school for the elite, had by 1980 qualified for inclusion in *Who's Who*. The effects of unemployment of 6–12 percent in the industrial nations, if sustained through the 1980s, may well solidify a similar intergenerational closure at the bottom end of the social hierarchy. In short, economic recession may well ossify existing inequalities in the absence of vigorous government action.

But such action in areas like housing or the provision of public services faces serious obstacles. Coleman and others have noted an inherent tension in government urban policy between the liberal ideals of liberty and equality. The achievement of equality may only be approached by imposition, that is, by the infringement of individual rights. In the American city this tension has been exposed acutely in such public policies as compulsory school busing or scattered-site public housing. As Coleman (1976) observes, "By moving in the direction of equality, we lose individual liberty to a central authority which imposes equality; and by moving in the direction of individual liberty, we lose equality to the accidents of birth reinforced by the market and the institution of private property." Coleman seeks to find a difficult middle ground between the extremes posed by this conundrum, but in practice a series of constraints removes the issue from the realm of moral philosophy.

Financial constraints on state intervention to establish equality in the city are real, though frequently overlooked in the literature. There is a limit to potential state expenditure for social programs which is set not only by political will but also by the performance of the economy. By 1978, the British government was already committing $11 billion to the redirection of the housing market (*The Economist,* 1980; also Downs, 1980). There are clearly limits to this form of reallocation, and in Britain, economic recession has suggested to politically conservative groups that these limits have already been exceeded. There are also political limits to state social programs. By the late 1970s there was ample evidence of a consumer tax revolt, beginning with the middle-class rejection of increased taxation in California in 1978. The locus of conflict in California is instructive, for it did not occur between workers and employers in the workplace but between consumer factions concerning the size and the allocation of the state budget. Subsequent elections in the United States, Britain, and elsewhere have reinforced a period of government disengagement in the face of popular protest at the seemingly stifling presence of the state, a protest that has both material and ideological causes. In an age of existential powerlessness, the continuous expansion of government bureaucracy is not always seen as liberating. Max Weber's great question remains unanswered: "The great question thus is . . . what can we set against this mechanisation to preserve a certain section of humanity from this fragmentation of the soul, this complete ascendancy of the bureaucratic ideal of life?" (Giddens, 1971:236).

Cultural Limits

The erosion of the social life-world, that is, the private realm of culture and meaning, before the advance of bureaucracy and technical rationality is a repetitive theme of Weber's that has been taken up by influential contemporary theorists (e.g., Habermas, 1970). The rise of the technocracy, of technology and technical solutions, in public administration has accompanied its supremacy in the economy. Frederick Taylor's program of scientific management, appropriated by industry early in this century, also had an important influence on local politics, as the restructuring of urban government and even urban planning itself was urged in order to extend efficient and rational management to municipal administration (Anderson, 1978; van Nus, 1978). The result of the extension of the rational mind to urban administration was the installation of a tenacious and seemingly inaccessible bureaucracy; as W. H. Cox (1976) has put it, "The central fact of urban government in Britain in this century is its increasing bureaucratisation." Consequently, the singular world view of career bureaucrats, the "experts" of urban management, has been imposed on the city. To the extent that their world view is characterized by efficiency and rationality, the urban landscape they produce may be technically correct but humanly devastating—to which the urban freeway and high-rise public housing are the most recent testimony. Until recently the authority granted the technocrat on account of his expert status has blunted opposition and suppressed the presentation of alternative values to rationality and efficiency in urban planning. Habermas (1970) has made the relevant observation that "technocratic consciousness reflects not the sundering of an ethical situation but the repressions of 'ethics' as such as a category of life" (p. 112).

However, recently the case for more humane planning has been made, a case which argues that neither efficiency nor even equity are fully sufficient criteria for urban planning. Humane planning reflects an ideology of what Cotgrove and Duff (1980) have called "postmaterial values." These values are critical of the emphasis on economic growth for ecological and humanistic reasons: their orientation is rather toward a society favoring ecological harmony, conservation, greater participation by people in the circumstances that affect their daily lives, less individualism and greater attention to community goals, and a more cultured and aesthetic existence. Daniel Bell outlines the politics of the future as turning on such issues as "instilling a social ethos in our leaders, the demand for more amenities, for greater beauty and a better quality of life in the arrangement of our cities, a more differentiated and intellectual education system, and an improvement in the character of our culture" (Bell, 1976a:366–367).

As the tone of the program suggests, its principal lobbyists are frequently well-educated professionals, the new middle class, who often fall outside the strict market system, working for government or nonprofit groups and concentrated in such professions as the arts, health, education, and welfare. Criticism of existing technical and rational thought and planning, of theoretical blueprints unmindful of social and cultural realities, provides an important ingredient of the ideology of the new class (Disco, 1979). Within the city, Gans (1962a) demonstrated the human devastation wrought by urban renewal that disregarded the experience of place, and Rainwater (1970) showed similar negative effects proceeding from sterile low-income public housing projects. Sommer (1974) extended the indictment to a variety of public institutions, including libraries, hospitals, and prisons characterized by what he called "hard" architecture, which paid scarce attention to the needs and values of users. So, too, the disregard or ignorance of existing community values was exposed and criticized in the program of urban freeway building. Jane Jacobs, perhaps the most celebrated opponent of technical planning in cities, describes her major book as an "attack on current city planning and rebuilding" (Jacobs, 1961:16). She saw a faulty logic in the detached, technical plans for city development, a rationality which in its destructive human effects became irrational.

In its place Jacobs and others espoused planning that incorporated social as well as physical components, a style that was attentive to the social and cultural needs of people and communities. This program included such items as mixed land use, the encouragement of group diversity and place vitality, transit and other forms of transportation alternative to the private automobile, pedestrian malls, activity parks, lively public open spaces, alternatives to high-rise public housing, the favoring of neighborhood renovation over massive demolition and renewal, the preservation of neighborhoods and heritage buildings, and, as much as possible, the decentralization of social planning to permit participation by neighborhood units. To a remarkable extent these proposals were taken up in city planning in the 1970s.

Though innovative and necessary, these principles are not without their limitations. They imply active if enlightened state management of development, and particularly with rapid transit and subsidized housing, they require substantial government expenditure. Unless carefully monitored, they also contain a potential elitism, for as we have already noted, arguments that challenge economic growth are likely to penalize poorer households. Third, they require a level of creativity, openness, and pluralism in decision making which strains the capacity of bureaucracies and which they may therefore be unwilling to sustain. But, most important, humane planning assumes that urban residents are indeed disillusioned with the individualism of economic growth and a consumer society, and will actively support more communal solutions. The evidence suggests otherwise, that residents in the industrial nations are reluctant collectivists (Lemon, 1978). In transportation, for example, public transit falls a poor second to the private automobile in most household preferences. Although it may be true that "a new humanism has appeared concerned with enjoying life and people and leisure and art and inner experience and nature and living for oneself, rather than conforming for success" (Gartner and Riessman, 1974:102), yet it is not clear whether this trend is necessarily socially progressive, for it may turn not only to collective notions of common good but also to a lifestyle of personal indulgence (Lasch, 1978).

Kierkegaard, the nineteenth-century existentialist, drew a distinction in his philosophy between the aesthetic, the ethical, and the religious personality. The aesthetic personality for Kierkegaard was responsive to the senses rather than to ethics or will power, controlled by immediate experience, and guided by gratification of the self. It is not difficult to discern such traits within the culture of consumption. The liberation of the pleasure principle unleashes what Bell (1976a) called the enhancement of the self and what Tom Wolfe (1976) rather more dramatically labelled the ego-extension of the me-decade, a world committed to the celebration of the self. In such circumstances,

Habermas' call for ethics to be rediscovered as a category of life takes on a particular urgency, and Bell may not be too mistaken in his observation that "the lack of a deeply rooted moral belief system is the cultural contradiction of the society, the deepest challenge to its survival" (Bell, 1976a:480). The limits to a livable city are to be found in the urban dweller as well as in the contexts of urbanization, and attaining a livable city is therefore a problem of human responsibility as well as a problem of context and constraint. Both values and bounding conditions are part of the conundrum of the city as the home of man; each must therefore be included in analysis and integrated in public policy. In this venture, the mandate for urban geography to become human geography in theory and in application is self-evident; indeed, for a mature science it could not be otherwise.

References

Abler, R. F. 1974. *Employment Shifts and Transportation Policy: Changes in the Locations of Corporate Headquarters in Pennsylvania, 1950–1970.* University Park, Pa.: Pennsylvania Transportation Institute, Pennsylvania State University.

_____ and J. S. Adams 1976. *A Comparative Atlas of America's Great Cities.* Minneapolis: University of Minnesota Press and Association of American Geographers.

Abrahams, R. D. 1970. *Positively Black.* Englewood Cliffs, N.J.: Prentice-Hall.

Adams, C. 1978. "Federal Housing Policy and Neighborhood Change." Paper presented to the Association of American Geographers meeting in New Orleans.

Adams, J. S. 1969. "Directional Bias in Intra-Urban Migration," *Economic Geography* 45, pp. 302–323.

_____ 1970. "Residential Structure of Midwestern Cities," *Annals, Association of American Geographers* 60, pp. 37–62.

_____ 1972. "The Geography of Riots and Civil Disorders in the 1960s," *Economic Geography* 48, pp. 24–42.

_____ and K. Gilder 1976. "Household Location and Intra-Urban Migration." Pp.159–192 in D. T. Herbert and R. J. Johnston (eds.), *Social Areas in Cities.* Vol. 1. London: Wiley.

_____ and R. Sanders 1969. "Urban Residential Structure and the Location of Stress in Ghettos," *Earth and Mineral Sciences* 38, no. 4, pp. 29–33.

Alao, N. 1976. "On Some Determinants of the Optimum Geography of an Urban Place." Pp. 199–214 in G. Papageorgiou (ed.), *Mathematical Land Use Theory.* Lexington, Mass.: D. C. Heath.

Alcaly, R. E. 1976. "Transportation and Urban Land Values: A Review of the Theoretical Literature," *Land Economics* 52, pp. 42–53.

Alexander, C. et al. 1975. *The Oregon Experiment.* New York: Oxford University Press.

Alexander, I. 1979. *Office Location and Public Policy*. London: Longman.

Alford, R. 1972. "Critical Evaluation of the Principles of City Classification." Pp. 331–358 in B. J. L. Berry (ed.), *City Classification Handbook*. New York: Wiley.

Almasi, M. 1965. "Alienation and Socialism." Pp. 125–142 in H. Aptheker (ed.), *Marxism and Alienation*. New York: Humanities Press.

Alonso, W. 1960. "A Theory of the Urban Land Market," *Papers and Proceedings of the Regional Science Association* 6, pp. 149–157.

———— 1964. *Location and Land Use*. Cambridge, Mass.: Harvard University Press.

Ambrose P. and R. Colenutt 1975. *The Property Machine*. Harmondsworth, Middx., Penguin.

Anas, A. and D. Dendrinos 1976. "The New Urban Economics: A Brief Survey." Pp. 23–51 in G. Papageorgiou (ed.), *Mathematical Land Use Theory*. Lexington, Mass.: D. C. Heath.

Anderson, J. 1971. "Space-Time Budgets and Activity Studies in Urban Geography and Planning," *Environment and Planning* 3, pp. 353–368.

Anderson, J. D. 1979. "The Municipal Government Reform Movement in Western Canada, 1880–1920." Pp. 73–111 in A. Artibise and G. Stelter (eds.), *The Usable Urban Past: Planning and Politics in the Modern Canadian City*. Toronto: Macmillan.

Anderson, T. and J. Egeland 1961. "Spatial Aspects of Social Area Analysis," *American Sociological Review* 26, pp. 392–398.

Andrews, R. B. 1971. *Urban Land Economics and Public Policy*. New York: Free Press.

Andrus, A. et al. 1976. *Seattle*. Cambridge, Mass.: Ballinger.

Appelbaum, R. 1976. "City Size and Urban Life," *Urban Affairs Quarterly* 12, pp. 139–170.

Appleyard, D. 1981. *Livable Streets*. Berkeley: University of California Press.

Artibise, A. J. 1975. *Winnipeg: A Social History of Urban Growth, 1874–1914*. Montreal: McGill-Queens University Press.

Aubin, H. 1977. *City for Sale*. Toronto: James Lorimer.

Auf der Maur, N. 1976. *The Billion Dollar Game*. Toronto: James Lorimer.

Axelrod, M. 1956. "Urban Structure and Social Participation," *American Sociological Review* 21, pp. 13–19.

Babchuck, N. and A. Booth 1969. "Voluntary Association Membership: A Longitudinal Analysis," *American Sociological Review* 34, pp. 31–45.

Bachelard, G. 1969. *The Poetics of Space*. Boston: Beacon Press.

Bachrach, P. and M. Baratz 1970. *Power and Poverty*. New York: Oxford University Press.

Backler, A. 1974. *A Behavioral Study of Locational Changes in Upper Class Residential Areas: The Detroit Example*. Geography Monograph Series No. 5. Bloomington, Ind.: University of Indiana, Dept. of Geography.

Baerwald, T. 1978. "Locational Constraints on Large Suburban Residential Builders." Paper presented to the Association of American Geographers meeting at New Orleans.

Ball, M. and R. Kirwan 1977. "Accessibility and Supply Constraints in the Urban Housing Market," *Urban Studies* 14, pp. 11–32.

Banham, R. 1971. *Los Angeles: The Architecture of Four Ecologies*. Harmondsworth, Middx.: Penguin.

Banton, M. 1960. "Social Distance: A New Appreciation," *Sociological Review* 8, pp. 169–183.

Barabba, V. 1975. "The National Setting: Regional Shifts, Metropolitan Decline, and Urban Decay." Pp. 39–76 in G. Sternlieb and J. Hughes (eds.), *Post-Industrial America*. New Brunswick, N.J.: Rutgers University, Center for Urban Policy Research.

Barker, R. G. 1963. "On the Nature of the Environment," *Journal of Social Issues* 19, pp. 17–38.

Barnett, A. et al. 1970. "Some Factors Underlying Racial Discrimination in Housing," *Race* 12, pp. 75–85.

Barrett, F. 1973. *Residential Search Behaviour*. Geographical Monographs No. 1. Toronto: York University, Dept. of Geography.

Barrows, H. 1923. "Geography as Human Ecology," *Annals, Association of American Geographers* 13, pp. 1–14.

Bartholomew, H. 1955. *Land Uses in American Cities*. Cambridge, Mass.: Harvard University Press.

Bassett, K. and D. Hauser 1975. "Public Policy and Spatial Structure: Housing Improvement in Bristol." Pp. 20–66 in R. Peel, M. Chisholm, and P. Haggett (eds.), *Processes in Physical and Human Geography*. London: Heinemann.

_____ and J. Short 1980. "Patterns of Building Society and Local Authority Mortgage Lending in the 1970s" *Environment and Planning* A, 12, pp. 279–300.

Baudrillard, J. 1975. *The Mirror of Production*. St. Louis: Telos Press.

Bederman, S. 1974. "The Stratification of 'Quality of Life' in the Black Community of Atlanta, Georgia" *Southeastern Geographer* 14, pp. 26–37.

_____ and J. Adams 1974. "Job Accessibility and Underemployment," *Annals, Association of American Geographers* 64, pp. 378–386.

Bell, C. and H. Newby 1976. "Community, Communion, Class and Community Action: The Social Sources of the New Urban Politics." Pp. 189–207 in D. Herbert and R. Johnston (eds.), *Social Areas in Cities*. Vol. 2. London: Wiley.

Bell, D. 1976a. *The Coming of Post-Industrial Society*. New York: Basic Books.

_____ 1976b. *The Cultural Contradictions of Capitalism*. New York: Basic Books.

Bell, W. 1958. "Social Choice, Life Styles, and Suburban Residence." Pp. 225–247 in W. Dobriner (ed.), *The Suburban Community*. New York: Putnam.

_____ 1959. "Social Areas: Typology of Urban Neighborhoods." Pp. 61–92 in M. Sussman (ed.), *Community Structure and Analysis*. New York: Crowell.

Ben-Arieh, Y. 1975. "The Growth of Jerusalem in the Nineteenth Century," *Annals, Association of American Geographers* 65, pp. 252–269.

Bennett, R. J. 1980. *The Geography of Public Finance*. London: Methuen.

Berdoulay, V. 1978. "The Vidal-Durkheim Debate." Pp. 77–90 in D. F. Ley and M. S. Samuels (eds.), *Humanistic Geography*. Chicago: Maaroufa Press.

Berger, P. 1963. *Invitation to Sociology*. Garden City, N.Y.: Doubleday-Anchor.

_____ and T. Luckmann 1966. *The Social Construction of Reality*. Garden City, N.Y.: Doubleday.

Bergman, E. M. 1974. *Eliminating Exclusionary Zoning*. Cambridge, Mass.: Ballinger.

Berry, B. J. L. 1959. "The Spatial Organization of Business Land Uses." Chapter 3 in W. L. Garrison et al., *Studies of Highway Development and Geographic Change*. Seattle: University of Washington Press.

———— 1970. "The Geography of the United States in the Year 2000," *Transactions, Institute of British Geographers* 51, pp. 21–54.

———— 1973. "Contemporary Urbanization Processes." Pp. 94–107 in F. Horton (ed.), *Geographical Perspectives and Urban Problems*. Washington, D.C.: National Academy of Sciences.

———— 1975a. "Monitoring Trends, Forecasting Change and Evaluating Goal Achievements: The Ghetto v. Desegregation Issue in Chicago as a Case Study." Pp. 196–221 in C. Peach (ed.), *Urban Social Segregation*. London: Longman.

———— 1975b. "Short-Term Housing Cycles in a Dualistic Metropolis." Pp. 165–182 in G. Gappert and H. Rose (eds.), *The Social Economy of Cities*. Beverly Hills, Cal.: Sage.

———— 1976a. "Progress Toward Environmental Goals for Metropolitan America." Pp. 163–215 in J. S. Adams (ed.), *Urban Policymaking and Metropolitan Dynamics: A Comparative Geographical Perspective*. Cambridge, Mass.: Ballinger.

———— 1976b. "Ghetto Expansion and Single-Family Housing Prices: Chicago, 1968–1972." *Journal of Urban Economics* 3, pp. 397–423.

———— 1979. *The Open Housing Question*. Cambridge, Mass.: Ballinger.

———— 1980. "Inner City Futures: An American Dilemma Revisited," *Transactions, Institute of British Geographers* N.S. 5, pp. 1–28.

———— and Y. Cohen 1973. "Decentralization of Commerce and Industry: The Restructuring of Metropolitan America." Pp. 431–455 in L. Masotti and J. Hadden (eds.), *The Urbanization of the Suburbs*. Beverly Hills, Cal.: Sage.

———— and F. E. Horton 1970. *Geographic Perspectives on Urban Systems*. Englewood Cliffs, N.J.: Prentice-Hall.

———— and J. Kasarda 1977. *Contemporary Urban Ecology*. Riverside, N.J.: Macmillan.

———— et al. 1974. *Land Use, Urban Form and Environmental Quality*. Chicago: University of Chicago, Dept. of Geography Research Paper No. 155.

———— et al. 1976. "Attitudes Toward Integration: the Role of Status in Community Response to Racial Change." Pp. 221–264 in B. Schwartz (ed.), *The Changing Face of the Suburbs*. Chicago: University of Chicago Press.

Beshers, J. 1962. *Urban Social Structure*. New York: Free Press.

Bingham, R. 1977. "The Diffusion of Innovation among Local Governments," *Urban Affairs Quarterly* 13, pp. 223–232.

Binzen, P. 1970. *Whitetown, U.S.A.* New York: Random House.

Birch, D. 1971. "Toward A Stage Theory of Urban Growth," *Journal, American Institute of Planners* 37, pp. 78–87.

Bird, H. 1976. "Residential Mobility and Preference Patterns in the Public Sector of the Housing Market," *Transactions, Institute of British Geographers* N.S. 1, pp. 20–33.

Blackaby, F. (ed.), 1979. *De-industrialisation*. London: Heinemann.

Blunden, J. 1972. "The Decision-Making Process." Pp. 57–81 in *Economic Geography-Industrial Locational Theory*. Bletchley, Bucks.: The Open University.

Boal, F. W. 1969. "Territoriality on the Shankill-Falls Divide, Belfast." *Irish Geography* 6, pp. 30–50.

———— 1970. "Social Space in the Belfast Urban Area." Pp. 373–393 in N. Stephens and R. Glasscock (eds.), *Irish Geographical Studies*. Belfast: Queen's University Press.

_____ 1971. "Territoriality and Class: A Study of Two Residential Areas in Belfast," *Irish Geography* 8, pp. 229–248.

_____ 1976. "Ethnic Residential Segregation." Pp. 41–79 in D. Herbert and R. Johnston (eds.), *Social Areas in Cities*. Vol. 1. London: Wiley.

_____ 1978. "Territoriality on the Shankill-Falls Divide, Belfast: The Perspective from 1976." Pp. 58–77 in D. Lanegran and R. Palm (eds.), *An Invitation to Geography*. New York: McGraw-Hill.

_____ W. P. Doherty and D. Pringle 1978. *Social Problems in the Belfast Urban Area*. Queen Mary College, University of London, Dept. of Geography, Occasional Papers No. 12.

_____ and D. Livingstone 1982. "An International Frontier in Microcosm: The Shankill-Falls Divide, Belfast." Paper presented to the International Seminar in Political Geography in Haifa.

Boddy, M. 1976. "The Structure of Mortgage Finance," *Transactions, Institute of British Geographers* N.S. 1, pp. 58–71.

Bogardus, E. 1925. "Measuring Social Distance," *Journal of Applied Sociology* 9, pp. 299–308.

_____ 1926. "Social Distance in the City." Pp. 48–54 in E. Burgess (ed.), *The Urban Community*. Chicago: University of Chicago Press.

_____ 1959. *Social Distance*. Yellow Springs, Ohio: Antioch Press.

Booth, A. 1976. *Urban Crowding and Its Consequences*. New York: Praeger.

_____ and N. Babchuk 1969. "Personal Influence Networks and Voluntary Association Affiliation," *Sociological Inquiry* 39, pp. 179–188.

Booth, C. 1967. *On the City: Physical Pattern and Social Structure*. H. Pfautz (ed.). Chicago: University of Chicago Press.

Booth, W. 1890. *In Darkest England and the Way Out*. London: The Salvation Army.

Borchert, J. R. 1967. "American Metropolitan Evolution," *Geographical Review* 57, pp. 301–332.

_____ 1978. "Major Control Points in American Economic Geography," *Annals, Association of American Geographers* 68, pp. 214–232.

Bottomley, J. 1977. *Experience, Ideology and the Landscape: The Business Community, Urban Reform and the Establishment of Town Planning in Vancouver, British Columbia, 1900–1940*. Unpublished dissertation, University of British Columbia, Dept. of Geography.

Bourne, L. S. 1967. *Private Redevelopment of the Central City*. Chicago: University of Chicago, Dept. of Geography, Research Paper No. 112.

_____ 1971. "Physical Adjustment Processes and Land Use Succession: A Conceptual Review and Central City Example," *Economic Geography* 47, pp. 1–15.

_____ 1975. *Urban Systems: Strategies for Regulation*. Oxford: Clarendon Press.

_____ 1976a. "Housing Supply and Housing Market Behaviour in Residential Development." Pp. 111-158 in D. T. Herbert and R. J. Johnston (eds.), *Social Areas in Cities*. Vol. 1. London: Wiley.

_____ 1976b. "Urban Structure and Land Use Decisions," *Annals, Association of American Geographers* 66, pp. 531–547.

_____ 1980. "Alternative Perspectives on Urban Decline and Population Deconcentration," *Urban Geography* 1, pp. 39–52.

_____ 1981. *The Geography of Housing*. London: Arnold.

—— and M. Doucet 1973. "Components of Urban Land Use Change and Physical Growth." Pp. 83–103 in L. S. Bourne et al. (eds.), *The Form of Cities in Central Canada*. Toronto: University of Toronto, Dept. of Geography.

Bowden, M. J. 1976. "The Great American Desert in the American Mind: The Historiography of a Geographical Notion." Pp. 119–147 in D. Lowenthal and M. J. Bowden (eds.), *Geographies of the Mind*. New York: Oxford University Press.

Boyce, R. 1969. "Residential Mobility and its Implications for Urban Spatial Change," *Proceedings, Association of American Geographers* 1, pp. 22–26.

Breton, R. 1964. "Institutional Completeness of Ethnic Communities and the Personal Relations of Immigrants," *American Journal of Sociology* 70, pp. 193–205.

Briggs, A. 1965. *Victorian Cities*. New York: Harper & Row.

Briggs, R. 1973. "Urban Cognitive Distance." Pp. 361–388 in R. Downs and D. Stea (eds.), *Image and Environment*. Chicago: Aldine.

Broadbent, T. 1977. *Planning and Profit in the Urban Economy*. London: Methuen.

Brody, E. (ed.) 1970. *Behavior in New Environments*. Beverly Hills, Cal.: Sage.

Brookings, 1977. "Issues in the 1978 Budget," *The Brookings Bulletin* 14, Spring-Summer, pp. 1–5.

Brown, C. 1965. *Manchild in the Promised Land*. New York: Signet Books.

Brown, C. J. F. and T. Sheriff 1979. "De-industrialisation: A Background Paper." Pp. 233–262 in F. Blackaby (ed.), *De-industrialisation*. London: Heinemann.

Brown, J. et al. 1963. "Kentucky Mountain Migration and the Stem Family," *Rural Sociology* 28, pp. 48–69.

Brown, L. and J. Holmes 1971. "Search Behaviour in an Intra-Urban Migration Context: A Spatial Perspective," *Environment and Planning,* 3, pp. 307–326.

—— and E. Moore 1970. "The Intra-Urban Migration Process: A Perspective," *Geografiska Annaler* 52B, pp. 1–13.

Brown, W. 1972. "Access to Housing: The Role of the Real Estate Industry," *Economic Geography* 48, pp. 66–78.

Browning, C. 1964. "Selected Aspects of Land Use and Distance From the City Center: The Case of Chicago," *Southeastern Geographer* 4, pp. 29–40.

—— 1973. *The Geography of Federal Outlays*. Chapel Hill: University of North Carolina, Studies in Geography No. 4.

Brunhes, J. 1920. *Human Geography*. Chicago: Rand McNally.

Buber, M. 1957. "Distance and Relation," *Psychiatry* 20, pp. 97–104.

Bunge, W. 1966. *Theoretical Geography*. University of Lund Studies in Geography, series C, no. 1. Lund, Sweden: C. W. K. Gleerup.

—— 1971. *Fitzgerald: Geography of a Revolution*. Cambridge, Mass.: Schenkman.

—— and R. Bordessa 1975. *The Canadian Alternative: Survival, Expeditions and Urban Change*. Geographical Monographs No. 2. Toronto: York University, Dept. of Geography.

Burgess, E. W. and D. J. Bogue (eds.) 1967. *Urban Sociology*. Chicago: University of Chicago Press.

Burgess, J. 1974. "Stereotypes and Urban Images," *Area* 6, pp. 167–171.

Burkhead, J. 1975. "The Political Economy of Urban America: National Urban Policy Revisited."

Pp. 49–68 in G. Gappert and H. Rose (eds.), *The Social Economy of Cities*. Beverly Hills, Cal.: Sage.

Burks, E. 1972. "Growth of Poverty in City Creating New Poor Zones," *New York Times*, April 10, 1972, p. C-1.

Burns, L. and W. Pang 1977. "Big Business in the Big City: Corporate Headquarters in the CBD," *Urban Affairs Quarterly* 12, pp. 533–544.

Burton, L. and D. Morley 1979. "Neighborhood Survival in Toronto," *Landscape* 23, no. 3, pp. 33–40.

Busteed, M. 1975. *Geography and Voting Behaviour*. London: Oxford University Press.

Butler, E. W. et al. 1969. *Moving Behavior and Residential Choice: A National Survey*. National Cooperative Highway Research Program Report No. 81. Washington, D.C.: Highway Research Board.

Buttimer, A. 1969. "Social Space in Interdisciplinary Perspective," *Geographical Review* 59, pp. 417–426.

———— 1971. *Society and Milieu in the French Geographic Tradition*. Association of American Geographers, Monograph Series No. 6. Chicago: Rand McNally.

———— 1972. "Social Space and the Planning of Residential Areas," *Environment and Behavior* 4, pp. 279–310.

———— 1974. *Values in Geography*. Washington, D.C.: Association of American Geographers Commission on College Geography Resource Paper No. 24.

———— 1976. "Grasping the Dynamism of Lifeworld," *Annals, Association of American Geographers* 66, pp. 277–292.

Byerly, K. 1961. *Community Journalism*. Philadelphia: Chilton.

Cairncross, A. 1979. "What is De-industrialisation?" Pp. 5–17 in F. Blackaby (ed.), *De-industrialisation*. London: Heinemann.

Calhoun, J. 1962. "Population Density and Social Pathology," *Scientific American* 206, pp. 139–148.

Canter, D. and T. Lee (eds.) 1974. *Psychology and the Built Environment*. London: Architecture Press.

Caplan, N. and J. Paige 1968. "A Study of Ghetto Rioters," *Science* 219, no. 2, pp. 15–21.

Caplovitz, D. 1963. *The Poor Pay More*. New York: Free Press.

Caplow, T. and R. Forman 1950. "Neighborhood Interaction in a Homogeneous Community," *American Sociological Review* 15, pp. 357–366.

Capozza, D. 1976. "The Efficiency of Speculation in Urban Land," *Environment and Planning A*, 8, pp. 411–422.

Carey, L. and R. Mapes 1972. *The Sociology of Planning: A Study of Social Activity on New Housing Estates*. London: Batsford.

Caro, R. 1974. *The Power Broker: Robert Moses and the Fall of New York*. New York: Knopf.

Carr, S. 1967. "The City of the Mind." Pp. 197–226 in W. Ewald (ed.), *Environment for Man: The Next Fifty Years*. Bloomington: Indiana University Press.

Carter, H. 1972. *The Study of Urban Geography*. London: Edward Arnold.

Carter, R. 1974. *The Criminal's Image of the City*. Unpublished dissertation, University of Oklahoma, Dept. of Geography.

Caruso, D. and R. Palm 1973. "Social Space and Social Place," *Professional Geographer* 25, pp. 221–225.

Carveth, D. 1977. "The Disembodied Dialectic: A Psychoanalytical Critique of Sociological Relativism," *Theory and Society* 4, pp. 73–102.

Castells, M. 1977. *The Urban Question: A Marxist Approach*. London: Arnold.

Cawson, A. 1977. "Pluralism, Corporatism and the Role of the State," *Government and Opposition* 13, pp. 178–198.

Champion, A. 1976. "Evolving Patterns of Population Distribution in England and Wales, 1951–71," *Transactions, Institute of British Geographers* N.S. 1, pp. 401–420.

Chapin, F. S. 1974. *Human Activity Patterns in the City*. New York: Wiley.

Chave, S. 1966. "Mental Health in Harlow New Town," *Journal of Psychosomatic Research* 10, July, pp. 38–44.

Chimbos, P. 1972. "A Comparison of the Social Adaptation of Dutch, Greek and Slovak Immigrants in a Canadian Community," *International Migration Review* 6, pp. 230–244.

Choldin, H. 1973. "Kinship Networks in the Migration Process," *International Migration Review* 7, pp. 163–175.

Christaller, W. 1966. *Central Places in Southern Germany*. C. W. Baskin (trans.). Englewood Cliffs, N.J.: Prentice-Hall.

Christian, C. 1975. "Emerging Patterns of Industrial Activity Within Large Metropolitan Areas and their Impact on the Central City Work Force." Pp. 213–246 in G. Gappert and H. Rose (eds.), *The Social Economy of Cities*. Beverly Hills, Cal.: Sage.

City of Los Angeles 1976. *Housing Price Trends in the City of Los Angeles*. Los Angeles: City of Los Angeles, Community Analysis Bureau.

Clark, A. 1977. "The Whole Is Greater Than the Sum of Its Parts: A Humanistic Element in Human Geography." Pp. 3–26 in D. Deskins et al. (eds.), *Geographic Humanism, Analysis and Social Action*. Ann Arbor: University of Michigan Press.

Clark, C. 1951. "Urban Population Densities," *Journal of the Royal Statistical Society* A, 114, pp. 490–496.

Clark, W. A. V. 1976. "Migration in Milwaukee," *Economic Geography* 52, pp. 48–60.

———— 1980. "Residential Mobility and Neighborhood Change: Some Implications for Racial Residential Segregation," *Urban Geography* 1, pp. 95–117.

Clawson, M. 1971. *Suburban Land Conversion in the United States*. Baltimore: Johns Hopkins University Press.

Clay, P. 1979. *Neighborhood Renewal*. Lexington, Mass.: Heath.

Clement, W. 1975. *The Canadian Corporate Elite*. Toronto: McClelland and Stewart.

Clout, H. 1974. "The Growth of Second-Home Ownership: An Example of Seasonal Suburbanisation." Pp. 101–128 in J. Johnson (ed.), *Suburban Growth*. London: Wiley.

Coates, B. E., R. J. Johnston and P. L. Knox 1977. *Geography and Inequality*. Oxford: Oxford University Press.

Coates, K. and R. Silburn 1970. *Poverty: The Forgotten Englishmen*. Harmondsworth, U.K.: Penguin.

Cockburn, A. and J. Ridgeway 1979. "The City the Bankers are Killing," *New Statesman* 9, February, pp. 178–181.

Code, W.R., et al. 1981. *The Decentralization of Office Space in Metropolitan Toronto.* University of Western Ontario, Department of Geography, Geographical Papers No. 47.

Cohen, S. 1973. "Living With Crime," *New Society* 26, pp. 330–333.

Coleman, J. 1976. "Rawls, Nozick, and Educational Equality," *The Public Interest* 43, pp. 121–28.

Colony, D. 1972. "Study of the Impact on Households of Relocation from a Highway Right of Way," *Highway Research Record* 399, pp. 12–26.

Committee on Government Relations 1968. *Staff Study of Major Riots and Civil Disorders, 1965–July 31, 1968.* Washington, D.C.: Government Printing Office.

Compton, P. 1976. "Religious Affiliation and Demographic Variability in Northern Ireland," *Transactions, Institute of British Geographers* N.S. 1, pp. 433–452.

Connell, J. 1973. "Social Networks in Urban Society." Pp. 41–52 in B. Clark and M. Gleave (eds.), *Social Patterns in Cities.* London: Institute of British Geographers, Special Publication No. 5.

_____ 1974. "The Metropolitan Village." Pp. 77–100 in J. Johnson (ed.), *Suburban Growth.* London: Wiley.

Conzen, M. P. 1974. "Town into Suburb: Boston's Expanding Fringe." Pp. 37–49 in C. Browning (ed.), *Population and Urbanized Area Growth in Megalopolis, 1950–1970.* University of North Carolina at Chapel Hill, Department of Geography, Studies in Geography No. 7.

Conzen, M. R. G. 1960. "Alnwick: A Study in Town Plan Analysis," *Transactions, Institute of British Geographers* 27.

Cooper, C. 1974. "The House as Symbol of the Self." Pp. 130–146 in J. Lang et al. (eds.), *Designing for Human Behavior.* Stroudsburg, Pa.: Dowden, Hutchinson, Ross.

_____ 1975. *Easter Hill Village.* New York: Free Press.

Cooper, M. 1971. *Residential Segregation of Elite Groups in Vancouver, B.C.* Unpublished thesis, University of British Columbia, Dept. of Geography.

Cotgrove, S. 1980. "Values that Call for the Greening of Industrial Society," *Times Higher Education Supplement,* no. 398, June 13, p. 12.

_____ and A. Duff 1981. "Environmentalism, Values, and Social Change," *British Journal of Sociology* 32, pp. 92–111.

Couper, M. and T. Brindley 1975. "Housing Classes and Housing Values," *Sociological Review* 23, pp. 563–576.

Cowper, W. 1785. "The Task." Pp. 143–144, in H. Milford (ed.), *The Poetical Works of William Cowper.* London: Oxford University Press, 1950.

Cox, K. R. 1969a. "The Voting Decision in a Spatial Context," *Progress in Geography* 1, pp. 81–117.

_____ 1969b. "The Spatial Structuring of Information Flow and Partisan Attitudes." Pp. 157–185 in M. Dogan and S. Rokkan (eds.), *Quantitative Ecological Analysis in the Social Sciences.* Cambridge, Mass.: M.I.T. Press.

_____ 1973. *Conflict, Power, and Politics in the City: A Geographic View.* New York: McGraw-Hill.

_____ 1978. "Local Interests and Urban Political Processes in Market Societies." Pp. 94–108 in K. R. Cox (ed.), *Urbanization and Conflict in Market Societies.* Chicago: Maaroufa.

———— and R. Golledge (eds.) 1981. *Behavioral Problems in Geography Revisited*. New York: Methuen.

———— and J. McCarthy 1980. "Neighborhood Activism in the American City," *Urban Geography* 1, pp. 22–38.

———— and D. Reynolds 1974. "Locational Approaches to Power and Conflict." Pp. 19–41, in K. R. Cox et al. (eds.), *Locational Approaches to Power and Conflict*. New York: Wiley.

Cox, W. H. 1976. *Cities: The Public Dimension*. Harmondsworth, Middx.: Penguin.

Craven, P. and B. Wellman 1973. *The Network City*. Toronto: University of Toronto, Centre for Urban and Community Studies Research Paper No. 59.

Cressey, P. F. 1938. "Population Succession in Chicago, 1898–1930," *American Journal of Sociology* 44, pp. 59–69.

Cressey, P. G. 1971. "The Taxi-Dance Hall as a Social World." Pp. 193–209 in J. Short (ed.), *The Social Fabric of the Metropolis*. Chicago: University of Chicago Press.

Crowe, P. R. 1938. "On Progress in Geography," *Scottish Geographical Magazine* 54, pp. 1–19.

Cullen, I. and V. Godson 1975. "The Structure of Activity Patterns," *Progress in Planning* 4, part I.

Cullingworth, J. 1965. *English Housing Trends*. London: Bell.

Cuomo, M. 1974. *Forest Hills Diary: The Crisis of Low-Income Housing*. New York: Random House.

Cybriwsky, R. A. 1976. "Fairmount Rules: Life in a Defended Neighborhood." Unpublished paper, Department of Geography, Temple University.

———— 1978. "Social Aspects of Neighborhood Change," *Annals, Association of American Geographers* 68, pp. 17–33.

Cyert, R. and J. March 1963. *A Behavioral Theory of the Firm*. Englewood Cliffs, N.J.: Prentice-Hall.

Damer, S. 1974. "Wine Alley: The Sociology of a Dreadful Enclosure," *Sociological Review* 22, pp. 221–248.

Damerell, R. G. 1968. *Triumph in a White Suburb*. New York: William Morrow.

Damesick, P. 1979. "Offices and Inner-Urban Regeneration," *Area* 11, pp. 41–47.

———— 1980. "The Inner City Economy in Industrial and Post-Industrial London," *The London Journal* 6, pp. 23–35.

Daniels, P. W. 1974. "New Offices in the Suburbs." Pp. 177–200 in J. Johnson (ed.), *Suburban Growth*. London: Wiley.

———— 1975. *Office Location*. London: Bell.

———— 1977. "Office Location in the British Conurbations: Trends and Strategies," *Urban Studies* 14, pp. 261–274.

Danielson, M. 1976. *The Politics of Exclusion*. New York: Columbia University Press.

Daon Development Corporation 1979. *Annual Report*. Vancouver, B.C.

Davies, C. S. and M. Albaum 1972. "Mobility Problems of the Poor in Indianapolis." Pp. 67–86 in R. Peet (ed.), *Geographical Perspectives on American Poverty*. Worcester, Mass.: Antipode Monographs in Social Geography No. 1.

———— and D. Huff 1972. "Impact of Ghettoization on Black Employment," *Economic Geography* 48, pp. 421–427.

Davies, W. 1978. "Alternative Factorial Solutions and Urban Social Character," *Canadian Geographer* 22, pp. 273–297.

Davis, A. F. and M. Haller (eds.), 1973. *The Peoples of Philadelphia*. Philadelphia: Temple University Press.

Dawson, J. 1974. "The Suburbanisation of Retail Activity." Pp. 155–175 in J. Johnson (ed.), *Suburban Growth*. London: Wiley.

Dear, M. 1976. "Abandoned Housing." Pp. 59–99 in J. S. Adams (ed.), *Urban Policymaking and Metropolitan Dynamics: A Comparative Geographical Analysis*. Cambridge, Mass.: Ballinger.

_____ 1977a. "Spatial Externalities and Locational Conflict." Pp. 152–167 in D. Massey and P. Batey (eds.), *London Papers in Regional Science* 7. London: Pion.

_____ 1977b. "Psychiatric Patients and the Inner City," *Annals, Association of American Geographers* 67, pp. 588–594.

Dennis, N. 1978. "Housing Policy Areas: Criteria and Indicators in Principle and Planning," *Transactions, Institute of British Geographers* N.S. 3, pp 2–22.

Deskins, D. 1972. *Residential Mobility of Negroes in Detroit 1837–1965*. Ann Arbor: University of Michigan, Dept. of Geography Publication No. 5.

Deutsch, K. 1961. "On Social Communication and the Metropolis," *Daedalus* 90, pp. 99–110.

Dicken, P. 1971. "Some Aspects of the Decision-Making Behavior of Business Organizations," *Economic Geography* 47, pp. 426–437.

Diggins, J. 1977. "Reification and the Cultural Hegemony of Capitalism: The Perspectives of Marx and Veblen," *Social Research* 44, pp. 354–383.

Dingemans, D. 1979. "Redlining and Mortgage Lending in Sacramento," *Annals, Association of American Geographers* 69, pp. 225–239.

Disco, C. 1979. "Critical Theory as Ideology of the New Class," *Theory and Society* 8, pp. 159–214.

Donaldson, B. 1973. "An Empirical Investigation into the Concept of Sectoral Bias in the Mental Maps, Search Spaces and Migration Patterns of Intra-Urban Migrants," *Geografiska Annaler* 55B, pp. 13–33.

Downs, A. 1980. "Too Much Capital for Housing?" *The Brookings Bulletin* 17 (summer), pp. 1–5.

Downs, R. and D. Stea 1977. *Maps in Minds*. New York: Harper & Row.

Driedger, L. and G. Church 1974. "Residential Segregation and Institutional Completeness: A Comparison of Ethnic Minorities," *Canadian Review of Sociology and Anthropology* 11, pp. 30–52.

Duncan, J. S. 1973. "Landscape Taste as a Symbol of Group Identity," *Geographical Review* 63, pp. 334–355.

_____ 1978a. "Men Without Property: The Tramp's Classification and Use of Space," *Antipode* 10, no. 1, pp. 24–34.

_____ 1978b. "The Social Construction of Unreality: An Interactionist Approach to the Tourist's Cognition of Environment." Pp. 269–282 in D. Ley and M. Samuels (eds.), *Humanistic Geography*. Chicago: Maaroufa.

_____ 1980. "The Superorganic in American Cultural Geography," *Annals, Association of American Geographers* 70, pp. 181–198.

_____ (ed.) 1981. *Housing and Identity*. London: Croom Helm.

Duncan, O., R. Cuzzort and B. Duncan 1961. *Statistical Geography*. Glencoe, Ill.: Free Press.

―――― and B. Duncan 1955a. "A Methodological Analysis of Segregation Indexes," *American Sociological Review* 20, pp. 210–217.

―――― and B. Duncan 1955b. "Occupational Stratification and Residential Distribution," *American Journal of Sociology* 50, pp. 493–503.

―――― and S. Lieberson 1959. "Ethnic Segregation and Assimilation," *American Journal of Sociology* 64, pp. 364–374.

Duncan, S. 1976a. "Research Directions in Social Geography: Housing Opportunities and Constraints," *Transactions, Institute of British Geographers* N.S. 1, pp. 10–19.

―――― 1976b. "Self-Help: The Allocation of Mortgages and the Formation of Housing Sub-Markets," *Area* 8, pp. 307–316.

Dunham, H. 1937. "The Ecology of Functional Psychoses in Chicago," *American Sociological Review* 2, pp. 467–479.

Dunleavy, P. 1979. "The Urban Basis of Political Alignment," *British Journal of Political Science* 9, pp. 409–444.

Dyos, H. 1961. *Victorian Suburb: A Study of the Growth of Camberwell*. Leicester: University of Leicester Press, 1961.

―――― 1968. "The Speculative Builders and Developers of Victorian London," *Victorian Studies* 11, pp. 641–690.

―――― and D. Reeder 1973. "Slums and Suburbs." Pp. 359–386 in H. Dyos and M. Wolff (eds.), *The Victorian City*. London: Routledge and Kegan Paul.

Dzus, R. and G. Romsa 1977. "Housing Construction, Vacancy Chains, and Residential Mobility in Windsor," *Canadian Geographer* 21, pp. 223–236.

Economic Geography 1975. Special Issue on Spatial Diffusion 51, no. 3.

Economist, The 1978. "Who Needs Merseyside?" Oct. 14, p. 63.

―――― 1979. "Feathering their Nests," Nov. 17, p. 78.

―――― 1980. "Unsafe as Houses," March 1, p. 16.

―――― 1982. "What Went Wrong with the Inner Cities?" April 10, p. 35.

Edel, M. and E. Sclar 1975. "The Distribution of Real Estate Value Changes: Metropolitan Boston, 1870–1970," *Journal of Urban Economics* 2, pp. 366–387.

Ellegård, K., T. Hägerstrand, and B. Lenntorp 1977. "Activity Organization and the Generation of Daily Travel: Two Future Alternatives," *Economic Geography* 53, pp. 126–152.

Elliott, B. and D. McCrone 1979. "Power and Protest in the City," Paper Presented to Centre for Environmental Studies Conference in Nottingham, U.K.

―――― and D. McCrone 1980. "Urban Development in Edinburgh: In Contribution to the Political Economy of Place," *Scottish Journal of Sociology* 4, pp. 1–26.

Ellul, J. 1964. *The Technological Society*. New York: Knopf.

―――― 1970. *The Meaning of the City*. Grand Rapids, Mich.: Eerdmans.

Engels, F. 1958. *The Condition of the Working Class in England*. W. Henderson and W. Chaloner (trans. and eds.). Oxford: Blackwell.

English, J. 1973. "Oatlands: An Area of Twilight Housing in Glasgow," *Urban Studies* 10, pp. 381–386.

Entrikin, J. N. 1980. "Robert Park's Human Ecology and Human Geography," *Annals, Association of American Geographers* 70, pp. 43–58.

Ermuth, F. 1974. *Residential Satisfaction and Urban Environmental Preferences*. Geographical Monographs No. 3. Toronto: York University, Dept. of Geography.

Evans, D. 1976. *A Critique of Locational Conflict*. Toronto: University of Toronto, Dept. of Geography Discussion Paper Series No. 20.

———— 1980. *Demystifying Suburban Landscapes: Localism in its Wider Context*. Loughborough University of Technology, Dept. of Geography, Occasional Paper No. 4.

Everitt, J. 1976. "Community and Propinquity in a City," *Annals, Association of American Geographers* 66, pp. 104–116.

Eyles, J. 1968. *The Inhabitants Perception of Highgate Village*. Discussion Paper No. 15. London School of Economics, Dept. of Geography.

———— 1979. "Area-Based Policies for the Inner City: Context, Problems, and Prospects." Pp. 226–243 in D. Herbert and D. Smith (eds.), *Social Problems and the City*. Oxford: Oxford University Press, 1979.

Faris, R. 1970. *Chicago Sociology 1920–1932*. Chicago: University of Chicago Press.

Farley, R. et al. 1978. "Chocolate City, Vanilla Suburbs: Will the Trend toward Racially Separate Communities Continue?" *Social Science Research* 7, pp. 319–344.

Fauset, A. 1971. *Black Gods of the Metropolis*. Philadelphia: University of Pennsylvania Press.

Festinger, L. 1967. "Informal Social Communication." Pp. 411–425 in F. Matson and A. Montagu (eds.), *The Human Dialogue*. New York: Free Press.

————, S. Schacter, and K. Back 1950. *Social Pressures in Informal Groups*. Stanford: Stanford University Press.

Fiddler, C. n.d. *Cornelius Reconcilio*. Unpublished poem.

Firey, W. 1945. "Sentiment and Symbolism as Ecological Variables," *American Sociological Review* 10, pp. 140–148.

Fischer, C. 1972. "Urbanism as a Way of Life: A Review and an Agenda," *Sociological Methods and Research* 1, pp. 187–242.

———— 1975. "Toward A Subcultural Theory of Urbanism," *American Journal of Sociology* 80, pp. 1319–1341.

———— 1976. *The Urban Experience*. New York: Harcourt Brace Jovanovich.

———— and R. Jackson 1976. "Suburbs, Networks, and Attitudes." Pp. 279–307 in B. Schwartz (ed.), *The Changing Face of the Suburbs*. Chicago: University of Chicago Press.

Flad, H. 1973. *The City and the Longhouse: A Social Geography of American Indians in Syracuse*. Unpublished dissertation, Syracuse University, Dept. of Geography.

Flax, M. 1972. *A Study in Comparative Urban Indicators: Conditions in 18 Large Metropolitan Areas*. Washington, D.C.: Urban Institute Paper 1206-4.

———— et al. 1975. "Social Indicators and Society: Some Key Dimensions." Pp. 535–560 in G. Gappert and H. Rose (eds.), *The Social Economy of Cities*. Beverly Hills, Cal.: Sage.

Fleming, K. 1968. "Comment." In J. Lyle (ed.), *The Black American and the Press*. Los Angeles: Ward Ritchie Press.

Ford, L. 1979. "Urban Preservation and the Geography of the City in the U.S.A." *Progress in Human Geography* 3, pp. 215–242.

———— and E. Griffin 1979. "The Ghettoization of Paradise," *Geographical Review* 69, pp. 140–158.

Form, W. 1954. "The Place of Social Structure in the Determination of Land Use," *Social Forces* 32, pp. 317–323.

Forman, R. 1971. *Black Ghettos, White Ghettos, and Slums*. Englewood Cliffs, N.J.: Prentice-Hall.

Forward, C. 1973. "The Immortality of a Fashionable Residential District: The Uplands." Pp. 1–39 in C. N. Forward (ed.), *Residential and Neighbourhood Studies in Victoria*. Victoria, B.C.: Western Geographical Series, No. 5.

Frankenberg, R. 1966. *Communities in Britain*. Harmondsworth, Middx.: Penguin.

Fried, M. and P. Gleicher 1961. "Some Sources of Residential Satisfaction in an Urban Slum," *Journal of the American Institute of Planners* 27, pp. 305–315.

Frieden, B. 1977. "The New Housing-Cost Problem," *The Public Interest* 40, pp. 70–87.

———— 1979. *The Environmental Protection Hustle*. Cambridge, Mass.: MIT Press.

Gad, G. 1973. "Crowding and Pathologies: Some Critical Remarks," *Canadian Geographer* 17, pp. 373–390.

———— 1979. "Face-to-Face Linkages and Office Decentralization Potentials: A Study of Toronto." Pp. 277–323 in P. Daniels (ed.), *Spatial Patterns of Office Growth and Location*. Chichester, U.K.: Wiley.

————, R. Peddie, and J. Punter 1973. "Ethnic Differences in the Residential Search Process." Pp. 168–180 in L. S. Bourne et al. (eds.), *The Form of Cities in Central Canada*. Toronto: University of Toronto, Dept. of Geography.

Gale, S. and E. Moore (eds.) 1975. *The Manipulated City*. Chicago: Maaroufa.

Gans, H. 1962a. *The Urban Villagers*. New York: Free Press.

———— 1962b. "Urbanism and Suburbanism as Ways of Life." Pp. 625–648 in A. M. Rose (ed.), *Human Behaviour and Social Processes*. London: Routledge and Kegan Paul.

———— 1967. *The Levittowners*. New York: Pantheon Books.

———— 1972. *People and Plans*. Harmondsworth, Middx.: Penguin.

Gartner, A. and F. Riessman 1974. *The Service Society and the Consumer Vanguard*. New York: Harper & Row.

Gershuny, J. 1978. *After Industrial Society?* London: Macmillan.

Gerth, H. and C. W. Mills 1953. *Character and Social Structure: The Psychology of Social Institutions*. New York: Harcourt Brace Jovanovich.

Gibson, E. 1970. "Urban Geography as Human Geography." Paper presented to the Association of Pacific Coast Geographers meeting in Santa Cruz, California.

———— 1978. "Understanding the Subjective Meaning of Places." Pp. 138–154 in D. Ley and M. Samuels (eds.), *Humanistic Geography*. Chicago: Maaroufa.

Giddens, A. 1971. *Capitalism and Modern Social Theory*. Cambridge: Cambridge University Press.

———— 1973. *The Class Structure of the Advanced Societies*. London: Hutchinson.

Giggs, J. and P. Mather 1975. "Factorial Ecology and Factor Invariance: An Investigation," *Economic Geography* 51, pp. 366–382.

Gillespie, A. E. and D. W. Owen 1981. "Unemployment Trends in the Current Recession," *Area* 13, pp. 189–196.

Ginzberg, E. 1979. "The Professionalization of the U.S. Labor Force," *Scientific American* 240, pp. 48–53.

Glass, S. and J. Obler (eds.), 1977. *Urban Ethnic Conflict*. Monograph Series No. 3. Chapel Hill, N.C.: University of North Carolina, Institute for Research in Social Science.

Glenn, N. 1973. "Suburbanization in the United States Since World War II." Pp. 51–78 in L. Masotti and J. Hadden (eds.), *The Urbanization of the Suburbs*. Beverly Hills, Cal.: Sage.

Goddard, J. 1973. "Office Linkages and Location: A Study of Communications and Social Factors in Central London," *Progress in Planning* 1, pp. 109–232.

———— 1975. *Office Location in Urban and Regional Development*. London: Oxford University Press.

Godkin, M. 1977. *Space, Time and Place in the Human Experience of Stress*. Unpublished dissertation, School of Geography, Clark University.

Goering, J. 1979. "The National Neighborhood Movement," *Journal, American Planning Association* 45, pp. 506–514.

Goffman, E. 1959. *The Presentation of Self in Everyday Life*. Garden City, N.Y.: Doubleday.

———— 1961. *Asylums*. New York: Anchor.

Goheen, P. G. 1970. *Victorian Toronto, 1850 to 1900*. Chicago: University of Chicago, Dept. of Geography Research Paper No. 127.

———— 1974. "Interpreting the American City: Some Historical Perspectives," *Geographical Review* 64, pp. 362–384.

Golant, S. 1972. *The Residential Location and Spatial Behavior of the Elderly*. Chicago: University of Chicago, Dept. of Geography, Research Paper No. 143.

Goldberg, M. 1970. "Transportation, Urban Land Values, and Rents: A Synthesis," *Land Economics* 46, pp. 153–162.

———— and D. Ulinder 1976. "Residential Developer Behavior 1975: Additional Empirical Findings," *Land Economics* 52, pp. 363–370.

Goldsmith, W. and M. Derian 1979. "Towards a National Urban Policy—Critical Reviews: Is There an Urban Policy?" *Journal of Regional Science* 19, pp. 93–108.

Goldstein, J. and H. Rosenfeld 1969. "Insecurity and Preference for Persons Similar to Oneself," *Journal of Personality* 37, pp. 253–268.

Golledge, R. and A. Spector 1978. "Comprehending the Urban Environment: Theory and Practice," *Geographical Analysis* 10, pp. 403–426.

———— and G. Zannaras 1973. "Cognitive Approaches to the Analysis of Human Spatial Behavior." Pp. 59–94 in W. Ittelson (ed.), *Environment and Cognition*. New York: Seminar Press.

Goodchild, B, 1974. "Class Differences in Environmental Perception: An Exploratory Study," *Urban Studies* 11, pp. 157–169.

Gordon, M. 1964. *Assimilation in American Life*. New York: Oxford University Press.

Gottman, J. 1961. *Megalopolis*. New York: Twentieth Century Fund.

———— 1966. "The Rising Demand for Urban Amenities." Pp. 163–178 in S. Warner (ed.), *Planning For A Nation of Cities*. Cambridge, Mass.: M.I.T. Press.

Gould, P. R. 1969a. *Spatial Diffusion*. Washington, D.C.: Association of American Geographers, Commission on College Geography, Resource Paper No. 4.

———— 1969b. "Problems of Space Preference Measures and Relationships," *Geographical Analysis* 1, pp. 31–44.

———— 1973. "The Black Boxes of Jönköping: Spatial Information and Preference." Pp. 235–245 in R. Downs and D. Stea (eds.), *Image and Environment*. Chicago: Aldine.

———— 1975. "Acquiring Spatial Information," *Economic Geography* 51, pp. 87–99.

Granovetter, M. 1973. "The Strength of Weak Ties," *American Journal of Sociology* 78, pp. 1360–1380.

Graves, P. 1980. "Migration and Climate," *Journal of Regional Science* 20, pp. 227–237.

Gray, F. 1976. "Selection and Allocation in Council Housing," *Transactions, Institute of British Geographers* N.S. 1, pp. 34–46.

Graziano, A. 1972. "In the Mental Health Industry, Illness Is Our Most Important Product," *Psychology Today* 5, pp. 12, 14, 17–18.

Green, D. H. 1977. "Industrialists' Information Levels of Regional Incentives," *Regional Studies* 11, pp. 7–18.

Greenberg, M. and T. Boswell 1972. "Neighborhood Deterioration as a Factor in Intraurban Migration," *Professional Geographer* 24, pp. 11–16.

Gregory, D. 1978. *Ideology, Science and Human Geography*. London: Hutchinson.

Grier, G. and E. Grier 1977. *Movers to the City: New Data on the Housing Market for Washington, D.C.* Washington, D.C.: The Washington Center for Metropolitan Studies.

Grigg, D. 1967. "Regions, Models, and Classes." Pp. 461–509 in R. Chorley and P. Haggett (eds.), *Models in Geography*. London: Methuen.

Gripaios, P. 1977. "The Closure of Firms in the Inner City: The South-East London Case 1970–75," *Regional Studies* 11, pp. 1–6.

Gross, B. and J. Straussman 1974. "The Social Indicator Movement," *Social Policy* 53, September-October, pp. 43–54.

Gross, P. 1972. "Urban Health Disorders, Spatial Analysis, and the Economics of Health Facility Location," *International Journal of Health Sciences* 2, pp. 64–83.

Guardian, The 1979. "Inmos Moves to Colorado," January 24.

Guest, A. 1974. "Neighborhood Life Cycles and Social Status," *Economic Geography* 50, pp. 228–243.

Gunton, T. 1978. "The Urban Land Question: Who is Right?" *City Magazine* 3, no. 3, pp. 39–45.

Gurwitsch, A. 1962. "The Common-Sense World As Social Reality," *Social Research* 29, pp. 50–72.

Gutstein, D. 1975. *Vancouver Limited*. Toronto: James Lorimer.

Habermas, J. 1970. *Toward A Rational Society*. Boston: Beacon Press.

———— 1976. *Legitimation Crisis*. London: Heinemann.

Hadden, J. and J. Barton 1973. "An Image That Will Not Die: Thoughts on the History of Anti-Urban Ideology." Pp. 79–119 in L. Masotti and J. Hadden (eds.), *The Urbanization of the Suburbs*. Beverly Hills, Cal.: Sage.

Hägerstrand, T. 1957. "Migration and Area." Pp. 27–158 in D. Hannerberg et al. (eds.), *Migration in Sweden*. Lund: University of Lund Studies in Geography, Series B., No. 13.

———— 1965. "A Monte-Carlo Approach to Diffusion." *Archives Européenes de Sociologie* 6, pp. 43–67.

_____ 1967. *Innovation Diffusion as a Spatial Process*. Chicago: University of Chicago Press.

_____ 1970. "What About People in Regional Science?" *Papers and Proceedings of the Regional Science Association* 24, pp. 7–21.

_____ 1974. "The Domain of Human Geography." Pp. 67–87 in R. Chorley (ed.), *New Directions in Geography*. New York: Cambridge University Press.

Hall, P. (ed.) 1966. *Von Thünen's Isolated State*. C. M. Wartenberg (trans). Oxford: Pergamon Press.

_____ 1980. "Planning with a Human Face," *The Times Higher Education Supplement*, June 13, p. 14.

_____ et al. 1973. *The Containment of Urban England*. 2 vols. London: Allen and Unwin.

Hall, W. 1974. *Spatial Behaviour in Victory Square: The Social Geography of an Inner City Park*. Unpublished thesis, University of British Columbia, Dept. of Geography.

Hamilton, B. 1978. "Zoning and the Exercise of Monopoly Power," *Journal of Urban Economics* 5, pp. 116–130.

Hamilton, F. E. I. (ed.) 1974. *Spatial Perspectives on Industrial Organizations and Decision-Making*. New York: Wiley.

Hammond, R. and P. McCullagh 1974. *Quantitative Techniques in Geography*. Oxford: Clarendon Press.

Hamnett, C. 1972. "The Social Patterning of Cities." Pp. 25–63 in *Social Geography*. Bletchley, Bucks.: The Open University Press.

_____ 1973. "Improvement Grants as an Indicator of Gentrification in Inner London," *Area* 5, pp. 252–261.

_____ 1977. "Non-Explanation in Urban Geography," *Area* 9, pp. 143–145.

_____ 1979. "Area-Based Explanations: A Critical Appraisal." Pp. 244–260 in D. Herbert and D. Smith (eds.), *Social Problems and the City*. Oxford: Oxford University Press.

_____ 1982a. "The Changing Economic Basis of Private Renting and the Rent Acts," unpublished paper, Department of Geography, The Open University.

_____ 1982b. "Owner-Occupation in the 1970s: Home Ownership or Investment?" *Estates Gazette*, forthcoming.

Hardwick, W. G. 1974. *Vancouver*. Don Mills, Ont.: Collier-Macmillan.

Harloe, M. (ed.) 1977. *Captive Cities*. London: Wiley.

Harries, K. 1974. *The Geography of Crime and Justice*. New York: McGraw-Hill.

_____ 1976. "Cities and Crime: A Geographic Model," *Criminology* 14, pp. 369–386.

Harris, B. 1968. "Quantitative Models of Urban Development: Their Role in Metropolitan Policy-Making." Pp. 363–412 in H. Perloff and L. Wingo (eds.), *Issues in Urban Economics*. Baltimore: Johns Hopkins Press.

Harris, C. and E. Ullman 1945. "The Nature of Cities," *Annals of the American Academy of Political and Social Science* 242, pp. 7–17.

Harrison, R., P. Bull, and M. Hart 1979. "Space and Time in Industrial Linkage Studies," *Area* 11, pp. 333–338.

Hart, J. F. 1976. "Urban Encroachment on Rural Areas," *Geographical Review* 66, pp. 1–17.

Hart, R. and G. Moore 1973. "The Development of Spatial Cognition: A Review." Pp. 246–288 in R. Downs and D. Stea (eds.), *Image and Environment*. Chicago: Aldine.

Hartman, C. 1974. *Yerba Buena*. San Francisco: Glide.

_____ and R. Kessler 1978. "The Illusion and Reality of Urban Renewal: San Francisco's Yerba Buena Center." Pp. 153–178 in W. Tabb and L. Sawers, *Marxism and the Metropolis*. New York: Oxford University Press.

Hartshorn, T. 1980. *Interpreting the City: An Urban Geography*. New York: Wiley.

Harvey, D. W. 1969a. "Conceptual and Measurement Problems in the Cognitive-Behavioral Approach to Location Theory." Pp. 35–67 in K. Cox and R. Golledge (eds.), *Behavioral Problems in Geography*. Evanston, Ill.: Northwestern University, Studies in Geography No. 17.

_____ 1969b. *Explanation in Geography*. London: Arnold.

_____ 1971. "Social Processes, Spatial Form, and the Redistribution of Real Income in an Urban System." Pp. 267–300 in M. Chisholm (ed.), *Regional Forecasting*. London: Butterworths.

_____ 1973. *Social Justice and the City*. London: Edward Arnold.

_____ 1975. "The Political Economy of Urbanization in Advanced Capitalist Societies: The Case of the United States." Pp. 119–163 in H. Rose and G. Gappert (eds.), *The Social Economy of Cities*. Beverly Hills, Cal.: Sage.

_____ 1978. "Labor, Capital and Class Struggle Around the Built Environment in Advanced Capitalist Societies." Pp. 9–37 in K. Cox (ed.), *Urbanization and Conflict in Market Societies*. Chicago: Maaroufa.

_____ and L. Chatterjee 1974. "Absolute Rent and the Structuring of Space by Governmental and Financial Institutions," *Antipode* 6, no. 1, pp. 22–36.

Hatt, P. 1946. "The Concept of the Natural Area," *American Sociological Review* 11, pp. 423–427.

Hays, S. 1964. "The Politics of Reform in Municipal Government in the Progressive Era," *Pacific Northwest Quarterly* 55, pp. 157–169.

Hayward, D. G. 1975. "Home as an Environmental and Psychological Concept," *Landscape* 20, no. 1, pp. 2–9.

Headley, J. 1971. *The Great Riots of New York, 1712–1873*. New York: Dover.

Helper, R. 1969. *Racial Policies and Practices of Real Estate Brokers*. Minneapolis: University of Minnesota Press.

Heraud, B. 1968. "Social Class and the New Towns," *Urban Studies* 5, pp. 33–58.

Herbert, D. T. 1968. "Principal Components Analysis and British Studies of Urban Social Structure," *Professional Geographer* 20, pp. 280–283.

_____ 1970. "Principal Components Analysis and Urban Social Structure: A Study of Cardiff and Swansea." Pp. 79–100 in H. Carter and W. K. D. Davies (eds.), *Urban Essays: Studies in the Geography of Wales*. London: Longmans.

_____ 1971. *Urban Geography: A Social Perspective*. New York: Praeger.

_____ 1975a. "Urban Neighbourhoods and Social Geographical Research." Pp. 459–478 in A. Phillips and B. Turton (eds.), *Environment, Man and Economic Change*. London: Longmans.

_____ 1975b. "Urban Deprivation: Definition, Measurement and Spatial Qualities," *Geographical Journal* 141, pp. 362–372.

_____ 1976a. "The Study of Delinquency Areas: A Social Geographic Approach," *Transactions, Institute of British Geographers* N.S. 1, pp. 472–492.

—— 1976b. "Urban Education: Problems and Policies." Pp. 123–158 in D. Herbert and R. Johnston (eds.), *Social Areas in Cities*. Vol. 2. London: Wiley.

—— 1982. *The Geography of Urban Crime*. London: Longman.

—— and R. J. Johnston 1978. "Geography and the Urban Environment." Pp. 1–33 in D. T. Herbert and R. J. Johnston (eds.), *Geography and the Urban Environment*. Vol. 1. Chichester: John Wiley.

—— and J. Raine 1976. "Defining Communities Within Urban Areas," *Town Planning Review* 47, pp. 325–338.

Hirsch, F. 1976. *Social Limits to Growth*. Cambridge: Harvard University Press.

Hobkirk, A. 1974. "Eastside, Westside: Social Class Images of Vancouver." Pp. 11–24 in D. Ley (ed.), *Community Participation and the Spatial Order of the City*. B.C. Geographical Series No. 19. Vancouver: Tantalus.

Hodge, D. 1979. *Seattle Displacement Study*. Seattle: City of Seattle, Office of Policy Planning.

Hoggart, R. 1958. *The Uses of Literacy: Aspects of Working Class Life*. Harmondsworth, Middx.: Penguin.

Holdsworth, D. W. 1979. "House and Home in Vancouver." Pp. 186–211 in G. Stelter and A. Artibise (eds.), *The Canadian City: Essays in Urban History*. Toronto: Macmillan.

—— 1981. "Whose Past, Whose Present? Residential Landscape Changes in the City of Toronto." Paper presented to the Association of American Geographers meeting in Los Angeles.

Holtermann, S. 1975. "Areas of Urban Deprivation in Great Britain: An Analysis of 1971 Census Data," *Social Trends* 6, pp. 33–47.

Hoover, E. and R. Vernon 1959. *Anatomy of a Metropolis*. New York: Doubleday.

Horton, F. and D. Reynolds 1971. "Effects of the Urban Spatial Structure on Individual Behavior," *Economic Geography* 47, pp. 36–48.

Howard, E. 1965. *Garden Cities of Tomorrow*. Cambridge, Mass.: M.I.T. Press.

Hoyt, H. 1933. *One Hundred Years of Land Values in Chicago*. Chicago: University of Chicago Press.

—— 1939. *The Structure and Growth of Residential Neighborhoods in American Cities*. Washington, D.C.: Federal Housing Administration.

Hughes, E. C. 1971. "The Growth of an Institution: The Chicago Real Estate Board." Pp. 33–69 in J. Short (ed.), *The Social Fabric of the Metropolis*. Chicago: University of Chicago Press.

Hugill, P. 1975. "Social Conduct on the Golden Mile," *Annals, Association of American Geographers* 65, pp. 214–228.

Humphreys, J. and J. Whitelaw 1979. "Immigrants in an Unfamiliar Environment," *Geografiska Annaler* 61B, pp. 8–18.

Hunter, A. 1972. "Factorial Ecology: A Critique and Some Suggestions," *Demography* 9, pp. 107–118.

—— 1974. *Symbolic Communities*. Chicago: University of Chicago Press.

Hurd, R. 1903. *Principles of City Land Values*. New York: The Record and Guide.

Hyland, G. 1970. "Social Interaction and Urban Opportunity: The Appalachian In-Migrant in the Cincinnati Central City," *Antipode* 2, no. 2, pp. 68–83.

Jackson, J. B. 1956–1957. "Other-Directed Houses," *Landscape* 6, pp. 29–35.

Jackson, P. and S. J. Smith (eds.) 1981. *Social Interaction and Ethnic Segregation*. London: Academic Press, Institute of British Geographers Special Publication No. 12.

Jacobs, J. 1961. *The Death and Life of Great American Cities*. New York: Random House.

Jacoby, L. R. 1972. *Perception of Air, Noise and Water Pollution in Detroit*. Ann Arbor: University of Michigan, Dept. of Geography Publication No. 7.

Jacquette, T. 1968. "Comment." In J. Lyle (ed.), *The Black American and the Press*. Los Angeles: Ward Ritchie Press.

Jakle, J. and J. Wheeler 1969. "The Changing Residential Structure of the Dutch Population in Kalamazoo, Michigan," *Annals, Association of American Geographers* 59, pp. 441–460.

Janelle, D. G. 1977. "Structural Dimensions in the Geography of Locational Conflicts," *Canadian Geographer* 21, pp. 311–328.

———— and H. Millward 1976. "Locational Conflict Patterns and Urban Ecological Structure," *Tijdschrift voor Economische en Sociale Geografie* 67, pp. 102–113.

Johnson, C. S. 1930. *The Negro in American Civilization*. New York: Holt.

Johnston, N. 1973. "Harland Bartholomew: Precedent for the Profession," *Journal, American Institute of Planners* 39, pp. 115–124.

Johnston, R. J. 1966. "The Location of High Status Residential Areas," *Geografiska Annaler* 48B, pp. 23–35.

———— 1969a. "Population Movements and Metropolitan Expansion: London, 1960–1," *Transactions, Institute of British Geographers* 46, pp. 69–91.

———— 1969b. "Processes of Change in the High Status Residential Districts of Christchurch," *New Zealand Geographer* 25, pp. 1–15.

———— 1971. *Urban Residential Patterns*. New York: Praeger.

———— 1976a. "Residential Area Characteristics: Research Methods for Identifying Sub-Areas." Pp. 193–235 in D. Herbert and R. Johnston (eds.), *Social Areas in Cities*. Vol. 1. London: Wiley.

———— 1976b. "Political Behaviour and the Residential Mosaic." Pp. 65–88 in D. Herbert and R. Johnston (eds.), *Social Areas in Cities*. Vol. 2. London: Wiley.

———— 1976c. "Spatial and Temporal Variations in Land and Property Prices in New Zealand: 1953–1972," *New Zealand Geographer* 32, pp. 30–55.

———— 1981. *The Geography of Federal Spending in the United States*. London: Wiley.

Jonassen, C. 1949. "Cultural Variables in the Ecology of an Ethnic Group," *American Sociological Review* 14, pp. 32–41.

Jones, E. 1960. *The Social Geography of Belfast*. London: Oxford University Press.

———— 1972. "The Nature and Scope of Social Geography." Pp. 11–23 in *Social Geography*. Bletchley, Bucks.: The Open University.

Journal of Social Issues 1973. "Asian Americans: A Success Story." Vol. 29, no. 2.

Joy, R. 1976. "Languages in Conflict, Canada 1976," *American Review of Canadian Studies* 2, pp. 7–21.

Kaiser, E. and S. Weiss 1970. "Public Policy and the Residential Development Process," *Journal, American Institute of Planners* 36, pp. 30–37.

Kammeyer, K. and C. Bolton 1968. "Community and Family Factors Related to the Use of a Family Service Agency," *Journal of Marriage and the Family* 30, pp. 488–498.

Kariel, H. and L. Rosenvall 1978. "Circulation of Newspaper News Within Canada," *Canadian Geographer* 22, pp. 85–111.

Kariya, P. 1978. "Keepers and Kept: The Lifeworld Relations of British Columbia Indians and the Department of Indian Affairs." Paper presented to the Association of American Geographers meeting in New Orleans.

Kasarda, J. and M. Janowitz 1974. "Community Attachment in Mass Society," *American Sociological Review* 39, pp. 328–339.

Kasperson, R. 1971. "The Location of the Massachusetts State Medical School." Unit 6 in S. Natoli (ed.), *Activities Selected From the High School Geography Project*. Washington, D.C.: Association of American Geographers.

——— and M. Breitbart 1974. *Participation, Decentralization, and Advocacy Planning*. Washington, D.C.: Association of American Geographers, Commission on College Geography Resource Paper No. 25.

Katz, E. 1957. "The Two-Step Flow of Communication," *Public Opinion Quarterly* 21, pp. 61–78.

Kellogg, P. (ed.) 1914. *Wage Earning Pittsburgh*. New York: Russell Sage Foundation.

King, L. 1969. *Statistical Analysis in Geography*. Englewood Cliffs, N.J.: Prentice-Hall.

Kirmeyer, S. 1978. "Urban Density and Pathology: A Review of Research," *Environment and Behavior* 10, pp. 247–269.

Knos, D. 1962. *Distribution of Land Values in Topeka, Kansas*. Center for Research in Business. Lawrence, Kansas: University of Kansas Press.

Knox, P. L. 1975. *Social Well-Being: A Spatial Perspective*. Oxford: Clarendon Press.

——— 1982. "Symbolism, Styles and Settings: The Built Environment and the Imperatives of Urbanized Capitalism," *Architecture and Behavior* 2, forthcoming.

——— and J. Cullen 1981. "Planners as Urban Managers," *Environment and Planning* 13A, pp. 885–892.

——— and A. MacLaran 1978. "Values and Perceptions in Descriptive Approaches to Urban Social Geography." Pp. 197–247 in D. Herbert and R. Johnston (eds.), *Geography and the Urban Environment*. Vol. 1. Chichester: Wiley.

Kohl, H. 1968. *36 Children*. New York: Signet Books.

Kornblum, W. 1974. *Blue Collar Community*. Chicago: University of Chicago Press.

Kotler, M. 1969. *Neighborhood Government*. Indianapolis: Bobbs-Merrill.

Kucharczyk, J. 1978. "Canadian Science Policy," *C.A.U.T. Bulletin* 25, no. 9, pp 8–9.

Ladd, F. 1970. "Black Youths View Their Environment: Neighborhood Maps," *Environment and Behavior* 2, pp. 64–79.

Lai, C. -Y. 1974. "Human Crowding in Hong Kong." Pp. 141–180 in M. Edgell and B. Farrell (eds.), *Themes on Pacific Lands*. Victoria, B.C.: Western Geographical Series No. 10.

Lamb, R. 1975. *Metropolitan Impact on Rural America*. Chicago: University of Chicago, Department of Geography, Research Paper No. 162.

——— 1977. "Intra-Regional Growth in Nonmetropolitan America: Change in the Pattern of Change." Paper presented to the Association of American Geographers meeting in Salt Lake City.

Langner, T. and S. Michael 1963. *Life Stress and Mental Health*. New York: Free Press.

Langton, J. 1975. "Residential Patterns in Pre-Industrial Cities: Some Case Studies from Seventeenth Century Britain," *Transactions Institute of British Geographers* 65, pp. 1–27.

Lansing, J., C. Clifton, and J. Morgan 1969. *New Homes and Poor People: A Study of Chains of Moves*. Ann Arbor: University of Michigan, Institute for Social Research.

Laponce, J. 1977. "Bilingualism and the Bilingual City: The Case of Montreal." Paper presented to the Urban Networks Seminar in Brazilia.

Lasch, C. 1978. *The Culture of Narcissism*. New York: Norton.

Laumann, E. 1973. *Bonds of Pluralism*. New York: Wiley.

_____ and J. House, 1970. "Living Room Styles and Social Attributes: The Patterning of Material Artifacts in a Modern Urban Community," *Sociology and Social Research* 54, pp. 321–342.

Laurenti, L. 1960. *Property Values and Race*. Berkeley, Cal.: University of California Press.

Lee, T. 1977. "Choice and Constraint in the Housing Market: The Case of One-Parent Families in Tasmania," *Australia and New Zealand Journal of Sociology* 13, pp. 41–46.

Lee, T. R. 1968. "Urban Neighborhood as a Socio-Spatial Schema," *Human Relations* 21, pp. 241–267.

_____ 1970. "Perceived Distance as a Function of Direction in the City," *Environment and Behavior* 2, pp. 40–51.

Lefebvre, H. 1976. "Reflections on the Politics of Space," *Antipode* 8, no. 2, pp. 30–37.

Leigh, R. 1966. *Specialty Retailing: A Geographic Analysis*. B.C. Geographical Series No. 6. Vancouver: Tantalus.

Leiss, W. 1976. *The Limits to Satisfaction*. Toronto: University of Toronto Press.

Lemon, J. 1974. "Toronto: Is It a Model for Urban Life and Citizen Participation?" Pp. 41–58 in D. Ley (ed.), *Community Participation and the Spatial Order of the City*. B.C. Geographical Series No. 19. Vancouver: Tantalus.

_____ 1978. "The Urban Community Movement: Moving Toward Public Households." Pp. 319–337 in D. F. Ley and M. S. Samuels (eds.), *Humanistic Geography*. Chicago: Maaroufa.

Leven, C. L. et al. 1976. *Neighborhood Change: Lessons in the Dynamics of Urban Decay*. New York: Praeger.

Lewis, O. 1968. "The Culture of Poverty." Pp. 187–200 in D. Moynihan (ed.), *On Understanding Poverty*. New York: Basic Books.

Lewis, P. F. 1976. *New Orleans: The Making of an Urban Landscape*. Cambridge, Mass.: Ballinger.

_____ 1979. "Axioms for Reading the Landscape." Pp. 11–32 in D. Meinig (ed.), *The Interpretation of Ordinary Landscapes*. New York: Oxford University Press.

Ley, D. F. 1974a. *The Black Inner City as Frontier Outpost: Images and Behavior of a Philadelphia Neighborhood*. Washington, D.C.: Association of American Geographers, Monograph Series No. 7.

_____ 1974b. "Problems of Co-optation and Idolatry in the Community Group." Pp. 75–88 in D. Ley (ed.), *Community Participation and the Spatial Order of the City*. B.C. Geographical Series No. 19. Vancouver: Tantalus.

_____ 1975a. "Resident Efficacy and the Quality of Inner City Life," *Proceedings, Association of American Geographers* 7, pp. 117–121.

_____ 1975b. "The Street Gang in its Milieu." Pp. 247–273 in H. Rose and G. Gappert (eds.), *The Social Economy of Cities*. Beverly Hills, Cal.: Sage.

———— 1977a. "The Personality of a Geographical Fact," *Professional Geographer* 29, pp. 8–13.

———— 1977b. "Social Geography and the Taken-for-Granted World," *Transactions, Institute of British Geographers* N.S. 2, pp. 498–512.

———— 1978a. "Social Geography and Social Action." Pp. 41–57 in D. F. Ley and M. S. Samuels (eds.), *Humanistic Geography*. Chicago: Maaroufa Press.

———— 1978b. "Inner City Resurgence in its Societal Context." Paper presented to the Association of American Geographers meeting in New Orleans.

———— 1980. "Liberal Ideology and the Postindustrial City," *Annals, Association of American Geographers* 70, pp. 238–258.

———— 1981. "Inner City Revitalization in Canada: A Vancouver Case Study," *Canadian Geographer* 25, pp. 124–148.

———— 1982. "The Politics of Landscape in a Postindustrial City." Paper presented to the International Seminar of the Centre of Canadian Studies, University of Edinburgh.

———— and R. A. Cybriwsky 1974. "Urban Graffiti as Territorial Markers," *Annals, Association of American Geographers* 64, pp. 491–505.

———— and J. Mercer 1980. "Locational Conflict and the Politics of Consumption," *Economic Geography* 56, pp. 89–109.

———— and M. S. Samuels (eds.) 1978. *Humanistic Geography*. Chicago: Maaroufa Press.

Lieberson, S. 1965. "Bilingualism in Montreal: A Demographic Analysis," *American Journal of Sociology* 71, pp. 10–25.

Liebow, E. 1967. *Tally's Corner*. Boston: Little, Brown.

Linowes, R. and D. Allensworth 1973. *The Politics of Land Use*. New York: Praeger.

Lipowski, Z. 1974. "Surfeit of Attractive Information Inputs: A Hallmark of Our Environment." Pp. 484–490 in R. Moos and P. Insel (eds.), *Issues in Social Ecology*. Palo Alto, Cal.: National Press.

Lipton, S. G. 1977. "Evidence of Central City Revival," *Journal, American Institute of Planners* 43, pp. 136–147.

Little, B. 1972. "Psychological Man as Scientist, Humanist and Specialist," *Journal of Experimental Research in Personality* 6, pp. 95–118.

———— 1976. "Specialization and the Varieties of Environmental Experience." Pp. 81–116 in S. Wapner et al. (eds.), *Experiencing the Environment*. New York: Plenum Press.

Liu, B. -C. 1975. "Differential Net Migration Rates and the Quality of Life," *Review of Economics and Statistics* 57, pp. 329–337.

———— 1976. *Quality of Life Indicators in U.S. Metropolitan Areas*. New York: Praeger.

Lloyd, P. and C. Mason 1978. "Manufacturing Industry in the Inner City: A Case Study of Greater Manchester," *Transactions, Institute of British Geographers* N.S. 3, pp. 66–90.

Lloyd, R. 1976. "Cognition, Preference, and Behavior in Space," *Economic Geography* 52, pp. 241–253.

Lofland, L. 1973. *A World of Strangers*. New York: Basic Books.

Logan, M. 1964. "Manufacturing Decentralization in the Sydney Metropolitan Area," *Economic Geography* 40, pp. 151–162.

Lonsdale, R. and H. Seyler (eds.) 1979. *Nonmetropolitan Industrialization*. Washington, D.C.: V. H. Winston.

Lord, J. D. 1977. *Spatial Perspectives on School Desegregation and Busing*. Washington, D.C.: Association of American Geographers, Commission on College Geography Resource Paper No. 77-3.

Lorimer, J. 1970. *The Real World of City Politics*. Toronto: James Lewis and Samuel.

――― 1972. *A Citizen's Guide to City Politics*. Toronto: James Lewis and Samuel.

――― and M. Phillips 1971. *Working People*. Toronto: James Lewis and Samuel.

――― and E. Ross (eds.) 1976. *The City Book*. Toronto: James Lorimer.

Louder, F. 1975. "Montreal's Downtown Moves East," *City Magazine* 1, Nov., pp. 32–39.

Lovrich, N. 1974. "Differing Priorities in an Urban Electorate," *Social Sciences Quarterly* 55, pp. 704–717.

Lowenthal, D. 1961. "Geography, Experience, and Imagination: Towards a Geographical Epistemology," *Annals, Association of American Geographers* 51, pp. 241–260.

――― 1979. "Environmental Perception: Preserving the Past," *Progress in Human Geography* 3, pp. 549–559.

Lowman, J. 1982. "Crime, Criminal Justice Policy and the Urban Environment." Forthcoming in D. Herbert and R. Johnston (eds.), *Geography and the Urban Environment* Vol. 5. Chichester: Wiley.

Lowry, M. 1973. "Schools in Transition," *Annals, Association of American Geographers* 63, pp. 167–180.

Loyd, B. 1975. "Woman's Place, Man's Place," *Landscape* 20, no. 1, pp. 10–13.

Lubove, R. 1969. *Twentieth Century Pittsburgh: Government, Business, and Environmental Change*. New York: Wiley.

Lynch, K. 1960. *The Image of the City*. Cambridge, Mass.: M.I.T. Press.

McAfee, A. 1973. "Evolving Inner City Residential Environments: The Case of Vancouver's West End." Pp. 163–181 in J. Minghi (ed.), *Peoples of the Living Land*. B.C. Geographical Series No. 15. Vancouver: Tantalus.

McCann, L. D. 1975. *Neighbourhoods in Transition*. Edmonton: University of Alberta, Dept. of Geography, Occasional Papers No. 2.

McCarthy, K. 1976. "The Household Life Cycle and Housing Choices," *Papers, Proceedings Regional Science Association* 37, pp. 55–80.

McCracken, K. 1975. "Household Awareness Spaces and Intraurban Migration Search Behavior," *Professional Geographer* 27, pp. 166–170.

McDermott, P. and M. Taylor 1976. "Attitudes, Images, and Location: The Subjective Context of Decision Making in New Zealand Manufacturing," *Economic Geography* 52, pp. 325–347.

McDermott, R. 1975. *Toward an Embodied Map of Urban Neighborhoods*. Occasional paper, Anthropological Society of Washington, D.C.

McDonald, J. and H. Bowman 1979. "Land Value Functions: A Reevaluation," *Journal of Urban Economics* 6, pp. 25–41.

――― 1981. "Spatial Patterns of Business Land Values in Chicago," *Urban Geography* 2, pp. 201–215.

MacDonald, J. and L. MacDonald 1964. "Chain Migration, Ethnic Neighborhood Formation and Social Networks," *Milbank Memorial Fund Quarterly* 42, pp. 82–97.

McEntire, D. 1960. *Residence and Race*. Berkeley: University of California Press.

McKay, D. and A. Cox 1979. *The Politics of Urban Change*. London: Croom Helm.

McKenzie, R. 1933. *The Metropolitan Community*. New York: McGraw-Hill.

——— 1968. *On Human Ecology*. A. Hawley (ed.). Chicago: University of Chicago Press.

Mackinder, H. 1902. *Britain and the British Seas*. New York: Appleton.

Maher, C. 1974. "Spatial Patterns in Urban Housing Markets: Filtering in Toronto, 1953–71," *Canadian Geographer* 18, pp. 108–124.

Makielski, S. 1966. *The Politics of Zoning*. New York: Columbia University Press.

Mallowe, M. 1973. "The $75 Million Misunderstanding," *Philadelphia Magazine,* Feb., pp. 73–77, 173.

Manners, G. 1974. "The Office in Metropolis: An Opportunity for Shaping Metropolitan America," *Economic Geography* 50, pp. 93–110.

Manvel, A. 1968. "Land Use in 106 Large Cities." In *Three Land Research Studies*. National Commission on Urban Problems. Washington, D.C.: Government Printing Office.

Marble, D. and S. Bowlby 1968. "Shopping Alternatives and Recurrent Travel Patterns." Pp. 42–75 in F. Horton (ed.), *Geographic Studies of Urban Transportation and Network Analysis*. Evanston, Ill.: Northwestern University Studies in Geography No. 16.

March, J. G. and H. Simon 1958. *Organizations*. New York: Wiley.

Marcus, S. 1974. *Engels, Manchester, and the Working Class*. New York: Random House.

Marcuse, H. 1964. *One-Dimensional Man*. Boston: Beacon Press.

Markusen, J. and D. Scheffman 1977. *Speculation and Monopoly in Urban Development*. Toronto: University of Toronto Press.

Marx, K. 1964. *Karl Marx, Early Writings*. T. B. Bottomore (ed.). New York: McGraw-Hill.

——— 1967. *Capital*. New York: International Publishers.

——— and F. Engels 1970. *The German Ideology*. C. Arthur (ed.). New York: International Publishers.

Maslow, A. 1970. *Motivation and Personality*. New York: Harper & Row.

Mason, P. 1972. "Some Characteristics of a Youth Ghetto in Boulder, Colorado," *Journal of Geography* 71, pp. 526–532.

Massam, B. 1975. *Location and Space in Social Administration*. London: Edward Arnold.

——— 1980. *Spatial Search*. Oxford: Pergamon.

Massey, D. 1976. "Class, Racism and Busing in Boston," *Antipode* 8, no. 2, pp. 37–49.

Matoré, G. 1966. "Existential Space," *Landscape* 15, pp. 5–6.

Matthiasson, C. 1974. "Coping in a New Environment: Mexican Americans in Milwaukee, Wisconsin," *Urban Anthropology* 3, pp. 262–277.

Mead, G. H. 1964. *On Social Psychology*. A. Strauss (ed.). Chicago: University of Chicago Press.

Megee, M. 1976. "Restructuring the Health Care Delivery System in the United States." Pp. 293–329 in J. S. Adams (ed.), *Urban Policymaking and Metropolitan Dynamics: A Comparative Geographical Analysis*. Cambridge, Mass.: Ballinger.

Meier, R. L. 1962. *A Communications Theory of Urban Growth*. Cambridge, Mass.: M.I.T. Press.

——— 1968. "The Metropolis as a Transaction—Maximizing System," *Daedalus* 97, pp. 1292–1313.

Mellor, E. 1973. "A Case Study: Costs and Benefits of Public Goods and Expenditures for a Ghetto." Pp. 38–58 in K. Boulding et al. (eds.), *Transfers in an Urbanized Economy*. Belmont, Cal.: Wadsworth.

Melton, A. 1969. "Le Quartier: Etude Géographique et Psychosociologique," *Canadian Geographer* 13, pp. 299–316.

Mercer, D. 1970. "Urban Recreational Hinterlands: A Review and Example," *Professional Geographer* 22, pp. 74–78.

_____ and J. Powell 1972. *Phenomenology and Other Non-Positivist Approaches in Geography*. Melbourne: Monash University Publications in Geography No. 1.

Mercer, J. 1972. "Housing Quality and the Ghetto." Pp. 143–167 in H. Rose and H. McConnell (eds.), *Geography of the Ghetto*. Dekalb, Ill.: Northern Illinois University Press.

_____ 1974. "City Manager Communities in the Montreal Metropolitan Area," *Canadian Geographer* 18, pp. 352–366.

_____ 1976. "National Policy and the Geography of Housing: Canada and the United States." Unpublished paper, Department of Geography, University of British Columbia.

_____ 1979. "On Continentalism, Distinctiveness, and Comparative Urban Geography: Canadian and American Cities," *Canadian Geographer* 23, pp. 119–139.

_____ and J. Hultquist 1976. "National Progress Toward Housing and Urban Renewal Goals." Pp. 101–162 in J. S. Adams (ed.), *Urban Policymaking and Metropolitan Dynamics: A Comparative Geographical Analysis*. Cambridge, Mass.: Ballinger.

Merleau-Ponty, M. 1962. *Phenomenology of Perception*. New York: Humanities Press.

Mesnard, A. and A. Vigarié 1979. "Internal Linkages in the Upper Tertiary Sector of Nantes," *Ekistics* 46, pp. 53–66.

Meyer, J. W. 1976. "Diffusers and Social Innovations: Increasing the Scope of Diffusion Models," *Professional Geographer* 28, pp. 17–22.

_____ 1981. "Migration to Near-Metropolitan Areas: Characteristics and Motives," *Urban Geography* 2, pp. 64–80.

Michelson, W. 1970. *Man and His Urban Environment*. Reading, Mass.: Addison-Wesley.

_____ 1977. *Environmental Choice, Human Behavior, and Residential Satisfaction*. New York: Oxford University Press.

Milgram, S. 1970. "The Experience of Living in Cities," *Science* 167, pp. 1461–1468.

_____ et al. 1972. "A Psychological Map of New York City," *American Scientist* 60, pp. 194–200.

Mills, C. Wright 1966. *Sociology and Pragmatism: The Higher Learning in America*. I. Horowitz (ed.). New York: Oxford University Press.

Mills, E. 1969. "The Value of Urban Land." Pp. 231–253 in H. Perloff (ed.), *The Quality of the Urban Environment*. Baltimore: Johns Hopkins University Press.

Mitchell, J. 1979. "Social Violence in Northern Ireland," *Geographical Review* 69, pp. 179–201.

Mitchell, J. C. 1969. "The Concept and Use of Social Networks." Pp. 1–50 in J. C. Mitchell (ed.), *Social Networks in Urban Situations*. Manchester: University of Manchester Press.

Moles, A. and E. Rohmer 1972. *Psychologie de l'Espace*. Paris: Casterman.

Mollenkopf, J. 1978. "The Postwar Politics of Urban Development." Pp. 117–152 in W. Tabb and L. Sawers (eds.), *Marxism and the Metropolis*. New York: Oxford University Press.

_____ 1981. "Neighborhood Political Development and the Politics of Urban Growth," *International Journal of Urban and Regional Research* 5, pp. 15–39.

Molotch, H. 1969. "Racial Change in a Stable Community," *American Journal of Sociology* 75, pp. 226–238.

———— 1976. "The City as a Growth Machine: Toward a Political Economy of Place," *American Journal of Sociology* 82, pp. 309–332.

Morgan, B. 1974. "Social Distance and Spatial Distance: A Research Note," *Area* 6, pp. 293–297.

———— 1975. "The Segregation of Socio-Economic Groups in Urban Areas: A Comparative Analysis," *Urban Studies* 12, pp. 47–60.

Morrill, R. L. 1965. "The Negro Ghetto: Problems and Alternatives," *Geographical Review* 55, pp. 339–361.

———— 1974. "Efficiency and Equity of Optimum Location Models," *Antipode* 6, no. 1, pp. 41–46.

———— 1977. "What's Behind the Rural Recovery? Population Trends in the Pacific Northwest, 1970–75." Paper presented to the Association of American Geographers meeting in Salt Lake City.

———— 1980. "The Spread of Change in Metropolitan and Nonmetropolitan Growth in the United States, 1940–1976," *Urban Geography* 1, pp. 118–129.

———— and O. Donaldson 1972. "Geographical Perspectives on the History of Black America," *Economic Geography* 48, pp. 1–23.

————, R. Earickson, and P. Rees 1970. "Factors Influencing Distances Travelled to Hospitals," *Economic Geography* 46, pp. 161–171.

———— and F. R. Pitts 1967. "Marriage, Migration and the Mean Information Field," *Annals, Association of American Geographers* 57, pp. 401–422.

Morrison, P. 1974. "Urban Growth and Decline: San Jose and St. Louis in the 1960s," *Science* 185, pp. 757–762.

Moses, R. 1956. *Working For The People*. New York: Harper & Row.

Muller, E. and P. Groves 1979. "The Emergence of Industrial Districts in Mid-Nineteenth Century Baltimore," *Geographical Review* 69, pp. 159–178.

Muller, P. 1976a. *The Outer City: Geographical Consequences of the Urbanization of the Suburbs.* Washington, D.C.: Association of American Geographers, Commission on College Geography Resource Paper 75-2.

———— 1976b. "Transportation Geography II: Social Transportation," *Progress in Geography* 8, pp. 208–231.

———— 1981. *Contemporary Suburban America*. Englewood Cliffs, N.J.: Prentice-Hall.

Mumford, L. 1961. *The City in History*. New York: Harcourt Brace Jovanovich.

Murdie, R. A. 1969. *Factorial Ecology of Metropolitan Toronto, 1951–1961*. Chicago: University of Chicago, Dept. of Geography Research Paper No. 116.

Murphy, P. 1973. "Apartment Location: The Balance Between Developer and Community." Pp. 149–179 in C. Forward (ed.), *Residential and Neighbourhood Studies in Victoria*. Victoria, B.C.: Western Geographical Series No. 5.

Murphy, R. E. 1974. *The American City: An Urban Geography*. New York: McGraw-Hill.

Murray, D. and C. Spencer 1979. "Individual Differences in the Drawing of Cognitive Maps," *Transactions, Institute of British Geographers* N.S. 4, pp. 385–391.

Murray, R. and F. Boal 1979. ''The Social Ecology of Urban Violence.'' Pp. 139–157 in D. Herbert and D. Smith (eds.), *Social Problems and the City*. Oxford: Oxford University Press.

Muth, R. 1961. ''The Spatial Structure of the Housing Market,'' *Papers and Proceedings of the Regional Science Association* 7, pp. 207–220.

———— 1969. *Cities and Housing*. Chicago: University of Chicago Press.

Nathan, R. and P. Dommell 1977. ''Understanding the Urban Predicament,'' *The Brookings Bulletin* 14, Spring-Summer, pp. 9–13.

National Association of Realtors 1978. *Existing Home Sales 1977*. Chicago: National Association of Realtors.

Neenan, W. 1973. ''Suburban-Central City Exploitation Thesis: One City's Tale.'' Pp. 10–37 in K. Boulding et al. (eds.), *Transfers in an Urbanized Economy*. Belmont, Cal.: Wadsworth.

Nelson, H. and W. Clark 1976. *Los Angeles: The Metropolitan Experience*. Cambridge, Mass.: Ballinger.

Newcomb, T. 1966. ''An Approach to the Study of Communicative Acts.'' Pp. 66–79 in A. Smith (ed.), *Communication and Culture*. New York: Holt, Rinehart and Winston.

Newling, B. 1966. ''Urban Growth and Spatial Structure: Mathematical Models and Empirical Evidence,'' *Geographical Review* 56, pp. 213–225.

———— 1969. ''The Spatial Variation of Urban Population Densities,'' *Geographical Review* 59, pp. 242–252.

Newman, O. 1972. *Defensible Space*. New York: Macmillan.

Newton, K. 1978. ''Conflict Avoidance and Conflict Suppression: The Case of Urban Politics in the United States.'' Pp. 76–93 in K. R. Cox (ed.), *Urbanization and Conflict in Market Societies*. Chicago: Maaroufa.

Nichols, A. 1977. ''Baltimore, A City Preserved,'' *Preservation News* 17, May, p. 12.

Niedercorn, J. and E. Hearle 1964. ''Recent Land-Use Trends in Forty-Eight Large American Cities,'' *Land Economics* 40, pp. 105–109.

Norberg-Schulz, C. 1972. *Existence, Space, and Architecture*. New York: Praeger.

Nourse, H. and D. Phares 1975. ''Socioeconomic Transition and Housing Values: A Comparative Analysis of Urban Neighborhoods.'' Pp. 183–208 in G. Gappert and H. Rose (eds.), *The Social Economy of Cities*. Beverly Hills, Cal.: Sage.

Nus, W. van 1979. ''Toward the City Efficient: The Theory and Practice of Zoning.'' Pp. 226–246 in A. Artibise and G. Stelter (eds.), *The Usable Urban Past: Planning and Politics in the Modern Canadian City*. Toronto: Macmillan.

Ollman, B. 1971. *Alienation*. Cambridge: Cambridge University Press.

O'Loughlin, J. 1976. ''Malapportionment and Gerrymandering in the Ghetto.'' Pp. 539–565 in J. S. Adams (ed.), *Urban Policymaking and Metropolitan Dynamics: A Comparative Geographical Analysis*. Cambridge, Mass.: Ballinger.

Olsson, G. 1969. ''Inference Problems in Locational Analysis.'' Pp. 14–34 in K. Cox and R. Golledge (eds.), *Behavioral Problems in Geography*. Evanston, Ill.: Northwestern University Studies in Geography No. 17.

———— 1972. ''On Reason and Reasoning,'' *Antipode* 4, July, pp. 26–31.

———— 1974a. ''Servitude and Inequality in Spatial Planning: Ideology and Methodology in Conflict,'' *Antipode* 6, no. 1, pp. 16–21.

———— 1974b. ''The Dialectics of Spatial Analysis,'' *Antipode* 6, no. 3, pp. 50–62.

———— 1975. *Birds in Egg*. Ann Arbor: University of Michigan Geographical Publications No. 15.

Orleans, P. 1973. "Differential Cognition of Urban Residents." Pp. 115–130 in R. Downs and D. Stea (eds.), *Image and Environment*. Chicago: Aldine.

Ostergaard, P. 1975. *Quality of Life in a Northern City: A Social Geography of Yellowknife, N.W.T.* Unpublished thesis, Department of Geography, University of British Columbia.

Pahl, R. E. 1969. "Urban Social Theory and Research," *Environment and Planning* 1, pp. 143–153.

———— 1977. "Managers, Technical Experts, and the State." Pp. 49–60 in M. Harloe (ed.), *Captive Cities*. London: Wiley.

———— 1979. "Socio-Political Factors in Resource Allocation." Pp. 33–46 in D. Herbert and D. Smith (eds.), *Social Problems and the City*. Oxford: Oxford University Press.

Palm, R. I. 1973a. "The Telephone and the Organization of Urban Space," *Proceedings, Association of American Geographers* 5, pp. 207–210.

———— 1973b. "Factorial Ecology and the Community of Outlook," *Annals, Association of American Geographers* 63, pp. 341–346.

———— 1976. "The Role of Real Estate Agents as Information Mediators in Two American Cities," *Geografiska Annaler* 58B, pp. 28–41.

———— 1978. "Spatial Segmentation of the Urban Housing Market," *Economic Geography* 54, pp. 210–221.

———— and D. Caruso 1972. "Factor Labelling in Factorial Ecology," *Annals, Association of American Geographers* 62, pp. 122–133.

———— and A. Pred 1974. *A Time-Geographic Perspective on Problems of Inequality for Women*. Working Paper No. 236, Institute of Urban and Regional Development, University of California, Berkeley.

Park, R. E. 1916. "The City: Suggestions for the Investigation of Human Behavior in the Urban Environment," *American Journal of Sociology* 20, pp. 577–612.

———— 1924. "The Concept of Social Distance," *Journal of Applied Sociology* 8, pp. 339–344.

———— 1926. "The Urban Community as a Spatial Pattern and a Moral Order." Pp. 3–18 in E. Burgess (ed.), *The Urban Community*. Chicago: University of Chicago Press.

———— 1929. "The City as a Social Laboratory." Pp. 1–19 in T. Smith and L. White (eds.), *Chicago: An Experiment in Social Science Research*. Chicago: University of Chicago Press.

———— 1936. "Human Ecology," *American Journal of Sociology* 42, pp. 1–15.

Parkin, F. 1979. *Marxism and Class Theory: A Bourgeois Critique*. London: Tavistock.

Parsons, J. 1969. "Toward a More Humane Geography," *Economic Geography* 45, facing p. 189.

Patterson, J. M. 1974. *The Factorial Urban Ecology of Greater Vancouver*. Unpublished thesis, University of British Columbia, Dept. of Geography.

Peach, C. (ed.) 1975. *Urban Social Segregation*. London: Longmans.

———— 1980. "Ethnic Segregation and Intermarriage," *Annals, Association of American Geographers* 70, pp. 371–381.

Pendakur, S. 1972. *Cities, Citizens and Freeways*. Vancouver: V. S. Pendakur.

Peterson, R., G. Wekerle, and D. Morley 1978. "Women and Environments," *Environment and Behavior* 10, pp. 511–534.

Pettigrew, T. and R. Green 1976. "School Desegregation in Large Cities," *Harvard Educational Review* 46, pp. 1–53.

Peursen, C. van 1972. *Phenomenology and Reality*. Pittsburgh: Duquesne University Press.

Pfaff, A. 1973. "Transfer Payments to Large Metropolitan Poverty Areas." Pp. 93–129 in K. Boulding et al. (eds.), *Transfers in an Urbanized Economy*. Belmont, Cal.: Wadsworth.

Phillips, D. 1976. *Urban Housing Quality: The Importance of Attitudes in the Decision to Rehabilitate*. Unpublished thesis, University of British Columbia, Dept. of Geography.

———— 1979. "Information Diffusion Within an Inner City Neighbourhood," *Geografiska Annaler* 61B, pp. 30–42.

Phillips, P. and S. Brunn 1978. "Slow Growth: A New Epoch of American Metropolitan Evolution," *Geographical Review* 68, pp. 274–292.

Pickvance, C. G. (ed.) 1976. *Urban Sociology: Critical Essays*. London: Tavistock.

Pilcher, W. 1972. "The Dispersed Urban Community: The Case of the Portland Longshoremen," *Growth and Change* 3, pp. 3–10.

Pinch, S. 1979. "Territorial Justice in the City: A Case Study of the Social Services for the Elderly in Greater London." Pp. 201–203 in D. T. Herbert and D. M. Smith (eds.), *Social Problems and the City*. Oxford: Oxford University Press.

Pinter, H. 1968. *The Dwarfs*. London: Methuen.

Pitt, J. 1977. *Gentrification in Islington*. London: Barnsbury Peoples Forum.

Pollowy, A. M. 1973. *Children in the Residential Setting: A Discussion Paper Toward Design Guidelines*. Montreal: University of Montreal.

Poole, M. and F. W. Boal, 1973. "Religious Residential Segregation in Belfast in Mid-1969: A Multi-Level Analysis." Pp. 1–40 in B. Clark and M. Gleave (eds.), *Social Patterns in Cities*. London: Institute of British Geographers, Special Publication No. 5.

Popenoe, D. 1977. *The Suburban Environment*. Chicago: University of Chicago Press.

Porteous, J. D. 1974. "Social Class in Atacama Company Towns," *Annals, Association of American Geographers* 64, pp. 409–417.

———— 1976. "Home: The Territorial Core," *Geographical Review* 66, pp. 383–390.

———— 1977. *Environment and Behavior*. Reading, Mass.: Addison-Wesley.

Potter, R. 1979. "Perception of Urban Retailing Facilities: An Analysis of Consumer Information Fields," *Geografiska Annaler* 61B, pp. 19–29.

Pratt, G. 1982. "Class Analysis and Urban Domestic Property: A Critical Re-examination," *International Journal of Urban and Regional Research* 6, forthcoming.

Pred, A. 1967. *Behavior and Location*. Part I. Lund Studies in Geography Series B, No. 27. Lund, Sweden: C. W. K. Gleerup.

———— 1974. *Major Job-Providing Organizations and Systems of Cities*. Washington, D.C.: Association of American Geographers, Commission on College Geography Resource Paper No. 27.

———— 1977a. "The Choreography of Existence: Comments on Hägerstrand's Time Geography and its Usefulness," *Economic Geography* 53, pp. 207–221.

———— 1977b. *City-Systems in Advanced Economies*. London: Hutchinson.

———— 1981. "Of Paths and Projects: Individual Behavior and its Societal Context." Pp.

231–255 in K. Cox and R. Golledge (eds.), *Behavioral Problems in Geography Revisited*. New York: Methuen.

Proshansky, H. M. et. al. (eds.) 1970. *Environmental Psychology: Man and His Physical Setting*. New York: Holt, Rinehart and Winston.

Prottas, J. 1978. "The Power of the Street-Level Bureaucrat in Public Service Bureaucracies," *Urban Affairs Quarterly* 13, pp. 285–312.

Pyle, G. 1969. *Heart Disease, Cancer and Stroke in Chicago*. Chicago: University of Chicago, Dept. of Geography Research Paper No. 134.

———— 1976. "Geographic Perspectives on Crime and the Impact of Anticrime Legislation." Pp. 257–291 in J. S. Adams (ed.), *Urban Policymaking and Metropolitan Dynamics: A Comparative Geographical Analysis*. Cambridge, Mass.: Ballinger.

Quigley, J. and D. Weinberg 1977. "Intra-Urban Residential Mobility: A Review and Synthesis," *International Regional Science Review* 2, pp. 41–66.

Quinn, J. 1940. "The Burgess Zonal Hypothesis and Its Critics," *American Sociological Review* 5, pp. 210–218.

Radford, J. P. 1979. "Testing the Model of the Pre-Industrial City: The Case of Ante-Bellum Charleston, South Carolina," *Transactions Institute of British Geographers* N.S. 4, pp. 392–410.

Ragatz, R. 1970. "Vacation Homes in the Northeastern United States: Seasonality in Population Distribution," *Annals, Association of American Geographers* 60, pp. 447–455.

Rainwater, L. 1970. *Behind Ghetto Walls*. Chicago: Aldine-Atherton.

Ramsøy, N. 1966. "Assortive Mating and the Structure of Cities," *American Sociological Review* 31, pp. 773–785.

Rapkin, C. and W. Grigsby 1960. *The Demand for Housing in Racially Mixed Areas*. Berkeley: University of California Press.

Ratcliff, R. U. 1949. *Urban Land Economics*. New York: McGraw-Hill.

Ravage, M. 1971. *An American In The Making*. New York: Dover.

Redstone, L. 1976. *The New Downtowns*. New York: McGraw-Hill.

Rees, P. H. 1970. "Concepts of Social Space: Toward an Urban Social Geography." Pp. 306–394 in B. J. L. Berry and F. Horton, *Geographic Perspectives on Urban Systems*. Englewood Cliffs, N.J.: Prentice-Hall.

———— 1971. "Factorial Ecology: An Extended Definition, Survey, and Critique of the Field," *Economic Geography* 47 (Supplement), pp. 220–233.

Relph, E. 1970. "An Inquiry into the Relations between Phenomenology and Geography," *Canadian Geographer* 14, pp. 193–201.

Rex, J. 1968. "The Sociology of a Zone in Transition." Pp. 211–231 in R. E. Pahl (ed.), *Readings in Urban Sociology*. Oxford: Pergamon.

Richardson, H. W. 1971. *Urban Economics*. Harmondsworth, Middx.: Penguin.

———— 1976. "Relevance of Mathematical Land Use Theory to Applications." Pp. 9–22 in G. Papageorgiou (ed.), *Mathematical Land Use Theory*. Lexington, Mass.: D. C. Heath.

Rider Haggard, H. 1906. *Rural England*. Volume I. London.

Riis, J. 1971. *How The Other Half Lives*. New York: Dover.

Roberts, R. 1973. *The Classic Slum: Salford Life in the First Quarter of the Century*. Harmondsworth. Middx.: Penguin.

Robertson, A. 1977. *The Pursuit of Power, Profit and Privacy: A Study of Vancouver's West End Elite, 1886–1914.* Unpublished thesis, University of British Columbia, Dept. of Geography.

Robinson, I. et al. 1975. "Trade-Off Games." Pp. 79–118 in W. Michelson (ed.), *Behavioral Research Methods in Environmental Design.* Stroudsburg, Pa.: Dowden, Hutchinson and Ross.

Robson, B. T. 1969. *Urban Analysis.* Cambridge: The University Press.

———— 1975. *Urban Social Areas.* London: Oxford University Press.

Rogers, E. and P. Shoemaker 1971. *Communication of Innovation: A Cross Cultural Approach.* New York: Free Press.

Rose, A. (ed.) 1962. *Human Behavior and Social Processes.* London: Routledge and Kegan Paul.

Rose, H. M. 1970. "The Development of an Urban Subsystem: The Case of the Negro Ghetto," *Annals, Association of American Geographers* 60, pp. 1–17.

———— 1972. "The Spatial Development of Black Residential Subsystems," *Economic Geography* 48, pp. 43–65.

Roseman, C., C. Christian, and H. Bullamore 1972. "Factorial Ecologies of Urban Black Communities." Pp. 239–255 in H. Rose and H. McConnell (eds.), *Geography of the Ghetto.* Dekalb, Ill.: Northern Illinois University Press.

———— and J. Williams 1980. "Metropolitan to Nonmetropolitan Migration: A Decision-Making Perspective," *Urban Geography* 1, pp. 283–294.

Rosenthal, E. 1961. "Acculturation without Assimilation? The Jewish Community of Chicago, Illinois," *American Journal of Sociology* 66, pp. 275–288.

Rossi, P. H. 1955. *Why Families Move.* Glencoe, Ill.: Free Press.

Roszak, T. 1973. *Where the Wasteland Ends.* Garden City, N.Y.: Anchor.

Rothman, D. J. 1971. *The Discovery of the Asylum.* Boston: Little, Brown.

Rothman, R. 1973. "Access vs. Environment," *Traffic Quarterly* 27, pp. 111–132.

Roweis, S. and A. Scott 1976. *The Urban Land Question.* University of Toronto, Dept. of Urban and Regional Planning, Papers on Planning and Design No. 10.

Rowles, G. 1978. *Prisoners of Space? Exploring the Geographical Experience of Older People.* Boulder, Col.: Westview Press.

———— 1980. "Growing Old 'Inside': Aging and Attachment to Place in an Appalachian Community." Pp. 153–170 in N. Datan and N. Lohmann (eds.), *Transitions of Aging.* New York: Academic Press.

Royko, M. 1971. *Boss: Richard J. Daley of Chicago.* New York: Dutton.

Saarinen, T. F. 1973. "The Use of Projective Techniques in Geographic Research." Pp. 29–52 in W. Ittelson (ed.), *Environment and Cognition.* New York: Seminar Press.

Salisbury, H. 1971. "The State Within a State: Some Comparisons Between the Urban Ghetto and the Insurgent State," *Professional Geographer* 23, pp. 105–112.

Samuels, M. S. 1978. "Existentialism and Human Geography." Pp. 22–40 in D. Ley and M. Samuels (eds.), *Humanistic Geography.* Chicago: Maaroufa Press.

Sanford, N. and C. Comstock (eds.) 1971. *Sanctions For Evil.* San Francisco: Jossey-Bass.

Sant, M. 1978. "Issues in Employment." Pp. 84–105 in R. Davies and P. Hall (eds.), *Issues in Urban Society.* Harmondsworth, Middx.: Penguin.

Sarkissian, W. 1976. "The Idea of Social Mix in Town Planning," *Urban Studies* 13, pp. 231–246.

Sarre, P. 1972. "Intra-Urban Migration." Pp. 65–106 in *Social Geography.* Bletchley, Bucks.: The Open University.

Sartre, J. -P. 1955a. "American Cities." Pp. 107–117 in *Literary and Philosophical Essays*. London: Rider.

_____ 1955b. "New York, The Colonial City." Pp. 118–124 in *Literary and Philosophical Essays*. London: Rider.

Saunders, P. 1978. "Domestic Property and Social Class," *International Journal of Urban and Regional Research* 2, pp. 233–251.

_____ 1979. *Urban Politics: A Sociological Interpretation*. London: Hutchinson.

Scheuch, E. 1969. "Social Context and Individual Behavior." Pp. 133–155 in M. Dogan and S. Rokkan (eds.), *Quantitative Ecological Analysis in the Social Sciences*. Cambridge, Mass.: M.I.T. Press.

Schneider, M. 1973. "Public Participation in Local Traffic Engineering," *Highway Research Record* 470, pp. 12–21.

Schorr, A. 1964. *Slums and Social Insecurity*. Washington, D.C.: Department of Health, Education, and Welfare.

_____ 1968. "Housing the Poor." Pp. 115–150 in W. Bloomberg and H. Schmandt (eds.), *Urban Poverty*. Beverly Hills, Cal.: Sage.

Schorske, C. 1963. "The Idea of the City in European Thought: Voltaire to Spengler." Pp. 95–115 in O. Handlin and J. Burchard (eds.), *The Historian and the City*. Cambridge, Mass.: M.I.T. Press.

Schutz, A. 1944. "The Stranger: An Essay in Social Psychology," *American Journal of Sociology* 49, pp. 499–507.

_____ 1951. "Making Music Together: A Study in Social Relationships," *Social Research* 18, pp. 76–97.

_____ 1960. "The Social World and the Theory of Social Action," *Social Research* 27, pp. 205–221.

_____ 1970. *On Phenomenology and Social Relations*. H. Wagner (ed.). Chicago: University of Chicago Press.

Schwartz, B. 1976. "Images of Suburbia." Pp. 325–340 in B. Schwartz (ed.), *The Changing Face of the Suburbs*. Chicago: University of Chicago Press.

Schwartz, G. 1979. "The Office Pattern in New York City, 1960–75." Pp. 215–237 in P. Daniels (ed.), *Spatial Patterns of Office Growth and Location*. Chichester: Wiley.

Scott, A. J. 1971. *An Introduction to Spatial Allocation Analysis*. Washington, D.C.: Association of American Geographers, Commission on College Geography, Research Paper No. 9.

Seeley, J. R., R. Sim, and E. Loosley 1956. *Crestwood Heights*. New York: Basic Books.

Seeman, M. 1971. "The Urban Alienations: Some Dubious Theses from Marx to Marcuse," *Journal of Personality and Social Psychology* 19, pp. 135–143.

Seley, J. 1970. *Spatial Bias: The Kink in Nashville's I-40*. University of Pennsylvania, Dept. of Regional Science, Research on Conflict in Locational Decisions, Paper No. 2.

_____ 1974. "Towards a Paradigm of Community-Based Planning." Pp. 109–126 in D. Ley (ed.), *Community Participation and the Spatial Order of the City*. B.C. Geographical Series No. 19. Vancouver: Tantalus.

_____ and J. Wolpert 1974. "A Strategy of Ambiguity in Locational Conflicts." Pp. 275–300 in K. R. Cox et al. (eds.), *Locational Approaches to Power and Conflict*. New York: Wiley.

Seyfried, W. 1963. "The Centrality of Urban Land Values," *Land Economics* 39, pp. 275–284.

Shannon, G. and A. Dever 1974. *The Geography of Health Care*. New York: McGraw-Hill.

———— and J. Nystuen 1976. "Surrogate Measures of Urban Social Interaction," *Professional Geographer* 28, pp. 23–28.

Shaw, C. R. and H. McKay 1972. *Juvenile Delinquency and Urban Areas*. Chicago: University of Chicago Press.

Sheppard, H. and A. Belitsky 1966. *The Job Hunt*. Baltimore: Johns Hopkins University Press.

Shevky, E. and W. Bell 1955. *Social Area Analysis*. Stanford: Stanford University Press.

Short, J. 1978. "Residential Mobility in the Private Housing Market of Bristol," *Transactions, Institute of British Geographers* N.S. 3, pp. 533–547.

Short, J. F. (ed.) 1971. *The Social Fabric of the Metropolis*. Chicago: University of Chicago Press.

Siggins, M. 1982. "Madness in South Parkdale," *Today Magazine* (Toronto), March 6, pp. 6–10.

Silverman, D. 1970. *The Theory of Organizations*. London: Heinemann.

Simmons, J. W. 1968. "Changing Residence in the City," *Geographical Review* 58, pp. 622–651.

———— 1982. "The Public Sector and the Canadian Urban System." Paper presented to the Canadian Association of Geographers meeting in Ottawa.

———— and A. Baker 1973. "Household Relocation Patterns." Pp. 199–217 in L. S. Bourne et al. (eds.), *The Form of Cities in Central Canada*. Toronto: University of Toronto, Dept. of Geography.

Simon, H. 1965. *Aministrative Behavior*. New York: Free Press.

Singh, A. 1977. "U.K. Industry and World Economy: A Case of Deindustrialisation," *Cambridge Journal of Economics* 1, pp. 113–136.

Singh, D. 1978. *The East Indian Community of Vancouver*. Unpublished paper, University of British Columbia, Dept. of Geography.

Sitton, C. 1967. "Racial Coverage: Planning and Logistics." In P. Fisher and R. Lowenstein (eds.), *Race and the News Media*. New York: B'nai B'rith.

Sjoberg, G. 1960. *The Pre-Industrial City*. Glencoe, Ill.: Free Press.

Sloan, L. 1969. " 'Good Government' and the Politics of Race," *Social Problems* 17, pp. 161–175.

Smailes, A. E. 1955. "Some Reflections on the Geographical Description and Analysis of Townscapes," *Transactions, Institute of British Geographers* 21, pp. 99–115.

Smith, C. A. and C. J. Smith, 1978. "Locating Natural Neighbours in the Urban Community," *Area* 10, pp. 102–110.

Smith, C. D. 1974. "Ethnic Plurality, Competition and Discretion over Primary Education in Montreal." Pp. 25–40 in D. Ley (ed.), *Community Participation and the Spatial Order of the City*. B.C. Geographical Series No. 19. Vancouver: Tantalus.

Smith, C. J. 1976. *The Geography of Mental Health*. Washington, D.C.: Association of American Geographers, Commission on College Geography Resource Paper No. 76-4.

———— 1980. "Social Networks as Metaphors, Methods, and Models," *Progress in Human Geography* 4, pp. 500–524.

Smith, Constance and A. Freedman 1972. *Voluntary Associations*. Cambridge, Mass.: Harvard University Press.

Smith, D. M. 1970. "On Throwing Out Weber with the Bathwater: A Note on Industrial Location and Linkage," *Area* 1, pp. 16–17.

_____ 1973. *The Geography of Social Well-Being in the United States*. New York: McGraw-Hill.

_____ 1977. *Human Geography: A Welfare Approach*. London: Edward Arnold.

_____ 1979. "The Identification of Problems In Cities: Applications of Social Indicators." Pp. 13–32 in D. Herbert and D. Smith (eds.), *Social Problems and the City*. Oxford: Oxford University Press.

Smith, G. 1976. "The Spatial Information Fields of Urban Consumers," *Transactions, Institute of British Geographers* N.S. 1, pp. 175–189.

Smith, N. 1979. "Gentrification and Capital: Practice and Ideology in Society Hill," *Antipode* 11, no. 3, pp. 24–35.

Smith, P. J. 1971. "Change in a Youthful City: The Case of Calgary, Alberta," *Geography* 56, pp. 1–14.

_____ and L. D. McCann 1981. "Residential Land Use Change in Inner Edmonton," *Annals, Association of American Geographers* 71, pp. 536–551.

Smith, W. 1971. "Filtering and Neighborhood Change." Pp. 170–179 in L. Bourne (ed.), *Internal Structure of the City*. New York: Oxford University Press.

Smout, T. 1969. *A History of the Scottish People, 1560–1830*. London: Collins.

Sommer, R. 1974. *Tight Spaces: Hard Architecture and How To Humanize It*. Englewood Cliffs, N.J.: Prentice-Hall.

Sopher, D. 1979. "The Landscape of Home." Pp. 129–149 in D. Meinig (ed.), *The Interpretation of Ordinary Landscapes*. New York: Oxford University Press.

Sorre, M. 1957. *Rencontres de la Géographie et de la Sociologie*. Paris: Rivière.

Southworth, M. 1969. "The Sonic Environment of Cities," *Environment and Behavior* 1, pp. 49–70.

Spector, A., L. Brown, and E. Malecki 1976. "Acquaintance Circles and Communication," *Professional Geographer* 28, pp. 267–276.

Springer, L. 1974. *Crime Perception and Response Behavior: Two Views of a Seattle Community*. Unpublished dissertation, Pennsylvania State University, Dept. of Geography.

Springer, M. 1970. "Social Indicators, Reports and Accounts: Toward the Management of Society," *The Annals* 388, pp. 1–13.

Spurr, P. 1976. *Land and Urban Development*. Toronto: James Lorimer.

Srole, L. 1972. "Urbanization and Mental Health: Some Reformulations," *American Scientist* 60, pp. 576–583.

Steed, G. P. F. 1973. "Intrametropolitan Manufacturing: Spatial Distribution and Locational Dynamics in Greater Vancouver," *Canadian Geographer* 17, pp. 235–258.

Stephens, J. 1976. "Daily Activity Systems and Time-Space Constraints." Pp. 21–69 in B. Holly (ed.), *Time Space Budgets and Urban Research*. Discussion Paper No. 1, Dept. of Geography, Kent State University.

_____ and B. Holly 1977. "Metropolitan Deconcentration and Trends in Location of Corporate Headquarters, 1955–74." Paper presented to the Association of American Geographers meeting in Salt Lake City.

Sternlieb, G. and J. Hughes (eds.) 1975. *Post-Industrial America: Metropolitan Decline and Inter-Regional Job Shifts*. New Brunswick, N.J.: Rutgers University, Center for Urban Policy Research.

Stetzer, D. 1975. *Special Districts in Cook County*. Chicago: University of Chicago, Dept. of Geography, Research Paper No. 169.

Stewart, J. et al. 1975. *Urban Indicators: Quality of Life Comparisons for Canadian Cities*. Ottawa: Ministry of State for Urban Affairs.

Stilwell, F. and J. Hardwick 1973. "Social Inequality in Australian Cities," *Australian Quarterly* 45, no. 4, pp. 18–36.

Stonequist, E. 1961. *The Marginal Man*. New York: Russell and Russell.

Strauss, A. (ed.) 1968. *The American City: A Sourcebook of Urban Imagery*. Chicago: Aldine.

Studer, R. 1972. "The Organization of Spatial Stimuli." Pp. 279–292 in J. Wohlwill and D. Carson (eds.), *Environment and the Social Sciences*. Washington, D.C.: American Psychological Association.

Stutz, F. P. 1973. "Distance and Network Effects on Urban Social Travel Fields," *Economic Geography* 49, pp. 134–144.

———— 1976a. *Social Aspects of Interaction and Transportation*. Washington, D.C.: Association of American Geographers, Commission on College Geography, Resource Paper No. 76-2.

———— 1976b. "Adjustment and Mobility of Elderly Poor Amid Downtown Renewal," *Geographical Review* 66, pp. 391–400.

———— 1982. "Spatial Variations in Housing Prices in the United States." Paper presented to the Association of American Geographers meeting in San Antonio.

Sullivan, J., P. Montgomery, and A. Farber 1973. *Evaluating Highway Environmental Impacts: Two Reports*. Washington, D.C.: Center for Science and the Public Interest.

Suttles, G. D. 1968. *The Social Order of the Slum*. Chicago: University of Chicago Press.

———— 1972. *The Social Construction of Communities*. Chicago: University of Chicago Press.

Tabb, W. 1978. "The New York City Fiscal Crisis." Pp. 241–266 in W. Tabb and L. Sawers (eds.), *Marxism and the Metropolis*. New York: Oxford University Press.

Taeuber, K. 1965. "Residential Segregation," *Scientific American* 213, no. 2, pp. 12–19.

Tannenbaum, D. 1974. *People With Problems: Seeking Help in an Urban Community*. Toronto: Centre for Urban and Community Studies, Research Paper No. 64.

Taylor, G. 1949. *Urban Geography*. London: Methuen.

Taylor, M. 1977. "Corporate Space Preferences: A New Zealand Example," *Environment and Planning* A, 9, pp. 1171–1177.

Thomas, D. 1954. *Quite Early One Morning*. London: J. M. Dent

Thomas, W. I. 1971. "The Immigrant Community." Pp. 120–130 in J. Short (ed.), *The Social Fabric of the Metropolis*. Chicago: University of Chicago Press.

Thompson, W. 1973. "A Preface to Suburban Economics." Pp. 409–430 in L. Masotti and J. Hadden (eds.), *The Urbanization of the Suburbs*. Beverly Hills, Cal.: Sage.

Thorsen, K. 1971. "The Cities Lock Up: Fortress on 78th Street," *Life Magazine*, Nov. 19.

Thrasher, F. 1963. *The Gang*. Chicago: University of Chicago Press.

Thrift, N. 1977. "Time and Theory in Human Geography: Part II," *Progress in Human Geography* 1, pp. 413–457.

———— 1979. "Unemployment in the Inner City: Urban Problem or Structural Imperative?" Pp.

125–226 in D. Herbert and R. Johnston (eds.), *Geography and the Urban Environment*. Vol. 2. Chichester: Wiley.

Timms, D. 1965. "Quantitative Techniques in Urban Social Geography." Pp. 239–265 in R. Chorley and P. Haggett (eds.), *Frontiers in Geographical Teaching*. London: Methuen.

―――― 1971. *The Urban Mosaic*. Cambridge: The University Press.

―――― 1976. "Social Bases to Social Areas." Pp. 19–39 in D. Herbert and R. Johnston (eds.), *Social Areas in Cities*. Vol. 1. London: Wiley.

Travers, J. and S. Milgram 1969. "An Experimental Study of the Small World Problem," *Sociometry* 32, pp. 425–443.

Triandis, H. and L. Triandis 1960. "Race, Social Class, Religion, and Nationality as Determinants of Social Distance," *Journal of Abnormal and Social Psychology* 61, pp. 110–118.

Tsang, E. 1981. "The Impact of High Interest Rates on Housing," *Habitat* 24 (no. 3), pp. 8–12.

Tuan, Yi-Fu 1974. *Topophilia*. Englewood Cliffs, N.J.: Prentice-Hall.

―――― 1975. "Place: An Experiential Perspective," *Geographical Review* 65, pp. 151–165.

Ullman, E. 1954. "Amenities as a Factor in Regional Growth," *Geographical Review* 44, pp. 119–132.

U.S. Commission on Civil Rights 1973. *Understanding Fair Housing*. Washington, D.C.: U.S. Government Printing Office.

U.S. Department of Health, Education and Welfare 1969. *Toward a Social Report*. Washington, D.C.: U.S. Government Printing Office.

Uyeki, E. 1964. "Residential Distribution and Stratification," *American Journal of Sociology* 69, pp. 491–498.

Vance, J. E. 1976. "The American City: Workshop for a National Culture." Pp. 1–49 in J. S. Adams (ed.), *Contemporary Metropolitan America*. Vol. 1. Cambridge, Mass.: Ballinger.

―――― 1977. *This Scene of Man*. New York: Harper & Row.

Vancouver Planning Department 1979. *Understanding Vancouver's Housing*. Vancouver, B.C.

Venturi, R., D. Brown, and S. Izenour 1973. "Learning from Las Vegas." Pp. 99–112 in W. Ittelson (ed.), *Environment and Cognition*. New York: Seminar Press.

Vise, P. de 1971. "Cook County Hospital," *Antipode* 3, no. 1, pp. 9–20.

―――― 1972. "Chicago, 1971: Ready for Another Fire?" Pp. 47–66 in R. Peet (ed.), *Geographical Perspectives on American Poverty*. Worcester, Mass.: Antipode Monographs in Social Geography No. 1.

―――― 1973. *Misused and Misplaced Hospitals and Doctors*. Washington, D.C.: Association of American Geographers, Commission on College Geography Resource Paper No. 22.

―――― 1976. "The Suburbanization of Jobs and Minority Employment," *Economic Geography* 52, pp. 348–362.

Visher, S. 1932. "Social Geography," *Social Forces* 10, pp. 351–354.

Vranicki, P. 1965. "Socialism and the Problem of Alienation." Pp. 275–287 in E. Fromm (ed.), *Socialist Humanism*. Garden City, N.Y.: Doubleday.

Walker, G. 1977. "Social Networks and Territory in a Commuter Village, Bond Head, Ontario," *Canadian Geographer* 21, pp. 329–350.

Wallace, I. 1978. "Towards a Humanized Conception of Economic Geography." Pp. 91–108 in D. Ley and M. Samuels (eds.), *Humanistic Geography*. Chicago: Maaroufa.

Walter, B. and F. Wirt 1972. "Social and Political Dimensions of American Suburbs." Pp. 97–123 in B. J. L. Berry (ed.), *City Classification Handbook*. New York: Wiley.

Ward, D. 1964. "A Comparative Historical Geography of Streetcar Suburbs in Boston, Massachusetts and Leeds, England: 1850–1920," *Annals, Association of American Geographers* 54, pp. 477–489.

———— 1968. "The Emergence of Central Immigrant Ghettoes in American Cities: 1840–1920," *Annals, Association of American Geographers* 58, pp. 343–359.

———— 1969. "The Internal Spatial Structure of Immigrant Residential Districts in the Late Nineteenth Century," *Geographical Analysis* 1, pp. 337–353.

———— 1971. *Cities and Immigrants*. New York: Oxford University Press.

———— 1975. "Victorian Cities: How Modern?" *Journal of Historical Geography* 1, pp. 135–151.

———— 1976. "The Victorian Slum: An Enduring Myth?" *Annals, Association of American Geographers* 66, pp. 323–336.

———— 1980. "Environs and Neighbours in the 'Two Nations': Residential Differentiation in Mid-Nineteenth-Century Leeds," *Journal of Historical Geography* 6, pp. 133–162.

Ware, C. 1935. *Greenwich Village 1920–1930*. New York: Harper & Row.

Warner, S. B. 1962. *Streetcar Suburbs*. Cambridge: Harvard University Press.

Watson, C. J. 1974. "Vacancy Chains, Filtering and the Public Sector," *Journal, American Institute of Planners* 40, pp. 346–352.

Watson, J. W. 1957. "The Sociological Aspects of Geography." Pp. 463–499 in G. Taylor (ed.), *Geography in the Twentieth Century*. London: Methuen.

Webber, M. 1963. "Order in Diversity: Community Without Propinquity." Pp. 23–54 in L. Wingo (ed.), *Cities and Space*. Baltimore: Johns Hopkins University Press.

Webber, M. J. 1972. *Impact of Uncertainty on Location*. Cambridge, Mass.: M.I.T. Press.

Weber, M. 1958. *The City*. New York: Free Press.

Weick, K. E. 1969. *The Social Psychology of Organizing*. Reading, Mass.: Addison-Wesley.

Weightman, B. 1976. "Indian Social Space: A Case Study of the Musqueam Band of Vancouver, B.C.," *Canadian Geographer* 20, pp. 171–186.

Weil, S. 1971. *The Need for Roots*. New York: Harper & Row.

Weiler, C. 1978. *Reinvestment Displacement: HUD's Role in a New Housing Issue*. Philadelphia: Temple University, Dept. of Political Science, unpublished report.

Weiner, P. and E. Deak 1972. *Environmental Factors in Transportation Planning*. Lexington, Mass.: D. C. Heath.

Wekerle, G., R. Peterson, and D. Morley (eds.) 1980. *New Space for Women*. Boulder, Col.: Westview Press.

Wellman, B. 1976. *Urban Connections*. Toronto: University of Toronto, Centre for Urban and Community Studies Research Paper No. 84.

Western, J. C. 1973. "Social Groups and Activity Patterns in Houma, Louisiana," *Geographical Review* 63, pp. 301–321.

———— 1978. "Knowing One's Place: 'The Coloured People' and the Group Areas Act in Cape Town." Pp. 297–318 in D. F. Ley and M. S. Samuels (eds.), *Humanistic Geography*. Chicago: Maaroufa.

———— 1981. *Outcast Cape Town*. Minneapolis: University of Minnesota Press.

Wheatley, P. 1963. "What the Greatness of a City Is Said To Be," *Pacific Viewpoint* 4, pp. 163–188.

Wheeler, J. 1968. "Residential Location by Occupational Status," *Urban Studies* 5, pp. 24–32.

_____ and F. P. Stutz 1971. "Spatial Dimensions of Urban Social Travel," *Annals, Association of American Geographers* 61, pp. 371–386.

White, H. 1971. "Multipliers, Vacancy Chains and Filtering in Housing," *Journal, American Institute of Planners* 37, pp. 88–94.

White, M. and L. White 1962. *The Intellectual Versus the City*. New York: Mentor.

Whyte, W. F. 1943. "Social Organization and the Slum," *American Sociological Review* 8, pp. 34–39.

_____ 1955. *Street Corner Society*. Chicago: University of Chicago Press.

Whyte, W. H. 1957. *The Organization Man*. Garden City, N.Y.: Doubleday.

Williams, C. H. 1980. "The Desire of Nations: Québecois Ethnic Separatism in Comparative Perspective," *Cahiers de Géographie du Québec* 24, no. 61, pp. 47–68.

Williams, O. 1975. "Technology, Location, and Access Strategies." Pp. 17–25 in S. Gale and E. Moore (eds.), *The Manipulated City*. Chicago: Maaroufa.

Williams, P. 1976. "The Role of Institutions in the London Housing Market," *Transactions, Institute of British Geographers* N.S. 1, pp. 72–82.

_____ 1978a. "Building Societies and the Inner City," *Transactions, Institute of British Geographers* N.S. 3, pp. 23–34.

_____ 1978b. "Urban Managerialism: A Concept of Relevance?" *Area* 10, pp. 236–240.

Wilner, D. et al. 1962. *The Housing Environment and Family Life*. Baltimore: Johns Hopkins University Press.

Wilson, R. 1962. "Livability of the City: Attitudes and Urban Development." Pp. 359–399 in F. Chapin and S. Weiss (eds.), *Urban Growth Dynamics*. New York: Wiley.

Winkler, J. 1976. "Corporatism," *European Journal of Sociology* 17, pp. 100–136.

_____ 1977. "The Corporate Economy: Theory and Administration." Pp. 43–58 in R. Scase (ed.), *Industrial Society: Class, Cleavage, and Control*. London: Allen & Unwin.

Winters, C. 1977. "The Geography of Rejuvenation in an Inner City Neighborhood; The Upper West Side of Manhattan, 1950–1975." Paper presented to the Association of American Geographers meeting in Salt Lake City.

_____ 1978. "Rejuvenation With Character." Paper presented to the Association of American Geographers meeting in New Orleans.

_____ 1979. "The Social Identity of Evolving Neighborhoods," *Landscape* 23, no. 1, pp. 8–14.

Wirt, F. 1974. *Power in the City: Decision-Making in San Francisco*. Berkeley: University of California Press.

Wirth, L. 1928. *The Ghetto*. Chicago: University of Chicago Press.

_____ 1938. "Urbanism as a Way of Life," *American Journal of Sociology* 44, pp. 3–24.

_____ 1964. *On Cities and Social Life*. A. Reiss (ed.). Chicago: University of Chicago Press.

Wiseman, J. 1970. *Stations of the Lost: The Treatment of Skid Row Alcoholics*. Englewood Cliffs, N.J.: Prentice-Hall.

Wohlwill, J. and D. Carson (eds.) 1972. *Environment and the Social Sciences*. Washington, D.C.: American Psychological Association.

Wolch, J. 1980. "Residential Location of the Service-Dependent Poor," *Annals, Association of American Geographers* 70, pp. 330–341.

Wolfe, T. 1969. *The Pump House Gang*. New York: Bantam Books.

———— 1976. *Mauve Gloves and Madmen, Clutter and Vine*. New York: Farrar, Straus and Giroux.

Wolforth, J. 1965. *Residential Location and Place of Work*. B.C. Geographical Series No. 4. Vancouver: Tantalus.

Wolpert, E. and J. Wolpert 1974. "From Asylum to Ghetto," *Antipode* 6, no. 3, pp. 63–76.

Wolpert, J. 1965. "Behavioral Aspects of the Decision to Migrate," *Papers and Proceedings of the Regional Science Association* 15, pp. 159–169.

———— 1966. "Migration as an Adjustment to Environmental Stress," *Journal of Social Issues* 22, no. 4, pp. 92–102.

———— 1976. "Opening Closed Spaces," *Annals, Association of American Geographers* 66, pp. 1–13.

———— , M. Dear, and R. Crawford 1975. "Satellite Mental Health Facilities," *Annals, Association of American Geographers* 65, pp. 24–35.

———— , A. Mumphrey, and J. Seley 1972. *Metropolitan Neighborhoods: Participation and Conflict Over Change*. Washington, D.C.: Association of American Geographers, Commission on College Geography, Resource Paper No. 16.

Wood, A. E. 1955. *Hamtramck, Then and Now: A Sociological Study of a Polish-American Community*. New York: Bookman.

Wood, C. 1971. "Some Characteristics of Searching by Municipal Governments," *Geografiska Annaler* 53B, pp. 138–145.

Wood, D. 1978. "Introducing the Cartography of Reality." Pp. 207–220 in D. Ley and M. Samuels (eds.), *Humanistic Geography*. Chicago: Maaroufa.

Wood, P. 1974. "Urban Manufacturing: A View from the Fringe." Pp. 129–154 in J. Johnson (ed.), *Suburban Growth*. London: Wiley.

Wood, R. C. 1961. *1400 Governments*. Cambridge, Mass.: Harvard University Press.

Wrong, D. 1961. "The Oversocialized Conception of Man in Modern Sociology," *American Sociological Review* 26, pp. 183–193.

Yeates, M. 1965. "Some Factors Affecting the Spatial Distribution of Chicago Land Values, 1910–1960," *Economic Geography* 41, pp. 55–70.

———— 1975. *Main Street*. Toronto: Macmillan.

———— and B. Garner 1980. *The North American City*. 3d edition. New York: Harper & Row.

Young, K. and J. Kramer 1978. "Local Exclusionary Policies in Britain: The Case of Suburban Defense in a Metropolitan System." Pp. 229–251 in K. Cox (ed.), *Urbanization and Conflict in Market Societies*. Chicago: Maaroufa.

Young, M. and P. Wilmott 1957. *Family and Kinship in East London*. London: Routledge & Kegan Paul.

Zehner, R. 1972. ''Neighborhood and Community Satisfaction: A Report on New Towns and Less Planned Suburbs.'' Pp. 169–183 in J. Wohlwill and D. Carson (eds.), *Environment and the Social Sciences*. Washington, D.C.: American Psychological Association.

_____ 1977. *Indicators of the Quality of Life in New Communities*. Cambridge, Mass.: Ballinger.

Zeigler, D. J. 1981. ''Changing Regional Patterns of Central City Credit Ratings,'' *Urban Geography* 2, pp. 269–283.

Zelinsky, W. 1975. ''Nonmetropolitan Pennsylvania: A Demographic Revolution in the Making?'' *Earth and Mineral Sciences* 45, no. 1, pp. 1–4.

Znaniecki, F. 1969. *On Humanistic Sociology*. R. Bierstedt (ed.). Chicago: University of Chicago Press.

Zorbaugh, H. 1929. *The Gold Coast and the Slum*. Chicago: University of Chicago Press.

_____ 1961. ''The Natural Areas of the City.'' Pp. 45–49 in G. Theodorson (ed.), *Studies in Human Ecology*. New York: Harper & Row.

Index

82 83 84 85 9 8 7 6 5 4 3 2 1